SAVE OVER 50% OFF T NEWS

D0729988

Each issue of **Collector Magazine & Price Guide** brings y depth look at the collecting hobby. Features from experts give y advice on what to collect, how to collect it, and where to find it. **Collector Magazine's** exclusive 25 page price guide section gives you the most current prices on thousands of antiques, and **Collector Magazine's** editors are constantly bringing you the information you need to be a more informed collector.

Just send in this card to have 12 issues of **Collector Magazine & Price Guide** delivered to you for only $14.95.

Subscribe Today!

☐ ***Yes!*** Start my 1 year subscription (12 issues) to *Collector Magazine & Price Guide* for just $14.95.

☐ Payment Enclosed ☐ Bill Me

Make payable to Collector Magazine
P.O. Box 1050, Dubuque, IA 52004

Name _____

Address _____

City _____ State _____ Zip _____

1 Year $14.95 (12 issues)

Credit Card Orders Call 1-800-334-7165

AH8997

COMPLETE THIS CARD FOR A **FREE** COPY!

Are you a:
- ☐ Collector
- ☐ Auctioneer
- ☐ Dealer
- ☐ Other

Your interests are:
- ☐ Furniture
- ☐ Ceramics
- ☐ Glassware
- ☐ Advertising
- ☐ Toys
- ☐ Sports Items
- ☐ Records
- ☐ Comics
- ☐ Military
- ☐ Western Collectibles
- ☐ Movie Collectibles
- ☐ Paper Collectibles

Collector Magazine & Price Guide

_____
Name

_____
Address

_____
City/State/Zip

_____
Area Code/Phone

FREE OFFER—SEND NO MONEY
NO POSTAGE NECESSARY

AH8997

COLLECTOR MAGAZINE & PRICE GUIDE

NO POSTAGE
NECESSARY
IF MAILED
IN THE
UNITED STATES

BUSINESS REPLY MAIL
FIRST CLASS MAIL PERMIT NO.50 DUBUQUE, IA

POSTAGE WILL BE PAID BY ADDRESSEE

Department 10
COLLECTOR MAGAZINE & PRICE GUIDE
PO BOX 1050
DUBUQUE IA 52004-9969

COLLECTOR MAGAZINE & PRICE GUIDE

NO POSTAGE
NECESSARY
IF MAILED
IN THE
UNITED STATES

BUSINESS REPLY MAIL
FIRST CLASS MAIL PERMIT NO.50 DUBUQUE, IA

POSTAGE WILL BE PAID BY ADDRESSEE

Department 10
COLLECTOR MAGAZINE & PRICE GUIDE
PO BOX 1050
DUBUQUE IA 52004-9969

Christmas '95

From: John

ANTIQUE TRADER BOOKS

American Pressed Glass & Bottles Price Guide

Edited by
Kyle Husfloen

Consulting Editors
Neila and Tom Bredehoft

An illustrated comprehensive price guide to all types of pressed glass & bottles.

Antique Trader Books
P.O. Box 1050
Dubuque, IA 52004

STAFF

Assistant Editor . . . . . .Marilyn Dragowick

Production Coordinator/Editorial Assistant . . . .Louise Paradis

Production Assistant/Editorial Assistant . . . . . .Ruth Willis

Production Assistant . . . . . .Kristen Bushman

Cover Design . . . . . .Jaro Sebek

Subscription Manager . . . . . .Bonnie Rojemann

Copyright © 1994 by The Antique Trader. All rights reserved. No part of this publication may be reproduced, stored in a retrieval system, or transmitted in any form or by any means, electronic, mechanical, photocopying, recording or otherwise, without prior permission in writing from the publisher.

ISBN: 0-930625-50-1
Library of Congress Catalog Card No. 94-79664

Other books and magazines published by Antique Trader Publications:

Antiques & Collectibles Annual Price Guide
Ceramics Price Guide
Toy Trader
Discoveries
Postcard Collector
The Antique Trader Weekly
Collector Magazine & Price Guide
Big Reel
Baby Boomer Collectibles
Military Trader

To order additional copies of this book or other publications listed above, contact:

Antique Trader Publications
P.O. Box 1050
Dubuque, Iowa 52004
1-800-334-7165

Introduction

For twenty-five years The Antique Trader has been publishing a periodical price guide covering the whole realm of antiques and collectibles, first as a semi-annual and then a quarterly publication and then, from 1984 to 1993, a bi-monthly magazine. In 1985 we introduced a single annual edition to compliment the periodical issues and this yearly edition remains a mainstay of our publishing efforts today.

Earlier this year, we broadened our coverage of specialized collecting interests with the release of our new ANTIQUE TRADER BOOKS POTTERY AND PORCELAIN - CERAMICS PRICE GUIDE. This reference focuses on only pieces made from clay including fine porcelain and earthenware, stoneware pottery, Art pottery and 20th century collectible ceramics. We are now pleased to introduce our latest title - ANTIQUE TRADER BOOKS AMERICAN PRESSED GLASS AND BOTTLES PRICE GUIDE. In this volume we offer an in depth guide to all sorts of popular American-made glasswares of the 19th and 20th centuries.

For over sixty years Victorian pressed glass has been a passion for hundreds of collectors and in recent decades, a more diverse range of wares has joined the ranks of collectibility including Carnival glass and Depression glass, and the products of such well known 20th century American manufacturers as Heisey, Cambridge and Imperial.

In this volume we are covering all the most popular categories of glassware produced with the use of molds and machines. In general this includes all types of glasswares, both decorative and useful, which were originally marketed to attract the broadest spectrum of middle class consumers possible. Attractive and relatively inexpensive, such glasswares have been widely available to American housewives since the mid-19th century and have served to brighten the tables and sideboards of this country for generations. Today few of the great old glass-producing firms are still operating in the U.S. and the wares they marketed to our mothers, grandmothers and great-grandmothers are increasingly collectible.

Over 150 years of American glass manufacture are covered in this volume and I hope it will serve today's glass lover well. If, per chance, your favorite line of glass isn't included here, take heart as we are planning a sequel to this work which will cover in depth American and European Art and Decorative Glasswares of the 19th and 20th centuries, everything from

Bohemian to Tiffany and Custard glass to Venini. In the meantime, don't miss the chance to learn about mass-produced bottles and glasswares we're covering here.

My staff and I have worked diligently to gather a wide spectrum of accurate and in-depth descriptions for this expanded volume on American glass and we have also added a large selection of photographs to highlight our listings. To start you off we provide a chapter on "Collecting Guidelines" and a series of sketches of typical forms you may encounter in glass. Our price listings themselves are arranged alphabetically by the name of the type of glass or the producing company and each section begins with a brief introduction to that glassware. Although not many American companies permanently marked their pieces, a few did. So, where applicable, we include a sketch of the company marking or label. To round out our text we provide a "Glossary of Terms" relating to pressed and mold-blown glass and bottles as well as Appendices covering various collector clubs, associations and museums. Finally, we have carefully indexed and cross-referenced all of the listings included in this price guide.

We think you'll find this book a useful and informative guide to one of America's most popular collecting fields. It's hoped that our hard work will pay off in your greater understanding and appreciation of America's glassmaking heritage. In closing I wish to express sincere appreciation to my staff for their hard work and perseverance in producing this book and to Cecil Munsey, Poway, California, for his help in the Bottles section and Ruth Schinestuhl, Marmora, New Jersey, for her work on the Carnival Glass listings. A special thank you goes to Consulting Editors Neila and Tom Bredehoft who have reviewed a number of our categories and offered invaluable insights into how to make this the most comprehensive yet easy-to-use guide available. The Bredehofts are well known in glass collecting circles for their wide ranging knowledge and glass scholarship and it was a real pleasure to work with them on this project.

I hope you'll find this a useful guide to a fascinating and diverse collecting realm. We're always interested in comments from our readers, especially those of constructive critique, and we'll do our best to respond to your requests or suggestions. Sit back now and take an armchair tour of over 200 years of American glassmaking history.

Kyle Husfloen, Editor

Please note: Though listings have been double-checked and every effort has been made to insure accuracy, neither the compilers, editors nor publisher can assume responsibility for any losses that might be incurred as a result of consulting this guide, or of errors, typographical or otherwise.

Photography Credits

Photographers who have contributed to this issue include: E. A. Babka, East Dubuque, Illinois; Stanley L. Baker, Minneapolis, Minnesota; Donna Bruun, Galena, Illinois; Herman C. Carter, Tulsa, Oklahoma; J.D. Dalessandro, Cincinnati, Ohio; Jeff Grunewald, Chicago, Illinois; Kevin McConnell, Pilot Point, Texas; the late Don Moore, Alameda, California; Louise Paradis, Galena, Illinois; and Ruth Schinestuhl, Marmora, New Jersey.

For other photographs, artwork, data or permission to photograph in their shops, we sincerely express appreciation to the following auctioneers, galleries, museums, individuals and shops: The Burmese Cruet, Montgomeryville, Pennsylvania; Burns Auction Service, Bath, New York; Collector's Auction Services, Oil City, Pennsylvania; Collector's Sales and Service, Middletown, Rhode Island; DeFina Auctions, Austinburg, Ohio; T. Ermert, Cincinnati, Ohio; Garth's Auctions, Inc., Delaware, Ohio; Glass-Works Auctions, East Greenville, Pennsylvania; Glick's Antiques, Galena, Illinois; and Grunewald Antiques, Hillsborough, North Carolina.

Also to the Gene Harris Antique Auction Center, Marshalltown, Iowa; the late William Heacock, Marietta, Ohio; The House in the Woods Auction Gallery, Eagle, Wisconsin; International Carnival Glass Assoc., Mentone, Indiana; Jewel Johnson, Tulsa, Oklahoma; Sherry Klabo, Seattle, Washington; Peter Kroll, Sun Prairie, Wisconsin; James Lehnhardt, Galena, Illinois; J. Martin, Mt. Orab, Ohio; Randall McKee, Kenosha, Wisconsin; Jim Ludescher, Dubuque, Iowa; Joy Luke Gallery, Bloomington, Illinois; Dr. James Measell, Berkley, Michigan; Jane Rosenow, Galva, Illinois; Tammy Roth, East Dubuque, Illinois; Robert W. Skinner, Inc., Bolton, Massachusetts; Sotheby's, New York, New York; Temples Antiques, Minneapolis, Minnesota; Lee Vines, Hewlett, New York; Woody Auctions, Douglass, Kansas; The Yankee Peddler Antiques, Denton, Texas; and Yesterday's Treasures, Galena, Illinois.

ON THE COVER: Upper left: Amber Imperial 'Loganberry' pattern 10" h. vase. Lower left: Consolidated 'Dogwood' pattern 10½" h. vase. Lower right: Daisy & Button pattern 7¾" l. canoe in sapphire blue.

Cover design by Jaro Sebek.

Collecting Guidelines

It has been over 25 years since I first became enamored with early American glass and I still remember the piece that set my pulse racing - a tall clear pressed whale oil lamp with a large band of hearts encircling the font. "It's Sandwich," my dealer friend informed me, "and quite rare." I thought it was one of the loveliest antiques I'd seen in my budding collecting career and, if my meager allowance had allowed I would have certainly added it to my collection. However, it was priced out of my range so, as an alternative I soon discovered later 19th century pressed glass and began a collection of this much more affordable and available glassware. Today my love of American glass continues unabated and, although I still have to watch my budget, I've been able to add quite a few nice pieces to my collection.

I will admit that when I first got interested in American glass I found it a very daunting prospect...there are so many types available in so many styles and colors. I wasn't sure I'd ever understand all the intricacies of this diverse field. However, year by year and book by book my understanding and knowledge grew. About the time I first discovered pattern glass the interest in Depression era glassware developed, spurred on by Hazel Marie Weatherman's first book. That reference became one of the first in my library. Soon after I discovered the pioneering works on American pressed glass by Ruth Webb Lee who, in the early 1930s, became the moving force behind the collecting mania for 19th century American pressed glass. Other books on glass and other antiques topics have gradually found their way into my library but it's still a long way from complete.

Anyone who collects anything should know that building a good reference library is vital to the success of your collecting forays and an investment which will pay big dividends over the years. Today there are dozens of fine books available on all types of American glass and there's still glass available in a style and price range to fit nearly every pocketbook. If you are fortunate, like I was, to have a knowledgeable antiques dealer who is also a good friend, you're well ahead of the game. Learning firsthand from a dealer or fellow collector can give you many valuable insights into collecting which books alone may not.

Today there are also any number of national glass collecting clubs which anyone is free to join. These groups have become vital links between collectors and serve as a major source of important research information through their newsletters, books and conventions. The National Early American Glass Club was the first such organization, founded over 60 years ago. It has been joined in the last twenty years by many other groups formed to focus on such popular glasswares as Depression era glass, Heisey, Fostoria, Milk Glass, Cambridge and many others. In a special Appendix at the back of this book we list these clubs for easy reference.

Although each glass collecting topic has its own specialized vocabulary and methodology for collecting, certain guidelines apply to most glass specialties. First and foremost, as I mentioned above, is to begin building your reference library. Second, make contact with others who share your passion and become an avid student of the field. Finally, start out conservatively and try to specialize in one company, pattern, piece or even color of glass. Focusing your collecting is helpful to the novice collector, no matter what your interest, and this is especially true in a field as broad as American glass.

I have found, over the years, that certain factors will affect the collectibility and value of American glass, and they hold true for all types of glass, from Lacy glass to Depression or Lalique to Venini. The first factor is the *condition* of a piece. Glass, unlike ceramic wares, can not be easily and invisibly repaired or restored. Once a piece is chipped or cracked it will stay that way and such damages will greatly affect its market value unless it is exceedingly rare or unique. Buy only perfect pieces, especially if you are just starting out, since they will undoubtedly maintain their value and appreciate over time.

A second factor which determines overall value is *rarity of form*. In glassware very large or very small pieces are often the scarcest, and unusual forms can bring premium prices. For example, in early Lacy glass from the 1820-1850 era, some common clear cup plates can sell for a few dollars since they were produced in such abundance, whereas a rare set of green Cherry Blossom salt and pepper shakers in Depression Glass (ca. 1930s) may bring over $1,000.

It's a matter of the rarity of the piece as well as a third factor of value: *color*. Over the past two hundred years a vast majority of the glass produced for everyday use was made in clear glass and, in fact, early manufacturers strove to make the clearest and brightest glass possible. It wasn't until around the 1880s that it became possible to more inexpensively produce pressed glass in various bright hues. Since then glass tablewares in shades of blue, purple, green, yellow and amber have become more common although clear wares still lead production.

Since it required certain chemicals in the glass batch to produce certain colors, these additives added to the cost of production and some colors, such as a true red, were very difficult to produce. This is still true today and that is why red remains one of the scarcer and most expensive colors to collect in most glass patterns. The popularity of the color blue with the general public has meant that more of it was produced than red, but it is always a choice color for collectors today. The varied hues of purple, green, yellow and amber also have their following, but blue generally leads in collector appeal, no matter what type of glass it is.

Keep in mind, of course, that certain colors or pieces may be rare in one pattern of glass but common in another pattern of the same vintage. Sorting out what makes one piece or pattern unique and desirable is the challenge of glass collecting. This hunt for hidden treasure is one of the great pleasures in any collecting field and the broad realm of American-made glass means the likelihood of making such a discovery is even greater.

The collecting of American glass, no matter the type or age, is an exciting and fascinating pastime but, unfortunately there are some pitfalls which need to be touched upon. The biggest frustration today for collectors and dealers in glass is dealing with reproductions. This is not a new problem but one that continues to haunt us. Luckily for today's collector it is much easier to share information on troublesome pieces using the numerous trade publications, newsletters and magazines which serve the collecting market When author Ruth Webb Lee released her book, ***Antique Fakes and Reproductions,*** over fifty years ago it was one of the few publications to address the problem, especially as it pertains to American 19th century pressed glass. Although no longer in print, Mrs. Lee's pioneering volume is still an invaluable source of information.

In more recent years many other books have been published which deal with this problem. In my 1992 book, ***Collector's Guide to American Pattern Pressed Glass, 1825-1915***, I provided as much detail as possible on what patterns and pieces have been reproduced in pressed glass made before World War I. Other books which have added greatly to this field of knowledge include ***Early American Pattern Glass, 1850-1910 - Major Collectibles Table Settings*** by Bill Jenks and Jerry Luna (Wallace-Homestead, 1990) and a more recent release, ***Identifying Pattern Glass Reproductions, by*** Bill Jenks, Jerry Luna and Darryl Reilly (Wallace-Homestead, 1993). Many other glass categories have been covered in reference books which offer some coverage of reproductions to avoid. For the many collectors interested in Depression era glass, ***The Collector's Encyclopedia of Depression Glass,*** by Gene Florence (Collector Books) is especially helpful in guiding collectors through the repro maze.

Although the thought of being stung by reproductions may at first discourage some new collectors, they should know that it really isn't as big an obstacle to building a fine collection as they may think. Armed with some key reference books and the support and enthusiasm of fellow collectors you can quite easily maneuver your way through that mine field. With the enormous volume of American pressed and mold-blown glass produced in the past 150 years, everyone should be able to find a line of glass that fits their budget and taste. We hope this new book will help prepare you for an exciting and fulfilling collecting career, an adventure sure to bring you hours of satisfaction and enjoyment.

Kyle Husfloen

TYPICAL FORMS
Bowls in Pressed Glass

Candy Dish, 6" - 8" d.

A. Deeply ruffled openwork (latticework) sides with a lightly scalloped rim

B. Footring

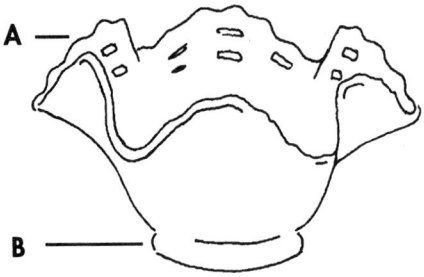

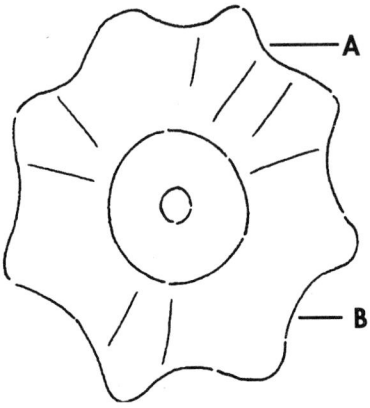

Bowl, 8" to 9" d.

A. Gently ruffled sides with (B.) Smooth rim.

Bowl, 8" to 9" d.

A. Gently ruffled rim

B. Tiny scallops at the edge. A rim with evenly spaced small crimps is sometimes called a "piecrust" rim, while one with multiple rounded looping crimps is sometimes called a "ribbon candy" rim.

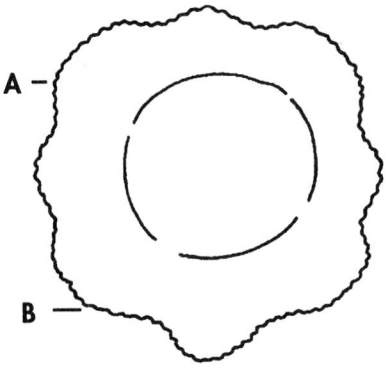

Rose Bowl, 4" d.

A. Incurved (or "closed") rim with small ruffles

B. Spherical, bulbous body

C. Knob feet

TYPICAL FORMS

Creamers & Pitchers
Blown & Pressed Glass

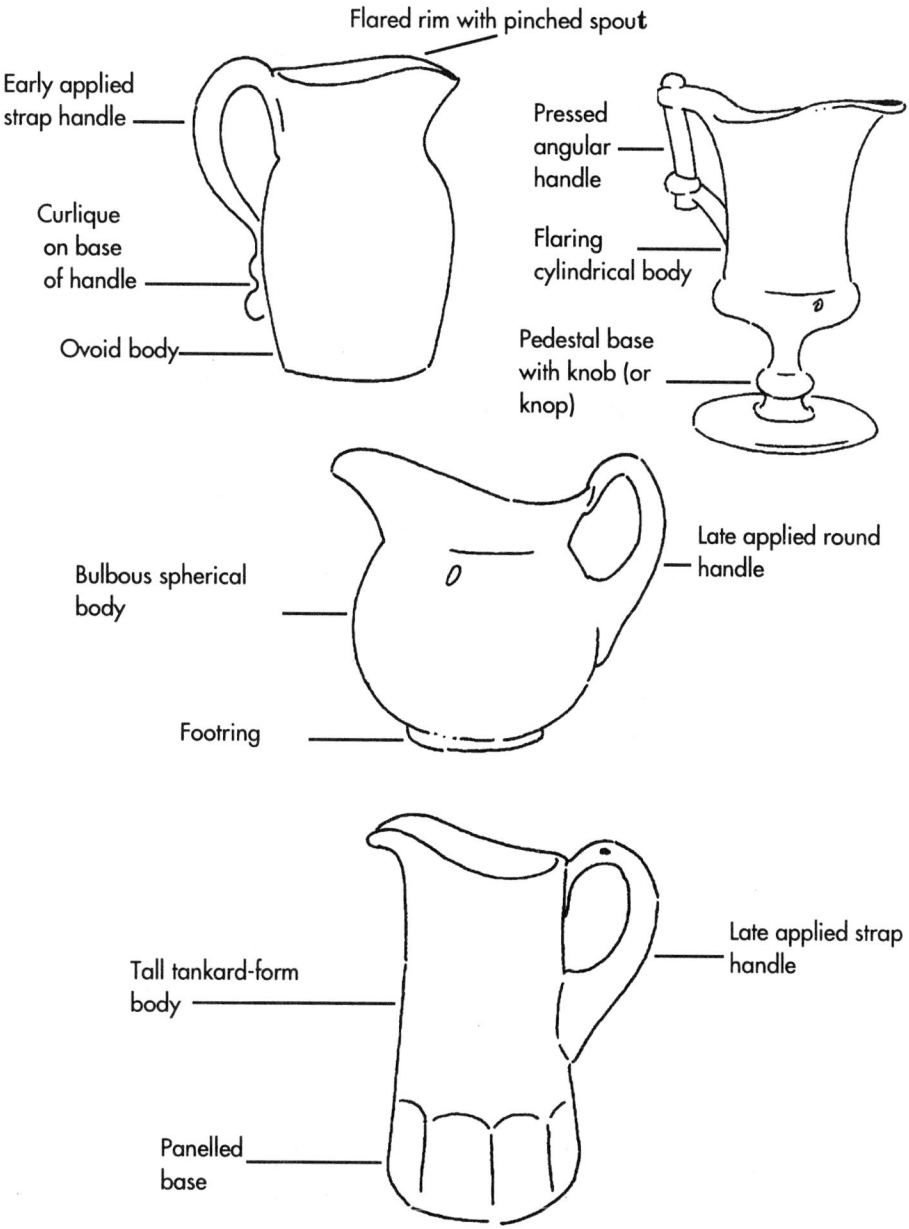

TYPICAL FORMS

Celery Vases, Spillholders & Spooners in Pattern Glass

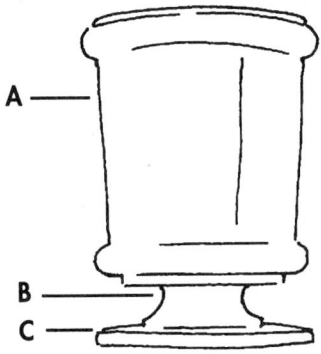

Flint Spillholder (Spooner)
ca. 1850-60, 5" - 5½" h.

A. Heavy, thick nearly cylindrical body
B. Short, thick applied pedestal
C. Thick, round applied foot

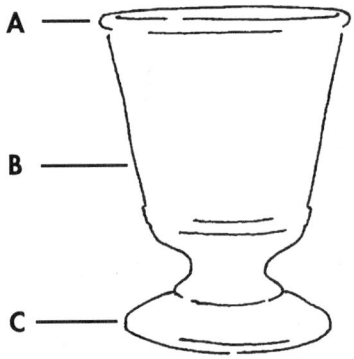

Non-flint Spooner
ca. 1880, 4½" - 6" h.

A. Flaring, flat rim
B. Tapering cylindrical body
C. Short pressed pedestal and round foot

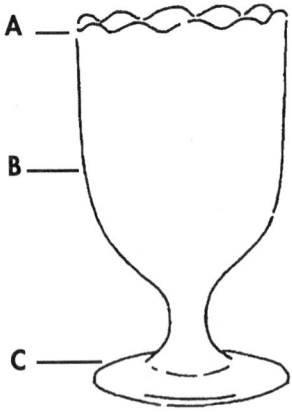

Non-flint Spooner
ca. 1880, 4½" - 6" h.

A. Scalloped rim
B. Bell-form rounded body
C. Slender pressed pedestal on round foot

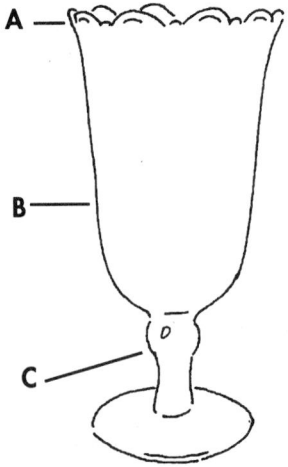

Non-flint Celery Vase
ca. 1885, 8" - 10" h.

A. Flaring and scalloped rim
B. Tall bell-form body
C. Slender pressed pedestal with knob (or knop), on round foot

AKRO AGATE

This glass was made by the Akro Agate Company in Clarksburg, West Virginia between 1932 and 1951. The company was famous for their marble production but also produced many novelty items in various colors of marbleized glass and offered a popular line of glass children's dishes in plain colors and marbleized glass. Most articles bear the company mark of a crow flying through a capital letter A.

Akro Agate Trademark

GENERAL LINE

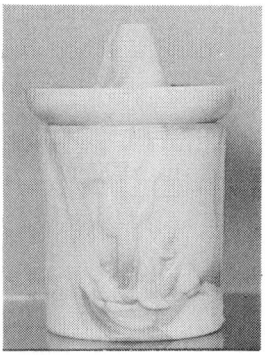

Mexicali Powder Jar

Cup & saucer, demitasse, marbleized orange & white $15.00
Flowerpot, miniature, ribbed rim, green opaque, 2¾" h. 9.00
Flowerpot, miniature, ribbed rim, orange opaque, 2¾" h. 14.00
Flowerpot, scalloped rim, black amethyst, 3" h. 35.00
Flowerpot, scalloped rim, embossed graduated dart decoration, white, No. 297, 3" h. 15.00
Flowerpot, royal blue w/floral decoration, No. 1310 .....75.00
Flowerpot, scalloped rim, cobalt blue, large 18.00
Flowerpot, white w/floral decoration, No. 1311 .....75.00
Jardiniere, ribbed & fluted rim, pumpkin opaque, No. 306CF, 5" h. 30.00
Lamp, marbleized orange & white, 9" h. 65.00
Planter, rectangular, blue w/decoration, No. 653, 8" l. 20.00
Powder jar, Colonial Lady cover, pink opaque, 6¼" h. 75.00
Powder jar, Colonial Lady cover, powder blue opaque base, white cover, 6¼" h. 65.00
Powder jar, Colonial Lady cover, turquoise opaque, 6¼" h. 95.00
Powder jar, cov., Concentric Ring patt., marbleized blue & yellow 22.00
Powder jar, Mexicali w/sombrero cover, marbleized orange & white (ILLUS.) 42.50
Powder jar, Mexicali w/sombrero cover, milk white opaque 40.00
Powder jar, Scottie Dog cover, white opaque 75.00
Smoking set: four ashtrays & cov. box; marbleized green & white, 5 pcs. 35.00
Vase, 6¼" h., scalloped rim, embossed graduated dart decoration, pumpkin opaque, No. 316 ..... 40.00
Vase, 6¼" h., tab handles, marbleized orange & white 30.00

CHILDREN'S DISHES

Bowl, cereal, Interior Panel patt., marbleized green & white 23.50
Bowl, cereal, Interior Panel patt., marbleized oxblood & lemon 35.00
Bowl, cereal, Stacked Disc & Panel patt., transparent cobalt blue 50.00
Creamer, Chiquita patt., transparent cobalt blue 24.50
Creamer, Interior Panel patt., azure blue 30.00
Creamer, large, Octagonal patt., transparent green 6.00
Creamer, small, Raised Daisy patt., yellow opaque 45.00
Cup, small, Interior Panel patt., marbleized blue & white..... 31.00
Cup, Octagonal patt., pumpkin 18.00
Cup, Raised Daisy patt., green opaque 35.00
Cup & saucer, Chiquita patt., transparent cobalt blue 14.50
Cup & saucer, Stippled Band patt., blue opaque 39.00
Plate, dinner, 3¼" d., Interior Panel patt., marbleized blue & white 16.00
Plate, dinner, 3¼" d., Raised Daisy patt., blue opaque 14.50
Plate, dinner, 4¼" d., Concentric Rings patt., transparent cobalt blue 12.00
Plate, dinner, 4¼" d., Interior Panel patt., marbleized green & white 13.00
Plate, dinner, 4¼" d., Interior Panel patt., marbleized oxblood & white.....14.00
Plate, dinner, 4¼" d., Octagonal patt., marbleized green & white 10.00

Saucer, Interior Panel patt., marbleized oxblood & white.....9.00
Sugar bowl, cov., Interior Panel patt., marbleized green & white 42.00
Sugar bowl, cov., Raised Daisy patt., yellow opaque 85.00
Sugar bowl, cov., Stacked Disc & Panel patt., transparent cobalt blue.....85.00
Teapot, cov., Interior Panel patt., marbleized green & white 40.00
Teapot, cov., Octagonal-O patt., marbleized blue & white 23.00
Teapot, cov., Raised Daisy patt., medium blue opaque 52.50
Teapot, cov., Stippled Band patt., blue opaque 75.00
Tumbler, small, Octagonal patt., yellow opaque 10.00
Tumbler, Raised Daisy patt., yellow opaque 26.00
Tumbler, Stacked Disc & Panel patt., transparent cobalt blue, 2" h. 20.00

ANIMALS

Americans evidently like to collect glass animals and, for the past fifty years, American glass manufacturers have turned out a wide variety of animals to please the buying public. Some were produced for long periods and some were later reproduced by other companies, while others were made for only a short period of time and are rare. We have not included late productions in our listings and have attempted to date the productions where possible. Evelyn Zemel's book, American Glass Animals A to Z *will be helpful to the novice collector.*

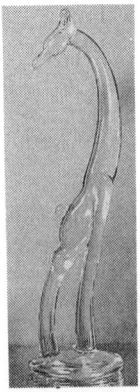

Giraffe by Heisey

Airedale Dog, clear frosted, unmarked, 6½" l., 5¾" h..... $250.00
Angelfish book end, clear, A.H. Heisey & Co., 2¼ x 3½" wave base, 7" h. 115.00
Bear, Mama, clear, New Martinsville Glass Mfg. Co., 6" l., 4½" h. .....165.00 to 180.00
Chinese Pheasant, blue, Paden City Glass Mfg. Co., ca. 1940, 13¾" l., 5¾" h. .....125.00 to 150.00
Deer sitting, clear, Fostoria Glass Co., 1940-43, 1 x 2" base, 2¼" h. 45.00
Deer standing, clear, Fostoria Glass Co., 1 x 2" base, 4½" h. 42.00
Elephant book end, clear, New Martinsville Mfg. Co., 3¼ x 5¼" base, 6¼" l., 5¼" h. 80.00
Elephant figure w/trunk up, clear, A.H. Heisey & Co., 1944-53, large, 6½" l., 4¼" h..... 425.00
Giraffe w/head turned, clear, A.H. Heisey & Co., 1942-52, 11" h.(ILLUS.) .....175.00 to 200.00
Goose, wings up, clear, A.H. Heisey & Co., 1942-53, 7½" l., 6½" h..... 90.00 to 125.00
Hen, clear, A.H. Heisey & Co.,1948-49, 2¾ x 2½" base, 4½" h. 425.00
Horses, Clydesdale, clear, A.H. Heisey & Co., 1942-48, 8" l., 8" h., pr. .....400.00 to 450.00
Horse, Pony ashtray, clear, K.R. Haley, 5½" d. tray, pony 2½" h. at ears 23.00
Horse, Plug (Sparky), clear, A.H. Heisey & Co., 1941-46, 3½" l., 4¼" h.....95.00
Horse, Pony, standing, clear, A.H. Heisey & Co., 1940-52, 1½ x 2¼" base, 3" l., 5" h.....75.00 to 100.00
Horse rearing book ends, clear, A.H. Heisey & Co., 3¼ x 6½ " base, 7¾" h., pr. 235.00
Horse rearing book ends, black, L.E. Smith, 1940s, 3 x 5¼" base, 5¾" l., 8" h., pr. 120.00
Horse Head (double heads) ashtray, clear, A.H. Heisey & Co. 45.00
Horse Head book ends, clear, A.H. Heisey & Co., 1937-55, 2¾ x 4¾" base, 7¼" h., pr.....250.00 to 300.00
Pelican, clear, New Martinsville Glass Mfg. Co., 8¼" h. 85.00
Pouter Pigeon book ends, clear, Cambridge Glass Co., 4 x 5" base, 6" h., pr. 160.00
Pouter Pigeon book ends, clear, Paden City Glass Mfg. Co., 3 x 3¾" base, 6½" h., pr.....140.00
Rabbit, Bunnies, clear, ears up, ears back or ears lying down, New Martinsville Glass Mfg. Co., 1", each .....55.00 to 65.00

Seal w/ball candleholders, clear, New Martinsville Glass Mfg. Co., 7¼" h., pr. ....100.00 to 125.00
Starfish book end, clear, New Martinsville Glass Mfg. Co., 2¾ x 6¼" base, 7¾" h. 50.00
Swan dish, green opalescent, Imperial Swan, Imperial Glass Co., 1930s, 4½" h. 28.00
Swan dish, clear w/cobalt blue neck & head, New Martinsville Glass Co., 11" l. 85.00
Swan figure, wings up, clear, A.H. Heisey & Co., 1947-53, 7" h. ....475.00 to 525.00
Swan figure, Pall Mall patt., clear, Duncan & Miller Glass Co.,10½" h. ...60.00
Swordfish, blue opalescent frosted, Duncan & Miller Glass Co., 3¼" l., 5" h. 395.00
Tiger book end, head up, clear, New Martinsville Glass Mfg.Co., 3¼" x 5¾" base, 6½" h. 165.00
Tiger paperweight, black opaque, Imperial Glass Co. (Heisey mold), 1982-83, 8" l., 2⅔" h. 75.00

BLOWN THREE MOLD

This type of glass was entirely or partially blown in a mold from about 1820 to 1840 in the United States. The object was formed and the decoration impressed upon it by blowing the glass into a metal mold, usually of three but sometimes more sections, hinged together. Mold-blown glass actually dates back to ancient times. Recent research reveals that certain geometric patterns were reproduced in the 1920s and collectors are urged to read all recent information available. Reference numbers are from George L. and Helen McKearin's book, American Glass.

Blown Three Mold Bottle

Bottle, miniature, geometric, chestnut flask-shaped w/flattened sides, sheared & fire-polished lip, clear, 4¼" h., probably GII-2 (slight interior residue) $2,805.00
Bottle, geometric, spherical body tapering to a slender cylindrical neck w/applied collared rim, pale green, 7¾" h., minor interior stain, minor open blisters inside neck, similar to GII-7 (ILLUS.) 3,740.00
Bottle, geometric, barrel-shaped body w/ribbed medial band, slender tall neck w/applied sloping lip, grass green, 8¼" h., GII-7 (slight roughness on bottom) 2,750.00
Bowl, 4⅛" d., 1½" h., geometric, folded rim, sixteen diamond base w/pontil, clear (GII-19) 121.00
Bowl, 4⅛" d., geometric, shallow sides w/folded rim, rayed base, clear (GIII-24) 88.00
Bowl, 4⅞" d., 2½" h., geometric, deep conical sides w/flared & folded rim, sixteen diamond base w/pontil, clear (GII-21) 302.50
Bowl, 5" d., 2" h., overall diamond point design w/folded rim & rayed base, clear (GII-18) 148.50
Bowl, 5 1/16" d., 1⅝" h., geometric, folded rim, rayed base, clear (GIII-21) 88.00
Bowl, 5¼" d., 1¾" h., geometric, shallow rounded sides w/folded rim, rayed base, clear (GIII-21) 143.00
Bowl, 5½" d., 1⅜" h., shallow upright sides w/a folded rim, ringed base w/pontil, clear (GIII-25) 99.00
Bowl, 5½" d., 2" h., geometric, folded rim, rayed base, clear (GIII-20) 99.00
Bowl, 5⅞" d., 1½" h., shallow flaring sides w/folded rim, rayed base w/pontil, clear, shape D-6 (GIII-19) ..121.00
Bowl, 8½" d., 1¼" h., geometric, low sides w/folded rim, clear, probably Boston & Sandwich (GIII-6) 297.00
Bowl, 9" d., 5½" h., geometric, deep rounded sides w/folded rim, on applied round foot, clear, GII-18 (minor wear, small broken blister on bottom interior) 3,630.00
Bowl, 10⅝" d., 1½" h., wide shallow sides w/folded rim, geometric, clear (GIII-5) 990.00
Celery vase, geometric, tall bell-form bowl on an applied foot, clear, 7¼" h. (GII-18) 1,430.00
Celery vase, geometric, cylindrical bowl w/deeply rolled rim, on applied knopped stem & round disc foot, clear, probably Pittsburgh, 7½" h. (GII-27) 1,320.00

Celery vase, tall flaring cylindrical bowl w/molded swirled scrolls, applied knopped stem & round foot, clear, 8¼" h., GV-21 (wear) 1,375.00
Celery vase, geometric, flaring cylindrical shape w/diamond point band design, on applied solid base, clear (GIII-34).....1,200.00
Cologne bottle w/original Tam O'Shanter stopper, swirled ribs, sapphire blue, 5¾" h. (GI-3, type 2).....522.50
Cologne bottle w/old blue Tam O'Shanter stopper, ribbed, deep amethyst (GI-7, type III).....330.00
Cordial, geometric, small tapering conical bowl on an applied round foot, plain rim, clear, 2⅝" h. (GI-6) 302.50
Creamer, toy-size, geometric, applied strap handle, clear, 2⅝" h. 368.50
Creamer, geometric, applied strap handle, brilliant sapphire blue, 3⅞" h. (GIII-24) 2,750.00
Creamer, ovoid body tapering to a flared rim, applied strap handle, geometric, probably Boston & Sandwich, clear, 4" h. (GII-18).....313.50

Blown Three Mold Creamer

Creamer, geometric, ovoid body w/widely flaring rim w/pinched spout, applied strap handle, cobalt blue, 4¼" h., tool mark on tip of spout, GIII-6 (ILLUS.) 1,980.00
Creamer, wide center band of bold ribs flanked by narrow bands, applied strap handle, sapphire blue, 4½" h., GI-29 (roughness at stone in tip of spout) 2,310.00
Cruet stand bottle w/pressed wheel stopper, geometric, bulbous body above a cylindrical base, clear, pint (GII-18) 324.50
Cup plate, geometric, folded rim, rayed base w/pontil, clear, 4¼" d. (GII-16) 142.00
Decanter w/original pressed wheel stopper, miniature, geometric, clear, 3⅞" h., ¼ pint (GIII-21) 418.00
Decanter w/original bulbous ribbed stopper, ribbed sides flank center band w/embossed "BRANd/y," clear (GI-8).....522.50
Decanter w/original Tam O'Shanter stopper, ribbed, purplish blue, 6¼" h. (GI-29) 715.00
Decanter w/Tam O'Shanter stopper, wide ribs on sides & paneled shoulder, Boston & Sandwich, medium greyish blue, half pint (GI-29) 935.00
Decanter w/pressed wheel stopper, geometric, three-ringed neck, clear, 8⅜" h. (GII-18) 192.50

Square Blown Three Mold Decanter

Decanter w/original flattened bulbous stopper, geometric, square sides & paneled shoulders, emerald green, probably Keene, New Hampshire, pinpoint flake on lip, GII-28 (ILLUS.) 4,455.00
Decanter w/original bulbous patterned stopper, swirled ribs w/a body band molded "R U M," clear, quart (GIII-2, type 2).....302.50
Decanter w/original bulbous swirled rib stopper, swirled ribs above a wide body band embossed "BRANDY," flanged lip, clear, quart, GIII-2 (slight interior haze) 385.00
Decanter w/original bulbous patterned stopper, geometric, sixteen molded vertical ribs, three applied neck rings, clear, quart (GIII-5).....990.00
Decanter w/pressed wheel stopper, rounded arch design, flanged & folded rim, clear, 7⅜" h. (GIV-5) 247.50
Decanter w/original bulbous ribbed stopper, baroque, clear, half-pint, GV-8 (slight interior haze).....302.50
Decanter w/original patterned stopper, Gothic arch w/oval panel embossed "G I N," clear, pint (GIV-7).....357.50
Decanter, no stopper, geometric, cylindrical body w/paneling around

bottom edge, diamond quilted w/a wide ringed shoulder tapering to a cylindrical neck w/flared mouth, clear w/distinct brownish amethyst tint, probably New England Glass Company, quart (GII-10) 192.50

Decanter, no stopper, geometric, wide starburst in diamond band between ribbed base & long twisted ribs up the shoulder, Mt. Vernon Glass Works, Vernon, New York, ca. 1830, olive green, quart (GIII-2, type 1) ..2,200.00

Decanter, no stopper, geometric, wide diamond band below swirling ribbing on the shoulder & neck, flattened flared rim, grass green, 8" h. (GIII-2, type 2) 5,720.00

Decanter, no stopper, narrow sloping lip, geometric, olive amber, Keene, New Hampshire, quart (GIII-20)....2,200.00

Dish, footed, geometric, made from a tumbler, flattened sides w/upturned folded rim, clear, ⅝" h. (GII-18).....143.00

Dish, geometric, round w/shallow sides & folded rim, clear, 5¾" d., 1" h. (GII) 93.50

Dish, geometric, round w/shallow sides & folded rim, clear, 6" d., 1⅛" h. (GIII) 66.00

Dish, geometric, round w/low sides & folded rim, clear, 6½" d., 1⅜" h. (GII).....82.50

Dish, geometric, round w/low sides & folded rim, clear, 7¼" d., 2⅛" h. (GIII).....137.50

Dish, round w/low sides & folded rim, ringed base, clear, 5½" d. (GI-6).....132.00

Flip glass, geometric, tapering cylindrical form, clear, 3¾" d., 4½" h. (GII-21) 170.50

Flip glass, geometric, slightly tapering cylindrical form, diamond point band, rayed base, 4¾" d., 5¾" h. (GIII-22) 198.00

Flip glass, geometric, tall slightly flaring cylindrical body, clear, 6" h., GIII-22 (flakes on pontil) 192.50

Flip glass, slightly tapering cylindrical form, geometric, tooled rim, plain base, clear, 4½" d., 6" h. (GIII-22) ...225.50

Inkwell, geometric, low cylindrical form w/rounded edges, clear (GIII-25) ..1,800.00

Inkwell, cylindrical drum shape, geometric, olive amber, 2¼" d., 1½" h. (GIII-29) 176.00

Lamp, whale oil, table-type, a ribbed 'light bulb' shaped font above a ringed knop & an applied pressed lacy octagonal base w/an acanthus leaf design, original tin drop burner, clear, 8" h., GI-7 (unseen chip on underside of base, usual mold roughness) 1,650.00

Pitcher, miniature, 2⅛" h., geometric, applied handle, clear (GIII-12) 550.00

Pitcher, miniature, 3" h., geometric, applied handle, clear (GIII-21) 412.50

Pitcher, 6" h., geometric, wide ovoid body tapering to a flared rim w/pinched spout, applied strap handle, clear, quart (GIII-5).....990.00

Blown Three Mold Pitcher

Pitcher, 6½" h., geometric, ovoid body tapering to a flaring neck w/pinched spout, applied strap handle, clear, GIII-5 (ILLUS.) 1,457.50

Pitcher, 6¾" h., 5" d., Gothic arch, applied strap handle, tooled rings around the mouth, rayed & ringed base w/pontil, clear, GIV-7 (slight residue in bottom) 2,090.00

Pitcher, 7" h., Arch & Fern patt., applied solid handle w/a medial rib & curled end, clear (GIV-6) 950.00

Salt dip, geometric, round bowl w/incurved sides raised on a short applied pedestal foot, cobalt blue, probably Boston & Sandwich, 3⅛" d., 1⅞" h. (GIII-25) 522.50

Salt dip, geometric, round bowl on low pedestal foot, clear, 2" h. (GIII-3).....275.00

Salt dip, miniature, geometric, wide flat-rimmed & flat-sided bowl tapering to an applied foot, clear, 2½" h. (GII-18) 247.50

Salt dip, geometric, cylindrical bowl w/tapering base to applied round foot, cobalt blue, 2⅝" h. (GIII-24)..1,072.50

Salt dip, miniature, geometric, bell-form bowl w/galleried rim, applied foot, clear, 2¾" h. (GII-18) 302.50

Salt dip, geometric, ovoid bowl tapering to a low pedestal w/applied round foot, a widely flaring galleried rim, clear, 2¾" h. (GIII-13).....412.50

Sugar bowl, cov., geometric, cylindrical bowl w/galleried rim raised on a trumpet foot, the tapering domed cover w/a button finial, clear, 5" d., 7¾" h. (GII-21)..3,850.00

Toddy glass, geometric, tapering conical bowl on an applied crimped foot, clear, 4¼" h., GIV-2 (rim lightly ground) 550.00

Tumbler, barrel-shaped, geometric, probably Boston & Sandwich, very pale blue, 3" d., 3⅛" h. (GII-18) 280.50
Tumbler, cylindrical, geometric, clear, 3¼" d., 3¼" h. (GII-18) 143.00
Tumbler, geometric, cylindrical, clear, 3¼" h. (GII-22) 225.50
Tumbler, barrel-shaped, geometric, clear, 3½" h. (GII-21) 209.00
Tumbler, geometric, tapering cylindrical body, clear, 4¾" h. (GIII-16) 99.00
Whimsey, model of a top hat, geometric, wide cylindrical bowl, rolled & folded rim, clear, 2⅞" d., 2" h. (GIII-8) 143.00
Whimsey, model of a top hat, folded rim, geometric, clear, 2¼" h. (GIII)...137.50
Whimsey, model of a top hat, geometric, folded rim, rayed base, clear, 2¼" h. (GIII-3) 495.00
Whimsey, model of a top hat, geometric, tall conical crown, rolled & folded rim, clear, 2⅛" d., 2¼" h. (GIII-4) 176.00
Whimsey, model of a top hat, unrecorded geometric variation, clear, 2⅜" h. (GII-44) 522.50
Whiskey taster, geometric, tapering cylindrical body, tooled rim, clear, 2⅛" h. (GII-16) 110.00
Whiskey taster, geometric, conical body, tooled rim, clear, 2¼" h., GII-19 (two small rim flakes) 88.00
Wine glass, geometric, conical bowl w/ribbed band, applied ringed stem & round foot, clear, 3⅞" h., GI-6 (small ground spot on foot) 253.00
Wine glass, geometric, tapering conical bowl on applied ringed stem & round foot, 3⅞," h. (GII-19).....440.00

BOTTLES & FLASKS

BITTERS

(Numbers with some listings below refer to those used in Carlyn Ring's For Bitters Only.)

African Stomach Bitters, Spruance, Stanley & Co., round, light amber, 9⅝" h.....$125.00
Angostura Bark Bitters, Eagle Liqueur Distiller, globe-shaped, amber, 7" h.....75.00
Atwood (Moses F.) in script - None Genuine Without My Signature, round, aqua, 6¼" h. 25.00
Atwood's - Vegetable Dyspeptic - Bitters, rectangular, aqua, 6¾" h. 85.00
Baker's Orange Grove - Bitters, square w/roped corners, reddish amber, 3 x 9½".....335.00
Beggs' Dandelion Bitters, rectangular w/beveled edges, smooth base, tooled lip, yellow w/olive tone, 7¾" h.....231.00
Berliner Magen Bitters Co., square, amber, 9" h. 260.00
Big Bill Best Bitters, tapering square, golden amber, ca. 1870-90, 12⅛" h.....110.00
Boyce's (Dr.) Tonic Bitters, 12-sided, deep aqua, 7¾" h.....45.00
Brady's (Dr.) Mandrake Bitters, Honesdale, Pennsylvania, paper label only, rectangular, smooth base, tooled lip, clear, 8⅛" h.....77.00
Brown's Celebrated Indian Herb Bitters - Patented 1867, figural Indian Queen, golden amber, 12¼" h.....605.00

Brown's Celebrated Herb Bitters

Brown's Celebrated Indian Herb Bitters - Patented Feb. 11, 1868, figural Indian Queen, medium amber, 12¼" h. (ILLUS.) 550.00
Caldwells Herb Bitters (below) The Great Tonic, triangular, amber, 12⅜" h.....187.00
Caldwell's (Dr.) Herb Bitters (below) The Great Tonic, triangular, golden amber, ca. 1860-80, 12¾" h. 263.00
California Fig Bitters - California Extract of Fig Co., San Francisco, Cal., square, amber, 10" h. 88.00
California Fig & Herb Bitters - California Fig Products Co., San Francisco, Cal., square, amber, 4½" h.....195.00
California Herb Bitters, Pittsburgh, Pa., G.W. Frazier, square, amber, 9½" h.....200.00
Capuziner Stomach Bitters, Spellman Distilling Co., Peoria, Illinois, square, amber, w/paper label, qt., 8¼" h. 500.00
Celebrated Crown Bitters - F.

Chevalier & Co., Sole Agents, square, light honey amber, 2¾ x 8⅞" 265.00
Clotworthy's - Oriental Tonic Bitters, square, amber, 2⅞ x 9½" 345.00
Clotworthy's - Oriental Tonic Bitters, square, honey amber, 2⅞ x 9¾" 285.00
Cole Bros. - Vegetable Bitters - Binghamton N.Y. - G.L. Cole Prop'r, rectangular, aqua, 7⅞" h. 95.00
Demuth's Stomach Bitters, Philada, square, light golden amber, 9⅜" h. ..165.00
Doyle's - Hop - Bitters - 1872 (on shoulders), square, amber, 9⅝" h. 52.00
Drakes Plantation Bitters - Patented 1862, cabin-shaped, five-log, chocolate amber w/a hint of puce, 10" h. (D-109) 275.00
Drakes Plantation Bitters - Patented 1862, cabin-shaped, five-log, golden yellowish amber, 10" h. (D-106) 357.50
Drakes Plantation Bitters - Patented 1862, cabin-shaped, five-log, lemon amber, 10" h. (D-109) 175.00
Drakes Plantation Bitters - Patented 1862, cabin-shaped, five-log, strawberry puce, 10" h. (D-109) 325.00
Drakes Plantation Bitters - Patented 1862, arabesque variant, square w/six embossed logs above label panels, medium puce, 10" h. (D-102) 325.00
Drake's (S T) 1860 Plantation Bitters - Patented 1862, no "X," cabin-shaped, four-log, light honey amber (D-110) 100.00
Drake's (S T) 1860 Plantation Bitters - Patented 1862, no "X," cabin-shaped, four-log, orange amber (D-110) 60.00
Drake's (S T) 1860 Plantation Bitters - Patented 1862, no "X," cabin shaped, four-log, yellow (D-110) 475.00
Drake's (S T) 1860 Plantation Bitters - Patented 1862, no "X," cabin-shaped, six-log, deep puce, 10" h. (D-103) 160.00
Drake's (S T) 1860 Plantation X Bitters - Patented 1862, cabin-shaped, six-log, deep cherry puce, 10" h. (D-105) 93.50
Drake's (S T) 1860 Plantation X Bitters - Patented 1862, cabin-shaped, six-log, deep puce, 10" h., D-105 ....110.00
Drake's (S T) 1860 Plantation X Bitters - Patented 1862, cabin-shaped, six-log, medium amber, 10" h. (D-105) 66.00
Drake's (S T) 1860 Plantation X Bitters - Patented 1862, cabin-shaped, six-log, bright yellow w/hint of olive, 10" h. (D-108) 495.00
Drake's (S T) 1860 Plantation X Bitters - Patented 1862, cabin-shaped, six-log, dark burgundy puce, 10" h. (D-108) 165.00
Drake's (S T) 1860 Plantation X Bitters - Patented 1862, cabin-shaped, six-log, light pinkish puce, 10" h. (D-108) 395.00
Drake's (S T) 1860 Plantation X Bitters - Patented 1862, cabin-shaped, six-log, medium pinkish puce, 10" h. (D-108) 231.00
Eagle Angostura Bark Bitters, globe-shaped, amber, 4" h. 62.50
Electric Bitters - H.E. Bucklen & Co., Chicago, Ill., square, amber, 9⅞" h. 30.00
"Electric" Brand Bitters - H.E. Bucklen & Co., Chicago, Ill., square, original label, amber, 8⅞" h. 25.00
Ferro Quina Bitters, D.P. Rossi, Dogliani, Italia, square, light amber, 1 x 2½" 125.00
Fischs (Doctor) Bitters - W.H. Ware, Patent 1866, figural fish, golden amber, ca. 1860-80, 11¾" h. 308.00
Fischs (Doctor) Bitters - W.H. Ware, Patent 1866, figural fish, light amber, 11¾" h. 225.00
Fischs (Doctor) Bitters - W.H. Ware, Patented 1866, figural fish, medium amber, 11¾" h. 195.00
Fish (The) Bitters - W.H. Ware, Patented 1866, figural fish, medium root beer amber, 11½" h. 165.00
Fisher's N.E. Cough Bitters, Atlanta, GA., rectangular, aqua, 5¾" h. 125.00
Genuine Bull Wild Cherry Bitters, rectangular, clear, 8¾" h. 150.00
Globe (The) Tonic - Bitters, square, golden amber, 9⅝" h. 132.00
Grand Prize Bitters, square, amber, 9¼" h. 325.00
Greeley's Bourbon Bitters, barrel-shaped, ten rings above & below center band, copper puce, 9⅜" h. 264.00
Greeley's Bourbon Bitters, barrel-shaped, ten rings above & below center band, deep wine, 9⅜" h. 412.50
Greeley's Bourbon Bitters, barrel-shaped, ten rings above & below center band, medium smoky puce, 9⅛" h. 357.50
Greeley's Bourbon Bitters, barrel-shaped, ten rings above & below center band, smoky greyish green, 9⅜" h. 1,045.00
Hall's Bitters - E.E. Hall New Haven, Established 1842, barrel-shaped, ten-rib, yellow, 9⅛" h. 210.00
Herb (H.P.) Wild Cherry Bitters, Reading, Pa., square, cabin-shaped w/cherry tree motif & roped corners, golden amber, ca. 1860-80, 10" h. 286.00

Highland Bitters and Scotch Tonic, barrel-shaped, ten-rib, light reddish amber, 9⅝" h. 1,900.00
Holtzermann's - Patent Stomach Bitters, cabin-shaped, stylized logs like hoops on barrels, golden orangish amber, 9¼" h..... 1,800.00

Holtzermans Patent Stomach Bitters

Holtzermans Patent Stomach Bitters (on shoulder), cabin-shaped w/four roofs, golden amber, w/paper label, ca. 1870-90, 9⅝" h. (ILLUS.) 330.00
Home Bitters - St. Louis, Mo. - Prepared Black - Berry Brandy, round, amber, 3¼" d., 11½" h. 250.00
Hostetter's (Dr. J.) Stomach Bitters, square, bright green, 9" h. (H-195) ..475.00
Hostetter's (Dr. J.) Stomach Bitters, square, smooth base, applied mouth, yellow, 9" h. (H-195) 165.00
Iron & Quinine Bitters - Burlington, Vt. - N.K. Brown, rectangular, aqua, 7⅛" h.....190.00
Johnson's Calisaya Bitters - Burlington, Vt., square, collared mouth w/ring, amber, 10" h.....90.00
Kelly's Old Cabin Bitters - Patd March 1870, cabin-shaped, dark root beer amber, 9¼" h. 2,420.00
Kelly's Old Cabin Bitters - Patd March 1870, cabin-shaped, medium amber, 9¼" h. 1,155.00
Kimball's Jaundice - Bitters - Troy, N.H., rectangular, yellowish amber, 7" h.....450.00 to 550.00
King's 25 Cent Bitters, oval, aqua, 6¾" h.....110.00
King Solomon's Bitters, Seattle, Wash., rectangular, 8⅜" h. 75.00
Lacour's Bitters - Sarsapariphere, round, lettering in sunken side panels, lime green, 9" h. 5,060.00
Lacour's Bitters - Sarsapariphere, round, lettering in sunken side panels, yellowish root beer amber, 9" h.....1,650.00
Landsberg (M.G.) Chicago (bitters), square, amber, 11" h. 742.50
Landsberg (M.G.) Chicago (bitters), square, light golden amber, 11" h. ...687.50
Langley's (Dr.) Root & Herb Bitters - 76 Union St., Boston, round aqua.....55.00
Leipziger Burgunder Wein Bitter, The Hockstadter Co., round, green, 11¾" h.....200.00

Litthauer Stomach Bitters

Litthauer Stomach Bitters (paper label), Hartwig Kantorowicz, Posen, Berlin, Hamburg, Germany, square case gin shape, milk white, 9½" h. (ILLUS.) 135.00
Litthauer Stomach Bitters Invented 1864 by Josef Loewenthal, Berlin, square case gin shape, milk white, 9½" h.....176.00
Loew's (Dr.) Celebrated Stomach Bitters & Nerve Tonic - The Loew & Sons Co., Cleveland, O., square, emerald green, 9¼" h. 325.00
Mack's Sarsaparilla Bitters - Mack & Co. Prop'rs. San Francisco, rectangular w/concave corners, medium amber, 9¼" h.....242.00
Mills' Bitters - A.M. Gilman - Sole Proprietor, lady's leg shape, yellowish amber, 11¼" h.....1,540.00
Moffat (John) - Phoenix Bitters - Price $1.00 - New York, rectangular w/wide beveled corners, olive green, ½ pt., 5½" h.....412.50
Moffat (Jno.) - Price $1 - Phoenix Bitters - New York, rectangular w/wide beveled corners, pontil scarred base, applied mouth, olive green, 5½" h. 385.00
National Bitters, embossed "Pat. Applied For" on base, figural ear of corn, amber, 12½" h. 275.00
National Bitters - Patent 1867, figural ear of corn, aqua, 12⅝" h. 3,400.00
National Bitters - Patent 1867, figural ear of corn, deep golden amber, 12⅝" h.....262.00

National Bitters - Patent 1867, figural ear of corn, light shading to medium pinkish puce, 12⅝" h. 3,300.00

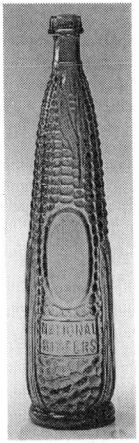

National Bitters

National Bitters - Patent 1867, figural ear of corn, yellowish amber, 12⅝" h. (ILLUS.) 1,265.00
Niagara Star (John W. Steele's), square w/roofed shoulders, three stars on roof & 1864, collared mouth w/ring, golden amber, 10" h. 715.00
Niagara Star (John W. Steele's), square w/roofed shoulders, three stars on roof & 1864, collared mouth w/ring, deep golden amber, 10¼" h. 385.00
Nibol Kidney and Liver Bitters, The Best Tonic Laxative & Blood Purifier, square, amber, 9½" h. 165.00
Old Homestead Wild Cherry Bitters - Patent (on shoulders), cabin-shaped, deep strawberry puce, 9⅞" h. 3,080.00
Old Homestead Wild Cherry Bitters - Patent (on shoulders), cabin-shaped w/shingles, yellowish amber, 9⅞" h. 412.50
Old Sachem Bitters and Wigwam Tonic, barrel-shaped, ten-rib, bright golden amber, ca. 1860-80, 9½" h. 550.00
Old Sachem Bitters and Wigwam Tonic, barrel-shaped, ten-rib, ginger ale yellow, ca. 1860-80, 9½" h. 770.00
Old Sachem Bitters and Wigwam Tonic, barrel-shaped, ten-rib, golden amber, ca. 1860-80, 9½" h. (ILLUS. top next column) 175.00
Old Sachem Bitters and Wigwam Tonic, barrel-shaped, ten-rib, light yellowish amber, 9½" h. 450.00
Old Sachem Bitters and Wigwam Tonic, barrel-shaped, ten-rib, medium copper color, 9½" h. 467.50

Old Sachem Bitters

Old Sachem Bitters and Wigwam Tonic, barrel-shaped, ten-rib, medium orangish amber, 9½" h. 742.50
Old Sachem Bitters and Wigwam Tonic, barrel-shaped, ten-rib, medium pinkish strawberry puce, 9½" h. 715.00
Old Sachem Bitters and Wigwam Tonic, barrel-shaped, ten-rib, orangish amber, 9½" h. 325.00
Old Sachem Bitters and Wigwam Tonic, barrel-shaped, ten-rib, yellowish amber, 9½" h. 154.00
Old Sachem Bitters and Wigwam Tonic, barrel-shaped, ten-rib, aqua, 10⅛" h. 4,620.00
Original Pocahontas Bitters, Y. Ferguson, barrel-shaped w/ten horizontal ribs above & below embossing, narrow square collar, aqua, 2¼" d., 9 5/16" h. 2,695.00
Orruro - Bitters (on shoulders), cylindrical, green, ¾ qt., 10⅝" h. 25.00
Oxygenated for Dyspepsia, Asthma & General Debility, rectangular, aqua, ½ pt., 7⅝" h. 140.00
Pepsin Bitters - R.W. Davis Drug Co., Chicago, U.S.A., rectangular, apple green, 1⅜ x 2¼", 4⅛" h. 200.00
Pepsin Calisaya Bitters, Dr. Russell Med. Co., rectangular, green, pt., 7⅞" h. 105.00
Peruvian Bitters. w/"P.B.Co." monogram in shield, square, amber, 9¼" h. ..... 50.00 to 70.00
Peychaud's American Aromatic Cocktail Bitters (paper label), cylindrical, amber, 6" h. 40.00
Pierce's (Dr. Geo.) - Indian Restorative Bitters - Lowell, Mass, greenish aqua, 7⅞" h. 135.00
(Pineapple), W. & Co., N.Y., pineapple-shaped, bright yellowish green, 8⅞" h. 4,510.00

(Pineapple), W. & Co., N.Y., pineapple-shaped, medium orangish amber, 8⅞" h. 125.00
Reed's Bitters (repeated on shoulder), cylindrical, lady's leg neck, light orange amber, 12½" h. ....250.00 to 300.00
Richardson's (S.O.) - Bitters - South Reading - Mass., rectangular w/wide beveled corners, aqua, pt., 6⅞" h. .....65.00 to 85.00
Richardson's (W.L.) - Bitters - South Reading - Mass., rectangular, aqua, 7" h. 98.00
Roback's (Dr. C.W.) Stomach Bitters, Cincinnati, O, barrel-shaped, golden amber, 9⅜" h. 231.00
Root's (John) Bitters - Buffalo, N.Y. - 1867 (on two sides), rectangular, amber, 9¾" h. 1,595.00
Royal Italian Bitters, Registered, Trade Mark, A.M.F. Gianella, Genova, round, brilliant medium amethyst, 2¾" d., 13½" h. (some minor interior wear) 484.00
Royal Italian Bitters, Registered, Trade Mark, A.M.F. Gianella, Genova, round, light to medium pinkish amethyst, 2¾" d., 13½" h. 2,640.00
Royal Italian Bitters, Registered, Trade Mark, A.M.F. Gianella, Genova, round, pinkish amethyst, 2¾" d., 13½" h. 990.00
Royce's Sherry Wine Bitters, rectangular, smooth base, aqua, 8" h. 90.00
Rush's - Bitters - A.H. Flanders M.D., New York, square, amber, 8⅞" h. 40.00
Russ' St. Domingo Bitters - New York, rectangular, light yellowish amber, 9⅞" h. 275.00
Sanborn's Kidney and Liver Vegetable Laxative Bitters, rectangular, amber, 10" h. 150.00
Sazarac Aromatic Bitters, lady's leg neck, milk white, 10⅛" h. 522.50
Sazarac Aromatic Bitters, w/"PHD & Co." monogram, lady's leg neck, milk white, 12½" h. .....225.00 to 250.00
Schroeder's Bitters, Louisville, KY - S. B. & G. Co., lady's leg neck, tooled lip, smooth base, orangish amber, 9" h. 467.50
Severa (W.F.) - Stomach Bitters, square, amber, 9⅝" h. 70.00
Simon's Centennial Bitters - Trade Mark, figural bust of Washington on pedestal, aqua, ¾ qt., 9¾" h. 650.00
Solomons' Strengthening & Invigorating Bitters - Savannah, Georgia, square, cobalt blue, 3/16" stress crack, 9⅝" h. (S-140) 1,072.00
Specialitat Richter's Rossbacher Magen Bitter, Patentamtlich Christof Richter & Bruder, Hof in Baiern, applied mouth, smooth base, olive green, 11" h., ca. 1870-80 (tiny flake on one corner) 231.00
Swiss - Stomach Bitters - WM. F. Zoeller - Pittsburgh, PA., w/paper label, rectangular, applied mouth, smooth base, yellowish amber, 9¼" h. 220.00

Tippecanoe Bitters

Tippecanoe (birch bark & canoe motif), H.H. Warner & Co., cylindrical, amber, 9" h. (ILLUS.) .....80.00 to 100.00
Tonic Bitters, J.T. Higby, Milford, Ct., square, amber, 9½" h. 55.00
Von Hopfs (Dr.) - Curacoa Bitters - Chamberlain & Co., Des Moines Iowa, rectangular, amber, w/labels, ½ pt., 7½" h. .....60.00 to 80.00
Wakefield's Strengthening Bitters, rectangular w/beveled corners, aqua, 8" h. 70.00
Wear & Upham & Ostrom - Julien's Imperial - Aromatic Bitters, N.Y., lady's leg-shaped, yellowish amber, 12½" h. 3,035.00
Wheeler's - Berlin - Bitters - Baltimore, hexagonal, lettering reading reversed & base to shoulder, iron pontil, yellowish olive green, 9½" h. 7,150.00
Wonser's (Dr.) U.S.A., Indian Root Bitters, round w/fluted shoulder, dark aqua, ¾ qt., 11" h. 3,080.00
Wonser's (Dr.) U.S.A., Indian Root Bitters, round w/fluted shoulder, root beer amber, ¾ qt., 11" h. 4,730.00
Yerba Buena - Bitters, S.F. Cal., flask-shaped, amber, 8½" h. 80.00
Zu Zu Bitters, square, amber, 8⅜" h. 310.00

FIGURALS

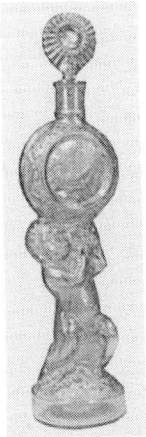

Cherub & Medallion Bottle

Bust of George Washington, applied sloping collared mouth, pontil scar, aqua, 10½" h. 27.50
Busts of three people, two men & one woman, atop of waisted paneled column, probably Europe, ca. 1880-1900, milk white cased in clear, 13½" h. 220.00
Cherub holding a medallion on his shoulder w/pressed wheel stopper in the short cylindrical neck, tooled lip, American-made, ca. 1890-1910, emerald green, 11" h. (ILLUS.) 192.50
Cherub holding a medallion on his shoulder w/pressed wheel stopper in the short cylindrical neck, tooled lip, American-made, ca. 1890-1910, medium purplish amethyst, 11" h. 198.00
Cigar, amber glass, 5¼" l. ....25.00 to 35.00
Cigar, ground top w/screw cap, amber glass 82.50

Dutchman Bottle

Cucumber, horizontal ribbing, pontil scar on one end, applied knob on other, American-made, ca. 1880-1900, medium sapphire blue, 7¾" l. 77.00
Dutchman standing wearing baggy pants, jacket w/kerchief & hat, holding a long pipe, probably from Germany, ca. 1890-1910, amber, 11½" h. (ILLUS. previous column) 825.00
Ham, amber glass 60.00
Klondyke gold nugget flask, milk white glass, 6" h. 62.50
Potato, sponge-daubed earthenware pottery, blue sponging on white, 8" l. 165.00

FLASKS

GI-2 - Washington bust below "General Washington" - American Eagle w/shield w/seven bars on breast, head turned to right, edges w/horizontal beading w/vertical medial rib, plain lip, pontil, aqua, pt. 245.00
GI-19 - "Washington" above bust - "Baltimore Glass Works." in semicircle around Battle Monument, Baltimore, smooth edges, plain lip, pontil, copper w/puce tones, ca. 1830-50, pt. 1,980.00
GI-22 - Washington bust (facing right) below "Baltimore X Glass Works" (all S's reversed) - classical bust facing right, three vertical ribs w/heavy medial rib, plain lip, pontil, clear, ca. 1820-40, pt. 1,210.00
GI-25 - Washington bust (facing right) below "Bridgetown New Jersey," - Classical bust below "Bridgetown New Jersey," plain lip, aqua, qt., 8¼" h., light inside haze 220.00
GI-28 -Washington bust below "Albany Glass Works," "Albany N Y" below bust - full-rigged ship sailing to right, plain lip, vertically ribbed edges, pontil, medium amber, pt. 660.00
GI-34 - "Washington" above bust (facing right) - "Jackson" above bust, plain lip, vertically ribbed edges w/heavy medial rib, pontil, light yellow olive green, ½ pt. 230.00
GI-37 - Washington bust below "The Father of His Country" - Taylor bust, "Gen. Taylor Never Surrenders, Dyottville Glass Works, Philad.a," smooth edges, plain lip, pontil, citron, qt. 375.00
GI-37 - Washington bust below "The Father of His Country" - Taylor bust, "Gen. Taylor Never Surrenders, Dyottville Glass Works, Philad.a," plain lip, smooth edge, pontil, topaz, qt. 1,450.00

GI-40 - Washington bust below "The Father of His Country" - Taylor bust, "Gen. Taylor Never Surrenders," smooth edges, sheared lip, pontil, aqua, pt. 70.00

GI-40 - Washington bust below "The Father of His Country" - Taylor bust, "Gen. Taylor Never Surrenders," smooth edges, sheared lip, pontil, bright medium green, pt. 253.00

GI-42 - Washington bust below "The Father of His Country" - Taylor bust, "A little More Grape Captain Bragg, Dyottville Glass Works, Philad.a," smooth edges, plain lip, pontil, aqua, qt. 85.00

GI-42 - Washington bust below "The Father of His Country" - Taylor bust, "A little More Grape Captain Bragg, Dyottville Glass Works, Philad.a," smooth edges, plain lip, pontil, cobalt blue, ca.1840-60, qt. 3,740.00

GI-42 - Washington bust below "The Father of His Country" - Taylor bust, "A little More Grape Captain Bragg, Dyottville Glass Works, Philad.a," smooth edges, plain lip, pontil, peacock blue, qt. 325.00

GI-43 - Washington bust below "The Father of His Country" - Taylor bust below "I Have Endeavour,d To Do My Duty," plain lip, smooth edges, pontil, dark golden amber, ca. 1840-60, qt. 1,210.00

GI-43 - Washington bust below "The Father of His Country" - Taylor bust below "I Have Endeavour,d To Do My Duty," plain lip, smooth edges, pontil, yellow w/slight olive tone, ca. 1840-60, qt. 495.00

GI-65 - "General Jackson" surrounding bust - American Eagle w/shield on oval frame, "J.T. & Co." below oval frame, thirteen small five-pointed stars above eagle, horizontal beading w/vertical medial rib, plain lip, pontil mark, aqua, 1829-32, pt. 363.00

GI-77 - Taylor bust below "Rough & Ready" - American Eagle w/shield w/eight vertical & three horizontal bars on breast, head turned left, "Masterson" above 13 five-pointed stars above eagle, plain lip, open pontil, aqua, ca. 1830-40, qt. 1,045.00

GI-80 - "Lafayette" above & "T.S." & bar below - "DeWitt Clinton" above bust & "Coventry C-T" below, plain lip, horizontally corrugated edges, pontil, light yellowish olive, ca. 1824-25, pt. 630.00

GI-80 - "Lafayette" above bust & "T.S." & bar below - "DeWitt Clinton" above bust & "Coventry C-T" below, plain lip, horizontally corrugated edges, pontil, yellowish olive, ca. 1824-25, pt. 550.00

GI-85 - "Lafayette" above bust & "Covetry (sic) - C-T" below - French liberty cap on pole & semicircle of eleven five-pointed stars above, "S & S" below, fine vertical ribbing, two horizontal ribs at base, plain lip, pontil mark, yellowish olive, ca. 1824-25, pt. 242.00

GI-86 - "Lafayette" above bust & "Coventry - C-T" below - French liberty cap on pole & semicircle of eleven five-pointed stars above, "S & S" below, fine vertical ribbing, two horizontal ribs at base, plain lip, pontil mark, yellowish olive green, ca. 1824-25, ½ pt. 440.00

GI-92 - Lafayette bust facing right below Masonic Arch & a fleur-de-lis, "Genl Lafayette" along sides - American Eagle w/shield on breast below seven stars all in an oval & "Wheeling" in semicircle above upper part of panel & "Knox & McKee" in semicircle around lower panel, smooth edges, plain lip, pontil mark, brilliant pale green, ca. 1820-40, pt. 4,070.00

GI-95 - Franklin bust below "Benjamin Franklin" - Dyott bust below "T.W. Dyott, M.D.," three vertical ribs w/heavy medial rib, plain lip, pontil mark, aqua, ca. 1820-40, pt. 242.00

GI-96 - Franklin bust below "Benjamin Franklin" - Dyott bust below "T.W. Dyott, M.D.," edges embossed "Eripuit Coelo Fulmen. Sceptrumque Tyrannis" and "Kensington Glass Works, Philadelphia," plain lip, pontil, aqua, qt. 200.00

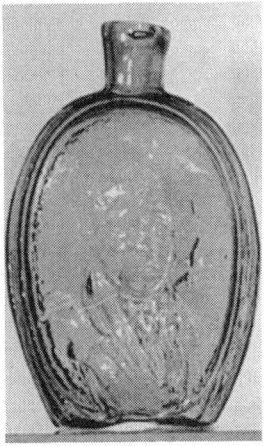

Benjamin Franklin Flask

GI-98 - Franklin bust below "Benjamin Franklin" - "Wheeling Glassworks" in semi-circle above bust of Thomas Dyott, vertically ribbed edges, plain neck, aqua, pt. (ILLUS.) 2,750.00

GI-104 - "Jeny (sic) Lind" above bust - View of Glasshouse, calabash, vertically ribbed edges, rounded collar, pontil, brilliant light powder blue, ca. 1845-60, qt. 396.00

GI-113 - "Kossuth" above bust - tall tree in foliage, calabash, smooth edges, iron pontil, light greyish blue, ca. 1840-60, qt. 495.00

American Eagle Flask

GII-1a - American Eagle on oval, head turned to right & 10 stars in semi-circle above eagle (eight 5-pointed stars & two 6-pointed stars) obverse & reverse, beaded edges w/narrow vertical medial rib, plain sheared lip, open pontil, amber, pt. (ILLUS.) 23,650.00

GII-6 - American Eagle w/head turned right on oval w/inner band of tiny pearls, nine pearls above eagle - large Cornucopia with Produce, horizontally ribbed edges, plain lip, greenish aqua, pt. 250.00

GII-18 - American Eagle w/head turned to right above oval frame enclosing "Zanes - Ville" - Cornucopia with Produce, vertically ribbed edges, plain lip, pontil mark, aqua, ½ pt. 30.50

GII-23 - American Eagle above oval, ribbon & two semi-circular rows of stars above, oval w/elongated eight-point star - large floral medallion above oval containing an elongated eight-pointed star, edges corrugated horizontally w/vertical medial rib, plain lip, pontil, aqua, ca. 1850-55, pt. 495.00

GII-26 - American Eagle above stellar motif obverse & reverse, horizontally corrugated edges, plain lip, aqua, qt. 115.00

GII-30 - American Eagle in a small circular medallion obverse & reverse, overall heavy vertical ribbing except for medallions, plain lip, pontil, brilliant aqua, ca. 1855-60, ½ pt. 374.00

GII-31 - American Eagle in large oval medallion obverse & reverse, overall heavy vertical ribbing except for medallions, pontil, aqua, qt. 180.00

GII-48 - American Eagle on oval - American flag w/"Coffin & Hay." above & "Hammonton" below, vertically ribbed edges, plain lip, pontil, aqua, qt. 190.00

GII-61 - American Eagle below "Liberty" - inscribed in four lines, "Willington - Glass, Co - West Willington - Conn," smooth edges, deep olive green, qt. 187.00

GII-61 - American Eagle below "Liberty" - inscribed in four lines, "Willington - Glass, Co - West Willington - Conn," smooth edges, orange amber, ca. 1860-72, qt. 209.00

GII-62 - American Eagle below "Liberty" - "Willington Glass, Co West, Willington Conn," smooth edges, plain lip, emerald green, ca. 1860-72, pt. 330.00

GII-62 - American Eagle below "Liberty" - "Willington Glass, Co West, Willington Conn," smooth edges, plain lip, reddish amber, pt. ..308.00

GII-63 - American Eagle below "Liberty" - inscription in five lines, "Willington - Glass - Co - West Willington - Conn.," smooth edges, plain lip, deep reddish amber, ½ pt. 198.00

GII-64 - American Eagle below "Liberty" - inscription in four lines, "Willington - Glass, Co - West Willington - Conn," smooth edges, plain lip, pontil, golden amber, pt. 187.00

GII-65 - American Eagle below "Liberty" - inscribed in five lines "Westford - Glass - Co - Westford - Conn.," smooth edges, plain lip, deep yellowish olive, ca. 1860-73, ½ pt. 253.00

GII-67 - American Eagle below nine five-pointed stars standing on large laurel wreath - large anchor w/"New London" in a banner above & "Glass Works" in a banner below, smooth edges, plain lip, pontil, aqua, ca. 1860-66, ½ pt. 286.00

GII-67 - American Eagle below nine five-pointed stars standing on large laurel wreath - large anchor w/"New London" in a banner above & "Glass Works" in a banner below, smooth edges, plain lip, pontil, medium orangish amber, ½ pt. 467.50

GII-68 - American Eagle in flight below seven five-pointed stars - large anchor w/"New London" in a banner above & "Glass Works" in a banner below, smooth edges, plain lip, pontil, bright orangish amber, ca. 1860-66, pt. 467.50

GII-70 - American Eagle lengthwise obverse & reverse, vertically ribbed edges, plain lip, pontil, yellowish olive, ca. 1830-48, pt. 165.00

GII-71 - American Eagle lengthwise obverse & reverse, vertically ribbed edges, plain lip, pontil, bright yellowish olive, ½ pt. 176.00

GII-73 - American Eagle w/head turned to the right & standing on rocks - Cornucopia with Produce & "X" on left, vertically ribbed edges, plain lip, pontil, deep golden yellow, pt. 220.00

GII-105 - American Eagle above oval obverse & reverse, w/"Pittsburgh, Pa." in oval obverse & reverse, narrow vertical ribbing on edges, sheared lip w/applied flat collar, smooth base, deep green, pt. 250.00

GII-106 - American Eagle above oval obverse & reverse, w/"Pittsburgh, PA" in oval on obverse, narrow vertical rib on edges, honey amber, pt. 185.00

GII-115 - American Eagle above oval obverse & reverse, w/"Louisville KY." in oval obverse & "Glass Works" in oval on reverse, narrow vertical ribbing on edges, applied rounded collar & seamed base w/depression, aqua, pt. 195.00

GIII-1 - Cornucopia with Produce surrounded by an oval beaded panel - large circular beaded medallion enclosing a star-shaped design w/six ribbed points & a small eight-petaled rosette center, above a symmetrical palm motif, edges w/horizontal beading, plain lip, pontil mark, pale yellowish green, ca. 1820-40, ½ pt. 412.50

GIII-2 - Cornucopia with Produce obverse & reverse, vertically ribbed edges, sheared, tooled lip, pontil, aqua, ½ pt. 105.00

GIII-4 - Cornucopia with Produce - Urn with Produce, vertically ribbed edges, plain lip, pontil, bright medium green, pt. (some exterior high point wear, inner mouth flake)..319.00

GIII-7 - Cornucopia with Produce - Urn with Produce, vertically ribbed edges, sheared lip, pontil, aqua, ½ pt. 126.50

GIII-12 - Cornucopia with Produce & curled to right - Urn with Produce, plain lip, vertically ribbed edges, pontil, yellowish olive, ½ pt. 88.00

GIII-16 - Cornucopia with Produce & curled to right - Urn with Produce & w/"Lancaster.Glass.Works N.Y" above, sheared mouth, vertically ribbed edges, iron pontil, yellowish olive amber, pt. 770.00

GIV-1 - Masonic Emblems - American Eagle w/ribbon reading "E Pluribus Unum" above & "IP" (old-fashioned J) below in oval frame, tooled mouth, five vertical ribs, bright bluish green, pt. .....275.00 to 300.00

GIV-1 - Masonic Emblems - American Eagle w/ribbon reading "E Pluribus Unum" above & "IP" (old-fashioned J) below in oval frame, tooled mouth, five vertical ribs, medium bluish green, pt. 192.50

GIV-3 - Masonic Emblems - American Eagle w/heavily crimped ribbon above & "J.K. - B." below in oval frame, tooled lip, five vertical ribs, light bluish green, pt. 412.50

GIV-7 - Masonic Arch - American Eagle holding shield w/twelve dots (representing stars), open pennant ribbon above, oval frame w/eight-pointed star below, vertically ribbed sides, pontil, aqua, pt. 220.00

GIV-14 - Masonic Arch, pillars & pavement w/Masonic emblems inside the arch - American Eagle above oval frame w/elongated eight-pointed star, plain rim, vertically ribbed sides, light green, ½ pt. 440.00

GIV-17 - Masonic Arch, pillars & pavement w/Masonic emblems - American Eagle w/oval frame enclosing "KEENE" below, edges smooth w/single vertical rib, plain lip, pontil, olive green, pt. 187.50

GIV-20 - Masonic Arch, pillars & pavement w/Masonic emblems - American Eagle w/"KCCNC" in oval frame below, edges w/single vertical rib, plain lip, pontil, yellowish olive, pt. 165.00

GIV-24 - Masonic Arch, pillars & pavement w/Masonic emblems - American Eagle grasping large balls in talons & without shield on breast, plain oval frame below, smooth edges w/single medial rib, plain lip, pontil, bright light yellow amber, ½ pt. 132.00

GIV-24 - Masonic Arch, pillars & pavement w/Masonic emblems - American Eagle grasping large balls in talons & without shield on breast, plain oval frame below, smooth edges w/single medial rib, plain lip, pontil, light yellowish olive green, ½ pt. 187.00

GIV-27 - Masonic Arch, pillars & pavement w/Masonic emblems & radiating triangle enclosing the letter "G" - American Eagle w/"NEG Co" in oval frame below, vertically ribbed edges, tooled lip, pontil mark, light green, pt. 325.00

GIV-32 - Masonic Arch w/"Farmer's Arms," sheaf of rye & farm implements within arch - American Eagle, w/shield w/seven bars on breast, head turned to right, "Zanesville" above, eagle stands on oval frame w/"Ohio" inside & "J. Shepard & Co." beneath, vertically ribbed edges, open pontil, amber, pt. 330.00

GIV-32 - Masonic Arch w/"Farmer's Arms," sheaf of rye & farm implements within arch - American Eagle, w/shield w/seven bars on breast, head turned to right, "Zanesville" above, eagle stands on oval frame w/"Ohio" inside & "J. Shepard & Co." beneath, vertically ribbed edge, open pontil, aqua, pt. ....225.00 to 250.00

GIV-32 - Masonic Arch w/"Farmer's Arms," sheaf of rye & farm implements within arch - American Eagle w/shield w/seven bars on breast, head turned to right, "Zanesville" above, eagle stands on oval frame w/"Ohio" inside & "J. Shepard & Co." beneath, vertically ribbed edge, open pontil, golden yellow w/olive tone, ca. 1820-30, pt. 1,980.00

GIV-34 - Masonic Arch w/"Farmer's Arms," sheaf of rye & farm implements within arch & "Kensington Glass Works Philadelphia" around edge - Sailing frigate above "Franklin" w/"Free Trade and Sailors Rights" around edge, aqua, pt. 192.50

GIV-36 - Masonic Arch w/"Farmer's Arms," sheaf of rye & farm implements within arch - full rigged frigate sailing to right, "Franklin" below, edges horizontally beaded w/medial rib, plain lip, pontil, aqua, pt. 550.00

GV-3 - "Success to the Railroad" around embossed horse pulling cart - similar reverse, sheared lip, pontil, yellowish olive amber, pt. 132.00

GV-3 - "Success to the Railroad" around embossed horse pulling cart - similar reverse, sheared lip, pontil, yellowish olive green, pt. 627.00

GV-5 - "Success to the Railroad" around embossed horse pulling cart - similar reverse, plain lip, pontil, vertically ribbed edges, aqua, ca. 1840-60, pt. 374.00

GV-5 - "Success to the Railroad" around embossed horse pulling cart - similar reverse, plain lip, pontil, vertically ribbed edges, forest green, ca. 1840-60, pt. 247.50

GV-6 - "Success to the Railroad" around embossed horse pulling cart obverse & reverse, w/"Success" above scene, plain lip, pontil, vertically ribbed edges, golden amber, ca. 1840-60, pt. 198.00

GV-6 - "Success to the Railroad" around embossed horse pulling cart obverse & reverse, w/"Success" above scene, plain lip, pontil, vertically ribbed edges, olive amber, pt. 192.50

GV-6 - "Success to the Railroad" around embossed horse pulling cart obverse & reverse, w/"Success" above scene, plain lip, pontil, vertically ribbed edges, yellowish olive ca. 1830-48, pt. 253.00

GV-8 - "Success to the Railroad" around embossed horse pulling cart - large American Eagle w/head turned left & holding a shield w/seven vertical & two horizontal bars on breast, seventeen large five-pointed stars surround eagle, three vertically ribbed edges w/heavy medial rib, plain lip, pontil mark, yellowish olive amber, pt. 165.00

GV-9 - "Success to the Railroad" around embossed horse pulling cart - large eagle & seventeen five-pointed stars, vertically ribbed edges w/heavy medial rib, plain lip, pontil mark, bright yellowish olive, pt. 264.00

GV-9 - "Success to the Railroad" around embossed horse pulling cart - large eagle & seventeen five-pointed stars, vertically ribbed, heavy medial rib, plain lip, pontil mark, deep olive green, pt. 192.50

GV-9 - "Success to the Railroad" around embossed horse pulling cart - large eagle & seventeen five-pointed stars, vertically ribbed, heavy medial rib, plain lip, pontil mark, medium olive amber, pt. 176.00

GV-10 - "Railroad" above horse-drawn cart on rail & "Lowell" below - American Eagle lengthwise & 13 five-point stars, vertically ribbed edges , sheared lip, pontil , yellowish olive, ½ pt. 253.00

GVI-2 - "Balto" below monument - "Fells" above & "Point" below a small sloop w/pennant flying & sailing to the right, vertically ribbed edges w/three heavy medial ribs, plain lip, pontil mark, pale aqua, ½ pt. 247.50

GVI-4a - Washington Monument in large oval panel - "Corn For The World" in semicircle above ear of corn, plain lip, smooth edges, aqua, qt. (flake on mouth) 275.00

GVIII-2 - Sunburst w/twenty-four triangular sectioned rays obverse & reverse, plain lip, pontil, clear, ca. 1826-30, pt. 687.50

GVIII-2 - Sunburst w/twenty-four triangular sectioned rays obverse & reverse, plain lip, pontil, light green, ca. 1815-30, pt. 440.00

Scarce Sunburst Flask

GVIII-3 - Sunburst w/twenty-four rounded rays obverse & reverse, horizontal corrugated edges, plain lip, pontil mark, olive amber, pt. (ILLUS.) 605.00

GVIII-5 - Sunburst w/twenty-four rounded rays obverse & reverse, horizontal corrugated edges, plain lip, pontil mark, bright yellowish olive, ca. 1815-30, pt 880.00

GVIII-8 - Sunburst w/twenty-eight triangular sectioned rays obverse & reverse, center raised oval w/"KEEN" on obverse & w/"P & W" on reverse, pontil, yellowish olive, pt. 247.50

GVIII-9 - Sunburst w/twenty-nine triangular sectioned rays obverse & reverse, center raised oval w/"KEEN" reading from top to bottom on obverse & w/"P & W" on reverse, sheared lip, pontil, olive green, ½ pt. ....250.00 to 300.00

GVIII-9 - Sunburst w/twenty-nine triangular sectioned rays obverse & reverse, center raised oval w/"KEEN" reading from top to bottom on obverse & w/"P & W" on reverse, sheared lip, pontil, yellowish olive, ca. 1815-30, ½ pt. 258.50

GVIII-16 - Sunburst w/twenty-one triangular sectioned rays obverse & reverse, plain lip, open pontil, bright yellowish olive green, ca. 1815-30, ½ pt. 286.00

GVIII-18 - Sunburst w/twenty-four rounded rays obverse & reverse, horizontal corrugated edges, plain lip, pontil mark, olive green, ½ pt. 275.00

GVIII-18 - Sunburst w/twenty-four rounded rays obverse & reverse, horizontal corrugated edges, plain lip, pontil mark, yellowish olive amber, ca. 1815-30, ½ pt. 577.50

GVIII-18 - Sunburst w/twenty-four rounded rays obverse & reverse, horizontal corrugated edges, plain lip, pontil mark, yellowish olive green, ½ pt. 302.50

GVIII-22 - Sunburst w/thirty-six slender rays forming a scalloped ellipse w/five small oval ornaments in center obverse & reverse, smooth sides, pontil, pale green, pt. 159.50

GVIII-25 - Sunburst w/twenty-four slender rays tapering to rounded ends obverse & reverse, five oval-shaped ornaments forming five-petaled flower in middle of sunburst, plain lip, pontil, aqua, ½ pt. 192.50

GVIII-25 - Sunburst w/twenty-four slender rays tapering to rounded ends obverse & reverse, five oval-shaped ornaments forming five-petaled flower in middle of sunburst, plain lip, pontil, medium to deep burgundy, ½ pt. 3,960.00

GVIII-28 - Sunburst w/sixteen rays obverse & reverse, rays converging to a definite point at center & covering entire side of flask, horizontally corrugated edges, plain lip, open pontil, light aqua, ½ pt. 220.00

GVIII-29 - Sunburst in small sunken oval w/twelve rays obverse & reverse, panel w/band of tiny ornaments around inner edge, entire flask except panels covered w/heavy, narrow widely spaced vertical ribbing, pontil, deep aqua, ¾ pt. ....300.00 to 315.00

GVIII-29 - Sunburst in small sunken

oval w/twelve rays obverse & reverse, panel w/band of tiny ornaments around inner edge, entire flask except panels covered w/heavy, narrow widely spaced vertical ribbing, pontil, greenish aqua, ¾ pt. 140.00

GVIII-29 - Sunburst in small sunken oval w/twelve rays obverse & reverse, panel w/band of tiny ornaments around inner edge, entire flask except panels covered w/heavy, narrow, widely spaced vertical ribbing, pontil, medium bluish green, ¾ pt. .....165.00 to 185.00

GIX-2 - Scroll w/two six-point stars obverse & reverse, vertical medial rib, long neck w/plain lip, deep sapphire blue, qt., 9" h. (small mouth flake) 2,310.00

GIX-6 - Scroll w/two six-point stars obverse & reverse, one side w/"Louisville KY," the other w/"Glassworks," vertical medial rib, plain lip, pontil mark, light yellowish green, qt. 269.50

GIX-10 - Scroll w/two eight-point stars obverse & reverse, golden amber, ca. 1840-60, pt. 352.00

GIX-10 - Scroll w/two eight-point stars obverse & reverse, golden amber w/olive tones, ca. 1840-60, pt. 385.00

GIX-10c - Scroll w/two eight-point stars, a small one in upper space & medium sized one in midspace obverse - seven-point upper star reverse, vertical medial rib, plain neck, bluish green, ½ pt. 352.00

GIX-11 - Scroll w/two eight-point stars obverse & reverse, emerald green, pt. (minor interior stain) 935.00

GIX-11 - Scroll w/two eight-point stars obverse & reverse, golden amber, pt. 319.00

GIX-11 - Scroll w/two eight-point stars obverse & reverse, sapphire blue, pt. (pinpoint flakes) 1,760.00

GIX-12 - Scroll w/two seven-point stars above "Louisville" in straight line near base obverse & reverse, vertical medial rib, plain neck, bright medium olive green, ca. 1840-60, pt. 605.00

GIX-14 - Scroll w/two six-pointed stars above seven-pointed star obverse & reverse, vertical medial on edge, plain lip, pontil, aqua, pt. 82.50

GIX-20 - Scroll w/large oval ornament above large eight-point star above large six-petaled flower obverse & reverse, vertical medial rib, plain lip, pontil, medium green, pt. ...192.50

GIX-27 - Scroll w/two eight-point large stars in upper & mid-space w/slightly sunken rectangular panel near base obverse - a large nine-point star above large eight-point star reverse, vertical medial rib, plain neck, aqua, pt. 660.00

Early Scroll Flasks

GIX-34 - Scroll w/large eight-point star above a large pearl over a large fleur-de-lis obverse & reverse, vertical medial rib on edge, tooled broad rounded collar w/lower bevel, iron pontil, aqua, ½ pt., rough lip, 5⅝" h. ((ILLUS. left) 55.00

GIX-34a - Scroll w/large eight-point star above a medium-sized pearl over a large fleur-de-lis similar to obverse w/very small pearl, vertical medial rib, plain lip, aqua, ½ pt. 104.50

GIX-36 - Scroll w/medium-sized eight-point star above a large fleur-de-lis & a medium-sized pearl below obverse & reverse, vertical medial rib on edge, tooled broad collar w/lower bevel, iron pontil, aqua, ½ pt., 5⅞" h. (ILLUS. right) 93.50

GIX-39 - Scroll w/knobbed shoulder & nine-petaled flower at top & embossed initials "BP & B" near bottom obverse & reverse, vertical medial rib, plain lip, clear, ca. 1845-60, ½ pt. 495.00

GIX-43 - Scrolls w/large pearl below each curved line at base of inner frame, above a long oval finial containing a large pearl above "JR & SON" & two large pearls below scrolls at top of outer frame - fleur-de-lis w/two large pearls below top scroll left & right, vertical medial rib, plain lip, pontil mark, aqua, pt. ...495.00

GIX-45 - Scroll w/elaborate scroll decoration forming acanthus leaves w/four-petal flower at the top & diamond at center obverse & reverse, vertical medial ribs, bluish aqua, pt. 330.00

GIX-47 - Scroll w/four graduated

finger-like ribs following the pear-shaped contour, large eight-point star in upper center & "R. Knowles & Co." (follow left rib), "Union Factory" (follow right rib) & "South Wheeling" in circle around "VA" - similar scroll w/large fleur-de-lis between inner ribs, plain lip, pontil mark, aqua, pt. 852.50

GX-2 - Stag standing above "Good" & "Game" at right of stag - Weeping willow tree, vertically ribbed edges, plain lip, aqua, ½ pt. 332.50

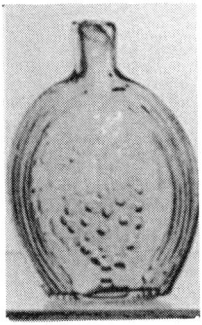

Sheaf of Rye Flask

GX-3 - Sheaf of Rye - Bunch of Grapes w/stem & three large leaves, vertically ribbed edges, sheared lip, pontil, aqua, ½ pt. (ILLUS.) 140.00

GX-4 - Cannon, "Genl Taylor Never Surrenders" inscribed in semicircle around cannon - vine & grape form a semicircular frame containing the inscription "A Little More Grape Capt Bragg," vertically ribbed w/heavy medial ribbing, plain lip, pontil, aqua, pt. 302.50

GX-4 - Cannon, "Genl Taylor Never Surrenders" inscribed in semicircle around cannon - vine & grape form a semicircular frame containing the inscription "A Little More Grape Capt Bragg," vertically ribbed w/heavy medial ribbing, plain lip, pontil, olive green, pt. 2,805.00

GX-8A - Sailboat (sloop) w/pennant on waves surrounded w/large oval frame - eight-point star w/three-pointed ornaments surrounded w/large oval frame, smooth edges, plain lip, pontil, aqua, ½ pt. 220.00

GX-14 - "Murdock" in semi-circle - "& - Cassel" in two straight lines, beneath rectangular band of heavy diagonal ribbing & below that a wider band of heavy vertical ribs extend to the base - "Zanesville" in semi-circle & "Ohio" in straight line, below ribbing similar to obverse, vertically ribbed edges w/narrow medial rib, plain lip, pontil, light bluish green, ca. 1830-37, pt. 1,760.00

GX-15 - "Summer" Tree - "Winter" Tree, plain lip, smooth edges, pontil, light olive green, pt. 324.50

GX-19 - Summer Tree - Winter Tree, plain lip, smooth edges, pontil, golden olive amber, qt. 770.00

GX-21 - Early American steamboat w/paddle wheel & "The American" above & "System" below in the water - "Use Me But Do Not Abuse Me" in semicircle above sheaf of grain, herringbone ribbing on edges, plain lip, pontil mark, pale yellowish green, pt. 4,180.00

GXI-11 - Prospector w/tools & cane standing on oblong frame - American Eagle w/pennant above oval frame, aqua, pt. 70.00

GXI-22 - "For Pike's Peak" above prospector w/short staff & pack standing on oblong frame - American Eagle w/long pennant above oblong frame, aqua, pt. 82.50

GXI-50 - "For Pike's Peak" above prospector w/tools & cane - Hunter shooting stag, molded collar, plain edges, olive green, pt. 550.00

GXII-2 - Clasped hands, all inside shield, w/ "Waterford" above - American Eagle above oval frame, light yellow w/an olive tone, qt. 852.50

GXII-6 - Clasped hands above oval, all inside shield - American Eagle above oval frame, yellowish green, qt. 137.50

GXII-15 - Clasped hands above oval, all inside shield, w"Union" above - American Eagle above frame w/"E. Wormser C ("o" of Co just outside frame), flat collar, narrow beveled edge, aqua, qt. 110.00

GXII-31 - Clasped hands above oval, all inside shield - American Eagle above oval, golden amber, ½ pt. 154.00

GXII-37 - Clasped hands above oval all inside shield w/ "Union" above shield obverse & reverse, aqua, qt. ...55.00

GXII-38 - Clasped hands above oval, all inside shield w/ "Union" above - large cannon & American flag, smooth base, collared lip, aqua, qt. 52.50

GXII-40 - Clasped hands above oval w/ "FA & Co.," all inside shield w/"Union" above - Small cannon & large American flag, smooth base, aqua, pt. 90.00

GXII-43 - Clasped hands above square & compass above oval

w/"Union" all inside shield - American Eagle, calabash, round collar, deep golden amber, qt. 242.00

GXIII-3 - Girl wearing a full-length skirt & hat & riding a bicycle - American Eagle w/head turned right above oval frame embossed w/"A & DH.C," smooth edges, collared lip, aqua, qt. 137.50

GXIII-8 - Sailor dancing a hornpipe on an eight-board hatch cover, above a long rectangular bar - banjo player sitting on a long bench, smooth edges, plain lip, pontil mark, aqua, ½ pt. 115.00

GXIII-13 - Soldier wearing a spiked helmet - rectangular frame enclosing "Balt. MD." below, smooth edges, plain lip, pontil mark, yellowish olive green, ca. 1860-80, pt. 825.00

GXIII-22 - Flora Temple obverse, plain reverse, smooth edges, small handle, ginger ale w/olive tone, ca. 1860-80, pt. 467.50

GXIII-35 - Sheaf of Grain w/rake & pitchfork crossed behind sheaf - "Westford Glass Co., Westford Conn," smooth sides, reddish amber, pt. 110.00

GXIII-35 - Sheaf of Grain w/rake & pitchfork crossed behind sheaf - "Westford Glass Co., Westford Conn," plain lip, smooth edges, yellowish amber, ca. 1860-72, pt. 132.00

GXIII-36 - Sheaf of Grain w/rake & pitchfork crossed behind sheaf & five-pointed star centered between rake & pitchfork handles - "Westford Glass Co., Westford Conn," plain lip, smooth edges, reddish amber, pt. ...143.00

GXIII-37 - Sheaf of Grain w/rake & pitchfork crossed behind sheaf - "Westford Glass Co., Westford Conn," smooth sides, deep yellowish olive, ca. 1857-60, ½ pt. 907.50

GXIII-37 - Sheaf of Grain w/rake & pitchfork crossed behind sheaf - "Westford Glass Co., Westford Conn," smooth sides, deep golden amber, ca. 1860-73, ½ pt. 121.00

GXIII-55 - Anchor w/fork-ended pennants inscribed "Isabella" & "Glass Works" on obverse - three-quarter view of glasshouse, plain lip, smooth edges, aqua, qt. 121.00

GXIII-64 - Anchor w/cable - plain reverse, smooth edges, round collar w/lower bevel, amber, qt. 55.00

GXIII-75 - Key at center, plain reverse, wide bevel each side to mold seam, narrow round collar, aqua, pt. 65.00

GXIV-1 - "Traveler's Companion" arched above & below star formed by a circle of eight small triangles - Sheaf of Grain w/rake & pitchfork crossed behind, applied flat collar, seamed base, deep golden amber, ca. 1860-72, qt. 132.00

GXIV-1 - "Traveler's Companion" arched above & below star formed by a circle of eight small triangles - Sheaf of Grain w/rake & pitchfork crossed behind, crude sloping collared mouth, smooth base, olive amber, qt. 104.50

GXIV-1 - "Traveler's Companion" arched above & below star formed by a circle of eight small triangles - Sheaf of Grain w/rake & pitchfork crossed behind, applied flat collar, seamed base, yellowish olive, ca. 1860-73, qt. 143.00

GXIV-2 - "Traveler's Companion" arched above & below star formed by a circle of eight small triangles - Star like obverse & "Ravenna" above & "Glass Co" below, applied flat collar, brilliant golden amber, qt. 852.00

GXIV-3 - "Traveler's Companion" arched above & below star formed by a circle of eight small triangles - Sheaf of Grain w/rake & pitchfork crossed behind, deep aqua, pt. .....110.00 to 160.00

GXIV-8 - "Traveler's" arched above & "Companion" arched below - plain reverse, plain lip, aqua, ½ pt. 165.00

GXV-7 - "Granite - Glass - Co." inscribed in three lines - "Stoddard - NH" inscribed in two lines, smooth edges, plain lip w/applied double collar, smooth base, golden amber, ca. 1860-70, pt. 176.00

GXV-7 - "Granite - Glass - Co." inscribed in three lines - "Stoddard - NH" inscribed in two lines, smooth edges, plain lip w/applied double collar, smooth base, golden olive amber, pt. 90.00

GXV-23 - "Union Glass Works" in an arc & - "New London - Ct" in straight lines below, plain reverse, round collar w/lower bevel, smooth base, light bluish green, ca. 1815-30, pt....473.00

Chestnut, forest green, free-blown, applied mouth, pontil, New England, ca. 1780-1830, 8⅝" h. 187.00

Chestnut, yellowish olive, collared mouth, pontil, New England, ca. 1780-1830, 5¾" h. 132.00

Chestnut, yellowish olive, collared mouth, pontil, New England, ca. 1780-1830, 9⅝" h. 154.00

Chestnut, ten-diamond, amber, short cylindrical neck w/flat flared rim, Zanesville, Ohio, 4¾" h. 3,410.00
Chestnut, ten-diamond, amber, short flaring cylindrical neck, fire polished pontil, 4⅝" h. 1,210.00

Ten-Diamond Chestnut Flask

Chestnut, ten-diamond, light green, short flaring cylindrical neck, sheared lip, fire polished pontil, 4⅝" h. (ILLUS.) 3,410.00
Chestnut, 16 swirled ribs, aqua, Mantua, Ohio, 6" h. 165.00
Chestnut, 16 vertical ribs, aqua, 5⅝" h. 137.50
Chestnut, 18 swirled ribs, pale green, Midwestern, 6½" h. 192.50

Ribbed Chestnut Flask

Chestnut, 18 vertical ribs, pale green, sheared lip, Midwestern, minor stains, wear & scratches, 7" h. (ILLUS.) 126.50
Chestnut, 24 broken swirled ribs, amber, applied lip, pontil, 7¼" h. 660.00
Chestnut, 24 swirled ribs, red amber, sheared lip, 4⅞" h. 130.00
Chestnut, 24 swirled ribs, aqua, Zanesville, Ohio, 7½" h. 550.00
Chestnut, 24 swirled ribs, golden honey amber, applied lip, pontil, 8" h. 1,760.00
Chestnut, 24 vertical ribs, deep amber, sheared lip, Zanesville, Ohio, 4⅞" h. 247.50
Chestnut, 24 vertical ribs, dark amber brown, sheared & fire polished lip, pontil, 6½" h. 275.00
Chestnut, 24 vertical ribs, golden amber, Zanesville, Ohio, 4¾" h. 275.00
Chestnut, checkered diamond design, clear, sheared lip, 6⅞" h. 1,100.00
Pitkin, 16 slightly swirled ribs, amber, half post neck w/sheared lip, pontil, 5½" h. 275.00
Pitkin, 24 vertical ribs, golden amber, sheared mouth, pontil, Midwestern, 1820-40, 5" h. 209.00
Pitkin, 24 vertical ribs, light olive brown, sheared mouth, pontil scar, Zanesville, 7⅞" h. 385.00
Pitkin, 30 broken ribs swirled to the left, yellowish olive green, slightly flared sheared mouth, pontil, 7¼" h. 357.50
Pitkin, 30 broken ribs swirled to the right, light bluish green, sheared neck, pontil, New England, ca. 1780-1830, 5⅛" h. (some light interior base stain, tiny mouth flake) 286.00
Pitkin, 32 broken ribs swirled to the right, bright medium green, sheared neck, pontil, ca. 1800-30, 6⅝" h. 467.50
Pitkin, 35 broken ribs swirled, pale green, sheared lip, pontil, Midwestern, ca. 1800-30, 7⅛" h. 330.00

Ribbed Pitkin Flask

Pitkin, 36 broken swirled ribs, amber, half post neck w/sheared & fire polished lip, tubular pontil, 6" h. (ILLUS.) 770.00
Pitkin, 36 broken swirled ribs, golden olive amber, half post neck w/sheared & fire polished lip, pontil, 5¾" h. 880.00

Pitkin, 36 broken ribs swirled to the left, yellowish olive, sheared lip, pontil, New England, ca. 1780-1830, 5⅛" h. 506.00
Pitkin, 36 broken ribs swirled to the left, yellowish olive green, sheared lip, 5¼" h. 440.00
Pitkin, 36 broken ribs swirled to the right, bright olive green, sheared lip, pontil, New England, ca. 1780-1830, 5 1/16" h. 357.50
Pitkin, 36 broken ribs swirled to the right, yellow olive, sheared lip, pontil, New England, ca. 1780-1830, 5⅛" h. 385.00
Pitkin, 36 broken ribs swirled to the right, bright yellowish olive, sheared lip, pontil, New England, ca. 1780-1830, 6⅜" h. 341.00
Pitkin, 36 broken ribs swirled to the right, olive green, sheared lip, pontil, New England, ca. 1780-1830, 6⅝" h. 330.00
Pitkin, 36 broken swirled ribs, olive, half-post neck, ½ pt., 4⅞" h. 313.50

INKS

Bulbous Master Ink Bottle

Bulbous, master ink, clear glass nearly spherical body w/raised rings flanking the paper label w/"Paul's Safety Ink...," tall stick neck w/tooled rim & original pour spout, ca. 1880-1900, 8¼" h. (ILLUS.) 110.00
Cathedral, six Gothic arch panels, cobalt blue glass, embossed "Carter" around bottom edge, smooth base, qt., 9¾" h. 110.00
Cylindrical, medium sapphire blue, embossed "Harrison's Columbian Ink," applied flared mouth, 1 13/16" d., 4⅛" h. 577.50
Cylindrical, medium green glass, embossed "S. Fine, Blk Ink," inward rolled mouth & pontil scar, ca. 1830-50, 2⅞" h. 467.50
Cylindrical, master size, light to medium bluish green glass, rounded shoulder embossed "Hover - Phila.," cylindrical neck w/flared lip, 6" h. (professionally cleaned) 176.00
Domed octagonal w/offset neck, aqua glass, "Harrisons - Columbian - Ink," sheared & tooled lip, dug, ca. 1860-75, 1½" h. (light outside & inside content stain) 176.00
Domed w/central neck, medium amber glass, sheared & ground lip, ca. 1870-80, 1⅞" h. (tiny iridescent bruise on inside of lip) 132.00
Domed w/central neck, olive amber, mold blown glass, embossed "Bertinguiot," 2½" d., 2" h. 154.00
House-shaped, aqua glass, embossed "NE - Plus - Ultra - Fluid" on the roof, crudely sheared mouth, pontil, ca. 1860-80, 2⅝" h. 385.00
Octagonal, yellowish olive glass, tooled collared mouth, pontil scar, New England, ca. 1780-1830, 2⅜" d., 2¼" h. 242.00
Square w/central neck, clear glass, "Tinta - American," tooled & rolled lip, ca. 1840-55, 1¾" h. 253.00
Teakettle-type fountain inkwell w/neck extending up at angle from base, cobalt blue glass, ground mouth w/original lid, smooth base, 2" h. 550.00
Teakettle-type fountain inkwell w/neck extending up at angle from base, lime sherbet clambroth opaque glass, ground mouth, smooth base, 3½" d., 2¼" h. 715.00
Teakettle-type fountain inkwell w/neck extending up at angle from base of the tapering hexagonal body, ground lip, deep amethyst glass, ca. 1870-90, 2" h. (two flat chips on lip) 412.50
Teakettle-type fountain inkwell w/neck extending at angle from base of the tapering domical mushroom-form body w/six panels w/bull's-eyes divided by thin ribs, medium yellowish green glass, ground lip w/original metal neck ring, ca. 1870-90, 2¾" h. 935.00
Teakettle-type fountain inkwell w/angled neck extending from base of double-stepped domical octagonal body, attributed to Boston & Sandwich Glass Co., ca. 1870, opaque lime green glass, 2" h. 715.00
Teakettle-type fountain inkwell w/neck extending up at angle from base of tapering hexagonal body, each

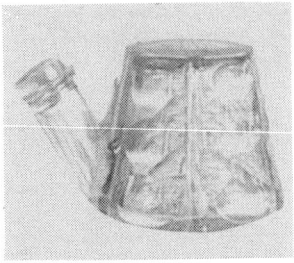

Rare Cut Teakettle-form Inkwell

panel cut & polished w/a diamond design, ground lip w/original brass lid, turquoise blue glass, ca. 1875-90, 2⅜" h. (ILLUS.) 715.00

Umbrella-type (8-panel cone shape), amber glass, sheared lip, open pontil, ca. 1830-50, 2½" h. 175.00

Umbrella-type (8-panel cone shape), medium amber glass, rolled lip, open pontil, ca. 1840-55, 2⅜" h. (few spots of haze) 132.00

Eight-Sided Umbrella Ink

Umbrella-type (8-panel cone shape), yellow w/amber tone glass, rolled lip, pontil-scarred base, ca. 1840-55, minor spotty stain inside, partially open discolored bubble on base edge, 2⅜" h. (ILLUS.) 825.00

Umbrella-type (8-panel cone shape), yellowish olive glass, rolled lip, open pontil, ca. 1830-50, 2⅜" h. 357.50

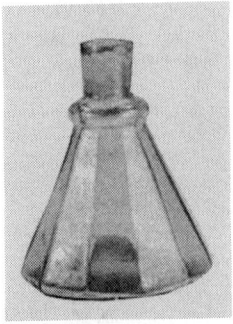

Twelve-Sided Umbrella Ink

Umbrella-type (12-panel cone shape), light green glass, rolled lip, open pontil, ca. 1840-55, few minor spots of inside haze, 2⅝" h. (ILLUS.) 242.00

MEDICINES

American (embossed bottle) Compound - Phila, rectangular w/paneled sides, aqua, applied mouth, open pontil, ca. 1845-55, 5⅞" h. (lightly cleaned) 93.50

Angell's (Dr. N.) Rheumatic Gun, rectangular, deep aqua, applied mouth, pontiled base, ca. 1850-60, 7⅜" h. (light spotty interior haze) 302.50

Baker's (Dr.) - Pain Panacea, rectangular, pontil, aqua, 5" h. 100.00

Balsam of Honey, rounded, aqua, 3⅛" h. 55.00

Barnett (E.I.) Magic Cure Liniment, Easton, PA, rectangular, aqua, 6⅜" h. 26.00

Barrell's Indian Liniment - H.G.O. Cary, rectangular, aqua, 1 x 1 9/16 x 4¾" 70.00

Bears Oil, pictures walking bear above "Oil," flared lip, open pontil, rectangular, aqua, 2¾" h. 450.00

Bennett's (Dr.) Quick Cure - A.L. Scovill & Co, rectangular, rolled lip, aqua, 4⅝" h. 31.00

Dr. Blendigo's Celery Tonic

Blendigo's (Dr.) Celery Tonic - Peptonized - John Schweyer & Co., Sole Distributors, Chicago, Ill., rectangular w/paneled sides, amber, tooled lip, ca. 1880-1900, 9½" h. (ILLUS.) 255.00

Brinkerhoff's Health Restorative, New York, rectangular, pontil, emerald green, 7" h. 650.00

Brown's (F.) Ess of Jamaica Ginger Philada., oval, aqua, 5½" h. 25.00

Brown's Blood Cure - Philadelphia - M.B.W., U.S.A., yellowish green, 6⅛" h. 130.00

Brunet's Universal Remedy

Brunet's Universal Remedy - Philada, cylindrical, aqua, applied mouth, open pontil, overall interior stain, ca. 1845-60, 8" h. (ILLUS.) 264.00

Brunet's (Dr.) Worm Syrup, rectangular w/beveled corners, aqua, applied mouth, open pontil, ca. 1840-55, 6¾" h. (some faint inside haze) 275.00

Burton's (Dr. W.) Syrup - Philada, cylindrical, pale green, applied mouth, pontiled base, ca. 1845-60, 6¼" h. (light inside haze spots) 440.00

Callan's (Prof.) World Renowned Brazillian (sic) Gum," rectangular, orangish amber, 4¼" h. 35.00

Cann's Kidney Cure, 1876, clear, 8½" h. 24.00

Celery Compound - Compound (over a stack of celery), square w/paneled sides, yellowish amber, tooled lip, ca. 1880-90, 10" h. 88.00

Clarke's World Famed Blood Mixture, blue 65.00

Davis' (Perry) Pain Killer, rectangular, pontil, aqua, 8¼" h. 25.00

Davis Vegetable Pain Killer, rectangular, aqua, 4⅝" h. 35.00

Dewitts Colic & Cholera Cure - E. C. Dewitt & Co., Chicago, U.S.A., aqua, paper label, 4⅞" h. 30.00

Dewitts (Dr.) Eclectic Cure, W J Parker & Co, Baltimore, MD, rectangular, 5⅝" h. 26.00

Fahrney's (Dr.) Health Restorer, Hagerstown, MD., amber, 7⅛" h. 17.50

Fenner's (Dr. M.M.) Kidney & Backache Cure, oval, amber, 90% label, 10⅜" h. 68.00

Fenner's (Dr. M.M.) Peoples Remedies - Fredonia, N.Y. - U.S.A. 1872-1891, rectangular, blown in mold, aqua, 1¼ x 2¼ x 7¾" 32.00

Foley's Kidney & Bladder Cure - Foley & Co. - Chicago, U.S.A., rectangular, amber, paper label, 9½" h. 38.00

Folger's Olosaonian - (Dr Robt. B. - New-York, rectangular w/deeply beveled corners, pontil, aqua, 1½ x 2½ x 7¾" 55.00

Freeman's (Dr. Clarkson) Indian Specific, square, aqua, 5" h. 125.00

Gesteria (Dr. J.), Regulator Gesteria, amber, 5" h. 20.00

Gould (L.A.), Portland, ME., paper label w/"White Clover Cream for Chapped Hands, Sunburn, etc...," rectangular, clear, 4½" h. 16.00

Grove's (Dr.) Anodyne for Infants, Philada., rectangular, aqua, 5½" h. (w/paper label) 22.00

Hagan's Magnolia Balm, rectangular, milk white, 5" h. 9.00

Hall's Balsam for the Lungs, John F. Henry & Co., New York, rectangular, aqua, 7¾" h. 25.00

Hall's Catarrh Cure, round, aqua, 1⅝" d., 4⅝" h. 15.00

Hanford's (Dr.) Celery Cure or Nerve Food Cures Rheumatism - Neuralgia - Insomnia - & C & C, rectangular w/beveled corners, rolled lip, pontil, aqua, 1¾ x 2½", 7⅝" h. 45.00

Healy & Bigelow's Kickapoo Cough Syrup, cylindrical, aqua, 1¼" d., 6¼" h. 20.00

Hills (embossed H w/arrow) Trade Mark Dys Pep Cu, Cures Chronic Dyspepsia, Indiana Drug Specialty Co., St. Louis & Indianapolis, rectangular w/fluted corners, amber, 8⅛" h. 110.00

Hobensack's Medicated Worm Syrup, Philada., rectangular w/indented panels, aqua, 4½" h. 39.00

Hollis' (Thomas) Balm of America, round, aqua, 5" h. 18.00

Hooker's (Dr.) Cough and Croup Syrup, round, aqua, 5⅝" h. 89.00

Hough's (Dr.) Anti Scrofula Syrup, rectangular, aqua, applied mouth, open pontil, ca. 1845-60, 9½" h. (light inside stain, small stress fissure in neck) 176.00

Hunter's (H.C:) Palm Lotion, Marlboro, Mass., paper label reading "Chapped Hands, Sunburn, Chafing & ...," rectangular, amber, 5¼" h. 38.00

Hyatt's - Infallible - Life Balsam, N.Y., rectangular w/beveled corners, smooth base, deep aqua, 9½" h. (minor lip bruise) 140.00

James' (Dr.) Cherry Tar Syrup, Pittsburgh, Penna, U.S.A., aqua, 5¾" h. 12.50

James (Dr. H.) Cannabis Indica, Crabbock & Co., Proprietors, No. 1032 Pace St. Phila. Pa., cylindrical, aqua, applied lip, 7¾" h. 302.50

Kauffman's (Dr. J.) Angeline Internal Rheumatism Cure, Hamilton, Ohio, deep amethyst, 7⅝" h. 25.00

Kilmer's (Dr.) Female Remedy, Binghamton, N.Y., rectangular, aqua, w/paper label & contents, 8⅜" h. 300.00

Kilmer's (Dr.) Indian Cough Remedy Consumption Oil, Binghamton, N.Y. U.S.A., rectangular, aqua, 5½" h. 25.00

Kilmer's (Dr.) Ocean Weed Heart Remedy, The Blood Specific, rectangular, embossed heart, aqua, 8½" h. 175.00

Kilmer's (Dr.) Swamp-Root Kidney Cure, Binghamton, N.Y., Sample Bottle, cylindrical, aqua, 3⅛" h. 20.00

Kilmer's (Dr.) Swamp-Root Kidney, Liver & Bladder Cure, Binghamton, N.Y., Sample Bottle, round, 3¼" h. 12.00

Kilmer's (Dr.) Swamp-Root Kidney, Liver & Bladder Cure, London, E.C., rectangular w/beveled corners, aqua, 7" h. 25.00

Kilmer's (Dr.) Swamp-Root Kidney, Liver & Bladder Cure, rectangular, amethyst, 7" h. 45.00

K.K. Cures Bright's Disease and Cystitis, rectangular, aqua, 7½" h. 25.00

Lindsey's - Blood + Searcher - Hollidaysburg (Pennsylvania), rectangular, aqua, qt. 89.00

Lorman's (Prof.) Indian Oil Philada., PA., rectangular, aqua, 5¼" h. 21.00

Low's (Prof.) Magnetic Liniment, Philada, Pa., rectangular, aqua, 6⅛" h. 18.00

McLean's (Dr. J.H.) Strengthening Cordial & Blood Purifier, oval, aqua, 8" h. 45.00

Miles' (Dr.) Restorative Nervine, aqua, 8½" h. 15.00

Myers (Dr.) Bilious King - Smith Myers & Co., square w/beveled corners, amber, applied mouth, ca. 1870-80, 9" h. (ILLUS. top next column) 93.50

National Remedy Company, New York, rectangular, amber, w/paper label, 7⅝" h. 25.00

Pierce's (Dr.) Anuric Tablets for Kidneys and Backache, cylindrical, aqua, 3½" h. 15.00

Pierce's (Dr.) Golden Medical Discovery - R.V. Pierce, M.D. - Buffalo, N.Y., rectangular, amber, 8⅜" h. 40.00

Dr. Myers Bilious King

Polar Star Cough Cure, embossed star, aqua 25.00

Ransom's Hive Syrup & Tolu, square, aqua, 3½" h. 15.00

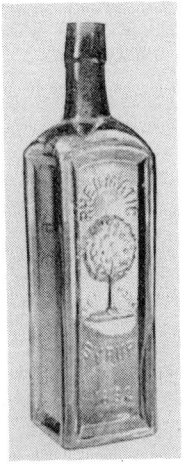

Rheumatic Syrup

Rheumatic (embossed tree) Trade Mark Syrup 1882 - R.S. Co., Rochester, N.Y., rectangular w/paneled sides, medium amber, slightly tilted applied mouth, ca. 1870-80, 9¾" h. (ILLUS.) 176.00

Richter (F.A.) & Co., New York (embossed anchor) Pain-Expeller, Reg. U.S. Patt. Off. For Rheumatism, Gout, Neuralgia, Colds, etc., rectangular w/beveled corners, aqua, 4⅞" h. 12.50

Rowand's - Tonic Mixture - Vegetable - Febrifuge - Philad, six-sided, open pontil, aqua, 5¾" h. ....140.00 to 180.00

Schrage's Rheumatic Cure, Swanson Rheumatic Cure Company, Chicago, aqua 39.00

Seabury's Cough Balsam, open pontil, aqua, 1¼" d., 4¾" h...40.00 to 50.00
Simonds Pain Cure, rectangular, aqua, 4¾" h.....15.00
Sparks Perfect Health (embossed man) for Kidney & Liver Diseases, amber, 9⅜" h. 50.00
Swaim's Vermifuge - Fever - Dysentery - Cholera Morbus - Dyspepsia, paneled sides, aqua, thin flared lip, open pontil, ca. 1835-45, 4¼" h. 247.50
Sykes' (Dr.) Sure Cure For Catarrh, medium apple green, 6⅝" h.....65.00
Thatcher's (Dr.) Liver & Blood Syrup, Chattanooga, Tenn., amber, sample size, 3" h. 28.00
Thatcher's (Dr.) Liver & Blood Syrup, Chattanooga, Tenn., amber, 8⅜" h....45.00
Thomson's - Compound - Syrup of Tar for Consumption - Philada, rectangular w/paneled sides, aqua, applied mouth, open pontil, ca. 1840-55, 5¾" h. 60.50
Turlington's (Robt.) Balsam of Life, paneled pear-shape, flared lip, open pontil, aqua, England, 2⅝" h.....93.50
(Warner's) Log Cabin - Extract, Rochester, NY., three indented panels on front, flat back, dark yellow amber, 8⅛" h. 95.00
Warner's Safe Cure, London, emerald green, ½ pt., 7½" h. 80.00
Warner's Safe Cure, Melbourne, w/safe, oval tooled blob lip, smooth base, amber, 1880-90, 7" h. 85.00
Warner's Safe Cure, Melbourne, w/safe, reddish amber, 9½" h. 45.00
Warner's Safe Cure (safe) Pressburg, oval, olive green, 9½" h. 1,925.00

Warner's Safe Diabetes Cure

Warner's Safe Diabetes Cure - Pressburg, w/safe, amber, applied mouth, tiny lip ding, 9½" h. (ILLUS.) 2,640.00
Warner's Safe Kidney & Liver Cure, Rochester, N.Y., w/reversed (or "left-handed") picture of safe, oval, amber, 9¾" h. 80.00
Warner's Safe Nervine, Frankfurt A/M, w/safe, oval, amber, applied mouth, 9¼" h.....1,375.00
Warner's Safe Rheumatic Cure Rochester, NY., U.S.A., w/safe, oval, light yellow, 9½" h. (spotty haze).....40.00
Wishart's (L.Q.C.) - Pine Tree Tar Cordial Phila. - (embossed pine tree) Patent 1859, square w/beveled corners, emerald green, 8" h. 242.00

Wishart's Pine Tree Tar Cordial

Wishart's (L.Q.C.) - Pine Tree Tar Cordial Phila. - (embossed pine tree) Patent 1859, square w/beveled corners, medium bluish green, 8" h. (ILLUS.) 100.00
Wishart's (L.Q.C.) - Pine Tree Tar Cordial Phila. - (embossed pine tree) Patent 1859, square w/beveled corners, yellowish green, 8" h.....121.00
Wishart's (L.Q.C.) Pine Tree Tar Cordial Phila. - Trade (embossed pine tree) Mark, square w/beveled corners, sapphire blue, tooled lip, 9¾" h. (some light scratching on back panel) 797.50
Wistar's (Dr.) - Balsam of - Wild Cherry - John D. Park - Cincinnati, Ohio, octagonal, deep aqua, 6½" h.....30.00
Wynkoop's Katharismic Sarsaparilla - New York, rectangular, medium sapphire blue, applied mouth, iron pontil, lightly cleaned, ca. 1845-60, 10" h. (ILLUS. top next page) 7,150.00
Zollickoffer's Anti Rheumatic Cordial - Philada, rectangular w/paneled sides, yellowish olive amber, applied

Wynkoop's Katharismic Sarsaparilla

mouth, open pontil, ca. 1840-50, 6⅜" h. 1,595.00

MILK

Individual Cream-Size Bottles

Amber, embossed "Golden Royal," ½" gal. 8.50
Brilliant grass green, embossed "Return to - H.B. Day," tapering cylindrical-form w/tooled square collared mouth, smooth base, 10¼" h. 198.00
Clear, individual cream-size, enameled "Blanding's - Greenville, Mich. (ILLUS. left) 21.00
Clear, individual cream-size, enameled "Country Club Dairy" (ILLUS. right) 24.00
Clear, individual cream-size, enameled "McDonald's White House Dairy" (ILLUS. left, top next column) .. 21.00
Clear, individual cream-size, enameled "Suncrest Farms and Mowrer's, Inc." (ILLUS. right, top next column) 26.00
Clear, "Maui - Haleakala Dairy," qt. 30.00
Clear, "Oahu - Moanaloa Dairy," 12 oz. 12.00

McDonald's & Suncrest Bottles

Clear, embossed "Registered Strictly Pure Milk - Bottled by the Empire State Dairy Company (state seal) - 502 & 506 Broadway, Brooklyn - Trade Mark," tooled lip, smooth base, ca. 1900-20, qt., 9" h. 66.00

Robinson & Woolworth Bottle

Clear, embossed "Robinson & Woolworth - 1667 B'way, N.Y. - This Bottle to be Washed and Returned Not to be Bought or Sold," base w/"Whiteman Maker - 144 Chamber St., New York," tooled lip w/original metal lid stamped "Jan. 5.1875, Patd. April 3.1889," wire closure, smooth base, qt., 8½" h. (ILLUS.) 99.00
Clear, embossed "F.K. Wards - Milk Preserving Jar - Sealed Stopper - Patents 1890 & 1892 - When Empty Return to - Ward's Alderney Milk P & C Association - Washington, D.C. - Wash Clean When Empty," embossed on smooth base "This Jar Has Been Stolen If Offered For Sale" & on lip "Refuse A Broken Seal" & cow's head, w/original glass lid & wire bail, ca. 1890-95, pt. 1,155.00

Clear, embossed "Woodrow Wilson Dairy, Palmyria, WI.," pt. 10.00
Clear, "Your Dairy New London, WI," red paint, qt. 10.00

MINERAL WATERS

Congress & Empire Spring Co.

Caladonia (sic) Spring, Wheelock, Vt., Saratoga-type, yellowish amber, qt., 9½" h. 660.00
Congress & Empire Spring Co., Hotchkiss' Sons, "C," New York, Saratoga, N.Y., Congress Water, smooth base, applied mouth, emerald green, ca. 1865-75, pt., 7¾" h. (ILLUS.) 170.00
Congress & Empire Spring Co., "C," Saratoga, N.Y., Congress Water, smooth base, applied mouth, deep emerald green, ca. 1865-75, pt. 7⅝" h. (dug, fair amount of scratching & scuffing on the outside) 121.00
Geyser Spring. Saratoga Springs. State of New York. - "The Saratoga" Spouting Spring, smooth base, applied mouth, bluish aqua, ca. 1865-75, qt., 9⅜" h. 99.00
Highrock Congress Spring - motif of rock - C & W, Saratoga, N.Y., smooth base, applied mouth, teal blue, ca. 1850-70, pt., 7⅝" h. 253.00
Hutchinson & Co., Celebrated Mineral Water, Chicago, iron pontil, applied mouth, medium cobalt blue w/tiny seed bubbles, ca. 1845-55, 7¼" h. 253.00
Knowlton (D.A.), Saratoga, N.Y., smooth base, applied mouth, deep olive amber, ca. 1860-70, qt. 110.00
Meincke & Ebberwein, 1882, Savannah, Geo., Mineral "M&E," Water, smooth base, applied mouth, electric cobalt blue, ca. 1865-75, 7⅞" h. (lightly cleaned) 66.00

John Ryan Excelsior Mineral Water

Ryan (John) Excelsior Mineral Water, Savannah, Ga., 1859, Union Glass Works, Phila. This bottle is never sold, smooth base, applied mouth, cobalt blue, lightly cleaned, ca. 1865-75, 7⅛" h. (ILLUS.) 121.00
Weston (G.W.) & Co., Saratoga, N.Y., pontil mark, applied mouth, olive green, ca. 1855-65, qt., 9⅝" h. 187.00

NURSING

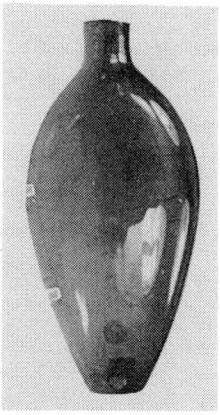

Blown Nursing Bottle

Aqua, mold-blown glass w/eighteen swirled ribs, Midwestern, 6½" l. 66.00
Aqua, mold-blown glass w/twelve vertical ribs, flattened ovoid shape tapering at base, slightly flared lip, Midwestern, 8¼" l. 60.50
Aqua, pressed glass, "Burr - Boston," embossed medallion 82.50
Clear, mold-blown glass, thick & heavy flask-form, pontil mark, sheared lip, 6¾" h. 55.00
Clear, pressed glass, "Corning - Pyrex," 4 oz., w/original wrapper 10.00

Clear, pressed glass, tilted neck, embossed "Empire," ca. 1910.....12.00
Clear, pressed glass, embosssed "Rexall" & w/a stork.....15.00
Deep cobalt blue, mold-blown glass, flask-form, pontil mark, sheared lip, America, ca. 1830-50, 7¼" h. (ILLUS.) 231.00
Greenish aqua, mold-blown glass, flask-form, diamond pattern, pontil mark, sheared lip, America, ca. 1830-50, 6½" h. 88.00
Pale green, mold-blown glass w/expanded ogival pattern, flattened ovoid shape tapering at base, slightly flared lip, Midwestern, 6¼" l. 27.50
Pale green, mold-blown glass w/twenty vertical ribs, flattened ovoid shape tapering at base, slightly flared lip, Midwestern, 7" l. 192.50
Yellowish green w/black amber neck & shoulder, mold-blown glass, flattened ovoid shape tapering at base, slightly flared lip, sheared & fire polished lip, 7⅛" l. 225.50

PICKLE BOTTLES & JARS

Cathedral Pickle with Lattice Windows

Aqua, four-sided, cathedral-type w/Gothic arch windows, rolled lip, smooth base, Willington Glass Works, West Willington, Connecticut, ca. 1860-72, 11⅞" h. (light interior haze) 247.50
Aqua, four-sided, cathedral-type w/Gothic arch windows w/diamond lattice, smooth base, rolled lip, America, ca. 1865-75, small open bubble on one corner at base, 13¾" h. (ILLUS.) 203.50
Bright yellow green, barrel-shaped w/embossed rows of rings at top & base, pontil mark, tooled lip, America, ca. 1860-70, 9½" h. (ILLUS.) 148.50
Clear, cathedral-type, 13" h. 165.00
Deep aqua, four-sided, cathedral-type w/Gothic arch windows w/diamond lattice, smooth base, rolled lip, America, ca. 1865-75, 11" h. (overall milky stain inside) 198.00
Deep aqua, four-sided, cathedral-type w/Gothic arch windows w/diamond lattice, smooth base, rolled lip, America, ca. 1865-75, 13¾" h. 275.00

Barrel-Shaped Pickle Jar

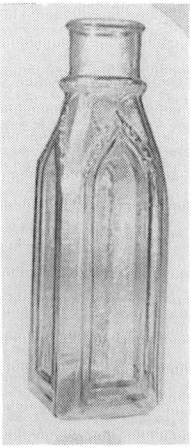

Large Cathedral Pickle Jar

Greenish aqua, four-sided, cathedral-type w/Gothic arch windows, smooth base, rolled lip, America, ca. 1865-75, 8¾" h. (ILLUS.) 143.00
Light green, four-sided, cathedral-type w/Gothic arch windows, iron pontil, rolled lip, America, ca. 1855-65, 11½" h. 297.00
Medium green, four-sided, cathedral-type w/Gothic arch windows, rolled collared mouth, pontil scar, Willing-

ton Glass Works, West Willington, Connecticut, ca. 1840-60, 13⅝" h. 2,310.00

POISONS

Poison Bottle with Hobnails

Clear, blown half post w/hobnails, applied flared lip, 4¾" h. (ILLUS.) 27.50
Clear, flattened flask shape w/overall small square raised knobs, sheared mouth, pontil, pint, ca. 1850....231.00
Cobalt blue, six-sided, embossed "POISON" & ribbed design, 3½" h. 28.00
Cobalt blue, six-sided, embossed "POISON" & ribbed design, 5½" h. 29.00
Cobalt blue, rectangular, embossed "POISON" & ribbed design, 6" h. 29.00
Green, six-sided, embossed "POISON" & ribbed design, 3¼" h. 21.00
Green, six-sided, embossed "POISON" & ribbed design, 6" h. 24.00

WHISKEY & OTHER SPIRITS

Black Label Beer

Beer, "American Brewing Co., Bennett, PA," embossed w/eagle & flags, blob top, light amber, pt. 25.00
Beer, "Black Label Beer," slightly rounded cylindrical form w/tapering neck, paper label, w/screw cap, amber, 18" h. (ILLUS.) 5.50
Beer, "Bunker Hill Lager, Charlestown, Mass.," w/lightning stopper, golden amber, pt. 20.00
Beer, "Golden Gate Bottling Works, San Francisco," embossed bear holding a glass, blob top, reddish amber, ½ pt. 240.00
Beer, "Gold Medal, C. Maurer," applied lip, golden amber, ½ pt. 85.00

Heineken Lager Beer

Beer, "Heineken Lager Beer," green w/paper labels, 18" h. (ILLUS.) 5.50
Beer, "Hinckel Brewing, Albany, Manchester, Boston" embossed in script, smoky golden amber, pt. 25.00
Beer, "Kerns (E.L.)," w/embossed moose head, greenish aqua, pt. 25.00
Beer, D. Lagrange, Moravia, NY.," whittled neck, lightning stopper, honey amber, pt. 20.00
Beer, "Norfolk Brewing Co., Boston," amber, pt. 25.00
Beer, "Rainier Beer, Seattle," blob top, light amber, miniature bottle 80.00
Beer, "Seitz Bros., Easton PA," embossed w/large "S" on back, blob top, light amber, pt. 20.00
Bourbon, "Old Crow Bourbon Rawlins Wyoming Robt. Freedman," flask-shape, amber, pt. 300.00
Bourbon, "Phoenix Old Bourbon, Naber, Alfs and Brune, San Francisco, Sole Proprts," & an embossed eagle, orangish amber, ½ pt. 200.00
Case gin, "Wistar's Club House," iron pontil, single collared lip, red puce, qt. 750.00

Case gin, blown half post, polychrome floral enameling, light olive green, pewter lip & cap, 6⅝" h. (minor stain) 495.00

Case gin, dip-molded, square tapered-form, mushroom mouth, pontil scar, yellowish olive, ca. 1780-1830, 9½" h. 104.50

Case gin, dip-molded, tapering square-form, w/rolled & flared mouth, pontil, deep yellow olive, 5¼" d., 16⅞" h. 770.00

Gin, "London Jockey Club House Gin," embossed horse & jockey, square w/beveled corners, sloping collared mouth, smooth base, bright green, 9" h. 275.00

Gin, "Olive Tree," tapered square-form, crude sloping collared mouth, smooth base, Netherlands, olive green, ca. 1860-80, 9¾" h. 242.00

Schnapps, "Udolpho Wolfe's," yellowish amber 35.00

Schnapps, "Udolpho Wolfe's - Aromatic - Schnapps - Schiedam," Stoddard-type, open pontil, crude, sandy amber, qt. 65.00

Spirits, applied seal w/"David Provost 1723," squat onion-form, free blown, applied collar, olive green, 7⅜" h. 1,925.00

Spirits, demijohn,"Saml Bowne 1759" on applied seal, pontil, applied lip, olive green, 8¾" h. (rough lip, minor wear & scratches) 880.00

Spirits, free-blown, bladder-shaped, "Thomas Morley 1730" on applied seal, green 1,500.00

Globular Spirits Bottles

Spirits, globular, tall neck, twenty-four swirled ribs, pontil mark, applied lip, Zanesville, Ohio, amber, 7¼" h. (ILLUS. left) 660.00

Spirits, globular, tall neck, twenty-four swirled ribs, pontil mark, applied lip, Zanesville, Ohio, golden honey amber, 8" h. (ILLUS. right) 1,760.00

Spirits, pumpkin seed, marked "Union Pacific Tea Company 1873" & embossed w/two men on an elephant, clear, ½ pt. 135.00

Spirits, rectangular w/beveled corners, ground mouth w/pewter collar & cap, pontil scar, clear ground decorated w/red, blue, yellow & white enameled bird & florals, 5½" h. 313.50

Spirits, squat, cylindrical-form w/sheared mouth w/string rim, free-blown, pontil scar, olive green, Netherlands, 1700-30, 4½" d., 5⅝" h. 385.00

Spirits, squat onion-form, free-blown, sheared mouth w/string rim, pontil scar, dark yellowish olive, England, ca. 1700-30, 6" d., 6" h. 418.00

Spirits, squat onion-form, free-blown, tooled mouth w/an applied wide neck ring, pontil scar, yellowish olive, Netherlands, 1700-30, 5½" d., 7⅛" h. 2,530.00

Whiskey, "Ambrosial" on applied seal, flattened chestnut-form w/applied mouth w/ring, pontil scar, golden amber, 9" h. (interior stain spots throughout) 132.00

Whiskey, "E.G. Booz's Old Cabin Whiskey," cabin-shaped, golden amber, 7⅞" h. 440.00

Whiskey, "Chapin & Gore Chicago Sour Mash 1867," barrel-shaped, inside threaded neck, amber (no stopper) 125.00

Whiskey, "Chestnut Grove," chestnut flask-shaped w/applied handle, open pontil, dark amber 170.00

Whiskey, "Chestnut Grove Whiskey," flattened globular-form, pontil, applied mouth ring & handle, golden amber, 8⅞" h. 143.00

Whiskey, "Cyrus Eaton Denver - One Quart You Bet," blob top, light amber, qt. 750.00

Whiskey, Goodman (Geo.) Wholesale, Paducah, KY, embossed w/sign of the Red Rock, clear, ½ gal. 90.00

Whiskey, Pierce (S.S.) Co., Est., 1831, Inc. 1891, Boston, embossed shield w/lion & eagle logo, clear, ½ gal. 45.00

Whiskey, mold-blown, globular form, 14 swirled ribs, light blue, Zanesville, Ohio, 8¼" h. 605.00

Whiskey, mold-blown, globular form, 16 swirled ribs, aqua, Midwestern, 7⅛" h. 148.50

Whiskey, mold-blown, globular form, 24 melon ribs, aqua, Zanesville, Ohio, 7½" h. 192.50

Whiskey, mold-blown, globular form, 24 swirled ribs, amber, Zanesville, Ohio, 7¼" h. 660.00

Whiskey, mold-blown, globular form, 24 swirled ribs, cornflower blue, Zanesville, Ohio, 8¼" h. 5,170.00
Whiskey, mold-blown, globular form, 24 swirled ribs, golden honey amber, Zanesville, Ohio, 8" h. 1,760.00

(End of Bottles Section)

CAMBRIDGE

Statuesque Line Compote

The Cambridge Glass Company was founded in Ohio in 1901. Numerous pieces are now sought, especially those designed by Arthur J. Bennett, including Crown Tuscan. Other productions included crystal animals, "Black Amethyst," "blanc opaque," and other types of colored glass. The firm was finally closed in 1954. It should not be confused with the New England Glass Co., Cambridge, Massachusetts.

Various Cambridge Marks

Ashtray, shell-shaped, pressed Caprice patt., Moonlight (pale blue) $9.00
Ashtray, Statuesque line, Royal Blue (dark blue) bowl, clear Nude Lady stem 135.00
Banana bowl, pressed Caprice patt., Crystal 195.00
Basket, etched Rose Point patt., Crystal, 7" h. 750.00
Bonbon, upright handles, pressed Caprice patt., Crystal, 5" sq. 12.00
Bonbon, handled, Inverted Strawberry patt., clear, 5½" 40.00
Bowl, 5 x 12½", Decagon line, etched Vintage patt., Crystal 65.00
Bowl, 5¾" d., Strawberry (No. 2780) line, clear 38.00
Bowl, 6" d., Inverted Strawberry patt., clear 15.00
Bowl, 10½" d., pressed Caprice patt., clear & frosted 35.00
Bowl, 11", etched Chantilly patt., No. 400, Crystal 85.00
Bowl, 11" d., rolled rim, etched Rose Point patt., No. 3400/2, Crystal 125.00
Bowl, 12" d., footed, etched Apple Blossom patt., Amber 70.00
Bowl, 12" d., crimped rim, footed, Caprice patt., Cobalt Blue 85.00
Bowl, 12" oval, pressed Caprice patt., Mandarin Gold (medium yellow) 125.00
Bowl, 12" d., etched Rose Point patt., Crystal 85.00
Bowl, 12½" d., bell-shaped, four-footed, pressed Caprice patt., No. 62, Moonlight 85.00
Bowl, 13½" d., crimped rim, footed, pressed Caprice patt., Mandarin Gold 75.00
Bowl, salad, 13½" d., pressed Caprice patt., Cobalt Blue 110.00
Bowl w/underplate: 9½" d. bowl w/ruffled rim, 10½" d. underplate; Strawberry (No. 2780) line, clear, 2 pcs. 98.00
Brandy, Tally-Ho line, Carmen (ruby red) bowl, clear stem 38.00
Bridge set: four tumblers & tray w/center handle; etched Rose Point patt., Crystal, 5 pcs. 250.00
Butter dish, cov., pressed Caprice patt., Crystal 359.00
Butter dish, cov., Gadroon (No. 3500) line, Crystal 40.00
Butter dish, cov., Thistle (No. 2766) line, green 90.00
Cake plate, handled, etched Rose Point patt., Crystal, 12" d. 85.00
Candleholders, two-light, etched Apple Blossom patt., Mandarin Gold, pr. 50.00
Candleholders, two-light, pressed Caprice patt., w/prisms, Crystal, 6" h., pr. 140.00
Candlesticks, Pristine line, No. 499 Calla Lily design, Amber, 6" h., pr. 75.00
Candlesticks, Pristine line, No. 499, Calla Lily design, Crystal, 6" h., pr. 54.00
Candlesticks, etched Diane patt., Crystal, 2½" h., pr. 35.00
Candlesticks, three-light, etched Rose Point patt., Crystal, pr. .....150.00 to 200.00

Candlesticks w/rams' heads, etched Rose Point patt., No. 3500/74, Crystal, 4" h., pr. 180.00
Candlesticks, two-light, keyhole stem, etched Wildflower patt., Crystal, pr. ...75.00
Candy box, cover w/sterling silver finial, etched Chantilly patt., Crystal, three-part, 7" l. 90.00
Candy box, cov., footed, Sea Shell line, Charleton decoration, milk white, 6" h. 85.00
Candy dish, heart-shaped, pressed Caprice patt., Moonlight, 5".....35.00
Candy dish, cov., Honeycomb line, Rubina 245.00
Champagne, etched Portia patt., Crystal.....21.00
Champagne, etched Rose Point patt., Crystal.....24.50
Champagne, Statuesque line, Carmen bowl, clear Nude lady stem.....125.00
Champagne, etched Wildflower patt., Crystal, 6 oz.....24.50
Champagnes, hollow stem, etched Laurel Wreath patt., Crystal, set of 6.....90.00
Cigarette holder, Mt. Vernon line, No. 66 on No. 1066 stem, Carmen 88.00
Cigarette set: cov. box & two ashtrays; Statuesque line, Cobalt Blue box & ashtrays, clear Nude Lady stem, 3 pcs.....825.00
Claret, etched Rose Point patt., Crystal.....55.00
Claret, etched Wildflower patt., Crystal.....40.00
Cocktail, etched Chantilly patt., Crystal.....9.50
Cocktail, Mt. Vernon line, Crystal, 3½ oz. 9.00
Cocktail, Statuesque line, Carmen bowl, clear Nude Lady stem 120.00
Cocktail, Statuesque line, Dianthus (light pink) bowl, clear Nude Lady stem, 3 oz. 150.00
Cocktail, Statuesque line, Royal Blue bowl, clear Nude Lady stem 110.00
Cocktail, etched Wildflower patt., Crystal.....20.00
Cocktail shaker w/original glass top, etched Blossom Time patt., Crystal.....85.00
Cocktail shaker w/original glass top, etched Rose Point patt., Crystal, 32 oz. 185.00
Cocktail shaker w/original top, Tally-Ho line, Cobalt Blue 175.00
Compote, open, 5½" d., etched Chantilly patt., Crystal.....30.00
Compote, open, 6½" d., 5" h., Tally-Ho line, Amber 30.00
Compote, open, 7" d., 9½" h., Statuesque line, Carmen bowl, clear Nude Lady stem (ILLUS.) 150.00
Compote, open, 8" d., Statuesque line, Cobalt Blue bowl, clear Nude Lady stem 295.00
Console bowl, pressed Caprice patt., Mandarin Gold w/silver overlay.....32.00
Console bowl, etched Diane patt., Crystal.....65.00
Console set: bowl & pair of candleholders; Everglade line, Crystal, 3 pcs. 250.00
Console set: 9" d., ram's head-handled bowl & pair 9½" h. Doric Column candlesticks; Jade (blue-green opaque), 3 pcs.....300.00 to 350.00
Cordial, etched Apple Blossom patt., Topaz (vaseline) bowl w/amber stem 95.00
Cordial, etched Rose Point patt., No. 3121, Crystal, 1 oz. 70.00
Cordial, etched Rose Point patt., Carmen bowl w/clear embossed base 150.00
Cordial, Statuesque line, Topaz bowl, clear Nude Lady stem.....140.00
Cordials, pressed Caprice patt., Moonlight, 1 oz., set of 12.....149.00
Cordials, etched Wildflower patt., No. 3121, Crystal, 1 oz., set of 6 .....325.00
Creamer, individual size, etched Chantilly patt., Crystal.....12.00

Child's Colonial Creamer

Creamer, child's, Colonial patt., Emerald (ILLUS.) 25.00
Creamer & open sugar bowl, individual size, pressed Caprice patt., No. 40, Crystal, pr. 27.00
Creamer & open sugar bowl, individual size, pressed Caprice patt., Moonlight, pr. 40.00
Creamer & open sugar bowl, Decagon line, Crystal, 2 pcs. 34.00
Creamer & open sugar bowl, individual size, Gadroon (No. 3500) line, Crystal, 2 pcs. 16.00

Creamer & open sugar bowl, etched Wildflower patt., No. 3900/41, Crystal, pr. 30.00
Creamer, sugar bowl & underplate, Decagon line, Ebony, 3 pcs. 65.00
Crown Tuscan cake plate w/open handles, Gadroon (No. 3500) line, 13" d. 98.00
Crown Tuscan candy dish, cov., three-part, Gadroon (No. 3500/57) line 50.00

Crown Tuscan Center Bowl

Crown Tuscan center bowl, footed, Seashell line ("Flying Lady"), shell-shaped bowl w/nude lady at one end, gold & floral trim, 10" d. (ILLUS.) 265.00
Crown Tuscan cocktail, Statuesque line, Nude Lady stem, Mandarin Gold 110.00
Crown Tuscan compote, open, 7" w., Sea Shell line 25.00
Crown Tuscan compote, open, 8" d., Statuesque line, Nude Lady stem, "Charleton" (roses) decoration 200.00
Crown Tuscan vase, 7" h., Sea Shell line 110.00
Cruet w/original stopper, pressed Caprice patt., Crystal, 5 oz. 85.00
Cruet w/original stopper, Strawberry (No. 2780) line, clear 38.00
Cruet w/original stopper & undertray, pressed Caprice patt., Moonlight, 2 pcs. 95.00
Cruet set: two cruets w/original stoppers & underplate; pressed Caprice patt., Crystal, 3 pcs. 60.00
Cup & saucer, etched Cleo patt., Emerald (light green) 18.00
Cup & saucer, Mt. Vernon line, Crystal ..8.00
Decanter w/original stopper, etched Rose Point patt., No. 1321, Crystal 275.00
Decanter w/original stopper, footed, No. 1321, Crystal, 28 oz. 30.00
Decanter w/original stopper, Mt. Vernon line, Crystal, 40 oz. 65.00
Decanter w/original stopper, Nautilus line, Cobalt Blue, 80 oz. 120.00
Figure flower holder, "Bashful Charlotte," Emerald, 13" h. 275.00
Figure flower holder, "Draped Lady," Amber, 8½" h. 165.00
Figure flower holder, "Draped Lady," yellow, 8½" h. .....250.00 to 275.00
Figure flower holder, "Draped Lady," Crystal, 13" h. 140.00
Figure flower holder, "Draped Lady," frosted Amber, 13" h. 265.00
Figure flower holder, "Draped Lady," pink, 13" h. .....250.00 to 275.00
Figure flower holder, "Mandolin Lady," Forest Green (dark green), 9" h. 350.00
Figure flower holder, "Two-Kid," La Rosa (light to medium pink), 8¾" h. 210.00
Figure flower holder, "Two-Kid," Emerald (light green), 8¾" h. 240.00
Finger bowl, Martha Washington line, No. 4, Royal Blue 18.00
Flower holder, Sea Gull, Crystal, 9½" h. 50.00
Flower holder, Sea Gull, Dianthus (pink), 10½" h. 350.00
Goblet, pressed Caprice patt., Crystal, 7½" h. 14.00
Goblet, pressed Caprice patt., No. 300, Moonlight, 9 oz. 38.50
Goblet, Martha Washington line, Crystal 8.00
Goblet, Mt. Vernon line, Crystal, 12 oz. 14.00
Goblet, No. 1401, Mandarin Gold 12.00
Goblet, etched Rose Point patt., No. 3121, Crystal, 10 oz. 25.00
Goblet, Statuesque line, Amber bowl, clear Nude Lady stem 155.00
Goblet, water, etched Wildflower patt., Crystal w/gold trim 28.00
Honey dish, cov., Gadroon (No. 3500) line, Crystal, Farberware cover w/embossed peony design, 5½" sq. 16.50
Ice bucket w/tongs, etched Apple Blossom patt., Topaz (vaseline) 140.00
Ice bucket, etched Cleo patt., blue 135.00
Ice bucket, etched Cleo patt., pink 80.00
Ice bucket w/bail handle, etched Diana patt., Crystal 70.00
Ice bucket w/chrome handle & tongs, etched Rose Point patt., Crystal, 2 pcs. 150.00
Ice bucket, etched Wildflower patt., Crystal 75.00
Ice bucket & six tumblers, Decagon line, Royal Blue, 7 pcs. 175.00
Ivy ball w/keyhole stem, Carmen 60.00
Ivy ball, Statuesque line, Royal Blue bowl, clear Nude Lady stem 150.00
Lemon plate, handled, pressed Caprice patt., Crystal, 6½" d. 10.00

Marmalade jar, cov., etched Chantilly patt., Crystal, silver plate cover & base 80.00
Mayonnaise dish & ladle, etched Rose Point patt., Crystal, 2 pcs. 55.00
Mayonnaise dish & underplate, etched Cleo patt., Crystal, 2 pcs. 45.00
Model of a swan, Dianthus, 6½" l. 85.00
Model of a swan, Ebony, 6½" l. 75.00
Mug, beer, Everglade line, milk white 45.00
Mustard jar, cov., etched Rosepoint patt., Crystal 135.00
Oyster cocktail, etched Rose Point patt., Crystal 38.00
Perfume bottle w/original stopper, Nautilus line, Cobalt Blue, 1½ oz. 85.00
Pitcher, Gadroon (No. 3500) line, Amber, Farber chrome holder, 76 oz. 55.00
Pitcher, ball-shaped, etched Rose Point patt., Amber, 80 oz. 45.00
Pitcher w/ice lip, etched Rose Point patt., Crystal, 80 oz. 180.00
Plate, bread & butter, 6½" d., etched Rose Point patt., Crystal 15.00
Plate, 7½" d., Decagon line, Moonlight 10.00
Plates, 7½" d., etched Wildflower patt., Crystal 11.00
Plate, 7¾" d., etched Cleo patt., blue 20.00
Plate, 7¾" d., etched Cleo patt., Crystal 20.00
Plate, 7¾" w., Decagon line, Moonlight 7.00
Plate, 8" d., etched Elaine patt., Crystal 12.50
Plate, 8½" d., etched Apple Blossom patt., yellow 18.00
Plate, 8½" d., Mt. Vernon line, Crystal 7.00
Plate, 8½" d., etched Rose Point patt., Crystal 40.00
Plate, sandwich, 11½" d., tab handles, etched Rose Point patt., Amber 16.00
Plate, torte, 13" d., three-footed, etched Chantilly patt., Crystal 42.00
Plate, 14" d., Mt. Vernon line, Crystal 19.00
Plates, salad, 7½" d., Caprice patt., Crystal, set of 7 ....62.50
Platter, 11½" oval, three-footed, pressed Caprice patt., Crystal 25.00
Relish dish, etched Apple Blossom patt., Crystal, 9" l. 13.00
Relish, pressed Caprice patt., Crystal, 12" l. 40.00
Relish dish, five-part, etched Chantilly patt., Crystal 35.00
Relish, three-part, etched Diane patt., No. 3400/91, Crystal, 8" l. 22.00
Relish, two-part, etched Elaine patt., Crystal, 9" l. 32.00
Relish dish, five-part, etched Portia patt., Crystal, 12" 80.00
Relish dish, five-part, Pristine line, Crystal, 10" l. 20.00
Relish, three-part, etched Rose Point patt., Crystal, 12" l. 85.00
Salt & pepper shakers w/original tops, etched Chantilly patt., Crystal, pr. 25.00
Salt & pepper shakers w/original tops, tilt-type, Nautilus line, Cobalt Blue, pr. 55.00
Salt & pepper shakers, footed, No. 3400/77 line, etched Rose Point patt., Crystal, pr. 60.00
Sherbet, pressed Caprice patt., Crystal 18.00
Sherbet, pressed Caprice patt., Moonlight, 5¾" h. 20.00
Sherbet, tall, etched Cleo patt., Crystal 22.00
Sherbet, high stem, Mt. Vernon line, Crystal, 6½ oz. 9.00
Sherbet, low, etched Rose Point patt., Crystal 16.00
Sherbet, sq., No. 3797, Crystal "crackle" 55.00

Child's Colonial Pattern Spooner

Spooner, child's, Colonial patt., Emerald (ILLUS.) 30.00
Tumbler, Apple Blossom etching, Emerald, 12 oz. 45.00
Tumbler, footed, pressed Caprice patt., Moonlight, 12 oz. 40.00
Tumbler, whiskey, pressed Caprice patt., Crystal 20.00
Tumbler, footed, etched Cleo patt., Crystal, 5½" h., 12 oz. 45.00
Tumbler, iced tea, etched Grape patt., Crystal, 10 oz. 20.00
Tumbler, Mt. Vernon line, Crystal 10.00
Tumbler, footed, etched Rose Point patt., Crystal, 12 oz. 30.00
Tumbler, iced tea, etched Rose Point patt., Crystal 40.00
Urn, cov., Mt. Vernon line, Carmen 105.00
Vase, 3½" h., pressed Caprice patt., Amber 80.00
Vase, bud, 5" h., etched Rose Point patt., Crystal w/gold trim 70.00

Vase, 10" h., keyhole base, etched Rose Point patt., Crystal 65.00
Vase, 10½" h., pressed Block Optic patt., Rubina 155.00
Vase, 12" h., etched Wildflower patt., Crystal.....85.00
Water set: 32 oz. pitcher & six 5 oz. tumblers; pressed Caprice patt., Moonlight, 7 pcs.....575.00
Wine, etched Rose Point patt., Crystal.....43.00
Wine, Statuesque line, Carmen bowl, clear Nude Lady stem, 7¾" h.....125.00
Wine set: decanter & six wines; Mt. Vernon line, Crystal w/gold trim, 7 pcs. 150.00

CARNIVAL GLASS

Earlier called Taffeta glass, the Carnival glass now being collected was introduced early in this century. Its producers gave it an iridescence that attempted to imitate that of some Tiffany glass. Collectors will find available books by leading authorities Donald E. Moore, Sherman Hand, Marion T. Hartung and Rose M. Presznick.

ACANTHUS (Imperial)

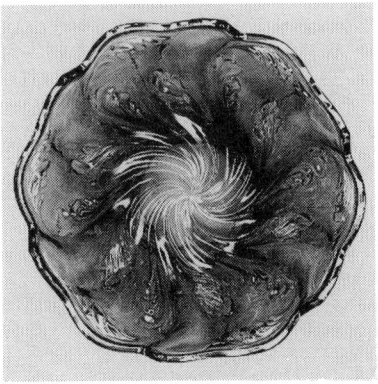

Acanthus Bowl

Bowl, 7" d., green $20.00
Bowl, 7" d., marigold.....46.50
Bowl, 7½" d., purple.....80.00
Bowl, 7¾" d., smoky 45.00
Bowl, 8" to 9" d., green 88.00
Bowl, 8" to 9" d., marigold (ILLUS.) 62.00
Bowl, 8" to 9" d., purple 95.00
Bowl, 8" to 9" d., smoky.....85.00
Plate, 9" to 10" d., marigold 193.00
Plate, 9" to 10" d., smoky.....250.00

ACORN (Fenton)

Bowl, 3½" d., marigold.....50.00
Bowl, 5" d., milk white w/marigold overlay 322.00
Bowl, 6" d., aqua.....128.00
Bowl, 6" d., blue.....45.00
Bowl, 6" d., ruffled, sapphire blue.....90.00
Bowl, 6" d., vaseline 40.00
Bowl, 7" d., ruffled, amber 98.00
Bowl, 7" d., aqua.....82.50
Bowl, 7" d., blue.....44.00
Bowl, 7" d., green 68.00
Bowl, 7" d., ice blue 150.00
Bowl, 7" d., lime green.....55.00
Bowl, 7" d., marigold.....35.00
Bowl, 7" d., peach opalescent 185.00
Bowl, 7" d., ruffled, peach opalescent.....300.00
Bowl, 7" d., purple.....45.00
Bowl, 7" d., red .....550.00 to 600.00
Bowl, 7" d., vaseline 170.00
Bowl, 7" d., ruffled, vaseline .....100.00 to 125.00
Bowl, 8" to 9" d., blue.....55.00
Bowl, 8" to 9" d., ice blue.....350.00
Bowl, 8" to 9" d., marigold.....35.00
Bowl, 8" to 9" d., ribbon candy rim, purple.....115.00
Bowl, 8" to 9" d., ruffled, red.....700.00 to 750.00
Bowl, ice cream shape, aqua 125.00
Bowl, ice cream shape, blue.....35.00
Bowl, ice cream shape, green 65.00
Bowl, ice cream shape, ice blue w/marigold overlay.....75.00
Bowl, ice cream shape, moonstone 185.00
Bowl, ice cream shape, red slag.....650.00
Bowl, ice cream shape, teal blue.....75.00
Bowl, ruffled, aqua opalescent 125.00
Bowl, ruffled, green.....70.00
Bowl, ruffled, marigold.....30.00
Bowl, ruffled, moonstone.....450.00
Bowl, ruffled, peach opalescent.....362.00
Bowl, white 180.00

ACORN BURRS (Northwood)

Berry set: master bowl & 5 sauce dishes; purple, 6 pcs.....350.00 to 400.00
Berry set: master bowl & 6 sauce dishes; green, 7 pcs.....350.00
Bowl, master berry, 10" d., green 80.00
Bowl, master berry, 10" d., marigold 78.00
Bowl, master berry, 10" d., purple 175.00
Butter dish, cov., green.....300.00 to 375.00
Butter dish, cov., marigold.....178.00
Butter dish, cov., purple.....175.00 to 200.00
Creamer, green 90.00
Creamer, marigold.....100.00
Creamer, purple.....100.00
Creamer & sugar bowl, purple, pr.....250.00
Pitcher, water, marigold.....325.00
Pitcher, water, purple.....350.00 to 400.00
Punch bowl & base, purple, 2 pcs. 795.00

Punch cup, aqua opalescent 1,800.00
Punch cup, blue 85.00
Punch cup, green 40.00
Punch cup, ice blue 100.00
Punch cup, ice green 97.00
Punch cup, marigold 21.00
Punch cup, purple 30.00
Punch cup, white 55.00
Punch set: bowl, case & 5 cups; green, 7 pcs. .....1,200.00 to 1,600.00
Punch set: bowl, base & 6 cups; ice blue, 8 pcs. 7,000.00
Punch set: bowl, base & 6 cups; marigold, 8 pcs. 1,000.00
Punch set: bowl, base & 6 cups; purple, 8 pcs. 1,500.00
Punch set: bowl, base & 6 cups; white, 8 pcs 4,000.00
Sauce dish, green 37.50
Sauce dish, marigold 30.00
Sauce dish, purple 45.00
Spooner, green 150.00
Spooner, marigold 88.00
Spooner, purple .....100.00 to 125.00
Table set: cov. sugar bowl, creamer, spooner & cov. butter dish; marigold, 4 pcs. 900.00
Table set, purple, 4 pcs 1,000.00
Tumbler, green 78.00
Tumbler, marigold 50.00
Tumbler, purple 58.00
Water set: pitcher & 4 tumblers; marigold, 5 pcs. .....600.00 to 650.00
Water set: pitcher & 6 tumblers; green, 7 pcs. 1,200.00
Water set: pitcher & 6 tumblers; purple, 7 pcs. .....750.00 to 800.00

ADVERTISING & SOUVENIR ITEMS

BPOE Elks Plate

Basket, "Feldman Bros. Furniture, Salisbury, Md.," open edge, marigold .....50.00 to 75.00
Basket, "John H. Brand Furniture Co., Wilmington, Del.," marigold 60.00
Bell, souvenir, BPOE Elks, "Atlantic City, 1911," blue 2,250.00
Bell, souvenir, BPOE Elks, "Parkersburg, 1914," blue 1,250.00
Bowl, "Isaac Benesch," 6¼" d., purple (Millersburg) .....300.00 to 325.00
Bowl, "Bernheimer Brothers," blue 1,000.00
Bowl, "Dreibus Parfait Sweet," ruffled, smoky lavender 400.00
Bowl, "Horlacher," Peacock Tail patt., green 100.00
Bowl, "Horlacher," Thistle patt., green 100.00
Bowl, "Ogden Furniture Co.," purple 225.00
Bowl, "Sterling Furniture," purple 600.00
Bowl, souvenir, BPOE Elks, "Atlantic City, 1911," blue, one-eyed Elk 675.00
Bowl, souvenir, BPOE Elks, "Detroit, 1910," blue, one-eyed Elk 550.00
Bowl, souvenir, BPOE Elks, "Detroit, 1910," green, one-eyed Elk 1,000.00
Bowl, souvenir, BPOE Elks, "Detroit, 1910," ruffled, green 250.00
Bowl, souvenir, BPOE Elks, "Detroit, 1910," marigold 845.00
Bowl, souvenir, BPOE Elks, "Detroit, 1910," purple, one-eyed Elk 385.00
Bowl, souvenir, BPOE Elks, "Detroit, 1910," purple, two-eyed Elk (Millersburg) .....775.00 to 825.00
Bowl, souvenir, "Brooklyn Bridge," marigold .....300.00 to 325.00
Bowl, souvenir, Brooklyn Bridge, unlettered, marigold .....475.00 to 550.00
Bowl, souvenir, "Millersburg Courthouse," purple 550.00
Bowl, souvenir, Millersburg Courthouse, unlettered, purple 965.00
Card tray, "Fern Brand Chocolates," turned-up sides, 6¼" d., purple 175.00
Card tray, "Isaac Benesch," Holly Whirl patt., marigold .....50.00 to 70.00
Dish, "Compliments of Pacific Coast Mail Order House, Los Angeles, California" 700.00
Hat, "Arthur O'Dell," green 75.00
Hat, "General Furniture Co." 1910, Peacock Tail patt., green 75.00
Hat, "Horlacher," Peacock Tail patt., green 70.00
Hat, "John Brand Furniture," green 42.00
Hat, "John Brand Furniture," open edge, marigold 45.00
Hat, "Miller's Furniture - Harrisburg," basketweave, marigold 75.00
Paperweight, souvenir, BPOE Elks, green 625.00
Paperweight, souvenir, BPOE Elks, purple (Millersburg) .....600.00 to 700.00
Plate, "Ballard, California," purple (Northwood) 900.00
Plate, "Bird of Paradise," purple 220.00

Plate, "Brazier Candies," w/handgrip, 6" d., purple....500.00 to 600.00
Plate, "Davidson Chocolate Society," 6¼" d., purple....230.00
Plate, "Dreibus Parfait Sweets," 6¼" d., purple....400.00
Plate, "Eagle Furniture Co.," purple....750.00
Plate, "Fern Brand Chocolates," 6" d., purple....700.00
Plate, "Gervitz Bros., Furniture & Clothing," w/handgrip, 6" d., purple....1,350.00
Plate, "Greengard Furniture Co.," purple....625.00
Plate, "F.A. Hudson Furniture Co.," 7" d., purple (Northwood)....225.00
Plate, "Jockey Club," w/handgrip, 6" d., purple....500.00
Plate, "Old Rose Distillery," Grape & Cable patt., stippled, 9" d., green....370.00
Plate, "Roods Chocolate, Pueblo," purple....750.00
Plate, "Season's Greetings - Eat Paradise Soda Candies," 6" d., purple....178.00
Plate, "Spector's Department Store," Heart & Vine patt., 9" d., marigold....450.00
Plate, "Utah Liquor Co.," w/handgrip, 6" d., purple....950.00
Plate, "We Use Brocker's," 7" d., purple....495.00
Plate, souvenir, BPOE Elks, "Atlantic City, 1911," blue (ILLUS.)....800.00 to 900.00
Plate, souvenir, BPOE Elks, "Parkersburg, 1914," 7½" d., blue....1,050.00
Vase, "Howard Furniture," Four Pillars patt., green....80.00

AMARYLLIS (Dugan)
Compote, tri-corner, miniature, marigold....225.00 to 275.00
Compote, marigold....143.00
Compote, purple....112.00

APPLE BLOSSOMS
Bowl, 5½" d., purple....42.50
Bowl, 6" d., marigold....22.00
Bowl, 6" d., deep, purple....30.00
Bowl, 7" d., collared base, marigold....32.00
Bowl, 7" d., collared base, purple....70.00
Bowl, 7" d., ribbon candy rim, marigold....25.00
Bowl, 7" d., ribbon candy rim, white....135.00
Lamp, kerosene-type, small, green....1,200.00
Lamp, kerosene-type, large w/pattern on interior of lamp base, green....3,100.00
Rose bowl, marigold....65.00
Tumbler, enameled, blue....120.00

APPLE BLOSSOM TWIGS
Banana boat, ruffled, peach opalescent....175.00
Bowl, 8" to 9" d., blue....80.00
Bowl, 8" to 9" d., marigold....55.00 to 75.00
Bowl, 8" to 9" d., peach opalescent....143.00
Bowl, 8" to 9" d., purple....115.00
Bowl, 8" to 9" d., white....90.00
Bowl, 9" d., ice cream shape, white....150.00 to 175.00
Plate, 9" d., blue....265.00
Plate, 9" d., ruffled, blue....210.00
Plate, 9" d., marigold....100.00
Plate, 9" d., ruffled, marigold....130.00
Plate, 9" d., peach opalescent....400.00
Plate, 9" d., purple....200.00 to 300.00
Plate, 9" d., flat, smooth edge, purple....900.00
Plate, 9" d., white....200.00 to 250.00
Plate, 9" d., ruffled, white....165.00
Plate, chop, peach opalescent....375.00 to 400.00

APPLE TREE
Pitcher, water, marigold....115.00
Pitcher, water, white....350.00
Tumbler, blue....70.00
Tumbler, marigold....42.00
Tumbler, white....250.00
Water set: pitcher & 6 tumblers; blue, 7 pcs.....820.00

APRIL SHOWERS (Fenton)
Vase, 8" h., green....40.00
Vase, 8½" h., Peacock Tail interior, purple....85.00
Vase, 11" h., blue....47.00
Vase, 11½" h., marigold....35.00
Vase, 12" h., Peacock Tail interior, marigold....35.00
Vase, 12" h., Peacock Tail interior, purple....50.00
Vase, 12" h., vaseline....110.00
Vase, green....45.00
Vase, purple opalescent....700.00 to 750.00

AUSTRALIAN
Berry set: master bowl & 6 sauce dishes; Magpie, marigold, 7 pcs.....325.00
Bowl, 5½" d., Swan, marigold....45.00
Bowl, 9" to 10" d., Emu, aqua....550.00
Bowl, 9" to 10" d., Emu, marigold....145.00
Bowl, 9" to 10" d., Kangaroo, marigold....100.00
Bowl, 9" to 10" d., Kangaroo, purple....150.00 to 170.00
Bowl, 9" to 10" d., Kingfisher, purple....150.00

Bowl, 9" to 10" d., Kiwi, ruffled, marigold 250.00
Bowl, 9" to 10" d., Kiwi, purple 250.00
Bowl, 9" to 10" d., Kookaburra, marigold 98.00
Bowl, 9" to 10" d., Magpie, marigold 115.00
Bowl, 9" to 10" d., Magpie, purple 110.00
Bowl, 9" to 10" d., Swan, purple 175.00
Bowl, 9" to 10" d., Thunderbird, marigold 200.00
Bowl, 9" to 10" d., Thunderbird, purple 165.00
Bowl, 11" d., ice cream shape, Kookaburra, marigold 135.00
Bowl, 11" d., ice cream shape, Kookaburra variant, marigold 135.00
Bowl, 11" d., ice cream shape, Kookaburra variant, purple 300.00
Bowl, pin-up, purple 65.00
Cake plate, Butterfly & Bells, marigold 78.00
Compote, Butterflies & Waratah, aqua 135.00
Compote, Butterflies & Waratah, marigold ....175.00 to 200.00
Compote, Butterflies & Waratah, purple 210.00
Compote, Butterfly & Bush, marigold 86.00
Sauce dish, Kangaroo, marigold 70.00
Sauce dish, Kangaroo, purple 64.00
Sauce dish, Kingfisher, marigold 60.00
Sauce dish, Kookaburra, marigold 65.00
Sauce dish, Kookaburra, purple 45.00
Sauce dish, Swan, marigold 65.00
Sauce dish, Thunderbird, marigold 65.00
Sauce dish, Thunderbird, purple 85.00

BANDED DRAPE

Mug, marigold 25.00
Pitcher, water, green 450.00
Pitcher, water, marigold w/enameled iris 600.00
Water set: tankard pitcher & 6 tumblers; h.p. decoration, marigold, 7 pcs. 395.00

BASKET (Fenton's Open Edge)

Amber ....200.00 to 250.00
Amberina, w/two rows, two sides turned up 125.00
Aqua 74.00
Aqua, w/two rows, jack-in-the-pulpit shape ....100.00 to 125.00
Aqua, w/two rows, two sides turned up 110.00
Aqua opalescent 145.00
Black amethyst 365.00
Blue 50.00
Celeste blue 92.00
Green 53.00
Green, hat shape 85.00
Green, low sides ....125.00 to 175.00
Ice blue 195.00
Ice blue, w/two rows, open edge, six ruffled ....225.00 to 295.00
Ice blue, w/three rows 600.00
Ice green 240.00
Ice green, w/three rows 450.00
Marigold, 5" h., w/applied crystal handle 75.00
Marigold 40.00
Purple 110.00
Red 340.00
Red, hat shape ....400.00 to 450.00
Red, jack-in-the-pulpit shape ....425.00 to 450.00
Red, w/two rows, small 325.00
Reverse Amberina 650.00
Vaseline ....75.00 to 100.00
Vaseline, plain interior 275.00
Vaseline, w/two rows, large 75.00
White, w/two rows 150.00
White, 6" ....200.00 to 250.00

BASKET (Northwood) or BUSHEL BASKET

Aqua, 4½" d., 4¾" h. 425.00
Aqua opalescent, 4½" d., 4¾" h. ....450.00 to 500.00
Blue 147.00
Blue w/electric iridescence 160.00
Celeste blue 1,900.00
Clambroth 400.00
Cobalt blue ....150.00 to 200.00
Green 540.00
Honey amber ....400.00 to 500.00
Horehound, variant 1,250.00
Ice blue ....600.00 to 800.00
Ice green ....275.00 to 300.00
Lavender 190.00
Lime green 350.00
Lime green opalescent 1,500.00
Marigold 108.00
Olive green 550.00
Purple ....100.00 to 125.00
Sapphire blue 1,750.00
Smoky 750.00
Teal blue 450.00
Vaseline 2,600.00
White ....125.00 to 150.00

BEADED BULL'S EYE (Imperial)

Vase, 8" h., marigold 38.00
Vase, 10½" h., marigold 50.00
Vase, 10½" h., purple 195.00
Vase, green 35.00
Vase, marigold 35.00
Vase, purple 38.00

BEADED CABLE (Northwood)

Bowl, 7" d., three-footed, green 50.00
Bowl, 7" d., three-footed, ruffled, marigold 35.00
Candy dish, green 50.00

Candy dish, marigold.....30.00
Candy dish, purple.....55.00
Rose bowl, aqua.....350.00
Rose bowl, aqua opalescent 305.00
Rose bowl, blue.....100.00 to 125.00
Rose bowl, blue w/electric iridescence.....300.00
Rose bowl, green.....108.00
Rose bowl, ice blue .....850.00 to 1,000.00
Rose bowl, ice green.....950.00 to 1,300.00
Rose bowl, lime green opalescent...1,200.00
Rose bowl, marigold.....75.00

Beaded Cable Rose Bowl

Rose bowl, purple (ILLUS.) 97.00
Rose bowl, white .....450.00 to 550.00

BEADED SHELL (Dugan or Diamond Glass Co.)

Bowl, 8½" d., footed, purple.....165.00
Creamer, marigold.....65.00
Mug, blue.....150.00 to 200.00
Mug, marigold.....120.00
Mug, purple.....91.00
Mug, purple, souvenir.....150.00
Mug, white 1,000.00
Sauce dish, marigold.....30.00
Spooner, footed, marigold 60.00
Sugar bowl, cov., marigold 55.00
Table set, marigold, 4 pcs. 275.00
Tumbler, blue.....118.00
Tumbler, lavender.....80.00
Tumbler, marigold.....55.00
Tumbler, purple 62.00

BEAUTY BUD VASE

Purple, 6½" h.....75.00 to 100.00
Marigold, 8" h.....30.00
Purple, 8" h.....40.00
Marigold, 9½" h.....35.00

BIG FISH BOWL (Millersburg)

Green.....595.00
Green, square.....900.00 to 1,000.00
Marigold.....507.00
Marigold, ice cream shape 550.00
Marigold, square.....850.00
Purple, ice cream shape.....660.00

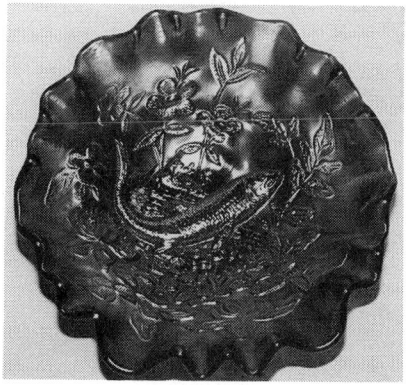

Big Fish Bowl

Purple, ruffled (ILLUS.).....704.00
Purple, square 700.00

BIRD WITH GRAPES

Bird with Grapes Wall Vase

Wall vase, marigold, 7½" w., 8" h. (ILLUS.) 60.00

BLACKBERRY (Fenton)

Basket, aqua.....150.00
Basket, blue.....42.00
Basket, clambroth.....45.00
Basket, green 95.00
Basket, marigold.....65.00
Basket, purple.....72.00
Basket, red 250.00
Basket, smoky w/marigold overlay 75.00
Bowl, 5" d., purple.....30.00
Bowl, 7" d., purple.....80.00
Bowl, 8" to 9" d., ruffled, green 90.00
Bowl, 8" to 9" d., ruffled, marigold.....50.00
Bowl, 8" to 9" d., ruffled, purple 58.00
Bowl, 10" d., ruffled, blue.....650.00
Bowl, nut, open edge, Basketweave exterior, purple.....60.00
Plate, openwork rim, marigold.....550.00
Vase, whimsey, open edge, blue opalescent 900.00

Vase, whimsey, open edge, marigold 650.00

BLACKBERRY BRAMBLE
Compote, ruffled, green 54.00
Compote, ruffled, lavender 50.00
Compote, ruffled, marigold 45.00
Compote, ruffled, purple 46.00

BLACKBERRY MINIATURE COMPOTE
Blue 113.00
Blue, flat top 325.00
Blue, w/red stem 350.00
Green 200.00
Marigold 87.00
Purple 85.00
White 448.00

BLACKBERRY SPRAY
Bonbon, marigold 30.00
Bowl, 7" d., marigold 20.00
Compote, 5½" d., purple 95.00
Hat shape, amber ....100.00 to 150.00
Hat shape, Amberina ....280.00 to 300.00
Hat shape, aqua 75.00
Hat shape, jack-in-the-pulpit, crimped rim, aqua 85.00
Hat shape, aqua opalescent 475.00
Hat shape, jack-in-the-pulpit, aqua opalescent 300.00
Hat shape, blue 40.00
Hat shape, blue opalescent 585.00
Hat shape, jack-in-the-pulpit, crimped rim, blue 50.00
Hat shape, jack-in-the-pulpit, crimped rim, clambroth 27.00
Hat shape, green 75.00
Hat shape, ice green opalescent 350.00
Hat shape, jack-in-the-pulpit, lime green w/marigold overlay 35.00
Hat shape, lime green opalescent 325.00
Hat shape, marigold 32.50
Hat shape, purple 50.00
Hat shape, red 388.00
Hat shape, red slag 475.00
Hat shape, Reverse Amberina 450.00
Hat shape, vaseline 70.00
Hat shape, jack-in-the-pulpit, crimped rim, vaseline 65.00
Hat shape, vaseline w/marigold overlay 54.00

BLACKBERRY WREATH (Millersburg)
Bowl, 5" d., green 52.00
Bowl, 5" d., marigold 35.00
Bowl, 5" d., ruffled, marigold 100.00 to125.00
Bowl, 5" d., purple 55.00
Bowl, 5" d., candy ribbon edge, purple ....75.00 to 100.00
Bowl, 7" d., green 68.00
Bowl, 7" d., marigold 50.00
Bowl, 7" d., purple 70.00
Bowl, 7½" d., three-in-one edge, clambroth 75.00
Bowl, 8" to 9" d., green 93.00
Bowl, 8" to 9" d., marigold 55.00
Bowl, 8" to 9" d., purple 85.00
Bowl, 10" d., blue ....850.00 to 950.00
Bowl, 10" d., green 82.00
Bowl, 10" d., marigold 90.00
Bowl, 10" d., purple 165.00
Bowl, ice cream, large, marigold 68.00
Bowl, ice cream, large, purple ....200.00 to 225.00

BOUQUET
Pitcher, water, blue 550.00
Tumbler, blue 57.00
Tumbler, marigold 32.00
Water set: pitcher & 1 tumbler; blue, 2 pcs. 400.00
Water set: pitcher & 4 tumblers; marigold, 5 pcs. 375.00

BROKEN ARCHES (Imperial)

Broken Arches Punch Cup

Punch bowl, purple, 12" d. 500.00
Punch bowl & base, marigold, 12" d., 2 pcs. 300.00
Punch bowl & base, purple, 12" d., 2 pcs. 450.00
Punch cup, marigold 25.00
Punch cup, purple (ILLUS.) 38.00
Punch set: bowl, base & 6 cups; purple, 8 pcs. 915.00

BUSHEL BASKET - See Basket (Northwood) Pattern

BUTTERFLY (Northwood)
Bonbon, threaded exterior, blue ....250.00 to 270.00
Bonbon, handled, threaded exterior, blue w/electric iridescence 450.00
Bonbon, threaded exterior, ice blue 2,200.00
Bonbon, green 88.00
Bonbon, marigold 50.00
Bonbon, purple 74.00
Bonbon, threaded exterior, purple ....225.00 to 250.00
Bonbon, smoky 350.00

BUTTERFLY & BERRY (Fenton)

Butterfly & Berry Pitcher

Berry set: master bowl & 5 sauce dishes; marigold, 6 pcs. 240.00
Bowl, 7" d., three-footed, marigold 65.00
Bowl, 8" to 9" d., footed, blue....55.00
Bowl, 8" to 9" d., footed, marigold 72.00
Bowl, 8" to 9" d., footed, purple 175.00
Bowl, master berry or fruit, four-footed, blue 95.00
Bowl, master berry or fruit, four-footed, green....150.00
Bowl, master berry or fruit, four-footed, marigold 82.00
Bowl, master berry or fruit, four-footed, purple....120.00
Bowl, master berry or fruit, four-footed, white ....250.00 to 275.00
Butter dish, cov., blue 250.00
Butter dish, cov., green....280.00
Butter dish, cov., marigold 126.00
Centerpiece bowl, purple....500.00
Creamer, blue....85.00
Creamer, marigold....70.00
Creamer, purple....145.00
Creamer & cov. sugar bowl, marigold, pr. 190.00
Hatpin holder, blue 1,900.00
Hatpin holder, marigold 1,550.00
Nut bowl, purple....437.00
Pitcher, water, blue....425.00
Pitcher, water, marigold (ILLUS.) ....225.00 to 275.00
Sauce dish, blue....42.00
Sauce dish, green....45.00
Sauce dish, marigold....30.00
Sauce dish, purple....50.00 to 75.00
Spooner, blue 120.00
Spooner, marigold 62.00
Spooner, purple 140.00
Sugar bowl, cov., blue 120.00
Sugar bowl, cov., marigold 82.00
Tumbler, blue....60.50
Tumbler, green 85.00
Tumbler, marigold....39.50
Tumbler, purple 325.00
Vase, 6" h., marigold 35.00
Vase, 7" h., blue 65.00
Vase, 7" h., green 145.00
Vase, 7" h., marigold 30.00
Vase, 8" h., blue 65.00
Vase, 8" h., marigold 35.00
Vase, 9" h., blue 80.00
Vase, 9" h., marigold 50.00
Vase, 9" h., purple 50.00
Vase, 10" h., blue 50.00
Vase, amber 130.00
Vase, green 170.00

BUTTERFLY & FERN (Fenton)

Pitcher, water, blue....425.00
Pitcher, water, green 425.00
Pitcher, water, marigold....275.00 to 325.00
Tumbler, blue....45.00
Tumbler, green 59.00
Tumbler, marigold....32.00
Tumbler, pastel marigold 35.00
Tumbler, purple 45.00
Water set: pitcher & 6 tumblers; blue, 7 pcs. 775.00
Water set: pitcher & 6 tumblers; green, 7 pcs. 850.00
Water set: pitcher & 6 tumblers; marigold, 7 pcs. 515.00

BUZZ SAW - See Double Star Pattern

CAPTIVE ROSE

Bonbon, two-handled, blue, 7½" d....125.00
Bowl, 6" d., blue....35.00
Bowl, 8" to 9" d., blue....77.00
Bowl, 8" to 9" d., green 60.00
Bowl, 8" to 9" d., marigold....68.00
Bowl, 8" to 9" d., purple 46.00
Bowl, 8" to 9" d., ribbon candy rim, green....70.00
Bowl, 8" to 9" d., ribbon candy rim, marigold 67.00
Bowl, 8" to 9" d., ribbon candy rim, purple....68.00
Bowl, 8" to 9" d., ruffled rim, blue....80.00
Bowl, 8" to 9" d., ruffled rim, green....125.00
Bowl, 8" to 9" d., ruffled rim, marigold 35.00
Compote, blue 75.00
Compote, marigold 55.00
Compote, white....125.00
Compote, ribbon candy rim, purple....100.00
Plate, 6" d., marigold 65.00
Plate, 9" d., blue ....425.00 to 525.00
Plate, 9" d., green 975.00
Plate, 9" d., marigold 321.00
Plate, 9" d., purple 485.00

CARNIVAL HOLLY - See Holly Pattern

CAROLINE

Banana bowl, peach opalescent.....65.00
Basket w/applied handle, peach opalescent .....375.00 to 400.00
Bowl, 8" d., handgrip, ruffled, peach opalescent 140.00
Bowl, 8" to 9" d., peach opalescent 65.00
Bowl, 8" to 9" d., tricornered, peach opalescent .....125.00 to 150.00
Bowl, 9" d., ruffled, peach opalescent 160.00
Bowl, 9" sq., peach opalescent.....65.00
Plate, w/handgrip, peach opalescent 125.00

CATTAILS & WATER LILY - See Water Lily & Cattails Pattern

CHATELAINE

Chatelaine Pitcher

Pitcher, purple (ILLUS.) 2,500.00
Tumbler, purple 255.00

CHERRY (Dugan)

Bowl, 6" d., clambroth opalescent 30.00
Bowl, 6" d., Jeweled Heart exterior, purple 45.00
Bowl, 6" d., purple.....60.00
Bowl, 7" d., three-footed, crimped rim, peach opalescent.....95.00
Bowl, 8" d., ruffled, purple.....125.00
Bowl, 8" to 9" d., three-footed, marigold 135.00
Bowl, 8" to 9" d., three-footed, peach opalescent .....250.00 to 300.00
Bowl, 8" to 9" d., three-footed, purple 116.00
Bowl, 10" d., Jeweled Heart exterior, purple 260.00
Bowl, large, peach opalescent.....240.00
Bowl, large, Jeweled Heart exterior, purple 275.00
Dish, ruffled, marigold, 6" d. 80.00
Dish, ruffled, purple, 6" d. 50.00
Plate, 6" d., ruffled, purple 150.00
Plate, 6½" d., candy ribbon rim, purple .....225.00 to 250.00
Plate, 6½" d., ruffled, Jeweled Heart exterior, purple 95.00
Sauce dish, peach opalescent.....65.00
Sauce dish, Jeweled Heart exterior, ruffled, peach opalescent.....75.00
Sauce dish, purple 45.00

CHERRY or CHERRY CIRCLES (Fenton)

Red Cherry Bonbon

Bonbon, two-handled, aqua.....280.00
Bonbon, two-handled, blue.....50.00
Bonbon, two-handled, marigold.....38.00
Bonbon, two-handled, red (ILLUS.) 7,250.00
Bowl, 5" d., fluted, blue 30.00
Bowl, 5" d., marigold.....32.00
Bowl, 5" d., purple.....40.00
Bowl, 7" d., three-footed, marigold 42.50
Bowl, 7" d., three-footed, peach opalescent w/plain interior 90.00
Bowl, 10" d., vaseline w/ marigold overlay 75.00
Bowl, 10" d., ruffled, white 100.00
Card tray, aqua.....125.00
Plate, 6" d., blue 100.00
Plate, 6" d., Orange tree exterior, marigold 80.00
Plate, 6" d., purple 275.00

CHERRY or HANGING CHERRIES (Millersburg)

Banana compote (whimsey), blue 625.00
Banana compote (whimsey), green.....1,500.00
Bowl, 4" d., green 75.00
Bowl, 5" d., blue.....825.00 to 875.00
Bowl, 5" d., green 62.00
Bowl, 5" d., ruffled, marigold.....50.00
Bowl, 5" d., piecrust rim, purple 49.00
Bowl, 6" d., ruffled, green 95.00
Bowl, 7" d., marigold.....80.00
Bowl, 7" d., purple.....88.00

Bowl, 7" d., ice cream shape, marigold 112.00
Bowl, 8" to 9" d., ruffled, green 264.00
Bowl, 8" to 9" d., ice cream shape, green....175.00 to 200.00
Bowl, 8" to 9" d., dome-footed, marigold 70.00
Bowl, 8" to 9" d., purple 60.00
Bowl, 9" d., Hobnail exterior, marigold 795.00
Bowl, 10" d., ice cream shape, green....194.00
Bowl, 10" d., ice cream shape, marigold 125.00
Bowl, 10" d., ice cream shape, purple....175.00 to 200.00
Bowl, 10" d., three-in-one rim, marigold 245.00
Bowl, 10" d., purple....310.00
Bowl, 10½" d., ruffled, white 125.00
Bowl, ruffled, Hobnail exterior, marigold, large 468.00
Butter dish, cov., green....227.00
Butter dish, cov., marigold....190.00
Compote, green....1,400.00
Creamer, green 77.00
Creamer, marigold....70.00
Creamer, purple....75.00
Pitcher, milk, marigold 600.00
Pitcher, milk, purple 418.00
Pitcher, water, marigold....200.00
Pitcher, water, purple....600.00
Plate, 7" d., purple 225.00
Spooner, green....68.00
Spooner, marigold 75.00
Sugar bowl, cov., marigold 85.00
Tumbler, green 290.00
Tumbler, marigold....200.00

CHERRY CIRCLES - SEE CHERRY (Fenton) Pattern

CHRISTMAS COMPOTE

Christmas Compote

Marigold (ILLUS.) 4,000.00
Purple 3,500.00

CHRYSANTHEMUM or WINDMILL & MUMS

Bowl, 8" to 9" d., three-footed, blue 125.00
Bowl, 8" to 9" d., three-footed, green....78.00
Bowl, 8" to 9" d., three-footed, marigold 46.00
Bowl, 9" d., ruffled, blue....115.00
Bowl, 9" d., ruffled, green ...175.00 to 200.00
Bowl, 9" d., marigold....52.00
Bowl, 9" d., ruffled, marigold....120.00
Bowl, 9" d., ruffled, purple....150.00
Bowl, 9" d., red w/amber center....4,100.00
Bowl, 10" d., three-footed, marigold 82.00
Bowl, 10" d., three-footed, purple 75.00
Bowl, 10" d., collared base, red....5,000.00
Bowl, 11" d., three-footed, blue 200.00
Bowl, 11" d., three-footed, green 250.00
Bowl, 11" d., three-footed, marigold 52.00
Bowl, 12" d., three-footed, ruffled, black amethyst....575.00
Bowl, 12" d., three-footed, vaseline 275.00
Bowl, collared base, green 238.00
Bowl, collared base, purple....300.00 to 350.00
Bowl, orange, footed, vaseline 350.00

COBBLESTONES BOWL (Imperial)

Marigold, 7" d....67.00
Green, 9" d. 100.00
Purple, 9" d. 112.00

COIN DOT

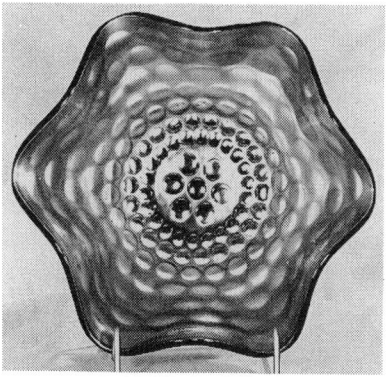

Coin Dot Bowl

Bowl, 6" d., green 25.00
Bowl, 6" d., ice cream shape red....1,500.00
Bowl, 6½" d., lavender....30.00
Bowl, 6½" d., stippled, purple 32.00
Bowl, 7" d., blue....30.00
Bowl, 7" d., green 30.00
Bowl, 7" d., marigold....38.00
Bowl, 7" d., red 1,500.00
Bowl, 7" d., ribbon candy rim, green....50.00
Bowl, 7" d., ribbon candy rim, marigold 40.00
Bowl, 7" d., ribbon candy rim, purple 40.00
Bowl, 8" to 9" d., amber 65.00
Bowl, 8" to 9" d., stippled, aqua 46.00
Bowl, 8" to 9" d., blue....32.00
Bowl, 8" to 9" d., blue opalescent 300.00

Bowl, 8" to 9" d., green 42.50
Bowl, 8" to 9" d., stippled, green.....25.00
Bowl, 8" to 9" d., lavender.....75.00
Bowl, 8" to 9" d., marigold.....35.00
Bowl, 8" to 9" d., stippled, marigold 75.00
Bowl, 8" to 9" d., peach opalescent 173.00
Bowl, 8" to 9" d., purple (ILLUS.) 43.00
Bowl, 8" to 9" d., ruffled, vaseline 55.00
Bowl, 9½" d., ruffled, purple 68.00
Bowl, 9½" d., stippled, purple 35.00
Bowl, 10" d., green 35.00
Bowl, 10" d., stippled, marigold 28.00
Bowl, 10" d., ruffled, peach opalescent 165.00
Bowl, aqua.....65.00
Bowl, red.....1,700.00
Pitcher, water, marigold.....150.00
Plate, 9" d., aqua 80.00
Plate, 9" d., purple 90.00
Rose bowl, green.....80.00
Rose bowl, stippled, green 75.00
Rose bowl, marigold.....50.00
Rose bowl, large, marigold.....78.00
Rose bowl, purple.....52.00
Rose bowl, stippled, purple 80.00
Tumbler, marigold.....50.00

COIN SPOT (Dugan)
Compote, 7" d., marigold.....35.00
Compote, 7" d., peach opalescent.....60.00
Compote, 7" d., fluted, peach opalescent .....85.00 to 100.00
Compote, 7" d., fluted, purple.....65.00
Vase, 10" h., purple 25.00
Water set: lemonade pitcher & 4 tumblers; marigold, 5 pcs.....365.00

COMET or RIBBON TIE (Fenton)

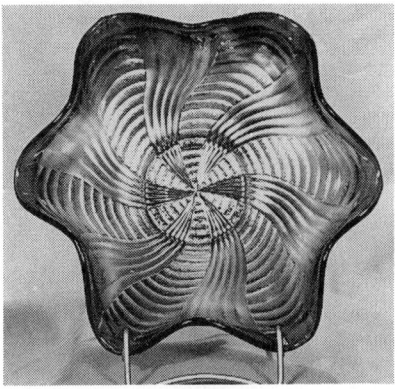

Comet Bowl

Bowl, 8" to 9" d., blue (ILLUS) 70.00
Bowl, 8" to 9" d., green 45.00
Bowl, 8" to 9" d., ribbon candy rim, lavender 90.00
Bowl, 8" to 9" d., marigold.....45.00
Bowl, 8" to 9" d., purple 55.00
Plate, 9" d., ruffled, blue 173.00
Plate, 9" d., ruffled, purple 180.00

CONCAVE DIAMOND - See Diamond Concave Pattern

CONSTELLATION (DUGAN)
Compote, green.....95.00
Compote, marigold 100.00
Compote, purple 275.00
Compote, white.....113.00

CORAL (Fenton)
Bowl, 8" to 9" d., collared base, blue ..250.00
Bowl, 8" to 9" d., collared base, green.....125.00 to 150.00
Bowl, 8" to 9" d., collared base, marigold 125.00
Plate, 9" d., marigold 700.00

CORN BOTTLE
Green.....230.00
Ice green.....250.00 to 275.00
Marigold.....250.00 to 275.00
Smoky.....210.00

CORN VASE (Northwood)
Aqua opalescent.....1,500.00
Aqua w/light marigold overlay.....1,975.00
Green.....800.00
Ice blue 1,400.00
Ice green.....375.00
Marigold.....800.00 to 900.00
Pastel marigold.....475.00
Purple 625.00
White 308.00

CORNUCOPIA
Candlestick, ice blue.....75.00
Vase, 5" h., marigold 25.00

COSMOS
Bowl, 5" d., green 50.00
Bowl, 5" d., ice cream shape, green.....40.00
Bowl, 6" d., clambroth.....35.00
Bowl, 6" d., green 45.00
Bowl, 9" d., blue.....85.00 to 110.00
Bowl, 9" d., green 50.00
Bowl, 9" d., marigold.....30.00
Bowl, 10" d., marigold.....45.00
Bowl, 10" d., purple.....48.00
Bowl, 10½"d., ice cream shape, blue .....75.00 to 100.00
Plate, 6" d., green 75.00
Plate, chop, 10½" d., marigold.....245.00

CRAB CLAW (Imperial)
Bowl, 8" to 9" d., clambroth.....100.00
Bowl, 8" to 9" d., fluted, smoky 40.00
Bowl, 10" d., ruffled, marigold.....70.00
Bowl, fruit, w/base, marigold.....90.00
Pitcher, marigold (ILLUS.) 255.00

Crab Claw Pitcher

Sauce dish, marigold.....29.00
Tumbler, marigold.....52.00

CRACKLE

Automobile vase w/bracket, marigold...25.00
Automobile vases, marigold, pr. (no brackets).....20.00
Bowl, 7½" d., marigold.....15.00
Plate, 6" d., marigold.....40.00
Plate, 8" d., marigold.....20.00
Rose bowl, low, marigold.....25.00
Salt & pepper shakers, w/original tops, light blue, pr. 25.00
Tumbler, green.....37.00
Tumbler, dome-footed, marigold 12.00
Vase, fan-shaped, marogold 20.00
Wall pocket, marigold.....30.00
Water set: pitcher & 6 footed tumblers; marigold, 7 pcs.....150.00
Water set: pitcher & 8 footed tumblers; marigold, 9 pcs.....195.00

CRUCIFIX

Candlesticks, marigold, pr. 1,000.00

CUT COSMOS

Tumbler, marigold.....258.00

DAISY & PLUME

Daisy & Plume Rose Bowl

Bowl, 8" to 9" d., three footed, green..150.00
Bowl, 8" to 9" d., three footed, marigold.....90.00
Candy dish, footed, blue.....185.00
Candy dish, footed, marigold.....50.00
Candy dish, footed, peach opalescent (Dugan).....100.00
Candy dish, footed, purple.....75.00
Candy dish, footed, white 125.00
Compote, green.....50.00
Compote, marigold 38.00
Compote, purple.....55.00
Rose bowl, three-footed, blue.....250.00
Rose bowl, three-footed, green (ILLUS.) 92.00
Rose bowl, three-footed, ice blue.....900.00
Rose bowl, three-footed, ice green.....900.00
Rose bowl, three-footed, marigold.....56.00
Rose bowl, three-footed, purple 85.00
Rose bowl, three-footed, white 850.00

DAISY CUT BELL

Daisy Cut Bell

Marigold (ILLUS.) .....425.00 to 450.00

DAISY SQUARES

Compote, green.....575.00 to 675.00
Compote, marigold 400.00
Goblet, purple.....800.00
Rose bowl, stemmed, green.....550.00 to 650.00
Rose bowl, jack-in-the-pulpit type, light green w/marigold overlay 725.00
Rose bowl, marigold.....550.00

DAISY WREATH (Westmoreland)

Bowl, 8" to 9" d., blue opalescent.....400.00 to 500.00
Bowl, 8" to 9" d., moonstone .....200.00 to 220.00
Bowl, 8" to 9" d., peach opalescent.....95.00

DANDELION (Northwood)

Mug, aqua opalescent.....475.00 to 500.00
Mug, blue.....440.00 to 480.00
Mug, green .....500.00 to 600.00
Mug, ice blue opalescent.....895.00
Mug, marigold.....375.00 to 400.00

Mug, pastel marigold .....275.00 to 300.00
Mug, purple.....200.00 to 275.00
Mug, Knights Templar, ice blue 1,000.00
Mug, Knights Templar, ice green.....1,100.00
Mug, Knights Templar, marigold.....500.00
Mug, Knights Templar, purple 295.00
Pitcher, water, tankard, blue.....260.00
Pitcher, water, tankard, green.....1,000.00 to 1,200.00

Dandelion Pitcher

Pitcher, water, tankard, marigold (ILLUS.) .....400.00 to 450.00
Pitcher, water, tankard, purple.....650.00 to 750.00
Tumbler, blue.....60.00
Tumbler, green .....75.00 to 100.00
Tumbler, ice blue.....200.00
Tumbler, ice green.....900.00
Tumbler, lavender.....225.00
Tumbler, marigold.....45.00
Tumbler, purple 60.00
Tumbler, smoky 250.00
Tumbler, white 195.00
Water set: pitcher & 1 tumbler; white, 2 pcs. 2,500.00
Water set: pitcher & 2 tumblers; pastel marigold, 3 pcs. 875.00
Water set: pitcher & 5 tumblers; green, 6 pcs. 1,400.00
Water set: pitcher & 6 tumblers; blue, 7 pcs. 695.00
Water set: pitcher & 6 tumblers; purple, 7 pcs. .....925.00 to 975.00

DANDELION, PANELED (Fenton)

Pitcher, water, blue.....450.00
Pitcher, water, green 475.00
Pitcher, water, marigold.....350.00
Pitcher, water, purple.....400.00 to 500.00
Tumbler, blue.....65.00
Tumbler, green 40.00
Tumbler, marigold.....40.00
Tumbler, purple 50.00
Water set: pitcher & 1 tumbler; blue, 2 pcs. 130.00
Water set: pitcher & 6 tumblers; blue, 7 pcs. .....800.00 to 850.00

DIAMOND & RIB VASE (FENTON)

Vase, 6" h., green 40.00
Vase, 7" h., marigodl 25.00
Vase, 7" h., purple 34.00
Vase, 8" h., white.....75.00
Vase, 10" h., green 40.00
Vase, 10" h., marigold 35.00
Vase, 10" h., purple 35.00
Vase, 10" h., white.....85.00
Vase, 11" h., aqua 40.00
Vase, 11" h., green 38.00
Vase, 11" h., ice green 80.00
Vase, 11" h., marigold 70.00
Vase, 12" h., purple 32.50
Vase, 13" h., blue 35.00
Vase, 15" h., marigold 55.00
Vase, 16" h., purple .....50.00 to 75.00
Vase, 19" h., purple 95.00
Vase, 19" h., funeral, purple 1,150.00

DIAMOND CONCAVE or CONCAVE DIAMOND (Dugan)

Pitcher w/cover, blue 100.00
Tumbler, celeste blue 35.00
Tumbler, olive green.....165.00
Tumbler, vaseline .....130.00 to 160.00

DIAMOND LACE (Imperial)

Diamond Lace Tumbler

Bowl, 8" to 9" d., clambroth.....65.00
Bowl, 8" to 9" d., marigold.....40.00
Bowl, 8" to 9" d., purple 50.00
Bowl, 10" d., purple.....76.00
Pitcher, water, purple.....250.00
Sauce dish, marigold, 5" d.....25.00
Sauce dish, purple, 5" d.....35.00
Tumbler, marigold.....425.00
Tumbler, purple (ILLUS.) 50.00
Water set: pitcher & 4 tumblers; purple, 5 pcs. 450.00

DIAMOND POINT COLUMNS

Bowl, 5" d., 2½" h., marigold.....20.00
Butter dish, cov., marigold 40.00
Vase, 6" h., green 42.00
Vase, 6" h., marigold 30.00
Vase, 7" h., green 125.00
Vase, 7" h., purple 40.00

Vase, 7½" h., white.....150.00 to 200.00

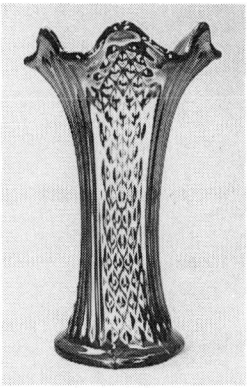

Diamond Point Columns Vase

Vase, 8" h., green (ILLUS.).....40.00
Vase, 9" h., purple.....75.00
Vase, 10" h., green.....80.00
Vase, 10" h., purple.....62.00
Vase, 10" h., white.....65.00
Vase, 11" h., green.....30.00
Vase, 11" h., ice blue.....240.00
Vase, 12" h., marigold.....28.00
Vase, 12" h., purple.....35.00
Vase, 16" h., blue.....250.00 to 300.00

DIAMOND RING (Imperial)

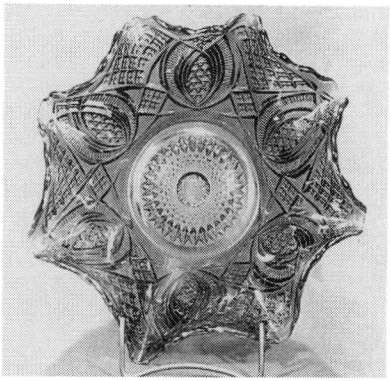

Diamond Ring Bowl

Bowl, 8" to 9" d., marigold.....60.00
Bowl, 8" to 9" d., purple.....75.00
Bowl, 8" to 9" d., smoky (ILLUS.).....40.00
Rose bowl, marigold.....300.00
Sauce dish, marigold.....22.50
Sauce dish, smoky.....28.00

DIAMONDS (Millersburg)

Pitcher, water, aqua.....225.00
Pitcher, water, green.....225.00
Pitcher, water, marigold.....125.00 to 150.00
Pitcher, water, purple.....160.00
Punch bowl & base, green, 2 pcs.....2,000.00
Tumbler, aqua.....85.00
Tumbler, green.....55.00
Tumbler, lavender.....70.00
Tumbler, marigold.....40.00
Tumbler, purple.....55.00
Water set: pitcher & 1 tumbler; marigold, 2 pcs.....250.00
Water set: pitcher & 4 tumblers; purple, 5 pcs.....475.00
Water set: pitcher & 6 tumblers; green, 7 pcs.....600.00

DIVING DOLPHINS FOOTED BOWL (Sowerby)

Diving Dolphins Bowl

Aqua blue, embossed scroll interior.....325.00
Marigold.....150.00
Purple (ILLUS.).....500.00

DOGWOOD SPRAYS

Bowl, 7" d., collared base, peach opalescent.....60.00
Bowl, 8" to 9" d., dome-footed, marigold.....36.00
Bowl, 8" to 9" d., dome-footed, peach opalescent.....80.00
Bowl, 8" to 9" d., dome-footed, purple.....65.00
Bowl, blue opalescent.....300.00

DOUBLE DUTCH BOWL

Marigold, 5" d.....20.00
Marigold, 8" to 9" d., footed.....40.00
Purple, 8" to 9" d., footed.....135.00
Clambroth, 10" d., ruffled.....69.00

DOUBLE STAR or BUZZ SAW (Cambridge)

Cruet w/stopper, green, small, 4".....500.00
Cruet w/stopper, green, large, 6".....400.00 to 425.00
Cuspidor whimsey (made from tumbler mold), green.....2,500.00
Pitcher, water, green.....300.00 to 325.00
Pitcher, water, marigold.....1,500.00
Tumbler, green.....65.00
Tumbler, purple.....130.00
Water set: pitcher & 6 tumblers, green, 7 pcs.....775.00

DOUBLE STEM ROSE

Bowl, 7" d., dome-footed, marigold.....35.00
Bowl, 8" to 9" d., dome-footed, aqua.....450.00
Bowl, 8" to 9" d., dome-footed, celeste blue.....600.00
Bowl, 8" to 9" d., dome-footed, lavender.....250.00
Bowl, 8" to 9" d., dome-footed, marigold.....45.00
Bowl, 8" to 9" d., dome-footed, peach opalescent.....125.00 to 150.00
Bowl, 8" to 9" d., dome-footed, purple..60.00
Bowl, 8" to 9" d., dome-footed, white.....100.00 to 125.00
Bowl, 10" d., peach opalescent.....175.00
Plate, dome-footed, purple.....145.00
Plate, dome-footed, white.....150.00

DRAGON & LOTUS (Fenton)

Dragon & Lotus Bowl

Bowl, 7" to 9" d., three-footed, blue.....68.00
Bowl, 7" to 9" d., three-footed, green....75.00
Bowl, 7" to 9" d., three-footed, lavender.....125.00
Bowl, 7" to 9" d., three-footed, lime green opalescent.....300.00
Bowl, 7" to 9" d., three-footed, marigold.....45.00
Bowl, 7" to 9" d., three-footed, peach opalescent.....500.00
Bowl, 7" to 9" d., three-footed, purple...70.00
Bowl, 8" to 9" d., collared base, amber.....200.00 to 225.00
Bowl, 8" to 9" d., collared base, blue..117.00
Bowl, 8" to 9" d., collared base, green.....108.00
Bowl, 8" to 9" d., collared base, lime green.....325.00
Bowl, 8" to 9" d., collared base, lime green opalescent.....550.00 to 650.00
Bowl, 8" to 9" d., collared base, marigold.....60.00
Bowl, 8" to 9" d., collared base, moonstone.....1,100.00
Bowl, 8" to 9" d., collared base, peach opalescent.....550.00
Bowl, 8" to 9" d., collared base, purple.....150.00
Bowl, 8" to 9" d., red.....1,750.00
Bowl, 9" d., ice cream shape, collared base, amber.....150.00 to 200.00
Bowl, 9" d., ice cream shape, collared base, aqua opalescent.....3,400.00
Bowl, 9" d., ice cream shape, collared base, blue.....103.00
Bowl, 9" d., ice cream shape, collared base, marigold.....50.00
Bowl, 9" d., ice cream shape, collared base, moonstone w/peach marigold overlay.....1,250.00
Bowl, 9" d., ice cream shape, collared base, red (ILLUS.).....4,500.00
Bowl, 9" d., ice cream shape, collared base, Reverse Amberina.....675.00 to 725.00
Bowl, 9" d., marigold.....82.00
Bowl, 9" d., three-in-one edge, green.....135.00
Bowl, ice cream shape, spade-footed, purple.....100.00
Bowl, ruffled, blue.....86.00
Bowl, ruffled, lavender.....195.00
Bowl, ruffled, marigold.....55.00
Bowl, ruffled, marigold opalescent.....675.00
Bowl, ruffled, purple.....75.00
Bowl, vaseline.....200.00
Plate, 9" d., marigold.....2,600.00
Plate, collared base, blue.....1,500.00 to 2,000.00
Plate, collared base, ruffled, marigold.....2,200.00
Plate, edge turned up, blue.....250.00
Plate, spatula-footed, marigold.....638.00

DRAGON & STRAWBERRY BOWL or DRAGON & BERRY (Fenton)

Bowl, 9" d., blue.....600.00
Bowl, 9" d., green.....682.00
Bowl, 9" d., marigold.....350.00 to 375.00
Bowl, 9" d., purple.....625.00

DRAPERY (Northwood)

Candy dish, tricornered, ice blue.....175.00 to 195.00
Candy dish, tricornered, ice green.....150.00 to 200.00
Candy dish, tricornered, marigold.....62.50
Candy dish, tricornered, purple.....400.00
Candy dish, tricornered, white.....135.00
Rose bowl, aqua opalescent.....325.00
Rose bowl, blue.....250.00 to 300.00
Rose bowl, blue w/electric iridescence.....600.00
Rose bowl, ice blue.....800.00 to 1,000.00
Rose bowl, lavender.....110.00
Rose bowl, marigold.....325.00 to 375.00
Rose bowl, pastel marigold.....385.00
Rose bowl, purple.....200.00 to 250.00
Rose bowl, white.....225.00 to 275.00

Vase, 4" h., ice blue.....170.00
Vase, 7" h., blue 67.50
Vase, 7" h., ice green 95.00
Vase, 7" h., marigold 50.00
Vase, 8" h., blue 50.00
Vase, 8" h., ice blue.....60.00
Vase, 8" h., ice green 150.00
Vase, 8" h., marigold 42.50
Vase, 8" h., white.....100.00
Vase, 9" h., blue 95.00
Vase, 9" h., purple 150.00
Vase, 10" h., ice blue.....425.00
Vase, 10" h., ice green 185.00
Vase, 10" h., marigold .....75.00 to 100.00
Vase, squatty, purple.....85.00

EMBROIDERED MUMS (Northwood)
Bonbon, stemmed, white 1,150.00
Bowl, 8" to 9" d., amber 1,000.00
Bowl, 8" to 9" d., ruffled, aqua opalescent 3,400.00
Bowl, 8" to 9" d., blue.....350.00 to 400.00
Bowl, 8" to 9" d., ruffled, blue.....1,350.00
Bowl, 8" to 9" d., blue w/electric iridescence.....500.00
Bowl, 8" to 9" d., ice blue 900.00
Bowl, 8" to 9" d., ice green.....900.00 to 1,000.00
Bowl, 8" to 9" d., marigold.....500.00
Bowl, 8" to 9" d., ruffled, marigold.....230.00
Bowl, 8" to 9" d., pastel marigold.....500.00
Bowl, 8" to 9" d., purple .....350.00 to 400.00
Bowl, aqua.....1,400.00
Bowl, lavender.....1,600.00
Bowl, lime green opalescent.....1,800.00
Bowl, piecrust rim, sapphire blue.....2,700.00
Plate, ice green.....2,000.00 to 2,500.00

ESTATE (Westmoreland)
Creamer, peach opalescent 60.00
Creamer & sugar bowl, peach opalescent, pr. 250.00
Mug, marigold, souvenir 150.00
Mug, marigold.....88.00
Mug, peach opalescent 125.00
Perfume bottle & stopper, smoky 1,100.00
Sugar bowl, marigold, souvenir 50.00
Sugar bowl, peach opalescent 75.00
Sugar bowl, peach opalescent, souvenir 40.00

FAN (Dugan)
Sauceboat, peach opalescent 137.00
Sauceboat, purple 60.00

FANCIFUL (Dugan)
Bowl, 8" to 9" d., blue.....85.00
Bowl, 8" to 9" d., marigold.....24.00
Bowl, 8" to 9" d., piecrust rim, marigold .....100.00 to 125.00
Bowl, 8" to 9" d., peach opalescent 192.00
Bowl, 8" to 9" d., ruffled, purple 135.00
Bowl, 8" to 9" d., ruffled, white .....160.00 to 190.00
Bowl, 10" d., ruffled, white ..150.00 to 175.00
Bowl, ice cream shape, marigold.....60.00
Bowl, ice cream shape, peach opalescent 144.00
Bowl, ice cream shape, purple 325.00
Bowl, ice cream shape, white 95.00
Plate, 9" d., blue .....250.00 to 275.00
Plate, 9" d., marigold .....100.00 to 150.00
Plate, 9" d., peach opalescent .....275.00 to 325.00
Plate, 9" d., purple .....250.00 to 275.00
Plate, 9" d., white.....245.00
Plate, 9½" d., ruffled, white.....200.00

FANTAIL
Bowl, 9" d., footed, blue.....185.00
Bowl, 9" d., shallow, footed, w/Butterfly & Berry exterior, blue 175.00
Bowl, 9" d., ice cream shape, w/Butterfly & Berry exterior, marigold 200.00
Bowl, 9" d., footed, marigold.....70.00

FARMYARD (Dugan)

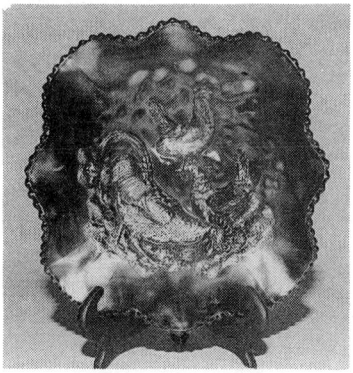

Farmyard Square Bowl

Bowl, purple.....2,600.00
Bowl, fluted, purple 3,900.00
Bowl, ribbon candy rim, purple 3,500.00
Bowl, square, purple (ILLUS.) 2,900.00
Plate, 10" d., purple 6,000.00

FASHION (Imperial)
Bowl, 9" d., marigold.....25.00
Bowl, 9" d., ruffled, smoky 40.00
Creamer, marigold.....25.00
Creamer, smoky 130.00
Creamer & sugar bowl, marigold, pr.....60.00
Creamer & sugar bowl, purple, pr.....325.00
Pitcher, water, marigold, (ILLUS. top next page).....100.00 to 125.00
Pitcher, water, purple.....950.00
Punch bowl & base, marigold, 12" d., 2 pcs. 104.00
Punch cup, marigold.....15.00
Punch cup, red 325.00
Punch cups, marigold, set of 6 .....105.00
Punch set: bowl, base & 8 cups; marigold, 10 pcs. 325.00

Fashion Pitcher

Rose bowl, green.....425.00
Rose bowl, marigold, 7" d.....90.00
Tumbler, marigold.....20.00
Tumbler, purple 175.00
Tumbler, smoky.....90.00
Water set: pitcher & 3 tumblers; smoky, 4 pcs.....700.00
Water set: pitcher & 6 tumblers; marigold, 7 pcs. .....300.00 to 350.00

FEATHER & HEART

Feather & Heart Pitcher

Pitcher, water, green (ILLUS.) 450.00
Pitcher, water, marigold.....300.00 to 350.00
Tumbler, green 200.00
Tumbler, marigold.....70.00
Water set: pitcher & 1 tumbler; purple, 2 pcs. 975.00

FEATHER STITCH BOWL

Aqua 225.00
Blue 236.00
Green.....100.00
Marigold.....55.00
Vaseline, three-in-one edge 995.00

FEATHERED SERPENT

Bowl, 8" to 9" d., green 60.00
Bowl, 8" to 9" d., marigold.....40.00
Bowl, 8" to 9" d., purple 70.00
Bowl, 10" d., ruffled, blue.....65.00
Bowl, 10" d., fluted, green.....55.00
Bowl, 10" d., marigold.....60.00
Bowl, 10" d., flared, purple.....55.00
Bowl, 12½" d., ruffled, blue.....95.00
Sauce dish, blue 27.50
Sauce dish, green.....28.00
Sauce dish, marigold 15.00
Sauce dish, purple.....35.00
Whimsey, tricornered, marigold.....45.00

FENTONIA

Berry set: master bowl & 4 sauce dishes; marigold, 5 pcs. 175.00
Bowl, master berry, blue.....275.00
Bowl, master berry, marigold.....55.00
Butter dish, cov., footed, marigold.....137.50
Creamer, blue.....100.00
Creamer, marigold.....60.00
Sugar bowl, cov., blue 115.00
Table set: creamer, cov. sugar bowl & spooner; blue, 3 pcs. 350.00
Tumbler, blue.....65.00
Tumbler, marigold.....44.00

FENTON'S FLOWERS ROSE BOWL - See Orange Tree Pattern

FERN

Compote, w/Daisy & Plume exterior, green (Northwood) 95.00
Compote, w/Daisy & Plume exterior, marigold (Northwood) 78.00
Compote, w/Daisy & Plume exterior, purple (Northwood) 75.00
Dish, hat-shaped, marigold (Fenton) 27.00

FIELD FLOWER (Imperial)

Pitcher, water, amber 350.00
Pitcher, water, green 325.00
Pitcher, water, marigold.....165.00
Pitcher, water, purple.....400.00 to 425.00
Tumbler, amber 39.00
Tumbler, blue.....100.00
Tumbler, green 70.00
Tumbler, marigold.....32.00
Tumbler, purple 55.00

FIELD THISTLE (English)

Bowl, 5" d., berry, marigold.....40.00
Compote, marigold 275.00
Plate, 6" d., marigold 190.00
Plate, 9" d., marigold 435.00
Tumbler, marigold.....46.00

FILE (Imperial)

Bowl, 8" d., marigold.....40.00
Pitcher, water, marigold.....650.00
Spooner, marigold 70.00
Tumbler, marigold.....175.00 to 200.00

Vase, marigold.....250.00

FILE & FAN

Compote, blue opalescent..250.00 to 300.00
Compote, marigold 45.00
Compote, milk white w/marigold overlay 225.00
Compote, peach opalescent.....80.00

FINECUT & ROSES (Northwood)

Candy dish, three-footed, aqua opalescent .....400.00 to 450.00
Candy dish, three-footed, blue w/electric iridescence.....67.50
Candy dish, three-footed, green.....65.00
Candy dish, three-footed, ice blue .....300.00 to 350.00
Candy dish, three-footed, ice green ...175.00
Candy dish, three-footed, marigold 40.00
Candy dish, three-footed, purple 50.00
Candy dish, three-footed, white .....125.00 to 150.00
Rose bowl, amber.....550.00
Rose bowl, aqua opalescent .....1,000.00 to 1,300.00
Rose bowl, green.....250.00
Rose bowl, ice blue 315.00
Rose bowl, ice green 200.00
Rose bowl, marigold 88.00
Rose bowl, purple.....75.00
Rose bowl, white .....425.00 to 450.00
Rose bowl/whimsey, straight top, lavender 650.00
Rose bowl/whimsey, purple.....195.00

FINECUT FLOWERS

Compote, marigold 35.00
Compote, marigold, clear stem, 5 x 6½".....20.00

FINE RIB (Northwood & Fenton)

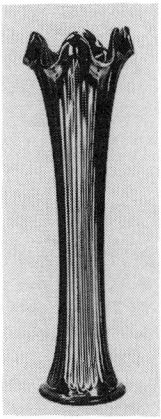

Fine Rib Vase

Bowl, master berry, 9" d., marigold.....35.00
Bowl, 10½" d., green 50.00
Bowl, purple.....35.00
Compote, ruffled, green.....45.00
Plate, 9" d., eight-sided, marigold.....85.00
Sauce dish, vaseline.....25.00
Vase, 6½ h., 5" d., blue 25.00
Vase, 6½ h., 5" d., green 30.00
Vase, 6½ h., 5" d., marigold 25.00
Vase, 7" h., green 42.50
Vase, 7" h., marigold 35.00
Vase, 7½" h., white.....80.00
Vase, 8" h., aqua 62.50
Vase, 8½" h., blue 38.00
Vase, 8½" h., red 195.00
Vase, 9" h., green 65.00
Vase, 9" h., purple 55.00
Vase, 9" h., red (Fenton) 275.00
Vase, 9½" h., blue 45.00
Vase, 9½" h., vaseline (Fenton) 50.00
Vase, 10" h., amber (Fenton) 40.00
Vase, 10" h., aqua (Northwood) 70.00
Vase, 10" h., blue (ILLUS.) 40.00
Vase, 10" h., purple 45.00
Vase, 10" h., red (Fenton) 500.00
Vase, 12" h., red (Fenton) 650.00
Vase, 12" h., vaseline (Fenton) .....50.00 to 75.00
Vase, 14" h., marigold 36.00
Vase, 15" h., blue 60.00
Vase, 16" h., marigold 45.00
Vase, 17" h., marigold 85.00

FISHERMAN'S MUG

Marigold.....190.00 to 210.00
Marigold opalescent 1,200.00
Pastel marigold.....200.00 to 250.00
Peach opalescent.....1,100.00 to 1,250.00
Purple 125.00

FISHSCALE & BEADS

Banana boat, peach opalescent, 7" l. ...73.00
Bonbon, marigold, 6" 45.00
Bonbon, peach opalescent, 6".....55.00
Bowl, 7" d., marigold.....21.00
Bowl, 7" d., ribbon candy rim, purple 40.00
Card tray, peach opalescent, 4 x 7".....70.00
Plate, 7" d., marigold 79.00
Plate, 7" d., pastel marigold.....75.00
Plate, 7" d., ruffled rim, peach opalescent .....125.00 to 150.00
Plate, 7" d., purple 375.00
Plate, 7" d., white.....115.00
Plate, 7½" d., marigold 95.00
Plate, 7½" d., purple 130.00
Plate, 8" d., purple 1,000.00

FLEUR DE LIS (Millersburg)

Bowl, 8" to 9" d., dome-footed, marigold 200.00
Bowl, 8" to 9" d., dome-footed, purple.....225.00 to 250.00
Bowl, 10" d., green .....175.00 to 200.00

Fleur-de-Lis Bowl

Bowl, 10" d., marigold (ILLUS.) 180.00
Bowl, 10" d., purple.....300.00 to 400.00
Bowl, dome-footed, ruffled, marigold..150.00
Bowl, dome-footed, purple.....350.00
Bowl, tricornered, footed, marigold.....300.00
Bowl, tricornered, footed, purple.....245.00
Rose bowl, dome-footed, purple.....3,300.00

FLORAL & GRAPE (Dugan or Diamond Glass Co.)

Pitcher, water, blue.....395.00
Pitcher, water, green 275.00
Pitcher, water, marigold.....90.00
Pitcher, water, purple.....150.00 to 200.00
Pitcher, water, white 350.00
Pitcher, water, variant, white 750.00
Tumbler, black amethyst 80.00
Tumbler, blue.....35.00
Tumbler, green 175.00
Tumbler, marigold.....25.00
Tumbler, purple 40.00
Tumbler, white 70.00
Water set: pitcher & 4 tumblers; white, 5 pcs. 695.00
Water set: pitcher & 6 tumblers; marigold, 7 pcs. .....225.00 to 250.00
Whimsey, hat-shaped (from tumbler mold), marigold 80.00

FLORAL & WHEAT COMPOTE (Dugan)

Marigold.....45.00
Peach opalescent.....50.00 to 75.00
Purple 40.00
White 135.00

FLOWERS & BEADS

Card tray, tricornered, purple, 7" w.....62.00
Plate, 7½" w., six-sided, peach opalescent 65.00
Plate, flat, purple.....55.00
Plate, six-sided, purple 80.00

FLOWERS & FRAMES

Bowl, 7" d., single handle, peach opalescent 33.00
Bowl, 7" d., dome-footed, purple 100.00
Bowl, 9" d., dome-footed, green 275.00
Bowl, 9" d., dome-footed, peach opalescent 145.00
Bowl, 9" d., dome-footed, fluted, purple.....150.00 to 200.00
Bowl, tricornered, peach opalescent.....100.00 to 125.00
Bowl, tricornered, dome-footed, purple.....125.00

FLUTE (Imperial)

Berry set: master bowl & 6 sauce dishes; marigold, 7 pcs. 135.00
Bowl, 8" to 9" d., marigold.....28.00
Bowl, 8" to 9" d., purple 65.00
Butter dish, cov., marigold 60.00
Compote, green.....25.00
Creamer, breakfast size, marigold.....50.00
Creamer, breakfast size, purple 60.00
Creamer & open sugar bowl, breakfast size, purple, pr. 130.00
Match holder, purple.....900.00
Pitcher, water, clambroth.....175.00
Pitcher, water, marigold.....275.00
Pitcher, water, purple.....293.00
Punch cup, green 25.00
Punch cup, marigold.....35.00
Punch cup, purple.....25.00

Flute Punch Set

Punch set: bowl, base & 6 cups; purple, 8 pcs. (ILLUS.).....750.00 to 850.00
Rose bowl, marigold 24.00
Sauce dish, green.....34.00
Sauce dish, marigold 15.00
Sauce dish, purple.....50.00
Sugar bowl, open, breakfast size, amber.....65.00
Sugar bowl, open, breakfast size, green.....60.00
Sugar bowl, open, breakfast size, purple.....60.00
Toothpick holder, green.....48.00
Toothpick holder, lavender ...75.00 to 100.00

Toothpick holder, marigold 65.00
Toothpick holder, purple 80.00
Tumbler, aqua 175.00
Tumbler, cobalt blue 400.00
Tumbler, marigold.....40.00
Tumbler, purple 82.00
Tumbler, red 275.00
Tumbler, smoky 425.00
Vase, 9" h., aqua 70.00
Vase, 9" h., purple 82.00
Vase, 12" h., funeral, green 32.00
Vase, 17" h., green 65.00
Water set: pitcher & 6 tumblers; marigold, 7 pcs. 650.00

FLUTE (Northwood)
Pitcher, milk, marigold 20.00
Pitcher, water, clambroth.....175.00
Salt dip, master size, blue 45.00
Salt dip, master size, vaseline 95.00
Tumbler, dark marigold.....95.00
Tumbler, marigold.....55.00
Tumbler, marigold, variant.....85.00
Vase, 13" h., funeral, marigold 35.00
Vase, funeral, green 175.00

FLUTE & CANE
Compote, marigold, 6½" d., 6" h.....125.00
Goblet, marigold 55.00
Pitcher, marigold.....200.00
Pitcher, milk, marigold 140.00

FLUTED SCROLL
Cuspidor, purple 2,500.00
Tumbler, blue opalescent 75.00

FORMAL
Vase, marigold.....125.00
Vase, rolled top, purple.....425.00
Vase, jack-in-the-pulpit, marigold 350.00
Vase, jack-in-the-pulpit, purple 500.00

FOUR FLOWERS - See Pods & Posies Pattern

FOUR SEVENTY FOUR (Imperial)
Compote, green.....95.00
Goblet, water, marigold 75.00
Pitcher, milk, green.....400.00
Pitcher, milk, marigold 162.00
Pitcher, water, marigold.....150.00
Pitcher, water, purple.....725.00
Punch cup, green 60.00
Punch cup, marigold.....22.00
Punch cup, purple.....50.00
Punch cup, teal blue 40.00
Punch set: bowl, base & 6 cups; marigold, 8 pcs. 425.00
Tumbler, blue.....200.00
Tumbler, marigold.....35.00
Tumbler, purple 75.00
Water set: pitcher & 6 tumblers; marigold, 7 pcs. 385.00

FROLICKING BEARS (U.S. Glass)
Pitcher, green .....5,000.00 to 7,000.00
Tumbler, green 9,500.00

FROSTED BLOCK
Bowl, 6" d., marigold.....19.00
Bowl, 8" to 9" d., scalloped & fluted, clambroth 35.00
Bowl, square, clambroth 30.00
Bowl, square, marigold 40.00
Bowl, square, "USA," white.....45.00
Compote, clambroth 100.00
Compote, white.....150.00
Nut dish, clambroth.....55.00
Pitcher, milk, marigold 50.00
Plate, 7¾" sq., marigold.....30.00
Plate, 7¾" sq., smoky 100.00
Plate, 9" d., clambroth 70.00
Plate, 9" d., marigold 50.00
Plate, 9" d., smoky 50.00
Relish, marigold.....35.00
Rose bowl, clambroth 280.00
Rose bowl, marigold 50.00
Rose bowl, white 55.00
Vase, smoky 35.00

FRUIT SALAD
Punch bowl (no base), marigold 95.00
Punch cup, marigold.....28.00
Punch set: bowl, base & 6 cups; marigold, 8 pcs. 350.00

FRUITS & FLOWERS (Northwood)

Fruits & Flowers Bonbon

Berry set: master bowl & 4 sauce dishes; purple, 5 pcs. 395.00
Bonbon, stemmed, two-handled, amber.....375.00
Bonbon, stemmed, two-handled, aqua opalescent .....475.00 to 500.00
Bonbon, stemmed, two-handled, blue 163.00
Bonbon, stemmed, two-handled, electric blue.....250.00
Bonbon, stemmed, two-handled, green.....125.00
Bonbon, stemmed, two-handled, ice blue .....700.00 to 750.00

Bonbon, stemmed, two-handled, ice green....450.00
Bonbon, stemmed, two-handled, lavender....650.00
Bonbon, stemmed, two-handled, marigold (ILLUS.)....90.00
Bonbon, stemmed, two-handled, olive green....135.00
Bonbon, stemmed, two-handled, pastel marigold....115.00
Bonbon, stemmed, two-handled, purple....95.00
Bonbon, stemmed, two-handled, white....375.00 to 400.00
Bowl, 6" d., ruffled, green....48.00
Bowl, 6" d., ruffled, marigold....60.00
Bowl, 6" d., ruffled, purple....48.00
Bowl, 7" d., blue....85.00
Bowl, 7" d., blue w/electric iridescence....300.00 to 350.00
Bowl, 7" d., green....53.00
Bowl, 7" d., purple....60.00
Bowl, 7" d., ruffled, blue....200.00 to 275.00
Bowl, 7" d., ruffled, ice green....350.00
Bowl, 7" d., ruffled, marigold....15.00
Bowl, 9½" d., ruffled, Basketweave exterior, purple....61.00
Bowl, master berry, 10" d., green....82.00
Bowl, master berry, 10" d., marigold....45.00
Bowl, master berry, 10" d., purple....66.00
Bowl, 10" d., ruffled, ice green....475.00
Bowl, 10" d., ruffled, purple....150.00
Bowl, piecrust rim, purple....225.00
Card tray, green....125.00
Plate, 7" d., green....170.00
Plate, 7" d., marigold....125.00
Plate, 7" d., purple....175.00
Plate, 7½" d., handgrip, green....165.00
Plate, 7½" d., handgrip, purple....150.00 to 175.00
Sauce dish, marigold....31.00
Sauce dish, purple....45.00

GARDEN PATH

Garden Path Chop Plate

Bowl, 6" d., peach opalescent, variant....60.00
Bowl, 6" d., ruffled, purple....45.00
Bowl, 6" d., ruffled, white....45.00
Bowl, 9" d., ice cream shape, marigold....60.00
Bowl, 9" d., ice cream shape, purple..700.00
Bowl, 10" d., ruffled, marigold....80.00
Bowl, 10" d., ruffled, peach opalescent....282.00
Bowl, 10" d., ruffled, white..300.00 to 325.00
Bowl, fruit, peach opalescent, variant....550.00
Bowl, white, variant....120.00
Plate, 6" d., peach opalescent....625.00
Plate, 6½" d., white....400.00
Plate, chop, 11" d., peach opalescent....4,200.00
Plate, chop, 11" d., purple (ILLUS.)....7,500.00
Plate, peach opalescent, variant....500.00
Sauce dish, peach opalescent....80.00

GARLAND ROSE BOWL (Fenton)

Garland Rose Bowl

Blue (ILLUS.)....60.00
Marigold....50.00 to 75.00

GOD & HOME

God & Home Tumbler

Pitcher, blue....1,130.00

Tumbler, blue (ILLUS.) 275.00
Water set: pitcher & 6 tumblers; blue, 7 pcs. 2,500.00

GODDESS OF HARVEST (FENTON)
Bowl, 8" d., piecrust rim, purple 6,750.00

GOLDEN HARVEST or HARVEST TIME (U.S. Glass)
Decanter w/stopper, marigold.....146.00
Wine, marigold.....25.00
Wine, purple 40.00

GOOD LUCK (Northwood)

Good Luck Ruffled Bowl

Bowl, 8" d., ruffled, blue.....285.00
Bowl, 8" d., ruffled, stippled, blue 374.00
Bowl, 8" d., ruffled, blue w/electric iridescence.....285.00
Bowl, 8" d., ruffled, stippled, blue w/electric iridescence.....375.00 to 400.00
Bowl, 8" d., ruffled, green 263.00
Bowl, 8" d., ruffled, Basketweave exterior, green.....250.00 to 300.00
Bowl, 8" d., ruffled, marigold.....125.00
Bowl, 8" d., ruffled, Basketweave exterior, marigold .....150.00 to 200.00
Bowl, 8" d., ruffled, stippled, marigold 169.00
Bowl, 8" d., ruffled, purple...200.00 to 225.00
Bowl, 8" d., ruffled, Basketweave exterior, purple 225.00
Bowl, 8" to 9" d., piecrust rim, aqua opalescent 1,800.00
Bowl, 8" to 9" d., piecrust rim, blue.....403.00
Bowl, 8" to 9" d., piecrust rim, stippled, blue.....321.00
Bowl, 8" to 9" d., piecrust rim, clambroth 450.00
Bowl, 8" to 9" d., piecrust rim, green.....375.00 to 425.00
Bowl, 8" to 9" d., piecrust rim, marigold 170.00
Bowl, 8" to 9" d., piecrust rim, stippled, marigold.....190.00
Bowl, 8" to 9" d., piecrust rim, purple..322.00
Bowl, 8" to 9" d., piecrust rim, teal blue .....2,500.00 to 3,000.00
Bowl, 8" to 9" d., ruffled, aqua opalescent 1,300.00
Bowl, 8" to 9" d., ruffled, green 800.00
Bowl, 8" to 9" d., ruffled, ice blue.....4,200.00
Bowl, 8" to 9" d., ruffled, lavender.....200.00 to 250.00
Bowl, 8" to 9" d., ruffled, marigold (ILLUS.) 125.00
Bowl, 8" to 9" d., ruffled, purple 297.00
Bowl, 8" to 9" d., ruffled, teal blue .....1,200.00 to 1,500.00
Bowl, aqua.....1,200.00
Bowl, piecrust rim, stippled, ribbed exterior, blue w/electric iridescence 775.00
Bowl, ruffled, sapphire blue 1,300.00
Plate, 9" d., blue 425.00
Plate, 9" d., blue w/electric iridescence.....1,250.00 to 1,275.00
Plate, 9" d., green.....700.00
Plate, 9" d., marigold 500.00
Plate, 9" d., purple 475.00
Plate, 9" d., stippled, purple.....600.00
Plate, 9" d., Basketweave exterior, purple.....525.00

GRAPE & CABLE

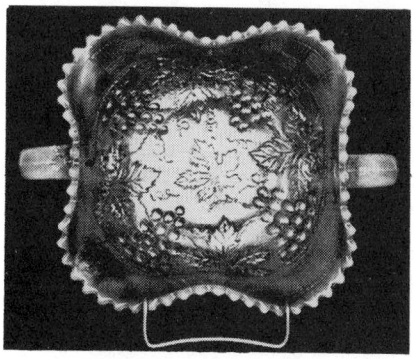

Grape & Cable Bonbon

Banana boat, banded rim, stippled, blue .....1,000.00 to 1,200.00
Banana boat, green 525.00
Banana boat, ice blue.....550.00 to 600.00
Banana boat, ice green 750.00
Banana boat, marigold 140.00
Banana boat, stippled, marigold.....225.00
Banana boat, purple 225.00
Banana boat, white.....650.00 to 685.00
Berry set: master bowl & 6 sauce dishes; green, 7 pcs.....300.00
Berry set: master bowl & 6 sauce dishes; marigold, 7 pcs. 275.00

Berry set: master bowl & 6 sauce dishes; purple, 7 pcs. .....375.00 to 400.00
Bonbon, two-handled, stippled, aqua opalescent (ILLUS.) 3,900.00
Bonbon, two-handled, blue 95.00
Bonbon, two-handled, stippled, blue .....200.00 to 225.00
Bonbon, two-handled, green 58.00
Bonbon, two-handled, stippled, green .....100.00 to 125.00
Bonbon, two-handled, marigold 75.00
Bonbon, two-handled, stippled, marigold 45.00
Bonbon, two-handled, purple 68.00
Bonbon, two-handled, white .....650.00 to 750.00
Bowl, 5" d., blue (Fenton) 50.00
Bowl, 5" d., green 40.00
Bowl, 5" d., marigold 38.00
Bowl, 5" d., purple 32.00
Bowl, 6" d., ruffled, purple 40.00
Bowl, 6½" d., marigold 38.00
Bowl, 7" d., ice cream shape, aqua (Fenton) 300.00
Bowl, 7" d., ice cream shape, ice green 315.00
Bowl, 7" d., ice cream shape, marigold (Fenton) 125.00
Bowl, 7" d., ice cream shape, milk white w/marigold overlay (Fenton) .....150.00 to 250.00
Bowl, 7" d., ice cream shape, red (Fenton) 750.00
Bowl, 7" d., blue (Fenton) 40.00
Bowl, 7" d., ice blue 750.00
Bowl, 7" d., red (Fenton) 500.00
Bowl, 7" d., ruffled, purple 42.50
Bowl, 7" d., ruffled, teal blue 250.00
Bowl, 7" d., ruffled, vaseline (Fenton) ...47.50
Bowl, 8" to 9" d., piecrust rim, aqua opalescent (Northwood) 3,200.00
Bowl, 8" to 9" d., piecrust rim, blue w/electric iridescence 350.00
Bowl, 8" to 9" d., piecrust rim, stippled, blue 340.00
Bowl, 8" to 9" d., piecrust rim, green 147.00
Bowl, 8" to 9" d., piecrust rim, Basket-weave exterior, green 60.00
Bowl, 8" to 9" d., piecrust rim, ice blue 1,000.00
Bowl, 8" to 9" d., piecrust rim, marigold 100.00
Bowl, 8" to 9" d., piecrust rim, purple .....250.00 to 275.00
Bowl, 8" to 9" d., piecrust rim, Basketweave exterior, purple 160.00
Bowl, 8" to 9" d., ball-footed, blue (Fenton) 85.00
Bowl, 8" to 9" d., ball-footed, green (Fenton) 76.00
Bowl, 8" to 9" d., ball-footed, pastel marigold (Fenton) 50.00
Bowl, 8" to 9" d., ball-footed, purple (Fenton) 50.00
Bowl, 8" to 9" d., ball-footed, smoky (Fenton) 275.00
Bowl, 8" to 9" d., ball-footed, teal blue 275.00
Bowl, orange, 10½" d., footed, Persian Medallion interior, blue (Fenton) .....225.00 to 250.00
Bowl, orange, 10½" d., footed, Persian Medallion interior, green (Fenton) .....225.00 to 250.00
Bowl, orange, 10½" d., footed, Persian Medallion interior, marigold (Fenton) 140.00
Bowl, orange, 10½" d., footed, Persian Medallion interior, purple (Fenton) 267.00
Bowl, orange, 10½" d., footed, blue .....350.00 to 450.00
Bowl, orange, 10½" d., footed, stippled, blue w/electric iridescence (Northwood) 895.00
Bowl, orange, 10½" d., footed, clambroth 350.00
Bowl, orange, 10½" d., footed, green .....300.00 to 350.00
Bowl, orange, 10½" d., footed, ice blue 1,250.00
Bowl, orange, 10½" d., footed, ice green .....950.00 to 1,150.00
Bowl, orange, 10½" d., footed, marigold 202.00
Bowl, orange, 10½" d., footed, stippled, marigold 300.00
Bowl, orange, 10½" d., footed, purple 325.00
Bowl, orange, 10½" d., footed, white 1,250.00
Bowl, orange, 10½" d., lavender 395.00
Bowl, 10½" d., ruffled, Basketweave exterior, green 100.00
Breakfast set: individual size creamer & sugar bowl; green, pr. 123.00
Breakfast set: individual size creamer & sugar bowl; purple, pr. .....200.00 to 250.00
Bride's basket, purple 2,975.00
Butter dish, cov., amber 155.00
Butter dish, cov., green 180.00
Butter dish, cov., ice green 250.00
Butter dish, cov., marigold 165.00
Butter dish, cov., purple 190.00
Candle lamp, green .....650.00 to 700.00
Candle lamp, marigold .....500.00 to 550.00
Candle lamp, purple .....500.00 to 600.00
Candle lamp shade, green 750.00
Candlestick, green 135.00
Candlestick, marigold 72.00
Candlestick, purple .....100.00 to 125.00
Candlesticks, blue, pr. 275.00
Candlesticks, marigold, pr. 235.00

Card tray, green.....350.00
Card tray, horehound.....80.00
Card tray, marigold.....50.00
Card tray, purple.....80.00
Centerpiece bowl, green.....775.00
Centerpiece bowl, ice blue.....825.00
Centerpiece bowl, ice green.....910.00
Centerpiece bowl, marigold.....260.00
Centerpiece bowl, purple.....425.00
Centerpiece bowl, white.....632.00
Cologne bottle w/stopper, green.....225.00 to 250.00
Cologne bottle w/stopper, ice blue.....950.00
Cologne bottle w/stopper, marigold....165.00
Cologne bottle w/stopper, purple.....259.00
Cologne bottle w/stopper, sapphire blue.....795.00
Cologne bottle w/stopper, white.....625.00 to 650.00
Compote, cov., large, green.....425.00
Compote, cov., large, marigold.....1,450.00
Compote, cov., small, purple.....325.00 to 350.00
Compote, cov., large, purple.....450.00
Compote, open, large, green.....795.00
Compote, open, large, marigold.....300.00 to 350.00
Compote, open, small, purple.....225.00
Compote, open, large, purple.....425.00 to 525.00
Cracker jar, cov., ice green.....800.00
Cracker jar, cov., marigold.....300.00
Cracker jar, cov., purple.....400.00
Cracker jar, cov., white.....875.00
Creamer, green.....125.00
Creamer, marigold.....90.00
Creamer, purple.....88.00
Creamer, individual size, green.....65.00
Creamer, individual size, marigold.....68.00
Creamer, individual size, purple.....65.00
Creamer & cov. sugar bowl, purple, pr.....278.00
Cup & saucer, blue.....275.00
Cup & saucer, marigold.....250.00
Cup & saucer, purple.....450.00
Cuspidor, purple.....3,000.00
Decanter w/stopper, whiskey, marigold.....600.00 to 625.00
Dresser set, purple, 7 pcs.....2,500.00
Dresser tray, blue.....250.00
Dresser tray, green.....250.00 to 275.00
Dresser tray, ice blue.....1,500.00
Dresser tray, marigold.....150.00
Dresser tray, purple.....195.00
Fernery, ice blue.....1,300.00
Fernery, purple.....650.00 to 700.00
Hatpin holder, blue.....1,300.00
Hatpin holder, green.....285.00
Hatpin holder, ice blue.....2,500.00
Hatpin holder, ice green.....1,700.00
Hatpin holder, lavender.....400.00 to 450.00
Hatpin holder, marigold.....256.00
Hatpin holder, purple.....250.00 to 275.00

Grape & Cable Hatpin Holder

Hatpin holder, white (ILLUS.).....1,800.00
Hat shape, green.....225.00 to 250.00
Hat shape, marigold.....50.00
Hat shape, purple.....50.00 to 60.00
Humidor (or tobacco jar), cov., blue.....1,000.00
Humidor, cov., stippled, blue.....1,500.00
Humidor, cov., marigold.....275.00 to 300.00
Humidor, cov., stippled, marigold.....160.00
Humidor, cov., purple.....700.00 to 900.00
Ice cream set: master bowl & 1 individual dish; marigold, 2 pcs.....425.00
Ice cream set: master bowl & 6 individual dishes; white, 7 pcs.....1,500.00
Nappy, single handle, green.....75.00
Nappy, single handle, ice blue.....600.00
Nappy, single handle, marigold.....47.00
Nappy, single handle, purple.....130.00
Nappy, cup whimsey, hairpin, purple....50.00
Perfume bottle w/stopper, marigold....417.00
Perfume bottle w/stopper, purple.....650.00 to 675.00
Pin tray, green.....225.00
Pin tray, ice blue.....900.00
Pin tray, marigold.....140.00 to 150.00
Pin tray, purple.....250.00 to 275.00
Pitcher, water, 8¼" h., green.....400.00
Pitcher, water, 8¼" h., marigold.....205.00
Pitcher, water, 8¼" h., purple.....319.00
Pitcher, tankard, 9¾" h., marigold.....540.00
Pitcher, tankard, 9¾" h., purple.....600.00
Plate, 5" to 6" d., purple (Northwood).....130.00 to 140.00
Plate, 7½" d., turned-up handgrip, green.....95.00
Plate, 7½" d., turned-up handgrip, marigold.....100.00 to 125.00
Plate, 7½" d., turned-up handgrip, purple.....114.00
Plate, 8" d., clambroth.....850.00
Plate, 8" d., footed, green (Fenton)....185.00
Plate, 8" d., green (Northwood).....140.00
Plate, 8" d., footed, marigold.....92.00

Plate, 8" d., footed, purple 84.00
Plate, 8" d., purple .....225.00 to 275.00
Plate, 9" d., spatula-footed, blue.....150.00
Plate, 9" d., stippled, blue 600.00
Plate, 9" d., green .....300.00 to 400.00
Plate, 9" d., marigold 250.00

Grape & Cable Plate

Plate, 9" d., spatula-footed, green (ILLUS.) 165.00
Plate, 9" d., spatula-footed, ice green .....850.00 to 875.00
Plate, 9" d., marigold 109.00
Plate, 9" d., spatula-footed, marigold....85.00
Plate, 9" d., purple 128.00
Plate, 9" d., spatula-footed, purple 125.00
Plate, 9" d., Basketweave exterior, green.....150.00
Plate, 9" d., Basketweave exterior, marigold .....100.00 to 125.00
Plate, 9" d., Basketweave exterior, purple 179.00
Plate, 9" d., stippled, green.....302.00
Plate, 9" d., stippled, green, variant....900.00
Plate, 9" d., stippled, marigold 150.00
Plate, 9" d., stippled, marigold, variant 750.00
Plate, 9" d., stippled, purple.....525.00
Plate, 9" d., stippled, sapphire blue .....3,500.00 to 3,800.00
Plate, 9" d., stippled, teal 2,700.00
Plate, chop, 12" d., white 5,000.00
Plate, olive green.....900.00
Plate, pastel marigold 300.00
Powder jar, cov., blue 600.00
Powder jar, cov., green.....160.00
Powder jar, cov., marigold 125.00
Powder jar, cov., purple.....129.00
Punch bowl & base, green, 11" d., 2 pcs. 1,100.00
Punch bowl & base, marigold, 11" d., 2 pcs. 250.00
Punch bowl & base, purple, 11" d., 2 pcs. 450.00
Punch bowl & base, purple, 14" d., 2 pcs. .....500.00 to 525.00
Punch bowl & base, marigold, 17" d., 2 pcs. 1,100.00
Punch cup, aqua opalescent 895.00
Punch cup, blue.....50.00
Punch cup, stippled, blue .....50.00 to 75.00
Punch cup, green 38.00
Punch cup, stippled, green 45.00
Punch cup, ice blue 90.00
Punch cup, ice green.....80.00
Punch cup, lavender.....25.00
Punch cup, marigold.....30.00
Punch cup, purple.....25.00
Punch cup, white .....60.00 to 75.00
Punch set: 11" bowl & 6 cups; blue, 7 pcs. 1,550.00
Punch set: 11" bowl & 6 cups; white, 7 pcs. 1,750.00
Punch set: 11" bowl, base & 8 cups; green, 10 pcs. 600.00
Punch set: 14" bowl & 10 cups; ice green, 11 pcs. 2,300.00
Punch set: 14" bowl, base & 5 cups; purple, 7 pcs. 895.00
Punch set: 14" bowl, base & 6 cups; marigold, 8 pcs. 585.00
Punch set: 14" bowl, base & 6 cups; white, 8 pcs. 3,500.00
Punch set: 14" bowl, base & 8 cups; blue, 10 pcs. 2,300.00
Punch set, master: 17" bowl, base & 6 cups; purple, 8 pcs.....2,000.00
Punch set, master: 17" bowl, base & 8 cups; green, 10 pcs. 3,800.00
Punch set, master: 17" bowl, base & 10 cups; white, 12 pcs. 6,000.00
Punch set, master: 17" bowl, base & 12 cups; marigold, 14 pcs. 2,500.00
Spooner, green.....125.00
Spooner, marigold 42.00
Spooner, purple 100.00
Sugar bowl, cov., green.....85.00
Sugar bowl, cov., marigold 85.00
Sugar bowl, cov., purple 104.00
Sugar bowl, individual size, green 60.00
Sugar bowl, individual size, marigold ...35.00
Sugar bowl, individual size, purple 68.00
Sweetmeat jar, cov., marigold 1,800.00
Sweetmeat jar, cov., purple .....225.00 to 275.00
Table set, green, 4 pcs. 525.00
Tumbler, green .....45.00 to 65.00
Tumbler, ice green.....700.00 to 800.00
Tumbler, marigold.....36.00
Tumbler, stippled, marigold 60.00
Tumbler, purple 45.00
Tumbler, stippled, purple 50.00
Tumbler, tankard, blue.....72.00
Tumbler, tankard, green .....200.00 to 225.00
Tumbler, tankard, marigold.....48.00
Tumbler, tankard, stippled, marigold 65.00
Tumbler, tankard, purple .....45.00 to 55.00
Tumbler, tankard, stippled, purple 89.00

Water set: pitcher & 2 tumblers; blue, 3 pcs. 450.00
Water set: pitcher & 4 tumblers; purple, 5 pcs. 625.00
Water set: pitcher & 6 tumblers; green, 7 pcs. 1,150.00
Water set: pitcher & 6 tumblers; marigold, 7 pcs. .....500.00 to 550.00
Water set: tankard pitcher & 6 tumblers; marigold, 7 pcs. .....700.00 to 800.00
Whimsey compote (sweetmeat base), purple 135.00
Whimsey punch cup, green 100.00
Whimsey punch cup, marigold 125.00
Whimsey teacup, purple .....100.00 to 125.00
Whiskey shot glass, marigold 165.00
Whiskey shot glass, purple 173.00

GRAPE & GOTHIC ARCHES (Northwood)

Grape & Gothic Arches Pitcher

Berry set: master bowl & 6 sauce dishes; marigold, 7 pcs. 140.00
Bowl, master berry, blue 70.00
Bowl, master berry, marigold 43.00
Butter dish, cov., blue 300.00
Creamer, blue 85.00
Creamer, green 200.00
Creamer, marigold 45.00
Creamer & cov. sugar bowl, marigold, pr. 100.00
Pitcher, water, blue .....350.00 to 375.00
Pitcher, water, marigold (ILLUS.) 190.00
Sauce dish, blue 30.00
Sauce dish, green 35.00
Sauce dish, marigold 15.00
Sauce dish, pearl pastel milk white 45.00
Spooner, blue 65.00
Spooner, green 200.00
Spooner, marigold 45.00
Sugar bowl, cov., blue 100.00
Sugar bowl, cov., marigold 55.00
Sugar bowl, cov., purple 90.00
Table set, blue, 4 pcs. .....350.00 to 450.00
Table set, marigold, 4 pcs. 300.00
Tumbler, amber 50.00
Tumbler, blue 49.00
Tumbler, clambroth 150.00
Tumbler, green 75.00
Tumbler, marigold 35.00
Tumbler, pearl pastel milk white .....125.00 to 150.00
Tumbler, purple 50.00
Water set: pitcher & 4 tumblers; blue, 5 pcs. 600.00
Water set: pitcher & 6 tumblers; green, 7 pcs. 700.00
Water set: pitcher & 6 tumblers; marigold, 7 pcs. 375.00
Water set: pitcher & 6 tumblers; purple, 7 pcs. 600.00

GRAPE ARBOR (Northwood)

Bowl, 10" d., footed, marigold (Dugan) 90.00
Bowl, 10" d., footed, purple (Dugan) .....350.00 to 375.00
Hat shape, blue 75.00
Hat shape, marigold .....75.00 to 100.00
Hat shape, white 110.00
Pitcher, tankard, marigold...250.00 to 275.00
Pitcher, tankard, purple 600.00
Pitcher, tankard, white .....550.00 to 650.00
Tumbler, blue .....200.00 to 250.00
Tumbler, ice blue .....125.00 to 175.00
Tumbler, ice green .....400.00 to 500.00
Tumbler, lavender 175.00
Tumbler, marigold 30.00
Tumbler, pastel marigold 40.00
Tumbler, purple 62.50
Tumbler, teal blue 175.00
Tumbler, white .....125.00 to 150.00
Water set: tankard pitcher & 4 tumblers; white, 5 pcs. 1,250.00
Water set: tankard pitcher & 6 tumblers; marigold, 7 pcs. .....500.00 to 575.00

GRAPE DELIGHT

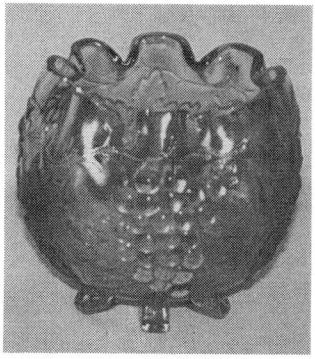

Grape Delight Rose Bowl

Nut bowl, six-footed, blue 85.00
Nut bowl, six-footed, ice blue 60.00
Nut bowl, six-footed, marigold 45.00
Nut bowl, six-footed, purple 80.00
Nut bowl, six-footed, white....80.00 to 100.00
Rose bowl, six-footed, amber 70.00
Rose bowl, six-footed, blue ....60.00 to 90.00

Rose bowl, six-footed, lavender 225.00
Rose bowl, six-footed, marigold (ILLUS.) 75.00
Rose bowl, six-footed, purple 90.00
Rose bowl, six-footed, white .....75.00 to 100.00

GRAPE LEAVES (Northwood)
Bonbon, handled, purple 26.00
Bowl, 8" d., green 90.00
Bowl, 8" d., ribbon candy rim, green...295.00
Bowl, ice blue 1,200.00
Bowl, 9" d., marigold.....50.00 to 75.00
Bowl, 9" d., purple.....120.00
Bowl, marigold (Millersburg) 500.00
Bowl, purple.....75.00

GRAPEVINE LATTICE
Bowl, 7" d., ruffled, ice white.....185.00
Bowl, 7" d., ruffled, white .....50.00 to 60.00
Bowl, fluted, white.....85.00
Hat shape, white.....150.00
Pitcher, water, blue.....287.00
Pitcher, water, purple.....450.00 to 475.00
Pitcher, water, white .....600.00 to 800.00
Plate, 6" to 7" d., marigold 58.00
Plate, 6" to 7" d., purple.....150.00 to 175.00
Plate, 6" to 7" d., white.....94.00
Plate, 8" d., ruffled, marigold 110.00
Tumbler, marigold.....40.00
Tumbler, purple .....50.00 to 70.00
Tumbler, smoky 40.00
Tumbler, white 165.00
Water set: pitcher & 1 tumbler; blue, 2 pcs. 800.00
Water set: pitcher & 1 tumbler; white, 2 pcs. 1,500.00
Water set: pitcher & 6 tumblers; marigold, 7 pcs. .....475.00 to 525.00

GREEK KEY (Northwood)

Greek Key Plate

Bowl, 8" to 9" d., blue.....500.00
Bowl, 8" to 9" d., fluted, green 185.00
Bowl, 8" to 9" d., ruffled, marigold.....85.00
Bowl, 8" to 9" d., purple 118.00
Bowl, 8" to 9" d., ruffled, purple.....150.00 to 200.00
Bowl, eight-sided, 6½" w., 4" h., purple.....75.00
Bowl, dome-footed, green 55.00
Bowl, piecrust rim, blue w/electric iridescence.....1,950.00
Bowl, piecrust rim, green.....400.00
Pitcher, water, green ....1,300.00 to 1,400.00
Pitcher, water, purple.....500.00 to 700.00
Plate, 9" d., blue 2,800.00
Plate, 9" d., green (ILLUS.).....1,100.00
Plate, 9" d., marigold 800.00
Plate, 9" d., purple .....300.00 to 400.00
Tumbler, green .....75.00 to 100.00
Tumbler, marigold.....60.00
Tumbler, purple .....75.00 to 100.00
Water set: pitcher & 4 tumblers; purple, 5 pcs. 1,250.00

HAMMERED BELL
Chandelier shade, white 40.00

HANGING CHERRIES - See Cherry (Millersburg) Pattern

HARVEST FLOWER (Dugan or Diamond Glass)
Pitcher, tankard, marigold .....1,200.00 to 1,500.00
Tumbler, amber 125.00
Tumbler, lime green.....395.00
Tumbler, marigold.....85.00
Tumbler, purple 900.00

HARVEST TIME See Golden Harvest Pattern

HATTIE (Imperial)

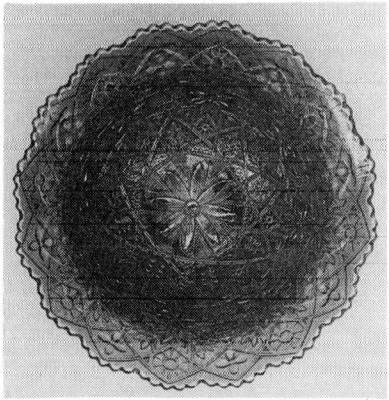

Hattie Bowl

Bowl, 8" to 9" d., green 69.00
Bowl, 8" to 9" d., marigold.....35.00

Bowl, 8" to 9" d., purple 70.00
Bowl, 8" to 9" d., smoky (ILLUS.).....63.00
Plate, chop, green .....650.00 to 750.00
Plate, chop, purple.....2,500.00
Rose bowl, amber.....325.00

HEART & HORSESHOE (Fenton's Good Luck)
Bowl, marigold.....1,000.00

HEART & VINE (Fenton)

Heart & Vine Plate

Bowl, 8" to 9" d., blue.....75.00 to 100.00
Bowl, 8" to 9" d., ribbon candy rim, blue 55.00
Bowl, 8" to 9" d., green 85.00
Bowl, 8" to 9" d., ribbon candy rim, green.....75.00
Bowl, 8" to 9" d., marigold.....45.00
Bowl, 8" to 9" d., ribbon candy rim, marigold 67.50
Bowl, 8" to 9" d., purple 81.00
Bowl, 8½" d., ribbon candy rim, purple 95.00
Plate, 9" d., blue (ILLUS.) ...350.00 to 450.00
Plate, 9" d., purple 450.00

HEARTS & FLOWERS (Northwood)
Bowl, 8" to 9" d., aqua opalescent .....1,000.00 to 1,500.00
Bowl, 8" to 9" d., blue.....600.00
Bowl, 8" to 9" d., piecrust rim, blue 500.00
Bowl, 8" to 9" d., piecrust rim, blue w/electric iridescence.....1,175.00
Bowl, 8" to 9" d., piecrust rim, ice blue .....550.00 to 650.00
Bowl, 8" to 9" d., piecrust rim, ice green.....2,600.00
Bowl, 8" to 9" d., piecrust rim, marigold .....450.00 to 550.00
Bowl, 8" to 9" d., piecrust rim, purple .....350.00 to 375.00
Bowl, 8" to 9" d., ruffled, blue.....454.00
Bowl, 8" to 9" d., ruffled, green 700.00
Bowl, 8" to 9" d., ruffled, ice blue .....450.00 to 475.00
Bowl, 8" to 9" d., ruffled, ice green.....800.00 to 1,000.00
Bowl, 8" to 9" d., ruffled, marigold.....350.00
Bowl, 8" to 9" d., ruffled, purple .....400.00 to 425.00
Bowl, 8" to 9" d., ruffled, white 275.00
Compote, 6¾" h., aqua opalescent .....500.00 to 600.00
Compote, 6¾" h., blue .....475.00 to 500.00
Compote, 6¾" h., blue opalescent 1,500.00
Compote, 6¾" h., blue w/electric iridescence.....270.00
Compote, 6¾" h., green.....2,250.00 to 2,700.00
Compote, 6¾" h., ice blue 950.00
Compote, 6¾" h., ice green 933.00
Compote, 6¾" h., lime green 2,000.00
Compote, 6¾" h., marigold 204.00
Compote, 6¾" h., moonstone 5,000.00
Compote, 6¾" h., purple.....450.00 to 500.00
Compote, 6¾" h., sapphire blue 895.00
Compote, 6¾" h., white .....150.00 to 175.00
Plate, green .....1,500.00 to 1,700.00
Plate, ice blue 4,000.00
Plate, ice green.....3,900.00
Plate, marigold.....700.00 to 1,000.00
Plate, purple .....900.00 to 1,000.00
Plate, white 2,500.00

HEAVY GRAPE (Dugan, Diamond Glass or Millersburg)
Bowl, 6" d., purple.....40.00
Bowl, 7" d., ruffled, green 35.00
Bowl, 7" d., ruffled, vaseline 40.00
Bowl, 8" sq., ruffled, blue w/electric iridescence.....325.00
Bowl, 8" d., marigold.....65.00
Bowl, 9" d., purple.....60.00
Bowl, 10" d., marigold.....45.00
Bowl, master berry, 10" d., purple .....350.00 to 400.00
Nappy, marigold 28.00
Nappy, purple 50.00
Sauce dish, blue w/electric iridescence, 5" sq.....95.00

HEAVY GRAPE (Imperial)
Bowl, 4" d., lavender.....25.00
Bowl, 5" d., purple.....150.00
Bowl, 6" d., green 32.50
Bowl, 6" d., marigold.....45.00
Bowl, 6" d., purple.....38.00
Bowl, 7" d., fluted, green.....30.00
Bowl, 7" d., marigold.....20.00
Bowl, 7" d., purple.....42.50
Bowl, 8" to 9" d., green 58.00
Bowl, 8" to 9" d., marigold.....55.00
Bowl, 8" to 9" d., purple 85.00
Bowl, 8" to 9" d., smoky 75.00
Bowl, 10" d., marigold.....80.00
Bowl, 10" d., purple.....335.00
Bowl, square, purple.....550.00

Nappy, handled, green 38.00
Nappy, handled, marigold.....28.00
Nut bowl, six-footed, purple.....75.00
Plate, 7" to 8" d., amber.....150.00 to 200.00
Plate, 7" to 8" d., blue-green.....195.00
Plate, 7" to 8" d., green.....55.00
Plate, 7" to 8" d., lavender 140.00
Plate, 7" to 8" d., marigold 56.00
Plate, 7" to 8" d., purple.....120.00
Plate, 7" to 8" d., smoky.....125.00
Plate, chop, 11" d., amber 462.00
Plate, chop, 11" d., blue.....400.00
Plate, chop, 11" d., green 235.00
Plate, chop, 11" d., marigold.....140.00
Plate, chop, 11" d.,
purple.....300.00 to 325.00
Plate, chop, 11" d., smoky 2,500.00

Heavy Grape Punch Bowl

Punch bowl & base, green, 2 pcs.
(ILLUS.) .....250.00 to 300.00
Punch cup, amber 50.00
Punch cup, green 45.00
Punch cup, marigold.....20.00
Punch cup, purple.....38.00
Punch set: bowl, base & 4 cups;
purple, 6 pcs. 800.00

HEAVY IRIS (Dugan or Diamond Glass)
Pitcher, water, marigold .....300.00 to 350.00
Pitcher, water, tankard,
marigold .....300.00 to 350.00
Tumbler, clambroth.....65.00
Tumbler, marigold.....68.00
Tumbler, pastel lavender.....350.00
Tumbler, purple 70.00
Tumbler, white.....200.00 to 250.00
Water set: pitcher & 5 tumblers;
marigold, 6 pcs. .....650.00 to 685.00
Water set: pitcher & 6 tumblers;
purple, 7 pcs. 2,000.00

HOBNAIL (Millersburg)
Butter dish, cov., marigold (ILLUS. top
next column) 895.00
Creamer, blue.....650.00

Hobnail Butter Dish

Cuspidor, marigold 700.00
Cuspidor, purple .....600.00 to 700.00
Rose bowl, green.....1,500.00
Rose bowl, marigold .....300.00 to 400.00
Rose bowl, purple.....300.00 to 400.00
Tumbler, blue .....700.00 to 900.00
Tumbler, purple 600.00

HOBNAIL, SWIRL - See Swirl Hobnail Pattern

HOBSTAR (Imperial)
Butter dish, cov., green.....245.00
Butter dish, cov., marigold.....110.00
Celery vase, two-handled, marigold 75.00
Compote, green.....60.00
Compote, purple.....110.00
Cracker jar, cov., marigold.....70.00
Creamer, marigold.....40.00
Creamer, purple.....75.00
Humidor, cov., marigold.....100.00
Punch set: bowl, base & 12 cups,
marigold, 14 pcs. 300.00
Spooner, marigold 35.00
Spooner, purple 90.00
Sugar bowl, cov., green.....70.00
Sugar bowl, cov., marigold 60.00

HOBSTAR & FEATHER (Millersburg)
Punch bowl & base, purple 3,300.00
Punch cup, blue.....65.00
Punch cup, marigold.....35.00
Punch cup, purple.....100.00
Punch set: bowl, base & 6 cups;
marigold, 8 pcs. 1,250.00
Whimsey, cuspidor-shaped,
purple.....5,000.00

HOBSTAR BAND
Pitcher, marigold .....150.00 to 200.00
Tumbler, marigold (ILLUS. top next
column) 40.00

Hobstar Band Tumbler

HOLLY, HOLLY BERRIES & CARNIVAL HOLLY (Fenton)

Holly Bowl

Bonbon, two-handled, green 55.00
Bonbon, two-handled, marigold.....110.00
Bonbon, two-handled, purple.....65.00
Bowl, 5" d., marigold.....25.00
Bowl, 5" d., scalloped, red 450.00
Bowl, 8" to 9" d., amber 125.00
Bowl, 8" to 9" d., aqua 550.00
Bowl, 8" to 9" d., blue.....65.00
Bowl, 8" to 9" d., celeste blue 500.00
Bowl, 8" to 9" d., green 70.00
Bowl, 8" to 9" d., lavender...175.00 to 200.00
Bowl, 8" to 9" d., light blue w/marigold overlay 200.00
Bowl, 8" to 9" d., marigold.....40.00 to 50.00
Bowl, 8" to 9" d., milk white w/marigold overlay.....1,050.00
Bowl, 8" to 9" d., purple 55.00
Bowl, 8" to 9" d., red, (Fenton) .....1,000.00 to 1,125.00
Bowl, 8" to 9" d., vaseline 85.00
Bowl, 8" to 9" d., white.....100.00 to 125.00
Bowl, 8" to 9" d., ice cream shape, blue 66.00
Bowl, 8" to 9" d., ice cream shape, celeste blue.....4,000.00
Bowl, 8" to 9" d., ice cream shape, clambroth 85.00
Bowl, 8" to 9" d., ice cream shape, cobalt blue 275.00
Bowl, 8" to 9" d., ice cream shape, green (ILLUS.) 103.00
Bowl, 8" to 9" d., ice cream shape, ice green 3,200.00
Bowl, 8" to 9" d., ice cream shape, marigold 80.00
Bowl, 8" to 9" d., ice cream shape, moonstone .....850.00 to 900.00
Bowl, 8" to 9" d., ice cream shape, purple 75.00
Bowl, 8" to 9" d., ice cream shape, red.....1,300.00
Bowl, 8" to 9" d., ice cream shape, vaseline.....130.00
Bowl, 8" to 9" d., ice cream shape, white 135.00
Bowl, 8" to 9" d., ribbon candy rim, amethyst .....100.00 to 125.00
Bowl, 8" to 9" d., ribbon candy rim, blue 55.00
Bowl, 8" to 9" d., ribbon candy rim, green.....135.00
Bowl, 8" to 9" d., ribbon candy rim, marigold 65.00
Bowl, 8" to 9" d., ribbon candy rim, pastel green 65.00
Bowl, 8" to 9" d., ribbon candy rim, purple.....100.00 to 125.00
Bowl, 8" to 9" d., ruffled, blue opalescent 1,400.00
Bowl, 8" to 9" d., ruffled, emerald green.....300.00
Bowl, 8" to 9" d., ruffled, green.....100.00 to 125.00
Bowl, 8" to 9" d., ruffled, marigold.....45.00
Bowl, 8" to 9" d., ruffled, pastel blue .....50.00 to 75.00
Bowl, 8" to 9" d., ruffled, peach opalescent 35.00
Bowl, 8" to 9" d., ruffled, purple 130.00
Bowl, 8" to 9" d., ruffled, red.....900.00 to 1,000.00
Bowl, 8" to 9" d., ruffled, vaseline 225.00
Compote, small, aqua w/marigold overlay .....100.00 to 125.00
Compote, small, blue.....40.00
Compote, small, green .....50.00 to 75.00
Compote, small, lavender.....50.00 to 75.00
Compote, small, lime green opalescent 735.00
Compote, small, marigold.....28.00
Compote, small, marigold w/vaseline stem 65.00
Compote, small, purple.....100.00 to 125.00
Compote, small, red .....450.00 to 550.00
Compote, small, vaseline 70.00
Compote, ice green opalescent.....625.00

Compote, red....1,000.00
Dish, hat-shaped, amber, 5¾"....75.00
Dish, hat-shaped, Amberina....450.00
Dish, hat-shaped, amethyst opalescent....425.00
Dish, hat-shaped, aqua, 5¾"....75.00
Dish, hat-shaped, aqua opalescent....275.00
Dish, hat-shaped, aqua w/marigold overlay....55.00
Dish, hat-shaped, blue, 5¾"....50.00
Dish, hat-shaped, green, 5¾"....36.00
Dish, hat-shaped, green w/marigold overlay....29.00
Dish, hat-shaped, ice blue w/marigold overlay, 5¾"....75.00
Dish, hat-shaped, lavender....85.00
Dish, hat-shaped, lime green, 5¾"....50.00 to 75.00
Dish, hat-shaped, marigold, 5¾"....30.00
Dish, hat-shaped, milk white w/marigold overlay....118.00
Dish, hat-shaped, moonstone....200.00
Dish, hat-shaped, purple, 5¾"....35.00
Dish, hat-shaped, purple opalescent, 5¾"....300.00
Dish, hat-shaped, red, 5¾"....430.00 to 450.00
Dish, hat-shaped, vaseline, 5¾"....72.00
Goblet, blue....35.00
Goblet, green....70.00
Goblet, marigold....27.00
Goblet, red (Fenton)....429.00
Plate, 9" to 10" d., amethyst....1,050.00
Plate, 9" to 10" d., blue....350.00 to 450.00
Plate, 9" to 10" d., celeste blue (Fenton)....9,500.00
Plate, 9" to 10" d., clambroth....125.00
Plate, 9" to 10" d., green....800.00 to 1,000.00
Plate, 9" to 10" d., marigold....125.00 to 175.00
Plate, 9" to 10" d., pastel marigold....200.00
Plate, 9" to 10" d., purple....400.00 to 600.00
Plate, 9" to 10" d., white....200.00 to 225.00
Sauceboat, handled, peach opalescent....102.00
Sauceboat, handled, purple....110.00
Sherbet, blue....40.00
Sherbet, green....25.00
Sherbet, lime green....75.00
Sherbet, lime green opalescent....675.00
Sherbet, marigold....35.00
Sherbet, red....425.00

HOLLY SPRIG - See Holly Whirl Pattern

HOLLY WHIRL or HOLLY SPRIG (Millersburg & Dugan)

Bowl, 6" w., tricornered, amethyst....125.00
Bowl, 6" w., tricornered, green....85.00
Bowl, 6" w., tricornered, purple....125.00
Bowl, 6" d., ruffled, marigold....95.00
Bowl, 6" d., ruffled, purple....92.50
Bowl, 7" d., green....60.00
Bowl, 7" d., marigold....55.00
Bowl, 7" d., ruffled, purple....60.00
Bowl, 8" d., ice cream shape, marigold, variant....68.00
Bowl, 8" d., ice cream shape, white....110.00
Bowl, 8" to 9" d., ruffled, blue....50.00
Bowl, 8" to 9" d., green....75.00 to 100.00
Bowl, 8" to 9" d., marigold....55.00
Bowl, 8" to 9" d., peach opalescent....75.00
Bowl, 8" to 9" d., purple....75.00 to 100.00
Bowl, 10" d., ruffled, marigold....50.00
Bowl, 10" d., ruffled, purple....100.00 to 125.00
Hat shape, green, 6"....38.00
Nappy, single handle, marigold....45.00
Nappy, single handle, peach opalescent (Dugan)....62.00
Nappy, single handle, purple (Dugan)....75.00 to 100.00
Nappy, tricornered, green (Dugan)....110.00
Nappy, tricornered, marigold (Millersburg)....110.00
Nappy, tricornered, purple (Dugan)....100.00
Nappy, tricornered, purple (Millersburg)....175.00 to 200.00

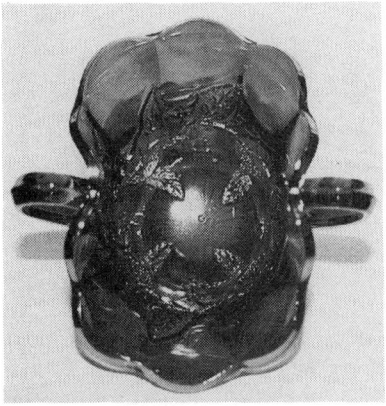

Holly Whirl Nappy

Nappy, two-handled, amethyst, Millersburg (ILLUS.)....68.00
Nappy, two-handled, green (Dugan)....75.00 to 100.00
Nappy, two-handled, green (Millersburg)....80.00
Nut dish, two-handled, green....75.00
Nut dish, two-handled, marigold....68.00
Nut dish, two-handled, purple....72.50
Rose bowl, blue....300.00
Rose bowl, small, marigold....325.00
Sauceboat, peach opalescent (Dugan)....135.00
Sauce dish, green, 6½" d. (Millersburg)....100.00 to 125.00
Sauce dish, deep, purple....350.00

HOMESTEAD - See NU-ART HOMESTEAD PLATE

HONEYCOMB

Honeycomb Rose Bowl

Bonbon, marigold 28.00
Bonbon, green 53.00
Rose bowl, peach opalescent (ILLUS.) .....200.00 to 250.00
Vase, 7" h., green 52.50

HORSE HEADS OR HORSE MEDALLION (Fenton)

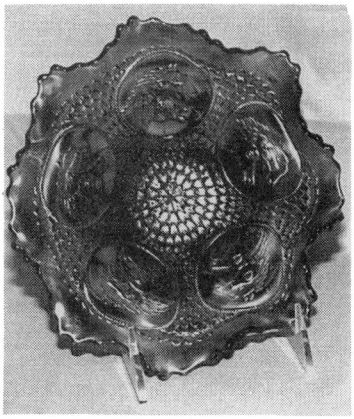

Horse Heads Bowl

Bowl, 5" d., footed, marigold.....57.00
Bowl, 6" d., blue.....60.00
Bowl, 6" d., collared base, marigold 85.00
Bowl, 7" to 8" d., amber 395.00
Bowl, 7" to 8" d., blue.....115.00
Bowl, 7" to 8" d., green (ILLUS.).....135.00
Bowl, 7" to 8" d., marigold.....75.00 to 100.00
Bowl, 7" to 8" d., purple 118.00
Bowl, 7" to 8" d., red .....1,250.00 to 1,500.00
Bowl, ice cream shape, amber 280.00
Bowl, ice cream shape, blue.....235.00
Bowl, 7" d., ice cream shape, marigold 85.00
Bowl, 7" d., ice cream shape, purple ..425.00
Bowl, ruffled, collared base, Amberina 450.00
Bowl, jack-in-the-pulpit shaped, amber.....495.00
Bowl, jack-in-the-pulpit shaped, blue .....150.00 to 175.00
Bowl, jack-in-the-pulpit shaped, green.....250.00 to 300.00
Bowl, jack-in-the-pulpit shaped, marigold 130.00
Bowl, jack-in-the-pulpit shaped, purple 265.00
Bowl, jack-in-the-pulpit shaped, teal green.....675.00
Bowl, jack-in-the-pulpit shaped, vaseline.....400.00 to 425.00
Bowl, 7" to 8" d., blue.....750.00
Bowl, 7" to 8" d., marigold...200.00 to 225.00
Nut bowl, three-footed, amethyst.....225.00
Nut bowl, three-footed, blue 150.00
Nut bowl, three-footed, green 195.00
Nut bowl, three-footed, marigold 85.00
Nut bowl, three-footed, red.....1,500.00 to 1,700.00
Nut bowl, three-footed, vaseline .....250.00 to 300.00
Rose bowl, blue 225.00
Rose bowl, marigold 136.00
Rose bowl, smoky blue.....400.00
Rose bowl, vaseline.....750.00

HORSESHOE CURVE - See Twins Pattern

ILLINOIS SOLDIER'S & SAILOR'S PLATE
Blue 1,000.00

ILLUSION (Fenton)

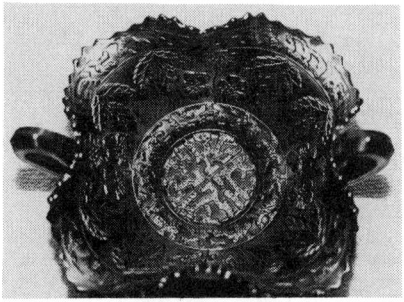

Illusion Bonbon

Bonbon, two-handled, blue (ILLUS.) 68.00
Bonbon, two-handled, marigold.....65.00
Bonbon, two-handled, purple.....150.00

IMPERIAL GRAPE (Imperial)
Basket, marigold.....80.00
Basket, smoky 118.00
Berry set: master bowl & 2 sauce dishes; purple, 3 pcs.....225.00
Berry set: master bowl & 4 sauce dishes; green, 5 pcs.....125.00 to 150.00
Bowl, 6" d., marigold.....35.00
Bowl, 6" d., ruffled, purple.....70.00
Bowl, 7" d., 2½" h., green 42.00

Bowl, 7" d., 2½" h., marigold.....20.00
Bowl, 7" d., 2½" h., ruffled, purple 70.00
Bowl, 8" to 9" d., aqua 75.00
Bowl, 8" to 9" d., green 48.00
Bowl, 8" to 9" d., marigold.....43.00
Bowl, 8" to 9" d., purple 120.00
Bowl, 10" d., green 40.00
Bowl, 10" d., marigold.....45.00
Bowl, 10" d., purple.....117.00
Bowl, 10" d., smoky 33.00
Bowl, 11" d., ruffled, purple.....100.00
Compote, amber.....60.00
Compote, clambroth 35.00
Compote, green.....45.00
Compote, lavender swirled w/amber ..140.00
Compote, purple 500.00
Compote, smoky.....35.00
Cup, purple 20.00
Cup & saucer, amber.....65.00
Cup & saucer, green.....85.00

Imperial Grape Cup & Saucer

Cup & saucer, marigold (ILLUS.).....80.00
Decanter w/stopper, green.....125.00 to 150.00
Decanter w/stopper, marigold.....94.00
Decanter w/stopper, purple.....225.00 to 250.00
Goblet, aqua teal 90.00
Goblet, clambroth 75.00
Goblet, green.....35.00
Goblet, marigold 35.00
Goblet, purple 55.00
Goblet, smoky.....75.00 to 100.00
Pitcher, water, amber 650.00
Pitcher, water, marigold.....75.00 to 100.00
Pitcher, water, smoky .....300.00 to 400.00
Plate, 6" d., amber.....125.00 to 150.00
Plate, 6" d., green 60.00
Plate, 6" d., marigold 48.00
Plate, 6" d., purple .....100.00 to 150.00
Plate, 7" d., green 85.00
Plate, 7" d., marigold 30.00
Plate, 8" d., green 50.00
Plate, 8" d., marigold 50.00
Plate, 8" d., purple .....75.00 to 100.00
Plate, 9" d., ruffled, clambroth 75.00
Plate, 9" d., flat, green 75.00
Plate, 9" d., ruffled, green 137.00
Plate, 9" d., flat, marigold.....75.00 to 100.00
Plate, 9" d., ruffled, marigold .....50.00 to 100.00
Plate, 9" d., ruffled, purple 100.00
Plate, 9" d., ruffled, smoky.....95.00
Rose bowl, amber.....675.00
Rose bowl, green.....65.00
Rose bowl, purple.....60.00
Rose bowl, white 70.00
Sauce dish, amber.....17.00
Sauce dish, green.....25.00
Sauce dish, ruffled, marigold 20.00
Tray, center handle, amber 30.00
Tray, center handle, clambroth.....45.00
Tray, center handle, marigold.....75.00
Tray, center handle, smoky 35.00
Tumbler, amber 98.00
Tumbler, aqua 130.00
Tumbler, green 28.00
Tumbler, lilac 59.00
Tumbler, marigold.....25.00
Tumbler, purple 50.00
Water bottle, green.....100.00 to 125.00
Water bottle, marigold .....75.00 to 100.00
Water bottle, purple .....150.00 to 175.00
Water bottle, smoky.....450.00
Water set: pitcher & 6 tumblers; marigold, 7 pcs. 225.00
Water set: pitcher & 6 tumblers; purple, 7 pcs. 700.00
Wine, clambroth.....18.00
Wine, green 33.00
Wine, marigold.....28.00
Wine, purple 35.00
Wine, smoky 75.00
Wine set: decanter w/stopper & 6 wines; marigold, 7 pcs. 260.00
Wine set: decanter w/stopper & 6 wines; purple, 7 pcs. .....475.00 to 500.00

INVERTED COIN DOT

Pitcher, marigold .....75.00 to 100.00
Tumbler, marigold.....60.00
Water set: pitcher & 1 tumbler; marigold, 2 pcs. .....250.00 to 300.00

INVERTED FEATHER (Cambridge)

Compote, jelly, marigold.....75.00
Cracker jar, cov., green .....200.00 to 250.00
Parfait, marigold 90.00
Pitcher, milk, pastel marigold 475.00
Tumbler, green 750.00
Vase, 6" h., marigold (Cambridge) 75.00
Vase, 6" h., marigold (Northwood).....45.00

INVERTED STRAWBERRY (Cambridge)

Bowl, 6½" d., green, marked Near-Cut 52.00
Bowl, 7" d., green 125.00
Candlestick, marigold 128.00
Candlesticks, green, 7" h., pr.....225.00
Compote, open, 5" d., 6" h., marigold 225.00
Compote, open, giant, marigold .....225.00 to 250.00
Creamer, blue.....300.00

Cuspidor, green 1,000.00
Cuspidor, marigold .....800.00 to 850.00
Pitcher, tankard, marigold.....950.00
Powder jar, cov., green.....150.00 to 200.00
Powder jar, cov., marigold.....100.00
Sherbet w/flared sides, blue 625.00
Spooner, green.....225.00
Sugar bowl, cov., green.....250.00
Table set, marigold, 4 pcs. 1,000.00
Table set, purple, 4 pcs. 1,500.00
Tumbler, green 275.00
Tumbler, marigold.....125.00 to 150.00
Tumbler, purple .....175.00 to 200.00
Water set: pitcher & 1 tumbler; green, 2 pcs. 1,500.00
Water set: pitcher & 6 tumblers; marigold, 7 pcs. 1,700.00

Inverted Strawberry Water Set

Water set: pitcher & 6 tumblers; purple, 7 pcs. (ILLUS.).....3,750.00
Whimsey, made from two-handled nappy, marked "Near-Cut," green.....1,400.00

INVERTED THISTLE (Cambridge)

Bowl, purple.....65.00
Pitcher, milk, purple 2,500.00
Tumbler, purple 225.00
Water set: pitcher & 6 tumblers; purple, 7 pcs. .....3,500.00 to 4,300.00

IRIS

Compote, 6¾" d., blue 285.00
Compote, 6¾" d., green.....68.00
Compote, 6¾" d., marigold.....40.00
Compote, 6¾" d., etched "Mother, 1909," marigold.....30.00
Compote, 6¾" d., purple.....55.00
Compote, 7½" d., wide top, marigold....55.00
Goblet, buttermilk, green 65.00
Goblet, buttermilk, marigold.....85.00
Goblet, buttermilk, marigold, souvenir ..80.00
Goblet, buttermilk, purple 80.00

IRIS, HEAVY - See Heavy Iris Pattern

JEWELED HEART (Dugan or Diamond Glass)

Basket, peach opalescent, 6" h.....525.00 to 625.00
Bowl, master berry, 10½" d., fluted, peach opalescent.....135.00
Bowl, 10" d., purple.....100.00
Bowl, white 165.00

Jeweled Heart Pitcher

Pitcher, marigold (ILLUS.) ..650.00 to 850.00
Sauce dish, peach opalescent.....38.00
Sauce dish, peach opalescent w/rayed interior 32.00
Tumbler, amber 115.00
Tumbler, green 35.00
Tumbler, marigold.....65.00

KITTENS (Fenton)

Bowl, cereal, blue .....450.00 to 500.00
Bowl, cereal, marigold 193.00
Bowl, ruffled, blue 775.00
Bowl, ruffled, marigold .....100.00 to 125.00
Bowl, four-sided, blue 350.00
Bowl, four-sided, ruffled, marigold.....159.00
Bowl, six-sided, ruffled, marigold .....175.00 to 200.00
Cup, blue 675.00
Cup, marigold 129.00
Cup & saucer, blue 2,600.00
Cup & saucer, marigold.....200.00 to 275.00
Dish, turned-up sides, blue.....550.00
Dish, turned-up sides, marigold .....125.00 to 150.00
Dish, turned-up sides, purple.....525.00
Plate, 4½" d., marigold .....125.00 to 150.00
Spooner, blue 280.00
Spooner, marigold 150.00
Toothpick holder, blue .....400.00 to 475.00
Toothpick holder, marigold 185.00
Vase, marigold.....250.00
Vase, child's, ruffled, marigold.....145.00

LATTICE & GRAPE (Fenton)

Pitcher, tankard, marigold .....200.00 to 250.00
Tumbler, blue.....46.00
Tumbler, marigold (ILLUS. top next page).....35.00
Tumbler, white 135.00

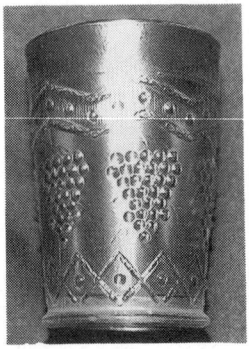

Lattice & Grape Tumbler

Water set: tankard pitcher & 1 tumbler; white, 2 pcs. 900.00
Water set: tankard pitcher & 6 tumblers; blue, 7 pcs. 685.00
Water set: tankard pitcher & 6 tumblers; marigold, 7 pcs. 685.00

LATTICE & POINSETTIA (Northwood)

Lattice & Poinsettia Bowl

Bowl, cobalt blue (ILLUS.) ..500.00 to 550.00
Bowl, ice blue 3,000.00
Bowl, marigold 425.00
Bowl, purple ....500.00 to 550.00

LATTICE & POINTS

Hat shape, clambroth 42.00
Hat shape, marigold 28.00
Vase, 3½" h., marigold 30.00
Vase, 8" h., purple 65.00
Vase, 15½" h., marigold 45.00
Vase, purple 85.00
Vase, white 55.00

LEAF & BEADS (Northwood)

Candy bowl, footed, green 48.00
Candy bowl, footed, marigold 45.00
Candy bowl, footed, purple 55.00
Nut bowl, aqua opalescent 575.00
Nut bowl, handled, green 60.00
Nut bowl, handled, marigold ....75.00 to 100.00
Nut bowl, handled, purple 95.00
Nut bowl, handled, white 275.00
Rose bowl, aqua 300.00
Rose bowl, aqua opalescent ....325.00 to 350.00
Rose bowl, blue ....200.00 to 250.00
Rose bowl, blue w/electric iridescence ....200.00 to 250.00
Rose bowl, green 114.00
Rose bowl, interior pattern, green ....75.00 to 85.00
Rose bowl, ice blue 1,400.00
Rose bowl, lime green 450.00
Rose bowl, marigold 96.00
Rose bowl, interior pattern, marigold ....75.00 to 100.00
Rose bowl, olive green ....225.00 to 275.00
Rose bowl, pastel marigold 50.00
Rose bowl, purple 96.00
Rose bowl, purple w/smooth rim ....350.00 to 375.00
Rose bowl, interior pattern, purple 150.00
Rose bowl, interior pattern, teal blue 1,000.00
Rose bowl, white 900.00

LEAF & FLOWERS or LEAF & LITTLE FLOWERS (Millersburg)

Compote, miniature, green 300.00
Compote, miniature, marigold 285.00
Compote, miniature, purple ....375.00 to 400.00

LEAF CHAIN (Fenton)

Leaf Chain Bowl

Bowl, 5" d., ruffled, marigold 45.00
Bowl, 6" d., ruffled, red 600.00
Bowl, 7" d., ruffled, Amberina 450.00
Bowl, 7" d., ruffled, green 75.00
Bowl, 7" d., aqua ....125.00 to 150.00
Bowl, 7" d., blue 52.00
Bowl, 7" d., lavender 150.00
Bowl, 7" d., marigold 48.00
Bowl, 7" d., red ....1,000.00 to 1,200.00

Bowl, 7" d., vaseline 100.00
Bowl, 7" d., white 62.00
Bowl, 8" to 9" d., blue (ILLUS.) 75.00
Bowl, 8" to 9" d., clambroth.....48.00
Bowl, 8" to 9" d., green 65.00
Bowl, 8" to 9" d., marigold.....50.00
Bowl, 8" to 9" d., vaseline 95.00
Bowl, 8" to 9" d., white 88.00
Plate, 7" to 8" d., blue 80.00
Plate, 7" to 8" d., marigold 75.00
Plate, 9" d., blue 180.00
Plate, 9" d., clambroth .....115.00 to 130.00
Plate, 9" d., green.....135.00
Plate, 9" d., marigold .....125.00 to 175.00
Plate, 9" d., pastel marigold.....370.00
Plate, 9" d., white.....200.00 to 225.00

LEAF RAYS NAPPY

Marigold.....25.00
Peach opalescent.....38.00
Purple 40.00
Purple, "Souvenir of Cedar City, Michigan" 60.00
White 50.00

LEAF SWIRL COMPOTE

Amber.....45.00
Marigold.....45.00
Purple 75.00
Teal blue.....100.00
Vaseline.....95.00

LEAF TIERS

Butter dish, cov., marigold.....150.00
Sauce dish, footed, marigold.....40.00
Shade, milk white w/marigold overlay 60.00
Tumbler, marigold.....62.00
Vase, purple 65.00

LILY OF THE VALLEY (Fenton)

Lily of the Valley Pitcher

Pitcher, water, blue (ILLUS.) 5,000.00

Tumbler, blue.....250.00 to 300.00
Tumbler, marigold.....400.00

LINED LATTICE VASE

Blue 68.00
Lavender, pastel.....100.00 to 150.00
Marigold.....45.00
Peach opalescent, 6" h.....95.00
Purple 47.00
White 76.00
White, 10" h., pr.....225.00

LION (Fenton)

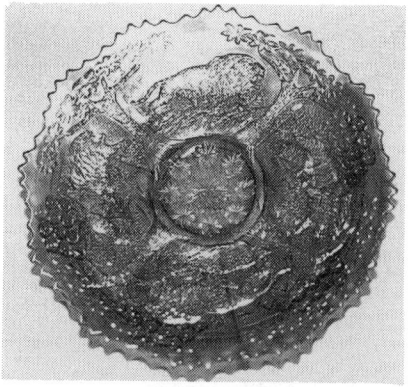

Lion Plate

Bowl, 5" d., marigold.....105.00
Bowl, 6" d., marigold.....100.00 to 140.00
Bowl, 7" d., blue.....250.00 to 300.00
Bowl, 7" d., marigold.....40.00
Bowl, 7" d., ice cream shape, blue 315.00
Bowl, 7" d., ice cream shape, marigold 104.00
Bowl, ruffled, red.....675.00
Plate, 7" d., marigold (ILLUS.) 700.00

LITTLE BARREL PERFUME

Little Barrel Perfume

Green (ILLUS.) 200.00
Marigold.....100.00 to 125.00
Smoky.....97.00

LITTLE DAISIES (Fenton)
Bowl, 9" to 10" d., marigold.....950.00

LITTLE FISHES (Fenton)
Bowl, 6" d., three-footed, marigold 62.50
Bowl, 8" to 9" d., three-footed, blue 245.00
Bowl, 8" to 9" d., three-footed, marigold 145.00
Bowl, 10" d., three-footed, blue .....175.00 to 225.00
Bowl, 10" d., three-footed, marigold 125.00
Bowl, 10" d., three-footed, white 1,000.00
Sauce dish, three-footed, aqua, 5" d.....210.00
Sauce dish, three-footed, blue, 5" d.....90.00
Sauce dish, three-footed, marigold, 5" d.....48.00
Sauce dish, three-footed, purple, 5" d.....100.00
Sauce dish, three-footed, vaseline, 5" d.....95.00

LITTLE FLOWERS (Fenton)

Little Flowers Chop Plate

Berry set: master bowl & 4 sauce dishes; purple, 5 pcs.....240.00
Berry set: master bowl & 6 sauce dishes; green, 7 pcs.....250.00
Bowl, 6" d., ice cream shape, blue .....30.00 to 40.00
Bowl, 6" d., ruffled, vaseline 35.00
Bowl, 6½" d., marigold.....20.00
Bowl, 6½" d., purple.....65.00
Bowl, 8" to 9" d., blue.....110.00
Bowl, 8" to 9" d., green 45.00
Bowl, 8" to 9" d., marigold.....58.00
Bowl, 8" to 9" d., purple 65.00
Bowl, 10" d., blue.....110.00
Bowl, 10" d., green 75.00
Bowl, 10" d., ruffled, green 110.00
Bowl, 10" d., ruffled, lavender.....116.00
Bowl, 10" d., ruffled, marigold.....75.00
Bowl, 10" d., purple.....95.00
Bowl, 10" d., spatula-footed, red.....750.00 to 800.00
Plate, 6" d., marigold 450.00
Plate, chop, footed, marigold (ILLUS.) 400.00
Sauce dish, 5" d., blue.....40.00
Sauce dish, 5" d., green 25.00
Sauce dish, 5" d., marigold.....32.00
Sauce dish, 5" d., purple.....40.00

LITTLE STARS BOWL (Millersburg)
Bowl, 7" d., green 97.00
Bowl, 7" d., marigold.....95.00
Bowl, 7" d., fluted, marigold.....95.00
Bowl, 7" d., purple.....140.00
Bowl, 7½" d., three-in-one edge, marigold 100.00
Bowl, 8" d., ruffled, green 181.00
Bowl, 8" d., ruffled, marigold.....90.00
Bowl, 8" d., ruffled, pastel marigold 135.00
Bowl, 8" d., ruffled, purple.....125.00
Bowl, ice cream, 8" d., marigold 95.00
Bowl, ice cream, 10" d., blue 300.00
Plate, 9" d., marigold 475.00

LOGANBERRY VASE (Imperial)
Amber 500.00
Green.....325.00
Marigold.....180.00
Purple .....550.00 to 600.00

LONG HOBSTAR
Bowl, fruit, marigold 60.00

LONG THUMBPRINTS
Creamer, marigold.....22.00
Creamer & sugar bowl, marigold, pr.....50.00
Sugar bowl, marigold.....37.00
Vase, 9½" h., purple 64.00

LOTUS & GRAPE (Fenton)

Lotus & Grape Plate

Bonbon, two-handled, green 90.00
Bonbon, two-handled, marigold.....45.00
Bonbon, two-handled, purple.....225.00

Bonbon, two-handled, red 1,800.00
Bonbon, two-handled, vaseline 90.00
Bowl, 5" d., footed, green 67.00
Bowl, 5" d., footed, marigold.....45.00
Bowl, 7" d., footed, marigold.....45.00
Bowl, 7½" d., ice cream shape, blue 65.00
Bowl, 8" d., collared base, ruffled, marigold on vaseline 75.00
Bowl, 8" to 9" d., blue.....105.00
Bowl, 8" to 9" d., green 95.00
Bowl, 8" to 9" d., marigold.....125.00
Bowl, 8" to 9" d., purple 95.00
Plate, 9" d., blue (ILLUS.) 1,400.00
Plate, 9" d., green 1,200.00

LOUISA (Westmoreland)

Louisa Rose Bowl

Bowl, 5" oval, footed, teal blue 20.00
Bowl, 7" d., footed, green 45.00
Bowl, 8" to 9" d., three-footed, amber...50.00
Bowl, 8" to 9" d., three-footed, peach opalescent 375.00
Bowl, 8" to 9" d., three-footed, purple...55.00
Bowl, 8" to 9" d., three-footed, teal blue 65.00
Nut bowl, footed, green 60.00
Nut bowl, footed, purple.....60.00
Plate, 9½" d., footed, amber.....137.50
Plate, 9½" d., footed, marigold 100.00
Plate, 9½" d., footed, purple 140.00
Rose bowl, footed, amber.....95.00
Rose bowl, footed, aqua.....90.00
Rose bowl, footed, blue 80.00
Rose bowl, footed, green (ILLUS.) 65.00
Rose bowl, footed, lavendar.....70.00
Rose bowl, footed, marigold.....40.00
Rose bowl, footed, purple.....78.00

LUSTRE FLUTE (Northwood)

Bowl, berry, green 45.00
Creamer, green 32.00
Creamer, purple.....50.00
Cup, green.....12.00
Hat shape, fluted, green, 5" d. 35.00
Hat shape, fluted, marigold, 5" d. 22.00
Hat shape, fluted, purple, 5" d. 55.00
Nappy, green .....45.00 to 50.00
Nappy, marigold 32.00
Punch cup, green .....25.00 to 30.00
Sugar bowl, green 45.00
Sugar bowl, marigold.....27.50
Tumbler, marigold.....25.00

LUSTRE ROSE (Imperial)

Lustre Rose Bowl

Bowl, 7" d., three-footed, clambroth 75.00
Bowl, 7" d., three-footed, green.....35.00
Bowl, 7" d., three-footed, marigold 42.00
Bowl, 7" d., three-footed, vaseline.....100.00
Bowl, 8" to 9" d., three-footed, clambroth .....50.00 to 75.00
Bowl, 8" to 9" d., three-footed, marigold (ILLUS.).....40.00
Bowl, 8" to 9" d., three-footed, purple.....117.00
Bowl, 8" to 9" d., three-footed, smoky 35.00
Bowl, 8" to 9" d., three-footed, vaseline.....125.00
Bowl, 10½" d., three-footed, clambroth 50.00
Bowl, 10½" d., three-footed, marigold 35.00
Bowl, 10½" d., three-footed, smoky.....74.00
Bowl, 11" d., ruffled, collared base, green.....85.00
Bowl, 11" d., ruffled, footed, marigold 50.00
Bowl, 11" d., ruffled, footed, purple.....650.00
Bowl, fruit, red.....2,400.00
Bowl, whimsey, centerpiece, amber...250.00
Bowl, whimsey, centerpiece, purple ...550.00
Butter dish, cov., marigold.....65.00
Butter dish, cov., purple.....110.00
Creamer, marigold.....37.00
Creamer, purple.....125.00
Fernery, amber 80.00
Fernery, blue 75.00
Fernery, green, 7½" d., 4" h.....60.00
Fernery, green w/marigold overlay 125.00
Fernery, marigold 45.00
Fernery, olive.....70.00
Fernery, red 1,000.00

Pitcher, water, clambroth.....65.00
Pitcher, water, green 90.00
Pitcher, water, marigold.....85.00
Plate, 9" d., green.....75.00
Plate, 9" d., marigold 60.00
Plate, 9" d., purple 600.00
Plate, 10½" d., marigold 85.00
Rose bowl, amber.....70.00
Rose bowl, green.....40.00
Rose bowl, marigold.....45.00
Rose bowl, purple.....30.00
Sauce dish, clambroth.....30.00
Sauce dish, marigold.....12.00
Spooner, purple.....125.00
Sugar bowl, cov., green.....50.00
Tumbler, amber 17.00
Tumbler, aqua 395.00
Tumbler, green 25.00
Tumbler, honey amber 45.00
Tumbler, marigold.....25.00
Tumbler, purple 50.00
Tumbler, white.....39.00
Water set: pitcher & 4 tumblers;
purple, 5 pcs. 700.00
Water set: pitcher & 6 tumblers;
marigold, 7 pcs. 250.00
Whimsey, flattened fernery, green.....110.00

MANY FRUITS (Dugan)
Punch bowl & base, marigold,
2 pcs. 400.00
Punch bowl & base, purple, 2 pcs. 715.00
Punch cup, green 35.00
Punch cup, purple.....28.00

MANY STARS (Millersburg)
Bowl, 8" to 9" d., ruffled, green 425.00
Bowl, 8" to 9" d., ruffled, marigold.....410.00
Bowl, 10" d., ruffled, blue.....2,800.00
Bowl, 10" d., ruffled, purple.....450.00
Bowl, ice cream, 10" d., green.....700.00
Bowl, ice cream, 10" d., purple.....800.00

MAPLE LEAF (Dugan)

Maple Leaf Creamer

Berry set: master bowl & 6 small berry
bowls; pedestaled, purple, 7 pcs. 300.00
Bowl, 6" d., small berry, marigold 25.00
Bowl, 6" d., small berry, purple.....30.00
Bowl, master berry or fruit, purple 100.00
Bowl, ice cream, footed, marigold 35.00
Butter dish, cov., blue.....82.50
Butter dish, cov., marigold.....175.00
Butter dish, cov., purple.....195.00
Creamer, marigold.....42.00
Creamer, purple (ILLUS.) 58.00
Pitcher, water, blue.....275.00
Spooner, blue 70.00
Spooner, marigold 43.00
Spooner, purple.....60.00
Table set, blue, 4 pcs. 295.00
Tumbler, amber 75.00
Tumbler, blue.....65.00
Tumbler, lavender.....150.00
Tumbler, marigold.....24.00
Tumbler, pastel marigold.....75.00
Tumbler, purple 38.00
Water set: pitcher & 6 tumblers;
purple, 7 pcs. 725.00

MARILYN (Millersburg)
Pitcher, water, marigold.....575.00
Tumbler, green 200.00
Tumbler, purple 92.00
Water set: 8½" h. pitcher & 3 tumblers;
marigold, 4 pcs. 675.00
Water set: pitcher & 6 tumblers;
purple, 7 pcs. 1,200.00

MARY ANN VASE (Dugan)
Marigold.....50.00 to 70.00
Purple 165.00

MAYAN (Millersburg)
Bowl, 8" to 9" d., green 116.00
Bowl, 8" to 9" d., purple 125.00

MEMPHIS (Northwood)

Memphis Punch Bowl

Bowl, master berry, marigold.....75.00
Fruit bowl & base, ice blue, 2 pcs....4,500.00
Fruit bowl & base, marigold,
2 pcs. .....150.00 to 200.00

Fruit bowl & base, purple, 2 pcs. .....425.00 to 475.00
Fruit bowl & base, white, 2 pcs.....700.00
Punch bowl & base, marigold, 2 pcs. 175.00
Punch bowl & base, purple, 2 pcs. (ILLUS.) 600.00
Punch cup, green 46.00
Punch cup, ice blue 65.00
Punch cup, ice green.....70.00
Punch cup, marigold.....25.00
Punch cup, purple.....38.00
Punch cup, white 40.00
Punch set: bowl, base & 4 cups; white, 6 pcs. 900.00
Punch set: bowl, base & 6 cups; green, 8 pcs. 1,250.00
Punch set: bowl, base & 6 cups; marigold, 8 pcs. 415.00
Punch set: bowl, base & 6 cups; purple, 8 pcs. 1,300.00

MIKADO (Fenton)
Compote, 10" d., blue 412.00
Compote, 10" d., marigold 154.00

MILADY (Fenton)
Pitcher, water, blue.....1,000.00
Pitcher, water, marigold.....675.00
Tumbler, blue.....89.00
Tumbler, green 675.00
Tumbler, marigold.....84.00
Tumbler, purple 116.00
Water set: pitcher & 6 tumblers; blue, 7 pcs. 800.00

MILLERSBURG PIPE HUMIDOR - See Pipe Humidor Pattern

MILLERSBURG TROUT & FLY - See Trout & Fly Pattern

MIRRORED LOTUS
Bowl, 7" d., blue.....55.00
Bowl, 7" d., ice green.....400.00
Bowl, 7" d., marigold.....55.00
Rose bowl, white 500.00

MORNING GLORY (Millersburg)
Pitcher, tankard, purple (ILLUS. top next column) .....6,350.00 to 7,500.00
Tumbler, green 1,000.00
Tumbler, marigold.....1,400.00
Tumbler, purple 1,300.00
Vase, 4¼" h., marigold 30.00
Vase, 5" h., marigold 48.00
Vase, 5½" h., marigold 72.00
Vase, 6" h., green.....79.00
Vase, 6" h., purple 73.00
Vase, 7" h., smoky.....95.00
Vase, 8" h., purple 75.00
Vase, purple 125.00
Vase, funeral, 10 x 12" , marigold.....280.00

Morning Glory Pitcher

Vase, funeral, 9½ x 13" , purple 300.00

MULTIFRUITS & FLOWERS (Millersburg)

Multifruits & Flowers Pitcher

Pitcher, water, marigold (ILLUS.) 3,300.00
Pitcher, water, purple.....4,500.00
Punch bowl & base, marigold, 2 pcs. 600.00
Punch bowl & base, purple, 2 pcs. 850.00
Punch cup, green 60.00
Punch cup, marigold.....70.00
Punch cup, purple.....40.00
Punch set: bowl, base & 5 cups; green, 7 pcs. 1,675.00
Tumbler, green 1,000.00
Tumbler, marigold.....1,000.00

MY LADY
Powder jar, cov., marigold 89.00

NAUTILUS (Dugan)
Bowl, peach opalescent.....200.00 to 250.00
Bowl, footed, purple.....175.00
Creamer, peach opalescent 295.00
Creamer, purple.....225.00 to 250.00

Dish, flattened boat shape, peach opalescent, 6 x 7½", 3" h. 295.00
Sugar bowl, open, peach opalescent 250.00
Sugar bowl, open, purple.....225.00

NESTING SWAN (Millersburg)
Bowl, 10" d., amber 325.00
Bowl, 10" d., green .....300.00 to 325.00
Bowl, 10" d., marigold.....220.00
Bowl, 10" d., purple.....300.00 to 350.00

NIGHT STARS (Millersburg)
Bonbon, green.....450.00 to 475.00
Bonbon, marigold 950.00
Bonbon, purple 450.00

NIPPON (Northwood)

Nippon Bowl

Bowl, 8" to 9" d., blue.....275.00
Bowl, 8" to 9" d., 3" h., green.....164.00
Bowl, 8" to 9" d., 2¼" h., ice blue (ILLUS) 286.00
Bowl, 8" to 9" d., ice green.....1,000.00
Bowl, 8" to 9" d., marigold.....100.00
Bowl, 8" to 9" d., purple 174.00
Bowl, 8" to 9" d., fluted, white 225.00
Bowl, 8" d., piecrust rim, ice blue.....325.00
Bowl, 8" d., piecrust rim, ice green 900.00
Bowl, 8" d., piecrust rim, marigold.....200.00 to 250.00
Bowl, 8" d., piecrust rim, pastel lime green w/opal tips.....3,000.00
Bowl, 8" d., piecrust rim, purple.....225.00
Bowl, 8" d., piecrust rim, white.....225.00
Plate, 9" d., ice blue.....5,000.00
Plate, 9" d., marigold 392.00
Plate, 9" d., purple 640.00

NU-ART CHRYSANTHEMUM PLATE (Imperial)
Amber 600.00
Marigold.....495.00
Purple (ILLUS. top next column) 1,200.00

Nu-Art Chrysanthemum Plate

White 700.00

NU-ART HOMESTEAD PLATE (Imperial)
Amber.....1,200.00 to 1,500.00
Blue 5,250.00
Emerald green.....3,000.00
Green.....750.00 to 850.00
Helios.....395.00
Lavender.....900.00
Marigold.....400.00
Purple .....875.00 to 975.00
White 758.00

OCTAGON (Imperial)

Octagon Goblet

Bowl, 8" to 9" d., marigold.....38.00
Butter dish, cov., marigold.....100.00
Creamer, marigold.....60.00
Creamer, purple.....165.00
Decanter w/stopper, green 700.00
Decanter w/stopper, marigold.....68.00
Decanter w/stopper, purple 230.00
Goblet, water, light blue w/marigold overlay 70.00
Goblet, water, marigold (ILLUS.) 40.00
Pitcher, milk, marigold 88.00
Pitcher, milk, purple.....250.00 to 275.00
Pitcher, water, 8" h., marigold.....89.00
Pitcher, water, 8" h., purple 525.00
Pitcher, water, tankard, 9¾" h., marigold 100.00

Pitcher, water, tankard, 9¾" h., purple 400.00
Punch set: bowl, ladle & 12 cups; marigold, 14 pcs. 2,400.00
Salt shaker, purple 95.00
Spooner, marigold 45.00
Spooner, purple 165.00
Sugar bowl, cov., marigold 50.00
Toothpick holder, marigold 135.00
Tumbler, green 150.00
Tumbler, marigold 25.00
Tumbler, purple ....125.00 to 175.00
Vase, 8" h., marigold 100.00
Water set: pitcher & 6 tumblers; purple, 7 pcs. 950.00
Wine, marigold 27.00
Wine set: decanter & 1 wine; purple, 2 pcs. 450.00
Wine set: decanter & 6 wines; marigold, 7 pcs. 275.00

OHIO STAR (Millersburg)

Vase, green 1,100.00
Vase, marigold 750.00
Vase, purple 1,150.00
Vase, white 550.00

ORANGE PEEL

Punch bowl, marigold 55.00
Punch cup, marigold 16.50
Punch cup, teal 40.00
Punch set: bowl & 12 cups; marigold, 13 pcs. 500.00

ORANGE TREE (Fenton)

Orange Tree Mug

Bowl, 8" to 9" d., blue 105.00
Bowl, 8" to 9" d., clambroth 83.00
Bowl, 8" to 9" d., green 155.00
Bowl, 8" to 9" d., marigold 57.00
Bowl, 8" to 9" d., pastel marigold 60.00
Bowl, 8" to 9" d., purple ....75.00 to 100.00
Bowl, 8" to 9" d., red 2,100.00
Bowl, 8" to 9" d., white 156.00
Bowl, 10" d., three-footed, blue 233.00
Bowl, 10" d., three-footed, green 235.00
Bowl, 10" d., three-footed, marigold 100.00
Bowl, 10" d., three-footed, purple 325.00
Bowl, 10" d., three-footed, white 200.00
Bowl, 10" d., Rose Tree interior, blue 1,100.00
Bowl, ice cream shape, blue 100.00
Bowl, ice cream shape, green 185.00
Bowl, ice cream shape, marigold 45.00
Bowl, ice cream shape, red 1,400.00
Bowl, ice cream shape, white 125.00
Bowl, moonstone 2,000.00
Bowl, peach opalescent 1,900.00
Breakfast set: individual size creamer & cov. sugar bowl; blue, pr. 130.00
Breakfast set: individual size creamer & cov. sugar bowl; marigold, pr. 195.00
Breakfast set: individual size creamer & cov. sugar bowl; purple, pr. 130.00
Breakfast set: individual size creamer & cov. sugar bowl; white, pr. 150.00
Butter dish, cov., blue 400.00
Butter dish, cov., blue w/electric iridescence 350.00
Butter dish, cov., marigold 250.00
Centerpiece bowl, footed, marigold, 12" d., 4" h. 80.00
Compote, 5" d., blue 62.50
Compote, 5" d., marigold 35.00
Creamer, footed, blue 80.00
Creamer, footed, purple 50.00
Creamer, individual size, blue 45.00
Creamer, individual size, purple 75.00
Creamer, individual size, white 85.00
Creamer & sugar bowl, footed, blue, pr. 100.00
Dish, ice cream, footed, blue 38.00
Dish, ice cream, footed, marigold 50.00
Goblet, amber 62.50
Goblet, blue 75.00
Goblet, green 190.00
Goblet, marigold 48.00
Hatpin holder, blue ....300.00 to 325.00
Hatpin holder, green 800.00
Hatpin holder, marigold 239.00
Loving cup, blue ....225.00 to 250.00
Loving cup, green 350.00
Loving cup, marigold ....175.00 to 200.00
Loving cup, purple 400.00
Mug, amber 114.00
Mug, Amberina 395.00
Mug, aqua 163.00
Mug, blue (ILLUS.) 57.00
Mug, lavender 135.00
Mug, lime green 500.00
Mug, lime green w/vaseline base 150.00
Mug, marigold 30.00
Mug, marigold, souvenir 75.00
Mug, marigold w/aqua base 75.00
Mug, marigold w/vaseline base 150.00
Mug, purple 80.00
Mug, red ....350.00 to 400.00
Mug, sapphire blue ....300.00 to 350.00
Mug, smoky blue 155.00
Mug, vaseline 100.00

Mug, white 1,000.00
Plate, 9" d., flat, blue.....350.00 to 400.00
Plate, 9" d., flat, clambroth.....215.00
Plate, 9" d., flat, green 2,000.00
Plate, 9" d., flat, marigold....225.00 to 250.00
Plate, 9" d., flat, pastel marigold 140.00
Plate, 9" d., flat, teal blue.....375.00
Plate, 9" d., flat, white 210.00
Plate, 9" d., flat, Beaded Berry exterior, blue 550.00
Plate, 9" d., trunk center, flat, Beaded Berry exterior, marigold 185.00
Plate, 9" d., trunk center, white .....250.00 to 275.00
Plate, 9" d., Blackberry exterior, "Souvenir of Hershey," blue 245.00
Powder jar, cov., blue 105.00
Powder jar, cov., green.....412.00
Powder jar, cov., marigold .....65.00 to 70.00
Powder jar, cov., purple.....160.00
Punch bowl & base, blue, 2 pcs. 255.00
Punch bowl & base, marigold, 2 pcs. 153.00
Punch bowl & base, white, 2 pcs. .....700.00 to 800.00
Punch cup, blue.....25.00
Punch cup, green 90.00
Punch cup, marigold.....12.00
Punch cup, white 35.00
Punch set: bowl, base & 4 cups; marigold, 6 pcs. .....300.00 to 350.00
Punch set: bowl, base & 6 cups; blue, 8 pcs. .....500.00 to 525.00
Rose bowl, blue 85.00
Rose bowl, green.....160.00
Rose bowl, marigold 58.00
Rose bowl, purple.....95.00
Rose bowl, red.....900.00 to 1,200.00
Rose bowl, white 275.00
Sauce dish, footed, blue 30.00
Sauce dish, footed, marigold 21.00
Sauce dish, footed, white 65.00
Shaving mug, Amberina 450.00
Shaving mug, blue.....50.00
Shaving mug, clambroth.....35.00
Shaving mug, marigold.....32.00
Shaving mug, marigold, large.....125.00
Shaving mug, purple.....265.00
Shaving mug, red 650.00
Shaving mug, vaseline 110.00
Spooner, marigold 50.00
Sugar bowl, cov., blue 60.00
Sugar bowl, cov., marigold 110.00
Sugar bowl, cov., white.....100.00
Sugar bowl, open, individual size, marigold 40.00
Sugar bowl, open, individual size, purple 52.00
Sugar bowl, open, individual size, white 75.00
Tumbler, blue.....55.00
Tumbler, clambroth.....55.00
Tumbler, marigold.....45.00
Tumbler, pastel marigold 49.00
Tumbler, purple 42.00
Tumbler, white 100.00
Water set: pitcher & 6 tumblers; blue, 7 pcs. 700.00
Wine, aqua 300.00
Wine, blue.....52.00
Wine, clambroth.....65.00
Wine, marigold.....25.00

ORANGE TREE ORCHARD (Fenton)

Pitcher, blue.....500.00
Pitcher, marigold.....250.00
Pitcher, white 515.00
Tumbler, blue.....50.00
Tumbler, marigold.....79.00

ORANGE TREE SCROLL

Pitcher, blue.....1,000.00
Tumbler, blue.....100.00
Tumbler, marigold.....65.00

ORIENTAL POPPY (Northwood)

Oriental Poppy Pitcher

Pitcher, water, green 1,250.00
Pitcher, water, marigold.....325.00
Pitcher, water, purple (ILLUS.) 950.00
Tumbler, blue.....200.00
Tumbler, green 60.00
Tumbler, ice blue 155.00
Tumbler, ice green.....475.00
Tumbler, lilac 39.00
Tumbler, marigold.....40.00
Tumbler, pastel marigold 45.00
Tumbler, purple 45.00
Tumbler, white 135.00
Water set: pitcher & 1 tumbler; white, 2 pcs. 1,900.00
Water set: pitcher & 6 tumblers; ice blue, 7 pcs. 5,000.00
Water set: pitcher & 6 tumblers; marigold, 7 pcs. 850.00
Water set: pitcher & 6 tumblers; purple, 7 pcs. 1,600.00

PALM BEACH (U.S. Glass Co.)

Bowl, 8½" d., marigold.....50.00

Butter dish, cov., white 250.00
Creamer, marigold.....68.00
Pitcher, water, white 700.00

Palm Beach Rose Bowl

Rose bowl, amber (ILLUS.) 125.00
Rose bowl, w/Gooseberry interior, white 225.00
Sauce dish, marigold.....30.00
Sauce dish, white 48.00
Spooner, marigold 80.00
Spooner, white.....125.00
Sugar bowl, cov., marigold 75.00
Table set, white, 4 pcs.....975.00
Tumbler, amber 175.00
Tumbler, white 125.00
Whimsey banana boat, marigold, 6".....75.00 to 90.00
Whimsey banana boat, purple, 6".....120.00

PANELED DANDELION - See Dandelion, Paneled Pattern

PANELED HOLLY (Northwood)

Bonbon, green 45.00
Bonbon, marigold 35.00
Candy, handled, green 80.00

PANTHER (Fenton)

Panther Centerpiece Bowl

Berry set: master bowl & 4 sauce dishes; marigold, 5 pcs. 325.00
Bowl, 5" d., footed, aqua.....425.00
Bowl, 5" d., footed, blue.....100.00
Bowl, 5" d., footed, clambroth.....35.00
Bowl, 5" d., footed, green 90.00
Bowl, 5" d., footed, marigold.....52.00
Bowl, 5" d., footed, red.....1,000.00 to 1,300.00
Bowl, 9" d., claw-footed, blue 390.00
Bowl, 9" d., claw-footed, green.....625.00 to 675.00
Bowl, 9" d., claw-footed, marigold .....200.00 to 250.00
Bowl, 9" d., claw-footed, white.....750.00
Bowl, berry, Butterfly & Berry exterior, marigold 35.00
Bowl, low, marigold.....300.00
Centerpiece bowl, marigold (ILLUS.) .....575.00 to 600.00

PEACH (Northwood)

Berry set: master bowl & 4 sauce dishes; white, 5 pcs. 395.00
Bowl, 7" d., w/hand enameling 60.00
Butter dish, cov., white 225.00

Peach Pitcher

Pitcher, water, blue (ILLUS.) 1,250.00
Pitcher, water, white 800.00
Sauce dish, white 45.00
Spooner, white.....150.00
Sugar bowl, cov., white.....175.00
Table set, white, 4 pcs.....450.00
Tumbler, blue.....85.00
Tumbler, white 95.00

PEACH & PEAR OVAL FRUIT BOWL

Marigold.....77.00
Purple 125.00

PEACOCK & DAHLIA (Fenton)

Bowl, 6" d., ice cream shape, marigold 45.00
Bowl, 6" d., ice cream shape, vaseline.....100.00
Bowl, 6¼" d., ice cream shape, green.....120.00
Bowl, 6½" d., 2" h., scalloped edge, green.....125.00
Bowl, 7" d., ice cream shape, vaseline.....110.00
Bowl, 7" d., ruffled, aqua opalescent ..125.00

Bowl, 7" d., ruffled, blue 85.00
Bowl, 7" d., marigold 50.00
Bowl, 7" d., ruffled, purple 75.00
Bowl, 7" d., vaseline 150.00
Bowl, 7½" d., purple w/blue base 100.00
Plate, 7½" d., marigold 550.00
Sauce dish, marigold 25.00

PEACOCK & GRAPE (Fenton)
Bowl, 8" d., collared base, amber 120.00
Bowl, 8" d., collared base, blue 53.00
Bowl, 8" d., collared base, ruffled, green 75.00
Bowl, 8" d., collared base, ruffled, ice green 225.00
Bowl, 8" d., collared base, marigold 40.00
Bowl, 8" d., collared base, peach opalescent 580.00
Bowl, 8" d., collared base, purple 76.00
Bowl, 8" d., collared base, ruffled, red 1,200.00
Bowl, 8" d., collared base, smoky 585.00
Bowl, 8" d., collared base, vaseline 275.00
Bowl, 8" d., collared base, ribbon candy rim, blue 80.00
Bowl, 8" d., collared base, ribbon candy rim, lavendar 75.00
Bowl, 8" d., spatula-footed, blue 50.00
Bowl, 8" d., spatula-footed, green 72.00
Bowl, 8" d., spatula-footed, ice green opalescent 418.00
Bowl, 8" d., spatula-footed, lavender .....150.00 to 200.00
Bowl, 8" d., spatula-footed, marigold 60.00
Bowl, 8" d., spatula-footed, milk white w/marigold overlay 360.00
Bowl, 8" d., spatula-footed, peach opalescent .....325.00 to 350.00
Bowl, 8" d., spatula-footed, purple 68.00
Bowl, 8" d., spatula-footed, red 934.00
Bowl, 8" d., spatula-footed, smoky 90.00
Bowl, 8" d., spatula-footed, vaseline opalescent .....450.00 to 550.00
Bowl, ice cream shape, Amberina 650.00
Bowl, 8" d., ice cream shape, green 85.00
Bowl, 8" d., ice cream shape, marigold 85.00
Bowl, 8" d., ice cream shape, red 1,650.00
Bowl, 9" d., ice cream shape, red 695.00
Bowl, ice cream shape, collared base, vaseline 185.00
Bowl, 9" d., ruffled, collared base, blue .....100.00 to 150.00
Bowl, 9" d., ruffled, ice blue w/marigold overlay 195.00
Bowl, 9" d., ruffled, ice blue w/smoky overlay 395.00
Bowl, 9" d., ruffled, purple 75.00
Bowl, 9" d., ruffled, red 300.00
Bowl, ruffled, iridized moonstone 325.00
Plate, 9" d., collared base, blue 325.00
Plate, 9" d., collared base, marigold 275.00
Plate, 9" d., flat base, marigold 525.00
Plate, 9" d., collared base, berry exterior, smoky ice blue 800.00
Plate, 9" d., spatula-footed, green .....150.00 to 175.00
Plate, 9" d., spatula-footed, marigold 350.00

PEACOCK & URN (Millersburg, Fenton & Northwood)
Berry set: master bowl & 5 sauce dishes; purple, 6 pcs. .....750.00 to 850.00
Bowl, 5½" d., ruffled, blue (Millersburg) 1,240.00
Bowl, 6" d., ice cream shape, blue, stippled 175.00
Bowl, 6" d., ice cream shape, green (Millersburg) 325.00
Bowl, 6" d., ice cream shape, ice green 315.00
Bowl, 6" d., ice cream shape, marigold (Millersburg) 75.00
Bowl, 6" d., ice cream shape, marigold (Northwood) 50.00
Bowl, 6" d., ice cream shape, purple 75.00
Bowl, 6" d., ice cream shape, purple (Millersburg) 162.00
Bowl, 6" d., ice cream shape, purple satin 195.00
Bowl, 6" d., ice cream shape, white 150.00
Bowl, 7" d., ruffled, blue (Millersburg) 400.00
Bowl, 7" d., ruffled, green (Millersburg) 250.00
Bowl, 7" d., ruffled, marigold (Millersburg) 395.00
Bowl, 7" d., ruffled, purple (Millersburg) 350.00
Bowl, 8" d., collared base, moonstone (Fenton) 1,825.00
Bowl, 8" d., ice cream shape, blue (Fenton) 195.00
Bowl, 8" d., ice cream shape, green (Fenton) 200.00
Bowl, 8" d., ice cream shape, marigold (Fenton) 108.00
Bowl, 8" d., ice cream shape, Beaded Berry exterior, purple 275.00
Bowl, 8" d., ice cream shape, white 350.00
Bowl, 8" to 9" d., blue (Fenton) 226.00
Bowl, 8" to 9" d., green (Fenton) 300.00
Bowl, 8" to 9" d., green (Millersburg) .....400.00 to 425.00
Bowl, 8" to 9" d., marigold (Fenton) 122.00
Bowl, 8" to 9" d., marigold (Millersburg) .....200.00 to 250.00
Bowl, 8" to 9" d., purple (Fenton) 180.00
Bowl, 8" to 9" d., purple (Millersburg) 275.00
Bowl, 8" to 9" d., white (Fenton) 349.00
Bowl, 10" d., ice cream shape, aqua opalescent 950.00
Bowl, 10" d., ice cream shape, blue (Northwood) 625.00

Bowl, 10" d., ice cream shape, blue, stippled 1,250.00
Bowl, 10" d., ice cream shape, blue w/electric iridescence (Northwood) 1,450.00
Bowl, 10" d., ice cream shape, green (Northwood) 2,500.00
Bowl, 10" d., ice cream shape, green, w/bee (Millersburg) .....825.00 to 850.00
Bowl, 10" d., ice cream shape, ice blue (Northwood) .....900.00 to 1,000.00
Bowl, 10" d., ice cream shape, ice green (Northwood).....1,200.00 to 1,300.00
Bowl, 10" d., ice cream shape, marigold (Millersburg) 375.00
Bowl, 10" d., ice cream shape, marigold (Northwood) 443.00
Bowl, 10" d., ice cream shape, pastel marigold (Northwood) .....650.00 to 700.00
Bowl, 10" d., ice cream shape, stippled, pastel marigold (Northwood) 485.00
Bowl, 10" d., ice cream shape, periwinkle blue (Northwood) 4.000.00
Bowl, 10" d., ice cream shape, purple (Millersburg) 465.00
Bowl, 10" d., ice cream shape, purple (Northwood) 700.00
Bowl, 10" d., ice cream shape, smoky (Northwood) 900.00
Bowl, 10" d., ice cream shape, white (Northwood) .....575.00 to 600.00
Compote, green (Millersburg Giant) .....1,350.00 to 1,400.00
Compote, marigold (Millersburg Giant) 1,900.00
Compote, purple (Millersburg Giant) 3,000.00
Goblet, Marigold (Fenton).....50.00
Ice cream dish, purple, 5¾" d. (Millersburg).....350.00 to 400.00
Ice cream dish, aqua opalescent, small (Northwood).....1,500.00
Ice cream dish, stippled, blue, small (Northwood) 145.00
Ice cream dish, blue, small (Northwood) 82.50
Ice cream dish, blue w/electric iridescence, small 175.00
Ice cream dish, ice blue, small 600.00
Ice cream dish, ice green, small 425.00
Ice cream dish, lavender, small (Northwood) 225.00
Ice cream dish, marigold, small 85.00
Ice cream dish, purple, small 86.00
Ice cream dish, white, small 200.00
Ice cream set: large bowl & 6 small dishes; purple, 7 pcs. (Millersburg) .....800.00 to 1,000.00
Plate, 6½" d., green (Millersburg)....3,600.00
Plate, 6½" d., marigold (Millersburg) 275.00
Plate, 6½" d., purple (Millersburg) 500.00
Plate, 9" d., blue (Fenton).....550.00
Plate, 9" d., marigold (Fenton).....408.00
Plate, 9" d., white (Fenton) .....450.00 to 500.00
Plate, chop, 11" d., marigold (Millersburg) 2,200.00
Plate, chop, 11" d., marigold (Northwood) 995.00
Plate, chop, 11" d., purple (Millersburg) 3,500.00
Plate, chop, 11" d., purple (Northwood) .....1,200.00 to 1,400.00
Sauce dish, blue (Millersburg).....250.00
Sauce dish, blue (Northwood) 120.00
Sauce dish, green (Millersburg).....75.00
Sauce dish, ice blue (Northwood).....200.00
Sauce dish, ice blue, 6" d. 70.00
Sauce dish, ice green, 6" d. (Northwood) 415.00
Sauce dish, lavender (Millersburg).....45.00
Sauce dish, marigold (Northwood) 50.00
Sauce dish, purple (Millersburg).....125.00
Sauce dish, purple (Northwood) 100.00
Sauce dish, white (Northwood).....185.00
Whimsey sauce dish, marigold, 5¼" d. (Millersburg).....175.00
Whimsey sauce dish, purple, 5¼" d. .....275.00 to 300.00

PEACOCK AT FOUNTAIN (Northwood)

Peacock at Fountain Water Set

Berry set: master bowl & 2 sauce dishes; ice blue, 3 pcs. 640.00
Berry set: master bowl & 4 sauce dishes; purple, 5 pcs.....450.00
Berry set: master bowl & 6 sauce dishes; blue, 7 pcs. 600.00
Bowl, master berry, blue.....325.00
Bowl, master berry, green 600.00
Bowl, master berry, ice blue 380.00
Bowl, master berry, marigold.....150.00
Bowl, master berry, purple.....200.00
Bowl, master berry, white 250.00
Bowl, orange, three-footed, aqua opalescent 1,100.00
Bowl, orange, three-footed, lavender.....525.00
Bowl, orange, three-footed, marigold 320.00

Bowl, orange, three-footed, purple 488.00
Butter dish, cov., green.....500.00
Butter dish, cov., marigold.....210.00
Butter dish, cov., purple.....275.00
Compote, aqua opalescent.....3,100.00
Compote, blue 587.00
Compote, ice blue.....1,200.00
Compote, ice green 1,400.00
Compote, marigold 400.00
Compote, purple 800.00
Compote, white.....550.00 to 650.00
Creamer, marigold.....65.00
Creamer, purple.....75.00 to 100.00
Pitcher, water, blue.....450.00
Pitcher, water, marigold.....250.00
Pitcher, water, white .....950.00 to 1,000.00
Punch bowl & base, blue,
2 pcs. 2,300.00
Punch bowl & base, ice blue,
2 pcs. 8,000.00
Punch bowl & base, ice green,
2 pcs. 9,500.00
Punch bowl & base, marigold,
2 pcs. 900.00
Punch bowl & base, purple,
2 pcs. 1,500.00
Punch cup, aqua opalescent 1,400.00
Punch cup, blue.....50.00
Punch cup, blue w/electric irides-
cence 95.00
Punch cup, ice blue 125.00
Punch cup, ice green.....525.00
Punch cup, lavender.....88.00
Punch cup, marigold.....45.00
Punch cup, purple.....38.00
Punch cup, white 75.00
Punch set: bowl, base & 2 cups;
marigold, 4 pcs. 675.00
Punch set: bowl, base & 5 cups;
ice green, 7 pcs. 10,750.00
Punch set: bowl, base & 6 cups;
purple, 7 pcs. 1,750.00
Punch set: bowl, base & 6 cups;
ice blue, 8 pcs. 7,000.00
Punch set: bowl, base & 6 cups;
white, 8 pcs. 6,000.00
Sauce dish, blue 40.00
Sauce dish, ice blue .....100.00 to 150.00
Sauce dish, marigold 21.00
Sauce dish, purple.....31.00
Sauce dish, white 50.00
Spooner, blue 150.00
Spooner, ice blue.....260.00
Spooner, marigold 76.00
Spooner, purple .....100.00 to 150.00
Spooner, white.....175.00
Sugar bowl, cov., ice blue.....265.00
Sugar bowl, cov., marigold 85.00
Table set, ice blue, 4 pcs. 2,600.00
Table set, marigold, 4 pcs. 475.00
Table set, purple, 4 pcs. .....450.00 to 500.00
Tumbler, amber 89.00
Tumbler, blue.....50.00
Tumbler, green .....300.00 to 350.00
Tumbler, ice blue .....400.00 to 425.00
Tumbler, lavender.....125.00
Tumbler, marigold.....45.00
Tumbler, purple 55.00
Tumbler, teal blue.....139.00
Tumbler, white 225.00
Water set: pitcher & 5 tumblers;
marigold, 6 pcs. 500.00
Water set: pitcher & 6 tumblers; blue,
7 pcs. 775.00
Water set: pitcher & 6 tumblers;
purple, 7 pcs. (ILLUS.) 900.00

PEACOCK, FLUFFY (Fenton)

Pitcher, water, green 750.00
Pitcher, water, marigold.....425.00
Pitcher, water, purple.....575.00 to 600.00
Tumbler, blue.....85.00
Tumbler, marigold.....63.00
Tumbler, purple 75.00

PEACOCK TAIL (Fenton)

Peacock Tail Plate

Berry set: 9" d. bowl & four 5" d. bowls;
green, 5 pcs. 140.00
Bonbon, two-handled, green 80.00
Bonbon, two-handled, marigold.....28.00
Bonbon, two-handled, purple.....65.00
Bonbon, tricornered, green.....55.00
Bonbon, tricornered, marigold 22.50
Bonbon, tricornered, purple 40.00
Bowl, 5" d., ruffled, marigold.....27.00
Bowl, 5" d., ruffled, purple.....28.00
Bowl, 6" d., blue.....45.00
Bowl, 6" d., ruffled, peach
opalescent 700.00
Bowl, 6" d., ruffled, red 1,850.00
Bowl, 7" d., green 35.00
Bowl, 7" d., purple.....37.00
Bowl, 8" d., green 75.00
Bowl, 8" d., purple.....40.00
Bowl, 9" d., crimped, green.....55.00
Bowl, 9" d., ribbon candy rim, green
w/electric iridescence.....175.00
Bowl, 9" d., ribbon candy rim, green...125.00

Bowl, 10" d., ribbon candy rim, green....225.00
Bowl, 10" d., green....75.00
Bowl, ice cream, green....35.00
Bowl, ice cream, purple....25.00
Compote, 6" d., 5" h., blue....38.00
Compote, 6" d., 5" h., green....69.00
Compote, 6" d., 5" h., marigold....68.00
Compote, 6" d., 5" h., purple....70.00
Plate, 6" d., blue....245.00
Plate, 6" d., green....100.00
Plate, 6" d., marigold (ILLUS.)....275.00
Whimsey, hat-shaped, green....75.00
Whimsey, hat-shaped, w/advertising, green....75.00
Whimsey, hat-shaped, purple....25.00

PEACOCKS ON FENCE (Northwood Peacocks)

Bowl, 8" to 9" d., piecrust rim, aqua opalescent....3,000.00
Bowl, 8" to 9" d., piecrust rim, blue....485.00
Bowl, 8" to 9" d., piecrust rim, blue, stippled w/ribbed back....795.00
Bowl, 8" to 9" d., piecrust rim, blue w/electric iridescence....995.00
Bowl, 8" to 9" d., piecrust rim, green....1,800.00 to 1,875.00
Bowl, 8" to 9" d., piecrust rim, ice blue....1,675.00
Bowl, 8" to 9" d., piecrust rim, ice green....1,850.00
Bowl, 8" to 9" d., piecrust rim, lavender....550.00

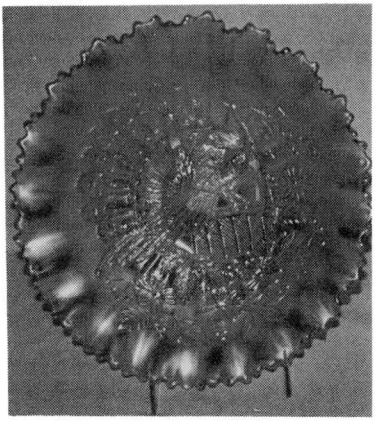

Peacocks on Fence Bowl

Bowl, 8" to 9" d., piecrust rim, marigold (ILLUS.)....288.00
Bowl, 8" to 9" d., piecrust rim, stippled, marigold....400.00 to 425.00
Bowl, 8" to 9" d., piecrust rim, pastel marigold....325.00 to 350.00
Bowl, 8" to 9" d., piecrust rim, purple....500.00
Bowl, 8" to 9" d., piecrust rim, white....850.00
Bowl, 8" to 9" d., ruffled rim, aqua opalescent....1,000.00
Bowl, 8" to 9" d., ruffled rim, blue....525.00
Bowl, 8" to 9" d., ruffled rim, green....1,100.00 to 1,200.00
Bowl, 8" to 9" d., ruffled rim, ice blue....1,750.00
Bowl, 8" to 9" d., ruffled rim, ice green....1,400.00
Bowl, 8" to 9" d., ruffled rim, marigold....243.00
Bowl, 8" to 9" d., ruffled rim, purple....395.00
Bowl, 8" to 9" d., ruffled rim, smoky....2,500.00
Bowl, 8" to 9" d., ruffled rim, white....650.00
Bowl, 9" d., stippled, green....1,100.00
Bowl, ruffled, lime green opalescent....4,000.00
Bowl, ruffled, ribbed back, white....875.00
Plate, 8" d., blue....700.00 to 750.00
Plate, 9" d., blue w/electric iridescence....1,050.00
Plate, 9" d., stippled, cobalt blue....650.00 to 700.00
Plate, 9" d., green....1,550.00 to 1,650.00
Plate, 9" d., ice blue....1,650.00 to 1,750.00
Plate, 9" d., ice green....450.00
Plate, 9" d., lavender....1,100.00 to 1,200.00
Plate, 9" d., marigold....456.00
Plate, 9" d., stippled, marigold....450.00 to 500.00
Plate, 9" d., purple....625.00 to 650.00
Plate, 9" d., white....450.00 to 470.00
Plate, 9" d., white, decorated....1,100.00

PERFECTION (Millersburg)

Pitcher, water, green....2,630.00
Pitcher, water, purple....3,100.00
Tumbler, green....400.00
Tumbler, purple....326.00

PERSIAN GARDEN (Dugan)

Bowl, 5" d., peach opalescent....45.00
Bowl, 5" d., white....83.00
Bowl, 6" d., ice cream shape, white....55.00
Bowl, 9" d., ruffled, marigold....150.00
Bowl, 11" d., ice cream shape, lavender tint....345.00
Bowl, 11" d., ice cream shape, peach opalescent....850.00 to 900.00
Bowl, 11" d., ice cream shape, purple....800.00
Bowl, 11" d., ice cream shape, white....300.00 to 325.00
Fruit bowl (no base), marigold, 11½" d....160.00
Fruit bowl (no base), peach opalescent, 11½" d....350.00
Fruit bowl (no base), white, 11½" d....250.00
Fruit bowl & base, marigold, 2 pcs....275.00
Fruit bowl & base, peach opalescent, 2 pcs....650.00

Fruit bowl & base, purple, 2 pcs. 800.00
Fruit bowl & base, white, 2 pcs. 500.00
Hair receiver, blue 115.00
Hair receiver, marigold 75.00
Plate, 6" to 7" d., marigold 92.00
Plate, 6" to 7" d., pastel marigold.....50.00
Plate, 6" to 7" d., purple 250.00
Plate, 6" to 7" d., white.....188.00
Plate, 9" d., marigold 125.00
Plate, chop, 11" d., purple 5,500.00

PERSIAN MEDALLION (Fenton)

Persian Medallion Chop Plate

Bonbon, two-handled, aqua.....215.00
Bonbon, two-handled, blue.....58.00
Bonbon, two-handled, celeste blue 500.00
Bonbon, two-handled, green 75.00
Bonbon, two-handled, lavender.....60.00
Bonbon, two-handled, marigold.....37.00
Bonbon, two-handled, purple..50.00 to 60.00
Bonbon, two-handled, red 1,000.00
Bonbon, two-handled, vaseline 230.00
Bowl, 5" d., aqua.....125.00 to 150.00
Bowl, 5" d., blue.....34.00
Bowl, 5" d., green 30.00
Bowl, 5" d., marigold.....35.00
Bowl, 5" d., purple.....58.00
Bowl, 6" d., ruffled, aqua.....95.00
Bowl, 6" d., ruffled, green 120.00
Bowl, 6" d., ruffled, marigold.....30.00
Bowl, 7" d., green 75.00
Bowl, 7" d., marigold.....45.00
Bowl, 7" d., ice cream shape, purple 32.50
Bowl, 7" d., ribbon candy rim, marigold 40.00
Bowl, 8" to 9" d., fluted, blue.....75.00
Bowl, 8" to 9" d., ice cream shape, green.....135.00
Bowl, 8" to 9" d., ribbon candy rim, blue 80.00
Bowl, 8" to 9" d., ribbon candy rim, green.....55.00
Bowl, 8" to 9" d., marigold.....50.00
Bowl, 8" to 9" d., purple 65.00
Bowl, 8" to 9" d., ribbon candy rim, purple 95.00
Bowl, 9½" d., purple.....100.00
Bowl, 10½" d., fluted, blue 85.00
Bowl, 10½" d., ruffled, green 100.00
Bowl, orange, marigold.....100.00
Compote, 6½" d., 6½" h., blue.....110.00
Compote, 6½" d., 6½" h., clambroth.....90.00
Compote, 6½" d., 6½" h., green 274.00
Compote, 6½" d., 6½" h., marigold.....66.00
Compote, 6½" d., 6½" h., purple .....75.00 to 100.00
Compote, 6½" d., 6½" h., white 500.00
Compote, ribbon candy rim, cobalt blue 275.00
Compote, ribbon candy rim, purple 350.00
Compote, three-in-one rim, purple.....575.00
Hair receiver, blue 100.00
Hair receiver, marigold 68.00
Hair receiver, white.....125.00
Plate, 6½" d., blue .....100.00 to 125.00
Plate, 6½" d., marigold 59.00
Plate, 6½" d., purple 175.00
Plate, 6½" d., white.....130.00
Plate, 7" d., blue 125.00
Plate, 7½" d., blue 100.00
Plate, 8" d., marigold 55.00
Plate, 9" d., blue 225.00
Plate, 9" d., clambroth 195.00
Plate, 9" d., marigold 275.00
Plate, 9" d., white.....2,800.00
Plate, chop, 10½" d., blue (ILLUS.) .....475.00 to 495.00
Rose bowl, blue 150.00
Rose bowl, clambroth 300.00
Rose bowl, marigold 80.00
Rose bowl, white 125.00

PETAL & FAN (Dugan)

Bowl, 5" d., peach opalescent 55.00
Bowl, 5" d., purple.....50.00
Bowl, 5⅜" d., black amethyst.....40.00
Bowl, 6" d., ruffled, peach opalescent 145.00
Bowl, 9" d., ruffled, dome base, peach opalescent.....145.00
Bowl, 10" d., ruffled, peach opalescent 150.00
Bowl, 11" d., marigold.....65.00
Bowl, 11" d., peach opalescent 250.00
Bowl, 11" d., ruffled, purple.....250.00 to 300.00
Bowl, 11" d., star-shaped, stippled, Jeweled Heart exterior, purple.....325.00
Bowl, 11" d., fluted, white ...500.00 to 600.00
Bowl, 12" d., Jeweled Heart exterior, white 125.00
Plate, 6" d., ribbon candy rim, Jeweled Heart exterior, peach opalescent 275.00
Plate, 6" d., ribbon candy rim, purple..700.00

PETALS (Northwood)

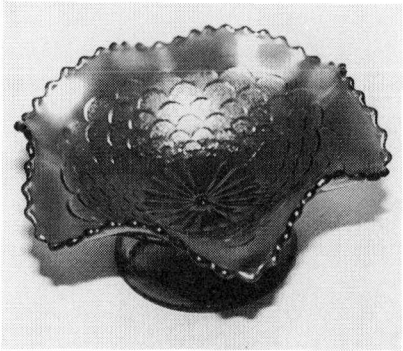

Petals Compote

Compote, green (ILLUS.) 60.00
Compote, marigold 37.00
Compote, purple 60.00

PETER RABBIT (Fenton)

Bowl, 8" d., blue .....700.00 to 1,000.00
Bowl, 8" d., green .....850.00 to 900.00
Bowl, 8" d., marigold 1,500.00
Plate, blue 1,900.00

PILLOW & SUNBURST (Westmoreland)

Bowl, purple 41.00
Bowl, teal blue 60.00

PINEAPPLE (Sowerby, England)

Bowl, 8" d., marigold 25.00
Compote, aqua 100.00
Compote, purple 72.00
Creamer, marigold, 4½" h. 35.00
Pitcher, miniature, purple 60.00
Plate, 8" d., stemmed, marigold 65.00
Rose bowl, marigold 75.00
Sugar bowl, marigold 38.00

PINE CONE (Fenton)

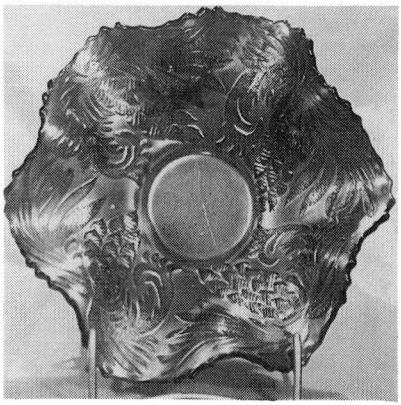

Pine Cone Bowl

Bowl, 5" d., blue (ILLUS.) 40.00
Bowl, 5" d., marigold 40.00
Bowl, 5" d., purple 35.00
Bowl, 6" d., ruffled, blue 45.00
Bowl, 6" d., marigold 25.00
Bowl, 7" d., ruffled, blue 50.00
Bowl, 7" d., marigold 28.00
Bowl, 7" d., ruffled, purple 65.00
Plate, 6½" d., blue 122.00
Plate, 6½" d., green 200.00
Plate, 6½" d., marigold 50.00
Plate, 6½" d., purple 110.00
Plate, 7½" d., amber 425.00
Plate, 7½" d., blue 125.00
Plate, 7½" d., marigold 100.00
Plate, 7½" d., purple 65.00
Plate, 7¾" d., blue 225.00

PIPE HUMIDOR (Millersburg)

Green 6,500.00
Marigold 5,000.00

PLAID (Fenton)

Bowl, 9" d., ruffled, blue .....300.00 to 325.00
Bowl, 9" d., ruffled, green ...325.00 to 425.00
Bowl, 9" d., ruffled, marigold .....100.00 to 125.00
Bowl, 9" d., ruffled, purple 1,500.00
Bowl, 9" d., ruffled, red .....3,250.00 to 3,750.00
Bowl, ice cream, 10" d., blue 300.00
Bowl, ice cream, 10" d., green .....800.00 to 900.00
Bowl, ice cream, 10" d., purple .....400.00 to 450.00
Bowl, ice cream, 10" d., purple w/gold overlay 800.00

PLUME PANELS VASE (Fenton)

Blue 65.00
Green 48.00
Marigold 44.00
Purple (amethyst) 35.00
Red .....750.00 to 950.00

PODS & POSIES or FOUR FLOWERS (Dugan)

Bowl, 6" d., peach opalescent 68.00
Bowl, 6" d., purple 55.00
Bowl, 8" to 9" d., marigold 45.00
Bowl, 8" to 9" d., purple 95.00
Bowl, 10" d., peach opalescent .....150.00 to 175.00
Bowl, 10" d., purple 145.00
Plate, 6" d., peach opalescent 150.00
Plate, 6" d., purple 295.00
Plate, 9" d., green 790.00
Plate, 9" d., purple 500.00
Plate, chop, 11" d., peach opalescent .....450.00 to 500.00

POINSETTIA (Imperial)

Pitcher, milk, green 245.00
Pitcher, milk, marigold 121.00
Pitcher, milk, smoky 135.00

POINSETTIA & LATTICE
Bowl, amethyst 400.00
Bowl, aqua opalescent 3,600.00
Bowl, blue w/electric iridescence.....850.00
Bowl, cobalt blue .....525.00 to 575.00
Bowl, ice blue 3,200.00
Bowl, marigold 575.00
Bowl, purple 500.00
Bowl, white 4,000.00

POLO
Ashtray, marigold.....35.00

POND LILY
Bonbon, blue 75.00
Bonbon, green 66.00
Bonbon, marigold 35.00
Bonbon, white.....90.00

PONY
Bowl, 8" to 9" d., aqua .....450.00 to 500.00
Bowl, 8" to 9" d., ice green.....932.00
Bowl, 8" to 9" d., marigold.....70.00
Bowl, 8" to 9" d., purple .....200.00 to 250.00
Plate, marigold.....275.00

POPPY (Millersburg)

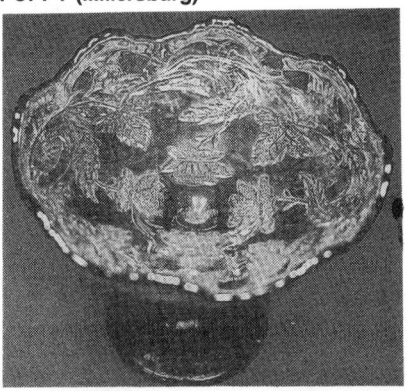

Millersburg Poppy Compote

Compote, green.....500.00
Compote, marigold 375.00
Compote, purple (ILLUS.).....1,200.00

POPPY (Northwood)

Northwood Poppy Pickle Dish

Pickle dish, amber 225.00
Pickle dish, aqua opalescent.....1,200.00
Pickle dish, blue (ILLUS.) 146.00
Pickle dish, green 325.00
Pickle dish, ice blue 700.00
Pickle dish, marigold.....80.00
Pickle dish, pastel marigold 50.00
Pickle dish, purple .....200.00 to 250.00
Pickle dish, white .....500.00 to 600.00

POPPY SHOW (Northwood)

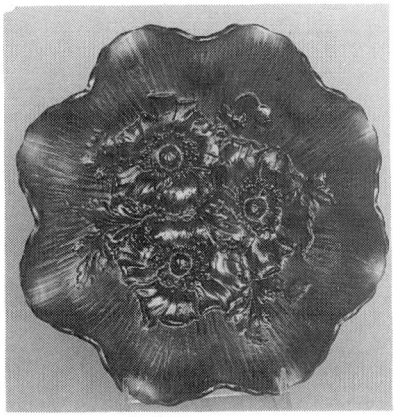

Poppy Show Bowl

Bowl, 8" to 9" d., aqua opalescent 18,500.00
Bowl, 8" to 9" d., blue (ILLUS.) 600.00
Bowl, 8" to 9" d., blue w/electric iridescence.....500.00 to 1,000.00
Bowl, 8" to 9" d., green 1,300.00
Bowl, 8" to 9" d., ice blue 1,800.00
Bowl, 8" to 9" d., ice green.....2,300.00
Bowl, 8" to 9" d., marigold...525.00 to 600.00
Bowl, 8" to 9" d., purple 650.00
Bowl, 8" to 9" d., white 375.00
Plate, blue.....3,000.00
Plate, blue w/electric iridescence 1,750.00
Plate, green 5,800.00
Plate, ice blue .....1,600.00 to 2,000.00
Plate, ice green.....3,800.00 to 4,200.00
Plate, marigold.....1,250.00
Plate, pastel marigold 1,000.00
Plate, purple .....1,200.00 to 1,400.00
Plate, white .....600.00 to 650.00

POPPY SHOW VASE (Imperial)
Green (ILLUS. top next column).....460.00
Marigold.....700.00 to 750.00
Pastel marigold.....325.00
Purple .....2,150.00 to 2,500.00
Smoky.....2,600.00 to 3,000.00

PRAYER RUG (Fenton)
Bonbon, milk white w/marigold overlay 425.00

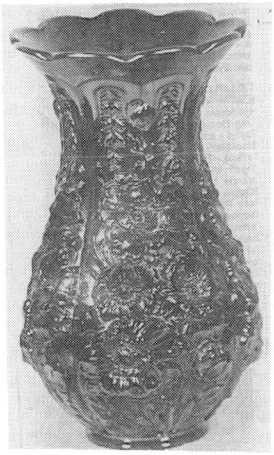

Poppy Show Vase

PRIMROSE BOWL (Millersburg)
Blue 2,400.00
Green....112.00
Marigold....77.00
Purple 125.00

PRINCESS LAMP
Purple, complete....1,700.00
Purple, base only....550.00

PRISMS
Bonbon, marigold ....40.00 to 60.00
Bonbon, purple 54.00
Bonbon, two-handled, purple....125.00
Bonbon, two-handled, white 40.00
Compote, 4½" d., two-handled, purple 95.00
Compote, 7¼" d., 2½" h., two-handled, marigold 48.00
Compote, 7¼" d., 2½" h., two-handled, purple 70.00

PULLED LOOP
Vase, 9½" h., peach opalescent....53.00
Vase, 10" h., marigold 20.00
Vase, 10" h., purple 37.00
Vase 10½" h., cobalt blue....90.00
Vase, 11" h., marigold ....30.00 to 35.00
Vase, 11" h., peach opalescent....30.00
Vase, 11½" h., celeste blue 500.00
Vase, 12" h., purple 42.50

PUZZLE
Bonbon, marigold ....30.00 to 50.00
Bonbon, stemmed, peach opalescent 55.00
Bonbon, two-handled, purple....80.00
Bonbon, white....65.00
Compote, marigold 25.00
Compote, peach opalescent....65.00
Compote, purple 58.00

QUESTION MARKS
Bonbon, footed, marigold, 6" d., 3¾" h. 38.00
Bonbon, footed, peach opalescent, 6" d., 3¾" h. 80.00
Bonbon, footed, purple, 6" d., 3¾" h. 45.00
Bonbon, footed, white, 6" d., 3¾" h. 130.00
Bonbon, stemmed, marigold....35.00
Bonbon, stemmed, peach opalescent 45.00
Bonbon, stemmed, purple 60.00
Bonbon, stemmed, white 48.00
Compote, crimped edge, marigold 45.00
Compote, crimped edge, peach opalescent 83.00
Plate, dome-footed, Georgia Peach exterior, purple....250.00
Plate, stemmed, marigold....80.00
Plate, stemmed, white 325.00

QUILL (Dugan or Diamond Glass Co.)
Pitcher, water, marigold....2,500.00
Pitcher, water, purple....950.00
Tumbler, blue....40.00
Tumbler, marigold....250.00
Tumbler, pastel marigold....195.00
Tumbler, purple 300.00
Water set: pitcher & 6 tumblers; purple, 7 pcs. 4,000.00

RAINDROPS (Dugan)

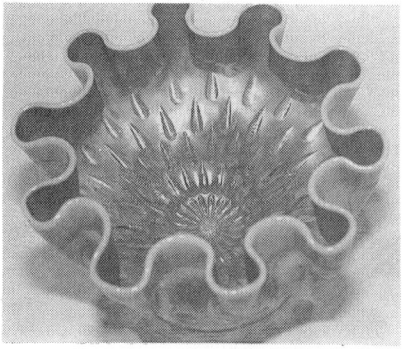

Raindrops Bowl

Bowl, 7" d., turned-up, fluted, peach opalescent 85.00
Bowl, 9" d., dome-footed, peach opalescent 126.00
Bowl, 9" d., dome-footed, ribbon candy rim, peach opalescent (ILLUS.) 85.00
Bowl, 9" d., dome-footed, ribbon candy rim, purple 225.00
Bowl, 9" d., dome-footed, purple....100.00 to 125.00

RAMBLER ROSE (Dugan)
Pitcher, water, blue....150.00
Tumbler, amber 29.00
Tumbler, blue....45.00
Tumbler, marigold....25.00
Tumbler, purple 36.00

Water set: pitcher & 6 tumblers; marigold, 7 pcs. 295.00

RANGER
Butter dish, marigold.....80.00
Pitcher, milk, marigold .....100.00 to 125.00
Pitcher, marigold.....60.00
Sherbet, marigold 20.00
Sugar bowl, marigold.....100.00
Whiskey shot glass, marigold 400.00

RASPBERRY (Northwood)

Raspberry Sauceboat

Pitcher, milk, green.....250.00
Pitcher, milk, ice blue....1,900.00 to 2,100.00
Pitcher, milk, marigold 136.00
Pitcher, milk, purple 290.00
Pitcher, milk, white.....1,000.00 to 1,200.00
Pitcher, water, green .....275.00 to 295.00
Pitcher, water, ice blue 2,100.00
Pitcher, water, marigold.....125.00
Pitcher, water, purple.....225.00 to 250.00
Sauceboat, green (ILLUS.).....225.00
Sauceboat, marigold.....70.00
Sauceboat, purple 80.00
Tumbler, green 48.00
Tumbler, ice blue .....275.00 to 300.00
Tumbler, ice green.....550.00 to 650.00
Tumbler, marigold.....35.00
Tumbler, purple 42.00
Tumbler, white 675.00
Water set: pitcher & 4 tumblers; green, 5 pcs. 495.00
Water set: pitcher & 4 tumblers; marigold, 5 pcs. 350.00
Water set: pitcher & 5 tumblers; purple, 6 pcs. 490.00

RAYS & RIBBONS (Millersburg)
Bowl, 8" to 9" d., green .....50.00 to 70.00
Bowl, 8" to 9" d., marigold.....80.00
Bowl, 8" to 9" d., purple 75.00
Bowl, 9" d., ruffled, three-in-one edge, marigold 150.00
Bowl, 10" d., green 85.00
Bowl, 10", ice cream shape, turned-down rim, green 125.00
Bowl, 10" d., marigold.....75.00
Bowl, 10" d., purple.....65.00
Bowl, 10" d., ice cream shape, purple 70.00
Bowl, ice cream shape, marigold.....135.00

RIBBED FUNERAL VASE
Aqua opalescent, 11" h.....175.00 to 200.00
Marigold, 6" h.....30.00
Olive green 125.00
Peach opalescent.....40.00
Purple, 13" h. 85.00

RIBBON TIE - See Comet Pattern

RIPPLE VASE
Amber, 7½" h.....58.00
Amber, 10" h.....60.00
Amber, 11½" h.....75.00
Amber, 15¼" h.....81.00
Aqua, 12" h. 78.00
Green, 6" h. 95.00
Green, 13" h. 45.00
Green, 14½" h. 75.00
Ice green, 14½" h. 245.00
Marigold, 5" h.....70.00
Marigold, 6" h.....100.00 to 150.00
Marigold, 6½" h.....55.00
Marigold, 8" h.....35.00
Marigold, 9½" h.....30.00
Marigold, 10½" h.....40.00
Marigold, 12" h.....50.00
Marigold, 15" h.....45.00
Marigold, 16½" h., funeral.....50.00
Marigold, 20" h.....150.00 to 200.00
Purple, 8" h. 40.00
Purple, 10" h. 45.00
Purple, 11" h. 55.00
Smoky, 12" h. 95.00
Teal blue, 6¾" h.....50.00
Teal blue, 10½" h.....100.00
White, 8" h. 155.00

RISING SUN
Pitcher, water, pedestal base, marigold 825.00
Tumbler, marigold.....442.00

ROBIN (Imperial)
Mug, green w/marigold overlay, green base 50.00
Mug, marigold.....42.00
Mug, smoky 275.00
Mug, smoky w/marigold overlay 158.00
Mug, unstippled, marigold 125.00
Pitcher, water, marigold.....250.00 to 300.00
Tumbler, marigold.....80.00

ROCOCO
Bowl, 8¼" d., dome-footed, ice cream shape, marigold 160.00
Candy dish, smoky 45.00
Vase, marigold.....119.00
Vase, smoky.....150.00 to 175.00
Vase, teal.....70.00

ROSALIND (Millersburg)
Bowl, 5½" d., purple.....800.00

Bowl, 9" d., ruffled, green 350.00
Bowl, 9" d., ruffled, purple...200.00 to 225.00
Bowl, 10" d., ruffled, green 200.00
Bowl, 10" d., marigold.....125.00 to 175.00
Bowl, 10" d., purple.....185.00
Bowl, 10½" d., ruffled, aqua teal.....450.00
Compote, 6" d., small, ruffled, purple 795.00

ROSE SHOW

Bowl, 9" d., aqua.....650.00 to 750.00
Bowl, 9" d., aqua opalescent 1,400.00
Bowl, 9" d., blue.....566.00
Bowl, 9" d., blue opalescent .....1,500.00 to 1,950.00
Bowl, 9" d., blue w/electric iridescence 1,250.00
Bowl, 9" d., green .....3,000.00 to 4,000.00
Bowl, 9" d., ice blue 1,600.00
Bowl, 9" d., ice green....1,500.00 to 2,000.00
Bowl, 9" d., ice green opalescent 2,150.00
Bowl, 9" d., lavender.....3,500.00
Bowl, 9" d., marigold.....552.00
Bowl, 9" d., purple.....1,275.00
Bowl, 9" d., sapphire blue 3,200.00
Bowl, 9" d., smoky 1,100.00
Bowl, 9" d., white .....350.00 to 400.00
Plate, 9" d., aqua opalescent.....8,000.00
Plate, 9" d., blue .....1,200.00 to 1,400.00
Plate, 9" d., clambroth 1,350.00
Plate, 9" d., custard 4,500.00
Plate, 9" d., green w/electric iridescence 7,500.00
Plate, 9" d., green 3,600.00
Plate, 9" d., ice blue.....1,800.00 to 2,000.00
Plate, 9" d., marigold .....600.00 to 650.00
Plate, 9" d., moonstone 7,000.00
Plate, 9" d., pastel marigold .....1,000.00 to 1,500.00
Plate, 9" d., purple 1,500.00
Plate, 9" d., vaseline 3,400.00
Plate, 9" d., white.....500.00

ROSES & FRUIT (Millersburg)

Bonbon, blue 2,600.00
Bonbon, green 900.00
Bonbon, marigold 375.00
Bonbon, pedestal, light marigold 850.00
Bonbon, purple 525.00
Compote, purple 1,450.00

ROSETTE

Bowl, 7" d., purple.....35.00
Bowl, footed, green.....110.00
Bowl, footed, purple (Northwood) 85.00

ROUND UP (Dugan)

Bowl, 9" d., low, fluted, blue.....110.00
Bowl, 9" d., white 225.00
Bowl, ice cream shape, marigold.....68.00
Bowl, ice cream shape, peach opalescent .....200.00 to 225.00
Bowl, ice cream shape, purple 225.00
Bowl, ice cream shape, white.....250.00

Round Up Plate

Plate, 9" d., blue (ILLUS.) 325.00
Plate, 9" d., ruffled, marigold 148.00
Plate, 9" d., flat, peach opalescent 425.00
Plate, 9" d., ruffled, peach opalescent 350.00
Plate, 9" d., flat, purple 250.00
Plate, 9" d., ruffled, purple ..250.00 to 350.00
Plate, 9" d., white.....350.00

RUSTIC VASE

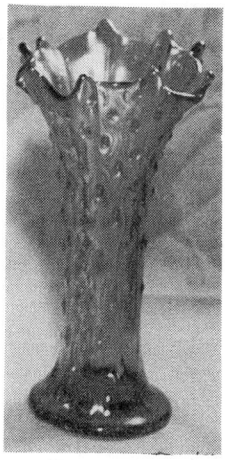

Rustic Vase

Blue, 9" h. 45.00
Blue, 10" h. 30.00
Blue, 10½" h. 35.00
Blue, 11" h. 45.00
Blue, 16" h. .....100.00 to 150.00
Blue, funeral, 18" h. .....475.00 to 500.00
Blue, funeral, 19½" h. 795.00
Green, 10½" h. 35.00
Green, 16" h. 95.00
Lime green opalescent, 11" h. 600.00
Marigold, 9½" h. (ILLUS.) 75.00
Marigold, 11" h.....30.00

Marigold, 15" h. 80.00
Marigold, 16" to 20" h. 250.00
Marigold, funeral, 21½" h. 300.00
Purple, 11" h. 50.00
Purple, 14" h. 90.00
Purple, 16" h. 195.00
Purple, 18½" h. 325.00
Purple, funeral 1,050.00
Red, 10" h., crimped top 3,700.00
White, 6" h. 46.00
White, 8" h. 80.00
White, 10" h. 85.00
White, 12½" h. 60.00
White, 14" h. 160.00
White, 16" h. 200.00

SAILBOATS (Fenton)

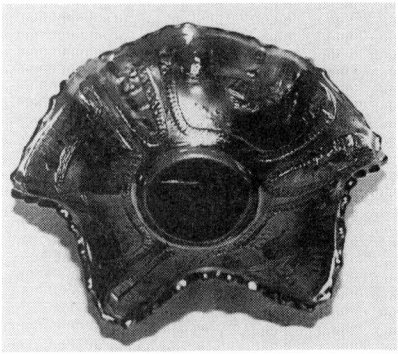

Sailboats Bowl

Bowl, 5" d., amber 250.00
Bowl, 5" d., aqua 110.00
Bowl, 5" d., ruffled, blue 55.00
Bowl, 5" d., green 125.00
Bowl, 5" d., marigold 28.00
Bowl, 5" d., ice cream shape, marigold 40.00
Bowl, 5" d., purple 120.00
Bowl, 5" d., ruffled, red ....500.00 to 550.00
Bowl, 5" d., vaseline 175.00
Bowl, 6" d., blue 60.00
Bowl, 6" d., ruffled, green (ILLUS.) 105.00
Bowl, 6" d., ruffled, marigold 32.00
Bowl, 6" d., Orange Tree exterior, marigold 60.00
Bowl, 6" d., ruffled, purple 150.00
Bowl, ruffled, vaseline 250.00
Compote, marigold 55.00
Dish, square, marigold 115.00
Goblet, water, green ....250.00 to 350.00
Goblet, water, marigold 125.00
Goblet, water, purple 300.00
Plate, 6" d., blue 195.00
Plate, 6" d., marigold 400.00
Wine, blue 120.00
Wine, marigold 35.00

SAILING SHIP PLATE

Amber, 8" d. 75.00
Marigold, 8" d. 25.00

SCALE BAND

Pitcher, marigold 85.00
Plate, 6" d., flat, marigold 22.00
Plate, 6½" d., flat, vaseline 65.00
Plate, 7" d., flat, marigold 38.00
Tumbler, blue 325.00
Tumbler, marigold 30.00
Tumbler, pastel marigold 19.00

SCALES

Bowl, 5" d., purple 30.00
Bowl, 6" d., peach opalescent 62.00
Bowl, 7" d., marigold 24.00
Bowl, 7" d., peach opalescent 43.00
Bowl, 7" w., tricornered, peach opalescent ....130.00 to 135.00
Bowl, 7" d., purple 57.50
Bowl, 8" to 9" d., aqua opalescent 308.00
Bowl, 8" to 9" d., marigold w/opalescent edge 40.00
Bowl, 8" to 9" d., milk white w/marigold overlay 225.00
Bowl, 8" to 9" d., peach opalescent ....80.00 to 100.00
Plate, 6½" d., amber 40.00
Plate, 6½" d., marigold 38.00
Plate, 6½" d., peach opalescent 60.00
Plate, 6½" d., purple 57.00
Plate, 9" d., turned-up sides (two), peach opalescent 125.00

SCOTCH THISTLE COMPOTE

Blue 55.00
Green ....50.00 to 70.00
Marigold 38.00
Purple ....55.00 to 60.00

SCROLL EMBOSSED

Bowl, 5½" d., File exterior, purple 25.00
Bowl, 7" d., aqua 85.00
Bowl, 7" d., purple 45.00
Bowl, 8" d., clambroth 35.00
Bowl, 8" to 9" d., green 39.00
Bowl, 8" to 9" d., marigold 40.00
Bowl, 8" to 9" d., pastel marigold 43.00
Bowl, 8" to 9" d., purple 55.00
Bowl, 8" to 9" d., File exterior, purple 68.00
Compote, green 75.00
Compote, marigold 49.00
Compote, File exterior, marigold 50.00
Compote, purple 76.00
Compote, miniature, purple 250.00
Plate, 9" d., green ....90.00 to 100.00
Plate, 9" d., marigold 125.00
Plate, 9" d., pastel marigold 125.00
Plate, 9" d., purple ....225.00 to 250.00
Sauce dish, purple, 5½" d. 35.00
Sauce dish, ruffled, purple, 5¾" d. 75.00

SEACOAST PIN TRAY (Millersburg)

Green 400.00

Marigold....450.00 to 500.00
Purple....575.00

SEAWEED (Millersburg)
Bowl, 6" d., purple....450.00
Bowl, 8½" d., ice cream shape, marigold....350.00
Bowl, 8¾" d., low, marigold....450.00 to 525.00
Bowl, 10" d., ruffled, green....275.00
Bowl, 10" d., ruffled, marigold....175.00 to 200.00
Bowl, ice cream shape, green....1,650.00
Lamp, marigold....300.00

SHELL (Imperial)
Bowl, 5" d., footed, green....35.00
Bowl, 5" d., purple....25.00
Bowl, 7¾" d., stippled, green....60.00
Bowl, 8" d., purple....100.00
Bowl, 8" d., ruffled, green....50.00
Bowl, footed, marigold....20.00
Bowl, footed, purple....45.00
Bowl, ruffled, green....35.00
Plate, smoky....300.00

SHELL & JEWEL
Creamer, cov., green....40.00
Creamer & cov., sugar bowl, green, pr....90.00
Sugar bowl, cov., marigold....35.00
Sugar bowl, open, green....11.00

SHELL & SAND
Bowl, 8" to 9" d., marigold....50.00
Bowl, 8" to 9" d., ruffled, purple....69.00
Plate, purple....725.00 to 1,025.00
Plate, smoky....450.00
Tumbler, purple....50.00

SHELL & WILD ROSE
Bowl, 8½" d., marigold....13.50
Bowl, small, purple....25.00
Dish, open heart-shaped rim, footed, green....32.50
Dish, open heart-shaped rim, footed, purple....41.00
Rose bowl, in-curved points, green....54.00

SHIP & STARS PLATE
Marigold....31.00

SINGING BIRDS (Northwood)
Berry set: master bowl & 3 sauce dishes; green, 4 pcs....132.00
Berry set: master bowl & 6 sauce dishes; purple, 7 pcs....325.00
Bowl, ice cream shape, green....48.00
Bowl, ice cream shape, marigold....48.00
Bowl, master berry, blue....225.00
Butter dish, cov., purple....350.00
Creamer, green....150.00
Creamer, marigold....52.00
Creamer, purple....125.00 to 150.00
Mug, aqua opalescent..1,000.00 to 1,550.00
Mug, blue....175.00
Mug, stippled, blue....575.00
Mug, blue w/electric iridescence....200.00 to 250.00
Mug, green....250.00
Mug, stippled, green....424.00
Mug, ice blue....750.00 to 800.00
Mug, lavender....400.00
Mug, marigold....134.00
Mug, stippled, marigold....129.00
Mug, purple....105.00
Mug, purple, w/advertising, "Amazon Hotel"....125.00
Mug, white....585.00
Pitcher, green....275.00 to 325.00
Pitcher, marigold....250.00 to 275.00
Pitcher, purple....350.00 to 400.00
Sauce dish, blue....65.00
Sauce dish, blue w/electric iridescence....90.00
Sauce dish, green....28.00
Sauce dish, marigold....32.00
Spooner, green....150.00
Spooner, marigold....62.00
Sugar bowl, cov., marigold...90.00 to 100.00
Table set, purple, 4 pcs....750.00
Tumbler, amber....60.00
Tumbler, green....45.00
Tumbler, green w/marigold overlay....60.00
Tumbler, marigold....40.00 to 45.00
Tumbler, purple....55.00
Water set: pitcher & 6 tumblers; green, 7 pcs....790.00
Water set: pitcher & 6 tumblers; purple, 7 pcs....795.00

SINGLE FLOWER
Basket, handled, ruffled, peach opalescent....750.00
Bowl, 7½" d., ribbon candy rim, peach opalescent....70.00
Bowl, 8¾" d., ruffled, peach opalescent....55.00
Bowl, 9", framed, tricornered, peach opalescent....65.00
Bowl, 9" d., peach opalescent....55.00
Bowl, 9" d., three-in-one edge, peach opalescent....110.00
Bowl, 9" d., purple....50.00
Bowl, ribbon candy rim, peach opalescent....125.00
Bowl, framed, ribbon candy rim, peach opalescent....110.00
Plate, crimped rim, peach opalescent....75.00
Plate, framed, w/hand grip, peach opalescent....85.00

SIX PETALS (Dugan)
Bowl, 7" d., crimped, peach opalescent....45.00

Bowl, 7" w., tricornered, peach opalescent 85.00
Bowl, 7" d., purple.....190.00
Bowl, 7" d., white 50.00
Bowl, 8" d., peach opalescent 80.00
Bowl, 8" d., purple.....75.00
Bowl, 8" d., white 85.00
Bowl, 9" d., dome-footed, peach opalescent 70.00

SKI STAR (Dugan)
Banana bowl, peach opalescent.....190.00
Basket, peach opalescent 520.00
Berry set: master bowl & 6 sauce dishes; peach opalescent, 7 pcs.....600.00
Bowl, 5" d., peach opalescent 40.00
Bowl, 5" d., fluted, peach opalescent....35.00
Bowl, 5" d., ruffled, peach opalescent 45.00
Bowl, 5" d., ruffled, purple.....55.00
Bowl, 6" d., ruffled, peach opalescent 50.00
Bowl, 8" d., ruffled, purple...425.00 to 450.00
Bowl, 8" to 9" d., dome-footed, peach opalescent 100.00
Bowl, 8" to 9" d., dome-footed, purple 130.00
Bowl, 10" d., marigold.....62.00
Bowl, 10" d., peach opalescent 75.00
Bowl, 10" d., purple.....175.00
Bowl, 11" d., peach opalescent .....125.00 to 175.00
Bowl, 11" d., purple.....185.00
Bowl, tricornered, dome-footed, peach opalescent 100.00
Plate, 6" d., crimped rim, peach opalescent .....150.00 to 200.00
Plate, 8½" d., dome-footed, w/hand-grip, peach opalescent.....165.00 to 185.00
Plate, 8½" d., dome-footed, w/hand-grip, purple 295.00

SOUTACHE (Dugan)
Bowl, 8" d., dome-footed, ruffled, peach opalescent.....95.00
Bowl, 8" to 9" d., dome-footed, pie-crust rim, peach opalescent.....145.00
Plate, 9½" d., dome-footed, peach opalescent .....250.00 to 300.00

SPRINGTIME (Northwood)
Butter dish, cov., green.....343.00
Butter dish, cov., marigold 250.00
Butter dish, cov., purple.....300.00
Creamer, purple.....100.00 to 150.00
Pitcher, green .....950.00 to 1,000.00
Pitcher, marigold.....300.00 to 400.00
Pitcher, purple 750.00
Sauce dish, 5" d., green 55.00
Sauce dish, 5" d., purple.....50.00
Spooner, green.....145.00
Spooner, pastel marigold.....140.00
Spooner, purple 425.00
Sugar bowl, cov., purple 200.00
Table set, green, 4 pcs. .....1,000.00 to 1,500.00
Table set, marigold, 4 pcs. .....500.00 to 800.00

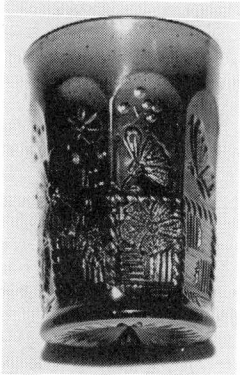

Springtime Tumbler

Tumbler, green (ILLUS.).....175.00
Tumbler, marigold.....80.00
Tumbler, purple 115.00

"S" REPEAT (Dugan)
Punch cup, purple.....100.00
Punch set: bowl, base & 8 cups; purple, 10 pcs. 2,850.00
Toothpick holder, blue 100.00
Toothpick holder, marigold 28.00
Tumbler, marigold.....450.00 to 500.00
Tumbler, w/advertising, dated 1910, marigold 350.00

STAG & HOLLY (Fenton)

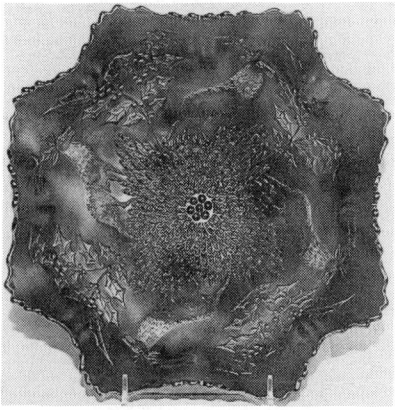

Stag & Holly Bowl

Bowl, 7" d., spatula-footed, blue .....125.00 to 175.00
Bowl, 7" d., spatula-footed, marigold 55.00
Bowl, 7" d., spatula-footed, purple 78.00
Bowl, 7" d., spatula-footed, red.....2,500.00

Bowl, 8" d., footed, ice cream shape, blue 185.00
Bowl, 8" d., footed, ice cream shape, green....255.00
Bowl, 8" to 9" d., spatula-footed, blue ....225.00 to 250.00
Bowl, 8" to 9" d., spatula-footed, green....228.00
Bowl, 8" to 9" d., spatula-footed, lavender ....175.00 to 200.00
Bowl, 8" to 9" d., spatula-footed, marigold 90.00
Bowl, 8" to 9" d., spatula-footed, peach opalescent....1,900.00
Bowl, 8" to 9" d., spatula-footed, purple 167.00
Bowl, 10" to 11" d., three-footed, amber....450.00 to 500.00
Bowl, 10" to 11" d., three-footed, aqua 800.00
Bowl, 10" to 11" d., three-footed, blue 300.00
Bowl, 10" to 11" d., three-footed, cobalt blue 125.00
Bowl, 10" to 11" d., three-footed, marigold ....100.00 to 125.00
Bowl, 10" to 11" d., three-footed, purple (ILLUS.) 435.00
Bowl, 10" to 11" d., three-footed, vaseline....175.00 to 275.00
Bowl, 11" d., flat, amber....750.00
Bowl, 11" d., flat, blue w/electric iridescence 450.00
Bowl, 11" d., flat, green....1,250.00
Bowl, 11" d., flat, marigold..100.00 to 125.00
Bowl, 11" d., ruffled, blue....232.00
Bowl, 11" d., ruffled, green w/marigold overlay 250.00
Bowl, 12" d., ice cream shape, blue ...325.00
Bowl, 12" d., ice cream shape, green....170.00
Bowl, 12" d., ice cream shape, marigold ....100.00 to 125.00
Bowl, spatula-footed, green....100.00
Plate, 9" d., marigold ....300.00 to 350.00
Plate, chop, 12" d., three-footed, marigold ....750.00 to 850.00
Rose bowl, blue, large 995.00
Rose bowl, marigold, large 275.00

STAR & FILE (Imperial)

Bowl, 5" d., marigold....22.00
Bowl, 7" d., marigold....22.00
Bowl, 8" d., ice cream shape, marigold 15.00
Bowl, 8" sq., marigold 50.00
Bowl, two-handled, marigold 35.00
Card tray, two turned-up sides, marigold, 6¼" d. 32.00
Celery vase, two-handled, clambroth ...35.00
Celery vase, two-handled, marigold 65.00
Compote, jelly, marigold 50.00
Compote, large, marigold 30.00
Creamer, marigold....30.00
Pitcher, milk, marigold 70.00
Pitcher, water, marigold....100.00 to 120.00
Plate, 6" d., marigold 95.00
Relish tray, two-handled, marigold 34.00
Rose bowl, marigold....50.00
Sherbet, marigold 25.00
Sugar bowl, marigold....12.00
Tumbler, marigold....106.00
Water set: pitcher & 6 tumblers; marigold, 7 pcs. 750.00
Wine, marigold....70.00
Wine decanter w/stoper, marigold 275.00

STARFISH

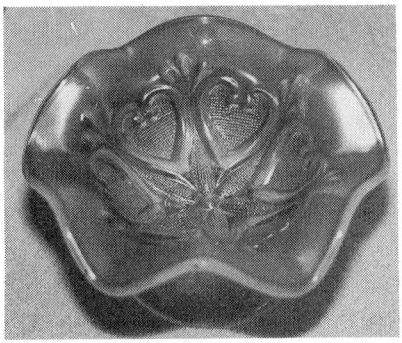

Starfish Compote

Bonbon, peach opalescent....120.00
Bonbon, purple 58.00
Compote, peach opalescent (ILLUS.) 65.00
Compote, purple 45.00

STAR FLOWER

Pitcher, blue....1,250.00 to 1,275.00
Pitcher, marigold....2,400.00

STAR MEDALLION

Bowl, 5" sq., marigold 25.00
Bowl, 8" d., marigold....22.50
Bowl, 8" d., smoky 40.00
Compote, marigold ....35.00 to 40.00
Goblet, marigold 35.00
Goblet, smoky....50.00
Pitcher, milk, clambroth ....50.00 to 75.00
Pitcher, milk, marigold 86.00
Pitcher, milk, smoky....75.00 to 100.00
Plate, 9" to 10" d., clambroth 50.00
Plate, 9" to 10" d., marigold 35.00
Punch cup, marigold....20.00
Sherbet, stemmed, marigold 35.00
Tumbler, marigold....25.00
Tumbler, tall, tankard form, marigold....28.00
Vase, 6" h., marigold 40.00

STAR OF DAVID (Imperial)

Bowl, 7" d., ruffled, purple....140.00
Bowl, 8" to 9" d., collared base, blue 75.00

Bowl, 8" to 9" d., collared base, green....85.00
Bowl, 8" to 9" d., collared base, marigold....48.00
Bowl, 8" to 9" d., collared base, purple....85.00
Bowl, 9" d., flat, ruffled, purple....80.00 to 100.00

STAR OF DAVID & BOWS (Northwood)

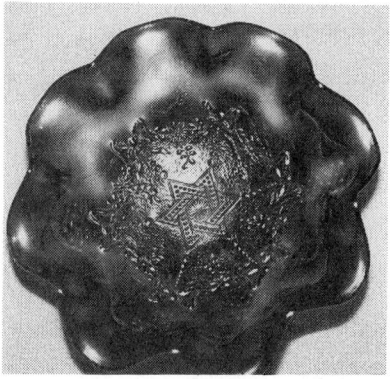

Star of David & Bows Bowl

Bowl, 7" d., dome-footed, green....60.00
Bowl, 7" d., dome-footed, marigold (ILLUS.)....38.00
Bowl, 7" d., dome-footed, purple....65.00
Bowl, 8" to 9" d., dome-footed, fluted, green....110.00
Bowl, 8" to 9" d., ome-footed, fluted, purple....72.00
Bowl, Embossed Scroll exterior, purple....105.00

STIPPLED FLOWER (Dugan)

Bowl, 8" d., peach opalescent....43.00
Bowl, 8½" w., tricornered, peach opalescent....65.00
Bowl, 8½" d., stippled, fluted, peach opalescent....60.00

STIPPLED PETALS

Bowl,peach opalescent....72.00
Bowl, purple....80.00

STIPPLED RAYS

Bonbon, two-handled, green....48.00
Bonbon, two-handled, lime green....200.00
Bonbon, two-handled, marigold....30.00
Bonbon, two-handled, purple....28.00
Bonbon, two-handled, red....350.00
Bowl, 5" d., Amberina....175.00
Bowl, 5" d., blue....50.00
Bowl, 5" d., green....33.00
Bowl, 5" d., marigold....20.00
Bowl, 5" d., purple....30.00
Bowl, 5" d., red....350.00 to 400.00
Bowl, 6" d., Amberina....225.00
Bowl, 6½" d., ruffled, red....300.00 to 350.00
Bowl, 7" d., dome-footed, green....32.00
Bowl, 7" d., red....250.00
Bowl, 7" d., ruffled rim, red....450.00
Bowl, 8" to 9" d., blue....225.00
Bowl, 8" to 9" d., green....55.00
Bowl, 8" to 9" d., ribbon candy rim, green....75.00
Bowl, 8" to 9" d., marigold....32.00
Bowl, 8" to 9" d., purple....46.00
Bowl, 8" to 9" d., ribbon candy rim, purple....70.00
Bowl, 8" to 9" d., red....605.00
Bowl, 10" d., green....65.00
Bowl, 10" d., ruffled, green....110.00
Bowl, 10" d., ruffled, lavender....75.00
Bowl, 10" d., white....150.00 to 200.00
Bowl, 10" w., tricornered, crimped rim, green....85.00
Bowl, 11" d., Basketweave exterior, ruffled, marigold....60.00
Bowl, 11" sq., dome-footed, ribbon candy rim, green....115.00
Bowl, dome-footed, Greek Key & Scales exterior, purple....90.00
Bowl, Wild Rose exterior, green....75.00
Bowl, Wild Rose exterior, purple....110.00
Creamer, blue....25.00
Creamer & sugar bowl, marigold, pr....45.00
Plate, 6" to 7" d., green....95.00
Plate, 6" to 7" d., marigold....32.00
Plate, 6" to 7" d., red....1,250.00
Rose bowl, green....80.00
Rose bowl, purple....65.00
Sherbet, Amberina....275.00
Sugar bowl, individual size, marigold....10.00
Sugar bowl, open, blue....25.00
Sugar bowl, open, marigold....18.00

STORK (Imperial)

Vase, marigold....45.00

STORK & RUSHES (Dugan or Diamond Glass Works)

Basket, handled, marigold....175.00
Berry set: master bowl & 6 sauce dishes, marigold, 7 pcs....245.00
Bowl, master berry or fruit, marigold....55.00
Butter dish, cov., marigold....135.00
Creamer, marigold....72.00
Hat shape, blue....40.00
Mug, amethyst....40.00
Mug, lavender....175.00
Mug, marigold....25.00
Mug, purple....125.00
Pitcher, water, blue....375.00
Pitcher, water, marigold....375.00
Pitcher, water, purple....575.00
Punch bowl & base, marigold, 2 pcs....225.00
Punch bowl & base, purple, 2 pcs....185.00
Punch cup, marigold....17.50
Punch cup, purple....35.00
Punch set: bowl, base & 6 cups; marigold, 8 pcs....300.00 to 325.00

Sauce dish, marigold 50.00
Sauce dish, purple 75.00
Spooner, marigold 80.00
Tumbler, blue 54.00
Tumbler w/lattice band, blue 55.00
Tumbler, marigold 28.00
Tumbler w/lattice band, marigold 30.00
Tumbler, purple 35.00
Tumbler w/lattice band, purple 69.00
Water set: pitcher & 1 tumbler; blue, 2 pcs. .....450.00 to 500.00

STRAWBERRY (FENTON)

Bonbon, Amberina 200.00
Bonbon, reverse Amberina .....325.00 to 400.00
Bonbon, one-handled, marigold 135.00
Bonbon, two-handled, amber 75.00
Bonbon, two-handled, blue 65.00
Bonbon, two-handled, ice green opalescent 450.00
Bonbon, two-handled, marigold 32.00
Bonbon, two-handled, vaseline w/marigold iridescence 155.00
Bonbon, two-handled, vaseline opalescent .....600.00 to 650.00

STRAWBERRY (Millersburg)

Bowl, 6" d., ruffled, purple 135.00
Bowl, 7" d., green 95.00
Bowl, 7".d., purple 115.00
Bowl, 8" to 9" d., marigold 260.00
Bowl, 8" to 9" d., purple .....225.00 to 250.00
Bowl, 8" to 9" d., vaseline 1,250.00
Bowl, 9" w., tricornered, marigold 200.00
Bowl, 9½" w., square, green 600.00
Bowl, 9½" w., square, ribbon candy rim, purple 400.00
Bowl, 9½" d., Basketweave exterior, marigold 55.00
Bowl, 9½" d., Basketweave exterior, purple .....75.00 to 100.00
Bowl, 10" w., tricornered, ribbon candy rim, purple 450.00
Compote, marigold 275.00
Compote, purple 225.00

STRAWBERRY (Northwood)

Bowl, 8" to 9" d., stippled, blue 900.00
Bowl, 8" to 9" d., stippled, ice green 1,100.00
Bowl, 8" to 9" d., stippled, purple .....200.00 to 250.00
Bowl, 8" to 9" d., ruffled, Basketweave exterior, green 95.00
Bowl, 8" to 9" d., ruffled, Basketweave exterior, marigold 60.00
Bowl, 8" to 9" d., ruffled, Basketweave exterior, purple .....100.00 to 125.00
Bowl, 8" to 9" d., ruffled, white 1,350.00
Bowl, 8" to 9" d., blue 80.00
Bowl, 8" to 9" d., piecrust rim, green .....100.00 to 150.00
Bowl, 8" to 9" d., marigold 40.00
Bowl, 8" to 9" d., purple 108.00
Bowl, 9" d., ruffled, stippled, ribbed exterior, purple 1,000.00
Bowl, 9" d., stippled, ribbed exterior, marigold 150.00
Plate, 9" d., green 135.00
Plate, 9" d., marigold 115.00
Plate, 9" d., pastel marigold 125.00
Plate, 9" d., purple 228.00
Plate, 9" d., Basketweave exterior, green .....200.00 to 275.00
Plate, 9" d., Basketweave exterior, marigold .....125.00 to 150.00
Plate, 9" d., Basketweave exterior, purple 213.00
Plate, 9" d., stippled, Basketweave exterior, green 400.00
Plate, 9" d., stippled, green 600.00
Plate, 9" d., stippled, marigold .....800.00 to 1,000.00
Plate, 9" d., stippled, purple 1,500.00

STRAWBERRY SCROLL (Fenton)

Strawberry Scroll Pitcher

Pitcher, water, blue (ILLUS.) 1,990.00
Pitcher, water, marigold 1,225.00
Tumbler. blue 200.00
Tumbler. marigold 175.00

STREAM OF HEARTS (Fenton)

Compote, marigold 100.00

SUNFLOWER BOWL (Northwood)

Bowl, 8" d., footed, blue (ILLUS. top next page) 650.00
Bowl, 8" d., footed, blue w/electric iridescence 650.00
Bowl, 8" d., footed, clambroth 350.00
Bowl, 8" d., footed, green .....75.00 to 95.00
Bowl, 8" d., footed, ice blue 200.00
Bowl, 8" d., footed, marigold 60.00
Bowl, 8" d., footed, purple 68.00

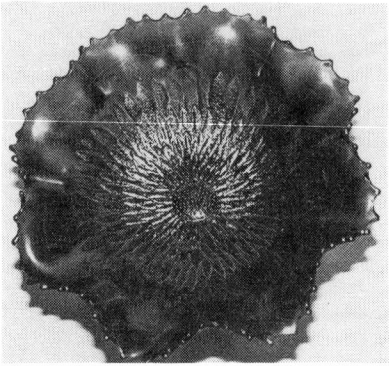

Sunflower Bowl

Bowl, 8" d., footed, Meander exterior, purple ..... 100.00 to 150.00

SUNFLOWER PIN TRAY (Millersburg)
Green ..... 175.00 to 200.00
Marigold 450.00
Purple ..... 450.00 to 475.00

SWAN PASTEL NOVELTIES (Dugan)
Salt dip, amber 125.00
Salt dip, celeste blue 38.00
Salt dip, ice blue 40.00
Salt dip, ice green 35.00
Salt dip, marigold ..... 100.00 to 125.00
Salt dip, peach opalescent ..... 300.00 to 325.00
Salt dip, pink 35.00
Salt dip, purple 272.00

SWIRL HOBNAIL (Millersburg)
Cuspidor, marigold 725.00
Cuspidor, purple 475.00
Rose bowl, marigold 300.00
Rose bowl, purple ..... 275.00 to 325.00
Vase, green 700.00
Vase, marigold 200.00
Vase, purple 225.00

SWIRL RIB
Tumbler, marigold 28.00
Vase, 8" h., 6" d., smoky 20.00
Vase, 10½" h., peach opalescent 60.00

TARGET VASE (Dugan)
7" h., white 75.00
10" h., peach opalescent 75.00
11" h., white 100.00
11½" h., marigold 15.00
11½" h., peach opalescent 60.00
12" h., white ..... 100.00 to 125.00

TEN MUMS (Fenton)
Bowl, 8" to 9" d., ribbon candy rim, blue 140.00
Bowl, 8" to 9" d., ribbon candy rim, green 125.00
Bowl, 8" to 9" d., ribbon candy rim, purple 180.00
Bowl, 10" d., ruffled, blue 130.00
Bowl, 10" d., footed, green 80.00
Bowl, 10" d., ribbon candy rim, green 175.00
Bowl, 10" d., footed, marigold 225.00
Bowl, 10" d., ribbon candy rim, marigold 300.00
Bowl, 10" d., ruffled, marigold 105.00
Bowl, 10" d., ribbon candy rim, purple 110.00
Bowl, 10" d., ruffled, purple 155.00

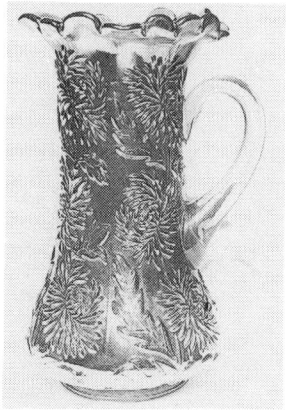

Ten Mums Pitcher

Pitcher, water, blue (ILLUS.) 1,650.00
Pitcher, water, marigold 475.00
Tumbler. amber 65.00
Tumbler. blue 75.00
Tumbler. marigold 50.00
Tumbler. white 153.00
Water set: pitcher & 1 tumbler; marigold, 2 pcs. 575.00

THIN RIB VASE
7" h., ice blue (Northwood) 500.00
8" h., green 30.00
9" h., aqua opalescent 85.00
9" h., blue 35.00
9" h., green 40.00
9" h., teal blue 105.00
9½" h., green (Northwood) 45.00
10" h., blue 35.00
10" h., green (Northwood) 40.00
10" h., marigold 48.00
10" h., purple (Northwood) 32.50
10" h., white 70.00
10½" h., peach opalescent 40.00
11" h., aqua opalescent 125.00
11" h., green 75.00
12" h., aqua 75.00
12" h., blue 40.00
12" h., green 85.00
12" h., purple 45.00
13" h., aqua opalescent (Northwood) 1,100.00

13" h., green .....100.00 to 125.00
13" h., purple 100.00
13" h., funeral, white 200.00
13" h., funeral, green (Northwood) 100.00
14" h., funeral, purple 135.00
16½" h., green 135.00

THISTLE (Fenton)
Banana boat, blue 400.00
Banana boat, celeste blue 350.00
Banana boat, green 285.00
Banana boat, marigold 224.00
Banana boat, purple .....350.00 to 400.00
Bowl, 7" d., purple 45.00
Bowl, 7½" d., ice cream shape, purple 85.00
Bowl, 8" to 9" d., ribbon candy rim, blue 80.00
Bowl, 8" to 9" d., ruffled, blue 90.00
Bowl, 8" to 9" d., flared, green 42.00
Bowl, 8" to 9" d., ribbon candy rim, green 112.00
Bowl, 8" to 9" d., ruffled, green 106.00
Bowl, 8" to 9" d., ruffled, lavender 45.00
Bowl, 8" to 9" d., ribbon candy rim, marigold .....50.00 to 75.00
Bowl, 8" to 9" d., ruffled, marigold 35.00
Bowl, 8" to 9" d., ribbon candy rim, purple 66.00
Bowl, 8" to 9" d., ruffled, purple 58.00
Bowl, ruffled, aqua 600.00
Centerpiece bowl, blue 380.00
Plate, 9" d., blue .....2,500.00 to 3,000.00
Plate, 9" d., green 3,000.00
Plate, marigold 3,500.00
Vase, 6" h., green 75.00

THISTLE & THORN (Sowerby's, England)
Bowl, 5" to 6" d., footed, marigold 60.00
Bowl, 9" d., footed, marigold 40.00
Creamer, marigold 30.00

THREE FRUITS (Northwood)
Bowl, 5" d., marigold 30.00
Bowl, 5" d., purple 30.00
Bowl, 6" d., green 40.00
Bowl, 6" d., marigold 30.00
Bowl, 8" d., ruffled, green 75.00
Bowl, 8" d., ruffled, marigold .....75.00 to 100.00
Bowl, 8" d., ruffled, purple 100.00
Bowl, 8" d., dome-footed, Basket-weave & Grapevine exterior, white ..350.00
Bowl, 8½" d., ruffled, blue 95.00
Bowl, 8½" d., collared base, Basket-weave & Grapevine exterior, green ...65.00
Bowl, 8½" d., dome-footed, green .....150.00 to 175.00
Bowl, 8½" d., piecrust rim, green 98.00
Bowl, 8½" d., piecrust rim, stippled, green 400.00
Bowl, 8½" d., piecrust rim, marigold 60.00
Bowl, 8½" d., purple 100.00
Bowl, 8½" d., piecrust rim, purple 70.00
Bowl, 9" d., footed, Meander reverse, black amethyst 750.00
Bowl, 9" d., piecrust rim, collared base, blue w/electric iridescence 700.00
Bowl, 9" d., ruffled, stippled, aqua opalescent 875.00
Bowl, 9" d., ruffled, blue 210.00
Bowl, 9" d., green 66.00
Bowl, 9" d., ruffled, green 100.00
Bowl, 9" d., stippled, marigold 75.00 to125.00
Bowl, 9" d., ruffled, pastel marigold 90.00
Bowl, 9" d., ruffled, collared base, marigold 60.00
Bowl, 9" d., purple 88.00
Bowl, 9" d., stippled, purple 200.00
Bowl, 9" d., stippled, white 762.50
Bowl, 9" d., dome-footed, Basket-weave & Grapevine exterior, green ...70.00
Bowl, 9" d., dome-footed, Basket-weave & Grapevine exterior, ice green 675.00
Bowl, 9" d., dome-footed, Basket-weave & Grapevine exterior, marigold 85.00
Bowl, 9" d., dome-footed, Basket-weave & Grapevine exterior, purple 60.00
Bowl, 9" d., dome-footed, Basket-weave & Grapevine exterior, white .....350.00 to 380.00
Bowl, 9" d., piecrust rim, stippled, ribbed exterior, green 795.00
Bowl, 9" d., spatula-footed, aqua opalescent .....500.00 to 550.00
Bowl, 9" d., spatula-footed, emerald green 425.00
Bowl, 9" d., spatula-footed, ruffled, green 60.00
Bowl, 9" d., spatula-footed, ice green 1,100.00
Bowl, 9" d., spatula-footed, marigold 95.00
Bowl, 9" d., spatula-footed, pastel honey amber (smoke tint) 350.00
Bowl, 9" d., spatula-footed, purple 152.00
Bowl, 9" d., spatula-footed, white 360.00
Bowl, 10" d., ruffled, ice green 375.00
Bowl, collared base, aqua opalescent .....1,100.00 to 1,200.00
Bowl, piecrust rim, stippled, green...1,425.00
Bowl, spatula-footed, stippled, purple 175.00
Bowl, stippled, ruffled, blue 700.00
Bowl, collared base, stippled, marigold 78.00
Bowl, collared base, stippled, white .....750.00 to 775.00
Bowl, piecrust rim, stippled, green .....1,000.00 to 1,200.00
Bowl, ruffled, stippled, footed, ice blue .....800.00 to 1,000.00
Bowl, ruffled, footed, Meander exterior, ice blue 450.00

Bowl, stippled, blue w/electric iridescence 475.00
Plate, 7½" d., Basketweave & Grapevine exterior, green 175.00
Plate, 8" d., w/handgrip, ribbed exterior, purple 150.00
Plate, 9" d., stippled, aqua opalescent ....1,850.00 to 2,000.00
Plate, 9" d., stippled, blue w/electric iridescence ....800.00 to 900.00
Plate, 9" d., green 168.00
Plate, 9" d., Basketweave exterior, green 100.00
Plate, 9" d., horehound 295.00
Plate, 9" d., lavender 325.00
Plate, 9" d., stippled, lavender ....1,250.00 to 1,400.00
Plate, 9" d., marigold 113.00
Plate, 9" d., stippled, marigold 230.00
Plate, 9" d., purple 173.00
Plate, 9" d., stippled, purple ....300.00 to 325.00
Plate, 9" d., stippled, ribbed exterior, purple 1,000.00
Plate, 9" d., stippled, teal blue 3,500.00
Plate, 9½" w., 12-sided, blue (Fenton) 100.00
Plate, 9½" w., 12-sided, green (Fenton) 150.00
Plate, 9½" w., 12-sided, marigold (Fenton) 150.00
Plate, 9½" w., 12-sided, purple (Fenton) 110.00
Plate, plain back, stretch "electric" finish, purple 275.00
Plate, two sides up, green 150.00
Plate, Basketweave exterior, green 195.00
Plate, Basketweave exterior, marigold 125.00
Plate, Basketweave exterior, purple 275.00

TIGER LILY (Imperial)

Pitcher, water, green ....150.00 to 200.00
Pitcher, water, purple 365.00
Tumbler, blue 250.00
Tumbler, clambroth 65.00
Tumbler, green 45.00
Tumbler, marigold 30.00
Tumbler, olive green 115.00
Tumbler, purple 80.00
Water set: pitcher & 4 tumblers; marigold, 5 pcs. 310.00
Water set: pitcher & 6 tumblers; aqua, 7 pcs. 2,205.00

TORNADO VASE (Northwood)

Blue 1,700.00
Green (ILLUS. top next column) 255.00
Marigold 425.00
Marigold, small, ribbed 600.00
Purple, ribbed 400.00

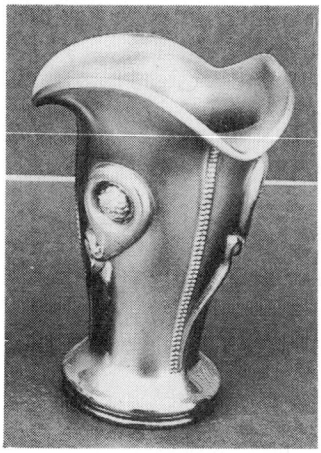

Tornado Vase

TOWN PUMP NOVELTY (Northwood)

Town Pump Novelty

Green (ILLUS.) 2,600.00
Marigold ....1,275.00 to 1,300.00
Purple 750.00

TRACERY (Millersburg)

Tracery Bonbon

Bonbon, handled, square, green (ILLUS.) 675.00
Bonbon, handled, oval, purple 550.00

TREE TRUNK VASE (Northwood)

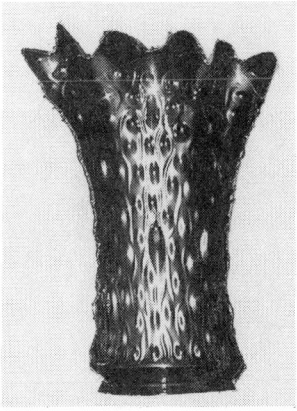

Tree Trunk Vase

6" h., purple, squatty.....150.00 to 175.00
6¼" h., squatty, marigold.....55.00 to 60.00
6¾" h., marigold.....75.00
7" h., green.....45.00
7" h., ice blue.....400.00
7½" h., squatty, green.....150.00
7" to 11" h., ice green.....134.00 to 220.00
8" to 10" h., blue.....92.00
8" to 10" h., ice blue.....250.00
8" to 11" h., green.....35.00 to 45.00
9" h., aqua.....95.00
9" h., white.....100.00
9" to 12" h., aqua opalescent.....475.00
9" to 10" h., marigold.....35.00
9" to 10" h., purple (ILLUS.).....52.50
10½" h., blue w/electric iridescence...115.00
11" h., ice blue.....350.00
11" h., purple.....85.00
11" h., white.....70.00
12" h., blue.....150.00 to 175.00
12" h., ice blue.....275.00
12" h., ice green.....440.00
12" h., marigold.....130.00 to 150.00
12" h., purple.....185.00
12" h., white.....175.00
13" h., green.....200.00 to 225.00
13" h., purple.....300.00
13½" h., blue.....375.00 to 400.00
14" h., purple.....125.00
15" h., purple, w/elephant foot.....1,300.00
17" h., white, funeral.....1,000.00
18" h., green.....550.00
18" h., purple.....975.00
19" h., purple, funeral.....1,800.00
20" h., cobalt blue, funeral.....1,300.00

TROUT & FLY (Millersburg)

Bowl, ice cream shape, green.....850.00
Bowl, ice cream shape, lavender.....1,350.00
Bowl, ice cream shape, marigold.....475.00 to 525.00
Bowl, ice cream shape, purple.....595.00 to 650.00
Bowl, ribbon candy rim, green.....712.00
Bowl, ribbon candy rim, lavender....1,400.00
Bowl, ribbon candy rim, marigold.....350.00
Bowl, ribbon candy rim, purple.....575.00
Bowl, ruffled, green.....450.00 to 500.00
Bowl, ruffled, lavender.....1,800.00
Bowl, ruffled, marigold.....400.00 to 475.00
Bowl, ruffled, marigold, satin finish.....385.00
Bowl, ruffled, pastel marigold, satin finish.....500.00
Bowl, ruffled, purple.....550.00 to 600.00
Bowl, ruffled, purple, satin finish.....675.00
Bowl, square, green.....1,400.00 to 1,500.00
Bowl, square, marigold.....700.00
Bowl, square, purple.....825.00

TULIP & CANE

Bowl, small, berry, marigold.....25.00
Compote, marigold.....50.00
Goblet, marigold, 4 oz.....60.00

TWIG VASE

3½" h., purple.....550.00 to 600.00
3½" h., pleated jack-in-the-pulpit rim, purple.....195.00
4" h., ruffled, purple.....425.00
9½" h., purple.....50.00
Bud, marigold.....29.00

TWINS or HORSESHOE CURVE (Imperial)

Bowl, 5" d., green.....42.00
Bowl, 6" d., green.....45.00
Bowl, 6" d., marigold.....22.50
Bowl, 10" d., marigold.....35.00
Fruit bowl & base, clambroth, 2 pcs.....80.00
Fruit bowl & base, marigold, 2 pcs.....80.00
Fruit bowl & base, white, 2 pcs.....650.00

TWO FLOWERS (Fenton)

Bonbon, stemmed. blue.....85.00
Bowl, 6" d., footed, blue.....75.00
Bowl, 6" d., footed, lime green.....45.00
Bowl, 6" d., footed, marigold.....26.00
Bowl, 6" d., footed, purple.....75.00
Bowl, 6" d., footed, vaseline.....100.00 to 125.00
Bowl, 7" to 8" d., footed, blue.....60.00
Bowl, 7" to 8" d., footed, clambroth.....90.00
Bowl, 7" to 8" d., footed, green.....80.00 to 100.00
Bowl, 7" to 8" d., footed, marigold.....60.00
Bowl, 7" to 8" d., footed, fluted, purple.....47.00
Bowl, 7" to 8" d., footed, red.....2,247.00
Bowl, 8" d., footed, Amberina.....1,500.00 to 1,900.00
Bowl, 8" d., collared base, marigold.....100.00 to 125.00
Bowl, 8" d., collared base, ice cream shape, marigold.....175.00
Bowl, 8½" d., footed, blue.....99.00
Bowl, 9" d., footed, marigold.....75.00
Bowl, 9" d., footed, ice cream shape, marigold.....125.00

Bowl, 9½" d., ruffled, purple.....150.00
Bowl, 10" d., footed, scalloped rim, blue.....85.00
Bowl, 10" d., footed, scalloped rim, green.....75.00
Bowl, 10" d., footed, scalloped rim, marigold.....60.00
Bowl, 10" d., footed, scalloped rim, purple.....135.00
Bowl, 10" d., footed, blue....100.00 to 125.00
Bowl, 10" d., footed, marigold.....80.00 to 100.00
Bowl, 10" d., ruffled, footed, red 2,000.00
Bowl, 10" d., footed, vaseline 350.00
Bowl, 10" d., footed, white 750.00
Bowl, 10½" d., ruffled, blue.....162.00
Bowl, 11" d., aqua.....650.00
Bowl, 11" d., green 1,050.00
Bowl, 11" d., footed, ruffled, purple.....750.00
Bowl, 11" d., ice cream shape, blue ...125.00
Bowl, 11" d., ice cream shape, marigold.....40.00
Bowl, 11½" d., footed, blue.....125.00
Bowl, 11½" d., ball-footed, marigold.....55.00
Plate, 6½" d., marigold 125.00
Plate, 9" d., footed, marigold 425.00
Plate, chop, 11½" d., three-footed, marigold.....350.00
Plate, chop, 13" d., three-footed, marigold.....575.00
Rose bowl, three-footed, blue.....175.00 to 225.00
Rose bowl, three-footed, marigold.....50.00 to 75.00
Rose bowl, three-footed, purple 257.00

TWO FRUITS

Banana boat, marigold 60.00
Bonbon, divided, blue.....100.00
Bonbon, divided, green.....130.00
Bonbon, divided, marigold.....60.00 to 65.00
Bowl, large, in metal holder, marigold.....165.00

VENETIAN GIANT ROSE BOWL (Cambridge)

Green.....1,200.00
Marigold.....1,700.00

VICTORIAN

Bowl, 11" d., purple.....325.00
Bowl, 11½" d., eight-ruffle, purple.....525.00

VINEYARD

Pitcher, water, marigold.....100.00
Pitcher, water, peach opalescent 1,200.00
Pitcher, water, purple.....315.00
Tumbler, amber 29.00
Tumbler, green 39.00
Tumbler, lavender.....79.00
Tumbler, marigold.....26.00
Tumbler, purple 55.00

VINTAGE or VINTAGE GRAPE

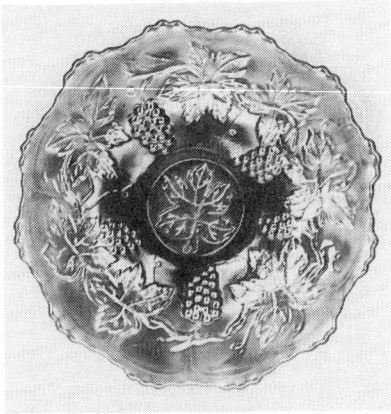

Vintage Plate

Bonbon, two-handled, blue (Fenton) 50.00
Bonbon, two-handled, green (Fenton)..50.00
Bonbon, two-handled, marigold (Fenton) 30.00
Bonbon, two-handled, purple (Fenton) 35.00
Bowl, 6" d., blue (Fenton) 35.00
Bowl, 6" d., green (Fenton).....45.00
Bowl, 6" d., purple (Fenton).....32.50
Bowl, 6½" d., ice cream shape, green 35.00
Bowl, 7" d., fluted, aqua opalescent (Fenton) 925.00
Bowl, 7" d., fluted, green (Fenton).....32.50
Bowl, 7" d., fluted, purple (Fenton) 28.00
Bowl, 7" d., purple (Millersburg) .....50.00 to 75.00
Bowl, 7" d., ruffled, vaseline 110.00
Bowl, 7½" d., ice cream shape, blue 36.00
Bowl, 7½" d., ice cream shape, green 32.00
Bowl, 7½" d., ice cream shape, purple 35.00
Bowl, 8" d., ribbon candy rim, aqua opalescent .....1,600.00 to 1,900.00
Bowl, 8" d., ribbon candy rim, Wide Panel exterior, blue.....55.00
Bowl, 8" to 9" d., aqua opalescent.....1,000.00 to 1,200.00
Bowl, 8" to 9" d., ruffled, aqua opalescent .....850.00 to 1,000.00
Bowl, 8" to 9" d., footed, blue (Fenton) 42.50
Bowl, 8" to 9" d., ruffled, blue 50.00
Bowl, 8" to 9" d., green (Fenton).....50.00
Bowl, 8" to 9" d., green (Millersburg) 30.00
Bowl, 8" to 9" d., marigold (Fenton).....35.00
Bowl, 8" to 9" d., fluted, Persian blue 630.00
Bowl, 8" to 9" d., footed, purple (Fenton) 38.00

Bowl, 8" to 9" d., ruffled, red ....1,700.00 to 1,800.00
Bowl, 8" to 9" d., fluted, teal blue 75.00
Bowl, 8" to 9" d., vaseline 225.00
Bowl, 9½" d., ruffled, dome-footed, marigold 68.00
Bowl, 10" d., blue ....75.00 to 100.00
Bowl, 10" d., green, Hobnail exterior (Millersburg) 950.00
Bowl, 10" d., marigold, Hobnail exterior (Millersburg) 575.00
Bowl, 10" d., ruffled, green 85.00
Bowl, 10" d., ruffled, purple 55.00
Bowl, 10" d., ruffled, red 3,250.00
Bowl, 10" d., ice cream shape, blue ...200.00
Bowl, 10" d., ice cream shape, red (Fenton) ....1,300.00 to 1,900.00
Bowl, 10" d., ice cream shape, vaseline (Fenton) 225.00
Bowl, 11" d., ice cream shape, marigold 600.00
Bowl, ruffled, domed base, celeste blue 825.00
Compote, 7" d., fluted, aqua opalescent 925.00
Compote, 7" d., blue (Fenton) 75.00
Compote, 7" d., fluted, green (Fenton) 46.00
Compote, 7" d., marigold (Fenton) 40.00
Compote, 7" d., purple (Fenton) 45.00
Cuspidor, marigold 2,300.00
Epergne, blue (Fenton) 110.00
Epergne, green, large 235.00
Epergne, green (Fenton) 150.00
Epergne, marigold (Fenton) 110.00
Epergne, purple, small 150.00
Epergne, purple, large 365.00
Epergne, purple (Fenton) 130.00
Fernery, footed, blue (Fenton) 85.00
Fernery, footed, green (Fenton) 75.00
Fernery, footed, marigold (Fenton) 42.50
Fernery, footed, purple (Fenton) 63.00
Fernery, footed, red (Fenton) ....1,400.00 to 1,600.00
Ice cream set: master ice cream bowl & four 6" d. bowls; cobalt blue, 5 pcs. 450.00
Nut dish, footed, blue, 6" d. (Fenton) 70.00
Nut dish, footed, green, 6" d. (Fenton) 110.00
Nut dish, footed, purple, 6" d. (Fenton) 62.00
Plate, 5" d., blue 75.00
Plate, 6" d., blue 140.00
Plate, 6" d., purple 65.00
Plate, 6½" d., stippled, marigold 50.00
Plate, 7" d., blue (Fenton) (ILLUS.) ....65.00 to 75.00
Plate, 7" d., green (Fenton) ....175.00 to 185.00
Plate, 7" d., marigold (Fenton) 125.00
Plate, 7" d., purple (Fenton) ....125.00 to 150.00
Plate, 7" d., purple 70.00
Plate, 8" d., blue 125.00
Plate, 8" d., green 165.00
Powder jar, cov., marigold (Fenton) 80.00
Powder jar, cov., marigold 75.00
Powder jar, cov., purple (Fenton) 100.00
Sandwich tray, handled, clambroth 28.00
Sandwich tray, handled, marigold 30.00
Sauce dish, blue 30.00
Sauce dish, blue, Hobnail exterior (Millersburg) 450.00
Sauce dish, green 25.00
Sauce dish, marigold (Fenton) 25.00
Sauce dish, ice cream shape, Hobnail exterior, marigold (Millersburg) 700.00
Tumbler, marigold (Fenton) 25.00
Wine, marigold (Fenton) 25.00
Wine, purple (Fenton) 32.00

VINTAGE BAND

Mug, marigold 28.00
Pitcher, water, marigold 175.00
Tumbler, marigold 695.00

VINTAGE GRAPE - See Vintage Pattern

WAFFLE BLOCK

Basket w/tall handle, clambroth, 10" h. 55.00
Basket w/tall handle, marigold, 10" h. 45.00
Basket w/tall handle, pastel marigold, 10" h. 145.00
Basket w/tall handle, teal, 10" h. 95.00
Basket w/tall handle, turquoise, 10" h. 100.00
Bowl, 7½" sq., marigold 36.00
Bowl, 8½" d., clambroth 55.00
Compote, clambroth 135.00
Creamer, clambroth 35.00
Punch cup, marigold 12.00
Sugar bowl, clambroth 30.00
Tumbler, marigold 215.00
Water set: pitcher & 2 tumblers; pastel marigold 350.00

WATER LILY (Fenton)

Banana boat, blue 160.00
Banana boat, marigold 70.00
Bonbon, blue, 7½" d. 65.00
Bonbon, white 60.00
Bowl, 5" d., aqua 95.00
Bowl, 5" d., marigold 28.00
Bowl, 6" d., aqua 140.00
Bowl, 6" d., ruffled, aqua 185.00
Bowl, 6" d., blue 37.00
Bowl, 6" d., footed, blue 58.00
Bowl, 6" d., green 160.00
Bowl, 6" d., footed, green 245.00
Bowl, 6" d., footed, lime green 45.00
Bowl, 6" d., footed, marigold 35.00
Bowl, 6" d., footed, purple 150.00
Bowl, 6" d., footed, red ....550.00 to 600.00

Bowl, 6" d., footed, red opalescent ....900.00 to 950.00
Bowl, 6" d., footed, vaseline 125.00
Bowl, 6" d., vaseline w/marigold overlay 85.00
Bowl, 8½" d., marigold 50.00
Bowl, 9" d., footed, black amethyst 75.00
Bowl, 9" d., footed, marigold 50.00
Bowl, 10" d., footed, fluted, blue 120.00
Bowl, 10" d., footed, green 115.00
Bowl, 10" d., footed, marigold 100.00
Bowl, 10" d., footed, purple 75.00

WATER LILY & CATTAILS

Bonbon, two-handled, marigold, large ..50.00
Bowl, 5" d., marigold 32.00
Bowl, 9" d., marigold 80.00
Bowl, 9" d., purple 60.00
Butter dish, cov., marigold 156.00
Dish, three turned up sides, marigold, 6" d. 29.00
Pitcher, water, marigold 548.00
Plate, 6" d., marigold 55.00
Rose bowl, marigold 20.00
Sauce dish, marigold 12.00
Sugar bowl, cov., marigold 75.00
Table set, marigold, 4 pcs. 675.00
Toothpick holder, marigold 65.00
Tumbler, blue 2,700.00
Tumbler, marigold 45.00
Tumbler, purple 22.50
Whimsey, marigold 32.50
Whimsey, purple 55.00

WHIRLING LEAVES BOWL (Millersburg)

9" d., green 70.00
9" d., marigold ....80.00 to 100.00
9" d., purple 75.00
9½" w., tricornered, green 345.00
9½" w., tricornered, marigold 140.00
9½" w., tricornered, vaseline 635.00
10" d., green ....50.00 to 75.00
10" d., marigold 75.00
10" d., purple ....100.00 to 150.00

WHITE OAK TUMBLER

Marigold 242.00

WIDE PANEL

Banana bowl, amber 40.00
Basket, green 80.00
Bowl, 8" to 9" d., marigold 19.00
Bowl, 8" to 9" d., purple 60.00
Bowl, 8½" d., Ragged Robin, 3 in l rim, blue 135.00
Bowl, 10" d., console, blue 40.00
Bowl, 10" d., console, vaseline 40.00
Bowl, 12" d., marigold 45.00
Candy dish, cov., marigold 30.00
Candy dish, cov., red 350.00
Candy dish, cov., white 55.00
Compote, miniature, marigold 25.00
Compote, vaseline 65.00

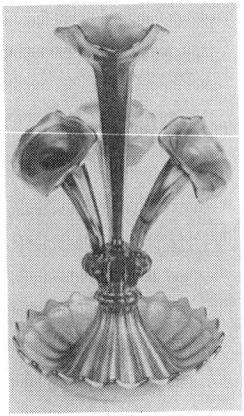

Wide Panel Epergne

Epergne, four-lily, green (ILLUS.) 1,250.00
Epergne, four-lily, ice blue 225.00
Epergne, four-lily, marigold 525.00
Epergne, four-lily, purple 950.00
Epergne, four-lily, white 2,600.00
Goblet, marigold 15.00
Goblet, red 175.00
Plate, 8" d., marigold 45.00
Plate, 8" d., red 57.00
Plate, chop, 12" d., vaseline 50.00
Plate, chop, 14" d., marigold 40.00
Plate, chop, 14" d., red 195.00
Plate, chop, 14" d., smoky 53.00
Plate, chop, 14" d., white 28.00
Rose bowl, clambroth 20.00
Rose bowl, marigold 25.00
Rose bowl, purple 29.00
Salt dip, marigold 50.00
Salt set: master pedestal salt dip & 6 individual size salt dips; marigold (Northwood), 7 pcs. 150.00
Vase, 6" h., marigold 55.00
Vase, 8½" h., 7½" d., smoke over milk white glass 185.00
Vase, 15" h., marigold 110.00

WILD ROSE

Bowl, 5½" d., three-footed, open heart rim, green 47.00
Bowl, 7" d., three-footed, open heart rim, green (Northwood) 48.00
Bowl, 7" d., three-footed, open heart rim, marigold (Northwood) 52.00
Bowl, 7" d., three-footed, open heart rim, purple (Northwood) ....50.00 to 70.00
Bowl, 8" to 9" d., marigold (Northwood) 32.50
Bowl, 8" to 9" d., green (Northwood) 38.00
Candy dish, open edge, blue, 5¾" d. 150.00
Candy dish, open edge, green 75.00
Candy dish, open edge, purple 90.00
Lamp, three portrait medallions, w/original burner & etched chimney shade, green, small (Millersburg) 850.00

Lamp, w/original burner & etched chimney shade, green, medium (Millersburg) .....1,250.00 to 1,450.00
Lamp, w/original burner & etched chimney shade, marigold, medium (Millersburg) .....1,100.00 to 1,300.00
Lamp, w/original burner & etched chimney shade, purple (Millersburg) 1,400.00
Syrup pitcher, marigold.....750.00 to 950.00

WILD STRAWBERRY (Northwood)
Bowl, 6" d., green 55.00
Bowl, 6" d., purple.....48.00
Bowl, 6" d., ruffled, purple.....100.00
Bowl, 7" d., marigold.....85.00
Bowl, 10" d., green .....175.00 to 225.00
Bowl, 10" d., ice green.....1,750.00
Bowl, 10" d., marigold.....85.00
Bowl, 10" d., purple.....185.00
Plate, 6" to 7" d., w/handgrip, green.....200.00 to 225.00
Plate, 6" to 7" d., w/handgrip, marigold .....125.00 to 150.00
Plate, 6" to 7" d., w/handgrip, purple 125.00
Plate, 8" d., w/handgrip, green 100.00
Plate, 8" d., w/handgrip, purple.....150.00

WINDFLOWER
Bowl, 8" to 9" d., blue.....60.00
Bowl, 8" to 9" d., ice green.....350.00
Bowl, 8" to 9" d., marigold.....32.00
Bowl, 8" to 9" d., pastel marigold.....75.00
Bowl, 8" to 9" d., purple 60.00
Bowl, 8" to 9" d., smoky 125.00
Plate, 8" d., marigold 130.00
Plate, 9" d., blue 175.00
Plate, 9" d., marigold .....75.00 to 100.00
Plate, 9" d., pastel marigold.....125.00
Sauceboat, ice green.....425.00
Sauceboat, marigold.....40.00
Sauceboat, purple 35.00
Tumbler, marigold.....200.00
Tumbler, purple 50.00

WINDMILL or WINDMILL MEDALLION (Imperial)
Bowl, 7" d., marigold.....40.00
Bowl, 7" d., purple.....56.00
Bowl, 8" to 9" d., green 35.00
Bowl, 8" to 9" d., ruffled, marigold.....75.00
Bowl, 8" to 9" d., ruffled, purple 145.00
Bowl, 8" to 9" d., ruffled, vaseline 65.00
Bowl, 8" to 9" d., ruffled, smoky 52.00
Bowl, 9" d., footed, marigold.....30.00
Bowl, 9" d., footed, purple.....115.00
Dresser tray, oval, marigold.....48.00
Pickle dish, aqua teal.....275.00
Pickle dish, green 50.00
Pickle dish, lavender.....70.00
Pickle dish, marigold.....28.00
Pickle dish, purple 50.00
Pitcher, milk, clambroth 45.00
Pitcher, milk, ice green 110.00
Pitcher, milk, marigold 60.00
Pitcher, milk, purple .....500.00 to 700.00
Pitcher, milk, smoky.....225.00
Pitcher, water, marigold.....78.00
Pitcher, water, purple.....450.00 to 500.00
Plate, 8" d., marigold 18.00
Sauce dish, clambroth.....35.00
Sauce dish, green.....32.00
Sauce dish, marigold.....20.00
Sauce dish, purple.....35.00
Tumbler, green 39.00

Windmill Tumbler

Tumbler, marigold (ILLUS.) 35.00
Tumbler, purple 100.00
Water set: pitcher & 1 tumbler; marigold, 2 pcs. 130.00
Water set: pitcher & 2 tumblers; purple, 3 pcs. 1,200.00

WINDMILL & MUMS - See Chrysanthemum Pattern

WINDMILL MEDALLION - See Windmill Pattern

WINE & ROSES

Wine & Roses Pitcher

Goblet, blue 75.00
Goblet, marigold 38.00
Goblet, vaseline 75.00
Pitcher, water, marigold (ILLUS.) 350.00
Wine, blue 60.00
Wine, marigold 25.00

WISHBONE (Northwood)

Wishbone Bowl

Bowl, 7" d., three-footed, ruffled rim, marigold 50.00
Bowl, 8" to 9" d., footed, blue 300.00
Bowl, 8" to 9" d., footed, clambroth 90.00
Bowl, 8" to 9" d., footed, green 103.00
Bowl, 8" to 9" d., footed, ice blue (ILLUS.) 2,200.00
Bowl, 8" to 9" d., footed, ice green...1,850.00
Bowl, 8" to 9" d., footed, lavender 200.00
Bowl, 8" to 9" d., footed, marigold .....50.00 to 75.00
Bowl, 8" to 9" d., footed, pastel marigold 85.00
Bowl, 8" to 9" d., footed, purple 111.00
Bowl, 8" to 9" d., footed, white 550.00
Bowl, 10" d., footed, blue....500.00 to 600.00
Bowl, 10" d., piecrust rim, blue w/electric iridescence 2,300.00
Bowl, 10" d., piecrust rim, green .....225.00 to 250.00
Bowl, 10" d., piecrust rim, Basket-weave exterior, green 1,175.00
Bowl, 10" d., piecrust rim, marigold 92.00
Bowl, 10" d., piecrust rim, Basket-weave exterior, marigold 140.00
Bowl, 10" d., ruffled, green 145.00
Bowl, 10" d., ruffled, marigold 150.00
Bowl, 10" d., ruffled, Basketweave exterior, purple 125.00
Bowl, 10" d., piecrust rim, purple .....125.00 to 150.00
Bowl, 10" d., footed, ruffled, purple.....135.00
Bowl, 10" d., footed, piecrust rim, smoky 1,300.00
Bowl, 10" d., footed, piecrust rim, white 750.00
Bowl, footed, clambroth 115.00
Epergne, green 675.00
Epergne, ice blue 2,500.00
Epergne, marigold .....400.00 to 450.00
Epergne, purple .....400.00 to 450.00
Epergne, white 1,950.00
Pitcher, water, green 1,800.00
Pitcher, water, marigold 1,500.00
Pitcher, water, purple....1,150.00 to 1,250.00
Plate, 8½" d., footed, marigold 475.00
Plate, 8½" d., footed, purple 300.00
Plate, 8½" w., footed, tricornered, green 675.00
Plate, 8½" w., footed, tricornered, purple .....350.00 to 400.00
Plate, chop, 11" d., marigold 500.00
Plate, chop, 11" d., purple 645.00
Tumbler, green 180.00
Tumbler, marigold 130.00
Tumbler, purple 135.00

WISHBONE & SPADES

Berry set: master bowl & 4 sauce dishes; purple, 5 pcs. 500.00
Bowl, 5" d., peach opalescent 80.00
Bowl, 5" d., purple 40.00
Bowl, 6" d., ruffled, peach opalescent ..55.00
Bowl, 10" d., peach opalescent 375.00
Bowl, 10" d., purple 270.00
Bowl, footed, green 85.00
Bowl, ruffled, purple 100.00
Plate, 6" d., purple 350.00
Plate, 6½" d., peach opalescent 325.00
Plate, chop, 11" d., purple .....775.00 to 800.00
Sauce dish, peach opalescent 70.00
Sauce dish, purple 45.00
Whimsey from 10½" ruffled chop plate, sides folded-up like a napkin holder, peach opalescent 1,400.00

WREATHED CHERRY (Dugan)

Berry set: master bowl & 4 sauce dishes; marigold, 5 pcs. 140.00
Berry set: master bowl & 4 sauce dishes; white, 5 pcs. 675.00
Bonbon, two-handled, green, 8" 45.00
Bonbon, two-handled, marigold, 8".....40.00
Bowl, berry, 9 x 12" oval, lavender 65.00
Bowl, berry, 9 x 12" oval, marigold 90.00
Bowl, berry, 9 x 12" oval, pastel marigold 150.00
Bowl, berry, 9 x 12" oval, peach opalescent .....200.00 to 250.00
Bowl, berry, 9 x 12" oval, purple 153.00
Bowl, berry, 9 x 12" oval, white 245.00
Butter dish, cov., marigold 70.00
Butter dish, cov., purple .....175.00 to 225.00
Compote, three-footed, peach opalescent 75.00
Creamer, blue 55.00
Pitcher, water, marigold 225.00
Pitcher, water, white w/gold cherries .....700.00 to 750.00

Sauce dish, 5" to 6" l., oval, marigold ...30.00
Sauce dish, 5" to 6" l., oval, peach opalescent 140.00
Sauce dish, 5" to 6" l., oval, purple 40.00
Sauce dish, 5" to 6" l., oval, white.....42.50
Spooner, marigold 65.00
Spooner, purple 60.00
Spooner, white.....95.00
Toothpick holder, marigold 100.00
Tumbler, marigold 32.50
Tumbler, purple 65.00
Tumbler, white 100.00
Tumbler, white w/red-stained cherries 115.00
Water set: pitcher & 4 tumblers; marigold, 5 pcs. 600.00

WREATH OF ROSES

Bonbon, two-handled, blue, 8" d.....75.00
Bonbon, two-handled, green, 8" d. 55.00
Bonbon, two-handled, marigold, 8" d....50.00
Bonbon, two-handled, purple, 8" d.....100.00 to 125.00
Bonbon, two-handled, white, 8" d. 150.00
Compote, 6" d., blue 65.00
Compote, 6" d., fluted, green.....50.00
Compote, 6" d., honey amber (variant).....35.00
Compote, 6" d., marigold 40.00
Compote, 6" d., fluted, purple 45.00
Punch bowl, Persian Medallion interior, blue 300.00
Punch bowl & base, Persian Medallion interior, marigold, 2 pcs. 225.00
Punch cup, blue.....22.00
Punch cup, Persian Medallion interior, blue 28.00
Punch cup, Vintage interior, blue.....25.00
Punch cup, green 25.00
Punch cup, Persian Medallion interior, green.....35.00
Punch cup, Vintage interior, green 37.00
Punch cup, marigold.....14.00
Punch cup, Persian Medallion interior, marigold 25.00
Punch cup, Vintage interior, marigold...30.00
Punch cup, purple.....25.00
Punch cup, Persian Medallion interior, purple 27.00
Punch cup, Vintage interior, purple 32.50
Punch set: bowl, base & 2 cups; green, 4 pcs. 425.00
Punch set: bowl, base & 4 cups; Persian Medallion interior, marigold, 6 pcs. 395.00
Punch set: bowl, base & 5 cups; Vintage interior, purple, 7 pcs. 800.00
Rose bowl, marigold (Dugan) 50.00
Rose bowl, purple (Dugan).....55.00
Whimsey, tricornered, marigold (Dugan) 45.00

ZIG ZAG (Millersburg)

Bowl, 9½" d., marigold.....195.00
Bowl, 9½" d., green 420.00
Bowl, 10" d., green .....250.00 to 275.00
Bowl, 10" d., marigold.....185.00
Bowl, 10" d., purple.....240.00
Bowl, 10" w., tricornered, piecrust rim, green.....200.00
Bowl, 10" w., tricornered, purple.....430.00
Bowl, ribbon candy rim, marigold 225.00
Bowl, ribbon candy rim, purple.....250.00 to 300.00

ZIPPERED HEART

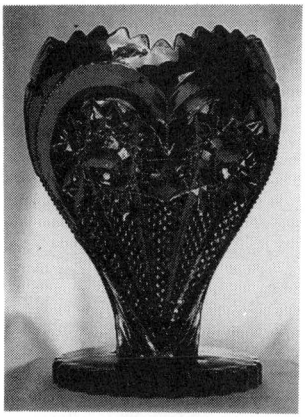

Zippered Heart Rose Bowl

Bowl, berry, 10" d., purple 130.00
Rose bowl, green (ILLUS.) 3,600.00
Sauce dish, purple, 5" d.....22.50
Vase, 9" h., green 2,100.00
Vase, marigold.....550.00

ZIPPERED LOOP LAMP (Imperial)

Zippered Loop Lamp

Hand, marigold, 4½" h. 1,200.00
Hand, marigold, medium 675.00
Sewing, marigold, small.....325.00
Sewing, marigold, medium .....600.00 to 675.00
Sewing, smoky, medium .....950.00 to 1,000.00
Sewing, marigold, large (ILLUS.) .....550.00 to 575.00

(End of Carnival Glass Section)

CONSOLIDATED

The Consolidated Lamp and Glass Company of Coraopolis, Pennsylvania was founded in 1894 and for a number of years was noted for its lighting wares but also produced popular lines of pressed and blown tablewares. Highly collectible glass patterns of this early era include the Cone, Florette and Guttate lines.

Lamps and shades continued to be good sellers but in 1926 a new "art" line of molded decorative wares was introduced. This "Martelé" line was developed as a direct imitation of the fine glasswares being produced by René Lalique of France and many Consolidated patterns resembled their French counterparts. Other popular lines produced during the 1920s and 1930s were "Dancing Nymph," the delightfully Art Deco "Ruba Rombic," introduced in 1928, and the "Catalonian" line, imitating 17th century Spanish glass, which debuted in 1927.

Although the factory closed in 1933, it was reopened under new management in 1936 and prospered through the 1940s. It finally closed in 1967. Collectors should note that many later Consolidated patterns closely resemble wares of other competing firms, especially the Phoenix Glass Company. Careful study is needed to determine the maker of pieces from the 1920-40 era.

A recent book which will be of help to collectors is Phoenix & Consolidated Art Glass, 1926-1980, *by Jack D. Wilson (Antique Publications, 1989).*

Consolidated Martelé Label

Bulging Loops

Pitcher, water, cased pink $360.00
Sugar shaker w/original top, blue opaque.....450.00
Tumbler, cased yellow.....45.00

Cone

Butter dish, cov., cased yellow 135.00
Pickle castor, cased pink, ornate silver plate frame, elaborate side & top trim, w/tongs 450.00
Pickle castor, cased yellow, silver plate frame.....275.00 to 325.00
Sugar shaker w/original top, cased blue satin .....125.00 to 150.00
Sugar shaker w/original top, green opaque.....165.00
Sugar shaker w/original top, cased pink, glossy finish.....145.00
Syrup pitcher w/original top, tall, blue opaque.....295.00
Syrup pitcher w/original top, squatty, cased blue 210.00
Syrup pitcher w/original top, squatty, cased pink.....250.00 to 275.00
Toothpick holder, cased pink.....75.00
Water set: pitcher & four tumblers; blue opaque, 5 pcs. 285.00

Florette

Florette Cracker Jar

Butter dish, cov., cased pink satin .....250.00 to 275.00
Cracker (or biscuit) jar w/original silver plate rim, lid & bail handle, cased pink (ILLUS.) 295.00
Cruet w/original stopper, pink.....185.00
Cruet w/original frosted stopper, frosted handle, cased pink satin 145.00
Lamp, kerosene-type, wall bracket-type, green opaque, 6" d.....175.00
Mustard pot w/hinged metal lid, cased yellow satin 75.00
Pitcher, water, pink satin 275.00
Salt shaker w/original top, cased pink .....75.00 to 100.00
Spooner, cased pink, metal rim & handles 50.00
Sugar bowl, cov., cased pink.....125.00

Sugar bowl, cov., cased pink satin 115.00
Syrup pitcher w/original ornate silver plate hinged lid & handle, cased pink satin.....250.00 to 290.00
Toothpick holder, cased blue.....65.00
Toothpick holder, cased green.....75.00 to 100.00
Toothpick holder, cased pink .....100.00 to 125.00

Guttate

Celery vase, cased pink .....150.00 to 175.00
Pitcher, water, 9½" h., applied clear handle, cased pink satin 395.00
Salt shaker w/brass top, cased blue.....52.00
Salt & pepper shakers, cased pink, pr.....75.00
Salt & pepper shakers w/original tops, cased pink satin, pr. 55.00
Spooner, cased pink.....75.00 to 100.00
Sugar shaker w/original top, cased pink satin.....200.00 to 300.00
Syrup pitcher w/original top, cranberry.....450.00

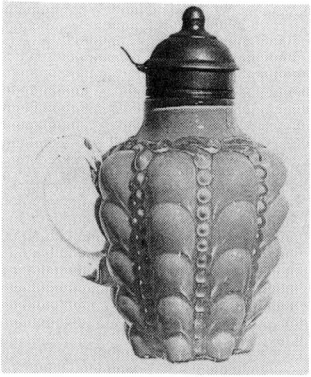

Guttate Syrup Pitcher

Syrup pitcher w/original top, cased pink (ILLUS.).....350.00 to 400.00
Table set: cov. butter dish, sugar bowl, creamer & spooner; white w/gold trim, 4 pcs.....225.00
Water set: pitcher & four tumblers; cased pink satin, 5 pcs. 595.00

Later Lines

Ruba Rombic Dresser Jar

Ashtray, oblong, Santa Maria line, amber.....45.00
Banana boat, oblong, Love Birds patt., Martelé line, three-color decoration on custard ground 500.00
Bowl, 9" d., 4" h., Catalonian line, yellow.....55.00
Bowl, 13" d., Cockatoo patt., Martelé line, gold wash 125.00
Bowl, 13" d., Cockatoo patt., Martelé line, green wash.....145.00
Bowl, 15" d., Fish patt., Martelé line, green wash 375.00
Candlesticks, Catalonian line, emerald green, pr. .....40.00 to 60.00
Cookie jar, cov., Con-Cora line, roses decoration on a milk white ground, 6½" h.....95.00
Cookie jar, cov., Con-Cora line, violets decoration on a milk white ground, 9" h. 145.00
Creamer & open sugar bowl, Catalonian line, pink, pr. 38.00
Dresser jar, cov., oblong, Ruba Rombic line, frosted amber, some staining, 5½" w., 4" h. (ILLUS.) 546.00
Lamp, table model, brass base & shade cap, Bittersweet patt., Martelé line, straw opal.....165.00
Lamp, table model, brass base & shade cap, Cockatoo patt., Martelé line, blue & brown on a custard ground, 9½" d., 8½" h. 295.00
Lamp, table model, brass base & shade cap, Foxglove patt., Martelé line, green wash.....145.00
Lamp, table model, brass base & shade cap, Foxglove patt., Martelé line, two-color decoration on a custard ground.....175.00
Lamp base, table model, brass fittings, baluster-form, Dogwood patt., Martelé line, salmon decoration on a milk white ground, 10½" h. glass insert, overall 15" h.....135.00
Lamp, table model, brass fittings, Thistle patt., Martelé line, umbrella vase-type, blue & irridescent white, overall 25" h. 550.00
Lamp base, table model, Cockatoo patt., Martelé line, matte blue on cream.....175.00
Lamp base, table model, Peony patt., peach w/green leaves, brown stems, factory drilled, 6¼" h. 65.00
Plate, 8½" d., Dancing Nymph line, clear frosted.....77.00
Plate, 10" d., Dancing Nymph line, green frosted.....150.00
Plate, 12" d., Five Fruits patt., Martelé line, milk white ground 95.00

Puff box, cov., Hummingbird patt., Martelé line, green wash, 4" d. 250.00
Snack plate, pear-shaped, Five Fruits patt., Catalonian line, jade green wash, 9¼" d. 18.00

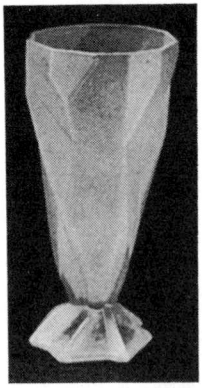

Ruba Rombic Tumbler

Tumblers, conical, Ruba Rombic line, opal green, one w/polished-down rim, 7¼" h., pr. (ILLUS. of one) 690.00
Vase, 6" h., ovoid, Dragonfly & Cattails patt., Martelé line, brown & coral decoration on a milk white ground ....95.00 to 110.00
Vase, 6" h., ovoid, Dragonfly & Cattails patt., Martelé line, milk white w/gold trim 70.00
Vase, 6" h., Hummingbird & Orchids patt., Martelé line, yellow cased 80.00
Vase, 6½" h., Chickadee patt., Martelé line, satin milk white ....95.00 to 110.00
Vase, 6½" h., Chickadee patt., Martelé line, tri-color highlighting on satin custard 195.00
Vase, 6½" h., Chickadee patt., Martelé line, yellow wash 125.00
Vase, 6½" h., flattened fan shape, shape No. 2201, Florentine line, green 185.00
Vase, 6½" h., 7" d., Pine Cone patt., Martelé line, ruby stain on crystal 195.00
Vases, 6¾" h., Ruba Rombic line, tall conical body on a flaring foot, green, pr. 770.00
Vase, 8" h., 9" d., Catalonian line, amethyst wash 65.00
Vase, 8½" h., 9" d., Cockatoo patt., Martelé line, three-color decoration on a white ground 225.00
Vase, 9" h., Tropical Fish patt., Martelé line, brown highlighting on satin milk white ground 175.00
Vase, 9½" h., Bittersweet patt., Martelé line, purple berries & brown leaves on a creamy white ground 125.00
Vase, 9½" h., baluster-form, Bittersweet patt., Martelé line, two-color decoration on a white ground 75.00
Vase, 9½" h., Bittersweet patt., Martelé line, three-color decoration on a custard ground 125.00
Vase, 10" h., triangular, Catalonian line, red wash ....100.00 to 115.00
Vase, 10" h., bulbous ovoid body, Line 700, French Crystal 260.00
Vase, 10½" h., Dogwood patt., Martelé line, tan decoration on a custard ground 150.00
Vase, 10½" h., Dogwood patt., Martelé line, three-color decoration on a white ground 135.00

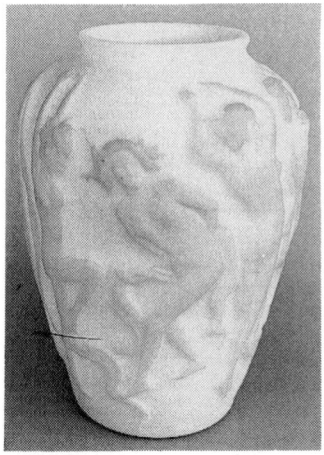

Dancing Girls Vase

Vase, 11½" h., Dancing Girls patt., Martelé line, blue figures on a custard ground (ILLUS.) ..495.00 to 525.00
Vase, 11½" h., Dancing Girls patt., Martelé line, clear figures on a frosted background ....400.00 to 425.00
Water set: pitcher & six tumblers; Five Fruits patt., Martelé line, yellow wash, 7 pcs. 375.00

CRUETS

Amber, blown, bulbous body, applied blue handle, blue stopper, ca. 1880s $140.00
Amber, pressed, I.O.U. patt., original faceted stopper 110.00
Amber lustre w/raised rounded swirled ribs, applied clear handle & original faceted stopper, polished pontil 150.00
Blue, blown, squared bulbous body, decorated w/enameled red, white & blue flowers & green leaves, all

outlined in gold, applied amber spun rope handle, original amber facet-cut stopper, 7¼" h., 3¼" d. 165.00

Blue opalescent, blown, Christmas Bead & Panel patt., applied blue handle, original stopper 225.00

Champagne, mold-blown, Inverted Thumbprint patt., bulbous body tapering to a cylindrical neck w/pinched lip, applied sapphire blue handle, sapphire blue facet-cut stopper, 3" d., 5¾" h. 75.00

Clear, blown, Swirl patt., applied clear closed round handle, original ball stopper, 4½" h. 22.50

Clear, pressed, Peacock Feather patt., original stopper, 10" h. 125.00

Cobalt blue, blown, ovoid body tapering to a cylindrical neck & pinched spout, upper body decorated w/pink flowers & green leaves on a enameled gold ground, the lower body decorated w/white lacy dotting, applied cobalt blue handle, cobalt blue teardrop-shaped stopper, 2⅝" d., 6¼" h. 85.00

Cobalt blue, blown, ovoid body tapering to a cylindrical neck w/pinched lip, enameled w/bands of sanded gold leaves & white dot decoration, applied cobalt blue handle, original cobalt blue ball stopper, 3½" d., 8" h. 165.00

Cobalt blue, pattern-molded, bulbous body tapering to a slender neck w/high arched spout, applied strap handle, hollow ball stopper, Midwest, early 19th c., 7½" h. plus stopper (minor residue, slight check at handle) 1,210.00

Cranberry, blown, Moire satin finish, applied clear frosted handle, clear bubble stopper 295.00

Cranberry, blown, baluster-form body, cylindrical neck w/tricorner rim, enameled w/blue & white flowers & yellow leaves, applied clear handle, original clear bubble stopper, 3⅛" d., 8¼" h. 195.00

Cranberry, blown, ovoid body tapering to long slender neck & applied clear handle, decorated w/overall gold enameled scrolling & dainty gold flowers, gold trim on original clear bubble stopper, 10½" h., 3⅜" d. 195.00

Emerald green, pressed, The Prize patt., w/original stopper 225.00

Green, pressed, Geneva patt., original stopper 290.00

Green, pressed, Georgia Gem patt., gold trim, original stopper 350.00

Light blue, mold-blown, square body, cylindrical neck w/flared spout, enameled w/rust, blue, white & yellow flowers & leaves, applied amber handle, original amber facet-cut stopper, 3½" d., 7½" h. 165.00

Lime green, blown, ovoid body tapering to a cylindrical neck w/pinched spout, decorated w/dainty enameled dot flowers & gold trim, applied clear handle, clear facet-cut stopper, 3⅛" d., 7¼" h. 100.00

Lime green, blown, bulbous body w/applied lime green handle, decorated w/small white daisies & gold foliage, original lime green bulbous stopper, 3¼" d., 8" h. 110.00

Orange, blown, Optic patt., tapering cylindrical body w/slender ringed neck w/petal-form spout, decorated w/dainty white enameled daisies, applied clear handle, original squatty bulbous stopper, 3" d., 8½" h. 165.00

Pink-stained, Blazing Cornucopia patt., original stopper 89.00

Enamel-Decorated Cruet

Sapphire blue, blown, ovoid body w/slender cylindrical neck w/pinched lip, decorated w/multicolored enameled Queen Anne's lace decoration, applied sapphire blue handle & original teardrop-shaped stopper, 7½" h. (ILLUS.) 375.00

Sapphire blue, blown, ovoid body tapering to a short rim & amber applied handle, decorated w/enameled white foliage, white w/yellow flowers & gold trim, original amber ball stopper, 3" d., 7½" h. 165.00

Sapphire blue, blown, bulbous body w/a slender cylindrical neck, decorated w/pink foliage w/deeper pink & white flowers, applied sapphire blue handle, original blue bubble stopper, 3½" d., 8" h. 165.00

Sapphire blue, blown, ovoid body w/slender neck & applied clear handle, decorated w/lavender flowers & green leaves, gold decoration & gold trim, original clear bubble stopper, 3¾" d., 9" h. 165.00

Sapphire blue, blown, ovoid shape tapering to a cylindrical neck, enameled w/rose pink florals w/green & gold foliage, applied light blue handle, original bubble-shaped stopper, 4" d., 9" h. 165.00

Sapphire blue, blown, white enameled decoration & matching enameled stopper, applied amber handle 55.00

Mold Blown Cruet

Sapphire blue, mold-blown, 16-rib globular body tapering to a narrow neck w/high arched spout, applied hollow handle, original stopper, Midwestern, 7" h. plus stopper (ILLUS.) 2,310.00

Sapphire blue, mold-blown, bulbous body tapering to a cylindrical neck w/pinched spout, decorated w/pink blossoms, orange flowers & pink branches, applied sapphire blue handle, original sapphire blue bubble stopper, 4" d., 8¼" h. 165.00

CUP PLATES

Produced in numerous patterns beginning some 160 years ago, these little plates were designed to hold a cup while the tea or coffee was allowed to cool in a saucer. Cup plates were also made of ceramics. Where numbers are listed below, they refer to numbers assigned these plates in the book, American Glass Cup Plates, *by Ruth Webb Lee and James H. Rose. Plates are of clear glass unless otherwise noted. A number of cup plates have been reproduced.*

L & R 87, plain round, 4 7/16" d. $16.00

L & R 95, octagonal, shields & tree-like devices in border, opal opaque 143.00

L & R 109, Thistle patt., octagonal w/incurved edges (some mold roughness on rim) 55.00

L & R 174, round w/petaled rim, eight-petaled design in center, opal opaque 385.00

L & R 243, round w/small rim scallops, quatrefoil in center surrounded by small blossomheads, scrolls in border, opalescent (underfill on one scallop, mold roughness) 148.50

L & R 388, diamond point border, eight-petal center flower (minor rim nip) 30.00

L & R 465F, Heart patt., round, violet blue (several scallops missing or tipped) 302.50

L & R 563, Henry Clay, no name variant, opalescent (three tipped scallops, mold roughness) 467.50

L & R 572, round w/small rim scallops, Queen Victoria bust design (mold roughness) 132.00

L & R 610B, Ship Cadmus patt. 30.00

L & R 655, Eagle patt., round, Pittsburgh (fin & mold roughness) ...126.50

L & R 691, round w/beaded rim, Lyre patt. (several beads tipped, overall mold roughness) 33.00

DEPRESSION GLASS

The phrase "Depression Glass" is used by collectors to denote a specific kind of transparent glass produced primarily as tablewares, in crystal, amber, blue, green, pink, milky-white, etc., during the late 1920s and 1930s when this country was in the midst of a financial depression. Made to sell inexpensively, it was turned out by such producers as Jeannette, Hocking, Westmoreland, Indiana and other glass companies. We compile prices on all the major Depression Glass patterns. Collectors should consult Depression Glass references for information on those patterns and pieces which have been reproduced.

ADAM (Process-etched)

Ashtray, clear, 4½" sq. $8.50

Ashtray, green, 4½" sq. 16.50

Ashtray, pink, 4½" sq. 24.50

Bowl, dessert, 4¾" sq., green 15.50

Bowl, dessert, 4¾" sq., pink 13.00

Bowl, cereal, 5¾" sq., green 37.00

Bowl, cereal, 5¾" sq., pink 41.00
Bowl, nappy, 7¾" sq., green.....21.50
Bowl, nappy, 7¾" sq., pink 18.50
Bowl, cov., 9" sq., green 75.00
Bowl, cov., 9" sq., pink.....53.00
Bowl, 9" sq., pink 18.00
Bowl, 10" oval vegetable, green 22.50
Bowl, 10" oval vegetable, pink.....27.50
Butter dish, cov., green.....265.00
Butter dish, cov., pink 76.00
Cake plate, footed, green or pink, 10" sq.....22.00
Candlesticks, green, 4" h., pr.....84.00
Candlesticks, pink, 4" h., pr 75.00
Candy jar, cov., green 96.50
Candy jar, cov., pink.....82.00
Coaster, green, 3¼" sq.....17.00
Coaster, pink, 3¼" sq. 21.00
Creamer, green 17.50
Creamer, pink.....16.00
Cup, green.....16.00
Cup, pink 20.00
Pitcher, 8" h., 32 oz., cone-shaped, green.....37.00
Pitcher, 8" h., 32 oz., cone-shaped, pink 30.00
Pitcher, 32 oz., round base, pink.....44.50
Plate, sherbet, 6" sq., green 7.00
Plate, sherbet, 6" sq., pink.....6.00
Plate, salad, 7¾" sq., green or pink.....10.50
Plate, salad, round, pink 60.00
Plate, salad, round, yellow.....110.00
Plate, dinner, 9" sq., green 19.00
Plate, dinner, 9" sq., pink.....26.00
Plate, grill, 9" sq., green or pink.....17.00
Platter, 11¾" l., green 18.00
Platter, 11¾" l., pink.....23.00
Relish dish, two-part, green or pink, 8" sq.....16.50
Salt & pepper shakers, footed, green, 4" h., pr. 75.00

Adam Salt & Pepper Shakers

Salt & pepper shakers, footed, pink, 4" h., pr. (ILLUS.) 60.00
Saucer, pink, 6" sq.....6.50
Saucer, round, green.....5.50
Saucer, round, pink 6.00
Sherbet, green, 3" h.....31.50
Sherbet, pink, 3" h. 25.00
Sugar bowl, cov., green..... 41.00
Sugar bowl, cov., pink 34.00
Tumbler, cone-shaped, green, 4½" h., 7 oz. 22.50
Tumbler, cone-shaped, pink,4½" h., 7 oz. 23.50
Tumbler, iced tea, green, 5½" h., 9 oz. 41.50
Tumbler, iced tea, pink, 5½" h., 9 oz. 55.00
Vase, 7½" h., green 53.00
Vase, 7½" h., pink.....185.00
Water set: pitcher & 6 tumblers; pink, 7 pcs.....162.50

AMERICAN SWEETHEART (Process-etched)

American Sweetheart Plate

Bowl, berry, 3¾" d., pink.....38.00
Bowl, cream soup, 4½" d., Monax.....106.00
Bowl, cream soup, 4½" d., pink 70.00
Bowl, cereal, 6" d., Cremax 8.00
Bowl, cereal, 6" d., Monax.....11.50
Bowl, cereal, 6" d., pink 12.50
Bowl, berry, 9" d., Cremax..... 28.50
Bowl, berry, 9" d., Monax.....55.00
Bowl, berry, 9" d., pink..... 35.00
Bowl, soup w/flange rim, 9½" d., Monax 70.00
Bowl, soup w/flange rim, 9½" d., pink...58.00
Bowl, 11" oval vegetable, Monax.....67.00
Bowl, 11" oval vegetable, pink..... 55.00
Console bowl, Monax, 18" d. 425.00
Creamer, footed, blue.....95.00
Creamer, footed, Monax.....8.50
Creamer, footed, pink 13.00
Creamer, footed, ruby red 93.00
Cup, Monax 9.00
Cup, pink 13.50
Cup & saucer, ruby red.....118.00
Lamp shade, Monax.....545.00
Pitcher, 7½" h., 60 oz., jug-type, pink 530.00
Pitcher, 8" h., 80 oz., pink.....440.00

Plate, bread & butter, 6" d., Monax or pink 4.50
Plate, salad, 8" d., blue 84.00
Plate, salad, 8" d., Monax 8.00
Plate, salad, 8" d., pink 11.00
Plate, salad, 8" d., ruby red 64.00
Plate, luncheon, 9" d., Monax 10.00
Plate, dinner, 9¾" d., Monax 22.00
Plate, dinner, 9¾" d., pink 30.00
Plate, dinner, 10¼" d., Monax 21.00
Plate, dinner, 10¼" d., pink 30.00
Plate, chop, 11" d., Monax 13.50
Plate, salver, 12" d., Monax 16.00
Plate, salver, 12" d., pink (ILLUS.) 15.00
Plate, salver, 12" d., ruby red 170.00
Plate, 15½" d., w/center handle, Monax 205.00
Platter, 13" oval, Monax 55.00
Platter, 13" oval, pink 40.00
Salt & pepper shakers, footed, Monax, pr. 270.00
Salt & pepper shakers, footed, pink, pr. 330.00
Saucer, Monax or pink 3.00
Sherbet, footed, pink, 3¾" h. 18.50
Sherbet, footed, Monax, 4¼" h. 19.00
Sherbet, footed, pink, 4¼" h. 13.50
Sherbet, metal holder, clear 6.00
Sugar bowl, cov., Monax (only) 265.00
Sugar bowl, open, Monax 7.50
Sugar bowl, open, pink 10.00
Sugar bowl, open, ruby red 100.00
Tidbit server, two-tier, Monax 70.00
Tidbit server, two-tier, pink 56.00
Tidbit server, two-tier, ruby red 220.00
Tumbler, pink, 3½" h., 5 oz. 67.00
Tumbler, pink, 4½" h., 9 oz. 68.00
Tumbler, pink, 4¾" h., 10 oz. 73.50

BLOCK or Block Optic (Press-mold)

Block Butter Dish

Bowl, berry, 4¼" d., green 6.50
Bowl, 4½" d., green 27.00
Bowl, cereal, 5¼" d., green 11.50
Bowl, cereal, 5¼" d., pink 19.50
Bowl, salad, 7" d., green 25.00
Bowl, large berry, 8½" d., green 22.00
Bowl, large berry, 8½" d., pink 19.00
Butter dish, cov., rectangular, green, 3 x 5" (ILLUS.) 42.00
Candlesticks, amber, 1¾" h., pr. 92.00
Candlesticks, green, 1¾" h., pr. 105.00
Candlesticks, pink, 1¾" h., pr. 67.00
Candy jar, cov., green, 2¼" h. 41.00
Candy jar, cov., pink, 2¼" h. 36.50
Candy jar, cov., yellow, 2¼" h. 48.00
Candy jar, cov., clear, 6¼" h. 24.50
Candy jar, cov., green, 6¼" h. 48.00
Candy jar, cov., pink, 6¼" h. 110.00
Compote, 4" d., cone-shaped, green 23.50
Creamer, various styles, green 14.00
Creamer, various styles, pink 9.00
Creamer, various styles, yellow 11.50
Cup, various styles, green 6.00
Cup, various styles, pink or yellow 7.00
Goblet, cocktail, pink, 4" h. 26.00
Goblet, wine, clear, 4½" h. 14.00
Goblet, wine, green or pink, 4½" h. 38.50
Goblet, clear, 5¾" h., 9 oz. 13.00
Goblet, green, 5¾" h., 9 oz. 19.50
Goblet, pink, 5¾" h., 9 oz. 26.00
Goblet, yellow, 5¾" h., 9 oz. 30.00
Goblet, clear, 7¼" h., 9 oz. 9.00
Goblet, green, 7¼" h., 9 oz. 21.00
Goblet, pink, 7¼" h., 9 oz. 18.00
Goblet, yellow, 7¼" h., 9 oz. 29.00
Ice bucket, w/metal bail handle, clear 17.50
Ice bucket, w/metal bail handle, green 35.00
Ice bucket, w/metal bail handle, pink 61.00
Ice tub, tab handles, green 40.00
Ice tub, tab handles, pink 76.00
Mug, green 32.00
Pitcher, 8" h., 80 oz., clear 25.00
Pitcher, 8" h., 80 oz., green 67.00
Pitcher, 8½" h., 54 oz., clear 16.00
Pitcher, 8½" h., 54 oz., green 42.00
Pitcher, 8½" h., 54 oz., pink 36.00
Plate, sherbet, 6" d., clear, green or pink 2.50
Plate, sherbet, 6" d., yellow 3.00
Plate, luncheon, 8" d., clear 3.50
Plate, luncheon, 8" d., green 4.50
Plate, luncheon, 8" d., pink or yellow 5.50
Plate, dinner, 9" d., green 16.00
Plate, dinner, 9" d., pink 21.00
Plate, dinner, 9" d., yellow 24.50
Plate, grill, 9" d., green 15.50
Plate, sandwich, 10¼" d., clear 15.50
Plate, sandwich, 10¼" d., green 21.00
Salt & pepper shakers, squat, green, pr. 71.00
Salt & pepper shakers, footed, clear, pr. 22.00
Salt & pepper shakers, footed, green, pr. 31.00
Salt & pepper shakers, footed, pink, pr. 73.00
Salt & pepper shakers, footed, yellow, pr. 65.00
Sandwich server w/center handle, green 42.00
Sandwich server w/center handle, pink 48.00

Saucer, green, 5¾" d. 10.50
Saucer, pink, 5¾" d. 6.00
Saucer, green, 6⅛" d. 8.50
Saucer, pink, 6⅛" d. 5.00
Saucer, yellow, 6⅛" d. 7.00
Sherbet, cone-shaped, footed, green 4.50
Sherbet, stemmed, clear, 3¼" h., 5½ oz. 3.00
Sherbet, stemmed, green, 3¼" h., 5½ oz. 5.00
Sherbet, stemmed, pink or yellow, 3¼" h., 5½ oz. 6.50
Sherbet, stemmed, clear, 4¾" h., 6 oz. 6.00
Sherbet, stemmed, green, pink or yellow, 4¾" h., 6 oz. 12.50
Sugar bowl, open, various styles, clear .. 7.00
Sugar bowl, open, various styles, green, pink or yellow 10.50
Tumbler, whiskey, pink, 1⅝" h., 1 oz. ... 32.00
Tumbler, whiskey, clear, 2¼" h., 2 oz. 8.00
Tumbler, whiskey, green, 2¼" h., 2 oz. 26.00
Tumbler, whiskey, pink, 2¼" h., 2 oz. ... 32.00
Tumbler, footed, green, 2⅝" h., 3 oz. ... 20.00
Tumbler, footed, pink, 2⅝" h., 3 oz. 30.00
Tumbler, juice, green, 3½" h., 5 oz. 17.50
Tumbler, juice, pink, 3½" h., 5 oz. 20.00
Tumbler, footed, clear, 9 oz. 5.00
Tumbler, footed, green, 9 oz. 16.50
Tumbler, footed, pink or yellow, 9 oz. ... 15.00
Tumbler, green, 3⅞" h., 9½ oz. 18.00
Tumbler, pink, 3⅞" h., 9½ oz. 11.00
Tumbler, iced tea, footed, green, 6" h., 10 oz. 26.00
Tumbler, iced tea, footed, pink, 6" h., 10 oz. 19.50
Tumbler, green, 5" h., 10 to 11 oz. 15.50
Tumbler, pink, 5" h., 10 to 11 oz. 14.50
Tumbler, green, 4⅞" h., 12 oz. 22.50
Tumbler, pink, 4⅞" h., 12 oz. 19.00
Tumbler, green, 5¼" h., 15 oz. 33.00
Tumbler, pink, 5¼" h., 15 oz. 30.00
Tumble-up bottle, green 14.50
Tumble-up set: bottle & 3" h. tumbler; green, 2 pcs. 52.00
Vase, 5¾" h., green 275.00

BUBBLE, Bullseye or Provincial (Press-mold)

Bowl, berry, 4" d., blue 15.00
Bowl, berry, 4" d., clear or milk white 3.00
Bowl, berry, 4" d., green 9.50
Bowl, fruit, 4½" d., blue 9.50
Bowl, fruit, 4½" d., clear or milk white 3.50
Bowl, fruit, 4½" d., green or ruby red 7.50
Bowl, cereal, 5¼" d., blue 10.50
Bowl, cereal, 5¼" d., clear 8.00
Bowl, cereal, 5¼" d., green 12.00
Bowl, soup, 7¾" d., blue 13.00
Bowl, soup, 7¾" d., clear 7.00
Bowl, soup, 7¾" d., pink 10.00
Bowl, 8⅜" d., blue 13.50
Bowl, 8⅜" d., clear or milk white 7.50
Bowl, 8⅜" d., green 14.00
Bowl, 8⅜" d., ruby red 24.00
Candlesticks, clear, pr. 12.00
Creamer, blue 29.00
Creamer, clear 6.00
Creamer, green 11.50
Creamer, milk white 4.00
Cup, blue 3.50
Cup, green 7.00
Cup, ruby red 6.50
Cup & saucer, clear 3.50
Cup & saucer, milk white 3.00
Lamps, clear (electric), pr. 56.00
Pitcher w/ice lip, 64 oz., clear 65.00
Pitcher w/ice lip, 64 oz., ruby red 48.00
Plate, bread & butter, 6¾" d., blue 3.50
Plate, bread & butter, 6¾" d., clear 2.00
Plate, bread & butter, 6¾" d., green 4.50
Plate, dinner, 9⅜" d., blue 6.00
Plate, dinner, 9⅜" d., clear 4.50
Plate, dinner, 9⅜" d., green 15.00
Plate, dinner, 9⅜" d., ruby red 12.50
Plate, grill, 9⅜" d., blue 16.50
Plate, grill, 9⅜" d., clear 7.50
Platter, 12" oval, blue 13.00
Platter, 12" oval, clear 11.50
Saucer, blue, green or ruby red 3.50
Sugar bowl, open, blue 17.50
Sugar bowl, open, clear 6.00
Sugar bowl, open, green 10.50
Sugar bowl, open, milk white 4.50
Tidbit server, two-tier, blue 44.00
Tumbler, juice, green, 6 oz. 10.50
Tumbler, juice, ruby red, 6 oz. 7.00
Tumbler, old fashioned, clear, 3¼" h., 8 oz. 6.00
Tumbler, old fashioned, ruby red, 3¼" h., 8 oz. 13.00
Tumbler, water, clear, 9 oz. 8.00
Tumbler, water, ruby red, 9 oz. 9.50
Tumbler, iced tea, clear, 4½" h., 12 oz. . 10.50

Bubble Iced Tea Tumbler

Tumbler, iced tea, ruby red, 4½" h., 12 oz. (ILLUS.) 9.00
Tumbler, lemonade, clear, 5⅞" h., 16 oz. 13.00

Tumbler, lemonade, ruby red, 5⅞" h., 16 oz. 16.00
Water set: pitcher & 8 tumblers; ruby red, 9 pcs. 130.00

CAMEO or Ballerina or Dancing Girl (Process-etched)

Bowl, sauce, 4¼" d., clear 6.50
Bowl, cream soup, 4¾" d., green....98.00
Bowl, cereal, 5½" d., clear 6.50
Bowl, cereal, 5½" d., green....27.00
Bowl, cereal, 5½" d., yellow....29.00
Bowl, salad, 7¼" d., green....54.00
Bowl, large berry, 8¼" d., green 35.00
Bowl, soup w/flange rim, 9" d., green ...47.00
Bowl, 10" oval vegetable, green 22.50
Bowl, 10" oval vegetable, yellow 37.00
Butter dish, cov., green....175.00

Cameo Footed Cake Plate

Cake plate, three-footed, green,10" d. (ILLUS.) 19.00
Candlesticks, green, 4" h., pr....100.00
Candy jar, cov., green, 4" h. 58.00
Candy jar, cov., yellow, 4" h. 64.00
Candy jar, cov., green, 6½" h. 160.00
Compote, mayonnaise, 5" d., 4" h., cone-shaped, green 28.00
Console bowl, three-footed, green, 11" d. 63.00
Console bowl, three-footed, pink, 11" d. 46.00
Console bowl, three-footed, yellow, 11" d. 75.00
Cookie jar, cov., green....44.00
Creamer, green, 3¼" h. 20.00
Creamer, yellow, 3¼" h. 16.00
Creamer, green, 4¼" h. 21.00
Creamer, pink, 4¼" h. 65.00
Cup, clear 5.50
Cup, green....13.50
Cup, yellow 7.50
Decanter w/stopper, green, 10" h. 135.00
Decanter w/stopper, green frosted, 10" h. 35.00
Domino tray, clear, 7" d. 85.00
Domino tray, green, 7" d. 145.00
Goblet, wine, green, 4" h. 59.00
Goblet, water, green, 6" h. 51.00
Goblet, water, pink, 6" h. 167.00
Ice bowl, tab handles, green, 5½" d., 3½" h. 165.00
Jam jar, cov., closed handles, green, 2" 155.00
Pitcher, syrup or milk, 5¾" h., 20 oz., green 200.00
Pitcher, juice, 6" h., 36 oz., green....48.00
Pitcher, water, 8½" h., 56 oz., jug-type, green 50.00
Plate, sherbet (or ringless saucer), 6" d., clear 2.00
Plate, sherbet (or ringless saucer), 6" d., green or yellow 3.50
Plate, salad, 7" d., clear....4.00
Plate, luncheon, 8" d., green or yellow 10.50
Plate, 8½" sq., green 37.00
Plate, dinner, 9½" d., green 15.50
Plate, dinner, 9½" d., yellow 7.50
Plate, sandwich, 10" d., green....14.00
Plate, sandwich, 10" d., pink....57.00
Plate, dinner, 10½" d., trimmed, green 12.50
Plate, 10½" d., closed handles, green 14.50
Plate, 10½" d., closed handles, yellow 24.00
Plate, grill, 10½" d., green 9.00
Plate, grill, 10½" d., yellow....6.50
Plate, grill, 10½" d., closed handles, green 78.00
Plate, grill, 10½" d., closed handles, yellow 6.50
Platter, 10½" oval, green 18.00
Platter, 10½" oval, yellow 36.00
Platter, 12", closed handles, green....21.00
Platter, 12", closed handles,yellow....36.00
Relish, footed, three-part, green, 7½"...25.00
Salt & pepper shakers, green, pr. 64.00
Salt & pepper shakers, pink, pr. 950.00
Saucer w/cup ring, green....155.00
Sherbet, green, 3⅛" h. 13.00
Sherbet, pink, 3⅛" h. 83.00
Sherbet, yellow, 3⅛" h. 35.00
Sherbet, thin, high stem, green, 4⅞" h. 26.00
Sherbet, thin, high stem, yellow, 4 ⅞" h. 30.00
Sugar bowl, open, green, 3¼" h. 15.50
Sugar bowl, open, yellow, 3¼" h. 13.00
Sugar bowl, open, green, 4¼" h. 20.00
Sugar bowl, open, pink, 4¼" h. 67.50
Tumbler, juice, footed, green, 3 oz. 61.00
Tumbler, juice, green, 3¾" h.,5 oz. 25.00
Tumbler, juice, pink, 3¾" h., 5 oz. 185.00
Tumbler, water, clear, 4" h., 9 oz. 10.00
Tumbler, water, green, 4" h., 9 oz. 25.00
Tumbler, water, pink, 4" h., 9 oz. 95.00
Tumbler, footed, green, 5" h., 9 oz. 25.00
Tumbler, footed, yellow, 5" h., 9 oz. 14.50

Tumbler, green, 4¾" h., 10 oz. 21.50
Tumbler, yellow, 4¾" h., 10 oz. 83.00
Tumbler, green, 5" h., 11 oz. 27.50
Tumbler, yellow, 5" h., 11 oz. 58.00
Tumbler, footed, green, 5¾" h., 11 oz. 56.00
Tumbler, green, 5¼" h., 15 oz. 46.00
Vase, 5¾" h., green 160.00
Vase, 8" h., green 27.50
Water bottle, dark green "White House Vinegar" base, 8½" h. 18.50

CHERRY BLOSSOM (Process-etched)

Cherry Blossom Pattern

Bowl, berry, 4¾" d., Delphite or pink 13.50
Bowl, berry, 4¾" d., green 15.50
Bowl, cereal, 5¾"d., green 30.00
Bowl, cereal, 5¾" d., pink 31.00
Bowl, soup, 7¾" d., green 54.00
Bowl, soup, 7¾" d., pink 57.00
Bowl, berry, 8½" d., Delphite 35.50
Bowl, berry, 8½" d., green 40.00
Bowl, berry, 8½" d., pink 41.00
Bowl, 9" d., two-handled, Delphite.....30.00
Bowl, 9" d., two-handled, green 27.50
Bowl, 9" d., two-handled, pink 26.00
Bowl, 9" oval vegetable, Delphite 38.00
Bowl, 9" oval vegetable, green 35.00
Bowl, 9" oval vegetable, pink 30.00
Bowl, fruit, 10½" d., three-footed, green or pink 72.00
Butter dish, cov., green 79.00
Butter dish, cov., pink 67.00
Cake plate, three-footed, green, 10¼" d. 22.50
Cake plate, three-footed, pink, 10¼" d. 25.00
Coaster, green 11.50
Coaster, pink 17.50
Creamer, Delphite or pink 17.50
Creamer, green 16.50
Cup, Delphite 18.00
Cup, green 17.00
Cup, pink 15.00
Mug, green, 7 oz. 195.00
Mug, pink, 7 oz. 180.00
Pitcher, 6¾" h., 36 oz., overall patt., Delphite 77.00
Pitcher, 6¾" h., 36 oz., overall patt., green 56.00
Pitcher, 6¾" h., 36 oz., overall patt., pink 54.00
Pitcher, 8" h., 36 oz., footed, cone-shaped, patt. top, Delphite 66.00
Pitcher, 8" h., 36 oz., footed, cone-shaped, patt. top, green 52.00
Pitcher, 8" h., 36 oz., footed, cone-shaped, patt. top, pink 48.50
Pitcher, 8" h., 42 oz., patt. top, green (ILLUS.) 51.00
Pitcher, 8" h., 42 oz., patt. top,pink 51.00
Plate, sherbet, 6" d., Delphite 8.50
Plate, sherbet, 6" d., green 6.00
Plate, sherbet, 6" d., pink 7.00
Plate, salad, 7" d., green or pink 18.00
Plate, dinner, 9" d., Delphite 17.50
Plate, dinner, 9" d., green or pink 20.00
Plate, grill, 9" d., green 21.00
Plate, grill, 9" d., pink.....22.00
Platter, 11" oval, green or pink 31.00
Platter, 13" oval, green 51.00
Platter, 13" oval, pink 49.00
Platter, 13" oval, divided, green 52.00
Platter, 13" oval, divided, pink 58.00
Salt & pepper shakers, green, pr. ...1,085.00
Sandwich tray, handled, Delphite or green, 10½" d. 21.00
Sandwich tray, handled, pink,10½"d. ..19.50
Saucer, Delphite or green 4.00
Saucer, pink 5.50
Sherbet, Delphite 12.00
Sherbet, green or pink 15.00
Sugar bowl, cov., clear 15.00
Sugar bowl, cov., Delphite 35.00
Sugar bowl, cov., green 32.00
Sugar bowl, cov., pink 27.50
Sugar bowl, open, Delphite 17.50
Sugar bowl, open, green or pink 13.00
Tumbler, patt. top, green, 3½" h.,4 oz. (ILLUS. right) 21.50
Tumbler, patt. top, pink, 3½" h., 4 oz. 16.50
Tumbler, juice, footed, overall patt., Delphite, 3¾" h., 4 oz. 18.00
Tumbler, juice, footed, overall patt., green or pink, 3¾" h., 4 oz. 16.00
Tumbler, footed, overall patt., Delphite, 4½" h., 8 oz. 20.00
Tumbler, footed, overall patt., green, 4½" h., 8 oz. 28.50
Tumbler, footed, overall patt., pink, 4½" h., 8 oz. 26.00
Tumbler, patt. top, green, 4¼" h., 9 oz. (ILLUS. left).....20.00
Tumbler, patt. top, pink, 4¼" h., 9 oz....17.50
Tumbler, footed, overall patt., Delphite, 4½" h., 9 oz. 19.00
Tumbler, footed, overall patt., green, 4½" h., 9 oz. 29.00

Tumbler, footed, overall patt., pink, 4½" h., 9 oz. 28.00
Tumbler, patt. top, green, 5"' h., 12 oz. 65.00
Tumbler, patt. top, pink, 5" h., 12 oz. 55.00
Water set: pitcher & 6 tumblers; green, 7 pcs. 165.00

JUNIOR SET:
Creamer, Delphite 36.00
Creamer, pink 38.00
Cup, pink 30.00
Cup & saucer, Delphite 37.00
Plate, 6" d., Delphite 10.50
Plate, 6" d., pink 7.50
Saucer, pink 4.00
Sugar bowl, Delphite or pink 35.00
14 pc. set, Delphite 260.00
14 pc. set, pink 270.00

CLOVERLEAF (Process-etched)

Cloverleaf Sugar Bowl

Ashtray w/match holder in center, black, 4" d. 64.00
Ashtray w/match holder in center, black, 5¾" d. 68.00
Bowl, dessert, 4" d., green 17.50
Bowl, dessert, 4" d., pink 12.50
Bowl, cereal, 5" d., green 23.00
Bowl, cereal, 5" d., yellow 25.00
Bowl, salad, 7" d., deep, green 36.50
Bowl, salad, 7" d., deep, yellow 47.00
Bowl, 8" d., green 47.00
Candy dish, cov., green 45.00
Creamer, footed, black, 3⅝" h. 16.00
Creamer, footed, green, 3⅝" h. 8.50
Creamer, footed, yellow, 3⅝" h. 14.50
Cup, black 13.00
Cup, green or pink 7.00
Cup, yellow 9.00
Plate, sherbet, 6" d., black 30.00
Plate, sherbet, 6" d., green or yellow 5.50
Plate, luncheon, 8" d., black 16.50
Plate, luncheon, 8" d., clear 4.00
Plate, luncheon, 8" d., green or pink 6.50
Plate, luncheon, 8" d., yellow 11.50
Plate, grill, 10¼" d., green 21.50
Salt & pepper shakers, black, pr. 75.00
Salt & pepper shakers, green, pr. 29.00
Salt & pepper shakers, yellow, pr. 86.00
Saucer, black, pink or yellow 4.50
Saucer, green 3.00
Sherbet, footed, black, 3" h. 16.50
Sherbet, footed, clear, 3" h. 3.00
Sherbet, footed, green or pink, 3" h. 5.50
Sherbet, footed, yellow, 3" h. 10.00
Sugar bowl, open, footed, black or yellow, 3⅝" h. 14.50
Sugar bowl, open, footed, green, 3⅝" h. (ILLUS.) 8.00
Tumbler, green, 4" h., 9 oz. 37.50
Tumbler, flared, green, 3¾" h., 10 oz. 32.50
Tumbler, flared, pink, 3¾" h., 10 oz. 20.50
Tumbler, footed, green, 5¾" h., 10 oz. 21.00
Tumbler, footed, yellow, 5¾" h., 10 oz. 27.00

COLONIAL or Knife & Fork, Hocking Glass Co., 1934-36 (Press-mold)

Colonial Cordial & Wine Goblets

Bowl, berry, 3¾" d., pink 40.00
Bowl, berry, 4½" d., clear 5.00
Bowl, berry, 4½" d., green 13.50
Bowl, berry, 4½" d., pink 11.50
Bowl, cream soup, 4½" d., clear 35.00
Bowl, cream soup, 4½" d., green 54.00
Bowl, cream soup, 4½" d., pink 48.00
Bowl, cereal, 5½" d., green 66.00
Bowl, soup, 7" d., green 48.50
Bowl, soup, 7" d., pink 51.50
Bowl, 9" d., clear 13.50
Bowl, 9" d., green or pink 25.00
Bowl, 10" oval vegetable, clear 17.00
Bowl, 10" oval vegetable, green 31.50
Bowl, 10" oval vegetable, pink 26.00
Butter dish, cov., clear 34.00
Butter dish, cov., green 52.50
Celery or spooner, clear 61.00
Celery or spooner, green 115.00
Celery or spooner, pink 104.50
Creamer or milk pitcher, clear, 5" h., 16 oz. 14.00
Creamer or milk pitcher, green, 5" h., 16 oz. 20.50
Cup, clear 7.00
Cup green 10.00
Cup, pink 10.50
Cup & saucer, clear 9.00
Cup & saucer, milk white 9.50
Goblet, cordial, clear, 3¾" h., 1 oz. 15.00

Goblet, cordial, green, 3¾" h., 1 oz. (ILLUS. left) 26.50
Goblet, wine, clear, 4½" h., 2½ oz. 15.50
Goblet, wine, green, 4½" h., 2½ oz. (ILLUS. right) 23.50
Goblet, cocktail, clear, 4" h., 3 oz. 12.00
Goblet, cocktail, green, 4" h., 3 oz. 22.50
Goblet, claret, clear, 5¼" h., 4 oz. 14.50
Goblet, claret, green, 5¼" h., 4 oz. 24.00
Goblet, clear, 5¾" h., 8½ oz. 14.50
Goblet, green, 5¾" h., 8½ oz. 25.50
Mug, green, 4½" h., 12 oz. 750.00
Pitcher, ice lip or plain, 7" h., 54 oz., clear 23.50
Pitcher, ice lip or plain, 7" h., 54 oz., green 44.00
Pitcher, ice lip or plain, 7" h., 54 oz., pink 49.50
Pitcher, ice lip or plain, 7¾" h., 68 oz., clear 122.50

Colonial Pitcher

Pitcher, ice lip or plain, 7¾" h., 68 oz., green (ILLUS. w/ice lip) 57.50
Pitcher, ice lip or plain, 7¾" h., 68 oz., pink 53.00
Plate, sherbet, 6" d., clear 3.50
Plate, sherbet, 6" d., green or pink 5.00
Plate, luncheon, 8½" d., clear 4.00
Plate, luncheon, 8½" d., green 8.00
Plate, luncheon, 8½" d., pink 9.00
Plate, dinner, 10" d., clear 21.50
Plate, dinner, 10" d., green 50.50
Plate, dinner, 10" d., pink 45.00
Plate, grill, 10" d., clear 12.00
Plate, grill, 10" d., green 24.50
Plate, grill, 10" d., pink 23.00
Platter, 12" oval, clear 16.50
Platter, 12" oval, green 22.50
Platter, 12" oval, pink 27.00
Salt & pepper shakers, clear, pr. 46.00
Salt & pepper shakers, pink, pr. 112.00
Saucer, green 5.50
Saucer, pink 6.00
Sherbet, pink, 3" h. 18.50
Sherbet, clear, 3⅜" h. 5.50
Sherbet, green, 3⅜" h. 12.50
Sherbet, pink, 3⅜" h. 10.00
Sugar bowl, cov., clear 19.00
Sugar bowl, cov., green 30.50
Sugar bowl, cov., pink 46.00
Tumbler, whiskey, clear, 2½" h., 1½ oz. 7.00
Tumbler, whiskey, green, 2½" h., 1½ oz. 12.00
Tumbler, whiskey, pink, 2½" h., 1½ oz. 10.50
Tumbler, cordial, footed, clear, 3¼" h., 3 oz. 11.00
Tumbler, cordial, footed, green, 3¼" h., 3 oz. 22.50
Tumbler, cordial, footed, pink, 3¼" h., 3 oz 15.00
Tumbler, juice, green, 3" h., 5 oz. 22.00
Tumbler, juice, pink, 3" h., 5 oz. 15.50
Tumbler, footed, clear, 4" h., 5 oz. 14.00
Tumbler, footed, green, 4" h., 5 oz. 34.50
Tumbler, footed, pink, 4" h., 5 oz. 23.50
Tumbler, water, clear, 4" h., 9 oz. 12.00
Tumbler, water, green, 4" h., 9 oz. 21.00
Tumbler, water, pink, 4" h., 9 oz. 18.50
Tumbler, footed, clear, 5¼" h., 10 oz. 22.50
Tumbler, footed, green, 5¼" h., 10 oz. 41.00
Tumbler, footed, pink, 5¼" h., 10 oz. 38.00
Tumbler, pink, 5⅛" h., 11 oz. 31.50
Tumbler, iced tea, green, 12 oz. 32.00
Tumbler, iced tea, pink, 12 oz. 45.00
Tumbler, lemonade, green, 15 oz. 72.50
Tumbler, lemonade, pink, 15 oz. 60.00

COLUMBIA, Federal Glass Co., 1938-42 (Press-mold)

Bowl, cereal, 5" d., clear 13.00
Bowl, soup, 8" d., clear 16.00
Bowl, salad, 8½" d., clear 17.00
Bowl, 10½" d., ruffled rim, clear 18.00
Butter dish, cov., clear 16.50
Cup & saucer, clear 10.00
Plate, bread & butter, 6" d., clear 3.00
Plate, bread & butter, 6" d., pink 14.50
Plate, luncheon, 9½" d., clear 8.00
Plate, luncheon, 9½" d., pink 33.00
Plate, chop, 11" d., clear 10.50
Saucer, pink 12.50
Snack plate, handled, clear 29.00
Snack plate, handled, w/cup, clear 38.50
Tumbler, juice, 2⅞" h., 4 oz., clear 10.00
Tumbler, water, clear, 9 oz. 25.00

CUBE or Cubist, Jeannette Glass Co., 1929-33 (Press-mold)

Bowl, dessert, 4½" d., clear 3.50
Bowl, dessert, 4½" d., green 6.50
Bowl, dessert, 4½" d., pink 5.00
Bowl, 4½" d., deep, clear 3.50
Bowl, 4½" d., deep, green 4.50
Bowl, 4½" d., deep, pink 6.50
Bowl, salad, 6½" d., clear 5.00

Bowl, salad, 6½" d., green.....11.50
Bowl, salad, 6½" d., pink 9.50
Bowl, salad, 6½" d., ultramarine.....55.00
Butter dish, cov., green.....50.00
Butter dish, cov., pink 51.50
Candy jar, cov., green, 6½" h. 25.50
Candy jar, cov., pink, 6½" h.....23.50
Coaster, green, 3¼" d.....6.50
Coaster, pink, 3¼" d. 5.50
Creamer, clear, 2⅝" h.....1.00

Cube Creamer

Creamer, pink, 2⅝" h. (ILLUS.) 3.50
Creamer, green, 3½" h. 8.00
Creamer, pink, 3½" h.....5.50
Cup & saucer, green.....17.00
Cup & saucer, pink 9.50
Pitcher, 8¾" h., 45 oz., green 211.00
Pitcher, 8¾" h., 45 oz., pink.....139.00
Plate, sherbet, 6" d., clear 1.00
Plate, sherbet, 6" d., green or pink 3.00
Plate, luncheon, 8" d., green or pink 5.50
Powder jar, cov., three-footed, green ...18.50
Powder jar, cov., three-footed, pink.....21.50
Salt & pepper shakers, green or pink, pr.....31.00
Sherbet, footed, green.....7.00
Sherbet, footed, pink 5.50
Sugar bowl, cov., green, 3" h.....18.50
Sugar bowl, cov., pink, 3" h. 16.00
Sugar bowl, open, clear, 2⅜" h.....1.00
Sugar bowl, open, green, 2⅜" h 4.00

Cube Sugar Bowl

Sugar bowl, open, pink, 2⅜" h. (ILLUS.) 3.00
Tray for 3½" h. creamer & open sugar bowl, clear, 7½" 4.00
Tumbler, green, 4" h., 9 oz. 59.50
Tumbler, pink, 4" h., 9 oz.....45.00

DAISY or Number 620, Indiana Glass Co., amber, 1940; clear, 1933 & red, late 1930s (Press-mold)

Daisy Vegetable Bowl

Bowl, berry, 4½" d., amber 7.50
Bowl, berry, 4½" d., clear.....5.00
Bowl, cream soup, 4½" d., amber.....9.50
Bowl, cream soup, 4½" d., clear.....6.50
Bowl, cereal, 6" d., amber.....25.00
Bowl, cereal, 6" d., clear 9.00
Bowl, berry, 7⅜" d., amber 15.00
Bowl, berry, 7⅜" d., clear.....6.00
Bowl, berry, 9⅜" d., amber 25.00
Bowl, 10" oval vegetable, amber (ILLUS.) 14.00
Creamer, footed, amber 6.50
Creamer, footed, clear.....4.50
Cup, amber.....5.50
Cup & saucer, clear.....3.50
Plate, sherbet, 6" d., amber.....2.50
Plate, salad, 7⅜" d., amber 7.50
Plate, salad, 7⅜" d., clear.....4.50
Plate, luncheon, 8⅜" d., amber 5.50
Plate, luncheon, 8⅜" d., clear.....3.50
Plate, dinner, 9⅜" d., amber.....7.50
Plate, dinner, 9⅜" d., clear 5.00
Plate, grill, 10⅜" d., amber 11.00
Plate, grill, 10⅜" d., clear.....6.50
Plate, 11½" d., amber (cake or sandwich).....12.50
Plate, 11½" d., clear (cake or sandwich).....11.00
Platter, 10¾" l., amber.....13.00
Relish dish, three-part, amber, 8⅜".....25.00
Relish dish, three-part, clear, 8⅜" 8.00
Saucer, amber 2.00
Sherbet, footed, amber.....7.00
Sherbet, footed, clear 4.00
Sugar bowl, open, footed, amber 7.00
Sugar bowl, open, footed, clear.....4.00
Tumbler, footed, amber, 9 oz. 17.50
Tumbler, footed, clear, 9 oz. 8.00
Tumbler, footed, amber, 12 oz. 35.50
Tumbler, footed, clear, 12 oz. 19.00

DIAMOND QUILTED or Flat Diamond, Imperial Glass Co., late 1920s - early 1930s (Press-mold)

Bowl, cream soup, 4¾" d., black 17.50

Bowl, cream soup, 4¾" d., blue 15.00
Bowl, cream soup, 4¾" d., green or pink 8.50
Bowl, 5½" d., single handle, black 15.00
Bowl, 5½" d., single handle, pink 7.00
Bowl, 7" d., crimped rim, black 21.50
Bowl, 7" d., crimped rim, blue 15.50
Bowl, 7" d., crimped rim, green 9.50
Bowl, 7" d., crimped rim, pink 8.00
Bowl, 7" d., crimped rim, red 18.00
Candlesticks, flat or domed base, black, pr. 35.00
Candlesticks, flat or domed base, green, pr. 23.50
Candlesticks, flat or domed base, pink, pr. 19.00
Candy jar, cov., footed, pink 85.00
Compote, open, 6" h., 7¼" d., green 40.00
Console bowl, rolled edge, pink 33.00
Creamer, black 16.50
Creamer, blue 13.50
Creamer, green 7.50
Creamer, pink 8.50
Cup & saucer, amber 7.50
Cup & saucer, green 10.00
Cup & saucer, pink 12.00
Ice bucket, black 72.50
Mayonnaise dish, three-footed w/plate, green, 2 pcs. 27.00
Pitcher, 64 oz., green 42.00
Plate, sherbet, 6" d., blue 4.50
Plate, sherbet, 6" d., green or pink 3.50
Plate, salad, 7" d., green 5.00
Plate, luncheon, 8" d., black 12.00
Plate, luncheon, 8" d., blue 13.50
Plate, luncheon, 8" d., green or pink 5.50
Plate, sandwich, 14" d., pink 18.00
Sherbet, black or blue 10.50
Sherbet, green 5.00
Sherbet, pink 6.50
Sugar bowl, open, amber 8.00
Sugar bowl, open, black or blue 14.50
Sugar bowl, open, green 7.50
Sugar bowl, open, pink 8.50
Tumbler, whiskey, green, 1½ oz. 6.50
Tumbler, iced tea, green, 12 oz. 9.00

DIANA, Federal Glass Co., 1937-41 (Press-mold)

Bowl, cereal, 5" d., amber 11.00
Bowl, cereal, 5" d., clear 3.50
Bowl, cereal, 5" d., pink 7.50
Bowl, cream soup, 5½" d., amber 14.00
Bowl, cream soup, 5½" d., clear or pink 4.00
Bowl, salad, 9" d., amber 11.00
Bowl, salad, 9" d., clear 5.00
Bowl, salad, 9" d., pink 19.00
Bowl, 12" d., scalloped rim, clear 7.50
Bowl, 12" d., scalloped rim, pink 15.00
Candy jar, cov., round, amber or pink ..31.00
Candy jar, cov., round, clear 13.00
Coaster, amber, 3½" d. 13.00
Coaster, clear, 3½" d. 4.50
Coaster, pink, 3½" d. 6.50
Console bowl, amber, 11" d. 12.00
Console bowl, clear, 11" d. 6.00
Console bowl, pink, 11" d. 8.00
Creamer, oval, amber 8.00
Creamer, oval, clear 3.00

Diana Demitasse Cup & Saucer

Cup & saucer, demitasse, clear (ILLUS.) 10.00
Cup & saucer, demitasse, pink 40.00
Cup & saucer, amber 8.00
Cup & saucer, clear 4.50
Cup & saucer, pink 15.00
Plate, bread & butter, 6" d., amber or clear 1.50
Plate, bread & butter, 6" d., pink 3.00
Plate, dinner, 9½" d., amber 7.50
Plate, dinner, 9½" d., clear 5.00
Plate, dinner, 9½" d., pink 13.00
Plate, sandwich, 11¾" d., amber 10.50
Plate, sandwich, 11¾" d., clear 5.00
Plate, sandwich, 11¾" d., pink 18.00
Platter, 12" oval, amber 11.00
Platter, 12" oval, clear 4.50
Salt & pepper shakers, amber, pr. 89.00
Salt & pepper shakers, clear, pr. 22.00
Salt & pepper shakers, pink, pr. 73.00
Sherbet, amber or pink 10.00
Sugar bowl, open, oval, amber or pink 7.50
Sugar bowl, open, oval, clear 2.00
Tumbler, amber, 4⅛" h., 9 oz. 22.00
Tumbler, clear, 4⅛" h., 9 oz. 25.00
Junior set: 6 cups, saucers & plates w/round rack; clear, set 76.50
Child's cup, clear 4.50
Child's cup & saucer, clear 11.00

DOGWOOD or Apple Blossom or Wild Rose, MacBeth-Evans, 1929-32 (Process-etched)

Bowl, cereal, 5½" d., green or pink 23.50
Bowl, berry, 8½" d., Cremax 31.00
Bowl, berry, 8½" d., green 85.00
Bowl, berry, 8½" d., Monax 44.00
Bowl, berry, 8½" d., pink 53.50
Bowl, fruit, 10½" d., green 133.00

Bowl, fruit, 10½" d., pink.....370.00
Cake plate, heavy solid foot, green, 13" d.....77.50
Creamer, thin, green, 2½" h. 37.00
Creamer, thin, footed, pink, 2¼" h.....17.50
Creamer, thick, footed, pink, 3¼" h. 18.00
Cup & saucer, green.....30.50
Cup & saucer, Monax.....39.00

Dogwood Pattern

Cup & saucer, pink (ILLUS.).....19.00
Pitcher, 8" h., 80 oz., American Sweetheart style, pink.....565.00
Pitcher, 8" h., 80 oz., decorated, green.....415.00
Pitcher, 8" h., 80 oz., decorated, pink 165.00
Plate, bread & butter, 6" d., green 4.50
Plate, bread & butter, 6" d., pink.....7.00
Plate, luncheon, 8" d., clear.....4.00
Plate, luncheon, 8" d., green 6.50
Plate, luncheon, 8" d., pink.....7.50
Plate, dinner, 9¼" d., pink.....28.50
Plate, grill, 10½" d., overall patt. or border design only, green 15.00
Plate, grill, 10½" d., border design, pink 16.00
Plate, grill, 10½" d., overall patt., pink (ILLUS.) 17.50
Plate, salver, 12" d., Monax.....20.50
Plate, salver, 12" d., pink.....31.00
Platter, 12" oval, pink.....400.00
Sherbet, low foot, green 40.00
Sherbet, low foot, pink.....27.00
Sugar bowl, open, thin, green, 2½" h.....40.00
Sugar bowl, open, thin, pink, 2½" h. 15.00
Sugar bowl, open, thick, footed, pink, 3¼" h.....15.00
Tumbler, decorated, green, 4" h., 10 oz. 75.00
Tumbler, decorated, pink, 4" h., 10 oz. 32.50
Tumbler, decorated, green, 4¾" h., 11 oz. 147.50
Tumbler, decorated, pink, 4¾" h., 11 oz. 46.00
Tumbler, decorated, pink, 5" h., 12 oz. 54.50
Tumbler, molded band, pink.....15.00
Water set: decorated pitcher & 6 decorated tumblers; pink, 7 pcs.....298.00

DORIC, Jeannette Glass Co., 1935-38 (Press-mold)

Doric Salt & Pepper Shakers

Bowl, berry, 4½" d., green or pink 7.00
Bowl, cereal, 5½" d., green.....55.00
Bowl, cereal, 5½" d., pink 44.00
Bowl, large berry, 8¼" d., green 17.50
Bowl, large berry, 8¼" d., pink.....16.50
Bowl, 9" d., two-handled, green or pink 13.50
Bowl, 9" oval vegetable, green 27.00
Bowl, 9" oval vegetable, pink.....24.50
Butter dish, cov., green.....75.00
Butter dish, cov., pink 58.00
Cake plate, three-footed, green, 10" d.....25.50
Cake plate, three-footed, pink, 10" d. ...20.50
Candy dish, three-section, Delphite or green, 6" 10.50
Candy dish, three-section, pink, 6".....9.00
Candy jar, cov., green, 8" h. 37.50
Candy jar, cov., pink, 8" h.....29.00
Coaster, green or pink, 3" d.....20.00
Creamer, green, 4" h. 16.50
Creamer, pink, 4" h.....11.50
Cup, green.....8.50
Cup, pink 10.00
Pitcher, 6" h., 36 oz., green or pink 32.00
Pitcher, 7½" h., 48 oz., footed, pink....425.00
Plate, sherbet, 6" d., green or pink 3.50
Plate, salad, 7" d., green 14.00
Plate, salad, 7" d., pink.....17.50
Plate, dinner, 9" d., green.....14.50
Plate, dinner, 9" d., pink.....13.00
Plate, grill, 9" d., green 15.00
Plate, grill, 9" d., pink.....17.00
Platter, 12" oval, green 21.50
Platter, 12" oval, pink.....20.00
Relish tray, green, 4 x 4" 11.50
Relish tray, pink, 4 x 4".....12.50
Relish tray, green, 4 x 8" 14.00
Relish tray, pink, 4 x 8".....11.50

Relish or serving tray, green, 8 x 8".....15.00
Relish or serving tray, pink, 8 x 8".....19.00
Relish, square inserts in metal holder, pink 48.00
Salt & pepper shakers, green, pr. (ILLUS.) 35.50
Salt & pepper shakers, pink, pr. 32.00
Sandwich tray, handled, green or pink, 10" d. 13.00
Saucer, green 4.00
Saucer, pink.....3.50
Sherbet, footed, Delphite.....5.00
Sherbet, footed, green.....12.50
Sherbet, footed, pink 11.00
Sugar bowl, cov., green.....28.50

Doric Sugar Bowl

Sugar bowl, cov., pink (ILLUS.) 23.00
Tumbler, green, 4½" h., 9 oz. 85.50
Tumbler, pink, 4½" h., 9 oz.....59.50
Tumbler, footed, green, 4" h., 10 oz. 52.50
Tumbler, footed, pink, 4" h., 10 oz.....48.00
Tumbler, footed, green, 5" h., 12 oz. 94.00
Tumbler, footed, pink, 5" h., 12 oz.....69.00

DORIC & PANSY, Jeannette Glass Co., 1937-38 (Press-mold)

Doric & Pansy Cup & Saucer

Bowl, berry, 4½" d., clear or pink.....8.00
Bowl, berry, 4½" d., ultramarine 17.00
Bowl, large berry, 8" d., clear.....25.00
Bowl, large berry, 8" d., pink.....18.00
Bowl, large berry, 8" d., ultramarine 68.00
Bowl, 9" d., handled, ultramarine.....35.00
Butter dish, cov., ultramarine.....470.00
Creamer, pink 32.00
Creamer, ultramarine.....160.00
Cup & saucer, clear 14.00
Cup & saucer, ultramarine (ILLUS.) 24.50
Plate, sherbet, 6" d., clear 8.00
Plate, sherbet, 6" d., pink.....6.50
Plate, sherbet, 6" d., ultramarine 10.00
Plate, salad, 7" d., ultramarine.....30.50
Plate, dinner, 9" d., ultramarine 27.50
Salt & pepper shakers, ultramarine, pr. 385.00
Sugar bowl, open, pink 32.00
Sugar bowl, open, ultramarine.....138.00
Tray, handled, ultramarine, 10" 24.00
Tumbler, ultramarine, 4½" h., 9 oz. 74.00

PRETTY POLLY PARTY DISHES
Creamer, pink 28.50
Creamer, ultramarine.....33.50
Cup, ultramarine 29.50
Cup & saucer, pink 33.50
Cup & saucer, ultramarine.....46.00
Plate, pink.....6.50
Plate, ultramarine 12.00
Saucer, pink.....5.50
Saucer, ultramarine 6.50
Sugar bowl, pink 27.50
Sugar bowl, ultramarine.....37.00
14 piece set, pink.....200.00
14 piece set, ultramarine 280.00

ENGLISH HOBNAIL, Westmoreland Glass Co., 1920s - '40s (Handmade - not true Depression)

English Hobnail Salt Dip

Ashtray, clear, various shapes 12.00
Basket, handled, clear, 5" h.....25.00
Bowl, nappy, 4½" d., clear.....7.00
Bowl, nappy, 4½" d., green.....9.50
Bowl, nappy, 4½" d., ice blue 43.00
Bowl, nappy, 4½" sq., clear 5.00
Bowl, nappy, 4½" sq., green.....8.00
Bowl, cream soup, 4¾" d., clear.....6.50
Bowl, cream soup, 4¾" d., green.....20.00
Bowl, 6" d., amber or clear 9.00
Bowl, grapefruit, 6½" d., clear.....14.50
Bowl, fruit, 8" d., two-handled, footed, cobalt blue 120.00

Bowl, fruit, 8" d., two-handled, footed, green....40.00
Bowl, nappy, 8" d., amber....17.00
Bowl, nappy, 8" d., clear....11.50
Bowl, nappy, 11" d., blue....38.00
Bowl, 12" d., flared, green....40.00
Candlesticks, amber, 3½" h., pr....19.00
Candlesticks, blue, 3½" h., pr....33.50
Candlesticks, clear, 3½" h., pr....14.50
Candlesticks, pink, 3½" h., pr....21.00
Candlesticks, clear, 8½" h., pr....58.00
Candlesticks, green, 8½" h., pr....67.50
Candlesticks, pink, 8½" h., pr....40.00
Candlesticks, turquoise, 8½" h., pr....61.00
Candy dish, cov., cone-shaped, amber, ½ lb....40.00
Candy dish, cov., cone-shaped, clear, ½ lb....26.00
Candy dish, cov., cone-shaped, green, ½ lb....61.00
Candy dish, cov., urn-shaped, green, 15" h....300.00
Celery tray, clear, 12" l....17.00
Cigarette box, cov., clear....35.50
Cologne bottle, clear or green....28.00
Cologne bottle, turquoise....36.00
Cologne bottles w/stoppers, blue, pr....55.00
Cologne bottles w/stoppers, cobalt blue, pr....91.50
Creamer, flat or footed, clear....11.00
Cup & saucer, demitasse, clear....25.50
Cup & saucer, clear....8.00
Cup & saucer, turquoise....23.00
Dish, cov., three-footed, amber....60.00
Dish, cov., three-footed, clear....33.00
Dish, cov., three-footed, green....57.00
Egg cup, clear....17.00
Goblet, cordial, clear, 1 oz....16.50
Goblet, wine, clear, 2 oz....17.00
Goblet, cocktail, amber or pink, 3 oz....15.00
Goblet, cocktail, clear, 3 oz....10.00
Goblet, cocktail, green, 3 oz....16.00
Goblet, claret, clear, 5 oz....7.00
Goblet, clear, 6¼ oz....16.00
Goblet, green, 6¼ oz....21.50
Goblet, pink, 6¼ oz....18.00
Goblet, turquoise, 6¼ oz....44.00
Goblet, water, green, 8 oz....22.00
Goblet, water, ice blue, 8 oz....50.00
Hat, high, clear....15.00
Ice tub, clear....65.00
Lamp, electric, clear, 6¼" h....30.50
Lamp, electric, amber, 9¼" h....71.00
Lamp, electric, blue, 9¼" h....85.00
Lamp, electric, clear, 9¼" h....27.00
Lamp, electric, pink, 9¼" h....89.00
Marmalade jar, cov., clear....29.50
Marmalade jar, cov., green....35.00
Marmalade jar, cov., pink....31.50
Oil bottle, clear, 2 oz....17.50
Parfait, footed, round, clear....19.00
Pitcher, 23 oz., clear....75.00
Pitcher, ½ gal., straight sides, clear....169.00
Pitcher, ½ gal., straight sides, green....235.00
Plate, sherbet, 5½" or 6½" d., clear....5.50
Plate, sherbet, 5½" or 6½" d., green....3.50
Plate, sherbet, 5½" or 6½" d., pink....2.50
Plate, luncheon, 8" round or square, amber....10.00
Plate, luncheon, 8" round or square, clear....6.50
Plate, luncheon, 8" round or square, green....9.00
Plate, luncheon, 8" round or square, ice blue....25.00
Plate, luncheon, 8" round or square, pink....8.00
Plate, luncheon, 8" round or square, turquoise....15.00
Plate, dinner, 10" d., clear....7.50
Puff box, cov., clear....27.50
Puff box, cov., green....34.50
Relish dish, three-part, clear, 8" oval....29.00
Rose bowl, clear, 6"....21.00
Salt & pepper shakers, amber, pr....72.50
Salt & pepper shakers, clear, pr....47.00
Salt & pepper shakers, green, pr....74.50
Salt & pepper shakers, turquoise, pr....110.00
Salt dip, footed, amber, 2"....13.00
Salt dip, footed, blue, 2"....10.50
Salt dip, footed, clear, 2"....10.00
Salt dip, footed, cobalt blue, 2"....31.00
Salt dip, footed, green, 2"....14.50
Salt dip, footed, pink, 2" (ILLUS.)....15.00
Salt dip, footed, turquoise, 2"....16.50
Sherbet, footed, amber....12.50
Sherbet, footed, clear....9.00
Sherbet, footed, green....13.00
Sherbet, footed, ice blue....23.00
Sugar bowl, open, footed or flat, clear....12.00
Sugar bowl, open, footed or flat, pink....19.50
Tumbler, whiskey, clear, 1½ oz....8.00
Tumbler, whiskey, clear, 3 oz....15.50
Tumbler, clear, 3¾" h., 5 oz....10.00
Tumbler, footed, clear, 7 oz....11.00
Tumbler, clear, 3¾" h., 9 oz....13.50
Tumbler, footed, clear, 9 oz....12.00
Tumbler, iced tea, clear, 4" h., 10 oz....8.50
Tumbler, iced tea, ice blue, 4" h., 10 oz....48.00
Tumbler, iced tea, clear, 5" h., 12 oz....13.50
Tumbler, footed, clear, 12½ oz....15.00
Vase, 7¼" h., amber....85.00
Vase, 7¼" h., clear....42.50
Vase, 7¼" h., pink....101.00

FLORAL or Poinsettia, Jeannette Glass Co., 1931-35 (Process etched)

Bowl, berry, 4" d., green or pink....16.00
Bowl, salad, 7½" d., green....20.00
Bowl, salad, 7½" d., pink....18.00

Butter dish, cov., green.....84.50
Butter dish, cov., pink.....86.50
Coaster, green, 3¼" d.....9.00
Coaster, pink, 3¼" d. 14.00
Creamer, green 12.50
Creamer, pink 14.50
Cup, pink 10.50
Cup & saucer, green.....21.50
Flower frog for vase, green.....1,200.00
Pitcher, 5½" h., 24 oz., green 630.00

Floral Pitcher & Tumblers

Pitcher, 8" h., 32 oz., cone-shaped, green (ILLUS.) 33.50
Pitcher, 8" h., 32 oz., cone-shaped, pink 32.00
Pitcher, lemonade, 10¼" h., 48 oz., green.....230.00
Pitcher, lemonade, 10¼" h., 48 oz., pink 285.00
Plate, sherbet, 6" d., green or pink.....6.00
Plate, salad, 8" d., green or pink.....10.00
Plate, dinner, 9" d., green 16.50
Plate, dinner, 9" d., pink.....15.50
Platter, 10¾" oval, green or pink 16.00
Platter, 11" oval, scalloped edge, pink..60.00
Salt & pepper shakers, footed, green, 4" h., pr 50.00
Salt & pepper shakers, footed, pink, 4" h., pr 44.00
Sherbet, green or pink.....15.00
Sugar bowl, cov., green.....26.50
Sugar bowl, cov., pink 20.00
Sugar bowl, open, green 10.00
Sugar bowl, open, pink.....9.50
Tray, closed handles, green, 6" sq. 21.00
Tray, closed handles, pink, 6" sq.....17.50
Tumbler, juice, footed, green or pink, 4" h., 5 oz.....18.50
Tumbler, water, footed, green, 4¾" h., 7 oz. (ILLUS.).....18.50
Tumbler, water, footed, pink, 4¾" h., 7 oz. 17.50
Tumbler, green, 4½" h., 9 oz. 170.00
Tumbler, lemonade, footed, green or pink, 5¼" h., 9 oz. 45.00
Vase, 6⅞" h., octagonal, clear.....300.00
Vase, 6⅞" h., octagonal, green 505.00

(OLD) FLORENTINE or Poppy No. 1
Hazel Atlas Glass Co., 1932-35
(Process-etched)

Ashtray, clear, 5½" 18.00
Ashtray, green, 5½".....20.00
Ashtray, pink or yellow, 5½" 27.50
Bowl, berry, 5" d., clear or pink.....10.00
Bowl, berry, 5" d., cobalt blue or yellow.....12.00
Bowl, berry, 5" d., green 11.00
Bowl, cereal, 6" d., clear or pink 20.00
Bowl, cereal, 6" d., yellow.....35.00
Bowl, 8½" d., clear.....15.00
Bowl, 8½" d., green 25.00
Bowl, 8½" d., pink.....31.00
Bowl, 8½" d., yellow.....27.50
Bowl, cov. vegetable, 9½" oval, clear...45.00
Bowl, cov. vegetable, 9½" oval, green..40.00
Bowl, cov. vegetable, 9½" oval, pink....60.00
Bowl, 9½" oval vegetable, green 22.50
Bowl, 9½" oval vegetable, pink.....26.00
Bowl, 9½" oval vegetable, yellow 27.50
Butter dish, cov., clear or green.....106.00
Butter dish, cov., pink 156.00
Butter dish, cov., yellow.....146.00
Coaster-ashtray, yellow, 3¾" d.....26.00
Creamer, plain rim, clear 8.00
Creamer, plain rim, green.....9.00
Creamer, plain rim, pink 15.50
Creamer, plain rim, yellow.....11.50
Creamer, ruffled rim, clear.....30.00
Creamer, ruffled rim, cobalt blue 60.00
Creamer, ruffled rim, green 23.00
Creamer, ruffled rim, pink.....26.00
Cup, clear 6.50
Cup, green.....8.00
Cup & saucer, pink or yellow.....13.50
Nut dish, handled, ruffled rim, clear or pink 15.00
Nut dish, handled, ruffled rim, cobalt blue 44.50
Nut dish, handled, ruffled rim, green 21.00
Pitcher, 6½" h., 36 oz., footed, clear.....37.50
Pitcher, 6½" h., 36 oz., footed, green ...39.00
Pitcher, 6½" h., 36 oz., footed, pink or yellow.....43.00
Pitcher, 7½" h., 48 oz., clear.....59.00
Pitcher, 7½" h., 48 oz., green 75.00
Pitcher, 7½" h., 48 oz., pink.....100.00
Plate, sherbet, 6" d., clear 3.00
Plate, sherbet, 6" d., green 6.00
Plate, sherbet, 6" d., pink.....5.00
Plate, salad, 8½" d., clear.....6.50
Plate, salad, 8½" d., green 7.50
Plate, salad, 8½" d., pink.....11.00
Plate, salad, 8½" d., yellow.....10.00
Plate, dinner, 10" d., clear 11.00
Plate, dinner, 10" d., green or yellow....15.00
Plate, dinner, 10" d., pink.....26.50
Plate, grill, 10" d., clear.....9.50

Plate, grill, 10" d., green 10.50
Plate, grill, 10" d., pink 15.50
Plate, grill, 10" d., yellow.....13.00
Platter, 11½" oval, green 15.50
Platter, 11½" oval, pink.....19.50
Platter, 11½" oval, yellow 21.00
Saucer, clear or green 3.50
Salt & pepper shakers, footed, clear, pr.....33.00
Salt & pepper shakers, footed, green, pr.....34.50
Salt & pepper shakers, footed, pink, pr.....46.00
Salt & pepper shakers, footed, yellow, pr.....52.00
Sherbet, footed, clear or green, 3 oz. 8.50
Sherbet, footed, pink, 3 oz.....9.00
Sherbet, footed, yellow, 3 oz. 10.00
Sugar bowl, cov., clear 19.50
Sugar bowl, cov., green or pink 25.50
Sugar bowl, cov., yellow 28.00
Sugar bowl, open, clear.....8.00
Sugar bowl, open, green 9.00
Sugar bowl, open, pink.....12.00
Sugar bowl, open, yellow.....10.50
Sugar bowl, open, ruffled rim, clear.....27.50
Sugar bowl, open, ruffled rim, cobalt blue 45.00
Sugar bowl, open, ruffled rim, green 30.00
Sugar bowl, open, ruffled rim, pink.....28.00
Tumbler, footed, green, 3¼" h., 4 oz. 8.00
Tumbler, juice, footed, clear, 3¾" h., 5 oz. 11.50
Tumbler, juice, footed, green, 3¾" h., 5 oz. 13.50
Tumbler, juice, footed, pink or yellow, 3¾" h., 5 oz. 19.00
Tumbler, ribbed, clear, 4" h., 9 oz.....12.00
Tumbler, ribbed, pink, 4" h., 9 oz.....15.00
Tumbler, water, footed, green, 4¾" h., 10 oz. 20.00
Tumbler, water, footed, pink, 4¾" h., 10 oz. 29.50
Tumbler, water, footed, yellow, 4¾" h., 10 oz. 19.00
Tumbler, iced tea, footed, green, 5¼" h., 12 oz. 16.00
Tumbler, iced tea, footed, pink, 5¼" h., 12 oz. 17.50
Tumbler, iced tea, footed, yellow, 5¼" h., 12 oz. 21.50

FLORENTINE or Poppy No. 2, Hazel Atlas Glass Co., 1932-35 (Process-etched)

Bowl, berry, 4½" d., clear.....9.00
Bowl, berry, 4½" d., green 11.00
Bowl, berry, 4½" d., pink.....13.00
Bowl, berry, 4½" d., yellow 17.50
Bowl, cream soup, plain rim, 4¾" d., clear 9.50
Bowl, cream soup, plain rim, 4¾" d., green.....11.50
Bowl, cream soup, plain rim, 4¾" d., pink 15.00
Bowl, cream soup, plain rim, 4¾" d., yellow.....19.00
Bowl, 5½" d., clear.....20.50
Bowl, 5½" d., green 45.00
Bowl, 5½" d., yellow.....41.00
Bowl, cereal, 6" d., yellow.....35.00
Bowl, 8" d., clear.....22.00
Bowl, cov. vegetable, 9" oval, green.....35.00
Bowl, cov. vegetable, 9" oval, yellow....60.00
Bowl, 9" oval vegetable, green 22.50
Bowl, 9" oval vegetable, yellow 26.00
Butter dish, cov., green.....96.00
Butter dish, cov., yellow.....137.00
Candlesticks, green, 2¾" h., pr.....47.00
Candlesticks, yellow, 2¾" h., pr.....56.50
Candy dish, cov., clear 67.50
Candy dish, cov., green.....95.00
Candy dish, cov., pink 114.00
Candy dish, cov., yellow.....145.00
Coaster-ashtray, clear, 3¾" d. 16.00
Coaster-ashtray, green, 3¾" d.....18.00
Coaster-ashtray, yellow, 3¾" d. 21.00
Coaster-ashtray, green, 5½"d.....19.00
Coaster-ashtray, yellow, 5½"d. 31.50
Compote, 3½", ruffled, clear 23.00
Compote, 3½", ruffled, cobalt blue 50.00
Compote, 3½", ruffled, pink 13.00
Condiment set: creamer, cov. sugar bowl, salt & pepper shakers & 8½" d. tray; yellow, 5 pcs. 161.00
Creamer, clear.....6.50
Creamer, green 8.00

Florentine Creamer

Creamer, yellow (ILLUS.) 9.00
Cup, clear 6.00
Cup, green.....7.50
Cup & saucer, pink 11.50
Cup & saucer, yellow.....12.50
Custard cup, green 70.00
Custard cup, yellow 79.00
Gravy boat, yellow 50.00
Gravy boat w/platter, yellow, 11½" oval 81.00
Pitcher, 6¼" h., 24 oz., cone-shaped, yellow 142.00
Pitcher, 7½" h., 28 oz., cone-shaped, green.....36.00
Pitcher, 7½" h., 48 oz., straight sides, green.....48.00
Pitcher, 7½" h., 48 oz., straight sides, pink 121.00
Pitcher, 7½" h., 48 oz., straight sides, yellow.....144.00
Pitcher, 8¼" h., 76 oz., clear.....61.00

Pitcher, 8¼" h., 76 oz., clear.....80.00
Pitcher, 8¼" h., 76 oz., pink.....219.00
Pitcher, 8¼" h., 76 oz., yellow 400.00
Plate, sherbet, 6" d., clear 3.00
Plate, sherbet, 6" d., green.....4.00
Plate, sherbet, 6" d., yellow 5.50
Plate, 6¼" d., w/indentation, yellow.....24.50
Plate, salad, 8½" d., clear or pink.....6.50
Plate, salad, 8½" d., green or yellow 8.00
Plate, dinner, 10" d., clear 10.50
Plate, dinner, 10" d., green.....13.50
Plate, dinner, 10" d., yellow 12.50
Plate, grill, 10¼" d., clear.....11.00
Platter, 11" oval, yellow 16.50
Platter, 11½", for gravy boat, yellow.....38.00
Relish dish, three-part or plain, clear, 10".....13.00
Relish dish, three-part or plain, yellow, 10".....26.00
Salt & pepper shakers, clear, pr. 27.50
Salt & pepper shakers, green, pr.....40.00
Salt & pepper shakers, yellow, pr. 44.00
Saucer, clear 3.00
Saucer, green.....4.00
Sherbet, clear, green or yellow.....9.50
Sugar bowl, cov., clear 22.00
Sugar bowl, cov., green.....19.00
Sugar bowl, cov., yellow.....29.00
Sugar bowl, open, clear.....6.50
Sugar bowl, open, green 7.50
Sugar bowl, open, yellow.....9.50
Tray, yellow, 8½" d. 83.00
Tumbler, footed, green, 3¼" h., 5 oz. ...11.50
Tumbler, footed, yellow, 3¼" h., 5 oz. ..13.00
Tumbler, juice, clear, 3½" h., 5 oz. 9.00
Tumbler, juice, green, 3½" h., 5 oz.....12.00
Tumbler, footed, green, 4" h., 5 oz. 11.50
Tumbler, footed, yellow, 4" h., 5 oz. 15.00
Tumbler, blown, clear, 3½" h., 6 oz. 16.00
Tumbler, blown, green, 3½" h., 6 oz.....12.50
Tumbler, water, clear, 4" h., 9 oz.....10.00
Tumbler, water, green, 4" h., 9 oz. 11.50
Tumbler, water, pink, 4" h., 9 oz. 13.50
Tumbler, water, yellow, 4" h., 9 oz.....19.00
Tumbler, footed, clear, 4½" h., 9 oz.....11.50
Tumbler, footed, green, 4½" h., 9 oz. ...21.00
Tumbler, footed, yellow, 4½" h., 9 oz. ..30.00
Tumbler, blown, clear, 5" h., 12 oz. 19.50
Tumbler, blown, green, 5" h., 12 oz.....16.00
Tumbler, iced tea, clear, 5" h., 12 oz. ...19.50
Tumbler, iced tea, green, 5" h., 12 oz...26.00
Tumbler, iced tea, yellow, 5" h., 12 oz. 41.00
Vase (or parfait), 6" h., clear.....26.00
Vase (or parfait), 6" h., green 36.50
Vase (or parfait), 6" h., yellow.....54.50

GEORGIAN or Lovebirds, Federal Glass Co., 1931-36 (Process-etched)
(All items in green only)
Bowl, berry, 4½" d. 7.50
Bowl, cereal, 5¾" d.....20.00
Bowl, 6½" d., deep.....64.00
Bowl, berry, 7½" d. 57.00
Bowl, 9" oval vegetable 61.00
Butter dish, cov.....70.00

Georgian Pattern

Creamer, footed, 3" h. (ILLUS.) 10.50
Creamer, footed, 4" h. 14.50
Cup (ILLUS.).....8.50
Hot plate, center design, 5" d. 44.50
Plate, sherbet, 6" d. 4.50
Plate, luncheon, 8" d.....8.00
Plate, dinner, 9¼" d. 26.50
Plate, 9¼" d., center design only.....18.50
Platter, 11½" oval, closed handles 58.50
Saucer (ILLUS.).....3.50
Sherbet.....11.50
Sugar bowl, cov., footed, 3" h.....42.00
Sugar bowl, cov., footed, 4" h.....76.00
Sugar bowl, open, footed, 3" h. (ILLUS.) 8.50
Sugar bowl, open, footed, 4" h. 10.00
Tumbler, 4" h., 9 oz. 52.00
Tumbler, 5¼" h., 12 oz. 103.00

HOBNAIL, Hocking Glass Co., 1934-36 (Press-mold)
Cup & saucer, clear.....5.00
Cup & saucer, pink 7.00
Decanter w/stopper, clear, 32 oz.....24.00
Decanter w/stopper, clear w/red trim, 32 oz. 22.00
Goblet, iced tea, clear, 13 oz.....7.50
Pitcher, milk, 18 oz., clear 17.50
Pitcher, 67 oz., clear.....24.00
Plate, sherbet, 6" d., clear 2.00
Plate, sherbet, 6" d., pink.....4.00
Plate, luncheon, 8½" d., clear.....3.00
Plate, luncheon, 8½" d., clear w/red trim 4.50
Plate, luncheon, 8½" d., pink.....5.50
Sherbet, clear 3.00
Sherbet, pink 6.00
Sugar bowl, open, footed, clear.....2.50
Tumbler, whiskey, clear, 1½ oz. 4.50
Tumbler, wine, footed, clear, 3 oz. 5.50
Tumbler, cordial, footed, clear, 5 oz. 4.00
Tumbler, water, clear, 9 oz. 5.00
Tumbler, water, clear, 10 oz. 5.50
Tumbler, iced tea, clear, 15 oz. 6.00
Wine set: decanter & 6 footed wines; clear, 7 pcs. 32.00

HOLIDAY or Buttons and Bows, Jeannette Glass Co., 1947-mid 50s (Press-mold)
(All items in pink unless otherwise indicated)

Holiday Berry Bowl

Bowl, berry, 5⅛" d. (ILLUS.) 11.00
Bowl, flat soup, 7¾" d. 43.00
Bowl, berry, 8½" d. 20.00
Bowl, 9½" oval vegetable 23.00
Butter dish, cov. 37.50
Cake plate, three-footed, 10½" d. 96.50
Candlesticks, 3" h., pr. 93.00
Console bowl, 10¾" d. 106.00
Creamer, footed 8.50
Cup 7.00
Pitcher, milk, 4¾" h., 16 oz., iridescent 23.50
Pitcher, milk, 4¾" h., 16 oz., pink 52.50
Pitcher, 6¾" h., 52 oz. 34.00
Plate, sherbet, 6" d. 5.00
Plate, dinner, 9" d. 15.00
Plate, chop, 13¾" d. 92.50
Platter, 8 x 11⅜" oval, iridescent 17.50
Platter, 8 x 11⅜" oval, pink 18.50
Sandwich tray, 10½" d. 16.00
Saucer 5.50
Sherbet 6.50
Sugar bowl, cov. 23.00
Sugar bowl, open 7.00
Tumbler, footed, iridescent, 4" h., 5 oz. ..8.50
Tumbler, footed, pink, 4" h., 5 oz. 35.00
Tumbler, footed, 6" h., 9 oz. 122.00
Tumbler, 4" h., 10 oz. 18.50

HOMESPUN or Fine Rib, Jeannette Glass Co., 1939-49 (Press-mold)
(All items in pink only, except child's tea set)

Bowl, 4½" d., closed handles 9.50
Bowl, cereal, 5" d. 17.00
Bowl, berry, 8¼" d. 11.50
Butter dish, cov. 48.00
Coaster-ashtray 9.50
Creamer, footed 7.50
Cup 7.00
Plate, sherbet, 6" d. 5.00
Plate, dinner, 9¼" d. 15.50
Platter, 13", closed handles 15.00
Saucer 3.50
Sherbet 15.50
Sugar bowl, open, footed 8.00
Tumbler, footed, 4" h., 5 oz. 7.00
Tumbler, water, 4" h., 9 oz. 17.00
Tumbler, footed, 6¼" h., 9 oz. 7.50
Tumbler, iced tea, 5¼" h., 13 oz. 35.00
Tumbler, footed, 6½" h., 15 oz. 23.00

CHILD'S TEA SET
Cup, clear 18.50
Cup & saucer, pink 20.50
Plate, clear 6.50
Plate, pink 12.50
Saucer, pink 8.00
14 piece set, pink 285.00

IRIS or Iris & Herringbone, Jeannette Glass Co., 1928-32, 1950s and 1970s (Press-mold)

Berry set: 11" d. ruffled fruit bowl & 6 sauce dishes; clear, 7 pcs. 68.00
Bowl, berry, 4½" d., beaded rim, amber iridescent 9.00
Bowl, berry, 4½" d., beaded rim, clear 37.00
Bowl, cereal, 5" d., clear 116.00
Bowl, sauce, 5" d., ruffled rim, amber iridescent 23.00
Bowl, sauce, 5" d., ruffled rim, clear 9.00
Bowl, soup, 7½" d., amber iridescent ...64.00
Bowl, soup, 7½" d., clear 150.00
Bowl, berry, 8" d., beaded rim, amber iridescent 23.50
Bowl, berry, 8" d., beaded rim, clear....85.00
Bowl, salad, 9½" d., amber iridescent ..12.50
Bowl, salad, 9½" d., clear 13.50
Bowl, fruit, 11" d., straight rim, clear 56.00
Bowl, fruit, 11½" d., ruffled rim, amber iridescent 14.00
Bowl, fruit, 11½" d., ruffled rim, clear....13.00
Butter dish, cov., amber iridescent 42.00
Butter dish, cov., clear 45.00
Candlesticks, two-branch, amber iridescent, pr. 41.00
Candlesticks, two-branch, clear, pr. 36.00
Candy jar, cov., clear 137.00
Coaster, clear 102.00
Creamer, footed, amber iridescent 12.00
Creamer, footed, clear 10.00
Cup, demitasse, clear 34.50
Cup & saucer, demitasse, clear 176.00
Cup & saucer, demitasse, ruby 250.00
Cup, amber iridescent 13.00
Cup, clear 15.50
Goblet, wine, amber iridescent, 4¼" h., 3 oz. 29.00
Goblet, wine, clear, 4¼" h., 3 oz. 15.50
Goblet, cocktail, clear, 4¼" h., 4 oz. 23.00
Goblet, clear, 5¾" h., 4 oz. 22.50
Goblet, amber iridescent, 5¾" h., 8 oz. 12.00
Goblet, clear, 5¾" h., 8 oz. 23.00
Lamp shade, blue 59.00
Lamp shade, clear 57.00
Lamp shade, clear frosted 83.50
Lamp shade, pink 62.00

Lamp shade, pink frosted 65.00
Nut set: 11½" d. ruffled bowl in metal holder, w/nutcracker & picks; amber iridescent, the set.....100.00
Nut set: 11½" d. ruffled bowl in metal holder, w/nutcracker & picks; clear, the set.....64.00
Pitcher, 9½" h., footed, amber iridescent 38.00
Pitcher, 9½" h., footed, clear 35.00
Plate, sherbet, 5½" d., amber iridescent 11.50
Plate, sherbet, 5½" d., clear 14.00
Plate, luncheon, 8" d., clear.....95.00
Plate, dinner, 9" d., amber iridescent....38.50
Plate, dinner, 9" d., clear 50.00
Plate, sandwich, 11¾" d., amber iridescent 29.00
Plate, sandwich, 11¾" d., clear 33.00
Saucer, amber iridescent.....10.00
Saucer, clear 11.50
Sherbet, footed, amber iridescent, 2½" h.....13.00
Sherbet, footed, clear, 2½" h. 23.50
Sherbet, footed, amber iridescent, 4" h.....13.00
Sherbet, footed, clear, 4" h. 19.50
Sugar bowl, cov., footed, amber iridescent or clear 23.00
Sugar bowl, open, footed, amber iridescent or clear 9.50
Tumbler, clear, 4" h. 135.00
Tumbler, footed, amber iridescent, 6" h.....16.00
Tumbler, footed, clear, 6" h. 17.50
Tumbler, footed, clear, 6½" h. 31.00
Vase, 9" h., amber iridescent.....23.00
Vase, 9" h., clear 25.00
Vase, 9" h., pink.....66.00
Water set: pitcher & 7 tumblers; clear, in original box, 8 pcs. 225.00

LACE EDGE or Open Lace, Hocking Glass Co., 1935-38 (Press-mold)

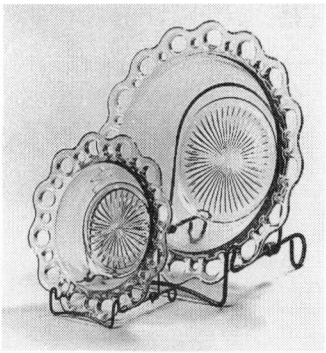

Lace Edge Bowls

Bowl, cereal, 6½" d., clear 5.50
Bowl, cereal, 6½" d., pink (ILLUS. front) 18.50
Bowl, 7¾" d., ribbed, pink 33.50
Bowl, salad or butter dish bottom, 7¾" d., pink 18.00
Bowl, 9½" d., plain or ribbed, clear 12.50
Bowl, 9½" d., plain or ribbed, pink (ILLUS. back) 20.00
Butter dish or bonbon, cov., pink 62.00
Candlesticks, pink, pr. 245.00
Candlesticks, pink frosted, pr. 50.00
Candy jar, cov., ribbed, pink, 4" h. 46.50
Compote, cov., 7" d., footed, pink.....44.00
Compote, open, 7" d., footed, pink 19.00
Console bowl, three-footed, pink, 10½" d.....186.00
Cookie jar, cov., pink, 5" h. 65.00
Creamer, pink 21.00
Cup, pink 22.00
Flower bowl w/crystal block, pink 22.50
Flower bowl without crystal block, pink 15.00
Plate, salad, 7¼" d., clear.....4.50
Plate, salad, 7¼" d., pink 18.50
Plate, luncheon, 8¾" d., pink 19.00
Plate, dinner, 10½" d., pink.....26.50
Plate, grill, 10½" d., pink 17.50
Plate, 13" d., solid lace, pink.....36.50
Platter, 12¾" oval, pink.....30.00
Platter, 12¾" oval, five-part, clear.....16.50
Platter, 12¾" oval, five-part, pink.....27.50
Relish dish, three-part, deep, pink, 7½" d.....63.00
Relish plate, three-part, pink, 10½" d. ..21.00
Relish plate, four-part, solid lace, pink, 13" d. 45.00
Saucer, pink.....12.50
Sherbet, footed, pink 79.00
Sugar bowl, open, pink 20.00
Tumbler, pink, 4½" h., 9 oz. 15.50
Tumbler, footed, pink, 5" h., 10½ oz. 63.00
Vase, 7" h., pink frosted.....49.50

LORAIN or Basket or Number 615, Indiana Glass Co., 1929-32 (Process-etched)

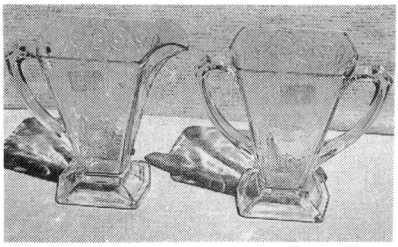

Lorain Creamer & Sugar Bowl

Bowl, cereal, 6", green.....36.50
Bowl, cereal, 6", yellow.....52.50
Bowl, salad, 7¼", green.....41.00
Bowl, salad, 7¼", yellow 55.00
Bowl, berry, 8", clear.....60.00
Bowl, berry, 8", green 97.00
Bowl, berry, 8", yellow 155.00
Bowl, 9¾" oval vegetable, green 45.00

Bowl, 9¾" oval vegetable, yellow 51.00
Creamer, footed, green 12.00
Creamer, footed, yellow (ILLUS. left) ...22.00
Cup, green.....9.50
Cup, yellow.....14.50
Cup & saucer, clear.....14.00
Plate, sherbet, 5½", green.....6.00
Plate, sherbet, 5½", yellow 10.50
Plate, salad, 7¾", clear.....9.00
Plate, salad, 7¾" green 11.00
Plate, salad, 7¾", yellow.....14.00
Plate, luncheon, 8⅜", green 10.50
Plate, luncheon, 8⅜", yellow.....25.00
Plate, dinner, 10¼", clear or green.....36.00
Plate, dinner, 10¼", yellow 49.00
Platter, 11½", green.....23.00
Platter, 11½", yellow.....40.00
Relish, four-part, clear, 8".....14.00
Relish, four-part, green, 8".....16.00
Relish, four-part, yellow, 8".....29.50
Saucer, green or yellow.....5.00
Sherbet, footed, green.....17.50
Sherbet, footed, yellow.....28.00
Sugar bowl, open, footed, green 10.50
Sugar bowl, open, footed, yellow
(ILLUS. right) 20.00
Tumbler, footed, green, 4¾" h., 9 oz. ...19.50
Tumbler, footed, yellow, 4¾" h., 9 oz. ..26.00

MADRID, Federal Glass Co., 1932-39 (Process-etched)

Madrid Sugar Bowl

Ashtray, amber, 6" sq. 221.00
Ashtray, green, 6" sq. 195.00
Bowl, cream soup, 4¾" d., amber.....13.50
Bowl, sauce, 5" d., amber or pink.....5.50
Bowl, sauce, 5" d., blue 35.00
Bowl, sauce, 5" d., green.....8.50
Bowl, soup, 7" d., amber.....13.50
Bowl, soup, 7" d., blue.....20.00
Bowl, soup, 7" d., clear.....6.00
Bowl, soup, 7" d., green.....15.50
Bowl, salad, 8" d., amber.....13.50
Bowl, salad, 8" d., blue 46.50
Bowl, salad, 8" d., green.....15.50
Bowl, large berry, 9⅜" d., amber 22.00
Bowl, salad, 9½" d., deep, amber.....27.50
Bowl, 10" oval vegetable, amber 16.00
Bowl, 10" oval vegetable, blue.....33.50
Bowl, 10" oval vegetable, green 22.00
Butter dish, cov., amber.....66.00
Butter dish, cov., clear 49.00
Butter dish, cov., green.....78.00
Cake plate, amber, 11¼" d. 15.00
Cake plate, pink, 11¼" d.....12.00
Candlesticks, amber, 2¼" h., pr.....16.00
Candlesticks, clear or pink, 2¼" h.,
pr.....14.50
Candlesticks, iridescent, 2¼" h., pr. 21.50
Console bowl, flared, amber or
iridescent, 11" d. 14.00
Console set: bowl & pair of candlesticks;
amber, 3 pcs. 37.00
Console set: bowl & pair of candlesticks;
iridescent, 3 pcs.....32.00
Console set: bowl & pair of candlesticks;
pink, 3 pcs.....36.00
Cookie jar, cov., amber.....39.50
Cookie jar, cov., clear 32.50
Cookie jar, cov., pink 36.50
Creamer, amber or clear 7.50
Creamer, blue.....14.00
Creamer, green 10.50
Cup, amber.....6.50
Cup, blue 19.50
Cup, green.....9.00
Cup & saucer, clear.....8.00
Cup & saucer, pink 9.00
Gelatin mold, amber, 2⅛" h. 11.50
Gravy boat & platter, amber 1,575.00
Gravy boat platter, amber.....500.00
Hot dish coaster, amber, 5" d. 39.50
Hot dish coaster, clear, 5" d.....23.00
Hot dish coaster, green, 5" d. 31.00
Hot dish coaster w/indentation, amber
or green 35.00
Hot dish coaster w/indentation, clear....26.50
Jam dish, amber, 7" d.....20.50
Jam dish, blue, 7" d. 31.50
Jam dish, clear, 7" d. 10.00
Jam dish, green, 7" d.....25.00
Lazy Susan, walnut base w/seven
clear hot dish coasters.....462.50
Pitcher, juice, 5½" h., 36 oz., amber.....38.00
Pitcher, 8" h., 60 oz., square, amber 43.00
Pitcher, 8" h., 60 oz., square, blue
or green 130.00
Pitcher, 8½" h., 80 oz., jug-type,
amber.....57.50
Pitcher, 8½" h., 80 oz., jug-type,
green.....188.50
Pitcher w/ice lip, 8½" h., 80 oz.,
amber.....55.50
Plate, sherbet, 6" d., amber, clear or
green.....4.50
Plate, sherbet, 6" d., blue 12.00
Plate, sherbet, 6" d., pink.....3.50
Plate, salad, 7½" d., amber, green or
pink 9.50
Plate, salad, 7½" d., blue.....17.00

Plate, luncheon, 8⅞" d., amber 7.50
Plate, luncheon, 8⅞" d., blue.....18.50
Plate, luncheon, 8⅞" d., clear.....5.50
Plate, luncheon, 8⅞" d., green 9.50
Plate, dinner, 10½" d., amber.....35.00
Plate, dinner, 10½" d., blue 54.50
Plate, dinner, 10½" d., clear 21.00
Plate, dinner, 10½" d., green.....32.50
Plate, grill, 10½" d., amber 10.50
Plate, grill, 10½" d., clear.....9.00
Plate, grill, 10½" d., green 16.00
Platter, 11½" oval, amber 14.00
Platter, 11½" oval, blue.....29.00
Platter, 11½" oval, green 16.50
Relish plate, amber, 10½" d. 13.50
Relish plate, clear, 10½" d.....7.00
Relish plate, pink, 10½" d. 12.00
Salt & pepper shakers, amber, 3½" h., pr. 40.00
Salt & pepper shakers, green, 3½" h., pr. 56.00
Salt & pepper shakers, footed, amber, 3½" h., pr. 52.00
Salt & pepper shakers, footed, blue, 3½" h., pr. 126.00
Salt & pepper shakers, footed, green, 3½" h., pr. 81.00
Saucer, amber.....4.00
Saucer, blue 8.00
Saucer, green.....5.00
Sherbet, amber.....7.50
Sherbet, blue or green.....10.00
Sherbet, clear 6.50
Sugar bowl, cov., amber (ILLUS.) 40.00
Sugar bowl, cov., clear 32.50
Sugar bowl, cov., green.....48.00
Sugar bowl, open, amber 7.50
Sugar bowl, open, blue.....15.00
Sugar bowl, open, green 9.00
Tumbler, juice, amber, 3⅞" h., 5 oz.....12.50
Tumbler, juice, blue, 3⅞" h., 5 oz. 32.50
Tumbler, juice, green, 3⅞" h., 5 oz.....48.00
Tumbler, footed, amber, 4" h., 5 oz. 21.50
Tumbler, blue, 4½" h., 9 oz.....25.00
Tumbler, green, 4½" h., 9 oz. 23.50
Tumbler, pink, 4½" h., 9 oz.....13.50
Tumblers, amber, 4½" h., 9 oz., set of 24 w/box 325.00
Tumbler, footed, amber, 5¼" h., 10 oz. 21.00
Tumbler, footed, clear, 5¼" h., 10 oz. 14.00
Tumbler, footed, green, 5¼" h., 10 oz. 33.50
Tumbler, amber, 5½" h., 12 oz. 19.50
Tumbler, blue, 5½" h., 12 oz.....39.00
Tumbler, clear, 5½" h., 12 oz.....20.00
Tumbler, green, 5½" h., 12 oz. 32.00

MANHATTAN or Horizontal Ribbed, Anchor Hocking Glass Co., 1938-43 (Press-mold)

Ashtray, clear, 4" d. 9.50
Ashtray, clear, 4½" sq.....16.50
Bowl, sauce, 4½" d., two-handled, clear 8.50
Bowl, berry, 5⅜" d., two-handled, clear or pink 17.00
Bowl, cereal, 5½" d., clear 28.50
Bowl, large berry, 7½" d., clear.....13.50
Bowl, 8" d., two-handled, clear 17.00
Bowl, salad, 9" d., clear 20.50
Bowl, fruit, 9½" d., clear.....31.50
Bowl, fruit, 9½" d., pink.....38.00
Candleholders, clear, 4½" sq., pr. 12.00
Candlesticks, double, clear, 4¼" h., pr. 32.00
Candy dish, cov., clear 31.50
Candy dish, open, three-footed, clear 6.50
Candy dish, open, three-footed, pink....10.50
Coaster, clear, 3½" d. 12.50
Coaster, pink, 3½" d. 7.00
Compote, 5¾" h., clear 26.50
Compote, 5¾" h., pink 29.00
Creamer, oval, clear 9.50
Creamer, oval, pink 10.00
Cup, clear 15.00
Pitcher, juice, 42 oz., ball tilt-type, clear 29.00
Pitcher w/ice lip, 80 oz., ball tilt-type, clear 36.00
Pitcher w/ice lip, 80 oz., ball tilt-type, pink 57.00
Plate, sherbet or saucer, 6" d., clear 5.50
Plate, sherbet or saucer, 6" d., pink.....12.00
Plate, salad, 8½" d., clear.....12.50
Plate, dinner, 10¼" d., clear 17.50
Plate, dinner, 10¼" d., pink.....12.50
Plate, sandwich, 14" d., clear 20.00

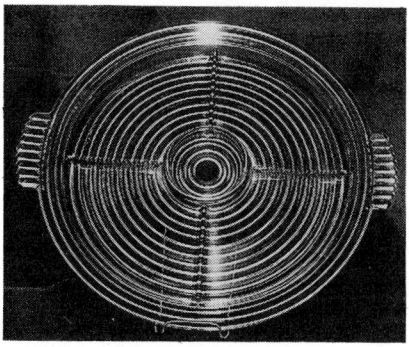

Manhattan Relish Tray

Relish tray, four-part, clear, 14" d. (ILLUS.) 16.00
Relish tray, five-part, clear w/clear inserts, 14" d. 43.00
Relish tray, five-part, clear w/pink inserts, 14" d. 27.00
Relish tray, five-part, clear w/ruby inserts, 14" d. 49.00
Relish tray, five-part, pink w/pink inserts, 14" d. 47.00

Relish tray insert, clear, pink or ruby 4.50
Salt & pepper shakers, square, clear, 2" h., pr. 23.00
Salt & pepper shakers, square, pink, 2" h., pr. 55.00
Saucer, clear 5.00
Sherbet, clear 8.00
Sherbet, pink 12.00
Sugar bowl, open, oval, clear or pink 9.50
Tumbler, footed, clear, green or pink, 10 oz. 17.00
Vase, 8" h., clear 10.50
Water bottle, cov., clear 15.50
Wine, clear, 3½" h. 5.50

MAYFAIR or Open Rose, Hocking Glass Co., 1931-37 (Process-etched)

Mayfair Plate

Bowl, cream soup, 5", blue 19.00
Bowl, cream soup, 5", pink 42.00
Bowl, cereal, 5½", blue 52.50
Bowl, cereal, 5½", pink 21.00
Bowl, vegetable, 7", blue 43.50
Bowl, vegetable, 7", pink 25.50
Bowl, vegetable, 7", pink frosted 18.00
Bowl, 9" d., 3⅛" h., three-footed console, green 7,250.00
Bowl, 9" d., 3⅛" h., three-footed console, pink 7,000.00
Bowl, 9½" oval vegetable, blue 62.00
Bowl, 9½" oval vegetable, pink 30.00
Bowl, 9½" oval vegetable, yellow 175.00
Bowl, 10", cov. vegetable, blue 130.00
Bowl, 10", cov. vegetable, pink 97.00
Bowl, 10", open vegetable, blue 62.00
Bowl, 10", open vegetable, pink 25.00
Bowl, 11¾" d., low, blue 63.50
Bowl, 11¾" d., low, green 32.00
Bowl, 11¾" d., low, pink 50.00
Bowl, fruit, 12" d., deep, scalloped, blue 81.00
Bowl, fruit, 12" d., deep, scalloped, green 36.50
Bowl, fruit, 12" d., deep, scalloped, pink 53.50
Bowl, fruit, 12" d., deep, scalloped, yellow 250.00
Butter dish, cov., blue 282.00
Butter dish, cov., pink 60.00
Candy jar, cov., blue 271.00
Candy jar, cov., pink 50.00
Celery dish, blue, 10" l. 41.50
Celery dish, pink, 10" l. 37.50
Celery dish, two-part, blue, 10" l. 51.00
Celery dish, two-part, pink, 10" l. 168.00
Cookie jar, cov., blue 275.00
Cookie jar, cov., green 541.00
Cookie jar, cov., pink 46.50
Creamer, footed, blue 70.00
Creamer, footed, pink 24.00
Creamer, footed, pink frosted 15.50
Cup, blue 43.50
Decanter w/stopper, pink, 10" h., 32 oz. 146.00
Decanter, no stopper, pink, 10" h., 32 oz. 93.00
Goblet, pink, 4" h., 2½ oz. 61.00
Goblet, wine, pink, 4½" h., 3 oz. 71.00
Goblet, cocktail, pink, 4" h., 3½ oz. 72.00
Goblet, claret, pink, 5¼" h., 4½ oz. 75.00
Goblet, water, pink, 5¾" h., 9 oz. 58.00
Goblet, water, thin, pink, 7¼" h., 9 oz. 121.00
Pitcher, juice, 6" h., 37 oz., blue 142.00
Pitcher, juice, 6" h., 37 oz., clear 14.50
Pitcher, juice, 6" h., 37 oz., pink 48.50
Pitcher, 8" h., 60 oz., jug-type, blue 184.00
Pitcher, 8" h., 60 oz., jug-type, pink 45.50
Pitcher, 8½" h., 80 oz., jug-type, blue 189.00
Pitcher, 8½" h., 80 oz., jug-type, pink 96.50
Plate, sherbet, 6½" d., pink 12.00
Plate, sherbet, 6½" d., off-center indentation, blue 24.00
Plate, sherbet, 6½" d., off-center indentation, pink 11.50
Plate, luncheon, 8½", blue 47.00
Plate, luncheon, 8½", pink 23.50
Plate, dinner, 9½", blue 76.00
Plate, dinner, 9½", pink (ILLUS.) 48.00
Plate, dinner, 9½", yellow 117.50
Plate, grill, 9½", blue 48.00
Plate, grill, 9½", pink 36.00
Platter, 12" oval, open handles, blue 62.00
Platter, 12" oval, open handles, clear 14.50
Platter, 12" oval, open handles, green or pink 25.50
Platter, 12" oval, open handles, yellow 232.00
Platter, 12½" oval, closed handles, yellow 200.00
Relish, four-part, blue, 8⅜" 48.50
Relish, four-part, pink, 8⅜" 27.50
Salt & pepper shakers, flat, blue, pr. 259.00
Salt & pepper shakers, flat, pink, pr. 57.00
Salt & pepper shakers, flat, pink frosted, pr. 39.00
Sandwich server w/center handle, blue, 12" 73.00

Sandwich server w/center handle, pink, 12" 43.50
Sandwich server w/center handle, pink frosted, 12" 20.50
Saucer w/cup ring, blue 20.00
Sherbet, flat, blue, 2¼" h. 127.00
Sherbet, flat, pink, 2¼" h. 153.00
Sherbet, footed, pink, 3" h. 16.00
Sherbet, footed, blue or pink, 4¾" h. 75.00
Sugar bowl, open, footed, blue 75.00
Sugar bowl, open, footed, pink 26.50
Sugar bowl, open, footed, pink frosted 16.00
Tumbler, whiskey, pink, 2¼" h., 1½ oz. 61.00
Tumbler, juice, footed, pink, 3¼" h., 3 oz. 80.00
Tumbler, juice, blue, 3½" h., 5 oz. 100.00
Tumbler, juice, pink, 3½" h., 5 oz. 38.50
Tumbler, water, blue, 4¼" h., 9 oz. 88.00
Tumbler, water, pink, 4¼" h., 9 oz. 26.50
Tumbler, footed, blue, 5¼" h., 10 oz. 123.00
Tumbler, footed, pink, 5¼" h., 10 oz. 34.50
Tumbler, water, blue, 4¾" h., 11 oz. 107.00
Tumbler, water, pink, 4¾" h., 11 oz. 128.50
Tumbler, iced tea, pink, 5¼" h., 13½ oz. 46.50
Tumbler, iced tea, footed, blue, 6½" h., 15 oz. 183.00
Tumbler, iced tea, footed, pink, 6½" h., 15 oz. 37.00
Vase, 5½ x 8½", sweetpea, hat-shaped, blue 93.00
Vase, 5½ x 8½", sweetpea, hat-shaped, pink 155.00

MISS AMERICA, Hocking Glass Co., 1935-38 (Press-mold)

Miss America Pitcher

Bowl, berry, 4½" d., green 10.00
Bowl, berry, 6¼" d., clear 9.50
Bowl, fruit, 8" d., curved in at top, pink 70.00
Bowl, fruit, 8¾" d., clear 36.00
Bowl, fruit, 8¾" d., pink 64.00
Bowl, 10" oval vegetable, clear 14.50
Bowl, 10" oval vegetable, pink 26.50
Butter dish, cov., clear 198.00
Butter dish, cov., pink 495.00
Cake plate, footed, clear, 12" d. 25.50
Cake plate, footed, pink, 12" d. 41.00
Candy jar, cov., clear, 11½" h. 58.00
Candy jar, cov., pink, 11½" h. 124.00
Celery tray, clear, 10½" oblong 14.50
Compote, 5" d., pink 25.00
Creamer, footed, clear 8.00
Creamer, footed, pink 15.50
Cup & saucer, pink 26.50
Goblet, wine, clear, 3¾" h., 3 oz. 18.50
Goblet, juice, pink, 4¾" h., 5 oz. 75.00
Goblet, water, clear, 5½" h., 10 oz. 18.00
Goblet, water, green, 5½" h., 10 oz. 14.00
Goblet, water, pink, 5½" h., 10 oz. 39.00
Pitcher, 8" h., 65 oz., clear 54.00
Pitcher, 8" h., 65 oz., pink 112.00
Pitcher w/ice lip, 8½" h., 65 oz., clear 55.00
Pitcher w/ice lip, 8½" h., 65 oz., pink (ILLUS.) 118.00
Plate, sherbet, 5¾" d., clear 5.50
Plate, sherbet, 5¾" d., pink 8.00
Plate, 6¾" d., green 7.50
Plate, salad, 8½" d., clear 7.00
Plate, salad, 8½" d., pink 21.50
Plate, dinner, 10¼" d., clear 13.00
Plate, dinner, 10¼" d., pink 29.00
Plate, grill, 10¼" d., clear 9.50
Plate, grill, 10¼" d., pink 22.50
Platter, 12¼" oval, clear 13.50
Platter, 12¼" oval, pink 23.50
Relish, four-part, clear, 8¾" d. 10.00
Salt & pepper shakers, clear, pr. 24.00
Salt & pepper shakers, green, pr. 180.00
Salt & pepper shakers, pink, pr. 58.50
Sherbet, clear 7.50
Sherbet, pink 14.00
Sugar bowl, open, footed, clear 7.00
Sugar bowl, open, footed, pink 17.50
Tumbler, juice, clear, 4" h., 5 oz. 15.50
Tumbler, juice, pink, 4" h., 5 oz. 42.50
Tumbler, water, clear, 4½" h., 10 oz. 15.00
Tumbler, water, green, 4½" h., 10 oz. 16.50
Tumbler, water, pink, 4½" h., 10 oz. 28.00

MODERNTONE, Hazel Atlas Glass Co., 1934-42, late 1940s and early 1950s (Press-mold)

Ashtray w/match holder, cobalt blue, 7¾" d. 195.00
Ashtray w/match holder, pink, 7¾" d. 42.50
Bowl, cream soup, 4¾" d., amethyst 16.00
Bowl, cream soup, 4¾" d., cobalt blue 19.00
Bowl, cream soup, 4¾" d., platonite 6.00
Bowl, berry, 5" d., amethyst or cobalt blue 21.00
Bowl, berry, 5" d., platonite 5.00
Bowl, cream soup w/ruffled rim, 5" d., cobalt blue 53.50

Bowl, cream soup w/ruffled rim, 5" d., platonite 5.00
Bowl, cereal, 6½" d., cobalt blue 70.00
Bowl, cereal, 6½" d., platonite 6.00
Bowl, soup, 7½" d., amethyst 10.00
Bowl, soup, 7½" d., cobalt blue 130.00
Bowl, soup, 7½" d., platonite 12.00
Bowl, large berry, 8¾" d., amethyst 44.00
Bowl, large berry, 8¾" d., cobalt blue 52.50
Bowl, large berry, 8¾" d., platonite 8.50
Butter dish w/metal lid, cobalt blue 93.50
Cheese dish w/metal lid, cobalt blue, 7" d. 411.00
Creamer, amethyst 9.00
Creamer, cobalt blue 11.00
Creamer, platonite 4.50
Cup, amethyst 9.00
Cup, cobalt blue 10.50
Cup, platonite 4.00
Custard cup, amethyst 11.50
Custard cup, cobalt blue 17.50
Plate, sherbet, 5⅞" d., amethyst 5.00
Plate, sherbet, 5⅞" d., cobalt blue 6.00
Plate, salad, 6¾" d., amethyst 5.00
Plate, salad, 6¾" d., cobalt blue 10.50
Plate, salad, 6¾" d., platonite 4.00
Plate, luncheon, 7¾" d., amethyst 10.00
Plate, luncheon, 7¾" d., cobalt blue 11.50
Plate, luncheon, 7¾" d., platonite 4.50
Plate, dinner, 8⅞" d., amethyst 12.00
Plate, dinner, 8⅞" d., cobalt blue 16.50
Plate, dinner, 8⅞" d., platonite 6.00
Plate, sandwich, 10½" d., amethyst 46.50
Plate, sandwich, 10½" d., cobalt blue 53.00
Plate, sandwich, 10½" d., platonite 13.50
Platter, 11" oval, cobalt blue 41.50
Platter, 11" oval, platonite 7.00
Platter, 12" oval, amethyst 42.50
Platter, 12" oval, cobalt blue 86.00
Platter, 12" oval, platonite 13.50
Salt & pepper shakers, amethyst, pr. 43.00
Salt & pepper shakers, cobalt blue, pr. 37.50
Salt & pepper shakers, platonite, pr. 12.50
Saucer, amethyst 4.00
Saucer, cobalt blue or platonite 5.00
Sherbet, amethyst 11.00
Sherbet, cobalt blue 12.00
Sherbet, platonite 4.00
Sugar bowl, open, amethyst or cobalt blue 10.00
Sugar bowl, open, platonite 6.00
Sugar bowl w/metal lid, cobalt blue 40.00
Tumbler, whiskey, clear, 1½ oz. 5.50
Tumbler, whiskey, cobalt blue, 1½ oz. 39.00
Tumbler, whiskey, platonite, 1½ oz. 11.50
Tumbler, juice, cobalt blue, 5 oz. 43.50
Tumbler, juice, platonite, 5 oz. 10.50
Tumbler, water, cobalt blue, 4" h., 9 oz. 33.00
Tumbler, water, platonite, 4" h., 9 oz. 8.00
Tumbler, iced tea, amethyst, 12 oz. 67.00

LITTLE HOSTESS PARTY SET

Creamer, 1¾" h., dark or pastel 11.00
Cup, 1¾" h., pastel 7.00
Cup & saucer, dark 16.00
Plate, 5¼" d., dark 10.00
Plate, 5¼" d., pastel 9.50
Saucer, 3⅞" d., pastel 8.50
Sugar bowl, 1¾" h., dark 10.50
Sugar bowl, 1¾" h., pastel 11.50
Teapot, cov., 3½" h., dark 89.00
Teapot, cov., 3½" h., pastel 60.00
Tea set, dark, 14 pcs. 120.00
Tea set, pastel, 14 pcs. 71.00
Tea set, pastel, 16 pcs. 220.00
Tea set, dark, 16 pcs. 210.00

MOONSTONE, Anchor Hocking Glass Corp., 1941-46 (Press-mold)

(All items clear to opalescent only. Also see Hobnail.)

Moonstone Vase

Bonbon, heart-shaped, w/handle, 6½" w. 11.50
Bowl, berry, 5½" d. 14.00
Bowl, dessert, 5½" d., crimped rim 8.50
Bowl, 6" w., three-part, cloverleaf-shaped 11.50
Bowl, 6½" d., two-handled, crimped rim 10.00
Bowl, 7¾" d., flat 12.00
Bowl, 9½" d., crimped rim 18.00
Candleholders, pr. 16.50
Candy dish, cov., two-handled, 6" d. 25.00
Cigarette box, cov., rectangular 20.00
Creamer, footed 8.00
Cup & saucer 13.00
Dinner set, service for four, 23 pcs. 275.00
Goblet, 10 oz. 18.50
Plate, sherbet, 6¼" d. 6.00
Plate, luncheon, 8" d. 13.00
Plate, sandwich, 10" d., crimped rim 23.50
Puff box, cov., 4¾" d. 20.50
Relish bowl, divided, 7¾" d. 10.00
Sherbet, footed 6.00
Sugar bowl, footed 8.00
Vase, bud, 5½" h. (ILLUS.) 11.00

MOROCCAN AMETHYST, Hazel Ware, Division of Continental Can, 1960's (not true Depression)

Moroccan Amethyst Cup & Saucer

Ashtray, 3¾" triangle 6.50
Ashtray, 6" triangle 10.00
Ashtray, 6⅞" triangle w/metal base 18.00
Ashtray set: round w/silver trim; two w/box & label 20.50
Bowl, fruit, 4¾" w. octagon 6.00
Bowl, cereal, 5¾" sq., deep 11.00
Bowl, 6" d. 10.50
Bowl, 6" d., w/metal center handle 33.00
Bowl, 6" sq., w/metal center handle 35.00
Bowl, 7¾" oval 16.00
Bowl, 7¾" oval w/center handle 18.00
Bowl, 7¾" rectangle 13.00
Bowl, 9½" oval, low 11.50
Bowl, 9½" oval, w/metal center handle 42.00
Candy jar, cov., short 25.50
Candy jar, cov., tall 29.00
Celery dish, 9½" l. 11.50
Chip & dip set, w/metal holder (5¾" & 10¾" bowls) 41.50
Cocktail set: cocktail stirrer w/pouring lip, stirring rod & two 2½" h. 4 oz. tumblers; w/original box, the set 37.00
Cocktail shaker w/chrome lid, 32 oz. 24.00
Cocktail stirrer, w/pouring lip, 6¼" h., 16 oz. 23.00
Compote 20.00
Cup (ILLUS.) 6.00
Dinner service for 12 w/serving pieces, 78 pcs. 425.00
Goblet, wine, 4" h., 4½ oz. 9.50
Goblet, juice, 4⅜" h., 5½ oz. 8.00
Goblet, water, 5½" h., 10 oz. 11.00
Ice bucket 25.50
Plate, 5¾" w. octagon 5.50
Plate, salad, 7¼" w. 7.00
Plate, dinner, 9¾" w. 9.50
Plate, sandwich, 12" w. 12.50
Punch cup 5.00
Punch set, bowl, base & 9 cups, 11 pcs. 95.00
Relish, 8" 8.50
Relish, 9½" 10.00
Relish server, two 5¾" sq. bowls in metal frame w/handle 28.00
Relish server, two 7¾" l. rectangular bowls in metal frame 35.00
Sandwich server, w/metal center handle, 12" 18.50
Saucer (ILLUS.) 2.00
Sherbet, footed, 4¼" h. 6.50
Snack set, four seashell-shaped plates, w/box 50.00
Tidbit server, two-tier 20.00
Tidbit server, three-tier 21.50
Tumbler, juice, 2½" h., 4 oz. 8.50
Tumbler, Old Fashioned, 3¼" h., 8 oz. 12.50
Tumbler, water, crinkled bottom, 4¼" h., 11 oz. 11.00
Tumbler, water, 4⅝" h., 11 oz. 12.50
Tumbler, iced tea, 6½" h., 16 oz. 15.50
Vase, 8½" h., ruffled 35.50

NORMANDIE or Bouquet and Lattice, Federal Glass Co., 1933-40 (Process-etched)

Bowl, berry, 5" d., amber or pink 6.00
Bowl, berry, 5" d., Sunburst iridescent 4.50
Bowl, cereal, 6½" d., amber or pink 18.00
Bowl, cereal, 6½" d., Sunburst iridescent 7.50
Bowl, large berry, 8½" d., amber 14.50
Bowl, large berry, 8½" d., pink 28.00
Bowl, large berry, 8½" d., Sunburst iridescent 13.50
Bowl, 10" oval vegetable, amber 15.00
Bowl, 10" oval vegetable, Sunburst iridescent 13.00
Creamer, footed, amber, pink or Sunburst iridescent 7.50
Cup, amber 7.50
Cup, Sunburst iridescent 5.50
Cup & saucer, pink 11.00
Luncheon set: 4 each 8" d. plates, cups & saucers plus creamer & sugar bowl; amber, 14 pcs. 80.00
Pitcher, 8" h., 80 oz., amber 70.00
Pitcher, 8" h., 80 oz., pink 100.00
Plate, sherbet, 6" d., amber 4.50
Plate, sherbet, 6" d., pink 3.50
Plate, sherbet, 6" d., Sunburst iridescent 2.50
Plate, salad, 8" d., amber 8.50
Plate, salad, 8" d., pink or Sunburst iridescent 10.50
Plate, luncheon, 9¼" d., amber 8.00
Plate, luncheon, 9¼" d., pink 12.00
Plate, dinner, 11" d., amber 19.50
Plate, dinner, 11" d., pink 116.00
Plate, dinner, 11" d., Sunburst iridescent 13.50
Plate, grill, 11" d., amber 13.50
Plate, grill, 11" d., Sunburst iridescent 7.50
Platter, 11¾" oval, amber 17.00

Platter, 11¾" oval, pink 29.00
Platter, 11¾" oval, Sunburst iridescent 12.50
Salt & pepper shakers, amber, pr. 43.00
Salt & pepper shakers, pink, pr. 81.50
Saucer, amber 4.00
Saucer, Sunburst iridescent 3.00
Sherbet, amber, clear or Sunburst iridescent 6.00
Sherbet, pink 9.00
Sugar bowl, cov., amber 81.00
Sugar bowl, open, amber 7.00
Sugar bowl, open, Sunburst iridescent...6.00
Tumbler, juice, amber, 4" h., 5 oz. 17.50
Tumbler, juice, pink, 4" h., 5 oz. 35.00
Tumbler, water, amber, 4½" h., 9 oz. ...15.00
Tumbler, water, pink, 4½" h., 9 oz. 41.00
Tumbler, iced tea, amber, 5" h., 12 oz. 19.00
Tumbler, iced tea, pink, 5" h., 12 oz. ..104.00

NUMBER 612 or Horseshoe, Indiana Glass Co., 1930-1933 (Process-etched)

Bowl, berry, 4½" d., green 21.00
Bowl, berry, 4½" d., yellow 18.00
Bowl, cereal, 6½" d., green 22.50
Bowl, cereal, 6½" d., yellow 19.50
Bowl, salad, 7½" d., green 18.50
Bowl, salad, 7½" d., yellow 19.50
Bowl, vegetable, 8½" d., green 19.00
Bowl, vegetable, 8½" d., yellow 30.00
Bowl, large berry, 9½" d., green 29.50
Bowl, large berry, 9½" d., yellow 31.50
Bowl, 10½" oval vegetable, green 18.50
Bowl, 10½" oval vegetable, yellow 22.50

Number 612 Butter Dish

Butter dish, cov., green (ILLUS.) 550.00
Creamer, footed, green or yellow 14.00
Cup, green 11.00
Cup, yellow 9.50
Pitcher, 8½" h., 64 oz., green 200.00
Pitcher, 8½" h., 64 oz., yellow 236.00
Plate, sherbet, 6" d., green 5.00
Plate, sherbet, 6" d., yellow 6.00
Plate, salad, 8⅜" d., green or yellow 8.50
Plate, luncheon, 9⅜" d., green 11.50
Plate, luncheon, 9⅜" d., yellow 13.00
Plate, dinner, 10⅜" d., green 16.50
Plate, grill, 10⅜" d., green 76.00
Plate, sandwich, 11" d., green 14.50
Plate, sandwich, 11" d., yellow 17.00
Platter, 10¾" oval, green 18.00
Platter, 10¾" oval, yellow 21.00
Relish, three-part, footed, green 15.00
Relish, three-part, footed, yellow 34.50
Saucer, green or yellow 4.50
Sherbet, green 14.00
Sherbet, yellow 15.50
Sugar bowl, open, footed, green 12.50
Sugar bowl, open, footed, yellow 14.00
Tumbler, footed, green or yellow, 9 oz. 20.00
Tumbler, footed, yellow, 12 oz. 102.50

OLD CAFE, Hocking Glass Co., 1936-40 (Press-mold)

Old Cafe Candy Dishes

Bowl, berry, 3¾" d., pink 7.50
Bowl, nappy, 5" d., handled, clear 3.50
Bowl, nappy, 5" d., handled, pink 7.00
Bowl, cereal, 5½" d., pink or ruby 11.50
Bowl, 9" d., handled, pink 7.50
Bowl, 9" d., handled, ruby 12.50
Candy dish, clear, 8" d. 7.50
Candy dish, pink, 8" d.(ILLUS. right) 10.00
Candy dish, ruby, 8" d.(ILLUS. left) 12.00
Cup, ruby 6.50
Cup & saucer, pink 11.00
Cup & saucer, ruby cup, clear saucer ..10.00
Lamp, pink 12.50
Olive dish, clear, 6" oblong 5.00
Olive dish, pink, 6" oblong 6.00
Pitcher, 6" h., 36 oz., clear 25.00
Pitcher, 6" h., 36 oz., pink 74.00
Pitcher, 8" h., 80 oz., pink 84.00
Plate, sherbet, 6" d., clear 4.00
Plate, sherbet, 6" d., pink 11.50
Plate, dinner, 10" d., pink 29.50
Sherbet, low foot, clear 3.50
Sherbet, low foot, pink 8.00
Tumbler, juice, clear or ruby, 3" h. 6.00
Tumbler, juice, pink, 3" h. 12.50
Tumbler, water, pink, 4" h. 13.00
Tumbler, water, ruby, 4" h. 12.00
Vase, 7¼" h., clear 9.00

OYSTER & PEARL, Anchor Hocking Glass Corp., 1938-40 (Press-mold)

Bowl, 5¼" heart-shaped, w/handle, clear or white w/green 7.00

Bowl, 5¼" heart-shaped, w/handle, pink 9.50
Bowl, 5¼" heart-shaped, w/handle, white w/pink 8.00
Bowl, 5½" d., w/handle, clear 8.50
Bowl, 5½" d., w/handle, ruby 13.00
Bowl, 6½" d., handled, pink 11.50
Bowl, 6½" d., handled, ruby 18.50
Bowl, fruit, 10½" d., clear 18.00
Bowl, fruit, 10½" d., pink 23.50
Bowl, fruit, 10½" d., ruby 44.00
Bowl, fruit, 10½" d., white w/green or white w/pink 13.00
Candleholders, clear, 3½" h., pr. 20.50
Candleholders, pink, 3½" h., pr. 17.00
Candleholders, ruby, 3½" h., pr. 41.50
Candleholders, white w/green, 3½" h., pr. 12.50
Candleholders, white w/pink, 3½" h., pr. 14.00
Plate, sandwich, 13½" d., clear 12.50
Plate, sandwich, 13½" d., pink 18.00
Plate, sandwich, 13½" d., ruby 32.00
Relish, divided, clear, 10¼" oval 8.00
Relish, divided, pink, 10¼" oval 10.00

PARROT or Sylvan, Federal Glass Co., 1931-32 (Process-etched)

Bowl, berry, 5" sq., amber 14.50
Bowl, berry, 5" sq., green 18.50
Bowl, soup, 7" sq., amber 29.50
Bowl, soup, 7" sq., green 38.50
Bowl, large berry, 8" sq., green 57.50
Bowl, 10" oval vegetable, green 46.50
Butter dish, cov., green 315.00
Creamer, footed, green 45.00
Cup & saucer, amber 39.00
Cup & saucer, green 50.00
Hot plate, green, scalloped edge 775.00
Jam dish, amber, 7" sq. 30.00
Plate, sherbet, 5¾" sq., amber 16.50
Plate, sherbet, 5¾" sq., green 18.00
Plate, salad, 7½" sq., green 31.50
Plate, dinner, 9" sq., green 43.50
Plate, grill, 10½" sq., amber 24.00
Plate, grill, 10½" d., green 28.00
Platter, 11¼" oblong, green 45.50
Salt & pepper shakers, green, pr. 205.00
Sherbet, footed, cone-shaped, amber 19.00
Sherbet, footed, cone-shaped, green 22.00
Sugar bowl, cov., green 150.00
Sugar bowl, open, green 21.00
Tumbler, green, 4¼" h., 10 oz. 97.50
Tumbler, footed, amber, 5½" h., 10 oz. 118.00
Tumbler, footed, cone-shaped, green, 5¾" h. 102.00

PATRICIAN or Spoke, Federal Glass Co., 1933-37 (Process-etched)

Bowl, cream soup, 4¾" d., amber 13.50
Bowl, cream soup, 4¾" d., clear, green or pink 15.00
Bowl, berry, 5" d., amber or green 10.00
Bowl, berry, 5" d., clear 9.00
Bowl, berry, 5" d., pink 11.00
Bowl, cereal, 6" d., amber or green 22.00
Bowl, cereal, 6" d., clear or pink 20.00
Bowl, large berry, 8½" d., amber 41.50
Bowl, large berry, 8½" d., clear 38.00
Bowl, large berry, 8½" d., green 30.00

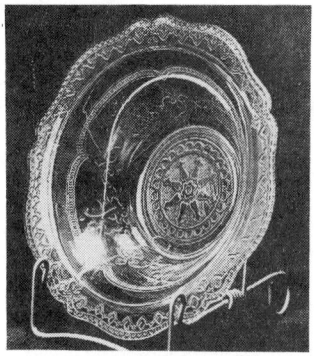

Patrician Berry Bowl

Bowl, large berry, 8½" d., pink (ILLUS.) 24.00
Bowl, 10" oval vegetable, amber or clear 27.50
Bowl, 10" oval vegetable, green 29.50
Bowl, 10" oval vegetable, pink 18.00
Butter dish, cov., amber or clear 81.50
Butter dish, cov., green 95.00
Butter dish, cov., pink 227.00
Cookie jar, cov., amber 80.00
Cookie jar, cov., clear 75.00
Cookie jar, cov., green 405.00
Creamer, footed, amber 8.00
Creamer, footed, clear or pink 9.00
Creamer, footed, green 11.50
Cup, amber or green 8.00
Cup & saucer, clear 13.00
Cup & saucer, pink 17.00
Jam dish, amber, 6" 26.50
Jam dish, green, 6" 29.00
Pitcher, 8" h., 75 oz., molded handle, amber 102.00
Pitcher, 8" h., 75 oz., molded handle, clear 95.00
Pitcher, 8" h., 75 oz., molded handle, green 107.00
Pitcher, 8" h., 75 oz., molded handle, pink 112.00
Pitcher, 8¼" h., 75 oz., applied handle, amber 95.00
Pitcher, 8¼" h., 75 oz., applied handle, clear 125.00
Pitcher, 8¼" h., 75 oz., applied handle, green 110.00
Plate, sherbet, 6" d., amber or pink 8.50
Plate, sherbet, 6" d., clear 5.50
Plate, sherbet, 6" d., green 6.50
Plate, salad, 7½" d., amber or green 13.50
Plate, salad, 7½" d., clear 12.00

Plate, luncheon, 9" d., amber, clear or green....10.00
Plate, luncheon, 9" d., pink....12.50
Plate, dinner, 10½" d., amber....6.50
Plate, dinner, 10½" d., green or pink....39.00
Plate, grill, 10½" d., amber or clear....11.50
Plate, grill, 10½" d., green or pink....10.50
Platter, 11½" oval, amber or clear....27.00
Platter, 11½" oval, green....23.50
Salt & pepper shakers, amber or clear, pr....52.50
Salt & pepper shakers, green, pr....51.00
Salt & pepper shakers, pink, pr....77.50
Saucer, amber or green....9.00
Sherbet, amber or clear....10.50
Sherbet, green or pink....12.50
Sugar bowl, cov., amber....61.00
Sugar bowl, cov., clear....54.00
Sugar bowl, cov., green....43.50
Sugar bowl, cov., pink....52.00
Sugar bowl, open, amber or clear....8.00
Sugar bowl, open, green....9.00
Sugar bowl, open, pink....10.50
Tumbler, amber or green, 4" h., 5 oz....27.00
Tumbler, clear, 4" h., 5 oz....20.00
Tumbler, footed, amber, 5¼" h., 8 oz....44.50
Tumbler, footed, clear, 5¼" h., 8 oz....34.00
Tumbler, footed, green, 5¼" h., 8 oz....47.50
Tumbler, amber or green, 4½" h., 9 oz....24.00
Tumbler, clear, 4½" h., 9 oz....26.00
Tumbler, pink, 4½" h., 9 oz....23.50
Tumbler, iced tea, amber, 5½" h., 14 oz....38.50
Tumbler, iced tea, clear, 5½" h., 14 oz....35.00
Tumbler, iced tea, green, 5½" h., 14 oz....27.00
Tumbler, iced tea, pink, 5½" h., 14 oz....40.00

PETALWARE, MacBeth-Evans Glass Co., 1930-40 (Press-mold)

Bowl, cream soup, 4½" d., clear....5.50
Bowl, cream soup, 4½" d., plain Cremax or Monax....10.50
Bowl, cream soup, 4½" d., decorated Cremax or Monax....10.50
Bowl, cream soup, 4½" d., Florette....10.00
Bowl, cream soup, 4½" d., pink....12.50
Bowl, cereal, 5¾" d., clear....5.00
Bowl, cereal, 5¾" d., plain Cremax or Monax....7.00
Bowl, cereal, 5¾" d., decorated Cremax or Monax....7.00
Bowl, cereal, 5¾" d., Florette....11.00
Bowl, cereal, 5¾" d., pink....9.50
Bowl, large berry, 9" d., plain Cremax or Monax....17.00
Bowl, large berry, 9" d., decorated Cremax or Monax....26.00
Bowl, large berry, 9" d., Florette....25.00
Bowl, large berry, 9" d., pink....17.50
Creamer, footed, clear....3.50
Creamer, footed, plain Cremax or Monax....7.50
Creamer, footed, decorated Cremax or Monax....8.50
Creamer, footed, Florette....11.00
Creamer, footed, pink....12.00
Cup, plain Cremax or Monax....5.00
Cup, decorated Cremax or Monax....6.50
Cup, Florette....9.00
Cup & saucer, clear....4.00
Cup & saucer, clear w/platinum trim....5.00
Cup & saucer, Red Trim Floral or pink....10.00
Lamp shade, Monax, 6" h....8.00
Lamp shade, Monax, 11" h....15.50
Lamp shade, pink, 12" h....21.00
Mustard jar w/metal cover, cobalt blue....15.00
Plate, sherbet, 6" d., clear....1.50
Plate, sherbet, 6" d., plain Cremax or Monax....2.50
Plate, sherbet, 6" d., decorated Cremax or Monax....4.00
Plate, sherbet, 6" d., pink....3.50
Plate, salad, 8" d., clear....2.50
Plate, salad, 8" d., plain Cremax or Monax....5.00
Plate, salad, 8" d., decorated Cremax or Monax....8.50
Plate, salad, 8" d., Florette....8.50
Plate, salad, 8" d., Red Trim Floral or pink....6.50
Plate, dinner, 9" d., clear....6.00
Plate, dinner, 9" d., plain Cremax or Monax....7.00
Plate, dinner, 9" d., decorated Cremax or Monax....13.00
Plate, dinner, 9" d., pink....8.50
Plate, salver, 11" d., clear w/platinum trim....5.00
Plate, salver, 11" d., plain Cremax or Monax....10.50
Plate, salver, 11" d., decorated Cremax or Monax`....19.50
Plate, salver, 11" d., Florette....15.50
Plate, salver, 11" d., Red Trim Floral....18.50
Plate, salver, 11" d., pink....14.00
Plate, salver, 12" d., plain Cremax or Monax....10.50
Plate, salver, 12" d., decorated Cremax or Monax....10.00
Plate, salver, 12" d., Florette....14.50
Plate, salver, 12" d., Red Trim Floral....40.00
Platter, 13" oval, plain Cremax or Monax....19.00
Platter, 13" oval, decorated Cremax or Monax....13.50
Platter, 13" oval, pink....15.50
Saucer, plain Cremax or Monax....2.00
Saucer, decorated Cremax or Monax....2.00
Saucer, Florette....3.50

Sherbet, low foot, clear, 4½" h.....6.00
Sherbet, low foot, cobalt blue, 4½" h. ...12.00
Sherbet, low foot, plain Cremax or Monax, 4½" h.....9.00
Sherbet, low foot, decorated Cremax or Monax, 4½" h.....11.00
Sherbet, low foot, Red Trim Floral, 4½" h.....30.00
Sherbet, low foot, pink, 4½" h.....7.50
Sugar bowl, open, footed, clear.....4.50
Sugar bowl, open, footed, plain Cremax or Monax.....7.00
Sugar bowl, open, footed, decorated Cremax or Monax 10.00
Sugar bowl, open, footed, Florette or pink 10.00
Tidbit server, plain Cremax or Monax...23.00
Tumbler, juice, pink 5.00
Tumbler, pink, 4¼" h.....29.00
Tumbler, pink, 4¾" h.....27.00

PINEAPPLE & FLORAL or Number 618 or Wildflower, Indiana Glass Co., 1932-37 (Press-mold)

Pineapple & Floral Plate

Ashtray, clear, 4½" l.....13.00
Bowl, berry, 4¾" d., amber 15.00
Bowl, berry, 4¾" d., clear.....24.50
Bowl, cream soup, 4⅝", amber or clear.....18.00
Bowl, cereal, 6" d., amber or clear.....21.00
Bowl, salad, 7" d., clear 3.50
Bowl, 10" oval vegetable, amber 18.00
Bowl, 10" oval vegetable, clear.....23.50
Compote, diamond-shaped, amber 5.00
Compote, diamond-shaped, clear 3.50
Creamer, diamond-shaped, amber.....9.50
Creamer, diamond-shaped, clear 5.50
Cup, amber.....6.00
Cup, clear 8.00
Plate, sherbet, 6" d., amber (ILLUS.).....4.00
Plate, sherbet, 6" d., clear 3.00
Plate, salad, 8⅜" d., amber or clear 7.00
Plate, dinner, 9⅜" d., amber.....12.00
Plate, dinner, 9⅜" d., clear 13.50
Plate, sandwich, 11½" d., amber.....15.50
Plate, sandwich, 11½" d., clear 12.50
Plate, 11½" d., w/indentation, clear 16.00
Platter, 11", closed handles, amber or clear.....15.50
Relish, divided, clear, 11½" 14.50
Saucer, amber or clear.....4.00
Sherbet, footed, amber or clear.....16.00
Sugar bowl, open, diamond-shaped, amber.....9.00
Sugar bowl, open, diamond-shaped, clear 6.00
Tumbler, clear, 4¼" h., 8 oz.....30.50
Tumbler, iced tea, clear, 5" h., 12 oz. ...42.50
Vase, 12½" h., cone-shaped, clear.....42.00
Vase, 12½" h., cone-shaped, clear w/holder 60.00

PRINCESS, Hocking Glass Co., 1931-35 (Process-etched)

Ashtray, green, 4½" 61.00
Ashtray, pink, 4½".....22.00
Bowl, berry, 4½", green 20.00
Bowl, berry, 4½", pink.....17.50
Bowl, berry, 4½", yellow 42.00
Bowl, cereal, 5", green or yellow 25.50
Bowl, cereal, 5", pink 22.00
Bowl, salad, 9" octagon, green or pink 36.00
Bowl, salad, 9" octagon, yellow 93.00
Bowl, 9½" hat shape, green.....38.00
Bowl, 9½" hat shape, pink 35.00
Bowl, 10" oval vegetable, green 24.00
Bowl, 10" oval vegetable, pink.....25.50
Bowl, 10" oval vegetable, yellow 49.00
Butter dish, cov., green or pink.....81.00
Butter dish, cov., yellow.....560.00
Cake stand, green, 10" 19.50
Cake stand, pink, 10".....23.50
Candy jar, cov., green 53.00
Candy jar, cov., pink 49.50
Coaster, green, 4".....31.50
Cookie jar, cov., green.....51.00
Cookie jar, cov., pink 48.00
Creamer, oval, green.....15.50
Creamer, oval, yellow 12.50
Cup, amber.....7.00
Cup, green.....9.50
Cup & saucer, pink 17.50
Cup & saucer, yellow.....10.50
Pitcher, 6" h., 37 oz., jug-type, green or pink 48.00
Pitcher, 8" h., 60 oz., jug-type, green or pink 49.50
Pitcher, 8" h., 60 oz., jug-type, yellow...78.00
Plate, sherbet, 5½", green 8.00
Plate, sherbet, 5½", pink.....9.00
Plate, sherbet, 5½", yellow 3.50
Plate, salad, 8", amber 8.00
Plate, salad, 8", green 12.50
Plate, salad, 8", pink.....11.00
Plate, salad, 8", yellow.....9.50
Plate, dinner, 9", green or pink 21.50
Plate, dinner, 9", yellow 12.00
Plate, grill, 9", green 11.00
Plate, grill, 9", pink.....12.50

Plate, grill, 9", yellow....5.50
Plate, grill, 10½", closed handles, green....11.00
Plate, grill, 10½", closed handles, pink....7.00
Plate, grill, 10½", closed handles, yellow....5.50
Plate, sandwich, 11¼", handled, green....15.00
Plate, sandwich, 11¼", handled, pink...24.00
Platter, 12" oval, closed handles, green....21.00
Platter, 12" oval, closed handles, pink..19.00
Relish, green, 7½"....103.00
Relish, pink, 7½"....300.00
Relish, divided, green, 7½"....24.50
Relish, divided, pink, 7½"....17.00
Salt & pepper shakers, green, 4½" h., pr....46.00
Salt & pepper shakers, pink, 4½" h., pr....42.50
Salt & pepper shakers, yellow, 4½" h., pr....65.00
Salt & pepper (or spice) shakers, green, 5½" h., pr....39.00
Saucer, green....9.00
Sherbet, footed, green or pink....17.50
Sherbet, footed, yellow....28.50
Sugar bowl, cov., green....27.50
Sugar bowl, cov., pink....44.00
Sugar bowl, cov., yellow....23.50
Sugar bowl, open, green....9.00
Sugar bowl, open, pink....7.50
Sugar bowl, open, yellow....8.50
Tumbler, juice, green, 3" h., 5 oz....27.50
Tumbler, juice, pink, 3" h., 5 oz....23.00
Tumbler, juice, yellow, 3" h., 5 oz....24.50
Tumbler, water, green or pink, 4" h., 9 oz....24.00
Tumbler, water, yellow, 4" h., 9 oz....20.50
Tumbler, footed, green, 5¼" h., 10 oz....28.00
Tumbler, footed, pink, 5¼" h., 10 oz....24.00
Tumbler, footed, yellow, 5¼" h., 10 oz....20.00
Tumbler, footed, green, 6½" h., 12½ oz....84.00
Tumbler, footed, pink, 6½" h., 12½ oz....67.50
Tumbler, footed, yellow, 6½" h., 12½ oz....22.50
Tumbler, iced tea, green, 5¼" h., 13 oz....35.00
Tumbler, iced tea, pink, 5¼" h., 13 oz....25.50
Tumbler, iced tea, yellow, 5¼" h., 13 oz....22.50
Vase, 8" h., green or pink....29.50
Vase, 8" h., pink frosted....20.00

QUEEN MARY or Vertical Ribbed, Hocking Glass Co., 1936-49 (Press-mold)

Ashtray, clear, 2 x 3¾" oval....3.00
Ashtray, clear, 3½" d....5.50
Ashtray, ruby, 3½" d....8.00
Bowl, nappy, 4" d., clear....3.50
Bowl, nappy, 4" d., pink....5.00
Bowl, nappy, 4" d., single handle, clear..4.00
Bowl, nappy, 4" d., single handle, pink...5.50
Bowl, berry, 5" d., clear or pink....5.50
Bowl, 5½" d., two-handled, pink....16.00
Bowl, cereal, 6" d., clear....6.00
Bowl, cereal, 6" d., pink....22.00
Bowl, nappy, 7" d., clear....9.50
Bowl, nappy, 7" d., pink....23.50
Bowl, large berry, 8¾" d., clear....10.00
Butter (or jam) dish, cov., clear....29.50
Candlesticks, two-light, clear, 4½" h., pr....15.50
Candy dish, cov., clear....23.50
Candy dish, cov., pink....33.00
Celery (or pickle) dish, clear, 5 x 10" oval....9.50
Celery (or pickle) dish, pink, 5 x 10" oval....17.00
Cigarette jar, clear, 2 x 3" oval....4.50
Coaster, clear, 3½" d....2.50
Coaster, pink, 3½" d....4.00
Coaster-ashtray, clear, 4¼" sq....3.50
Coaster-ashtray, pink, 4¼" sq....8.50
Compote, 5¾" d., clear....7.00
Creamer, oval, clear....4.50
Creamer, oval, pink....10.50
Cup, pink....7.50
Cup & saucer, clear....8.50
Plate, sherbet, 6" d., clear....3.50
Plate, sherbet, 6" d., pink....4.50
Plate, 6⅝" d., clear....4.00
Plate, 6⅝" d., pink....10.50
Plate, salad, 8½" d., clear....4.50
Plate, dinner, 9¾" d., clear....14.50
Plate, dinner, 9¾" d., pink....42.00
Plate, sandwich, 12" d., clear....8.50
Plate, sandwich, 12" d., pink....15.00
Plate, serving, 14" d., clear....9.00
Relish, three-part, clear, 12" d....10.50
Relish, four-part, clear, 14" d....10.00
Salt & pepper shakers, clear, pr....16.50
Saucer, pink....12.00
Sherbet, footed, clear....4.50
Sherbet, footed, pink....7.00
Sugar bowl, open, oval, clear....4.50
Sugar bowl, open, oval, pink....12.50
Tumbler, juice, pink, 3½" h., 5 oz....9.00
Tumbler, water, clear, 4" h., 9 oz....6.50
Tumbler, water, pink, 4" h., 9 oz....10.50
Tumbler, footed, clear, 5" h., 10 oz....17.50
Tumbler, footed, pink, 5" h., 10 oz....51.50

RAINDROPS or Optic Design, Federal Glass Co., 1929-33 (Press-mold)

(All items listed are green)

Bowl, cereal, 6" d....5.50
Bowl, berry, 7½" d....28.00
Cup & saucer....6.50
Plate, sherbet, 6" d....2.00

Plate, luncheon, 8" d. 5.00
Tumbler, whiskey, 1⅞" h., 1 oz. 5.50
Tumbler, 3" h., 4 oz. 4.00
Tumbler, 3⅞" h., 5 oz. 5.00
Tumbler, 4⅛" h., 9½ oz. 7.50

RIBBON, Hazel Atlas Glass Co., early 1930s (Press-mold)

(While pattern was also made in black, all items listed are green.)

Bowl, berry, 4" d. 12.00
Bowl, 8" d. 22.00
Candy dish, cov. 34.00
Creamer, footed 12.00
Cup & saucer 8.00
Plate, sherbet, 6¼" d. 3.50
Plate, luncheon, 8" d. 5.00
Salt & pepper shakers, pr. 23.50
Sherbet, footed 5.00
Sugar bowl, open, footed 12.00
Tumbler, 6" h., 10 oz. 24.50

RING or Banded Rings, Hocking Glass Co., 1927-33 (Press-mold)

Bowl, berry, 5" d., clear 3.50
Bowl, berry, 5" d., clear w/multicolored bands 6.00
Bowl, berry, 5" d., green 5.50
Bowl, soup, 7" d., clear 11.50
Bowl, soup, 7" d., clear w/platinum trim ..7.00
Bowl, soup, 7" d., clear w/multicolored bands 6.50
Bowl, soup, 7" d., green 8.50
Bowl, large berry, 8" d., green 10.50
Butter tub, clear w/multicolored bands 23.50
Cocktail shaker, clear 15.50
Cocktail shaker, clear w/multicolored bands 23.50
Cocktail shaker, clear w/platinum trim ..14.00
Cocktail shaker, green 12.00
Creamer, footed, clear 4.00
Creamer, footed, green 8.50
Cup, clear w/platinum trim 4.50
Cup, green 4.50
Cup & saucer, clear w/multicolored bands 5.00
Cup & saucer, green w/platinum trim 6.50
Decanter w/stopper, clear 19.00
Decanter w/stopper, clear w/multi-colored bands 28.00
Dinner set: four each 8" d. plates, cups & saucers, low sherbets & footed water tumblers plus center handled plate; green, 21 pcs. 170.00
Goblet, clear, 7¼" h., 9 oz. 7.00
Goblet, clear w/multicolored bands, 7¼" h., 9 oz. 10.50
Goblet, clear w/platinum trim, 7¼" h., 9 oz. 12.00
Goblet, green, 7¼" h., 9 oz. 10.50
Ice bucket w/tab handles, clear 12.50
Ice bucket w/tab handles, clear w/multicolored bands 17.00
Pitcher, 8" h., 60 oz., clear 14.00
Pitcher, 8" h., 60 oz., clear w/multi-colored bands 16.00
Pitcher, 8" h., 60 oz., green 17.00
Pitcher, 8½" h., 80 oz., clear 17.00
Pitcher, 8½" h., 80 oz., clear w/multi-colored bands 33.00
Pitcher, 8½" h., 80 oz., green 22.50
Plate, sherbet, 6¼" d., clear 1.50
Plate, sherbet, 6¼" d., clear w/multi-colored bands 2.00
Plate, sherbet, 6¼" d., green 2.00
Plate, 6½" d., off-center ring, clear w/multicolored bands 5.00
Plate, 6½" d., off-center ring, green 5.00
Plate, luncheon, 8" d., clear 4.00
Plate, luncheon, 8" d., clear w/multi-colored bands 2.50
Plate, luncheon, 8" d., clear w/platinum trim 4.50
Plate, luncheon, 8" d., green 4.50
Plate, luncheon, 8" d., green w/platinum trim 5.50
Salt & pepper shakers, clear, 3" h., pr. 18.00
Salt & pepper shakers, clear w/multi-colored bands, 3" h., pr. 24.00
Sandwich server w/center handle, clear 14.00
Sandwich server w/center handle, clear w/multicolored bands 16.00
Sandwich server w/center handle, green 19.50
Saucer, green 2.00
Sherbet, low, clear 6.00
Sherbet, low, clear w/multicolored bands 16.00
Sherbet, low, green 12.50
Sherbet, footed, clear, 4¾" h. 5.50
Sherbet, footed, clear w/multicolored bands, 4¾" h. 6.50
Sherbet, footed, green, 4¾" h. 8.00
Sugar bowl, open, footed, clear 4.50
Tumbler, whiskey, clear w/multicolored bands, 2" h., 1½ oz. 6.50
Tumbler, clear, 3½" h., 5 oz. 3.50
Tumbler, clear w/multicolored bands, 3½" h., 5 oz. 8.50
Tumbler, green, 3½" h., 5 oz. 12.50
Tumbler, clear, 3¾" h., 8 oz. 10.00
Tumbler, clear w/platinum trim, 3¾" h., 8 oz. 7.00
Tumbler, clear, 4¼" h., 9 oz. 5.50
Tumbler, clear w/multicolored bands, 4¼" h., 9 oz. 8.00
Tumbler, green, 4¼" h., 9 oz. 11.50
Tumbler, green, 4¾" h., 10 oz. 15.50
Tumbler, clear, 5⅛" h., 12 oz. 5.50
Tumbler, clear w/multicolored bands, 5⅛" h., 12 oz. 8.00
Tumbler, green, 5⅛" h., 12 oz. 13.50
Tumbler, pink, 5⅛" h., 12 oz. 7.00

Tumbler, cocktail, footed, clear, 3½" h. ..4.00
Tumbler, cocktail, footed, clear w/multicolored bands, 3½" h. 6.50
Tumbler, cocktail, footed, green, 3½" h. 12.00
Tumbler, water, footed, clear, 5½" h. 4.50
Tumbler, water, footed, clear w/multicolored bands, 5½" h. 6.00
Tumbler, water, footed, green, 5½" h. ..15.50
Tumbler, iced tea, footed, clear, 6½" h. ..6.50
Tumbler, iced tea, footed, clear w/multicolored bands, 6½" h. 8.50
Vase, 8" h., clear 12.50
Vase, 8" h., clear w/multicolored bands 25.00

ROULETTE or Many Windows, Hocking Glass Co., 1935-39 (Press-mold)

Bowl, fruit, 9" d., green 14.00
Cup, green 5.50
Pitcher, 8" h., 64 oz., green 30.00
Pitcher, 8" h., 64 oz., pink 26.50
Plate, sherbet, 6" d., green 3.00
Plate, luncheon, 8½" d., clear 4.00
Plate, luncheon, 8½" d., green 6.00
Plate, sandwich, 12" d., green 15.00
Saucer, green 4.00
Sherbet, green 5.50
Tumbler, whiskey, green, 2½" h., 1½ oz. 6.50
Tumbler, whiskey, pink, 2½" h., 1½ oz. 11.00
Tumbler, juice, green, 3¼" h., 5 oz. 18.50
Tumbler, juice, pink, 3¼" h., 5 oz. 7.00
Tumbler, Old Fashioned, pink, 3¼" h., 7½ oz. 19.00
Tumbler, water, green, 4⅛" h., 9 oz. 19.00
Tumbler, water, pink, 4⅛" h., 9 oz. 15.50
Tumbler, footed, green, 5½" h., 10 oz. 22.50
Tumbler, iced tea, green, 5⅛" h., 12 oz. 21.50
Tumbler, iced tea, pink, 5⅛" h., 12 oz. 14.50

ROYAL LACE, Hazel Atlas Glass Co., 1934-41 (Process-etched)

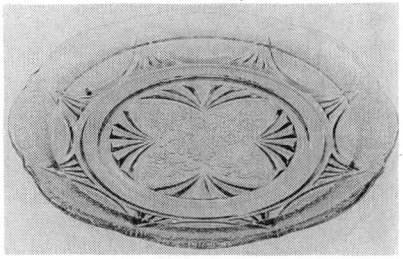

Royal Lace Plate

Bowl, cream soup, 4¾" d., blue 34.50
Bowl, cream soup, 4¾" d., clear 11.50
Bowl, cream soup, 4¾" d., green or pink 28.50
Bowl, berry, 5" d., blue 35.00
Bowl, berry, 5" d., clear 13.00
Bowl, berry, 5" d., green 28.00
Bowl, berry, 5" d., pink 22.50
Bowl, berry, 10" d., green 24.00
Bowl, berry, 10" d., pink 30.00
Bowl, 10" d., three-footed, rolled edge, blue 250.00
Bowl, 10" d., three-footed, rolled edge, clear 29.00
Bowl, 10" d., three-footed, rolled edge, pink 47.50
Bowl, 10" d., three-footed, ruffled edge, clear 35.00
Bowl, 10" d., three-footed, ruffled edge, green 65.00
Bowl, 10" d., three-footed, ruffled edge, pink 51.00
Bowl, 10" d., three-footed, straight edge, blue 70.00
Bowl, 11" oval vegetable, blue 43.50
Bowl, 11" oval vegetable, clear 14.00
Bowl, 11" oval vegetable, green 27.50
Bowl, 11" oval vegetable, pink 29.50
Butter dish, cov., blue 465.00
Butter dish, cov., clear 65.00
Butter dish, cov., green 250.00
Butter dish, cov., pink 139.00
Candlesticks, rolled edge, blue, pr. 167.50
Candlesticks, rolled edge, clear, pr. 25.00
Candlesticks, rolled edge, pink, pr. 42.50
Candlesticks, ruffled edge, blue, pr. ...132.00
Candlesticks, ruffled edge, clear, pr. 28.00
Candlesticks, ruffled edge, green, pr. ...42.50
Candlesticks, ruffled edge, pink, pr. 45.50
Candlesticks, straight edge, blue, pr. ...90.00
Candlesticks, straight edge, clear, pr. ..32.00
Cookie jar, cov., blue 348.00
Cookie jar, cov., clear 38.00
Cookie jar, cov., green 88.00
Cookie jar, cov., pink 44.00
Creamer, footed, blue 49.00
Creamer, footed, clear 12.50
Creamer, footed, green 24.00
Creamer, footed, pink 17.00
Cup, blue 35.50
Cup, clear 6.00
Cup & saucer, green 26.50
Cup & saucer, pink 18.50
Nut bowl, green 185.00
Pitcher, 48 oz., straight sides, blue 146.00
Pitcher, 48 oz., straight sides, clear 37.50
Pitcher, 48 oz., straight sides, green 95.50
Pitcher, 8" h., 64 oz., without ice lip, blue 156.00
Pitcher, 8" h., 68 oz., w/ice lip, clear 40.00
Pitcher, 8" h., 68 oz., w/ice lip, pink 53.50
Pitcher, 8" h., 86 oz., without ice lip, pink 70.00
Pitcher, 8½" h., 96 oz., w/ice lip, blue 257.00
Pitcher, 8½" h., 96 oz., w/ice lip, clear 59.00

Pitcher, 8½" h., 96 oz., w/ice lip, green....150.00
Plate, sherbet, 6" d., blue....14.00
Plate, sherbet, 6" d., clear....5.00
Plate, sherbet, 6" d., green or pink....8.00
Plate, luncheon, 8½" d., blue (ILLUS.)....31.00
Plate, luncheon, 8½" d., green or pink..15.50
Plate, dinner, 9⅞" d., blue....36.00
Plate, dinner, 9⅞" d., clear....17.00
Plate, dinner, 9⅞" d., green or pink....26.00
Plate, grill, 9⅞" d., blue....29.50
Plate, grill, 9⅞" d., pink....17.50
Platter, 13" oval, blue....46.50
Platter, 13" oval, clear....14.00
Platter, 13" oval, green....30.00
Platter, 13" oval, pink....32.50
Salt & pepper shakers, blue, pr....225.00
Salt & pepper shakers, clear, pr....39.50
Salt & pepper shakers, green, pr....120.00
Salt & pepper shakers, pink, pr....58.50
Saucer, blue....9.00
Saucer, clear....6.00
Sherbet, footed, blue....34.50
Sherbet, footed, clear or pink....12.50
Sherbet, footed, green....23.00
Sherbet in metal holder, amethyst....34.00
Sherbet in metal holder, blue....23.50
Sherbet in metal holder, clear....9.00
Sherbet in metal holder, green....5.50
Sugar bowl, cov., blue....198.00
Sugar bowl, cov., clear....23.50
Sugar bowl, cov., green....57.00
Sugar bowl, cov., pink....38.00
Sugar bowl, open, blue....31.00
Sugar bowl, open, clear....7.50
Sugar bowl, open, green....21.00
Sugar bowl, open, pink....15.50
Toddy or cider set: cookie jar w/metal lid & 6 roly-poly tumblers; blue, 7 pcs....125.00
Tumbler, blue, 3½" h., 5 oz....40.00
Tumbler, clear, 3½" h., 5 oz....12.50
Tumbler, green, 3½" h., 5 oz....21.50
Tumbler, pink, 3½" h., 5 oz....18.00
Tumbler, blue, 4⅛" h., 9 oz....37.00
Tumbler, clear, 4⅛" h., 9 oz....11.50
Tumbler, green, 4⅛" h., 9 oz....28.00
Tumbler, pink, 4⅛" h., 9 oz....18.00
Tumbler, blue, 4⅞" h., 10 oz....88.00
Tumbler, pink, 4⅞" h., 10 oz....35.00
Tumbler, blue, 5⅜" h., 12 oz....66.00
Tumbler, clear, 5⅜" h., 12 oz....21.00
Tumbler, green, 5⅜" h., 12 oz....42.00
Tumbler, pink, 5⅜" h., 12 oz....37.50
Water set: 68 oz. pitcher & six 9 oz. tumblers; blue, 7 pcs....360.00

ROYAL RUBY, Anchor Hocking Glass Co., 1939-60s (Press-mold)

(All items in ruby red.)

Ashtray, 4¼" sq....4.50
Bowl, berry, 4¼" d....6.00
Bowl, 4¾" sq....6.50
Bowl, 5¼" d....10.50
Bowl, 6½" d., scalloped....8.50
Bowl, 7⅜" sq....14.00
Bowl, soup, 7½" d....12.00
Bowl, 8" oval vegetable....35.00
Bowl, berry, 8½" d....17.50
Bowl, popcorn, 10" d., deep....45.00
Bowl, salad, 11½" d....30.50
Creamer, flat....7.00
Creamer, footed....8.00
Cup, round....4.50
Cup, square....6.00
Goblet, ball stem....10.00
Juice set, 22 oz. tilted pitcher & six 5 oz. tumblers, 7 pcs....67.50
Pitcher, 22 oz., tilted or upright....30.50
Pitcher, 3 qt., tilted or upright....41.50
Plate, sherbet, 6½" d....4.50
Plate, salad, 7" d....5.00
Plate, luncheon, 7¾" d....6.50
Plate, 8⅜" sq....7.50
Plate, dinner, 9" d....10.50
Plate, 13¾" d....21.50
Playing card or cigarette box, divided, clear base....69.00
Popcorn set, 10" d. serving bowl and six 5¼" d. bowls, 7 pcs....125.00
Punch bowl....37.50
Punch bowl & base....59.00
Punch cup....2.50
Punch set, punch bowl, base & 8 cups, 10 pcs....110.00
Saucer, round....2.50
Saucer, square....2.50
Sherbet, footed....7.00
Sugar bowl, flat....7.00
Sugar bowl, footed....8.00
Sugar bowl w/slotted lid, footed....15.50
Tumbler, cocktail, 3½ oz....10.50
Tumbler, juice, 5 oz....5.00
Tumbler, water, 9 oz....5.50
Tumbler, water, 10 oz....8.50
Tumbler, iced tea, footed, 6" h., 12 oz....11.50
Tumbler, iced tea, 13 oz....11.00
Vase, 4" h., ball-shaped....5.00
Vase, 5" h., ball-shaped....10.00
Vase, bud, 5½" h., ruffled top....6.50
Vase, 6½" h., bulbous....5.00
Vase, various styles, large....13.00
Wine, footed, 2½ oz....11.00

SAILBOATS or Ships or Sportsman Series, Hazel Atlas Glass Co., late 1930s

(All items in cobalt blue with white decoration)

Ashtray....27.50
Cocktail mixer w/stirrer....26.00
Cocktail shaker w/metal lid....48.00
Ice bowl....30.00
Pitcher without ice lip, 82 oz....62.50
Pitcher w/ice lip, 86 oz....72.50

Plate, bread & butter, 5⅞" d. 18.00
Plate, salad, 8" d.....35.00
Plate, dinner, 9" d. 33.50
Saucer 14.00
Tray, wooden handles (blue boat on white) 105.00
Tumbler, juice, 3¾" h., 5 oz. 10.50
Tumbler, roly poly, 6 oz. 9.50
Tumbler, Old Fashioned, 3⅜" h., 8 oz. .13.50
Tumbler, water, straight sides, 3¾" h., 9 oz. 10.50
Tumbler, water, 4⅝" h., 9 oz.....12.50
Tumbler, iced tea, 4⅞" h., 10½ oz.....12.50
Tumbler, iced tea, 12 oz. 21.00

SANDWICH, Anchor Hocking Glass Co., 1939-64 (Press-mold)

Sandwich Pattern

Bowl, 4⁵⁄₁₆" d., clear.....4.50
Bowl, 4⁵⁄₁₆" d., green 3.00
Bowl, berry, 4⅞" d., amber 3.00
Bowl, berry, 4⅞" d., clear.....12.50
Bowl, berry, 4⅞" d., pink.....6.50
Bowl, 5¼" d., scalloped, amber 5.00
Bowl, 5¼" d., scalloped, clear.....7.00
Bowl, 5¼" d., ruby.....17.00
Bowl, cereal, 6½" d., amber.....13.50
Bowl, cereal, 6½" d., clear 29.00
Bowl, salad, 7" d., clear 7.00
Bowl, salad, 7" d., green.....52.00
Bowl, 8" d., scalloped, clear.....9.50
Bowl, 8" d., scalloped, green 66.00
Bowl, 8" d., scalloped, pink.....12.00
Bowl, 8" d., scalloped, ruby 45.00
Bowl, 8½" oval vegetable, clear.....6.50
Bowl, salad, 9" d., amber.....23.50
Bowl, salad, 9" d., clear 21.00
Butter dish, cov., clear 40.00
Cookie jar, cov., amber.....35.00
Cookie jar, cov., clear 34.00
Cookie jar, green (no cover made) 17.00
Creamer, clear.....4.50
Creamer, green 23.00
Cup, amber.....3.00
Cup, clear 2.50
Cup & saucer, green.....28.00
Custard cup, clear 4.00
Custard cup, ruffled, clear 12.50
Custard cup, green 3.00
Custard cup liner, clear.....12.50
Custard cup liner, green 2.00
Pitcher, juice, 6" h., clear.....53.00
Pitcher w/ice lip, 2 qt., clear.....71.00
Pitcher w/ice lip, 2 qt., green 235.00
Plate, dessert, 7" d., amber 8.00
Plate, dessert, 7" d., clear.....9.00
Plate, 8" d., clear 5.00
Plate, dinner, 9" d., amber 7.00
Plate, dinner, 9" d., clear 15.50
Plate, dinner, 9" d., green 74.00
Plate, snack, 9" d., clear 5.00
Plate, sandwich, 12" d., amber.....14.00
Plate, sandwich, 12" d., clear 31.50
Punch bowl, clear 18.00
Punch bowl & base, clear (ILLUS.).....38.00
Punch bowl & base, opaque white 22.50
Punch cup, clear (ILLUS.) 2.50
Punch cup, opaque white 2.00
Punch set: punch bowl & 6 cups; clear, 7 pcs. 30.50
Punch set: punch bowl, base & 10 cups; opaque white, 12 pcs. 45.00
Sherbet, footed, clear 7.50
Sugar bowl, cov., clear 16.00
Sugar bowl, cov., green.....24.00
Sugar bowl, open, clear.....5.00
Sugar bowl, open, green 22.50
Tumbler, juice, clear, 3 oz. 5.50
Tumbler, juice, green, 3 oz. 3.50
Tumbler, clear, 5 oz. 6.50
Tumbler, green, 5 oz. 4.00
Tumbler, water, clear, 9 oz. 8.00
Tumbler, water, green, 9 oz.....4.00
Tumbler, footed, amber, 9 oz. 22.00
Tumbler, footed, clear, 9 oz. 27.00

SHARON or Cabbage Rose, Federal Glass Co., 1935-39 (Chip-mold)

Bowl, berry, 5" d., amber 7.00
Bowl, berry, 5" d., green or pink 11.00
Bowl, cream soup, 5" d., amber.....24.50
Bowl, cereal, 6" d., pink 22.50
Bowl, soup, 7½" d., amber.....42.00
Bowl, soup, 7½" d., pink 39.50
Bowl, berry, 8½" d., amber 5.00
Bowl, berry, 8½" d., green 23.50
Bowl, berry, 8½" d., pink.....28.50
Bowl, 9½" oval vegetable, amber 17.00
Bowl, fruit, 10½" d., green 31.00
Bowl, fruit, 10½" d., pink.....36.00
Butter dish, cov., amber.....42.00
Butter dish, cov., green.....74.50
Butter dish, cov., pink 49.00
Cake plate, footed, amber, 11½" d. 22.00
Cake plate, footed, clear, 11½" d. 11.00
Cake plate, footed, green, 11½" d. 48.50
Cake plate, footed, pink, 11½" d.....36.50
Candy jar, cov., amber 42.00
Candy jar, cov., green 177.50
Candy jar, cov., pink.....52.00
Cheese dish, cov., amber.....179.00
Cheese dish, cov., pink 805.00
Creamer, amber 12.00

Creamer, green 18.00
Creamer, pink 16.00
Cup, amber 7.50
Cup, pink 13.50
Cup & saucer, green 26.00
Jam dish, amber, 7½" d., 1½" h. 31.00
Jam dish, green, 7½" d., 1½" h. 34.50
Jam dish, pink, 7½" d., 1½" h. 150.00
Pitcher, 9" h., 80 oz., amber 110.00
Pitcher, 9" h., 80 oz., pink 116.00
Pitcher w/ice lip, 9" h., 80 oz., amber 115.00
Pitcher w/ice lip, 9" h., 80 oz., green 322.00
Pitcher w/ice lip, 9" h., 80 oz., pink 126.50
Plate, bread & butter, 6" d., amber 4.50
Plate, bread & butter, 6" d., green or pink 6.50
Plate, salad, 7½" d., amber 15.00
Plate, salad, 7½" d., green 20.50
Plate, salad, 7½" d., pink 25.50
Plate, dinner, 9¼" d., amber 10.00
Plate, dinner, 9¼" d., green or pink 17.00
Platter, 12¼" oval, amber 14.50
Platter, 12¼" oval, green 20.50
Platter, 12¼" oval, pink 26.50
Salt & pepper shakers, amber, pr. 35.00
Salt & pepper shakers, green, pr. 61.00
Salt & pepper shakers, pink, pr. 48.50
Saucer, amber 6.00
Saucer, pink 10.00
Sherbet, footed, amber 10.50
Sherbet, footed, green 30.50
Sherbet, footed, pink 14.50
Sugar bowl, cov., amber 30.50
Sugar bowl, cov., green 43.00
Sugar bowl, cov., pink 37.50
Sugar bowl, open, amber 8.00
Sugar bowl, open, green 14.00
Sugar bowl, open, pink 12.00
Tumbler, amber, 4" h., 9 oz. 23.50
Tumbler, green, 4" h., 9 oz. 60.50
Tumbler, pink, 4" h., 9 oz. 36.00
Tumbler, amber, 5¼" h., 12 oz. 49.00
Tumbler, green, 5¼" h., 12 oz. 87.00
Tumbler, pink, 5¼" h., 12 oz. 41.50
Tumbler, footed, amber, 6½" h., 15 oz. 90.00
Tumbler, footed, clear, 6½" h., 15 oz. 16.50
Tumbler, footed, pink, 6½" h., 15 oz. 44.50

SIERRA or Pinwheel, Jeannette Glass Co., 1931-33 (Press-mold)

Bowl, cereal, 5½" d., green or pink 12.50
Bowl, berry, 8½" d., green 25.00
Bowl, berry, 8½" d., pink 27.50
Bowl, 9½" oval vegetable, green 72.50
Bowl, 9½" oval vegetable, pink 39.50
Butter dish, cov., green 65.00
Butter dish, cov., pink 56.50
Creamer, green 19.50
Creamer, pink 11.50
Cup, green 13.50
Cup & saucer, pink 16.50
Pitcher, 6½" h., 32 oz., green 115.00
Pitcher, 6½" h., 32 oz., pink 78.50
Plate, dinner, 9" d., green 18.00
Plate, dinner, 9" d., pink 15.50
Platter, 11" oval, green 41.00
Platter, 11" oval, pink 37.50
Salt & pepper shakers, green, pr. 35.50
Salt & pepper shakers, pink, pr. 37.00
Saucer, green 6.00
Serving tray, two-handled, green or pink 17.00
Sugar bowl, cov., green 30.00
Sugar bowl, cov., pink 16.50
Tumbler, footed, green, 4½" h., 9 oz. ...69.50
Tumbler, footed, pink, 4½" h., 9 oz. 46.50

SPIRAL, Hocking Glass Co., 1928-30 (Press-mold)

Ice or butter tub, green 25.00
Pitcher, 7⅝" h., 58 oz., green 29.50
Plate, sherbet, 6" d., green 2.00
Plate, luncheon, 8" d., green 4.00
Platter, 12" l., oval, green 20.50
Preserve, cov., green 27.50
Sandwich server, w/center handle, green 30.00
Sherbet, green 4.50
Sherbet, pink 4.00
Sugar bowl, flat or footed, green 7.00
Tumbler, water, green, 5" h., 9 oz. 12.00

SWANKY SWIGS, early 1930s to early 1940s (Kraft cheese glasses)

Antique No. 1, black, blue, brown, green, orange or red 4.00
Band No. 1 .....3.50
Band No. 2 .....3.00
Band No. 3 .....3.00
Band No. 4 .....1.50
Bustlin' Betsy, blue, brown, green, orange, red or yellow 4.00
Carnival, cobalt blue or red 3.50
Carnival, yellow 7.00
Circles & Dot, blue or green 5.50
Daisy (or Bachelor Button), green, red or white 2.50
Forget-Me-Not, dark blue, light blue, red or yellow 3.00
Kiddy Kup, black, blue, brown, green, orange or red 4.50
Posy - Cornflower No. 1, 3½" h. 3.00
Posy - Cornflower No. 1, 4½" h. 15.00
Posy - Cornflower No. 2, dark blue, light blue, red or yellow 3.00
Posy - Jonquil 4.00
Posy - Tulip 3.50
Posy - Violet 4.00
Sailboat No. 1 (3 boats), blue 13.50
Sailboat No. 2 (4 boats), blue 12.50

Stars No. 1, black, blue, green, red or yellow....4.50
Texas Centennial, black....7.50
Texas Centennial, red....24.00
Tulip No. 1, black, dark blue, green or red, 3½" h. 2.50
Tulip No. 1, red or green, 4½" h. 6.00
Tulip No. 2, black, blue, green or red ...16.00
Tulip No. 3, dark blue, light blue or yellow....3.00

SWIRL or Petal Swirl, Jeannette Glass Co., 1937-38 (Press-mold)

Bowl, cereal, 5¼" d., Delphite....10.50
Bowl, cereal, 5¼" d., pink....8.50
Bowl, cereal, 5¼" d., ultramarine....13.50
Bowl, salad, 9" d., Delphite....25.00
Bowl, salad, 9" d., pink....15.00
Bowl, salad, 9" d., ultramarine....24.00
Bowl, 9" d., rimmed, ultramarine....22.00
Bowl, fruit, 10" d., closed handles, footed, ultramarine....27.50
Butter dish, cov., pink....153.00
Butter dish, cov., ultramarine....211.00
Candleholders, double, ultramarine, pr....35.50
Candy dish, cov., pink....100.00
Candy dish, cov., ultramarine....139.00
Candy dish, open, three-footed, pink, 5½" d. 12.00
Candy dish, open, three-footed, ultramarine, 5½" d....14.50
Coaster, pink, 3¼" d., 1" h....10.00
Coaster, ultramarine, 3¼" d., 1" h....13.50
Console bowl, footed, pink, 10½" d. 16.00
Console bowl, footed, ultramarine, 10½" d....23.50
Creamer, Delphite....9.00
Creamer, pink....7.50
Creamer, ultramarine....14.00
Cup, ultramarine....14.50
Cup & saucer, Delphite....11.00
Cup & saucer, pink....7.00
Plate, sherbet, 6½" d., Delphite or pink....4.50
Plate, sherbet, 6½" d., ultramarine....6.00
Plate, 7¼" d., ultramarine....12.00
Plate, salad, 8" d., Delphite....5.00
Plate, salad, 8" d., pink....6.00
Plate, dinner, 9½" d., Delphite....12.00
Plate, dinner, 9½" d., pink....8.50
Plate, dinner, 9½" d., ultramarine....15.50
Plate, sandwich, 12½" d., pink....18.00
Plate, sandwich, 12½" d., ultramarine ..23.00
Platter, 12" oval, Delphite....29.00
Salt & pepper shakers, Delphite, pr....95.00
Salt & pepper shakers, ultramarine, pr....37.50
Saucer, ultramarine....4.50
Sherbet, pink....10.00
Sherbet, ultramarine....16.00
Soup bowl w/lug handles, pink....18.50
Soup bowl w/lug handles, ultramarine..25.00
Sugar bowl, open, Delphite....8.00
Sugar bowl, open, pink....9.00
Sugar bowl, open, ultramarine....14.00
Tumbler, pink, 4" h., 9 oz....11.00
Tumbler, ultramarine, 4" h., 9 oz. 16.50
Tumbler, pink, 4⅝" h., 9 oz....18.50
Tumbler, footed, pink, 9 oz....14.00
Tumbler, footed, ultramarine, 9 oz....35.50
Tumbler, pink, 5⅛" h., 13 oz....25.50
Tumbler, ultramarine, 5⅛" h., 13 oz. 80.00
Vase, 6½" h., pink....11.00
Vase, 6½" h., ultramarine....17.00
Vase, 8½" h., ultramarine....25.00

TEA ROOM, Indiana Glass Co., 1926-31 (Press-mold)

Tea Room Creamer & Sugar Bowl

Banana split dish, flat, green, 7½"....98.00
Banana split dish, footed, clear, 7½"....46.00
Banana split dish, footed, green, 7½"...81.00
Bowl, salad, 8¾" d., green....80.00
Bowl, salad, 8¾" d., pink....52.00
Bowl, 9½" oval vegetable, green....69.00
Bowl, 9½" oval vegetable, pink....62.00
Candlesticks, green or pink, pr....50.50
Celery or pickle dish, green, 8½"....26.00
Creamer, green, 3¼" h. 14.50
Creamer, green, 4" h. 14.50
Creamer, pink, 4" h....11.00
Creamer, footed, green, 4½" h. 22.50
Creamer, rectangular, green....15.50
Creamer & open sugar bowl on center-handled tray, green....55.00
Creamer & open sugar bowl on center-handled tray, pink (ILLUS.)....86.00
Creamer & open sugar bowl on rectangular tray, green....108.00
Creamer & open sugar bowl on rectangular tray, pink....56.00
Cup & saucer, green....44.00
Cup & saucer, pink....63.50
Finger bowl, green....85.00
Finger bowl, pink....48.50
Goblet, green, 9 oz....77.50
Goblet, pink, 9 oz....74.00
Ice bucket, green....70.00
Ice bucket, pink....85.00

Lamp, electric, clear, 9" 95.00
Lamp, electric, green, 9" 61.50
Mustard, cov., clear 72.00
Parfait, clear 65.00
Parfait, green 63.50
Pitcher, 64 oz., green 160.00
Pitcher, 64 oz., pink 150.00
Plate, sherbet, 6½" d., pink 17.00
Plate, luncheon, 8¼" d., green 32.00
Plate, 10½" d., two-handled, green 50.00
Plate, sandwich, w/center handle, green 151.00
Plate, sandwich, w/center handle, pink 170.00
Relish, divided, green 22.50
Relish, divided, pink 13.00
Salt & pepper shakers, green, pr. 64.00
Salt & pepper shakers, pink, pr. 53.00
Sherbet, low footed, green 30.00
Sherbet, low footed, pink 23.00
Sherbet, low, flared edge, clear 18.00
Sherbet, low, flared edge, green 27.50
Sherbet, tall footed, clear 27.50
Sherbet, tall footed, green 37.00
Sherbet, tall footed, pink 31.00
Sugar bowl, cov., pink, 3" h. 130.00
Sugar bowl, cov., green, 3" h. 100.00
Sugar bowl, open, green, 4" h. 16.00
Sugar bowl, open, pink, 4" h. 14.00
Sugar bowl, open, footed, green, 4½" h. 17.50
Sugar bowl, open, footed, pink, 4½" h. 14.50
Sugar bowl, open, rectangular, green ..17.50
Sugar bowl, open, rectangular, pink 11.50
Sundae, footed, ruffled, clear 56.00
Sundae, footed, ruffled, green 135.00
Tray, rectangular, for creamer & sugar bowl, green 48.00
Tray, rectangular, for creamer & sugar bowl, pink 38.00
Tray w/center handle, for creamer & sugar bowl, green 209.00
Tray w/center handle, for creamer & sugar bowl, pink 74.00
Tumbler, footed, clear, 6 oz. 28.00
Tumbler, footed, green, 6 oz. 42.00
Tumbler, footed, pink, 6 oz. 30.00
Tumbler, green, 4³⁄₁₆" h., 8½ oz. 105.00
Tumbler, pink, 4³⁄₁₆" h., 8½ oz. 32.50
Tumbler, footed, green or pink, 5¼" h., 8 oz. 30.00
Tumbler, footed, green, 11 oz. 62.50
Tumbler, footed, clear, 12 oz. 45.00
Tumbler, footed, green, 12 oz. 82.00
Tumbler, footed, pink, 12 oz. 65.00
Vase, 6½" h., ruffled rim, green 109.00
Vase, 9½" h., ruffled rim, amber 150.00
Vase, 9½" h., ruffled rim, clear 19.00
Vase, 9½" h., ruffled rim, green 127.50
Vase, 11" h., ruffled rim, clear 110.00
Vase, 11" h., straight, green 153.00
Vase, 11" h., straight, pink 105.00

TWISTED OPTIC, Imperial Glass Co., 1927-30 (Press-mold)

Bowl, cream soup, 4¾" d., pink 8.50
Bowl, cereal, 5" d., amber 6.50
Candlesticks, yellow, 3", pr. 19.00
Candy jar, cov., green 23.50
Candy jar, cov., yellow 25.00
Creamer, green 7.00
Creamer, pink 8.00
Plate, sherbet, 6" d., amber 1.50
Plate, sherbet, 6" d., green 3.00
Plate, sherbet, 6" d., pink 2.00
Plate, luncheon, 8" d., amber or green ...3.00
Plate, luncheon, 8" d., pink 4.50
Preserve jar w/slotted lid, green 22.00
Sandwich server w/center handle, amber 17.00
Sandwich server w/center handle, green 16.00
Sandwich server w/center handle, yellow 29.00
Sherbet, amber, green or yellow 5.50
Sherbet, clear 3.00
Sherbet, pink 6.00
Sugar bowl, open, green 8.00
Sugar bowl, open, pink 6.00

WATERFORD or Waffle, Hocking Glass Co., 1938-44 (Press-mold)

Waterford Pattern

Ashtray, clear, 4" 5.00
Bowl, berry, 4¾" d., clear 5.50
Bowl, berry, 4¾" d., pink 11.00
Bowl, cereal, 5¼" d., clear 16.50
Bowl, cereal, 5¼" d., pink 26.50
Bowl, berry, 8¼" d., clear 10.00
Bowl, berry, 8¼" d., pink 17.00
Butter dish, cov., clear 24.00
Butter dish, cov., pink 195.00
Cake plate, handled, clear, 10¼" d. 8.00
Cake plate, handled, pink, 10¼" d. 12.00
Coaster, clear, 4" d. 3.50
Creamer, oval, clear 4.50
Creamer, oval, pink 12.00
Cup & saucer, clear (ILLUS.) 9.00
Cup & saucer, pink 20.50

Goblet, amber, 5¼" h. 125.00
Goblet, clear, 5¼" h. 15.50
Goblet, clear, 5½" h. (Miss America style) 32.50
Lamp, clear, 4" h. 29.00
Pitcher, juice, 42 oz., tilt-type, clear 22.50
Pitcher w/ice lip, 80 oz., clear 29.50
Pitcher w/ice lip, 80 oz., pink 147.50
Plate, sherbet, 6" d., clear 3.00
Plate, sherbet, 6" d., pink 7.00
Plate, salad, 7½" d., clear 4.50
Plate, salad, 7½" d., pink 10.00
Plate, dinner, 9⅝" d., clear 9.50
Plate, dinner, 9⅝" d., pink 18.00
Plate, sandwich, 13¾" d., clear 8.50
Plate, sandwich, 13¾" d., pink 24.50
Relish, five-section, clear, 13¾" d. 14.00
Salt & pepper shakers, clear, short or tall, pr. 7.50
Sherbet, footed, clear 3.50
Sherbet, footed, pink 11.50
Sugar bowl, cov., oval, clear 5.50
Sugar bowl, cov., oval, pink 27.50
Sugar bowl, open, footed, clear (Miss America style) 2.00
Tumbler, footed, clear, 5" h., 10 oz. (ILLUS.) 10.50
Tumbler, footed, pink, 5" h., 10 oz. 17.50

WINDSOR DIAMOND or Windsor, Jeannette Glass Co., 1936-46 (Press-mold)

Ashtray, Delphite, 5¾" d. 39.50
Ashtray, green, 5¾" d. 44.50
Ashtray, pink, 5¾" d. 34.00
Ashtray w/patterned rim, pink 475.00
Bowl, berry, 4¾" d., clear 5.00
Bowl, berry, 4¾" d., green 7.00
Bowl, berry, 4¾" d., pink 8.00
Bowl, 5" d., pointed edge, clear 5.00
Bowl, 5" d., pointed edge, pink 18.00
Bowl, cream soup, 5" d., green or pink 23.00
Bowl, cereal, 5⅛" or 5⅜" d., clear 7.00
Bowl, cereal, 5⅛" or 5⅜" d., green 22.00
Bowl, cereal, 5⅛" or 5⅜" d., pink 17.00
Bowl, 7" d., three-footed, clear 7.00
Bowl, 7" d., three-footed, pink 24.00
Bowl, 8" d., pointed edge, clear 11.00
Bowl, 8" d., pointed edge, pink 34.00
Bowl, 8" d., two-handled, clear 5.50
Bowl, 8" d., two-handled, green 21.00
Bowl, 8" d., two-handled, pink 19.50
Bowl, berry, 8½" d., clear 10.00
Bowl, berry, 8½" d., green 15.00
Bowl, berry, 8½" d., pink 17.00
Bowl, 9½" oval vegetable, clear 8.50
Bowl, 9½" oval vegetable, green 23.00
Bowl, 9½" oval vegetable, pink 19.00
Bowl, 10½" d., pointed edge, clear 25.00
Bowl, 10½" d., pointed edge, pink 107.50
Bowl, 7 x 11¾" boat shape, clear 17.50
Bowl, 7 x 11¾" boat shape, green 30.50
Bowl, 7 x 11¾" boat shape, pink 34.50
Bowl, fruit, 12½" d., clear 26.00
Bowl, fruit, 12½" d., pink 96.50
Butter dish, cov., clear 24.50
Butter dish, cov., green 76.50
Butter dish, cov., pink 48.50
Cake plate, footed, clear, 10¾" d. 7.50
Cake plate, footed, green or pink, 10¾" d. 19.00
Candlesticks, clear, 3" h., pr. 15.00
Candlesticks, pink, 3" h., pr. 81.00
Candy jar, cov., clear 11.00
Coaster, clear, 3¼" d. 7.00
Coaster, green, 3¼" d. 14.50
Coaster, pink, 3¼" d. 13.00
Creamer, flat, clear 4.00
Creamer, flat, green 12.50
Creamer, flat, pink 10.50
Creamer, footed, clear 5.50
Cup, clear 2.50
Cup, green 10.00
Cup, pink 9.50
Pitcher, 4½" h., 16 oz., Amberina red 600.00
Pitcher, 4½" h., 16 oz., clear 19.50
Pitcher, 4½" h., 16 oz., pink 113.00
Pitcher, 6¾" h., 52 oz., clear 11.50
Pitcher, 6¾" h., 52 oz., green 48.00
Pitcher, 6¾" h., 52 oz., pink 25.50
Plate, sherbet, 6" d., clear 2.00
Plate, sherbet, 6" d., green 6.00
Plate, sherbet, 6" d., pink 4.50
Plate, salad, 7" d., green 17.50
Plate, salad, 7" d., pink 19.50
Plate, dinner, 9" d., clear 5.00
Plate, dinner, 9" d., green or pink 19.00
Plate, sandwich, 10¼", handled, clear 7.00
Plate, sandwich, 10¼", handled, green 11.50
Plate, sandwich, 10¼", handled, pink 14.00
Plate, chop, 13⅝" d., clear 8.50
Plate, chop, 13⅝" d., green or pink 40.00
Platter, 11½" oval, clear 7.00
Platter, 11½" oval, green 19.50
Platter, 11½" oval, pink 18.50
Powder jar, cov., clear 10.00
Relish, divided, clear, 11½" 9.50
Relish, divided, pink, 11½" 187.50
Salt & pepper shakers, green, pr. 44.50
Salt & pepper shakers, pink, pr. 36.00
Saucer, clear 3.00
Saucer, green 5.00
Saucer, pink 5.00
Sherbet, footed, clear 4.50
Sherbet, footed, green 13.00
Sherbet, footed, pink 9.50
Sugar bowl, cov., flat, clear 6.00
Sugar bowl, cov., flat, green 23.00
Sugar bowl, cov., flat, pink 24.50
Sugar bowl, cov., footed, clear 6.00
Sugar bowl, cov., no lip, pink 110.00
Sugar bowl, open, clear 3.00
Sugar bowl, open, green 12.00
Sugar bowl, open, pink 8.50

Tray, clear, 4" sq., without handles.....5.00
Tray, pink, 4" sq., without handles.....37.00
Tray, green or pink, 4⅛ x 9", w/handles.....12.50
Tray, clear, 4⅛ x 9", without handles....10.00
Tray, pink, 4⅛" x 9", without handles....43.50
Tray, green, 8½ x 9¾", w/handles.....29.00
Tray, pink, 8½ x 9¾", w/handles.....22.00
Tray, clear, 8½ x 9¾", without handles.....12.00
Tray, pink, 8½ x 9¾", without handles.....75.00
Tumbler, clear, 3¼" h., 5 oz.....7.00
Tumbler, green, 3¼" h., 5 oz. 26.50
Tumbler, pink, 3¼" h., 5 oz.....22.00
Tumbler, clear, 4" h., 9 oz.....6.50
Tumbler, green, 4" h., 9 oz. 29.00
Tumbler, pink, 4" h., 9 oz.....17.00
Tumbler, footed, clear, 4" h., 9 oz.....7.00
Tumbler, footed, clear, 5" h., 11 oz.....9.00
Tumbler, clear, 5" h., 12 oz.....9.00
Tumbler, green, 5" h., 12 oz. 42.50
Tumbler, pink, 5" h., 12 oz.....26.00
Tumbler, footed, clear, 7¼" h. 12.50
Water set: pitcher & 6 each, 5 oz. tumblers, 9 oz. tumblers & 12 oz. tumblers; pink, in original box, 19 pcs. 400.00

(End of Depression Glass Section)

DUNCAN & MILLER

Duncan & Miller Glass Company, a successor firm to George Duncan & Sons Company, produced a wide range of pressed wares and novelty pieces during the late 19th century and into the early 20th century. During the Depression era and after, they continued making a wide variety of more modern patterns, including mold-blown types and also introduced a number of etched and engraved patterns. Many colors, including opalescent hues, were produced during this era and especially popular today are the graceful swan dishes they produced in the Pall Mall and Sylvan patterns. The numbers after the pattern name indicate the original factory pattern number. The Duncan factory was closed in 1955. Also see ANIMALS and PATTERN GLASS.

Ashtray, Caribbean patt. (No. 112), ruby.....$20.00
Ashtray, model of a duck, ruby.....110.00
Ashtray, Pall Mall patt. (No. 30), clear w/etched duck decoration, rectangular, 8" l.....66.00
Bowl, 4¾" d., Puritan patt., pink.....9.00
Bowl, 6" d., handled, Teardrop patt. (No. 301), clear.....4.00
Bowl, 7" d., Murano patt. (No. 127), pink opalescent.....28.00
Bowl, 9" oval., Canterbury patt. (No. 115), clear.....22.00
Bowl, 10" d., Murano patt., milk white 145.00
Bowl, 6½ x 11½", model of a Viking boat, clear.....150.00 to 175.00
Cake stand, miniature, Teardrop patt., 5½" d., 3¼" h. 55.00
Candelabrum, three-light, No. 14, w/prisms, clear, 10" h., 8" w.....50.00
Candlesticks, two-light, etched First Love patt., clear, pr. 110.00
Candlesticks, Terrace patt. (No. 111), amber, pr. 115.00
Candy dish, cov., etched First Love patt., clear 67.50

Teardrop Champagne

Champagne, saucer-type, Teardrop patt., clear (ILLUS.).....7.50
Cheese stand, Caribbean patt., blue, 3½" h.....35.00
Cigarette box, cov., Caribbean patt., blue 73.00
Cocktail shaker, Caribbean patt., blue 125.00
Cologne bottle w/original stopper, Hobnail patt. (No. 118), blue.....58.00
Compote, 5" d., 3" h., Teardrop patt., clear 35.00
Compote, 5½" h., Canterbury patt., ruby w/clear base.....85.00
Console set: bowl & candlesticks; American Way patt. (No. 71), ruby red, 3 pcs. 150.00
Cordial, Mardi Gras patt. (No. 42), clear 40.00
Cornucopia-vase, etched First Love patt., clear, 8" h. 65.00
Cornucopia-vase, Three Feathers patt. (No. 117), clear, 8" h. 45.00
Creamer & open sugar bowl, Georgian patt. (No. 103), pink, pr. 30.00
Creamer & open sugar bowl, individual, etched Language of Flowers patt., clear, pr. 30.00

Creamer & sugar bowl, large, etched Language of Flowers patt., clear, pr. 35.00
Creamer, open sugar bowl & 8" oblong tray, Early American Sandwich patt. (No. 41), clear, 3 pcs. 35.00
Cruet w/original stopper, Bag Ware (No. 800), vaseline, large, ca. 1880s 55.00
Cruet w/original stopper, Early American Sandwich patt., clear, 3 oz. 35.00
Cruet w/original stopper, Teardrop patt., clear, 3 oz. 12.00
Cup & saucer, Teardrop patt., clear 35.00
Deviled egg plate, Early American Sandwich patt., green, 12" d. 35.00
Goblet, Canterbury patt., clear 12.00
Goblet, Early American Sandwich patt., blue 17.00
Goblet, Early American Sandwich patt., clear, 9 oz., 6" h. 15.00
Goblet, etched First Love patt., clear....21.00
Goblet, water, Hobnail patt., clear 6.00
Goblet, water, Mardi Gras patt., clear...40.00
Ivy bowl, footed, Hobnail patt., blue opalescent, 6½" d. 48.00
Marmalade jar, cov., Teardrop patt., clear 37.00
Model of a goose, door stop-type, clear, 4 lb. 395.00
Model of a swan, Pall Mall patt. (No. 30), ruby, 7" l. 24.00
Model of a swan, Sylvan patt. (No. 122), blue opalescent, 7" l. 85.00
Model of a swan, Sylvan patt. (No. 122), milk white w/ruby neck & head, 7" l. 325.00
Model of a swan, nesting-type, teakwood, 10½" l. 60.00
Model of a swan, Sylvan patt., blue opalescent, 12" l. 350.00
Model of a swan, Sylvan patt., pink opalescent, 12" l. 350.00
Model of a swan, spread wing-type, green, 12" w., 11" h. 60.00
Mustard jar, cov., Caribbean patt., clear 20.00
Olive dish, Teardrop patt., clear, 7" l. ...15.00
Pitcher, 9½" h., w/ice lip, Canterbury patt., clear 90.00
Pitcher w/applied amber handle, Teardrop patt., clear 78.00
Plate, 8" d., Canterbury patt., amber 12.00
Plate, salad, 8" d., Early American Sandwich patt., clear 10.00
Plate, 8½" d., Spiral Flutes patt. (No. 40), clear 7.00
Plate, 8½" d., Spiral Flutes patt., green 4.00
Plate, 11" d., Teardrop patt., clear....45.00
Plate, 16" d., Early American Sandwich patt., clear 225.00
Punch set: punch bowl, 18" d. underplate & twelve cups; Caribbean patt., clear, cups clear w/applied ruby red handles, 14 pcs. 250.00
Relish dish, two-part, Caribbean patt., blue, 6" d. 22.50
Relish dish, three-part, etched First Love patt., clear, 10½" l. 45.00
Relish dish, three-part, Sylvan patt., yellow opalescent, 10 x 13" 80.00
Relish dish, four-part, Canterbury patt., clear, 12" d. 45.00
Relish dish, five-part, Teardrop patt., clear, 12" d. 18.00
Relish dish, Sylvan patt., milk white w/ruby handles, 10" l. 140.00
Relish dish, Terrace patt. (No. 111), clear w/gold, 10½" l. 32.00
Salt & pepper shakers w/original tops, Mardi Gras patt., clear, pr. 37.50
Salt & pepper shakers w/original tops, Teardrop patt., clear, pr. 50.00
Seafood sauce cup, Spiral Flutes patt., clear 20.00
Sherbet, crimped rim, Canterbury patt., clear, 5½" h. 22.00
Sherbet, Teardrop patt., clear, 3½" h. 4.00
Sugar bowl, cov., Bag Ware (No. 800), vaseline, ca. 1880s 80.00
Tumbler, Canterbury patt., clear, 5¼" h. 9.00
Tumbler, Canterbury patt., yellow opalescent, 5½" h. 50.00
Tumbler, old fashioned, Canterbury patt., clear, 8 oz. 7.50
Tumbler, footed, Caribbean patt., blue, 5½" h. 35.00
Tumbler, iced tea, Early American Sandwich patt., clear, 5¼" h. 14.00
Tumbler, juice, footed, cut Eternally Yours patt., clear, 5 oz. 20.00
Tumbler, water, footed, cut Eternally Yours patt., clear, 9 oz. 20.00
Tumbler, iced tea footed, cut Eternally Yours patt., clear, 13 oz. 22.00
Tumbler, bar, Mardi Gras patt., clear....20.00
Tumbler, hi-ball, flat, Teardrop patt., clear, 4¾" h. 9.00
Tumbler, juice, footed, Teardrop patt., clear, 4" h. 9.00
Tumbler, iced tea, Teardrop patt., clear, 6" h. 12.00
Tumbler, whiskey, footed, Teardrop patt., clear, 3" h. 16.50
Vase, 2½" h., Chanticleer patt., green opalescent 55.00
Vase (cigarette holder), 3½" h., Grecian Urn line (No. 538), clear 12.50
Vase, 5" h., Canterbury patt., clear....7.50

Vase, 8" h., ruffled rim, Hobnail patt., blue opalescent....62.50
Vase, 8" h., ruffled rim, Caribbean patt., blue....140.00
Vase, 10½" h., Teardrop patt., clear....24.00
Vase, 10½" h., Venetian patt. (No. 126), ruby red....145.00
Violet bowl, Canterbury patt., clear, 4½" d....18.00
Wine, Mardi Gras patt....25.00

Teadrop Wine

Wine, Teardrop patt., clear, 3 oz., 4¾" h. (ILLUS.)....13.50

FENTON

Fenton Art Glass Company began producing glass at Williamstown, West Virginia, in January 1907. Organized by Frank L. and John W. Fenton, the company began operations in a newly built glass factory with an experienced master glass craftsman, Jacob Rosenthal, as their factory manager. Fenton has produced a wide variety of collectible glassware through the years, including Carnival. Still in production today, their current productions may be found at finer gift shops across the country. William Heacock's three volumes on Fenton, published by Antique Publications, are standard references for collectors.

Modern Fenton Mark

Barber bottle, Coin Dot patt., cranberry opalescent....$225.00
Basket w/wicker handle, Big Cookies patt., No. 1681, Mandarin Red, 10½" d., 5" h....125.00
Basket, Aqua Crest, 7½" h....60.00
Basket, Coin Dot patt., French Opalescent, No. 1925, 6" h....85.00
Basket, Coin Dot patt., French Opalescent, 13" h....150.00
Basket, Hobnail patt., blue opalescent, 5½" h....39.00
Basket, Hobnail patt., French Opalescent, 6½" h....24.00
Basket, Hobnail patt., No. 3834, milk white, 12" h....40.00
Basket, Hobnail patt., No. 3839, Plum Opalescent, 12" oval....175.00
Basket, Hobnail patt., crimped rim, applied clear handle, Plum Opalescent, 12¾" h....165.00
Basket, No. 203, Blue Overlay, ca. 1943, 7¼" d....60.00
Basket, Rose Overlay, 8" h....48.00
Basket, No. 6437, Vasa Murrhina, blue & green spatter exterior, white interior, 11" h....125.00
Bowl, 6" d., low, Ruby Stretch glass....125.00
Bowl, 7½" d., Peach Crest, ca. 1940....40.00
Bowl, 8" d., footed, Silver Crest....28.00
Bowl, 8½" d., rolled rim, Celeste Blue Stretch glass....40.00
Bowl, 8½" d., footed, San Toy patt., clear satin....32.50
Bowl, 8½" d., w/metal handles, Silver Crest w/Violets in Snow decoration....35.00
Bowl, 9½" d., ruffled, No. 682, Emerald Crest....55.00
Bowl, 10" d., crimped edge, Black Rose....245.00
Bowl, 10" d., Diamond Optic patt., Mulberry....75.00
Bowl, 10" d., double crimped rim, Hobnail patt., French Opalescent....60.00
Bowl, 10" d., double crimped edge, No. 7224, Silver Crest....46.00
Bowl, 10" d., flared rim, No. 857, ruby, ca. 1933....40.00
Bowl, 12" d., Hobnail patt., milk white....20.00
Butter dish, cov., Hobnail patt., No. 3977, milk white....16.00
Cake stand, Silver Crest, 12½" d....46.00
Candleholders, cornucopia-shaped, Rose Crest, 6" h., pr....75.00
Candleholders, No. 7474, Silver Crest, 1968-71, 6" h., pr....70.00
Candlestick, Florentine Green Stretch glass, 8½" h....38.00
Candlesticks, Celeste Blue Stretch glass, 9½" h., pr....150.00
Candy dish, cov., footed, Hobnail patt., Topaz Opalescent, 7" h....110.00
Center bowl, three-footed, Pineapple patt., No. 2000A, clear w/satin finish, 12" d....35.00

Center bowl, oval, pedestal base, dolphin handles under wide flanged rim, No. 1608, Jade Green 45.00
Cigarette holder, round on dished base, No. 554, Celeste Blue Stretch glass 85.00
Compote, open, 6" d., Hobnail patt., green opalescent 35.00
Compote, open, 6" d., No. 206, Emerald Crest 25.00
Compote, footed, No. 7228, Silver Crest, ca. 1963 .....11.00
Console bowl, loop side handles, footed, No. 1563, Jade Green, 17" l. 65.00
Cookie jar, cov., Big Cookies (No. 1681) patt., Jade Green 125.00
Cookie jar, cov., Big Cookies (No. 1681) patt., Mandarin Red 130.00
Creamer, Coin Dot patt., No. 1942, cranberry opalescent, ca. 1944 .....55.00
Cruet, w/original stopper, Fenton's Drapery, Mulberry 80.00
Cruet, w/original stopper, Hobnail patt., No. 3863, clear 19.00
Cruet, w/original stopper, Hobnail patt., No. 3863, milk white 19.00
Cruet, w/original stopper, Spiral Optic patt., blue 29.00
Cup & saucer, Lincoln Inn patt., Jade Green 25.00
Dresser bottle w/clear teardrop stopper, No. 711, bulbous body w/lady's leg neck, Beaded Melon patt., Peach Crest, 5½" h. 35.00
Epergne, three-lily, ruffled rim, No. 1948A, Diamond Lace patt., blue opalescent 120.00
Epergne, three-lily, No. 4808, Diamond Lace patt., milk white 50.00
Ewer, ruffled rim, applied handle, No. 192, Rose Overlay, ca. 1943-48 .....38.00
Fairy light, Hobnail patt., ruby, 1975-80 .....15.00
Goblet, Hobnail patt., French Opalescent 12.00
Goblet, Thumbprint patt., Colonial Blue, 1960s, 6½" h. 16.00
Goblet, water, Lincoln Inn patt., Jade Green 25.00
Hen on Nest cov. dish, basketweave base, Blue Marble, 1971-73, 9" l. 45.00
Ice bucket w/metal handle, No. 1616, Ming patt., frosted clear, ca. 1936, 6" h. 35.00
Lamp, hurricane-type, No. 170, Diamond Optic patt., French Opalescent 125.00
Lamp, hurricane-type, emerald green Snowcrest w/milk white base, 11" h. 110.00
Lamps, Victorian style, Polka Dot patt., cranberry opalescent, 18" h., pr. 590.00
Lemonade set: cov. pitcher, six mugs, six coasters & six clear glass stirring spoons; Line 220, vaseline, w/applied cobalt handles, ca. 1926, 19 pcs. 395.00
Model of an egg, pedestal base, Violets in the Snow decoration, ca. 1980 .....30.00
Novelty, top hat, Peach Crest, 4½" h. 45.00
Novelty, top hat, Rib Optic patt., French Opalescent, 6" h. 165.00
Novelty, top hat, Spiral Optic patt., green, 4" h. 85.00
Novelty, top hat, crimped rim, No. 1492, Coin Dot patt., cranberry opalescent, ca. 1953 .....65.00
Perfume bottle w/atomizer, ovoid body w/molded blossoms, private mold made for Devilbiss, French Opalescent 65.00
Pitcher, 4" h., Coin Dot patt., green 45.00
Pitcher, 5½" h., squatty, Diamond Optic patt. 70.00
Pitcher, 6" h., Beaded Melon patt., Peach Crest 48.00
Pitcher, 6" h., Spiral Optic patt., cranberry opalescent 65.00
Pitcher w/applied black handle, Coin Dot patt., green opalescent 175.00
Pitcher, tankard, No. 8964, Hanging Heart patt., turquoise, 70 oz. .....150.00 to 175.00
Pitcher, ball-shaped w/ruffled rim, applied clear handle, Hobnail patt., cranberry opalescent, ca. 1948, 80 oz. 220.00
Pitcher, water, Daisy & Fern patt., vaseline opalescent 195.00
Pitcher-vase, No. 3760, Hobnail patt., ovoid body tapering to a cylindrical neck w/a spout pulled into a very long serrated point, milk white 30.00
Plate, 8½" d., Silver Crest 30.00
Plate, 11½" d., Ivory Crest 75.00
Plate, 12" d., Silver Crest 40.00
Plate, torte, 16" d., Silver Crest 59.00
Punch set: 10" d. bowl, underplate & eight punch cups; Hobnail patt., blue opalescent, 10 pcs. 500.00
Salt & pepper shakers w/original tops, Lincoln Inn patt., Jade Green, pr. 125.00
Tidbit tray, three-tier, Ivory Crest, 6", 8½" & 13" d. 45.00
Tumbler, Hobnail patt., French Opalescent, 15 oz. 35.00
Vase, 4½" h., No. 3874½, Hobnail patt., bulbous base, double-crimped rim, cranberry opalescent 45.00

Vase, 4½" h., crimped rim, Hobnail patt., blue opalescent.....20.00
Vase, 5" h., No. 3850, Hobnail patt., milk white.....10.00
Vase, 5" h., No. 187, triangular-shaped, Peach Crest.....47.00
Vases, 5½" h., Coin Dot patt., cranberry opalescent, pr.....65.00
Vase, 5½" h., Diamond Optic patt., Mulberry.....125.00
Vase, 6" h., No. 1925, Coin Dot patt., French Opalescent.....35.00
Vase, 6" h., No. 7551, fan-shaped w/figural dolphin handles, Jade Green, ca. 1980.....35.00
Vase, 6" h., footed, fan-shaped, Hobnail patt., blue opalescent.....28.00
Vase, 7" h., 5" d., ruffled rim, Burmese decorated w/maple leaves, 1970s.....72.00
Vase, 7" h., crimped edge, Diamond Optic patt., cranberry opalescent.....90.00
Vase, 7¾" h., 6" d., bulbous melon-ribbed body w/wide horizontal ribbed neck, double crimped rim, Blue Overlay.....45.00
Vase, 8" h., 9" d., No. 3859, pedestal base, fan-shaped w/crimped rim, Hobnail patt., cranberry opalescent...80.00
Vase, 8" h., pinched rim, Vasa Murrhina, gold, ruby & green, clear lining.....65.00
Vase, 8½" h., 8¾" d., No. 1458, corset-shaped w/flared double crimped rim, cranberry Snow Crest.....150.00
Vase, 10" h., No. 602, trumpet-form, Mongolian Green, ca. 1930s.....50.00
Vase, 10¾" h., No. 3752, Hobnail patt., bulbous base, double-crimped top w/three large ruffles, cranberry opalescent.....135.00
Vase, 11" h., jack-in-the-pulpit form, Coin Dot patt., cranberry opal-escent.....175.00
Vase, 12" h., swung-type, Hobnail patt., cranberry opalescent.....145.00
Vase, free-blown, wide cushion base tapering to a swelled body below a widely flaring rim, No. 3005, Mosaic Inlaid line, ca. 1926.....350.00
Water set: pitcher & two tumblers; Coin Dot patt., cranberry opalescent, 3 pcs.....270.00
Water set: 80 oz. pitcher & six 12 oz. tumblers; Hobnail patt., cranberry opalescent, 7 pcs.....525.00
Wine, Lincoln Inn patt., Jade Green.....20.00
Wine, Thumbprint patt., Colonial Blue, 1960s, 5" h.....8.00
Wine decanter or bottle w/clear pointed stopper, No. 1667, triple-lobe form, Rib Optic patt., cranberry, 13½" h.....80.00

FOSTORIA

Lido Goblet

Fostoria Glass Company, founded in 1887, produced numerous types of fine glassware over the years. Their factory in Moundsville, West Virginia closed in 1986. Also see ANIMALS.

Fostoria Label

Ashtray, American patt., clear, 2⅞" d. ..$6.00
Ashtray, Coin patt., olive green.....55.00
Bonbon, three-toed, American patt., clear.....17.50
Bouillon cup, Fairfax patt., pink.....10.00
Bouillon cup, footed, Versailles etching, blue.....40.00
Bowl, 4" w., tri-cornered, Sylvan patt., clear w/gold trim.....5.00
Bowl, 6¼" d., handled, Raleigh patt., Laurel cutting, clear.....12.50
Bowl, 6½" d., three-footed, Chintz etching, clear.....20.00
Bowl, 9¼" oval, Pioneer patt., green....22.00
Bowl, 10" d., Romance etching, clear...32.50
Bowl, 10½" d., three-footed, American patt., clear.....22.00
Bowl, 11" d., flared rim, Colony patt., clear.....32.00
Bowl, 11" d., flared rim, Navarre etching, clear.....55.00
Bowl, 11½" oval, American patt., clear.....43.00
Bowl, 11½" d., flared rim, Chintz etching, clear.....
Bowl, fruit, 12" d., footed, American patt., clear.....185.00
Bowl, 12" d., three-footed, Oak Leaf etching, pink.....55.00

Bowl, 12" d., flared rim, Shirley etching, clear 48.00
Bowl, 12½" oval, 2⅞" h., Flame patt., Navarre etching, clear....50.00
Bowl, 13" l., oblong, Heirloom cutting, blue 45.00
Bowl, cream soup, w/underplate, Fairfax patt., blue 22.50
Bowl, cream soup w/underplate, June etching, blue 54.00
Bowl, cov., fruit, footed, Coin patt., blue 75.00
Butter dish, cov., American patt., clear, 1 lb. 175.00
Cake plate, two-handled, Baroque patt., Meadow Rose etching, clear, 10" d. 40.00
Cake plate, two-handled, Chintz etching, clear, 10" d. 40.00
Cake stand (or salver), American patt., clear, 10" sq., 7¼" h. 75.00
Candelabra w/bobeches & prisms, two-light, Baroque patt., clear, pr. 145.00
Candlesticks, two-light, bell-shaped base, American patt., clear, pr. 220.00
Candlesticks, Baroque patt., Navarre etching, clear, pr. 50.00
Candlesticks, Coin Patt., emerald green frosted, 4½" h., pr. 80.00
Candlesticks, Coin patt., ruby, 8" h., pr. 100.00
Candlesticks, Heirloom cutting, green, 2¾" h., pr. 50.00
Candlesticks, two-light, Meadow Rose etching, clear, pr. 70.00
Candlesticks, Romance etching, clear, pr. 60.00
Candy box, cov., three-part, Meadow Rose etching, clear 80.00
Candy dish, cov., three-part, Chintz etching, clear 65.00
Candy dish, cov., Coin patt., clear....42.00
Candy dish, cov., three-part, Shirley etching, clear 85.00
Candy jar, cov., urn-shaped, Coin patt., emerald green, 12½" h. 200.00
Celery dish, Baroque patt., yellow, 11¼" l. 25.00
Celery dish, handled, Sunray patt., clear, 10" l. 12.00
Celery dish, Trojan etching, yellow, 11½" l. 50.00
Celery dish, Wistar patt., clear, 9½" oval 22.00
Champagne, Chintz etching, clear 20.00
Champagne, Holly cutting, clear....10.00
Champagne, Navarre etching, blue....24.00
Champagne, tall, Willow etching, clear 20.00
Cheese & cracker set, Navarre etching, clear, 2 pcs. 55.00
Cigarette box, cov., American patt., clear 45.00
Claret, Wheat cutting, clear 17.50
Cocktail, American patt., clear, 3½ oz. 14.00
Cocktail, Baroque patt., yellow, 3" h. 20.00
Cocktail, Colony patt., clear, 3½" oz. 12.50
Cocktail, Fairfax patt., pink 22.00
Cocktail, Holly cutting, clear, 5¼" h. 16.00
Compote, cov., jelly, 4½" d., 6¼" h., American patt., clear 25.00
Compote, 4", Sunray patt., clear....18.00
Compote, 6½", Colony patt., clear....30.00
Compote, 8½", Coin patt., frosted ruby 75.00
Condiment bottle w/original stopper, American patt., clear 95.00
Console bowl, footed, Versailles etching, blue 40.00
Console set: bowl & pair of 3½" h. candlesticks; June etching, blue, 3 pcs. 145.00
Cordial, Chintz etching, clear, 1 oz. 55.00
Cordial, Christiana cutting, clear....20.00
Cordial, Trojan patt., yellow 60.00
Cordial, Wheat cutting, clear 22.50
Creamer, individual size, Baroque patt., blue 24.00
Creamer, footed, Fairfax patt., pink 10.00
Creamer & open sugar bowl, flared rim, footed, American patt., clear, pr. 16.00
Creamer & open sugar bowl, individual size, Baroque patt., blue, pr. 50.00
Creamer & open sugar bowl, Queen Anne etching, clear, pr. 27.50
Creamer, open sugar bowl & undertray, Navarre etching, clear, 3 pcs. 50.00
Cruet w/original stopper, American patt., clear, 7 oz. 37.00
Cruet w/original stopper, Chintz etching, clear 87.00
Cruet w/original stopper, Fairfax patt., pink 95.00
Cruet w/original stopper, Raleigh patt., clear 25.00
Cup & saucer, demitasse, Vernon etching, green 28.00
Cup & saucer, Baroque patt., clear 9.00
Cup & saucer, Fairfax patt., pink 11.00
Goblet, Acanthus etching, amber 30.00
Goblet, American patt., clear, 5½" h., 9 oz. 14.00
Goblet, Arcady etching, clear, 9 oz. 25.00
Goblet, Buttercup etching, clear, 10 oz. 22.00
Goblet, Colony patt., clear, 5¼" h., 9 oz. 12.00
Goblet, Corsage etching, clear, 7⅜" h. 20.00

Goblet, Florentine etching, clear bowl w/yellow stem 12.00
Goblet, June etching, pink 55.00
Goblet, June etching, topaz 33.00
Goblet, Lido etching, clear, 12" h., 12 oz. (ILLUS.) 11.00
Goblet, Navarre etching, clear 28.00
Goblet, Queen Anne patt., clear, 10 oz. 18.00
Goblet, Romance etching, clear, 7⅜" h., 9 oz. 27.00
Ice bucket w/metal tongs, American patt., clear 48.00
Ice bucket w/metal tongs, Apple Blossom cutting, yellow 200.00
Ice bucket, Baroque patt., topaz 60.00
Ice bucket, Chintz etching, clear 125.00
Ice bucket, Colony patt., clear 275.00
Ice bucket w/metal handle, Navarre etching, clear 125.00
Ice bucket, Versailles etching, blue 100.00
Jam jar, cov., Chintz etching, clear, 7½" h. 80.00
Ketchup (condiment) bottle w/stopper, American patt., clear 45.00
Marmalade jar, cov., handled, American patt., clear, 5½" 80.00
Mayonnaise bowl & underplate, Baroque patt., topaz, 2 pcs. 45.00
Mayonnaise bowl, underplate & ladle, Chintz etching, clear, 3 pcs. 47.50
Mayonnaise bowl, underplate & ladle, Romance etching, clear, 3 pcs. 55.00
Nut cup, footed, Fairfax patt., blue 20.00
Oyster cocktail, Beverly etching, amber 4.00
Oyster cocktails, Willowmere etching, clear, set of 4 ....24.00
Parfait, Fairfax patt., topaz, 7 oz. 10.00
Pitcher, 5" h., American patt., clear 20.00
Pitcher w/ice lip, 6½" h., footed, American patt., clear, 3 pt. 50.00
Pitcher w/ice lip, Colony patt., clear, 2 qt. 125.00
Pitcher, water, Queen Anne etching, clear, 60 oz. 135.00
Plate, bread & butter, 6" d., Lido etching, clear 5.00
Plate, bread & butter, 6" d., Trojan etching, pink 6.00
Plate, bread & butter, 6" d., Versailles etching, green 7.00
Plate, salad, 7" d., American patt., clear 10.00
Plate, 7" d., Mayflower etching, clear 10.00
Plate, salad, 7½" d., Chintz etching, clear 14.00
Plate, salad, 7½" d., June etching, topaz 8.00
Plate, salad, 7½" d., Navarre etching, clear 14.00
Plate, salad, 7½" d., Versailles etching, blue 10.00
Plate, salad, 7½" d., Wheat cutting, clear 5.00
Plate, 8" d., Laurel cutting, clear 9.00
Plate, salad, 8½" d., American patt., clear 11.00
Plate, luncheon, 8½" d., Holly cutting, clear 12.00
Plate, luncheon, 8½" d., Meadow Rose etching, clear 15.00
Plate, dinner, 9" d., Colony patt., clear 17.50
Plate, 9½" d., Baroque patt., clear 12.00
Plate, dinner, 9½" d., Chintz etching, clear 45.00
Plate, luncheon, 9½" d., Fairfax patt., topaz 12.00
Plate, dinner, 9½" d., Navarre etching, clear 40.00
Plate, dinner, 10" d., Seville patt., amber 20.00
Plate, dinner, 10¼" d., Fairfax patt., blue 40.00
Plate, torte, 14" d., American patt., clear 30.00
Plate, torte, 20" d., American patt., clear 125.00
Platter, 12" oval, Pioneer patt., green 22.00
Punch bowl & base, American patt., clear, 14" d. bowl, 2 pcs. 235.00
Punch set: punch bowl, base & ten cups; Coin patt., clear, 12 pcs. 525.00
Relish dish, two-part, Baroque patt., blue, 6½" l. 20.00
Relish dish, two-part, Holly cutting, clear, 8½" l. 25.00
Relish dish, boat-shaped, American patt., clear, 8½" l. 19.00
Relish dish, divided, oval, Versailles etching, green, 8½" l. 26.00
Relish dish, three-part, American patt., clear, 6 x 9½" 37.50
Relish dish, three-part, Baroque patt., clear, 10" l. 20.00
Relish, three-part, Romance etching, clear, 10" l. 40.00
Relish dish, three-part, Fairfax patt., amber, 11½" l. 12.00
Relish dish, five-part, Navarre etching, clear, 13¼" l. 85.00
Salt & pepper shakers w/original tops, Baroque patt., topaz, pr. 90.00
Salt & pepper shakers w/original tops, Fairfax patt., pink, pr. 50.00
Salt & pepper shakers w/original tops, footed, Navarre etching, clear, pr. 95.00
Salt & pepper shakers w/original tops, Versailles etching, blue, pr. 225.00
Sandwich server w/center handle, Chintz etching, clear, 12" d. 40.00
Sandwich server w/center handle, Colony patt., clear 29.00

Sauceboat, Beverly etching, green.....55.00
Sauceboat & underplate, American patt., clear, 2 pcs. 45.00
Sauceboat & underplate, Fairfax patt., topaz, 2 pcs. 32.00
Sauceboat w/attached underplate, Pioneer patt., green 32.00
Sherbet, Coin patt., ruby.....50.00
Sherbet, low, Cynthia cutting, clear.....16.50
Sherbet, Colony patt., clear, 5 oz. 8.00
Sherbet, low, Florentine etching, clear, 7 oz. 8.00
Sherbet, Jamestown patt., green, 7 oz.. .....9.00
Sherbet, low, Laurel cutting, clear 10.00
Sherbet, Lido etching, clear, 6 oz. 7.00
Shrimp bowl, American patt., clear, 12¼" d.....325.00
Syrup pitcher w/original glass top & underplate, American patt., clear, 10 oz., 3 pcs. .....100.00 to 150.00
Toothpick holder, American patt., clear 35.00
Tumbler, whiskey, American patt., clear, 2 oz. 17.50

American Iced Tea Tumbler

Tumbler, iced tea, footed, American patt., clear, 5½" h., 12 oz. (ILLUS.). 15.00
Tumbler, footed, Arcady etching, clear, 12 oz. 25.00
Tumbler, cocktail, Baroque patt., yellow, 3" h., 3½ oz. 10.00
Tumbler, footed, Beverly etching, amber.....5.00
Tumbler, iced tea, footed, Chintz etching, clear, 12 oz.....20.00
Tumbler, old-fashioned, Coin patt., clear 55.00
Tumbler, juice, Colony patt., clear, 3⅝" h., 5 oz. 16.00
Tumbler, footed, Colony patt., clear, 5¾" h., 12 oz. 9.00
Tumbler, water, Cynthia cutting, clear..21.50
Tumbler, footed, Fairfax patt., blue, 6" h., 12 oz. 20.00
Tumbler, iced tea, Holly cutting, clear, 12 oz. 16.00
Tumbler, iced tea, Jamestown patt., clear 16.00
Tumbler, juice, Jamestown patt., green.....14.00
Tumbler, footed, June etching, clear, 6" h., 12 oz. 22.00
Tumbler, footed, Lido etching, clear, 9 oz. 10.00
Tumbler, iced tea, footed, Queen Anne patt., clear, 13 oz. 20.00
Tumbler, footed, Romance etching, clear, 6" h. 25.00
Tumbler, Versailles etching, green, 5¼" h., 9 oz. 25.00
Tumbler, iced tea, Wheat cutting, clear 15.00
Urn, cov., Coin patt., frosted emerald green, 12" h. 200.00
Vase, 7" h., Baroque patt., blue.....120.00
Vase, bud, 8" h., Coin patt., frosted blue 55.00
Vase, 8" h., Vesper etching, green.....70.00
Vase, 10" h., flared rim, American patt., clear 48.00
Water set: pitcher & six tumblers; Rosby patt., clear, 7 pcs. 180.00
Water set: pitcher & six stemmed goblets; Vesper etching, green, 7 pcs. 375.00
Wine, Acanthus etching, amber.....28.50
Wine, Alexis patt., clear 12.00
Wine, footed, American patt., clear, 4⅜" h., 2½ oz. 12.00
Wine, Coin patt. clear 55.00
Wine, Corsage etching, clear, 5½" h. ...17.50
Wine, Holly cutting, clear 30.00
Wine, Lido etching, clear, 3 oz. 20.00
Wine, Navarre etching, clear 35.00

FRY

Numerous types of glass were made by the H.C. Fry Company, Rochester, Pennsylvania. One of its art lines was called Foval and was blown in 1926-27. Cheaper was its milky-opalescent ovenware (Pearl Oven Ware) made for utilitarian purposes but also now being collected. The company also made fine cut glass.

Collectors of Fry Glass will be interested in the recent publication of a good reference book, The Collector's Encyclopedia of Fry Glassware, *by The H.C. Fry Glass Society (Collector Books, 1990).*

Bell, Foval bell w/Delft blue handle & rim trim, 6½" h.....$325.00

Bowl, 9¼" d., 5½" h., Foval, deep rounded & gently flaring white opal sides w/a jade green applied rim band & raised on a round applied jade green foot, No. 2504, w/a Fry company catalog No. 12, 2 pcs. 275.00
Bowl, 12" d., footed, Foval, w/applied Delft blue foot.....285.00
Cake pan, Pearl Oven Ware, 9" d. 18.00

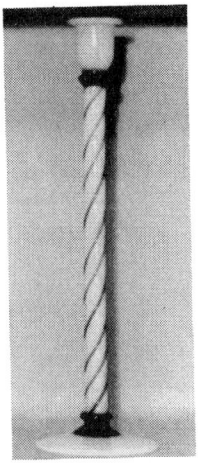

Fry Foval Candlestick

Candlesticks, Foval, bell-form socket above a blue connector to the twisted shaft wrapped w/a thin thread of blue, blue base connector to the round Foval foot, 16" h., pr. (ILLUS. of one) 495.00
Candlesticks, footed, clear & black striped decoration w/clear ball connector, pr. 500.00
Casserole dish, cov., Pearl Oven Ware, 8" d. 28.00
Coffeepot, cov., Foval w/applied jade green handle & finial on cover, 6½" h.....225.00
Compote, open, 6½" d., 9" h., Foval, Quilted patt. bowl, swirl stem w/open ring at the mid-point 350.00
Compote, open, 9" d., 5" h., Foval bowl w/Delft blue stem 235.00
Cup & saucer, Foval, applied green handle 59.00
Luncheon set: plate & goblet; Diamond Optic patt., clear w/black trim, 2 pcs. 150.00
Mug, iridescent green w/applied cobalt blue handle.....35.00
Perfume bottle w/original turquoise stopper, Foval bulbous base.....295.00
Pitcher, 9½" h., 5½" d., Diamond Optic patt., clear w/applied green handle 125.00
Platter, 9 x 12" oval, Foval, engraved w/flowers & ferns 65.00
Reamer, opaque green, embossed "F4/133/2/4" 30.00
Rose bowl, Foval w/three applied Delft blue feet.....250.00
Vase, cov., 5" h., 7½" d., footed, Foval, sterling silver cover 299.00
Vase, 7½" h., Diamond Optic patt. (No. 2565), clear w/azure blue trim 150.00
Vase, 23" h., bulbous base tapering to a long pulled neck, clear w/applied black lines decoration 85.00
Wine, royal blue bowl w/clear twisted stem 20.00

GOOFUS

This is a name collectors have given a pressed glass whose colors were sprayed on and then fired. Most pieces have intaglio or convex back designs. Several American glass companies, including Northwood Glass Co., produced this style ware early in the 20th century.

Bowl, 10¾" d., shallow, relief-molded red roses on gold $39.00
Bread tray, relief-molded Last Supper scene 50.00
Plate, 5¾" d., relief-molded rose & lattice decoration in red & gold 17.50
Plate, 7" d., relief-molded red on gold thistle design, advertising, molded into design "Henry Baack" 125.00
Vase, 7½" h., relief-molded red grapes on gold 20.00
Wall pocket, relief-molded bird & grapes decoration, 7¾".....55.00

GREENTOWN

Greentown glass was made in Greentown Indiana, by the Indiana Tumbler & Goblet Co. from 1894 until 1903. In addition to its famed Chocolate and Holly Amber glass, it produced other types of clear and colored glass. Miscellaneous pieces are listed here. Also see PATTERN GLASS.

Animal covered dish, rabbit, teal blue $185.00
Butter dish, cov., Holly patt., clear .....150.00 to 200.00
Cake stand, Austrian patt., clear 110.00
Compote, open, Austrian patt., clear, 8 x 8".....65.00

Cordial, Austrian patt., clear 75.00
Cordial, Shuttle patt., clear 25.00
Creamer, child size, Austrian patt., canary, 2⅛" d., 3¼" h.....90.00
Cruet w/original stopper, Cord Drapery patt., clear 115.00
Mug, Indoor Drinking Scene, clear 45.00
Mug, Outdoor Drinking Scene, Nile green.....85.00
Mug, Serenade (Troubador), amber, 4¾" h.....95.00
Nappy, cov., handled, Austrian patt., clear 20.00
Novelty, model of a dustpan, amber.....75.00
Novelty, model of a dustpan, blue (little roughness) 55.00
Pitcher, water, Fleur-de-lis patt.....35.00
Pitcher, water, Squirrel patt., clear 225.00
Sauce dish, footed, Herringbone Buttress patt., emerald green 85.00
Spooner, child's, Austrian patt., clear ...55.00
Toothpick holder, Holly patt., clear 85.00
Tumbler, Brazen Shield patt., cobalt blue 55.00
Vase, 6" h., Herringbone Buttress patt., emerald green.....175.00
Vegetable bowl, Cord Drapery patt., clear, 7½" l. 25.00
Wine, No. 11 patt., clear.....12.00

HEISEY

Heisey Puritan Pitcher

Numerous types of fine glass were made by A.H. Heisey & Co., Newark, Ohio, from 1895. The company's trade-mark -- an H enclosed within a diamond -- has become known to most glass collectors. The company's name and molds were acquired by Imperial Glass Co., Bellaire, Ohio, in 1958, and some pieces have been reissued. The glass listed below consists of miscellaneous pieces and types. Also see ANIMALS and PATTERN GLASS.

Heisey "Diamond H" Mark

Ashtray, Empress patt., Sahara (yellow) $100.00
Banana split dish, footed, Greek Key patt., clear.....33.00
Basket, Lariat patt., clear, 7½" h.....95.00
Bowl, cov., 5½" d., Ridgeleigh patt., clear 45.00
Bowl, 6" d., Pineapple & Fan patt., emerald green, late 1890s 65.00
Butter dish, cov., Lariat patt., clear.....50.00
Cake salver, Plantation patt., clear, 13".....135.00
Cake stand, Waverly patt., Orchid etching, clear, 12" 175.00
Candelabra, Old Williamsburg patt., Sahara, 20½" h., pr. 1,200.00
Candelabra, three-light, Old Williamsburg (No. 300) patt., Sahara w/clear prisms, pr. 950.00
Candlesticks, Empress patt. (No. 135), Alexandrite (orchid), pr.....895.00
Candlesticks, Oak Leaf patt., pink frosted, pr.....150.00
Candlesticks, Old Williamsburg patt., Sahara, 12" h., pr. 340.00
Candlesticks, two-light, Waverly patt., Orchid etching, clear, pr.....100.00
Candy dish, cov., w/seahorse handles, Waverly patt., Rose etching, clear 187.00
Celery tray, oval, Coarse Rib patt., clear, 9" l. 25.00
Champagne, Kohinoor patt., clear.....22.00
Champagne, Rose etching, clear 37.50
Champagne, Spanish patt., cobalt blue bowl w/clear stem, 5½ oz.....85.00
Champagne, saucer-type, Spanish patt., Killarney cutting, clear.....25.00
Champagne, saucer-type, Victorian patt., clear 12.50
Chip & dip set, Greek Key patt., clear, 2 pcs. 195.00
Cigarette box, cov., w/small horsehead finial, Puritan patt., No. 1489, clear 65.00
Coasters, Lariat patt., clear, set of 6.....60.00
Cocktail, Gascony patt., Tangerine (orange) 100.00
Cocktail, Orchid etching, clear, 5⅝" h., 4 oz.....50.00
Cocktail shaker, cov., Orchid etching, clear, sterling silver top & base.....160.00
Compote, jelly, 6¾" h., Rose etching, clear 40.00

Console set: bowl & pair of candle vases w/prisms & inserts; Ipswich patt., clear, bowl 11½" d., 5" h., 3 pcs. 375.00
Cordial, Carcassone patt., Old Colony etching, Sahara 145.00
Cordial, Lariat patt., w/Moonglo cutting, clear 110.00
Creamer & sugar bowl, Crystolite patt., clear, pr. 30.00
Creamer & sugar bowl, Petal patt., Moongleam (green), pr. 65.00
Creamer & sugar bowl, Queen Ann patt., Danish Princess etching, clear, pr. 85.00
Cruet w/original stopper, Empress patt., Sahara 135.00
Cruet w/original stopper, Lariat patt., clear 125.00
Cruet w/original stopper, Pleat & Panel patt., Flamingo 75.00
Crushed fruit jar, cov., Greek Key patt., clear 335.00
Cup & saucer, Orchid etching, clear 49.50
Decanter w/original stopper, Coronation patt., clear 65.00
Domino sugar tray, Narrow Flute patt., Moongleam 60.00
Goblet, Carcassonne patt., Sahara, 9 oz. 35.00
Goblet, Impromptu patt., clear 22.50
Goblet, Ipswich patt., clear, 8 oz. 18.00
Goblet, Kimberly patt., Belfast cutting, clear 42.50
Goblet, King Arthur patt., Moongleam 42.00
Goblet, Old Dominion patt., Alexandrite 315.00
Ice bucket, Empress patt., clear 52.50
Ice bucket, Empress patt., Orchid etching, clear 225.00
Ice bucket, Minuet etching, clear 150.00
Ice bucket, Waverly Orchid etching (No. 1519), clear 450.00
Ice bucket, cov. w/tongs, Empress patt., Alexandrite 495.00
Ice bucket, cov., Puritan patt. (No. 341), clear, 6" d. 57.50
Lamp, Windsor patt., clear, 9" h. 225.00
Lamps, hurricane-type, Plantation patt., clear, 15" h., pr. 675.00
Lemon dish, cov., w/dolphin finial, Queen Anne patt., clear, Farberware holder 70.00
Lemon dish, cov., Tudor patt., clear w/cutting 25.00
Luncheon set: four cups & plates & dolphin-footed creamer & sugar bowl; Empress patt., Sahara, 10 pcs. 195.00
Marmalade jar, cov., Crystolite patt., clear, 6" h. 38.00
Marmalade jar, cov., Minuet etching, clear 100.00
Marmalade jar, footed, handled, Pleat & Panel patt., Flamingo 35.00
Matchbox, cov., Banded Flute patt., clear 225.00
Mayonnaise bowl, three-handled, Provincial patt., Zircon 150.00
Mayonnaise bowl & spoon, Minuet etching, No. 1509, clear 85.00
Mayonnaise bowl & underplate, Lariat patt., clear, 2 pcs. 39.00
Mug, eight-sided w/elephant head & trunk forming handle, amber 895.00
Mugs, Pineapple & Fan patt., emerald green, set of 3 ....135.00
Mustard jar, cov., Crystolite patt., clear 20.00
Mustard jar, cov., Narrow Flute patt., clear 32.00
Mustard jar, cov., Twist patt., Flamingo 60.00
Nappy, Whirlpool (Provincial) patt., clear, 5½" 10.00
Nasturtium bowl, Twist patt., No. 1252, clear, 8" d. 25.00
Nut cup, Empress patt., Flamingo 28.00
Nut dish, individual, footed, Colonial patt., clear 10.00
Nut dishes, Octagon patt., green, set of 7 ....100.00
Oyster cocktail, Victorian patt. (No. 1425) clear, 5 oz. 11.00
Parfait, Old Glory patt., clear 27.50
Parfait, Plantation patt., clear 35.00
Perfume bottle w/stopper, Ridgeleigh patt., clear 69.00
Pitcher, tankard, Beaded Swag patt., ruby-stained, late 1890s 125.00
Pitcher, water, Charter Oak patt., clear 120.00
Pitcher, Colonial patt., clear, 1½ qt. 135.00
Pitcher, Empress patt., Sahara w/Old Colony etching, 73 oz. 195.00
Pitcher, Minuet etching, No. 4164, ½ gal., clear 295.00
Pitcher, Prince of Wales Plumes patt., clear w/gold trim, early 1900s 250.00
Pitcher, water, Puritan patt., clear, 3 qt. (ILLUS.) 115.00
Plate, 6" d., handled, Crystolite patt., clear 10.00
Plate, 6" d., Tudor patt., clear 7.00
Plate, 7" d., Empress patt., clear 25.00
Plate, 7" d., Minuet etching, clear 12.00
Plate, 7" sq., Empress patt., Tangerine 140.00
Plate, 7½" d., Queen Ann patt., Sahara 25.00
Plate, 8" d., Acorn & Leaves patt., Flamingo 25.00
Plate, 8" d., Orchid etching, clear 18.00
Plate, 8" d., Ipswich patt., Sahara 26.00

Plate, 8¼" d., Octagon Spiral patt., clear 20.00
Plate, 8¼" d., Rose etching, clear 25.00
Plate, 8½" d., Crystolite patt., clear 15.00
Plate, 8½" d., Empress patt., Tangerine 125.00
Plate, 8½" sq., Old Sandwich patt., Sahara 30.00
Plate, torte, 12" d., rolled rim, Lariat patt., clear 28.00
Plate, 13" d., Crystolite patt., clear 30.00
Plate, 13" d., Ridgeleigh patt., clear 32.00
Plate, torte, 14" d., Orchid etching, clear 65.00
Plate, torte, 14" d., Rose patt., clear 65.00
Plate, torte, 14" d., Waverly patt. w/Orchid etching, clear 42.50
Plate, dinner, square, Old Colony etching, Queen Ann patt., clear 60.00
Plates, 7" d., Pleat & Panel patt., Flamingo, set of 2 ....30.00
Plates, 8" d., Crystolite patt., clear, set of 8 ....75.00
Platter, 14" oval, Empress patt., Sahara 90.00
Platter, 14" l., Rose etching, clear 76.00
Pretzel jar, cov., etched Fisherman patt. 695.00
Puff box, cov., Winged Scroll patt., green, late 19th c. 50.00
Punch cup, Pillows patt., clear, ca. 1900 ....22.00
Punch cup, Pinwheel & Fan patt., clear..7.50
Punch cup, Prince of Wales patt., clear, early 1900s 9.00
Punch cup, Prison Stripe patt., No. 357, clear 20.00
Punch cup, Victorian patt., clear....12.00
Punch bowl & base, Banded Flute patt., clear, 2 pcs. 225.00
Punch bowl & base, Greek Key patt., clear, 2 pcs. ....350.00 to 450.00
Punch set: bowl, ten cups & ladle; Ridgeleigh patt., clear, 12 pcs. 200.00
Punch set: bowl, base & ten cups; Beaded Panel & Sunburst patt., No. 1235, clear, 12 pcs. 300.00
Punch set: bowl, ten cups & ladle; Ridgeleigh patt., clear, 12 pcs. 200.00
Punch set: bowl, twelve cups; Colonial patt., clear, 13 pcs. 225.00
Punch set: bowl, base & eleven cups; Greek Key patt., clear, 13 pcs. 500.00
Relish dish, Crystolite patt., clear, 6" oval 20.00
Relish dish, two-part, Waverly patt., clear, 6" 22.00
Relish dish, three-part, Lariat patt., clear, 10" l. 35.00
Relish dish, two-part, Ridgeleigh patt., clear, 10" d. 36.50
Relish dish, four-part, Whirlpool (Provincial) patt., Limelight (blue green), 10" l. 240.00
Relish dish, two-part, Fern patt., Zircon 275.00
Relish dish, two-part, Orchid etching, clear 40.00
Relish dish, three-part, Orchid etching, clear, 11¼" l. 50.00
Relish dish, Empress patt., clear, 13" l. 18.00
Relish dish, five-part, Colonial patt., clear 35.00
Relish dish, five-part, Williamsburg patt., clear 42.50
Relish tray, five-part, Crystolite patt., clear 25.00
Rose bowl, Fancy Loop patt., clear, late 1890s, 4" h. 45.00

Heisey Pillows Rose Bowl

Rose bowl, footed, Pillows patt. (No. 325), clear (ILLUS.) 225.00
Salt dip, individual size, Ridgeleigh patt., clear 8.00
Salt shaker w/original top, Beaded Swag patt., souvenir, milk white, late 1890s 35.00
Salt shaker w/original top, Winged Scroll patt., green w/gold trim, late 1890s 72.50
Salt & pepper shakers w/original sanitary tops, Banded Flute patt., clear, early 20th c., pr. 95.00
Salt & pepper shakers w/original tops, Beaded Swag patt., clear, late 1890s, pr. 50.00
Salt & pepper shakers w/original tops, Empress patt., Sahara, pr. 135.00
Salt & pepper shakers w/original metal tops, Pineapple & Fan patt., clear, late 1890s, pr. 40.00
Salt & pepper shakers w/original metal tops, Pineapple & Fan patt., emerald green w/gold, late 1890s, pr. 195.00

Salt & pepper shakers w/original tops, Rose etching clear, pr. 85.00
Salt & pepper shakers w/original sanitary tops, Victorian patt. (No. 1425), clear, pr. 85.00
Sherbet, Carcassone patt., clear w/cobalt bowl 55.00
Sherbet, Ipswich patt., Sahara 32.50
Sherbet, Jamestown patt., clear 6.00
Sherbet, low, Rose etching, clear 22.50
Sherbet, Whirlpool (Provincial) patt., clear 8.00
Spooner, Pineapple & Fan patt., emerald green w/gold trim, late 1890s 45.00
Spooner w/underplate, Queen Anne patt. (No. 365), clear, 2 pcs. 40.00
Sugar bowl, open, Minuet etching, clear 35.00
Sugar bowl, open, individual, Twist patt., Moongleam 35.00
Syrup pitcher w/original top, Beaded Swag patt., milk white, late 1890s ...160.00
Table set: creamer, cov. sugar bowl, cov. butter dish & spooner; Pineapple & Fan patt., emerald green w/gold trim, 4 pcs. 360.00
Toothpick holder, Beaded Swag patt., milk white w/floral decoration, late 1890s 85.00
Toothpick holder, Beaded Swag patt., ruby-stained, late 1890s 55.00
Toothpick holder, Fancy Loop patt., clear, late 1890s 60.00
Toothpick holder, Fancy Loop patt., emerald green w/gold trim, late 1890s 200.00
Toothpick holder, Fandango patt., clear, late 1890s 95.00
Toothpick holder, Pineapple & Fan patt., emerald green, late 1890s ....200.00 to 225.00
Toothpick holder, Punty Band patt., clear, late 1890s 50.00
Tray, Empress patt., Sahara, 13" d. 40.00
Tumbler, Banded Flute patt., clear, early 20th c. 55.00
Tumbler, footed, Barcelona cutting, clear, 6½" h. 18.00
Tumbler, old-fashioned, etched Sportsman scene, clear 55.00
Tumbler, Minuet etching, clear, 12 oz. 40.00
Tumbler, Pineapple & Fan patt., clear w/gold trim, late 1890s 30.00
Tumbler, iced tea, Plantation patt., clear, 12 oz. 47.00
Tumbler, juice, footed, Rose etching, clear, 5 oz. 35.00
Tumbler, iced tea, footed, Rose etching, clear, 12 oz. 40.00
Tumbler, iced tea, footed, Twist patt. (No. 1252), Marigold, 8 oz. 50.00
Tumbler, water, Victorian patt., clear, 3¾" d., 9 oz. 25.00
Tumbler, whiskey, Victorian patt., clear 39.00
Vase, 4" h., spherical, Empress patt. Sahara 145.00
Vase, 7" h., fan-shaped, Pineapple & Fan patt., emerald green w/gold trim, late 1890s 30.00
Vase, 8" h., dolphin-footed, Empress patt., Alexandrite 550.00
Vase, 8" h., Fancy Loop patt., clear, late 1890s 70.00
Vases, 7½" h., Ipswich patt., No. 1405, w/12 prisms each, clear, pr. 75.00
Water set: pitcher & four tumblers; Narrow Flute patt., clear, early 20th c., 5 pcs. 270.00
Wine, Gascony patt., Sportsman etching, clear 95.00
Wine, Minuet etching, clear, 2½ oz. 35.00
Wine, New Era patt., clear 18.00
Wine, Orchid etching, clear, 3 oz. 65.00
Wine, Spanish patt., cobalt blue 200.00

HISTORICAL & COMMEMORATIVE

Reference numbers are to Bessie M. Lindsey's book, American Historical Glass. *Also see MILK WHITE GLASS.*

Admiral Dewey Covered Dish

Battleship Maine dish, cov., milk white, 7¼" l., No. 466 ....$95.00
Bryan (William J.) cup, cov., bust portrait of Bryan, "The People's Money" above, clear, overall 5" h., No. 336 ....67.00
Bunker Hill platter, "Prescott 1776 Stark-Warren 1876 Putnam," clear, 9 x 13½", No. 44 ....80.00 to 90.00
Civil War liquor glass, shield, flag w/thirty-five stars, inscribed "A Bumper to the Flag," 3½" h., No. 480 ....115.00
Columbia bread tray, shield-shaped,

Columbia super-imposed against 13 vertical bars, amber, 11½ x 9½", No. 54 .....165.00
Columbus mugs, bust portraits of Columbus & George Washington, inscribed on base, "World's Columbian Exposition, 1893," clear, 2½" d., No. 2 .....80.00
Columbus mug, Columbus in landing scene front, reverse w/flagship "Santa Maria," inscribed on base, "World's Fair 1893," clear, 2½" d. 45.00
Columbus plate, bust portrait of Columbus center w/dates "1492-1892," pilot wheel border, clear, 9" d., No. 4 .....57.50
Columbus plate, bust portrait of Columbus center, openwork club border, milk white, 9½" d., No. 7.....64.00
Dewey (Admiral) dish, cov., ribbed base, amber, No. 387 .....230.00
Dewey (Admiral) dish, cov., tile base, milk white, 6¾" l., 4½" h., No. 390 (ILLUS.) 65.00
Emblem butter dish, cov., bullet finial, clear, No. 64 .....215.00

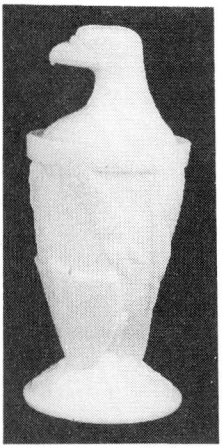

Emblem Tall Eagle Jar

Emblem Tall Eagle jar, cov., model of an eagle w/eagle head cover, American shield at front base under a banner w/"E Pluribus Unum," milk white, 6¾" h., No. 55 (ILLUS.) 195.00
Garfield cup plate, flaring rim, clear, 3" d., No. 297 .....100.00 to125.00
Golden Rule plate, "Do Unto Others, etc.," clear, 11" d., No. 221 .....83.00
Grant Peace plate, bust portrait of Grant center, maple leaf border, amber, 10½" d., No. 289.....55.00 to 70.00
Grant Peace plate, bust portrait of Grant center, maple leaf border, clear, 10½" d., No. 289 .....42.00
Grant Peace plate, bust portrait of Grant center, maple leaf border, vaseline, 10½" d., No. 289.....90.00
Harrison-Morton tray, bust portraits w/stippled ivy leaf border, clear, 8½ x 9½", No. 324 .....250.00 to 275.00
Indian match holder, milk white, 2¾" h., No. 12 .....65.00
Indian Chief plate, bust portraitof Indian center, milk white,7½" d. 60.00
Kaiser Wilhelm I plate, bust portrait of Kaiser center, laurel & oak leaf border, clear, 9¾" sq., No. 445 .....65.00
Kitchen stove dish, cov., amber, 4½ x 6¾", 4½" h., No. 149 .....300.00
Knights of Labor platter, amber, 11¾" l., No. 512 .....180.00 to 200.00
Liberty Bell plate, closed handles, scalloped rim w/thirteen original states & "100 Years Ago," clear, 8" d., No. 37 .....85.00
Louisiana Purchase Exposition plate, inscribed "World's Fair St. Louis, 1904," forget-me-not & openwork border, clear, 7¼" d., No. 105.....17.50
Louisiana Purchase Exposition plate, inscribed "World's Fair St. Louis, 1904," and "Festival Hall & Cascade Gardens," open work & forget-me-not border, clear w/frosted center scene, 7¼" d., No. 106 .....30.00
Louisiana Purchase Exposition tumbler, four features of St. Louis Exposition in relief, milk white, 5" h., No. 107 .....45.00

Martyr's Mug

Martyr's mug, Lincoln & Garfield bust portraits & inscription, clear, 2⅝" h., No. 272 (ILLUS.) 100.00
McKinley (William B.) cup, cov., bust portrait opposite handle, "Protection & Prosperity," clear, overall 5" h., No. 335 (ILLUS. top next column) .....80.00 to 100.00
McKinley Memorial platter, "It's God's Way" etc., clear, 8 x 10½", No. 356 ...60.00

McKinley "Protection & Prosperity" Cup

Moses in the Bulrushes dish, cov., lid w/full figure of an infant, base w/design resembling rushes, milk white, 4" w., 5½" l., No. 214 .....90.00
Old Abe (eagle) compote, cov., clear, No. 478 .....130.00
Old Glory plate, Betsy Ross making first flag pictured in center, clear, 5½" d., No. 52 .....38.00
Old Statehouse tray, shows Independence Hall above "Old Statehouse, Philadelphia, Erected 1735," amber, No. 32 .....55.00
Pickwick (Mr.) bottle, full figure of Mr. Pickwick (character created by Charles Dickens), marked "Mr. Pickwick," clear, 8¾" h., No. 408 .....22.50
Plymouth Rock paperweight, dated 1620, clear, 3¼" l., No. 17 .....95.00
Railroad train platter, Union Pacific Engine No. 350, amber, 9 x 12", No. 134 .....225.00

Rock of Ages Bread Tray

Rock of Ages bread tray, clear, No. 236 (ILLUS.) 85.00
Rock of Ages bread tray, clear w/translucent deep blue center, No. 236 .....165.00
Rock of Ages bread tray, clear w/milk white center, No. 236 .....155.00

Theodore Roosevelt Platter

Roosevelt (Theodore) platter, frosted portrait center, Teddy bears, etc. border, clear, 7¾ x 10¼", No. 357 (ILLUS.) 175.00
Ruth statuette, Ruth shown as gleaner resting on one knee w/wisps of grain in each hand, "Gillinder & Sons, Centennial Exhibition" inscribed on base, satin finish, clear, 4½" h., No. 216 .....75.00 to 100.00
Sampson pattern pitcher, honoring Rear Admiral William T. Sampson, leafy garlands, tassels & drops, clear w/partly stippled background, No. 402 .....135.00
Shakespeare statuette, frosted bust of Shakespeare, marked "Gillinder & Sons, Centennial Exhibition," 5" h., No. 405 .....85.00
Three Presidents platter, bust portraits of Garfield, Washington & Lincoln, inscribed "In Remembrance," clear, 10 x 12½", No. 249 .....70.00
Three Presidents platter, bust portraits of Garfield, Washington & Lincoln, inscribed "In Remembrance," clear w/frosted center, 10 x 12½", No. 249 (ILLUS. top next page) .....75.00 to 100.00
Uncle Sam dish, cov., battleship base, milk white, 6½" l. 80.00
Washington Centennial patt. platter w/bear paw handles, frosted center, "First in War," etc., clear, 8½ x 12", No. 27 .....130.00

Three Presidents Platter

Washington Bi-Centennial Bottle

Washington Bi-Centennial bottle, oval portrait medallion of Washington front & American eagle w/olive branches & thunderbolts in oval medallion reverse, "1732-1932," clear, qt., No. 262 (ILLUS.) 22.50
Washington Bi-Centennial plate, bust portrait of Washington center, large star border on stippled ground w/reserve at bottom w/"G. Washington - 1732-1932," clear, 8" d., No. 258 .....60.00
Washington Monument paperweight, milk white, 2¾" sq, base, 5½" h., No. 255 .....175.00
Whisk broom dish, Daisy & Button patt. below handle, amber, 5" w., 7½" l. 65.00

IMPERIAL

Imperial Glass Company, Bellaire, Ohio, was organized in 1901 and was in continuous production, except for very brief periods, until its closing in June 1984. It had been a major producer of Carnival Glass (which see) earlier in this century and also produced other types of glass, including an Art Glass line called "Free Hand Ware" during the 1920s and its "Jewels" about 1916. The company acquired a number of molds of other earlier factories, including the Cambridge and A.H. Heisey companies, and reissued numerous items through the years. Also see ANIMALS.

Imperial Nucut Mark

Early Imperial Cross Mark

Later Imperial Marks

CANDLEWICK PATTERN

Ashtray, heart-shaped, No. 400/172, clear, 4½" $10.00
Basket, No. 400/173, clear, 5" h. 250.00
Bonbon dish, heart-shaped, No. 51H, clear w/gold trim, 6" w. 15.00
Bonbon dish, heart-shaped, No. 51H, clear w/gold trim, 6" w. 15.00
Bowl, cream soup, 5", two-handled, No. 400/50, clear w/gold beads 55.00
Bowl, fruit, 5" d., 400/1F, clear 8.00
Bowl, 5", heart-shaped, No. 400/40H, clear 25.00
Bowl, 6" d., baked apple, No. 400/13B, clear 33.00
Bowl, 7" d., No. 400/5F, blue 55.00
Bowl, 7" d., two-handled, No. 400/62B, red 150.00
Bowl, 9" d., four-toed, square crimped, No. 400/74SC, black amethyst 200.00
Bowl, 9" d., heart-shaped, No. 400/49H, clear 140.00
Bowl, fruit, 10" d., footed, pedestal base, ruffled rim, No. 400/103C, clear 110.00
Bowl, 12" d., bell-shaped, No. 400/106B, clear 65.00
Cake plate, birthday, 72 candle holes, No. 400/160, clear, 13" d. 310.00
Cake stand, No. 400/103D, clear, 11" d. 73.00

Candleholders, No. 400/80, blue, 3½", pr. 165.00
Candleholders, mushroom, No. 400/86, clear w/gold beading, pr. 60.00
Candleholders w/applied handle, No. 400/90, clear, 5", pr. ....75.00 to 100.00
Candleholders, three-light, No. 400/115, clear, pr. 55.00
Candleholders, footed urn shape, No. 400/129R, clear, 6" h., pr. 125.00
Candy box, cov., No. 400/59, clear, 5½" d. 45.00
Candy box, cov., No. 400/259, clear, 7" d. 115.00
Champagne, saucer-type, No. 3400, clear, 6 oz. 11.50
Cheese & cracker server, No. 400/88, clear 30.00
Compote, 4½" d., No. 400/63B, clear ...16.00
Compote, 8", No. 400/48F, clear 75.00
Cordial, No. 3400, clear 35.00
Cream soup bowl w/underplate, two-handled, No. 400/50, clear, 5" d. bowl & 6¾" d. underplate, 2 pcs. 53.00
Creamer & open sugar bowl, No. 400/18, clear, pr. 50.00
Creamer & open sugar bowl, pedestal base, No. 400/31, clear, pr. 25.00
Cruet w/original stopper, applied handle, No. 400/279, clear, 6 oz. 40.00
Cup & saucer, clear 11.50
Goblet, water, No. 3400, clear, 9 oz. 15.00
Mayonnaise bowl & underplate, No. 40, blue, 2 pcs. 56.00
Mustard jar, spoon & underplate, No. 400/156, clear, 3 pcs. 45.00
Pitcher, water, 80 oz., No. 400/24, clear .....100.00 to 150.00
Pitcher, water, star-cut, No. 400/24, clear, 80 oz. 190.00
Plate, bread & butter, 6" d., No. 400/1D, clear 6.50
Plate, salad, 7" d., No. 400/3D, clear 7.00
Plate, luncheon, 8" d., No. 400/5D, clear 7.00
Plate, 8½" d., handled, crimped rim, No. 400/62C, clear 20.00
Plate, dinner, 10" d., No. 400/10D, clear 38.00
Plate, 10" d., two-handled, No. 400/72D, ruby 75.00
Plate, 10" d., two-handled, No. 400/72D, clear 25.00
Plate, 14" d., two-handled, No. 400/113D, clear 32.50
Platter, 16" oval, No. 400/131D, clear ..75.00
Punch bowl & underplate, 13" d. bowl No. 400/20B & 17" d. underplate No. 400/20V, clear, 2 pcs. 95.00
Relish dish, three-part, No. 400/208, clear, 10" l. 78.00
Relish dish, five-part, No. 400/209, clear, 13½" d. 65.00
Relish tray, three-part, No. 400/56, clear, 10½" d. 50.00
Relish tray, four-part, No. 400/55, clear, 8½" d. 16.50
Salt & pepper shakers, No. 400/96, clear, pr. 10.00
Sandwich server, center handle, No. 68D, clear, 11½" d. 38.00
Seafood cocktails, footed, 400/190, clear, set of 4 .....320.00
Sherbet, low, floral cutting, No. 400/19, clear, 5 oz. 15.00
Strawberry set: 7" d. plate & sugar dip bowl; No. 400/83, clear, 2 pcs. 55.00
Sugar bowl, open, No. 400/122, clear 6.50
Teacup & saucer, mallard cutting, No. 400/35, clear 15.00
Tray, heart-shaped center handle, No. 400/149D, clear, 9" d. 40.00
Tray, pastry, heart-shaped center handle, No. 400/68D, clear, 11½" d. ...30.00
Tumbler, juice, No. 400/19, clear, 5 oz. 12.00
Vase, bud, 5¾" h., No. 400/107, clear ..28.00
Vase, 8" h., No. 400/87C, clear 22.00
Vase, 8" h., fan-shaped, etched stars design, No. 400/87F, clear 40.00
Vase, 8" h., flip-type, ruffled rim, No. 400/143C, clear 66.00
Water set: 80 oz. pitcher No. 400/24 & six 12 oz. tumblers No. 400/19; clear, 7 pcs. 250.00

CAPE COD PATTERN

Ashtray, No. 160/134/1, clear, 4" d. 10.00
Bowl, cream soup, 5½", tab-handled, No. 160/198, clear 38.00
Bowl, fruit, 9" d., footed, No. 160/67F, clear 60.00
Bowl, 10" d., footed, No. 160/137B, clear 50.00
Box, cov., handled, clear 32.00
Cake plate, square, four-footed, No. 160/220, clear, 10" w. 80.00
Cake stand, round, footed, No. 160/67D, clear, 10½" d. 35.00
Candleholder, Aladdin style, No. 160/90, clear, 4" h. 125.00
Candleholders, two-light, No. 160/100, clear, pr. 100.00
Coaster w/spoon rest, clear 7.50
Comport, clear, 4½" d. 18.00
Compote, 6", cov., footed, No. 160/140, clear 55.00
Cruet w/original stopper, No. 160/119, amber, 4 oz. 30.00
Decanter w/original stopper, No. 160/163, clear, 30 oz. ....50.00 to 75.00
Egg cup, No. 160/225, clear 15.00
Epergne, plain center, No. 160/196, clear, 2 pcs. 175.00
Goblet, water, stemmed, No. 1600, clear, 10 oz. 10.00

Parfait, stemmed, No. 1602, clear, 6 oz. 16.00
Pitcher w/ice lip, No. 160/239, clear, 60 oz. 75.00
Plate, dinner, 10" d., No. 160/10D, clear 33.00
Plate, 16" d., cupped, No. 160/20V, clear 35.00
Platter, 13½" l. oval, No. 160/124D, clear 68.00
Punch cup, clear 5.00
Punch set: punch bowl, underplate & twelve cups; clear, 14 pcs. 150.00
Salt & pepper shakers w/original tops, cobalt blue, pr. 90.00
Sherbet, low, No. 1600, clear, 6 oz. 8.00
Tom & Jerry punch bowl, footed, No. 160/200, clear 275.00
Tumbler, flat, No. 160, clear, 10 oz. 8.00
Wine, No. 160/27, clear, 4½" h. 6.00

FREE HAND WARE

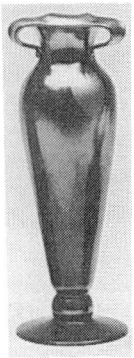

Graceful Free Hand Vase

Decanter w/original stopper, ship decoration, peach blow, w/original label 115.00
Vase, 7" h., iridescent orange w/dark threading 165.00
Vase, 7⅜" h., 3½" d., cushion footed baluster-form w/flared rim, overall white decoration on butterfly blue iridescent ground, ca. 1924 ....350.00
Vase, 8½" h., blue iridescent ground, gold iridescent interior 110.00
Vase, 8½" h., cylindrical shape, white drape design over mustard ground, orange iridescent interior 150.00
Vase, 9¾" h., iridescent orange over opaque white 50.00
Vase, 10" h., baluster-form w/flaring foot & rim, opaque white heart & vine decoration on a translucent cobalt blue ground 495.00
Vase, 10" h., iridescent yellow orange exterior, blue interior 125.00
Vase, 11½" h., footed slender body w/rounded shoulders & expanded tooled trefoil rim, dark iridescent body decorated w/orange hearts & vines (ILLUS.) 660.00

JEWELS LINE

Candlesticks, marigold, 8" h., pr. 38.00
Plate, 7¾" d., Pearl Green lustre 65.00

MISCELLANEOUS PATTERNS & LINES

Animal covered dish, lion on lacy base, caramel slag 135.00
Animal covered dish, rooster on lacy base, jade green 135.00
Animal covered dish, rooster on lacy base, purple slag 175.00
Bonbon, dolphin handled, cut florals on a pink ground, 6" d. 30.00
Bowl, Cathay line, Phoenix patt., blue satin 95.00
Bowl, 9" d., Rose patt., red slag 65.00
Compote, cov., Frosted Panels patt., Rubigold 60.00
Pitcher, Mt. Vernon patt. 23.00
Tumbler, Grape patt., ruby 12.00
Urn, Snake Dance patt., pink, 8½" h. 85.00
Vase, 8½" h., model of a dancing lady, red slag 98.00
Water set: pitcher & four tumblers; Frosted Panels patt., Rubigold, 5 pcs. 175.00

IOWA CITY GLASS

This ware, made by the Iowa City Glass Manufacturing Co., Iowa City, Iowa, from 1880 to about 1883, was produced in many shapes and patterns. The Frosted Stork pattern and pieces decorated with mottos and various animals are probably best known among collectors.

Goblet, Deer & Doe patt., clear $200.00
Goblet, Clear Stork patt. 150.00
Pickle castor, cov., Frosted Stork patt. 95.00
Plate, "Elaine," swan border 95.00
Platter, oval, "Be Industrious," clear beehive center, deer border 50.00
Platter, oval, "Be Industrious," clear beehive center, 1-0-1 border, 8 x 11½" 125.00
Platter, oval, Frosted Stork patt., 1-0-1 border, 8 x 11½" 58.00

LACY

Lacy Glass is a general term developed by collectors many years ago to cover the earliest type of pressed glass produced in this country. "Lacy" refers to the fact that most of these early patterns consisted of scrolls and geometric designs against a finely stippled background which gives the glass the look of fine lace. Formerly this glass was often referred to as "Sandwich" for the Boston & Sandwich Glass Company of Sandwich, Massachusetts which produced a great deal of this ware. Today, however, collectors realize that many other factories on the East Coast and in the Pittsburgh, Pennsylvania and Wheeling, West Virginia areas also made lacy glass from the 1820s into the 1840s. All pieces listed are clear unless otherwise noted. Numbers after salt dips refer to listings in Pressed Glass Salt Dishes of the Lacy Period, 1825-1850, *by Logan W. and Dorothy B. Neal. Also see SANDWICH GLASS.*

Rectangular Lacy Dish

Bowl, 5⅛" d., 1" h., round w/shallow sides and small rim scallops, starburst in center, hairpin border design (several scallops tipped, mold roughness) $33.00

Bowl, 5½" d., Acanthus & Tulip patt. 135.00

Bowl, 5¾" w., Roman Rosette patt., hexagonal finely scalloped rim (four scallops lightly tipped) 49.50

Bowl, 5⅝" d., Acanthus & Tulip patt., shallow sides w/finely scalloped rim, sapphire blue (three scallops lightly tipped, trace of mold roughness) 550.00

Bowl, 6" w., octagonal w/small rim scallops, American eagle & stars in center, acanthus leaves & shield border 330.00

Bowl, 6⅛" w., octagonal, Eagle patt., Boston & Sandwich (overall scallop roughness, section of jagged roughness on base rim) 330.00

Bowl, 6⅜" d., "Industry" patt., shallow sides, attributed to the New England Glass Co. (overall small spalls & rim flaking) 132.00

Bowl, 6½" d., shallow sides decorated w/grapes & leaves & tulips (eight lightly tipped scallops) 627.00

Bowl, 7¾" d., Lyre patt., shallow sides w/a finely scalloped rim line w/bull's eyes, Midwestern, ca. 1840 (light stippling, usual mold roughness) 104.50

Bowl, 8" l., 1⅝" h., shallow oblong sides w/triple end lobes, oak leaf scrolls in center & around the sides (several tipped scallops, mold roughness) 88.00

Bowl, 8¼" d., 1⅞" h., Acorn & Rose patt., shallow sides w/finely scalloped rim (mold roughness) 115.50

Bowl, 8⅜" l., 1⅝" h., oval w/scalloped rim, paired S-scrolls in center, tight S-scrolls around border (shallow spalls on two scallops, mold roughness) 77.00

Bowl, 9¼" d., shallow sides w/scalloped rim, Gothic Arch design, fire-polished (mold roughness) 302.50

Bowl, 9¼" d., shallow sides w/scalloped rim, S-scrolls & shells design w/bull's-eyes in rim, Midwestern, ca. 1835 (trace of tipping) 990.00

Bowl, 9½" d., Tulip patt., low sides w/scalloped rim (four scallops lightly tipped) 214.50

Bowl, 9½" oval, 2½" h., Crossed Peacock Feather patt., shallow flaring & scalloped sides, Midwestern, ca. 1840 (several shallow rim chips) 121.00

Bowl, cov., 7⅛" d., 5½" h., round flaring sides w/a galleried rim supporting a domed cover w/floraform finial, a band of Roman arches & thistles around the sides, Boston & Sandwich, ca. 1840 (one scallop slightly disfigured w/chip, two shallow spalls on top of rim) 715.00

Butter dish, cov., Roman Rosette patt., probably Pittsburgh, 6½" d., 4" h. (one rim chip, overall scallop tipping) 495.00

Candlestick, a lacy Peacock Eye socket attached by multiple wafers to a plain square stepped base, 5 11/16" h. (some corners w/shallow chips, others w/usual roughness) 1,100.00

Compote, cov., 6¼" d., 4¾" h., Peacock Feather patt., deep round bowl w/flared rim supporting the low domed cover w/floral-form finial, on a low domed base, Midwestern (base mold roughness, two points on rim tipped, shallow chips & severe roughness on edge of rim) 522.50

Compote, open, 4½" d., 4⅜" h., deep conical bowl w/scalloped rim & early

strawberry diamond design, on applied short pedestal & round foot (one rim bead w/shallow flake, mold roughness) 121.00
Compote, open, 4¾" d., 3½" h., round Heart patt. bowl, on applied knopped stem & round foot, attributed to Boston & Sandwich, ca. 1830 (shallow rim scallop flake, usual mold roughness) 660.00
Compote, open 6" d., 3¾" h., round w/deeply scalloped rim, Pine Tree & Shield patt., on applied short pedestal & plain round foot (base appears to be lightly polished) 357.50
Compote, open, 6½" w., 4" h., Eagle patt., octagonal bowl on a knopped stem & round lacy foot (roughness, chip on base) 880.00
Compote, open, 6½" d., 4¼" h., round bowl w/Heart & Sheaf of Wheat patt., small rim, on applied clear pedestal & plain round foot (mold roughness) 357.50
Compote, open, 10¾" l., 6⅛" h., shallow oblong bowl w/scalloped flanged rim in the Princess Feather patt., applied w/a wafer to the flaring Leaf patt. pedestal base, attributed to New England area, ca. 1830-40 (one scallop w/small flake).....2,475.00
Dish, miniature, oval, scroll design, scalloped rim, 2⅞" l. (minor chips).....60.50
Dish, oval w/scalloped rim & paneled sides, Constitution & Eagle patt., Boston & Sandwich Glass Co., 6¼" l., 1⅜" h. (two scallops flaked, usual mold roughness).....550.00
Dish, oval, Hairpin patt., attributed to Boston & Sandwich, 8½" l. (some roughess, small chips on underside of rim).....275.00
Dish, oblong w/angled sides, Pineapple & Gothic Arch patt., Boston & Sandwich Glass Co., 6½ x 9" (minor rim chipping) 192.50
Dish, rectangular w/notched corners, Peacock Eye patt., probably Boston & Sandwich, 7½ x 10" (ILLUS.) 1,430.00
Dish, round w/shallow sides, Princess Feather & Snail Shell design, attributed to New England, roughness, 9¼" d., (ILLUS. top next column).....385.00
Dish, oval, a band of diamonds, sheaves of wheat & acanthus leaves around the sides, 9⅜" l. (two scallops flaked) 495.00
Dish, shell-shaped w/wide loop end handle, attributed to New England, ca. 1830-40, 7¾ x 9½" (shallow non-disfiguring spalls on three scallops, usual mold roughness) 6,050.00

Large Lacy Dish

Honey dish, round w/scalloped rim, Roman Rosette patt., cobalt blue, 4" d. (three scallops lightly tipped) ...357.50
Honey dish, Nectarine patt. 40.00
Lamp, whale oil table-type, free-blown spherical font w/top opening tapering to a knopped stem applied w/a wide wafer to a pressed lacy Hairpin patt. foot, Midwestern, ca. 1830, 7¼" h. 1,870.00
Pitcher & bowl set, miniature, each piece w/tiny flowers against a stippled ground, ca. 1840, bowl 3¼" d., pitcher 2½" h., 2 pcs. (chips) 181.50
Plate, 5¼" d., round w/gently scalloped rim, Rose & Thistle patt. (light tipping on several scallops) 77.00
Plate, 5¾" d., Gothic Arch border, large center square divided into sixteen small squares, yellowish green (two scallops tipped).....330.00

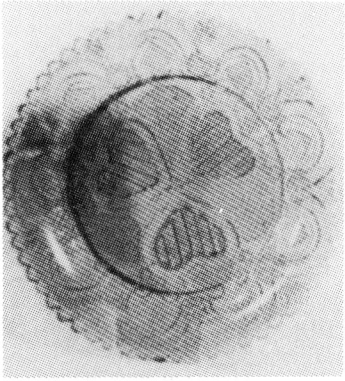

Triple-Heart Lacy Plate

Plate, 5¾" d., triple-heart center design, crescents w/diamonds border design, medium green, three scallops tipped (ILLUS.).....385.00
Plate, 5⅞" d., fan & star design (mold roughness).....55.00

Plate, 7" d., Waffle patt. center & fans around flanged rim (shallow spall on face) 44.00
Plate, 7½" w., octagonal Eagle patt. (usual mold roughness) 385.00
Plate, 7⅜" d., round w/scalloped rim, four-heart lobed center surrounded by strawberry diamond design, heart & blossom border band (shallow spalls on underside of scallops, mold roughness) 55.00
Plate, 8" d., round w/central flowers & leaves design framed w/concentric bands of intricate diamonds (mold roughness) 99.00
Plate, 10" w., octagonal, Beehive patt. (mold roughness, tipping on the scallops) 110.00
Salt dip, boat-shaped, BT-7 (heat check at stern) 220.00
Salt dip, boat-shaped, "Fayette" on stern, opalescent medium blue, Boston & Sandwich, BT 5 (flake on foot rim, usual mold roughness) ...1,045.00
Salt dip, boat-shaped, marked "Fayette" on stern, probably Boston & Sandwich, BT 4a (flaking, mold roughness) 385.00
Salt dip, flaring casket-form on a flaring base, shell design on sides, reddish amethyst, probably Boston & Sandwich (SL 1) 715.00
Salt dip, cov., sleigh-shaped w/scrolled sides & feet, domed cover w/knob finial, probably Boston & Sandwich, CD 2a (refracting small bubble on rim, some severe mold roughness on base & cover) 412.50
Salt dip, model of a small rowboat, bands of knobs down the sides, New England, cobalt blue (BT 9) 825.00
Salt dip, oblong octagonal, Eagle patt., Providence Flint Glass Co., EE 5 (one scallop tipped) 214.50
Salt dip, oval w/deeply serrated rim & overall heavy raised diamonds, Boston & Sandwich, blue opalescent, OL 15 (minute flake on one point) 412.50
Salt dip, oval bowl w/deeply fluted rim, diamonds around the sides, raised on an oblong footed base, probably Boston & Sandwich (OP 2b) 203.50
Salt dip, oval bowl w/finely scalloped rim, raised on four feet, opalescent, probably Boston & Sandwich, OP 17 (tiny flakes on tips of three feet) 302.50
Salt dip, oval, footed, Peacock Feather patt., probably Boston & Sandwich (PO 5) 88.00
Salt dip, rectangular w/columnar corners, Bird Bath patt., New England Glass Co., opalescent, BB 1 (flake on one corner) 385.00
Salt dip, rectangular w/columnar corners, Bird Bath patt., New England Glass Co., opaque white, BB 1 (annealing lines, one flake on corner, grey striations across interior bottom) 605.00
Salt dip, rectangular w/ringed columns at corners, Bird Bath patt., New England Glass Co., BB 2 (mold roughness on corners & lower rim) 227.50
Salt dip, rectangular w/columnar corners, Eagle patt., Boston & Sandwich, EE 1a (mold roughness) 104.50
Salt dip, rectangular w/slightly flaring sides, Hearts & Gothic Arches patt., Boston & Sandwich, opalescent medium blue w/striations, GA 4a (severe flaking & small chips along rim & sides) 275.00
Salt dip, rectangular w/columnar corners, finely waffled sides, New England Glass Co. (OG 2) 66.00
Salt dip, rectangular w/columnar corners, strawberry diamond point in sides, Boston & Sandwich, yellowish green (SD 7) 495.00
Salt dip, rectangular w/columnar corners & strawberry diamond design on the sides, cobalt blue, probably Boston & Sandwich, SD 7 variant (mold roughness) 104.50
Salt dip, rectangular casket-shape w/flared sides, on small knob feet, ornate scroll design around the sides, deep olive green, ca. 1840 (cooling crack on one side) 231.00
Salt dip, round flaring bowl on a short stem & round scalloped foot, silvery opaque mottled violet blue, probably Boston & Sandwich, RP 3 (unseen base flake, rim chip) 302.50
Salt dip, round bowl w/flaring paneled sides w/a scalloped rim, on a short round scalloped foot, New England (RP 10) 115.50
Salt dip, scrolled sofa shape w/scrolled rim & legs, Eagle patt., Boston & Sandwich, EE 7 (minor mold roughness) 357.50
Salt dip, sleigh-shaped, Eagle patt., molded eagles at each corner, Boston & Sandwich, EE 3b (mold roughness) 412.50
Salt dip, sleigh-shaped w/scroll feet, Lyre patt., peacock green, probably Boston & Sandwich, LE 3 (mold roughness, refracting annealing line on one scroll) 550.00
Salt dip, sleigh-shaped w/scrolled sides & rope-twist band around

base, Scroll patt., Providence Flint Glass Co., SC 1 (trace of mold roughness) 275.00
Salt dip, sleigh-shaped w/scrolled ends & feet, molded shell design, probably Boston & Sandwich, SL 15 (mold roughness, flaking on rim & feet) 88.00
Sauce dish, Oak Leaf patt., 4½" d. 60.00
Sugar bowl, cov., Acanthus patt., floral-form finial, 5⅜" h. (small chips on rims) 132.00

Rare Acanthus Leaf Sugar Bowl

Sugar bowl, cov., octagonal, Acanthus Leaf patt., Boston & Sandwich Glass Co., ca. 1830-40, unique deep emerald green, usual mold roughness, 5½" h. (ILLUS.) 17,600.00
Sugar bowl, cov., octagonal, Acanthus patt., flora-form finial on domed cover, canary yellow, 5½" h. (usual cover rim flaking, two shallow spalls on foot) 1,760.00
Sugar bowl, cov., early California patt., ca. 1850-60, medium amethyst, 6" h. (unseen chips on underside of base, minor mold roughness) 935.00
Sugar bowl, cov., octagonal, Gothic Arch patt., Boston & Sandwich Glass Co., ca. 1840-50, opaque starch blue, 5⅜" h. (small chips on rim of base, one on finial attachment of cover) 1,430.00
Sugar bowl, cov., Gothic Arch patt., petal foot, peacock blue, ca. 1840, 5¾" h. (tiny spall on base rim, multiple flakes on circular disk under lid finial) 1,045.00
Sugar bowl, cov., Gothic Arch patt., purplish blue, 5½" h. (usual flaking along cover edge) 1,320.00
Sugar bowl, cov., octagonal, footed, Gothic Arch patt., silvery white opaque, ca. 1840-60 ....750.00

Clear Lacy Sugar Bowl

Sugar bowl, cov., round flaring sides raised on a short pedestal base, tall domed cover w/a flora-form finial, Gothic Arch & Peacock Feather patt., probably Pittsburgh, 6" h. (ILLUS.) 880.00
Sugar bowl, cov., 'Ihmsen'-type, octagonal w/each panel featuring a relief-molded design of a piece of glassware produced by C. Ihmsen & Company of Pittsburgh, ca. 1851, opaque white, 5⅜" h. (shallow chip on base rim & four along rim) 4,290.00
Tray, oblong w/scalloped rim, Butterfly patt., 8¼" l. (one small rim chip) 176.00
Tray, oblong, an overall design of delicate scrolls w/shell-form fans at the ends & a curved diamond in the center all on a finely stippled ground, attributed to Boston & Sandwich, 8⅞ x 11⅝" (one scallop missing, another chipped) 1,100.00
Tray, rectangular, Peacock Eye & Shield patt., Boston & Sandwich, ca. 1835, 4⅝ x 8¼" (overall scallop roughness & flaking) 522.50

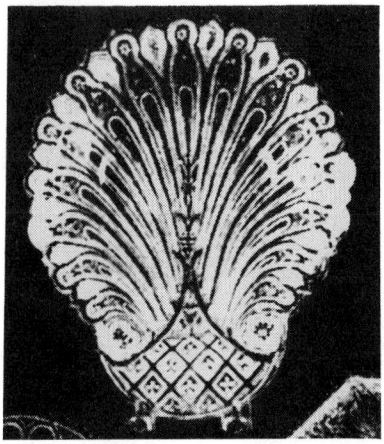

Shell-shaped Tray

Tray, shell-shaped w/Hairpin patt., closed tab handle w/diamonds, attributed to New England area, ca. 1830, 9½" l. (ILLUS.).....8,250.00
Tray, oval w/open loop end handles, open chain border, center diamond surrounded by scrolls, fans & leaf scrolls in border, ca. 1830, Boston & Sandwich Glass Co., 8½ x 11¾" (chip under one handle, minor rim roughness).....2,200.00
Tureen, cover & undertray, miniature, oval, raised scroll designs on a stippled ground, ca. 1840, 3" l., 3 pcs. (chips).....126.50
Vegetable dish, cov., Princess Feather patt., no grape clusters on flanged rim, domed cover w/loop handle, 10¾" l., 4¾" h. (mold roughness, some tipping, one shallow chip).....2,475.00
Window pane, rectangular, large diamond w/scrolls in center, quartered suns & rays at corners, Pittsburgh, 5 x 6⅞" (edge chips & roughness).....4,730.00

McKEE

The McKee name has been associated with glass production since 1834, first producing window glass and later bottles. In the 1850s a new factory was established in Pittsburgh, Pennsylvania, for production of flint and pressed glass. The plant was relocated in Jeannette, Pennsylvania in 1888 and operated there as an independent company almost continuously until 1951 when it sold out to Thatcher Glass Manufacturing Company. Many types of collectible glass were produced by McKee through the years including Depression, Pattern, Milk White (which see) and a variety of utility kitchenwares.

Early McKee Mark, ca. 1880

PRESCUT

McKee Prescut Mark

Kitchenwares
Bowl, 6" d., Chalaine Blue.....$45.00
Bowl, 7½" d., Chalaine Blue.....50.00
Bowl, 9" d., Skokie Green.....15.00
Canister w/original glass cover, round, Chalaine Blue, 10 oz.....50.00
Canister w/original glass cover, round, Chalaine Blue, 24 oz.....55.00
Canister w/original glass cover, round, "Flour," Chalaine Blue.....55.00
Canister w/original glass cover, round, French Ivory w/red polka dots, 10 oz.....16.00
Canister w/original glass cover, round, "Sugar," Chalaine Blue.....55.00
Measuring cup, Skokie Green, 2 cup...18.00
Mixing bowls, nesting-type, French Ivory w/red polka dots, 9" d., 8" d., 7" d., 6" d., set of 4.....60.00
Refrigerator dish, cov., rectangular, Chalaine Blue, 5 x 8".....85.00
Refrigerator dish, cov., rectangular, French Ivory w/blue polka dots, 4 x 5".....33.00
Salt & pepper shakers w/original metal lids, Chalaine Blue, pr.....100.00
Salt & pepper shakers w/original tops, French Ivory w/blue polka dots, pr.....32.00
Salt & pepper shakers w/original tops, Roman Arch patt., black, 4½" h., pr...45.00

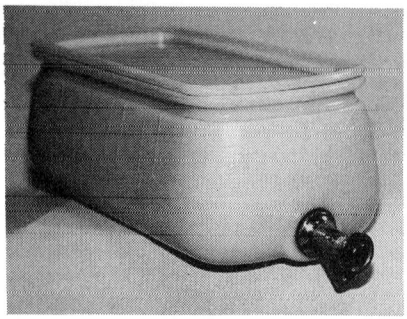

McKee Water Dispenser

Water dispenser w/glass top, Skokie Green, 4½ x 5 x 11" (ILLUS.).....225.00

Pres-Cut Lines
Bowl, 7" d., Rock Crystal patt., clear....15.00
Candlestick, Rock Crystal patt., amber, 8" h.....40.00
Champagne, Aztec patt., clear.....17.00
Cheese & cracker server, Rock Crystal patt., ruby.....175.00
Cocktail, Rock Crystal patt., clear, 3½ oz., 4¼" h.,.....13.50
Compote, 7" d., 3½" h., Rock Crystal patt., clear.....38.00
Cordial, Rock Crystal patt., clear, 1 oz.....20.00
Cordial, Rock Crystal patt., ruby, 1 oz.....60.00
Cracker jar, cov., Aztec patt., milk white.....60.00

Creamer & open sugar bowl, Sunbeam patt., blue w/gold trim, pr. 45.00
Cruet w/original stopper, Rock Crystal patt., clear 65.00
Goblet, footed, low, Rock Crystal patt., amber, 8 oz. 50.00
Goblet, footed, Rock Crystal patt., ruby, 8 oz. 45.00
Goblet, water, Rock Crystal patt., clear, 6½" h. 16.50
Goblet, water, Rock Crystal patt., green 20.00
Icer w/liner, Rock Crystal patt., clear 33.00
Mayonnaise bowl & underplate, Rock Crystal patt., pink, 2 pcs. 25.00
Nut bowl w/center handle, Rock Crystal patt., ruby, 8½" d. 135.00
Parfait, Rock Crystal patt., clear 25.00
Pitcher, water, cylindrical, Rock Crystal patt., amber, 2 qt. 150.00
Punch cup, Sunbeam patt., clear 25.00
Relish, five-part, Rock Crystal patt., clear, 12¼" d. 25.00
Sandwich server w/center handle, Rock Crystal patt., ruby 135.00
Sugar bowl, cov., footed, Rock Crystal patt., clear 36.00
Sundae, Rock Crystal patt., ruby, 6 oz. 33.00
Tumbler, Aztec patt., clear 10.00
Tumbler, juice, Rock Crystal patt., clear 12.00
Tumbler, Rock Crystal patt., clear, 5 oz. 12.50
Tumbler, iced tea, Rock Crystal patt., clear, 11 oz., 6½" h. 19.50
Tumbler, iced tea, Rock Crystal patt., ruby, 11 oz., 6½" h. 50.00
Tumbler, Rock Crystal patt., clear, 12 oz. 55.00
Vase, 11" h., footed, cylindrical, Rock Crystal patt., clear 55.00
Wine, Rock Crystal patt., clear, 4¾" h. 16.00

Miscellaneous Patterns & Pieces

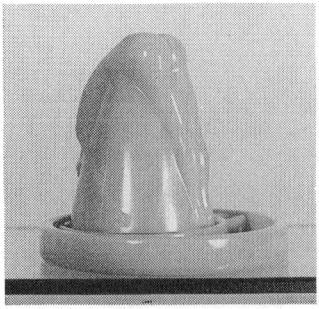

"Bottoms Up" Whiskey Tumbler

Animal covered dish, rabbit on split-ribbed base, milk white 325.00
Butter dish, cov., Wild Rose w/Bowknot patt., green (worn old gold) 100.00
Candlesticks, Laurel patt., French Ivory, pr. 25.00
Cruet, Wild Rose with Bowknot patt., frosted clear w/Goofus decoration 45.00
Egg cup, French Ivory 6.50
Mug, Outdoor Drinking Scene patt., green opaque 75.00
Mug, Serenade (Troubador) patt., blue opaque 55.00
Mug, Serenade (Troubador) patt., French Ivory 90.00
Mug, Serenade (Troubador) patt., green opaque 85.00
Pin tray, embossed scrolling patt., clear, decorated w/pink & blue trim, 2½ x 5" 10.00
Tom & Jerry set: bowl & twelve mugs; vaseline, all pieces signed, 13 pcs. 150.00
Tumbler, whiskey, w/coaster base, "Bottoms Up," French Ivory, 2 pcs. (ILLUS.) 50.00
Vase, 8" h., footed, triangular w/relief-molded nude on each side, opaque black 175.00
Vase, 10½" h., Rainbow patt., French Ivory 90.00

MILK WHITE

This is opaque white glass that resembles the color of and was used as a substitute for white porcelain. Opacity was obtained by adding oxide of tin to a batch of clear glass. It has been made in numerous forms and shapes in this country and abroad from about the first quarter of the last century. It is still being produced, and there are many reproductions of earlier pieces. Also see HISTORICAL and PATTERN GLASS.

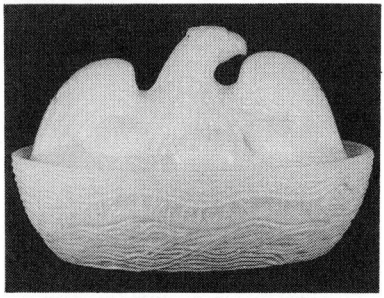

"American Hen" Covered Dish

Animal covered dish, "American Hen," eagle w/eggs inscribed "Porto Rico," "Cuba," & "Philippines," 6" l., 4" h. (ILLUS.) $66.00

Animal covered dish, Boar's Head w/glass eyes .....675.00 to 775.00
Animal covered dish, "The British Lion" on base, 6¼" l. 110.00
Animal covered dish, Camel resting, 6¼" l. .....100.00 to 125.00
Animal covered dish, Cat on coarse rib base, 5½" l., 4" h. 95.00
Animal covered dish, Cat on split-ribbed base, signed "McKee," 5½" (tiny ear fleck out) 295.00
Animal covered dish, Chick & Eggs on lacy-edge pedestal base, Atterbury, 1880s .....75.00 to 100.00
Animal covered dish, Chick in Egg cover on sleigh-shaped base, 5½" l. 70.00
Animal covered dish, Chicks on Round Basket, 4½" w., 3" h. 65.00
Animal covered dish, Cow on round paneled base, France, 5¾" l. 180.00
Animal covered dish, Deer on "fallen tree" base, Flaccus, 6¾" l. .....225.00 to 250.00
Animal covered dish, Dog (Chow) on wide ribbed base, Westmoreland Specialty Company, 5½" h. 65.00
Animal covered dish, Duck w/wavy base, glass eyes, Challinor, Taylor & Co., 5¼" h. 125.00
Animal covered dish, Pintail Duck on split-rib base, Kemple Glass Co., mid-20th c., 5½" l. 55.00
Animal covered dish, Fish, Entwined Fish (2) on lacy-edge base, shell finial, Atterbury, 7½" d. .....150.00 to 175.00
Animal covered dish, Fish on Skiff base, 7½" l. 32.50
Animal covered dish, Fish w/glass eyes, Challinor, Taylor & Co., 8¾" l. 75.00
Animal covered dish, Fish, Vallerysthal, 7" l. 100.00
Animal covered dish, Flat Fish, 8½" l. 200.00
Animal covered dish, Fox on ribbed top & lacy-edge base, Atterbury, 7¾" l. 160.00
Animal covered dish, Hen on Basketweave base, Kemple Glass Co., mid-20th c. 55.00
Animal covered dish, Hen on Basketweave base, signed "Vallerysthal," 7½" l. 125.00
Animal covered dish, Hen on Chick base, Flaccus, 6¼" l. .....250.00 to 300.00
Animal covered dish, Hen on flared Basketweave base, 5⅝" l. 75.00
Animal covered dish, Hen on ribbed flared base 100.00
Animal covered dish, Hen w/blue head on lacy base, amber glass eyes, Atterbury 140.00
Animal covered dish, Hen w/straight head w/glass eyes on lacy base, Westmoreland Specialty Company 50.00
Animal covered dish, Kittens (3) on square base, gold trim, 3½" sq. 40.00
Animal covered dish, Lamb on "Bo Peep" base, 6" l. base, 4¼" h. 295.00
Animal covered dish, Lion on Picket base, 5½" l. 65.00
Animal covered dish, Lamb on split-ribbed base, lamb facing right, McKee, 5½" l. .....75.00 to 100.00

Lion on Scroll Base Dish

Animal covered dish, Lion on scroll base, 5¾" l. (ILLUS.) 75.00
Animal covered dish, Majestic Lion, molded bird & foliage base, 6¾" h. 2,600.00

Ribbed Lion on Lacy Base

Animal covered dish, Ribbed Lion on lacy-edge base, patent dated, Atterbury (ILLUS.) 150.00
Animal covered dish, Ribbed Lion on ribbed base, Atterbury, 7½" l. 225.00
Animal covered dish, Mule-Eared Rabbit on ribbed octagonal base, 5½" l., 4½" h. .....80.00 to 100.00
Animal covered dish, Rabbit, original red glass eyes, patent date stamped on bottom, Atterbury, 9" l. .....250.00 to 275.00

Animal covered dish, Rabbit on Split Rib base, 5½" l. 65.00

Robin on Nest Dish

Animal covered dish, Robin on Nest, 6¼" d. (ILLUS.) 150.00
Animal covered dish, Robin with Berry, Kemple Glass Co., mid-20th c., 5½" l. 150.00
Animal covered dish, Rooster on wide rib base, Westmoreland Specialty Co., 5½" l. 60.00
Animal covered dish, Standing (Pedestal) Rooster, Westmoreland....55.00
Animal covered dish, Squirrel on acorn-shaped dish, Vallerysthal, 7¼" l. 50.00
Animal covered dish, "square block" Swan w/glass eyes, Atterbury, 8" l...240.00

Swan with Raised Wings Dish

Animal covered dish, Swan w/raised wings & glass eyes on lacy-edge base, Atterbury, 9½" l., 6" h. (ILLUS.) ....150.00 to 175.00
Animal covered dish, Turkey, Imperial Glass Co. 50.00
Animal covered dish, Turkey on split-ribbed base, McKee 90.00
Animal covered dish, Wooly Lamb on Octagon coarse ribbed base, 5¼" l....70.00
Basket, two-handled, chick emerging from egg on cover 95.00
Bottle, model of an Octopus, tentacles winding around a large American coin, 4½" h. (no metal cap) 650.00
Bottle, model of a Sitting Bear, 10¾" h. 85.00
Bowl, 7" d., 5" h., Chain & Petal Edge patt. 25.00
Bowl, 8" d., 3" h., Open Lattice Edge, apple blossom decoration in center, Atterbury 40.00
Bowl, 8" d., footed, Wide Weave Basket design 30.00
Bowl, 8¾ x 9¼", rectangular w/open edge border 40.00
Bowl, 8¾ x 12¾", 2⅞" h., Beaded Rib patt. w/interior floral design 60.00
Bowl, 10" d., 4" h., Daisy patt., unpainted 70.00
Bowl, 10" l., 5¾" h., oblong, Shell patt., two ribbed & two petal feet 25.00
Bowl, round, Daisy & Tree of Life patt. 40.00
Box, cov., heart-shaped, embossed floral design highlighted w/touches of blue & gold 35.00
Butter dish, cov., w/snowflake-shaped insert, Crossed Fern patt. w/Ball & Claw base 90.00
Butter dish, cov., Roman Cross patt. 50.00
Butter dish, cov., Versailles patt. w/pink decoration 45.00
Compote, open, 7¼" h., six-sided, Scroll patt. 60.00
Compote, open, 7½" h., Jenny Lind figural bust pedestal, ribbed bowl 85.00
Compote, open, 8¼" d., 8¼" h., Atlas stem, open-edge border, Atterbury..100.00
Covered dish, Admiral Dewey on Battleship base, 5½" l. 125.00

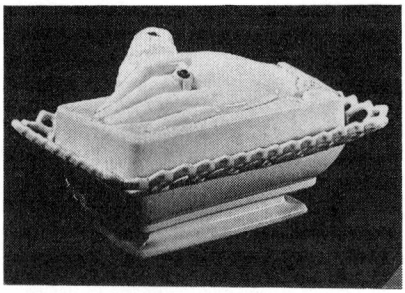

Hand & Dove Dish

Covered dish, Hand & Dove on lacy-edge base, Atterbury, 8¾" l., 4¾" h. (ILLUS.) ....100.00 to 150.00
Covered dish, pear-shaped lid resting in petalled leaf bowl, w/original fired paint & Westmoreland label underneath 35.00
Covered dish, Santa on Sleigh, 5½" l. 185.00
Covered dish, Snare Drum w/Cannon finial, 4½" d., 4" h. ....70.00 to 90.00
Creamer, Owl, miniature, 3½" h. 47.00

Dresser tray, Chrysanthemum patt., 7½ x 10" 35.00
Egg cup, cov., model of a Hen on Nest, 2½" w., 2½" h. 175.00

Blackberry Goblet

Goblet, Blackberry patt. (ILLUS.)....38.00
Match holder, model of a bulldog head w/striker on back of the head, 2¼" h. 85.00
Model of a cat, sitting, 8" h. 200.00
Model of a tramp's shoe, 2⅛" h. 42.00
Mug, Bleeding Heart patt., 3¼" h. 60.00
Plate, 5½" d., Woof Woof ....50.00 to 75.00
Plate, 6" d., Dog and Cats, open leaf border 100.00
Plate, 6" d., Three Puppies, open leaf border 85.00
Plate, 6¼" d., Easter Rabbits, old paint 35.00
Plate, 6¼" d., Mother Goose w/bunnies in relief 45.00
Plate, 7" w., diamond-shaped, Easter Chicks (2), openwork scroll & leaf border 38.00
Plate, 7" d., Ancient Castle (Garfield Monument) 50.00

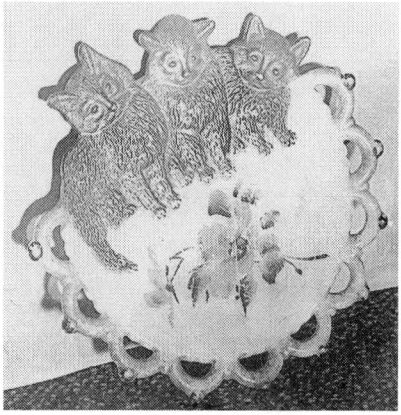

Three Kittens Plate

Plate, 7" d., Three Kittens (ILLUS.) 35.00
Plate, 7" d., Challinor's Forget-Me-Not patt. 40.00

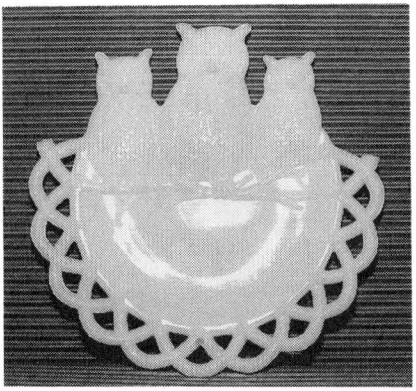

Three Owls Plate

Plate, 7" d., Three Owls (ILLUS.) 40.00
Plate, 7¼" d., Easter Bunny & Egg 60.00
Plate, 7¼" d., Lacy-Edge Indian, good paint 55.00
Plate, 7¼" d., Setting Hen & Chicks, openwork border 55.00
Plate, 7½" d., "Easter" ducks, scroll border 40.00

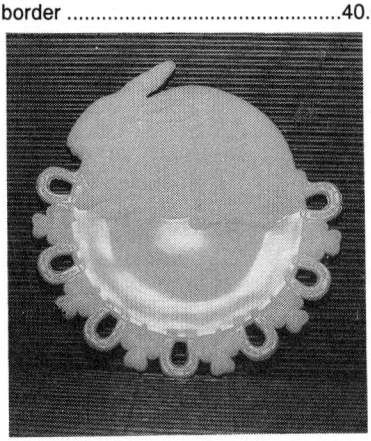

Rabbit & Horseshoe Plate

Plate, 7½" d., Rabbit & Horseshoe (ILLUS.) 55.00
Plate, 8" d., Diamond and Shell border 40.00
Plate, 8" d., Hearts & Anchor border 30.00
Plate, 8" d., Serenade 42.00
Plate, 8¼" d., Wicket border 35.00
Plate, 9" d., Angel Head, openwork border 30.00
Plate, 9" d., Gothic edge ....10.00 to 20.00
Plate, 10½" d., Closed Lattice Edge border, h.p. autumn leaves & grapes, sawtooth under base 35.00
Plate, 10½" d., Open Lattice Edge border, game bird in center 75.00

Platter, 9¾ x 13¼", Retreiver, lily pad border 110.00
Platter, 10½ x 13¾", flattened fish form w/scale details 125.00
Salt dip, figural turtle....45.00
Salt dip, model of a basket w/handle....35.00
Salt shaker w/original top, Chain & Swag patt. 35.00
Sugar shaker w/original top, h.p. Apple Blossom patt. 135.00
Sugar shaker w/original top, Grape patt., raised bunch of grapes w/leaf & vine decoration, old screw cap, 4½" h. 45.00
Sugar shaker w/original top, Little Shrimp patt. 75.00
Sugar shaker w/original top, Parian Swirl patt., enameled floral decoration, Northwood....110.00
Sugar shaker w/original top, Quilted Phlox patt., Northwood 125.00
Sugar shaker w/original top, Quilted Phlox patt., decorated w/blue flowers, Northwood 195.00
Syrup pitcher w/original hinged lid, Apple Blossom patt. 160.00
Syrup pitcher w/original metal top, Banded Shell patt., 5½" h. 65.00
Syrup pitcher w/original hinged tin cover, pressed Blackberry patt., applied strap handle, ca. 1860, 7¼" h. 137.50
Syrup pitcher w/original top, Catherine Ann patt. 125.00
Syrup pitcher w/original metal top, Challinor's Tree of Life patt. 80.00
Syrup pitcher w/original top, Petunia Swirl patt. 85.00
Table set: creamer, cov. sugar bowl, cov. butter dish, spooner; Versailles patt. w/h.p. rose decoration, 4 pcs...125.00
Tile, owl decoration in fired-on paint, 6" sq. 55.00
Water set: pitcher & four tumblers; Apple Blossom patt., 5 pcs. 160.00
Whimsey, Easter Egg with Emerging Chick, 3¼" l. 40.00
Whimsey, Straw Hat (College Hat), w/old paint, McKee, 4" d. 40.00

NEW MARTINSVILLE

The New Martinsville Glass Mfg. Co. opened in New Martinsville, West Virginia in 1901 and during its first period of production came out with a number of colored opaque pressed glass patterns and also developed an art glass line they named "Muranese" but which collectors today refer to as "New Martinsville Peach Blow." The factory burned in 1907 but reopened later that year and began focusing on production of various clear pressed glass patterns many of which were then decorated with gold or ruby staining or enameled decoration. After going through receivership in 1937 the factory again changed the focus of its production to more contemporary glass lines and figural animals. The firm was purchased in 1944 by The Viking Glass Company (now Dalzell-Viking) and some of the long-popular New Martinsville patterns are now produced by this still-active firm.

Ashtray, embossed w/"New Martinsville Centennial - 1838-1938" & a log cabin along the Ohio River, green ...$50.00
Book ends, model of an elephant, clear, pr. 185.00
Book ends, model of a prancing horse, clear, pr. 175.00
Bowl, 7 x 12" rectangle, Janice patt. (No. 4500 Line), ruby 40.00
Cordial, Moondrops patt. (No. 37 Line), cobalt blue 30.00
Dresser set: two cologne bottles w/original stoppers & cov. powder jar; Queen Ann patt. (No. 18 Line), clear, 3 pcs. 80.00
Liqueur set: decanter w/stopper & three liqueur tumblers; Moondrops patt., green, 4 pcs. 45.00
Pitcher, water, Moondrops patt., clear 50.00
Plate, torte, 18" d., Radiance patt. (No. 4200 Line), Prelude etching, clear 95.00
Relish dish, divided, Radiance patt., blue 24.00
Relish dish, five-part, Prelude etching, clear, 13" l. 85.00
Tumbler, Moondrops patt., ruby 12.00
Tumbler, water, footed, Prelude etching, clear 18.00

NORTHWOOD

Harry Northwood (1860-1919) was born in England, the son of noted glass artist John Northwood. Brought up in the glass business, Harry immigrated to the United States in 1881 and shortly thereafter became manager of the La Belle Glass Company, Bridgeport, Ohio. Here he was responsible for many innovations in colored and blown glass. After leaving La Belle in 1887 he opened The Northwood Glass Company in Martins Ferry, Ohio in 1888. The company moved to Ellwood City, Pennsylvania in 1892 and Northwood moved again to take over a glass plant in

Indiana, Pennsylvania in 1896. One of his major lines made at the Indiana, Pennsylvania plant was Custard glass (which he called "ivory"). It was made in several patterns and some pieces were marked on the base with "Northwood" in script.

Harry and his family moved back to England in 1899 but returned to the U.S. in 1902 at which time he opened another glass factory in Wheeling, West Virginia. Here he was able to put his full talents to work and under his guidance the firm manufactured many notable glass lines including opalescent wares, colored and clear pressed tablewares, various novelties and, probably best known of all, Carnival glass. Around 1906 Harry introduced his famous "N" in circle trade-mark which can be found on the base of many, but not all, pieces made at his factory. The factory closed in 1925.

In this listing we are including only the clear and colored tablewares produced at Northwood factories. Also see CARNIVAL, MILK WHITE and, under Pattern Glass, ROYAL IVY and ROYAL OAK.

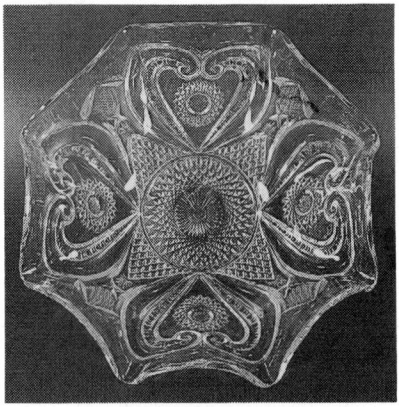

Northwood Valentine Bowl

Northwood Signature Mark, ca. 1898

Northwood "N" in Circle Mark, ca. 1906

Berry set: master bowl & five sauce dishes; Parian Swirl patt., ruby w/enameled decoration, 6 pcs. $145.00

Berry set: master bowl & nine sauce dishes; Leaf Medallion (Regent) patt., purple w/gold trim, 10 pcs. 625.00

Bowl, 9" w., crimped rim, Valentine (No. 14) patt., clear (ILLUS.) 49.00

Bowl, 11" d., rolled edge, Jade Blue 50.00

Bowl, master berry, Leaf Medallion (Regent) patt., purple w/gold 120.00

Bowl, master berry, Mikado (Flower & Bud) patt., clear w/gold & enameled trim 132.00

Butter dish, cov., Cherry & Cable (Cherry Thumbprints) patt., clear w/ruby & gold trim 100.00

Butter dish, cov., Gold Rose patt., green w/gold 100.00

Butter dish, cov., Panelled Holly patt., blue opalescent w/gold trim 375.00

Butter dish, cov., Peach patt., clear 95.00

Butter dish, cov., Strawberry & Cable patt., clear 110.00

Celery vase, Leaf Umbrella patt., ruby & white spatter 225.00

Compote, jelly, Leaf Medallion (Regent) patt., cobalt blue w/gold trim 120.00

Compote, jelly, Leaf Medallion (Regent) patt., purple w/gold trim 80.00

Creamer, Cherry & Cable (Cherry Thumbprints) patt., clear 45.00

Creamer, Panelled Holly patt., blue opalescent 95.00

Panelled Holly Creamer

Creamer, Panelled Holly patt., white opalescent w/gold & red (ILLUS.) 85.00

Creamer, Panelled Holly patt., green w/gold trim 75.00

Cruet w/original stopper, Parian Swirl mold, Daisy & Fern patt., blue opalescent 80.00

Cruet w/original stopper, Parian Swirl patt., ruby 450.00

Pickle castor, Leaf Mold patt. insert, rubina, w/silver plate frame 265.00

Pickle castor, Leaf Mold patt. insert, vaseline w/cranberry spatter, satin finish, ornate silver plate frame, cover & tongs (resilvered) 375.00
Pitcher, water, Grape & Gothic Arches patt., green w/gold trim 100.00
Pitcher, water, Leaf Medallion (Regent) patt., purple w/gold trim 350.00
Pitcher, water, Leaf Mold patt., cranberry & white spatter 395.00
Pitcher, water, Leaf Umbrella patt., cased blue 550.00
Pitcher, Leaf Umbrella patt., cased lemon yellow 495.00
Pitcher, water, Memphis patt., clear w/gold 90.00
Pitcher, water, Panelled Holly patt., white opalescent w/red & green.....225.00
Rose bowl, Jewel (Threaded Swirl) patt., rubina 90.00
Salt shaker w/original top, Leaf Mold patt., cranberry & white spatter.....125.00
Salt shaker w/original top, Leaf Umbrella patt., Rose du Barry (cased mauve) 125.00
Salt shaker w/original top, Leaf Umbrella patt., ruby 165.00
Salt & pepper shakers w/original tops, Leaf Medallion (Regent) patt., cobalt blue w/gold trim, pr. 200.00
Salt & pepper shakers w/original tops, Leaf Mold patt., cranberry & white spatter 125.00
Sauce dish, Leaf Medallion (Regent) patt., cobalt blue w/gold trim 30.00
Sauce dish, Memphis patt., green w/gold trim 20.00
Spooner, Cherry & Cable (Cherry Thumbprints) patt., clear w/ruby & gold trim 75.00
Spooner, Leaf Mold patt., vaseline w/cranberry spatter, satin finish 90.00
Spooner, Panelled Holly patt., blue opalescent 75.00
Sugar bowl, cov., Apple Blossom patt., milk white 125.00
Sugar bowl, cov., Leaf Medallion (Regent) patt., green w/gold trim 195.00
Sugar bowl, cov., Leaf Medallion (Regent) patt., purple w/gold trim 210.00
Sugar bowl, cov., Ribbed Pillar patt., pink spatter, satin finish 95.00
Sugar shaker w/original top, Aurora patt., Ring Neck mold, rubina (ILLUS. top next column) 265.00
Sugar shaker w/original top, Leaf Mold patt., blue 350.00
Sugar shaker w/original top, Leaf Mold patt., red & white spatter w/mica flecks 315.00
Sugar shaker w/original top, Leaf Mold patt., lemon yellow 325.00
Sugar shaker w/original top, Leaf Mold patt., ruby .....400.00 to 425.00

Aurora Rubina Sugar Shaker

Sugar shaker w/original top, Leaf Umbrella patt., cased blue 220.00
Sugar shaker w/original top, Leaf Umbrella patt., ruby 355.00
Sugar shaker w/original top, Parian Swirl patt., ruby 285.00
Sugar shaker w/original top, Quilted Phlox patt., amethyst 185.00
Sugar shaker w/original top, Ribbed Pillar patt., pink & white spatter, satin finish 160.00
Sugar shaker w/original top, Ring Neck mold, clear w/cranberry & white spatter, satin finish 269.00
Syrup pitcher w/original top, Leaf Mold patt., vaseline w/cranberry spatter 595.00
Syrup pitcher w/original top, Ribbed Pillar patt., pink & white spatter, satin finish 250.00
Table set: cov. butter dish, creamer & sugar bowl; Mikado patt., 3 pcs. 275.00
Table set: cov. butter dish, creamer & spooner; Leaf Medallion (Regent) patt., purple w/gold trim, 3 pcs. 500.00

Cherry & Cable Table Set

Table set: creamer, cov. sugar bowl, spooner & cov. butter dish; Cherry & Cable (Cherry Thumbprints) patt., clear w/ruby & gold trim, 4 pcs. (ILLUS.) 450.00
Table set: creamer, cov. sugar bowl, cov. butter dish & spooner; Leaf Medallion (Regent) patt., cobalt blue w/gold trim, 4 pcs. 675.00

Table set, Panelled Holly patt., white opalescent w/purple berries & green leaves decoration, 4 pcs. 475.00
Toothpick holder, Leaf Mold patt., vaseline w/cranberry spatter.....225.00
Toothpick holder, Leaf Umbrella patt., Rose du Barry (cased mauve) 225.00
Tumbler, Leaf Medallion (Regent) patt., purple w/gold trim 89.00
Tumbler, Leaf Mold patt., vaseline w/cranberry spatter 95.00
Tumbler, Netted Oak patt., milk white ..60.00
Tumbler, Panelled Holly patt., white opalescent 35.00
Tumbler, Parian Swirl patt., ruby 30.00
Tumbler, Strawberry & Cable patt., clear 35.00
Water set: pitcher & six tumblers; Memphis patt., clear w/gold trim, 7 pcs. .....175.00 to 200.00
Water set: pitcher & ten tumblers; Leaf Medallion (Regent) patt., purple w/gold trim, 11 pcs. 600.00

PADEN CITY

The Paden City Glass Manufacturing Company began operations in Paden City, West Virginia in 1916, primarily as a supplier of blanks to other companies. All wares were hand-made, that is, either hand-pressed or mold-blown. The early products were not particularly noteworthy but by the early 1930s the quality had improved considerably and the firm continued to turn out high quality glassware in a variety of beautiful colors until financial difficulties necessitated its closing in 1951. Over the years the firm produced in addition to tablewares, items for hotel and restaurant use, light shades, shaving mugs, perfume bottles and lamps.

Bowl, 9" d., pedestal foot, etched Peacock & Rose patt., pink.....$75.00
Bowl, cream soup, footed Crow's Foot (No. 412) line, red 20.00
Cheese & cracker set, Simplicity (No. 700) line, pink w/heavy silver trim, 13" d., 2 pcs. 45.00
Cheese stand, Crow's Foot (No. 412) line, clear, 5" d., 3" h. 8.00
Console bowl, footed, Triumph (No. 701) line, pink w/floral cutting & gold trim, 12" d. 45.00
Creamer, Party (No. 191) line, green 3.50
Cup & saucer, Crow's Foot (No. 412) line, amber 6.50
Cup & saucer, Crow's Foot (No. 412) line, red 10.00
Cup & saucer, Penny (No. 991) line, red 9.50
Goblet, Aristocrat line, red, 5¾" h. 12.00
Plate, 6" sq., Crow's Foot (No. 412) line, amber 1.25
Plate, 8½" sq., Crow's Foot (No. 412) line, amber 3.50
Platter, 6½ x 8¾" oval, Aristocrat line, red 18.00
Platter, 11¼" l., Crow's Foot (No. 412) line, amber 15.00
Platter, 9¼ x 12½" oval, Aristocrat line, red. 30.00
Rose bowl, footed, Gothic Garden etching, yellow 30.00
Salt & pepper shakers w/original tops, Party (No. 191) line, amber, pr. 18.00
Sandwich server w/center handle, Mrs. "B" line, amber 16.00
Sherbet, ball stem, Aristocrat line, ruby, 5 oz. 14.00
Tray w/handles, Crow's Foot (No. 412) line, amber, 10½" sq. 16.00
Vase, 5" h., elliptical-shaped, etched Lela Bird patt., ebony 95.00
Vase, 8¼" h., Crow's Foot (No. 412) line, red 62.50

PATTERN GLASS

Though it has never been ascertained whether glass was first pressed in the United States or abroad, the development of the glass pressing machine revolutionized the glass industry in the United States and this country receives the credit for improving the method to make this process feasible. The first wares pressed were probably small flat plates of the type now referred to as "lacy," the intricacy of the design concealing flaws.

In 1827, both the New England Glass Co., Cambridge, Massachusetts and Bakewell & Co., Pittsburgh, took out patents for pressing glass furniture knobs and soon other pieces followed. This early pressed glass contained red lead which made it clear and resonant when tapped (flint). Made primarily in clear, it is rarer in blue, amethyst, olive green and yellow.

By the 1840s, early simple patterns such as Ashburton, Argus and Excelsior appeared. Ribbed Bellflower seems to have been one of the earliest patterns to have had complete sets. By the 1860s, a wide range of patterns was available.

In 1864, William Leighton of Hobbs, Brockunier & Co., Wheeling, West Virginia, developed a formula for "soda lime" glass which did not require the expensive red lead for clarity. Although "soda lime" glass did not have the brilliance of the earlier flint glass, the formula came into widespread use because glass could be produced cheaply.

An asterisk (*) indicates a piece which has been reproduced.

ACTRESS

Bowl, cov. $110.00
Bowl, 6" d., flat....45.00
Bowl, 6" d., footed 50.00
Bowl, 7" d., footed 60.00
Bread tray, Miss Neilsen, 12½" l....87.50
Butter dish, cov., Fanny Davenport & Miss Neilson ....100.00 to 125.00
Cake stand, Maude Granger & Annie Pixley, 10" d., 7" h. 125.00
Cake stand, frosted stem....145.00 to 165.00
Celery vase, Pinafore scene....175.00
Cheese dish, cov., "Lone Fisherman" on cover, "The Two Dromios" on underplate....225.00 to 235.00
Compote, cov., 6" d., 10" h. 100.00
Compote, cov., 7" d., 8½" h. 145.00
Compote, cov., 8" d., 12" h. ....150.00 to 175.00
Compote, open, 7" d., 7" h., Miss Neilsen....150.00
Compote, open, 7" d., 7" h., Maggie Mitchell & Fanny Davenport....110.00
Compote, open, 8" d., 5" h....75.00
Compote, open, 10" d., 6" h....80.00
Compote, open, 10" d., 9" h....100.00
Creamer, clear....70.00
Creamer, frosted....125.00
Goblet, Lotta Crabtree & Kate Claxton....75.00 to 85.00
Marmalade jar, cov., Maude Granger & Annie Pixley....110.00
*Pickle dish, Kate Claxton, "Love's Request is Pickles," 5¼ x 9¼" 45.00
Platter, 7 x 11½", Pinafore scene 100.00
*Relish, Miss Neilson, 5 x 8"....40.00
Relish, Maude Granger, 5 x 9"....75.00 to 95.00
Sauce dish, Maggie Mitchell & Fanny Davenport, 4½" d., 2½" h. 24.00
Spooner, Mary Anderson & Maude Granger....74.00
Sugar bowl, cov., Lotta Crabtree & Kate Claxton 97.00

ADONIS (Pleat & Tuck or Washboard)

Celery 27.50
Creamer, blue....35.00
Creamer, clear....25.00
Plate, 10" d., clear 13.50
Plate, 10" d., green 35.00
Relish dish....9.50
Salt shaker w/original top 27.50
Sauce dish....7.00
Sugar bowl, cov. 28.00

ALABAMA (Beaded Bull's Eye with Drape)

Butter dish, cov. 50.00
Cake stand, 8" d. 100.00 to125.00
Castor set, 4-bottle, original silver plate stand, green 375.00
Celery tray, clear 38.00
Celery tray, ruby-stained 125.00
Compote, cov., 5" d. 125.00
Creamer....42.00
Creamer & cov. sugar bowl, individual size, pr. 100.00
Cruet w/original stopper....55.00
Pitcher, water....150.00
Relish, 5 x 8⅛"....25.00
Salt shaker w/original top 30.00
Sauce dish....17.50
Spooner....48.00
Sugar bowl, cov. 55.00
Sugar bowl, cov., miniature 48.00
Syrup pitcher w/original top ....85.00 to 95.00
Table set: creamer, cov. sugar bowl, spooner & cov. butter dish; 4 pcs. ...200.00
Toothpick holder....65.00
Tray, water, 10½" 125.00

ALASKA (Lion's Leg)

Alaska Butter Dish

Banana boat, blue opalescent....200.00 to 250.00
Banana boat, emerald green....165.00 to 185.00
Banana boat, vaseline opalescent....200.00
Banana boat, vaseline opalescent w/enameling....325.00
Berry set: master bowl & 4 sauce dishes; emerald green, 5 pcs. ....250.00 to 275.00
Bowl, 8" sq., blue opalescent....150.00 to 200.00
Bowl, 8" sq., clear opalescent w/enameled florals....65.00
Bowl, 8" sq., emerald green....55.00
Bowl, 8" sq., emerald green w/enameled florals....125.00
Bowl, 8" sq., emerald green w/gold & enameling, w/silver plate stand....145.00

Bowl, 8" sq., vaseline opalescent 140.00
Bowl, 8" sq., vaseline opalescent w/enameled florals 225.00
Butter dish, cov., blue opalescent (ILLUS.) .....350.00 to 375.00
Butter dish, cov., emerald green w/enameled florals .....200.00 to 250.00
Butter dish, cov., vaseline opalescent 268.00
Celery (or jewel) tray, blue opalescent 132.00
Celery tray, blue opalescent w/enameled florals 250.00
Celery tray, emerald green 75.00
Celery tray, emerald green w/gold.....85.00
Celery tray, vaseline opalescent w/enameled florals 170.00
Creamer, blue opalescent 75.00
Creamer, clear opalescent .....40.00 to 55.00
Creamer, emerald green 48.00
Creamer, vaseline opalescent 68.00
Cruet w/original stopper, blue opalescent 260.00
Cruet w/original stopper, emerald green.....275.00
Cruet w/original stopper, vaseline opalescent w/enameled florals .....200.00 to 250.00
Pitcher, water, blue opalescent 350.00
Pitcher, water, blue opalescent w/enameled florals 550.00
Pitcher, water, clear opalescent w/enameled florals & gold trim.....125.00
Pitcher, water, emerald green w/enameled florals 285.00
Pitcher, water, vaseline opalescent....350.00
Pitcher, water, vaseline opalescent w/enameled florals .....425.00 to 500.00
Salt shaker w/original top, blue opalescent 85.00
Salt shaker w/original top, emerald green.....70.00
Salt shaker w/original top, emerald green w/enameling 75.00
Salt shaker w/original top, vaseline opalescent 75.00
Sauce dish, blue opalescent.....47.00
Sauce dish, clear opalescent.....25.00
Sauce dish, clear opalescent w/enameled florals 35.00
Sauce dish, emerald green..... 20.00
Sauce dish, emerald green w/enameled florals & leaves.....38.00
Sauce dish, vaseline opalescent 38.00
Sauce dish, vaseline opalescent w/enameled florals 48.50
Spooner, blue opalescent.....65.00 to 75.00
Spooner, clear opalescent w/enameled florals 75.00
Spooner, emerald green.....34.00
Spooner, emerald green w/enameled florals 70.00
Spooner, vaseline opalescent 60.00
Spooner, vaseline opalescent w/enameled florals 75.00
Sugar bowl, cov., blue opalescent.....200.00
Sugar bowl, cov., emerald green w/enameled florals 73.00
Sugar bowl, cov., vaseline opalescent 210.00
Sugar bowl, cov., vaseline opalescent w/enameled florals 245.00
Table set, blue opalescent, 4 pcs. .....650.00 to 700.00
Table set, vaseline opalescent, 4 pcs. .....550.00 to 600.00
Tumbler, blue opalescent 70.00
Tumbler, emerald green 46.00
Tumbler, vaseline opalescent.....77.00
Tumbler, vaseline opalescent w/enameled florals 80.00
Water set: pitcher & 6 tumblers; vaseline opalescent, 7 pcs. .....800.00 to 850.00

ALEXIS - See Priscilla Pattern

ALMOND THUMBPRINT (Pointed Thumbprint)
Champagne, non-flint 40.00
Compote, cov., 6½" d., 8" h., flint .....75.00 to 85.00
Goblet 30.00
Salt dip, master size, flint.....20.00
Spooner, fluted, non-flint 20.00
Tumbler, footed, flint.....39.00
Wine, flint.....15.00

AMAZON (Sawtooth Band)
Banana stand 66.00
Bowl, 8" d., scalloped 24.00
Butter dish, cov.....90.00
Cake stand, 8" to 9½" d.....35.00 to 45.00
Champagne 30.00
Compote, open, jelly, 4½" d.....25.00
Compote, open, 9½" d., 8" h...45.00 to 55.00
Cordial, ruby-stained 38.00
Creamer.....48.00
Cruet w/bar in hand stopper, clear 75.00
Goblet 28.00
Pitcher, water.....60.00
Salt shaker w/original top 20.00
Sauce dish, flat or footed.....12.00
Spooner 30.00
Sugar bowl, cov. 47.50
Tumbler, engraved 35.00
Tumbler 20.00
Vase, double-bud 75.00
Wine 25.00

AMBERETTE - See Klondike Pattern

ANIMALS & BIRDS ON GOBLETS & PITCHERS

GOBLETS:
Bird & roses, acid-etched 30.00

Deer & Doe w/lily-of-the-valley, pressed 100.00
Dog w/rabbit in mouth, acid-etched 105.00
Flamingo Habitat, acid-etched 43.00
Giraffe, acid-etched 75.00
Ibex, acid-etched 86.00
Lion in the Jungle, acid-etched 90.00
Ostrich Looking at Moon, pressed 125.00
Owl-Possum, pressed 90.00
Stork & Flowers, acid-etched 65.00

PITCHERS:

Squirrel Pitcher

Bringing Home Cows, pressed 750.00
Flamingo Habitat, acid-etched 125.00
Fox & Crow, pressed 150.00
Heron, pressed 143.00
Squirrel, pressed, non-Greentown (ILLUS.) 150.00 to175.00

APOLLO

Bowl, 8" d. 22.50
Cake stand, engraved, 9" d. 47.50
Cake stand, plain, 9" to 10½" d. 50.00
Celery tray 16.00
Compote, cov., 4¾" d., 8¾" h. 45.00
Compote, cov., 6" d. 45.00
Compote, cov., 8" d. 65.00
Compote, open, 5" d. 25.00
Creamer, engraved 57.50
Creamer, plain 45.00
Goblet, engraved 35.00
Goblet, frosted 48.00
Goblet, plain 32.00
Lamp, kerosene-type, clear, 7" h. 60.00
Lamp, kerosene-type, blue, 9" h. 265.00
Lamp, kerosene-type, clear, 10" h. 72.00
Lamp, kerosene-type, blue base w/vaseline font 245.00
Sauce dish, flat or footed 14.00
Spooner 40.00
Sugar bowl, cov., etched 75.00
Sugar shaker w/original top 37.00
Syrup pitcher w/original top 90.00 to110.00
Toothpick holder 28.00
Tray, water 40.00
Tumbler, frosted 30.00

ARGUS (McKee & Brother, Pittsburgh)

Argus Spillholder

Celery vase, flint 70.00
Champagne, flint 75.00
Champagne, flint, cut panels w/gilt florals 95.00
Creamer, applied handle, flint 105.00
Egg cup, flint ....25.00 to 35.00
Egg cup, handled, flint 80.00
Goblet, flint 72.50
Goblet, Five-Row 55.00
Goblet, master size, flint 45.00
Mug, applied handle, flint 60.00
Salt dip, cov., master size, flint 90.00
Salt dip, open, master size, flint 35.00
Spillholder, flint (ILLUS.) ....45.00 to 55.00
Tumbler, footed, flint, 4" h. 40.00
Wine, flint, 4" h. 45.00
Wine (Hotel Argus), non-flint 18.00

ART (Job's Tears)

Banana stand 100.00
Bowl, 7" d., flared rim, footed 26.50
Bowl, 8" sq., shallow 34.00
Bowl, 8½" d. 40.00
Bowl, 9¾" d. 38.00
Bowl, rectangular 20.00
Butter dish, cov. 45.00
Cake stand, 9" to 10½" d. 63.00
Celery vase 46.00
Compote, cov., 6" d., 10" h. 54.00
Compote, cov., 7" d. 65.00
Compote, cov., 8" d., high stand 99.00
Compote, open, jelly, 5" d. 27.50
Compote, open, 9" d., 7¼" h. 48.00
Compote, open, 10" d., 9" h. 50.00
Cracker jar, cov., 7" d., 8" h., to top of finial 5.00
Creamer 42.00
Goblet 54.00
Pitcher, water, 9½" h. 150.00
Relish, 4¼" x 7¾" 18.50
Sauce dish, flat or footed 14.00
Spooner 27.00
Sugar bowl, cov., engraved 48.00
Sugar bowl, cov., plain 41.00
Tumbler 30.00

ASHBURTON

Ale glass, flint, 6½" h. 85.00
Bitters bottle w/original pewter lid 65.00
Celery vase, scalloped rim, canary yellow, flint .....700.00 to 850.00
Celery vase, scalloped rim, clear, flint 135.00
Champagne, barrel-shaped, flint 85.00
Claret, flint, 5¼" h. 68.00
Cordial, flint, 4¼" h. 45.00
Cordial, non-flint 55.00
Creamer, applied handle, flint .....275.00 to 325.00
Decanter, bar lip w/patent pewter stopper, canary yellow, flint 1,600.00
Decanter, bar lip w/patent pewter stopper, clear, flint 155.00
Decanter, bar lip & facet-cut neck, canary yellow, flint, qt. 600.00
Decanter, bar lip & facet-cut neck, clear, flint, qt. 55.00
Decanter w/original stopper, clear, flint, qt. 97.50
Egg cup, clambroth, flint 155.00
Egg cup, clear, flint 31.00
Egg cup, non-flint 15.50
Egg cup, disconnected ovals 35.00
Goblet, short, flint 42.00
Goblet, barrel-shaped, flint 44.00
Goblet, flared, flint, clear 52.50
Goblet, flared, flint, clear w/gold, 6" h. 100.00
Goblet, non-flint 30.00
Goblet, disconnected ovals 35.00
Honey dish, 3½" d. 9.00
Mug, applied handle, 3" h. 60.00
Pitcher, water, applied hollow handle, flint .....400.00 to 450.00
Pomade jar, cov., white opaque, flint..195.00
Sugar bowl, cov., flint 175.00
Tumbler, bar, flint 58.00
Tumbler, water, flint 59.00
Tumbler, water, footed .....75.00 to 85.00
Tumbler, whiskey, applied handle, flint 100.00 to125.00
Vases, 9¼" h., shaped pedestal base, flint, pr. 160.00
Wine, clear, flint 46.00
Wine, clear, knob stem 85.00
Wine w/cut design, clear w/gold trim ..125.00
Wine, peacock green, flint 650.00
Wine, non-flint 30.00

ATLANTA (Lion or Square Lion's Head)

Bowl, 5 x 8"' oblong, flat 50.00
Butter dish, cov. 125.00
Celery vase 60.00
Compote, cov., 5" sq., 6" h. 95.00
Compote, cov., 8" sq., 9½" h. 130.00
Compote, open, 4¼" sq., 4" h. 46.00
Compote, open, 6" sq., 7½" h. 75.00
Compote, open, 8" sq., high stand 95.00
Creamer 48.00
Egg cup 95.00
*Goblet 85.00
Marmalade jar, cov., w/lion's head finial 100.00
Relish, boat-shaped 30.00
Salt dip, individual size 35.00
Salt dip, master size, flint 20.00
Spooner, fluted, non-flint 20.00
Tumbler, footed, flint 39.00
Wine, flint 15.00

ATLAS (Crystal Ball or Cannon Ball)

Butter dish, cov. 50.00
Cake stand, 8" to 10" d. 28.00
Celery vase 39.50
Champagne, 5½" h. 37.00
Cordial 42.00
Creamer, flat or pedestal base 22.00
Goblet, engraved 30.00
Goblet, plain 30.00
Pitcher, milk, tankard, applied handle...45.00
Pitcher, water, tankard, applied handle 50.00
Salt dip, individual size 15.00
Salt dip, master size 20.00
Sauce dish, flat or footed 12.50
Spooner 30.00
Toothpick holder 25.00
Tray, water 65.00
Tumbler 28.00
Wine 25.00

AZTEC

Aztec Creamer

Bowl, cov., 8½" d., clear 72.50
Claret 40.00
Creamer (ILLUS.) 26.50
Cruet w/original stopper 48.00
Dresser bottle w/original stopper 37.50
Goblet 32.50
Pitcher, water 60.00
Salt & pepper shakers w/original tops, pr. 35.00
Sugar bowl, open 22.50
Toothpick holder 30.00
Wine 16.50

BABY THUMBPRINT - See Dakota Pattern

BALDER - See Pennsylvania Pattern

BALTIMORE PEAR

Baltimore Pear Creamer

Bowl, 4 x 8" 19.00
Bread plate, 12½" l. 48.00
*Butter dish, cov. 53.00
Cake plate, side handles, 10" octagon 38.00
*Cake stand, high pedestal 55.00
*Creamer (ILLUS.) ..... 25.00 to 35.00
*Goblet 35.00
*Plate, 9" d. 28.00
Relish, 8¼" l. 22.50
*Sauce dish, flat or footed 15.00
Spooner 45.00
*Sugar bowl, cov. 53.00
Tray, water 28.00

BAMBOO - See Broken Column Pattern

BANDED BEADED GRAPE MEDALLION

Creamer 41.00
Dish, open, 5 x 8" oval 15.00
Egg cup 25.00
Goblet 32.50
Spooner 30.00
Tumbler, footed 35.00

BANDED BUCKLE

Compote, cov., 6" 50.00
Egg cup 28.50
Goblet 28.00
Spooner 30.00

BANDED PORTLAND (Portland Maiden Blush, Portland with Diamond Point Band or Virginia)

Berry set: master bowl & 8 sauce dishes; pink-stained w/gold trim, 9 pcs. 295.00
Bowl, berry, 9" d. 30.00
Butter dish, cov., pink-stained 150.00
Candlesticks, pr. 75.00
Celery tray, pink-stained, 10" oval 75.00
Celery tray, clear, 5 x 12" 25.00
Celery vase, clear 32.00
Cologne bottle w/original stopper, clear 51.00
Compote, cov., 8" d., high stand 110.00
Creamer, individual size, clear 29.00
Cruet w/original stopper 60.00
Dresser jar, cov., clear, 3½" d. 36.00
Goblet, clear 35.00
Goblet, pink-stained 68.00
Pitcher, water, 9½" h. 95.00
Pitcher, child's, pink-stained 32.50
Pomade jar, cov. 27.50
Relish, pink-stained, 4 x 6½" 28.00
Relish, 4 x 8½" oval 14.00
Salt & pepper shakers w/original tops, clear, pr. 55.00
Salt & pepper shakers w/original tops, pink-stained, pr. ..... 85.00 to 100.00

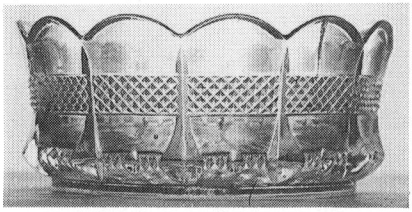

Banded Portland Sauce Dish

Sauce dish, 4½" d. (ILLUS.) 15.00
Spooner, pink-stained 75.00
Sugar bowl, cov., pink-stained 112.00
Sugar shaker w/original top 50.00
Syrup jug w/original top, pink-stained 365.00
Toothpick holder, clear 41.00
Toothpick holder, pink-stained 58.00
Tumbler 35.00
Vase, 6" h., flared, clear 32.00
Vase, 6" h., flared, pink-stained 35.00
Vase, 9" h. 42.00
Wine, clear 28.00
Wine, gold-stained 35.00
Wine, pink-stained 75.00

BARBERRY

Bowl, 6" oval 18.00
Butter dish, cov., shell finial 50.00
Butter dish, cov., pattern on base rim 110.00
Cake stand, 9½" d. 48.00
Cake stand, 11" d. 125.00
Celery vase 49.00
Compote, cov., 6" d., high stand, shell finial 42.50
Compote, cov., 8" d., high stand, shell finial 95.00
Compote, cov., 8" d., low stand, shell finial 77.50
Compote, open, 8½" d., 7" h. 42.00
Egg cup 20.00
Goblet 26.00

Pitcher, water, 9½" h., applied handle..84.00
Plate, 6" d., blue .....40.00 to 50.00
Plate, 6" d., clear 19.00
Sauce dish, flat or footed.....11.00
Spooner, footed.....32.00
Tumbler, footed 28.00
Wine 35.00

BARLEY

Barley Goblet

Bowl, 6¼ x 8½" oval, scalloped rim.....18.50
Bowl, 10" oval.....36.00
Butter dish, cov.....32.50
Cake stand, 8" to 10½" d. 37.50
Celery vase.....45.00
Compote, open, 7" d., 8" h.....25.00
Compote, open, 8½" d., 8" h.....33.00
Compote, open, 8¾" d., 6½" h., scalloped rim.....31.00
Creamer.....23.00
Goblet (ILLUS.).....25.00
Marmalade jar, cov. 50.00
Pickle castor w/silver plate frame & tongs 80.00
Pitcher, water.....46.00
Plate, 6" d. 30.00
Relish, 8" l., 6" w. 19.00
Relish, handled, 9½" l., 5¼" w. 17.50
Sauce dish, flat or footed.....12.50
Spooner 20.00
Wine, 3¾" h. 31.00

BASKETWEAVE

Bread plate, amber 30.00
Bread plate, blue 29.00
Creamer, amber 35.00
Cup, blue 40.00
Cup & saucer, vaseline.....37.50
*Goblet, blue.....35.00
*Goblet, clear.....27.00
*Goblet, vaseline 35.00
Mug, 3" h. 12.00
Pitcher, milk, blue 50.00
*Pitcher, water, amber 55.00
*Pitcher, water, blue 75.00
*Pitcher, water, vaseline 77.00
Plate, 8¾" d., handled, amber 27.50
*Tray, water, scenic center, amber, 12".....38.00
*Tray, water, scenic center, blue, 12"...55.00
*Tray, water, scenic center, vaseline, 12".....50.00
Vase, 8½" h. 12.50
Wine 22.00

BEADED BAND

Butter dish, cov. 36.00
Goblet.....28.00
Pitcher, water.....85.00
Relish, 5¼ x 8½".....10.00
Sauce dish, flat, 4¼" d. 12.50
Wine 27.00

BEADED BULL'S EYE WITH DRAPE - See Alabama Pattern

BEADED DEWDROP - See Wisconsin Pattern

BEADED GRAPE (California)

Beaded Grape Open Compote

Bowl, 6½" sq., green.....28.00
Bowl, 7½" sq., green.....30.00
Bowl, 8" sq. 28.00
Bowl, 6¼ x 8½" rectangle, green.....28.00
Bowl, 9" sq., four-footed 15.00
Bread tray, green, 7 x 10".....60.00
Butter dish, cov., square, clear 55.00
Butter dish, cov., square, green.....70.00 to 80.00
Cake stand, green, 9" sq., 6" h. .....75.00 to 85.00
Celery tray, green 40.00
Celery vase.....32.00
Compote, cov., 4⅞" sq., 6" h., green....55.00
*Compote, cov., 8½" sq., high stand ..125.00
Compote, open, 8½" sq., high stand, clear (ILLUS.).....72.50
Compote, open, 8½" sq., high stand, green.....85.00
Cordial 15.00
Creamer, clear.....35.00
Creamer, green 42.50
Cruet w/original stopper, green 115.00

*Goblet....35.00
Pitcher, water, round, green....78.00
Pitcher, water, square, green....125.00
Pitcher, water, tankard....78.00
*Plate, 8" sq., clear....27.50
*Plate, 8" sq., green....37.50
Relish, green w/gold, 4 x 7"....35.00
Salt shaker w/original top, clear....32.50
Salt & pepper shakers w/original tops, green, pr....75.00
*Sauce dish, green....15.00
Sauce dish, handled....15.00
Spooner....40.00
Sugar bowl, cov....54.00
Toothpick holder, clear....23.00
Toothpick holder, green....60.00
*Tumbler....27.50
*Wine, clear....35.00
*Wine, green....60.00

BEADED GRAPE MEDALLION

Butter dish, cov....50.00
Celery vase....55.00 to 65.00
Compote, cov., 8¼" d., low stand....85.00
Compote, open, 8¼" d., low stand....25.00
Creamer, applied handle....58.00
Egg cup....28.00
Goblet....30.00
Honey dish, 3½" d....8.00
Pitcher, water, applied handle....125.00
Salt dip, individual size....26.00
Salt dip, master size, footed, oval....55.00
Salt shaker w/original top....35.00
Sauce dish....11.00
Spooner....32.00
Wine....47.50

BEADED LOOP (Oregon, U.S. Glass Co.)

Berry set, master bowl & 6 sauce dishes, 7 pcs....65.00
Butter dish, cov....46.50
Cake stand, 9" to 10½" d....45.00
Celery vase, 7" h....29.00
Compote, cov., 7" d....95.00
Compote, open, jelly, clear....38.00
Compote, open, 7" d., clear....25.00
Compote, open, 7½" d., low stand, clear....38.00
Creamer....35.00
*Goblet....39.00
Goblet, w/gold trim....32.50
Mug, footed....38.00
Pickle dish, boat-shaped, 7¼" l....12.00
Pitcher, milk, 8½" h....35.00
Pitcher, water, tankard....50.00
Relish....18.00
Salt shaker w/original top....25.00
Sauce dish, flat or footed....10.00
Spooner, clear....26.00
Spooner, ruby-stained....65.00
*Sugar bowl, cov....39.00
Toothpick holder....60.00
Tumbler....50.00
Vase, small....37.00
Wine....57.50

BEADED TULIP

Bowl, 6⅝ x 9½" oval....20.00
Goblet....34.00
Pitcher, water....67.50
Tray, wine, 9" d....26.00
Wine, amber....55.00
Wine, clear....31.00

BEARDED HEAD - See Viking Pattern

BEARDED MAN - See Queen Anne Pattern

BELLFLOWER

Bellflower Goblet

Bowl, 7½" d., 2" h....110.00
Bowl, 8" d., 4½" h., scalloped rim....95.00
Butter dish, cov....125.00
Castor bottle w/original stopper....38.00
Celery vase, fine rib, single vine....130.00
Compote, open, 4½" d., low stand, scalloped rim....85.00 to100.00
Compote, open, 6" d., low stand....59.00
Compote, open, 7" d., low stand, scalloped rim....87.50
Compote, open, 8" d., 5" h., scalloped rim, single vine....100.00
Compote, open, 8" d., 8" h., dome-footed, single vine....125.00
Compote, open, 8" d., high stand, flint....285.00
Compote, open, 9½" d., 8½" h., scalloped rim, single vine....162.00
Cordial, barrel-shaped, knob stem, rayed base....95.00
Cordial, fine rib, single vine, knob stem....150.00
Cordial, fine rib, single vine, plain stem....60.00
Creamer, fine rib, double vine, applied handle....160.00
Creamer, fine rib, single vine, applied handle....190.00

Decanter w/bar lip, single vine, qt.....130.00
Decanter w/bar lip, patent stopper, double vine, qt. 385.00
Egg cup, fine rib, single vine.....50.00
Goblet, barrel-shaped, fine rib, single vine, knob stem.....54.00
*Goblet, barrel-shaped, fine rib, single vine, plain stem (ILLUS.) 48.00
Goblet, coarse rib 45.00
Goblet, double vine.....64.00
Goblet, single vine, fine rib, pale green, 5⅞" h. 210.00
Honey dish, rayed center, 3¼" d. 22.50
Honey dish, ringed center, 3½" d. 22.50
Lamp, kerosene-type, 8½" h.....175.00
*Pitcher, milk, double vine 350.00
Pitcher, water, 8¾" h., coarse rib, double vine 395.00
Plate, 6" d., fine rib, single vine 115.00
Salt dip, cov., master size, footed, beaded rim, fine rib, single vine 72.50
Salt dip, open, master size, footed, scalloped rim, single vine.....50.00
Sauce dish, double vine 20.00
Sauce dish, single vine.....20.00
Spooner, low foot, double vine 60.00
Spooner, scalloped rim, single vine.....40.00
Sugar bowl, cov., double vine.....55.00
Syrup pitcher w/original top, applied handle, fine rib, single vine, clear .....600.00 to 700.00
Syrup pitcher w/original top, applied handle, fine rib, single vine, fiery opalescent 1,100.00
Tumbler, bar, fine rib, single vine 90.00
Tumbler, coarse rib, double vine 105.00
Tumbler, fine rib, single vine, banded.....150.00
Tumbler, whiskey.....140.00 to 180.00
Wine, barrel-shaped, knob stem, fine rib, single vine, rayed base .....100.00 to 125.00
Wine, barrel-shaped, fine rib, double vine, w/cut bellflowers.....325.00
Wine, straight sides, plain stem, rayed base 55.00

BIRD & FERN - See Hummingbird Pattern

BIRD & STRAWBERRY (Bluebird)

Berry set: master bowl & 5 sauce dishes; w/color, 6 pcs. 525.00
Berry set: master bowl & 6 sauce dishes; footed, 7 pcs.....150.00 to 200.00
Bowl, 5½" d., clear.....24.00
Bowl, 5½" d., w/color 35.00
Bowl, 7½" d., footed, clear.....62.00
Bowl, 7½" d., footed, w/color 70.00
Bowl, 9" d., flat, w/color 75.00
Bowl, 9½" l., 6" w., oval, footed.....55.00 to 65.00
Bowl, 10" d., flat, clear.....60.00 to 70.00
Bowl, 10" d., flat, w/color & gold trim ..115.00
Butter dish, cov., clear 87.50
Butter dish, cov., w/color ....175.00 to 225.00
Cake stand, 9" to 9½" d. 60.00
*Compote, cov., 6½" d., 9½" h.....145.00
Compote, cov., jelly 130.00
Creamer, clear.....47.50
Creamer, w/color 125.00
Dish, heart-shaped 47.50
Pitcher, water.....287.50
Plate, 12" d. 75.00
Punch cup.....22.00
Sauce dish, flat or footed, clear 26.00
Sauce dish, w/color 34.00
Spooner, clear 49.00
Spooner, w/color.....100.00 to125.00
Sugar bowl, cov. 65.00
Sugar bowl, open.....32.00
Table set, 4 pcs. 225.00 to250.00
Tumbler, clear.....52.50
Tumbler, w/color 95.00
Wine 55.00

BLEEDING HEART

Bowl, cov., 7" d., 5" h. 110.00
Bowl, 8".....33.00
Butter dish, cov. 55.00
Cake stand, 9½" to 11" d. 115.00
Compote, cov., 8" d., high stand, w/Bleeding Heart finial .....150.00 to 175.00
Compote, open, 8½" d., high stand 37.50
Creamer.....50.00
Egg cup 44.00
Goblet, knob stem 40.00
Mug, 3" h. 57.50
Salt dip, master size, flat, oval.....92.00
Salt dip, master size, footed 68.00
Sauce dish, flat.....15.00
Spooner 35.00
Sugar bowl, cov. 78.00
Tumbler, bar 140.00
Tumbler, flat.....110.00
Wine, knob stem.....150.00 to175.00

BLOCK & FAN

Bowl, berry, 8" d., footed 27.50
Bowl, 9¾" d.....32.00
Butter dish, cov. 38.00
Cake stand, 9" to 10" d. 50.00
Celery tray 20.00
Celery vase.....35.00
Compote, open, 8" d., high stand 45.00
Cracker jar, cov. 75.00
Cruet w/original stopper, small, 6" h. 25.00
Cruet w/original stopper, medium.....45.00
Goblet, clear.....52.00
Goblet, ruby-stained 110.00
Ice bucket 45.00
Pitcher, water.....48.00
Plate, 10" d. 25.00
Relish, 11½" l.....45.00
Salt shaker w/original top 20.00
Sauce dish, flat or footed, clear 12.50

Sauce dish, flat or footed, ruby-stained 30.00
Spooner 28.00
Sugar shaker w/original top 40.00
Syrup pitcher w/original top, 7" h. 140.00
Wine, clear 50.00
Wine, ruby-stained 75.00

BLOCK & STAR - See Valencia Waffle Pattern

BLUEBIRD - See Bird & Strawberry Pattern

BOHEMIAN (Floradora)

Bohemian Cologne Bottle

Berry bowl, boat-shaped, green 47.50
Butter dish, cov., green w/gold trim 110.00
Cologne bottle w/original stopper, clear w/gold trim 100.00
Cologne bottle w/original stopper, green w/gold trim 225.00
Cologne bottle w/original stopper, rose-stained w/gold trim (ILLUS.) 130.00
Creamer, individual size, green 30.00
Creamer, clear w/rose & goldtrim 75.00
Mug, clear w/rose-stained leaves & gold trim 70.00
Spooner, clear w/rose-stained flowers & gold trim 55.00
Table set, green w/gold trim, 4 pcs. 350.00
Toothpick holder, green w/gold trim 225.00
Tumbler, clear w/rose-stained flowers 45.00

BOW TIE

Bowl, 6" d. 25.00
Bowl, berry, 8" d. 38.00
Bowl, 10" d., 5" h. 60.00
Butter dish, cov. 80.00
Compote, open, 6½" d., low stand 40.00
Compote, open, 8" d., low stand 45.00
Compote, open, 8¼" d., high stand 55.00
Creamer 35.00
Goblet 62.50
Marmalade jar, cov. 55.00
Pitcher, milk 55.00
Pitcher, water 95.00
Relish, rectangular 28.00
Salt dip, individual size 22.50
Spooner 34.00
Tumbler 55.00

BROKEN COLUMN (Irish Column, Notched Rib or Bamboo)

Bowl, 7" d. 40.00
Butter dish, cov. 85.00
Cake stand, 9" to 10" d. 90.00
Celery vase 55.00
Compote, cov., 5" d., high stand 80.00
Compote, open, jelly, w/red notches 195.00
Compote, open, 5" d., 6" h. 32.00
Compote, open, 6" d., high stand 35.00
Compote, open, 7" d., low stand 50.00
Cracker jar, cov. 100.00
*Creamer, clear 38.00
Creamer, w/red notches 245.00
Cruet w/original stopper 85.00
*Goblet 55.00
Marmalade jar w/original cover 100.00
Pickle castor, cov., clear, original ornate frame 250.00
Pickle castor, w/red notches, w/frame & tongs 400.00 to425.00
*Pitcher, water, clear 90.00
Pitcher, water, w/red notches 225.00
Plate, 5" d. 32.00
*Plate, 8" d. 40.00
Punch cup, blue 95.00
Punch cup, clear 25.00
Relish, w/red notches, 9" l., 5" w. 78.00
Salt shaker w/original top 55.00
*Sauce dish, clear 15.00
Sauce dish, w/red notches 32.00
*Spooner, w/red notches 125.00
*Sugar bowl, cov., clear 72.00
Sugar bowl, cov., w/red notches 250.00
Syrup pitcher w/metal top 130.00
Tumbler, clear 45.00
Tumbler, w/red notches 75.00
Vase, 6½" h. 30.00
Water set: pitcher & 5 tumblers; w/red notches, 6 pcs. 650.00
*Wine 85.00

BRYCE - See Ribbon Candy Pattern

BUCKLE

Butter dish, cov. 81.00
Champagne, flint 75.00
Compote, open, 8" d., low stand, flint 38.50
Compote, open, 8" d., low stand, non-flint 17.50
Creamer, applied handle, flint 95.00
Egg cup, flint 37.00
Egg cup, non-flint 25.00
Goblet, flint (ILLUS. top next column) 45.00
Goblet, non-flint 26.00
Lamp, kerosene-type, brass & iron base ....125.00 to 150.00

Buckle Goblet

Pitcher, water, bulbous, applied handle, flint .....550.00 to 600.00
Salt dip, master size, footed, flint.....35.00
Salt dip, master size, flat, oval, flint.....22.50
Spooner, non-flint.....30.00
Sugar bowl, cov., w/acorn finial, flint 95.00
Sugar bowl, cov., w/acorn finial, non-flint 43.00
Tumbler, bar, flint.....90.00

BUCKLE WITH STAR

Cake stand, 9" d. 35.00
Celery vase.....32.00
Compote, open, 8" d.....37.50
Creamer.....32.50
Goblet.....24.00
Sauce dish, flat or footed.....9.50
Spooner.....30.00
Sugar bowl, open.....24.00
Syrup pitcher w/metal top.....70.00
Tumbler, bar 65.00
Wine 24.00

BULL'S EYE

Ale glass.....45.00
Celery vase, flint.....75.00
Cordial, flint.....85.00
Cruet w/original stopper.....195.00
Decanter w/bar lip, flint, qt. 110.00
Egg cup, clear, flint, 3¾" h.....45.00 to 55.00
Egg cup, jade green 385.00
Goblet, flint 72.00
Salt dip, individual size, rectangular 35.00
Tumbler, flat, flint.....70.00
Wine, knob stem, flint 58.00

BULL'S EYE VARIANT - See Texas Bull's Eye Pattern

BULL'S EYE WITH DIAMOND POINT

Celery vase.....180.00
Champagne 687.50
Compote, cov., 5½" d. 50.00
Compote, open, jelly.....30.00
Cordial 357.50
Decanter w/bar lip, pt.....209.00
Goblet.....155.00
Honey dish.....25.00
Lamp, kerosene-type, applied strap handle, original burner & attached burner cover, 3" h. 250.00
Sauce dish.....22.50
Spillholder.....87.50
Spooner.....137.00
Sugar bowl, cov. 132.00
Tumbler, bar 135.00
Tumbler, water.....120.00
Tumbler, whiskey.....148.00

BULL'S EYE WITH FLEUR DE LIS

Compote, open, 8¼" d., low stand.....125.00
Creamer.....155.00
Decanter, bar lip, qt. 110.00
Goblet.....98.00
Pitcher, water, 9½" h. .....450.00 to 500.00
Sugar bowl, cov. 130.00
Vase, 8½" h., flared rim 145.00

BUTTON ARCHES

Berry set: 8" d. master bowl & 6 sauce dishes; ruby-stained, 7 pcs. 158.00
Bowl, 8" d., ruby-stained, souvenir 45.00
Compote, open, jelly, 4½" h., ruby-stained 40.00
*Creamer, ruby-stained 37.50
Creamer, ruby-stained, souvenir, 3½" h.....30.00
*Creamer, individual size, ruby-stained 28.00
Cruet w/original stopper, ruby-stained 175.00
Goblet, clambroth 26.00
Goblet, clear 24.00
Mug, clear.....18.00
Mug, ruby-stained.....30.00
Pitcher, tankard, 8¾" h. 117.00
Pitcher, water, tankard, ruby-stained, souvenir of Pan American Exposition 150.00
Punch cup, ruby-stained, souvenir 28.50
Salt dip.....18.50
Salt shaker w/original top, ruby-stained 25.00
Salt & pepper shakers, w/original tops, clear, pr. 35.00
Sauce dish, clear 15.00
Sauce dish, ruby-stained.....30.00
*Spooner, ruby-stained.....42.50
Spooner, ruby-stained w/clear band.....62.50
Spooner, ruby-stained & engraved.....44.00
Sugar bowl, cov., clear 45.00
*Sugar bowl, cov., ruby-stained.....85.00
Syrup pitcher w/original top, clear 40.00
*Toothpick holder, ruby-stained.....28.00
Toothpick holder, ruby-stained, souvenir 32.50
Tumbler, clambroth, souvenir 23.00
Tumbler, clear.....16.00
Tumbler, clear w/frosted band.....22.00
Tumbler, ruby-stained.....42.50

Tumbler, ruby-stained, souvenir 39.50
Wine, clear.....26.00
Wine, ruby-stained.....37.50

CABBAGE ROSE

Cabbage Rose Tumbler

Bitters bottle, 6½" h. 125.00
Butter dish, cov.....95.00
Cake stand, 9½" to 12½" d. 58.00
Celery vase.....62.00
Compote, cov., 6" d., low stand.....95.00
Compote, cov., 6" d., high stand.....110.00
Compote, cov., 7½" d., high stand.....115.00
Compote, cov., 8½" d., 7" h. 125.00
Compote, open, 7" d., low stand.....38.00
Compote, open, 7½" d., high stand 60.00
Creamer, applied handle 55.00
Egg cup 33.00
*Goblet.....45.00
Pickle or relish, 7½" to 8½" l. 20.00
Salt dip, master size 30.00
Sauce dish.....15.00
*Spooner.....40.00
Sugar bowl, cov. 70.00
Tumbler, bar 42.00
Tumbler (ILLUS.) 42.00
Wine .....35.00 to 45.00

CABLE

Butter dish, cov.....90.00
Celery vase.....82.00
Champagne 250.00
Compote, open, 7" d., 5" h.....52.50
Compote, open, 8" d., 4¾" h.....70.00
Decanter w/stopper, qt. .....300.00 to 325.00
Egg cup, clambroth, flint.....385.00
Egg cup, clear.....55.00
Goblet.....95.00
Honey dish, 3½" d., 1" h. 15.00
Lamp, whale oil, 11" h. 122.50
Plate, 6" d. 90.00
Salt dip, individual size 30.00
Salt dip, master size 36.00
Sauce dish.....26.00
Spooner, chartreuse green.....1,200.00
Spooner, clambroth w/gilt trim 850.00
Spooner, clear .....35.00 to 45.00
Spooner, starch blue w/original gilt decoration of grape leaves 1,500.00
Tumbler, footed 335.00
Tumbler, whiskey.....230.00

CABLE WITH RING

Creamer, applied handle, flint.....165.00
Lamp, kerosene-type, w/ring handle, flint 195.00
Sauce dish, flint 14.00

CALIFORNIA - See Beaded Grape Pattern

CAMEO - See Classic Medallion Pattern

CANADIAN

Bowl, berry, 7" d., 4½" h., footed 63.00
Bowl, 8" d., handled.....44.00
Bowl, 9½" d.....55.00
Bread plate, handled, 10" d. 48.00
Butter dish, cov.....80.00
Celery vase.....70.00
Compote, cov., 7" d., low stand.....125.00
Compote, cov., 7" d., 11" h. 125.00
Compote, cov., 8" d., low stand.....92.00
Compote, cov., 8" d., 11" h. 150.00
Compote, open, 8" d., 5" h.....55.00
Creamer.....55.00
Goblet.....57.00
Pitcher, milk, 8" h. .....100.00 to 125.00
Pitcher, water.....110.00
Plate, 6" d., handled 32.00
Plate, 7" d., handled 45.00
Plate, 8" d., handled 45.00
Sauce dish, flat or footed.....20.00
Spooner.....45.00
Sugar bowl, cov. 77.50
Wine .....40.00 to 50.00

CANE

Cane Water Pitcher

Bowl, 9½" oval, amber.....28.00
Bread platter, amber.....125.00
Cordial 18.00

Creamer, blue 42.00
Creamer, clear 25.00
Goblet, amber 34.00
Goblet, blue 55.00
Goblet, clear 20.00
Goblet, vaseline 37.00
Pickle castor w/tongs, amber 150.00
Pitcher, water, amber 68.00
Pitcher, water, blue 72.00
Pitcher, water, clear (ILLUS.) 40.00
Plate, 6" d., amber 12.00
Relish, blue 50.00
Spooner, amber 42.00
Sugar bowl, cov., apple green 47.50
Toddy plate, amber, 4½" d. 10.00
Tray, water, blue 53.00
Waste bowl, amber 35.00
Waste bowl, vaseline 30.00

CANNON BALL - See Atlas Pattern

CAPE COD
Bread platter 48.00
Compote, cov., 8" d., 12" h. 155.00
Compote, open, 8" d., 5½" h. 45.00
Cruet w/original stopper 43.00
Goblet 47.00
Marmalade jar, cov. 65.00
Pitcher, water 95.00
Plate, 6" d. 35.00
Plate, 10" d., open handles 48.00
Sauce dish, flat or footed 16.00

CARDINAL BIRD
Butter dish, cov. 90.00
Creamer 41.00
*Goblet 34.00
Sauce dish, flat or footed 16.00
Spooner 37.00
Sugar bowl, cov. 55.00

CATHEDRAL

Cathedral Compote

Bowl, 6" d., crimped rim, blue 25.00
Bowl, 6" d., clear 16.00
Bowl, 7" d., clear 20.00
Bowl, berry, 8" d., amber 48.00
Butter dish, cov. 44.00
Cake stand, amber 55.00
Cake stand, clear, 10" d., 4½" h. 38.00
Cake stand, vaseline 60.00
Compote, cov., 7¼" d., 10½" h. 85.00
Compote, cov., 8" d., high stand, blue 185.00
Compote, open, 9" d., 5½" h., amber 65.00
Compote, open, 9" d., 5½" h., blue 65.00
Compote. open, 10½" d., 8" h., shaped rim, clear (ILLUS.) 55.00
Compote, open, 10½" d., 8" h., ruby-stained 125.00
Creamer 35.00
Cruet w/original stopper, amber 100.00
Goblet, amber 37.00
Goblet, clear 38.00
Goblet, ruby-stained 65.00
Relish, fish-shaped, amber 40.00
Relish, fish-shaped, blue 42.50
Sauce dish, flat or footed, blue 25.00
Sauce dish, flat or footed, ruby-stained 22.00
Sauce dish, flat or footed, vaseline 20.00
Spooner, clear 28.00
Spooner, vaseline 48.00
Sugar bowl, cov. 50.00
Tumbler 24.00
Wine, amber 60.00
Wine, blue ....45.00 to 55.00
Wine, clear 26.00
Wine, vaseline 65.00

CERES (Goddess of Liberty)
Butter dish, cov., lady's head finial 125.00
Compote, open, 7½" d., low stand, woman in beaded oval 25.00
Creamer 42.00
Mug, clear 18.00
Mug, opaque-turquoise 60.00
Mug, purple-black 53.00
Spooner, milk white 22.00

CHAIN WITH STAR
Bread plate, handled 33.00
Cake stand, 8¾" to 10" d. 38.00
Creamer 28.00
Goblet 24.00
Pitcher, water 50.00
Plate, 7" d. 27.50
Relish 14.00
Sauce dish 12.50
Spooner 24.00
Tumbler 18.00
Wine 35.00

CHANDELIER (Crown Jewel)
Butter dish, cov. 100.00
Cake stand, 10" d. 75.00
Celery vase 40.00
Compote, open, 9¼" d., 7¾" h. 57.00
Creamer 55.00
Goblet 50.00
Goblet, engraved 60.00

Inkwell....55.00
Pitcher, water, tankard, ½ pt....65.00
Pitcher, water, tankard, ½ gal....125.00
Salt dip, footed....36.00
Sauce dish, flat....16.00
Spooner....45.00
Tumbler....40.00
Waste bowl....25.00

CHECKERBOARD (Barred Hobstar)
Bowl, 9" d., flat....16.00
Celery tray....35.00
Celery vase, footed, 6½" h....18.00
Compote, open, 8" d....15.00
Creamer....19.00
Goblet....30.00
Honey dish, cov., 5" w....30.00
Sauce dish, flat....15.00
Spooner....21.00
Tumbler....12.50
Wine....17.50

CLASSIC

Classic Goblet

Bowl, open, 8" hexagon, open log feet....100.00 to 125.00
Butter dish, cov., open log feet....225.00
Celery vase, collared base....150.00
Celery vase, open log feet....165.00
Compote, cov., 6½" d., collared base....200.00
Compote, cov., 7½" d., 8" h., open log feet....220.00
Compote, open, 7¾" d., open log feet....150.00
Creamer, collared base....125.00
Creamer, open log feet....150.00 to 175.00
Goblet (ILLUS.)....275.00 to 300.00
Pitcher, water, collared base....225.00 to 275.00
Pitcher, water, 9½" h., open log feet...425.00
Plate, 10" d., "Blaine" or "Hendricks," signed Jacobus, each....215.00
Plate, 10" d., "Cleveland"....200.00
Plate, 10" d., "Warrior"....150.00 to 175.00
Sauce dish, open log feet....40.00
Spooner, collared base....95.00
Spooner, open log feet....135.00
Sugar bowl, cov., open log feet....185.00

CLASSIC MEDALLION (Cameo)

Classic Medallion Spooner

Bowl, 6¾" d., 3½" h., footed....35.00
Bowl, 8" d., footed....40.00
Creamer....30.00
Sauce dish, footed....8.00
Spooner (ILLUS.)....25.00
Sugar bowl, cov....55.00
Table set, 4 pcs....130.00

COLLINS - See Crystal Wedding Pattern

COLONIAL (Empire Colonial)
Celery vase, flint....95.00
Champagne, flint....75.00
Claret, flint, 5½" h....70.00
Compote, open, 9" d., 3¾" h., flint....25.00
Egg cup, flint....45.00
Goblet, flint....55.00
Plate, 6¼" d., canary yellow, flint....250.00
Sugar bowl, cov., flint....125.00
Toothpick holder, flint....22.00

COLORADO (Lacy Medallion)
Banana bowl, two turned-up sides, blue....35.00
Banana stand, green....45.00
Berry set: 8" d. master bowl & five 4" d. sauce dishes; green w/gold, 6 pcs....160.00
Berry set: master bowl & 6 sauce dishes; clear w/gold, 7 pcs....125.00
Bowl, 5" d., ruffled rim, blue....40.00
Bowl, 7" d., footed....25.00
Bowl, 7½" d., footed, turned-up sides, blue w/gold....50.00
Bowl, 7½" d., footed, turned-up sides, green....29.00
Bowl, 9" d., green w/gold....45.00
Bowl, 10" d., footed, flared & scalloped rim....45.00
Bowl, 10" d., footed, fluted, green....48.00
Butter dish, cov., blue w/gold....260.00
Butter dish, cov., clear....85.00
Butter dish, cov., green....125.00
Cake stand....65.00

Celery vase, green w/gold 70.00
Cheese dish, cov., blue w/gold 70.00
Compote, open, 6" d., 4" h., crimped rim 22.00
Creamer, blue, souvenir 60.00
Creamer, clear 34.00
Creamer, green 42.50
Creamer, ruby-stained 54.00
Creamer, individual size, green w/gold 40.00
Cup, punch, green 28.00
Cup, punch, green, souvenir 25.00
Cup & saucer, green 45.00
Mug, green, souvenir, miniature 22.50
Mug, green 30.00
Mug, green souvenir 32.00
Mug, ruby-stained 55.00
Nappy, tricornered, blue w/gold 40.00
Nappy, tricornered, green w/gold 29.00
Rose bowl, blue 60.00
Salt shaker w/original top, ruby-stained, souvenir 75.00
Sauce dish, blue w/gold 30.00
Sauce dish, clambroth 20.00
Sauce dish, clear 13.00
Sauce dish, green w/gold 24.00
Sauce dish, green, souvenir 27.50
Sherbet, blue w/gold 48.00
Spooner, blue w/gold ....50.00 to 60.00
Spooner, clear 40.00
Spooner, green w/gold 60.00
Sugar bowl, cov., clear, large 53.00
Sugar bowl, cov., green, large 80.00
Sugar bowl, open, individual size, clear 20.00
Sugar bowl, open, individual size, green 35.00
Sugar bowl, open, individual size, ruby-stained 50.00
Table set, blue, 4 pcs. 525.00
Table set, green w/gold, 4 pcs. ....325.00 to 350.00
*Toothpick holder, blue w/gold 60.00
*Toothpick holder, clear w/gold 25.00
*Toothpick holder, green w/gold 35.00
*Toothpick holder, green w/gold souvenir 30.00
*Toothpick holder, ruby-stained, souvenir 55.00
Tumbler, green w/gold 32.00
Tumbler, green w/gold, souvenir 30.00
Vase, 2½" h., green 45.00
Vase, 10½" h., blue 78.00
Water set: pitcher & 6 tumblers; green w/gold, 7 pcs. 450.00
Wine, clear 26.00
Wine, green w/gold 40.00
Wine, green, souvenir 35.00
Wine, ruby-stained w/gold 40.00

COLUMBIAN COIN

Bowl, 8½" d., 3" h., frosted coins 75.00
Celery vase, frosted coins 110.00
Compote, cov., 8" d., frosted coins 157.00
Compote, open, 8" d., clear coins 68.00
Creamer, gilded coins 125.00
Cruet w/original stopper, frosted coins 195.00
*Goblet, gilded coins 80.00
Lamp, kerosene-type, milk white, 8" h. 400.00
Lamp, kerosene-type, frosted coins, 12" h. 180.00
Mug, frosted coins 120.00
Pitcher, milk, gilded coins 195.00
Relish, frosted coins, 5 x 8" 68.00
Sauce dish, flat or footed, frosted coins 42.00
Spooner, gilded coins 77.50
Syrup pitcher w/original top, frosted coins 335.00
*Tumbler, clear coins 30.00
*Tumbler, gilded coins 55.00
Wine, frosted coins 145.00

COMPACT - See Snail Pattern

CORD & TASSEL

Cord & Tassel Creamer

Cake stand, 9½" d. 65.00
Compote, cov., 8" d. 75.00
Creamer (ILLUS.) 36.00
Goblet 38.00
Lamp, kerosene-type, applied handle ..85.00
Pitcher, water 98.00
Salt shaker w/original top, blue 45.00
Spooner 23.00
Syrup pitcher w/original top, applied handle 110.00
Tumbler, water 50.00
Wine 38.00

CORD DRAPERY

Bowl, 6¼" d., footed, amber 175.00
Bowl, 10" d., 3½" h. 42.00
Butter dish, cov., clear 70.00
Butter dish, cov., green 175.00
Cake stand, amber 145.00
Cake stand, clear 40.00
Compote, cov., jelly 55.00
Compote, cov., 9" d. 70.00

Creamer, blue 125.00
Creamer, clear 40.00
Cruet w/original stopper ..... 80.00 to 90.00
Goblet 85.00
Mug 40.00
Pickle dish, amber, 5¼ x 9¼" oval 85.00
Pickle dish, clear, 5¼ x 9¼" oval 37.50
Pitcher, water, amber 185.00
Pitcher, water, clear 65.00
Pitcher, water, cobalt blue 225.00
Pitcher, water, green 235.00
Punch cup 15.00
Salt shaker w/original top 55.00
Sauce dish, flat or footed 15.00
Sugar bowl, cov., clear 60.00
Sugar bowl, cov., green 165.00
Toothpick holder 95.00

CORONA - See Sunk Honeycomb Pattern

COTTAGE (Dinner Bell or Finecut Band)

Bowl, master berry, 9¼" l., 6½" w. oval 25.00
Butter dish, cov., clear 36.00
Cake stand, amber 50.00
Cake stand, clear 35.00
Celery vase, amber 85.00
Celery vase, clear 35.00
Champagne 65.00
Compote, open, jelly, 4½" d., 4" h., clear 24.00
Compote, open, jelly, 4½" d., 4" h., green 42.50
Creamer, amber 60.00
Creamer, clear 27.00
*Goblet, amber 45.00
*Goblet, blue 48.00
*Goblet, clear 27.00
Pitcher, milk, clear 35.00
Pitcher, water, 2 qt. 72.50
Plate, 7" d. 22.50
Plate, 10" d. 42.50
Sauce dish 12.50
Tray, water 40.00
Tumbler 19.00
*Wine, amber 53.00
*Wine, blue 45.00

CROESUS

Berry set: master bowl & 6 sauce dishes; clear, 7 pcs. 300.00
Berry set: master bowl & 6 sauce dishes; green w/gold, 7 pcs. 395.00
Berry set: master bowl & 6 sauce dishes; purple, 7 pcs. ..... 400.00 to 425.00
Bowl, 7" d., 4" h., footed, purple 68.00
Bowl, 7" d., 4" h., footed, purple w/gold 225.00
Bowl, 8" d., purple 175.00
Bowl, berry or fruit, 9" d., green 108.00
Bowl, berry or fruit, 9" d., purple 165.00
*Butter dish, cov., clear 98.00
*Butter dish, cov., green ..... 150.00 to 165.00
*Butter dish, cov., purple ..... 200.00 to 225.00
Celery vase, gree w/gold 170.00
Celery vase, purple 300.00
Compote, open, jelly, green ..... 225.00 to 275.00
Compote, open, jelly, purple 280.00
Condiment tray, green 62.50
Condiment tray, purple 90.00
*Creamer, green ..... 80.00 to 100.00
*Creamer, purple 145.00
Creamer, individual size, purple, 3" h. 130.00
Cruet w/original stopper, green ..... 200.00 to 225.00
Cruet w/original stopper, purple 350.00
Pickle dish, green w/gold 35.00
Pitcher, milk, green 85.00
Pitcher, water, green 285.00
Pitcher, water, purple ..... 400.00 to 500.00
Relish, boat-shaped, green 60.00
Salt shaker w/original top, green w/gold 100.00
Sauce dish, clear 23.00
Sauce dish, green w/gold 37.00
Sauce dish, purple w/gold 42.00
*Spooner, green 73.00
*Spooner, green w/gold ..... 90.00 to 100.00
*Spooner, purple 80.00
*Spooner, purple w/gold 97.50
*Sugar bowl, cov., clear 78.00
*Sugar bowl, cov., green 110.00
Sugar bowl, cov., green w/gold 185.00
*Sugar bowl, cov., purple ..... 150.00 to 175.00
*Sugar bowl, cov., purple w/gold 180.00
Table set, purple, 4 pcs. 630.00
*Toothpick holder, green 65.00
*Toothpick holder, green w/gold 95.00
*Toothpick holder, purple ..... 100.00 to 125.00
Toothpick holder, purple w/gold 130.00
*Tumbler, green 42.00
*Tumbler, green w/gold 54.00
*Tumbler, purple w/gold 70.00
Water set: pitcher & 5 tumblers; green, 6 pcs. ..... 450.00 to 500.00
Water set: pitcher & 6 tumblers; purple, 7 pcs. ..... 850.00 to 900.00

CROWFOOT (Turkey Track, Yale)

Bowl, 10" d. 30.00
Butter dish, cov. 45.00
Cake stand, 9" d. 52.00
Compote, cov., 7" d. 68.00
Creamer 35.00
Goblet 35.00
Pitcher, water 60.00
Spooner 25.00
Sugar bowl, cov. 35.00
Tumbler 25.00

CROWN JEWEL - See Chandelier Pattern

CRYSTAL BALL - See Atlas Pattern

CRYSTAL WEDDING (Collins)

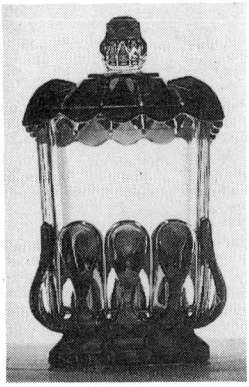

Crystal Wedding Sugar Bowl

Banana stand, 10" h. 110.00
Banana stand, low pedestal 108.00
Bowl, cov., 5" sq. 68.00
Bowl, cov., 7" sq. 67.00
Butter dish, cov., clear 110.00
Butter dish, cov., ruby-stained 130.00
Cake stand, 9" sq., 8" h. 60.00
Cake stand, 10" sq. 65.00
Celery vase.....45.00
Compote, cov., 4" sq., 6½" h. 37.50
Compote, cov., 5" sq. 58.00
Compote, cov., 7" sq., low stand 85.00
Compote, cov., 7" sq., high stand .....75.00 to 100.00
Compote, open, 5" sq. 45.00
Compote, open, 6" sq. 48.00
Compote, open, 6¼" sq., high stand, scalloped rim.....45.00
Compote, open, 7" sq., high stand .....50.00 to 75.00
Compote, open, 8" sq., low stand.....55.00
Creamer, clear.....38.00
Creamer, ruby-stained.....125.00
*Goblet, clear.....40.00
Goblet w/fern engraving 85.00
*Goblet, ruby-stained.....62.50
Honey dish, cov., 6" sq. 90.00
Lamp, kerosene-type, 7" h.....100.00
Lamp, kerosene-type, 9" h., frosted & clear 145.00
Lamp base, kerosene-type, square font, 10" h.....285.00
Lamp, kerosene-type, banquet-style, blue base, clear font 195.00
Pitcher, 12" h., tankard, water 85.00
Pitcher, water, square, engraved.....195.00
Pitcher, water, square, plain 175.00
Plate, 9" sq. 45.00
Salt dip.....45.00
Salt shaker w/original top 125.00
Sauce dish.....12.00
Spooner, clear 35.00
Spooner, ruby-stained 95.00
Sugar bowl, cov., amber-stained.....125.00
Sugar bowl, cov., clear 54.00
Sugar bowl, cov., ruby-stained (ILLUS.) 100.00
Table set: creamer, cov. sugar bowl & spooner; clear, 3 pcs. 185.00
Table set, ruby-stained, 4 pcs. 400.00
Tumbler 45.00
Wine 95.00

CUPID & VENUS (Guardian Angel)

Cupid & Venus Sauce Dish

Bowl, open, 8" d., footed.....28.00
Bowl, 9" oval 50.00
Bread plate, amber, 10½" d. 155.00
Bread plate, clear, 10½" d. 45.00
Bread plate, vaseline, 10½" d. 145.00
Butter dish, cov. 110.00
Cake plate, 11" d. 45.00
Celery vase.....55.00
Champagne 110.00
Compote, cov., 7" d., high stand.....110.00
Compote, cov., 7" d., low stand 65.00
Compote, cov., 9" d., low stand 82.00
Compote, open, 7" d., low stand.....30.00
Compote, open, 8½" d., low stand, scalloped rim.....40.00
Cordial 85.00
Creamer.....55.00
Goblet.....67.00
Honey dish, 3½" d. 15.00
Marmalade jar, cov. 125.00
Mug, 2½" h. 32.00
Mug, 3½" h. 40.00
Pitcher, milk 65.00
Pitcher, water.....90.00
Relish, oval, 4½ x 7" 30.00
Sauce dish, footed, 3½" to 4½" d. (ILLUS.) 14.00
Spooner 35.00
Sugar bowl, cov. 70.00
Wine 85.00

CURRIER & IVES

Bowl, master berry or fruit, 10" oval, flat w/collared base 35.00
Compote, cov., 7½" d., high stand.....90.00
Compote, cov., 11½" d., amber 145.00
Compote, open, 7½" d., high stand, scalloped rim.....50.00

Cup & saucer, blue 85.00
Cup & saucer, clear 42.50
Goblet, amber 95.00
Goblet, clear 30.00
Lamp, kerosene-type, 9½" h. 80.00
Pitcher, milk 65.00
Pitcher, water, amber 145.00
Pitcher, water, clear 75.00
Salt shaker w/original top, blue 75.00
Salt & pepper shakers w/original tops, pr. 65.00
Sauce dish, flat or footed 15.00
Spooner 35.00
Sugar bowl, cov. ..... 35.00 to 45.00
Syrup jug w/original top, amber 210.00
Syrup jug w/original top, blue 162.00
Syrup jug w/original top, clear 70.00

"Balky Mule" Water Tray

Tray, wine, Balky Mule on Railroad Tracks, clear, 9½" d. (ILLUS.) 49.00
Tray, water, Balky Mule on Railroad Tracks, blue, 12" d. 150.00
Tray, water, Balky Mule on Railroad Tracks, clear, 12" d. 65.00
Tumbler, footed 38.00
Waste bowl 42.00
Wine, clear 25.00
Wine, ruby-stained 85.00

CURTAIN

Bowl, cov., 7" d. ..... 100.00 to 125.00
Bowl, open, 7½" d. 20.00
Cake stand, 9½" d. 47.50
Celery vase 28.00
Compote, open 8" d., 6½" h. 47.50
Creamer 35.00
Goblet ..... 25.00 to 30.00
Mug, amber 65.00
Salt & pepper shakers w/original tops, pr. 65.00
Spooner 25.00
Sugar bowl, cov. 50.00

CURTAIN TIEBACK

Cake stand, 9" d., 6½" h. 23.00
Creamer 32.00

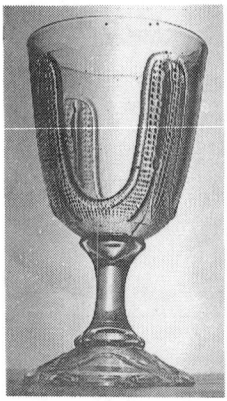

Curtain Tieback Goblet

Goblet (ILLUS.) 25.00
Pitcher, water 52.00
Sauce dish, flat or footed 12.00

CUT LOG

Cut Log Individual Creamer

Bowl, 7" d. 33.00
Bowl, master berry or fruit, 8" d., footed 40.00
Butter dish, cov. 64.00
Cake stand, 9¼" d., high stand 62.00
Cake stand, 10½" d., high stand 77.00
Celery tray 45.00
Celery vase 40.00
Compote, cov., jelly, 5½" d., high stand 65.00
Compote, cov., 7¼" d., high stand 95.00
Compote, open, jelly, 5" d. 30.00
Compote, open, 9¾" d., scalloped rim, high stand 65.00
Compote, open, 10¾" d., scalloped rim, high stand 75.00
Creamer 35.00
Creamer, individual size (ILLUS.) 18.00
Creamer & cov. sugar bowl, pr. 125.00
Cruet w/original stopper, small, 3¾" h. 36.00
Cruet w/original stopper, large, 5" h. 50.00
Goblet 55.00
Mug, small 18.00
Olive dish, handled, 5" d. 25.00
Pitcher, water, tankard, clear 96.00
Pitcher, water, tankard, ruby-stained 240.00

Relish, boat-shaped, 9¼" l. 23.00
Salt dip, master size 65.00
Salt shaker w/original tin top 60.00
Sauce dish, flat or footed 20.00
Spooner 40.00
Sugar bowl, cov. 60.00
Sugar bowl, cov., individual size 30.00
Tumbler, juice 40.00
Tumbler, water 40.00
Vase, 16" h. 58.00
Wine 23.00

DAHLIA

Dahlia Water Pitcher

Bread platter, 8 x 12" 45.00
Butter dish, cov., clear 52.00
Cake stand, amber, 9½" d. 75.00
Cake stand, blue, 9½" d. 52.50
Cake stand, clear, 9½" d. 30.00
Cordial 40.00
Creamer 28.00
Goblet 38.00
Mug, amber 45.00
Mug, blue 60.00
Mug, clear 32.00
Mug, child's 20.00
Pickle dish 15.00
Pitcher, milk, applied handle 55.00
Pitcher, water, blue (ILLUS.) 125.00
Pitcher, water, clear 50.00
Plate, 7" d. 18.00
Plate, 9" d., w/handles, apple green 42.50
Plate, 9" d., w/handles, clear 25.00
Plate, 9" d., w/handles, vaseline 42.50
Relish, blue, 5 x 9½" 25.00
Relish, clear, 5 x 9½" 13.00
Relish, green, 5 x 9½" 25.00
Sauce dish, flat, amber 22.00
Sauce dish, flat, clear 15.00
Sauce dish, footed 7.00
Spooner 35.00
Sugar bowl, cov., vaseline 60.00
Wine, amber 55.00
Wine, clear 32.00

DAISY & BUTTON

Banana boat, 14" l. 45.00
Basket, silver plate handle, 6" h 125.00
Berry set: triangular master bowl & 4 sauce dishes; vaseline, 5 pcs. 150.00
Berry set: octagonal master bowl & 10 sauce dishes; amber, 11 pcs. 140.00
Berry set: master bowl & 12 sauce dishes; vaseline, 13 pcs. 225.00
Bowl, 7 x 9½", sapphire blue 30.00
Bowl, 8" w., tricornered 45.00
Bowl, berry or fruit, 8½" d. 35.00
Bowl, 9" sq., amber 40.00
*Bowl, 10" oval, blue 65.00
Bowl, 10 x 11" oval, 7 ¾" h., flared, vaseline 95.00
Bowl, 11" d., amber 38.00
Bowl, 12" l., 9" w., shell-shaped oval, blue 75.00
Bowl, fruit, rectangular, ornate silver plate frame 250.00
*Bread tray, amber 25.00
*Butter chip, fan-shaped 9.50
*Butter chip, round 6.00
Butter chip, square, amber 15.00
Butter chip, square, Amberina 75.00
Butter chip, square, clear 7.50
Butter chip, square, purple 15.00
Butter chip, square, vaseline 25.00
Butter dish, cov., scalloped base 65.00
Butter dish, cov., square, clear 45.00
Butter dish, cov., square, green 60.00
Butter dish, cov., triangular, amber 60.00
*Butter dish, cov., model of Victorian stove, green 215.00
Cake stand, blue 50.00
Cake stand, clear, 9" sq., 6" h. 45.00
Canoe, vaseline, 4" l. 18.00

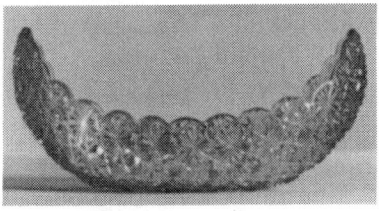

Daisy & Button Canoe

Canoe, amber, 8" l. (ILLUS.) 35.00
Canoe, blue, 8" l. 46.00
Canoe, vaseline, 8" l. 100.00
Canoe, amber, 11" l. 60.00
Canoe, blue, 11" l. 60.00
Canoe, amber, 12" l. 42.50
Canoe, green, 13" l. 48.00
Canoe, vaseline, 14" l. 85.00
Castor set, 4-bottle, blue, in glass frame 375.00
Castor set, 5-bottle, amber, blue & clear bottles, in original frame ....100.00 to 145.00
Castor set, 5-bottle, vaseline, in original frame 495.00
Celery tray, flat, boat-shaped, 4½ x 14" 90.00

Celery vase, square....65.00
Celery vase, triangular, amber....65.00
Celery vase, triangular, clear....45.00
Cheese dish, cov., clear....62.00
Cheese dish, cov., vaseline....165.00
Compote, cov., 8" d., high stand....55.00
Compote, cov., 8½" d., low stand, amber....60.00
Creamer, child's, amber....25.00
*Creamer, blue....40.00
*Creamer, clear....29.00
*Cruet w/original stopper, amber....100.00
*Cruet w/original stopper, blue....95.00
*Cruet w/original stopper, clear....45.00
Cuspidor, blue....38.00
Dish, 2½ x 6 x 9"....32.00
*Dish, fan-shaped, 10" w....35.00
Dresser tray, amber, 8 x 11"....75.00
*Goblet, amber....32.00
*Goblet, blue....25.00
*Goblet, clear....22.50
*Hat shape, amber, 2½" h....29.00
*Hat shape, blue, 2½" h....35.00
*Hat shape, vaseline, 2½" h....38.00
*Hat shape, from tumbler mold, 4½" widest d....55.00
*Hat shape, blue, from tumbler mold, 4¾" widest d....45.00
Hat shape, clear, 8 x 8", 6" h....85.00
Ice cream set: 2 x 7 x 9½" ice cream tray & two square sauce plates; amber, 3 pcs....85.00
Ice tub, amber 4¼ x 6¾"....60.00
Inkwell w/original insert, cat seated on cover....245.00
Inkwell, vaseline....175.00
Match holder, wall-hanging scuff, blue....75.00
Match holder, wall-hanging scuff, clear....65.00
*Pickle castor, sapphire blue insert, w/silver plate frame & tongs....238.00
*Pickle castor, vaseline insert, w/silver plate frame & tongs....185.00
Pitcher, 5⅛" h., applied handle, amber....55.00
Pitcher, water, tankard, 9" h., amber....125.00
Pitcher, water, bulbous, applied handle, clear....95.00
Pitcher, water, bulbous, applied handle, ruby-stained buttons....325.00
Plate, 9" d., vaseline....40.00
*Plate, 10" d., scalloped rim, amber....28.00
*Plate, 10" d., scalloped rim, blue....35.00
Powder jar, cov., amber, 3¾" d., 2" h....30.00
Powder jar, cov., blue....38.00
Relish, "Sitz bathtub"....145.00
*Rose bowl, vaseline....38.00
*Salt dip, canoe-shaped, vaseline, 2 x 4"....12.00
*Salt shaker w/original top, corset-shaped, blue....25.00
*Salt & pepper shakers w/original tops, vaseline, pr....50.00
Salt & pepper shakers, blue & amber, pr., w/clear glass stand....55.00
*Sauce dish, amber, 4" to 5" sq....15.00
Sauce dish, Amberina, 4" to 5" sq....115.00
*Sauce dish, blue, 4" to 5" sq....16.00
*Sauce dish, vaseline, 4" to 5" sq....20.00
Sauce dish, w/amber-stained buttons....20.00
Sauce dish, tricornered, clear....12.50
Sauce dish, tricornered, vaseline....16.00
*Slipper, "1886 patent," amber....46.00
*Slipper, "1886 patent," blue....47.00
Slipper, ruby-stained buttons....80.00
•Spooner, amber....40.00
Spooner, Amberina, 5" h....150.00
Spooner, amethyst....30.00
*Spooner, clear....30.00
Syrup pitcher, w/original pewter top, blue....175.00
Table set: creamer, open sugar bowl & spooner; vaseline, 3 pcs....65.00
Toothpick holder, fan-shaped, amber....35.00
Toothpick holder, square, blue....24.00
*Toothpick holder, three-footed, amber....30.00
Toothpick holder, three-footed, Amberina....170.00
*Toothpick holder, three-footed, electric blue....55.00
Toothpick holder, urn-shaped, clear....22.50
Toothpick holder, urn-shaped, vaseline....30.00
Tray, clover-shaped, amber....65.00
Tray, vaseline, 10 x 12"....89.00
Tray, ice cream, handled, blue, 9¼ x 16½"....30.00
Tray, water, amber, 11" d....95.00
Tray, water, triangular, vaseline....95.00
Tumbler, water, amber....22.50
Tumbler, water, blue....30.00
Tumbler, water, blue, pattern halfway up....30.00
Tumbler, water, clear....20.00
Tumbler, water, vaseline....30.00
Waste bowl, blue....28.00
Waste bowl, vaseline....30.00
Whimsey, "canoe," wall hanging-type, ruby-stained buttons, 11" l....110.00
Whimsey, "cradle," amber....45.00
*Whimsey, "dustpan," light blue....42.50
*Whimsey, "sleigh," amber, 4½ x 7¾"....225.00
Whimsey, "wheel barrow," vaseline....125.00
*Whimsey, "whisk broom" dish, amber....28.00
*Whimsey, "whisk broom" dish, blue....75.00
*Wine....20.00

DAISY & BUTTON WITH CROSSBARS (Mikado)

Bowl, 5 x 8"....20.00
Bread tray, amber, 9 x 12" (ILLUS.)....25.00

Daisy & Button w/Crossbars Bread Tray

Bread tray, canary yellow, 9 x 12" 52.00
Butter dish, cov., blue 58.00
Butter dish, cov., canary yellow 65.00
Butter dish, cov., clear 45.00
Celery vase, amber 38.00
Celery vase, clear 32.00
Compote, open, 7" d., low stand, amber 38.00
Compote, open, 7" d., high stand, blue 85.00
Compote, open, 7" d., high stand, canary yellow 45.00
Compote, open, 8" d., high stand, amber 45.00
Creamer, amber 37.00
Creamer, canary yellow 40.00
Creamer, clear 30.00
Creamer, individual size, amber 21.00
Creamer, individual size, blue 24.00
Creamer, individual size, canary yellow 22.00
Creamer, individual size, clear 14.00
Cruet w/original stopper, amber 115.00
Cruet w/original stopper, clear 55.00
Goblet, amber 40.00
Goblet, blue 45.00
Goblet, canary yellow 35.00
Goblet, clear 28.00
Mug, amber, 3" h. 25.00
Mug, clear, 3" h. 15.00

Daisy & Button w/Crossbars Pitcher

Pitcher, milk, amber (ILLUS.) 55.00
Pitcher, milk, blue 60.00
Pitcher, milk, canary yellow 45.00
Pitcher, water, amber 75.00
Pitcher, water, canary yellow 85.00
Pitcher, water, clear 52.00
Relish, amber, 4½ x 8" 30.00
Salt shaker w/original top, canary yellow 35.00
Salt & pepper shakers, blue & amber, pr., w/clear glass stand 85.00
Spooner, amber 32.00
Spooner, canary yellow 30.00
Sugar bowl, cov., amber 42.00
Sugar bowl, cov., blue 75.00
Syrup pitcher w/original top, clear 50.00
Tumbler, amber 25.00
Tumbler, canary yellow 24.00
Water set: pitcher & 6 tumblers; canary yellow, 7 pcs. 250.00
Wine, canary yellow 28.00
Wine, clear 25.00

DAISY & BUTTON WITH NARCISSUS

Daisy & Button w/Narcissus Wine

Bowl, 6 x 9½" oval, footed 46.00
Decanter w/original stopper 52.00
Goblet 20.00
Pitcher, water 60.00
Punch cup 10.00
Sauce dish, flat or three-footed 18.00
Sugar bowl, cov. 35.00
Tumbler 17.00
Water set: pitcher & 5 tumblers; cranberry-stained color, 6 pcs. 150.00
*Wine (ILLUS.) 22.00

DAISY & BUTTON WITH THUMBPRINT PANELS

Bowl, 7" w., heart-shaped, amber panels 42.50
Bowl, 8" sq., amber 28.00
Bowl, 9" sq., amber 28.00
Cake stand, vaseline, 10½" d., 7¼" h. 75.00
Celery vase, amber panels 125.00
Celery vase, clear 26.00

Creamer, applied handle, amber panels 68.00
*Goblet, amber panels 45.00
*Goblet, blue panels 55.00
Pitcher, water, vaseline 165.00
Salt shaker w/original top, amber panels 75.00
Spooner, amber panels 75.00
Tray, water, vaseline 95.00
Tumbler, amber panels 38.50
Tumbler, clear 25.00
Tumbler, vaseline 30.00

DAISY & BUTTON WITH "V" ORNAMENT
Bowl, 7" d., 2½" h., vaseline 19.00
Bowl, 9" d., blue 34.00
Celery vase, amber 40.00
Celery vase, clear 38.00
Celery vase, electric blue 70.00
Celery vase, vaseline 85.00
Creamer 30.00
Mug, amber 16.00
Mug, blue 23.00
Mug, miniature, vaseline 30.50
Pitcher, water 75.00
Salt & pepper shakers, amber, pr 55.00
Sauce dish, amber 15.00
Toothpick holder, amber 45.00
Toothpick holder, blue 45.00
Toothpick holder, clear 25.00
Tumbler, amber 26.00

DAISY IN PANEL - See Two Panel Pattern

DAKOTA (Baby Thumbprint)
Butter dish, cov., engraved 72.00
Butter dish, cov., plain 55.00
Cake stand, 8" d., engraved 50.00
Cake stand, 8" d., plain 45.00
Cake stand, 9½" d. 55.00
Cake stand, 10¼" d., engraved 67.00
Cake stand, 10¼" d., plain 58.00
Cake stand w/high domed cover 295.00

Dakota Engraved Celery Vase

Celery vase, flat base, engraved (ILLUS.) 42.00
Celery vase, flat base, plain 35.00
Celery vase, pedestal base, engraved 50.00
Celery vase, pedestal base, plain 42.00
Cologne bottle w/original stopper, 7" h. 135.00
Compote, cov., jelly, 5" d., 5" h. 45.00
Compote, cov., 6" d., high stand, engraved ....75.00 to 100.00
Compote, cov., 6" d., high stand, plain 58.00
Compote, cov., 8" d., high stand, engraved 190.00
Compote, open, jelly, 5" d., 5½" h., engraved 35.00
Compote, open, jelly, 5" d., 5" h., plain 36.00
Compote, open, 6" d. 30.00
Compote, open, 7" d., engraved 40.00
Compote, open, 7" d., plain 35.00
Compote, open, 8" d., high stand 55.00
Creamer, table, engraved 50.00
Creamer, table, plain 45.00
Creamer, hotel 110.00
Cruet w/original stopper, engraved 145.00
Goblet, clear, engraved 35.00
Goblet, clear, plain 24.00
Goblet, ruby-stained, engraved 95.00
Goblet, ruby-stained, plain 65.00
Pitcher, milk, jug-type, engraved, pt. 235.00
Pitcher, milk, tankard, engraved, pt. 145.00
Pitcher, milk, tankard, plain, pt. 90.00
*Pitcher, tankard, water, engraved, ½ gal. 254.00
Plate, 10" d. 63.00
Salt shaker w/original top 50.00
Sauce dish, flat or footed, clear, engraved 18.00
Sauce dish, flat or footed, clear, plain 15.00
Sauce dish, flat or footed, cobalt blue 55.00
Shaker bottle w/original top, 5" h. 68.00
Shaker bottle w/original top, hotel size, 6½" h. 65.00
Spooner, engraved 35.00
Spooner, plain 40.00
Sugar bowl, cov., engraved 62.50
Sugar bowl, cov., plain 48.00
Tray, water, piecrust rim, engraved, 13" d. 125.00
Tray, water, piecrust rim, plain, 13" d. 95.00
Tray, wine, 10½" d. 100.00
Tumbler, clear, engraved 45.00
Tumbler, clear, plain 30.00
Tumbler, ruby-stained 45.00
Waste bowl, engraved 75.00
Waste bowl, plain 58.00
Wine, clear, engraved 40.00
Wine, clear, plain 30.00
Wine, ruby-stained 50.00

DART
Butter dish, cov. 28.00

Compote, cov., 8½" d., high stand.....38.00
Compote, open, jelly.....13.50
Compote, open.....25.00

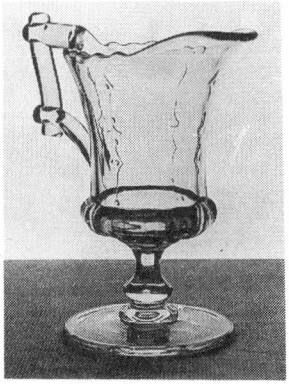

Dart Creamer

Creamer (ILLUS.).....31.00
Goblet.....25.00
Pitcher, water.....30.00
Salt shaker w/original top.....22.50
Sauce dish, footed.....7.00
Spooner.....25.00
Sugar bowl, cov.....32.00

DEER & DOG

Celery vase.....75.00
Compote, cov., 6" d., 8" h., frosted dog finial.....90.00
Compote, cov., 8" oval, 8¾" h., frosted dog finial.....155.00
Compote, cov., 8" d., 13" h., frosted dog finial.....225.00 to 250.00
Creamer.....90.00
Goblet, straight sides.....62.50
Goblet, U-shaped.....75.00
Mug, w/stacked ball handle.....50.00
Pitcher, water, applied reeded handle.....125.00 to 150.00
Sauce dish, footed.....16.00
Spooner.....92.00
Sugar bowl, cov., frosted dog finial.....150.00 to 175.00

DEER & PINE TREE

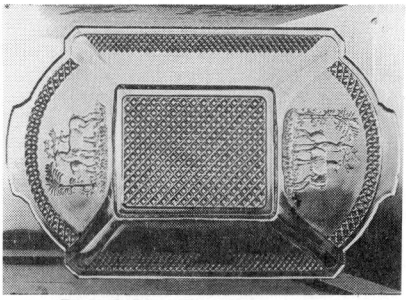

Deer & Pine Tree Bread Tray

Bowl, 5½ x 7¼".....45.00
Bowl, 5½ x 8".....55.00
Bread tray, amber, 8 x 13".....75.00
Bread tray, apple green, 8 x 13".....100.00
Bread tray, blue, 8 x 13".....110.00
Bread tray, canary yellow, 8 x 13".....100.00
Bread tray, clear, 8 x 13" (ILLUS.).....45.00
Butter dish, cov.....105.00
Cake stand.....110.00
Celery vase.....80.00
Compote, cov., 8" sq., high stand.....200.00
Creamer.....62.50
*Goblet.....50.00
Marmalade jar, cov.....110.00
Mug, child's, apple green.....45.00
Mug, child's, blue.....42.00
Mug, large, blue.....55.00
Mug, large, clear.....37.50
Pickle dish.....18.00
Pitcher, water.....125.00 to 150.00
Sauce dish, flat or footed.....18.00
Spooner.....45.00
Sugar bowl, cov.....62.50
Tray, water, handled, 9 x 15".....135.00
Vegetable dish, 5¾ x 9".....50.00

DELAWARE (Four Petal Flower)

Delaware Banana Boat

Banana boat, green w/gold, 11¾" l.....90.00
Banana boat, rose w/gold, 11¾" l. (ILLUS.).....120.00
Berry set: boat-shaped master bowl & 5 boat-shaped sauce dishes; rose w/gold, 6 pcs.....250.00 to 300.00
Berry set: round master bowl & 4 sauce dishes; rose w/gold, 5 pcs.....250.00
Bowl, 8" d., clear.....50.00
Bowl, 8" d., clear w/gold.....55.00
Bowl, 8" d., green w/gold.....50.00
Bowl, 8" d., rose w/gold.....57.50
Bowl, 9" d., scalloped rim, green w/gold.....70.00
Bride's basket, boat-shaped open bowl, green w/gold, in silver plate frame, 11½" oval.....160.00
Bride's basket, boat-shaped open bowl, rose w/gold in silver plate frame, 11½" oval.....200.00 to 225.00
Bride's basket, boat-shaped open bowl, green w/gold, miniature.....175.00
Bride's basket, rose w/gold, miniature.....85.00
Butter dish, cov., clear.....125.00
*Butter dish, cov., green w/gold.....125.00
Butter dish, cov., rose w/gold.....165.00

Celery vase, rose band w/gold 45.00
Celery vase, green w/gold 82.50
Celery vase, purple w/gold 59.00
Celery vase, rose w/gold 88.00
Claret jug, rose w/gold.....150.00 to 175.00
*Creamer, clear w/gold 45.00
Creamer, green w/gold 58.00
Creamer, rose w/gold 55.00
Creamer, individual size, clear w/gold..25.00
Creamer, individual size, green w/gold 50.00
Creamer, individual size, rose w/gold...60.00
Cruet w/original stopper, clear.....100.00
Cruet w/original stopper, green w/gold 185.00
Cruet w/original stopper, rose w/gold 325.00
Marmalade dish w/silver plate holder, green w/gold 45.00
Marmalade dish w/silver plate holder, rose w/gold 85.00
Pin tray, green w/gold.....55.00
Pin tray, rose w/gold.....90.00
Pitcher, milk, green w/gold 85.00
Pitcher, tankard, green w/gold.....150.00
Pitcher, tankard, rose w/gold .....200.00 to 225.00
Pitcher, water, clear w/gold ....50.00 to 75.00
Pitcher, water, green w/gold .....125.00 to 150.00
Pitcher, water, rose w/gold 175.00
Pomade jar w/jeweled cover, green w/gold .....185.00 to 200.00
Pomade jar w/jeweled cover, rose w/gold 335.00
Powder jar, cov., green w/gold 225.00
Punch cup, clear.....16.00
Punch cup, clear w/gold 30.00
Punch cup, green w/gold.....35.00
Punch cup, rose w/gold 45.00
Salt shaker w/original top 85.00
Sauce dish, boat-shaped, clear.....18.00
Sauce dish, boat-shaped, green w/gold 35.00
Sauce dish, boat-shaped, rose w/gold 40.00
Sauce dish, round, green w/gold.....22.50
Sauce dish, round, rose w/gold 24.00
Shade, gas, rose w/gold.....295.00
Spooner, green w/gold 50.00
Spooner, rose.....60.00
Spooner, rose w/gold.....75.00
Sugar bowl, cov., clear 62.50
*Sugar bowl, cov., green w/gold 90.00
Sugar bowl, cov., rose w/gold.....90.00
Sugar bowl, individual size, rose w/gold 95.00
Table set, green w/gold, 4 pcs.....400.00
Table set, rose w/gold, 4 pcs.....450.00
Toothpick holder, clear 45.00
Toothpick holder, green w/gold 101.00
Toothpick holder, rose w/gold.....125.00
Tumbler, green w/gold.....40.00
Tumbler, rose w/gold.....50.00
Vase, 6" h., green w/gold.....65.00
Vase, 8" h., clear 105.00
Vase, 8" h., green w/gold.....105.00
Vase, 8" h., rose w/gold.....105.00
Vase, 9½" h., amethyst.....100.00
Vase, 9½" h., green w/gold.....110.00
Vase, 9½" h., rose w/gold.....115.00
Water set: water pitcher & 3 tumblers; rose w/gold, 4 pcs.....295.00
Water set: water pitcher & 4 tumblers; green w/gold, 5 pcs.....550.00

DEW & RAINDROP

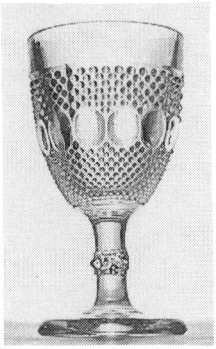

Dew & Raindrop Wine

Celery 11.00
Compote, cov., jelly 50.00
*Cordial.....30.00
*Goblet.....28.00
Pitcher, water.....50.00
*Punch cup 12.00
Spooner.....35.00
Sugar bowl, cov. 35.00
*Wine (ILLUS.).....20.00

DEWDROP

Bread tray 25.00
Compote, cov., 11" d. 60.00
Cordial 40.00
Goblet, amber.....25.00
Goblet, clear 25.00
Goblet, vaseline.....36.00
Mug, applied handle 26.00
Pitcher, water, collared base 50.00
Tumbler 15.00

DEWDROP WITH STAR

Bread tray, "Give Us This Day Our Daily Bread" 43.00
Butter dish, cov. 55.00
Cake stand, 11" d. 45.00
Cheese dish, cov. 130.00
Compote, cov., 7⅛" d., 9½" h. 82.50
Compote, cov., 11" h. 77.00
Honey dish.....13.50
*Plate, 7" d.....15.00
Plate, 9" d. 13.50
Relish, 9" l.....15.00
*Sauce dish, footed 7.00

DEWEY (Flower Flange)

Dewey Cruet

Bowl, 8" d. 35.00
*Butter dish, cov., amber 85.00
*Butter dish, cov., clear 55.00
*Butter dish, cov., green 80.00
Butter dish, cov., green, miniature 75.00
Creamer, cov., individual size 45.00
Creamer, amber 60.00
Creamer & cov. sugar bowl, individual size, canary yellow, pr. 150.00
Cruet w/original stopper, amber 125.00
Cruet w/original stopper, canary yellow (ILLUS.) 170.00
Cruet w/original stopper, green ....150.00 to 200.00
Mug, amber 60.00
Mug, clear 35.00
Mug, green 62.00
Parfait, amber 65.00
Parfait, clear 40.00
Pitcher, water, amber 110.00
Pitcher, water, canary yellow 145.00
Pitcher, water, clear 78.00
Plate, footed, canary yellow 85.00
Plate, footed, green 65.00
Salt shaker w/original top, amber 62.50
Sauce dish, canary yellow 35.00
Sauce dish, green 30.00
Sugar bowl, cov., clear 35.00
Sugar bowl, cov., green 75.00
Tray, serpentine shape, amber, small ..45.00
Tray, serpentine shape, clear, small 28.00
Tray, serpentine shape, amber, large ...55.00
Tumbler, amber 55.00
Tumbler, canary yellow 55.00
Tumbler, clear 45.00
Water set: pitcher & 6 tumblers; clear, 7 pcs. ....300.00 to 350.00

DIAGONAL BAND

Celery vase 30.00
Compote, open, 7½" d., high stand 18.00
Creamer 30.00
Goblet 20.00
Marmalade jar w/original lid 50.00
Pickle castor insert 35.00
Sauce dish, flat or footed ....7.00 to 10.00
Spooner 25.00
Tray, handled, 7¼ x 13" 20.00
Wine 22.00

DIAGONAL BAND & FAN

Celery 45.00
Compote, open, 6" d., 5¼" h. 35.00
Creamer 30.00
Creamer & cov. sugar bowl, pr. 75.00
Goblet 25.00
Pitcher, milk 38.00
Plate, 6" d. 15.00
Plate, 7" d. 24.50
Sauce dish, footed 12.50
Sauce dishes, set of 6 ....75.00
Spooner 35.00
Sugar bowl, cov. 30.00
Wine 25.00

DIAMOND & BULL'S EYE BAND - See Reverse Torpedo Pattern

DIAMOND & SUNBURST

Diamond & Sunburst Goblet

Bowl, cov., 8" d. 35.00
Cake stand, 8" d. 28.00
Compote, cov., 7" d., high stand 48.00
Creamer, applied handle 40.00
Goblet (ILLUS.) 25.00
Pitcher w/applied handle, milk 40.00
Sauce dish, handled, flat, 3¾" d. 10.00
Spooner 22.00
Toothpick holder 40.00
Tumbler 25.00

DIAMOND MEDALLION (Finecut & Diamond or Grand)

Bread plate, 10" d. 20.00
Cake stand, 9" d. 25.00
Cake stand, 10" d. 30.00
Celery vase 25.00
Compote, cov., 6" d., 9" h. 65.00
Compote, cov., 8" d., low stand 80.00
Creamer, footed 20.00
Goblet 30.00
Pitcher, water 38.00

Relish, 7½" oval 9.00
Salt shaker w/original top 32.50
Spooner 15.00
Wine 25.00

DIAMOND POINT

Diamond Point Creamer

Bar bottle, flint 125.00
Butter dish, cov., flint 82.50
Celery vase, pedestal base w/knob stem, flint 90.00
Champagne, flint ....125.00 to 150.00
Claret, flint 100.00
Compote, open, 6" d., high stand, flint 75.00
Compote, open, 7" d., low stand, flint 67.50
Compote, open, 7" d., high stand, milk white 175.00
Compote, open, 7½" d., high stand, flint 165.00
Compote, open, 8" d., shallow bowl, high stand, non-flint 65.00
Compote, open, 10¼" d., high stand, milk white 350.00
Cordial, flint 195.00
Creamer, applied handle, flint (ILLUS.) 165.00
Cup plate, flint 60.00
Decanter w/original stopper, pt. 100.00
Decanter w/original stopper, qt. 165.00
Decanter w/bar lip, qt. 65.00
Egg cup, cov., powder blue opaque, flint ....550.00 to 750.00
Egg cup, canary yellow, flint ....300.00 to 350.00
Egg cup, clambroth, flint 135.00
Egg cup, clear, flint 50.00
Egg cup, translucent sea green 650.00
Goblet, clear, flint 58.00
Goblet, amber, non-flint 25.00
Goblet, blue, non-flint 32.00
Goblet, clear, non-flint 35.00
Honey dish, clear, flint 18.00
Honey dish, milk white, flint 60.00
Honey dish, coarse points, non-flint 12.00
Lamp, whale oil, w/wafer connector, flint, 10⅛" h. 295.00
Pitcher, milk, applied handle, milk white, flint 550.00
Pitcher, water, bulbous, flint 350.00
Pitcher, water, non-flint 75.00
Plate, 8" d., milk white, flint 125.00
Salt dip, cov., master size, flint 195.00
Sauce dish, flint, 4¼" d. 20.00
Sauce dish, non-flint, 3½" to 5½" d. 10.00
Spillholder, clear, flint 42.50
Spillholder, clear w/gold rim, flint 165.00
Spooner, non-flint 28.00
Sugar bowl, cov., flint 95.00
Sugar bowl, cov., non-flint 45.00
Toothpick holder, non-flint 35.00
Tumbler, flint 45.00
Tumbler, bar, flint 95.00
Tumbler, whiskey, handled, flint, 3" h. 150.00
Wine, flint 100.00
Wine, non-flint 30.00

DIAMOND POINT WITH PANELS - See Hinoto Pattern

DIAMOND QUILTED

Bowl, 7" d., amber 25.00
Celery vase, blue 65.00
Champagne, amethyst 37.50
Champagne, turquoise blue 37.50
Champagne, vaseline 26.00
Claret, vaseline 18.00
Compote, open, 6" d., 6" h. 22.50
Compote, open, 8" d., low stand, amethyst 45.00
Compote, open, 9" d., low stand, vaseline 38.00
Cordial, amber 40.00
*Goblet, amber 40.00
*Goblet, amethyst 38.00
*Goblet, blue 37.50
*Goblet, vaseline 35.00
Pitcher, water, amber 52.00
Relish, amber, 4½ x 7½" 14.00
Relish, leaf-shaped, turquoise blue, 5½ x 9" 22.00
Relish, leaf-shaped, vaseline, 5½ x 9" 20.00
*Salt dip, amethyst, master size, rectangular 22.00
Sauce dish, flat or footed, amber 18.00
Sauce dish, flat or footed, turquoise blue 13.00
Sauce dish, flat or footed, vaseline 12.50
Spooner, amber 28.00
Spooner, turquoise blue 38.00
Spooner, vaseline 35.00
Sugar bowl, cov., vaseline 55.00
Tray, water, cloverleaf-shaped, amethyst, 10 x 12" 45.00
*Tumbler, amber 30.00
*Tumbler, vaseline 26.00
Wine, amethyst 42.00
Wine, clear 20.00
Wine, vaseline 38.00

DIAMOND THUMBPRINT

Bowl, 7" d., footed, scalloped rim 95.00
Bowl, 8" d., footed, scalloped rim 100.00
*Butter dish, cov. .....150.00 to 200.00
Celery vase.....175.00 to 200.00
Compote, open, 7" d., low stand, extended scalloped rim 125.00
Compote, open, 8" d., high stand 125.00
Compote, open, 8" d., low stand.....75.00
Compote, open, 10½" d., high stand .....200.00 to 250.00
Compote, open, 11½" d., high stand ..300.00
Cordial, 4" h. 295.00
*Creamer, applied handle.....200.00
Decanter w/bar lip, qt., 10½" h. 195.00
Decanter w/original stopper, qt.....225.00
*Goblet.....450.00
Honey dish.....25.00
Pitcher, water.....400.00 to 600.00
Sauce dish, flat.....20.00
*Spooner.....86.00
*Sugar bowl, cov.....150.00
Tray, serpentine shape, amber, small 45.00
*Tumbler.....50.00 to 90.00
Tumbler, bar, 3¾" h. 150.00
Tumbler, whiskey.....150.00
Wine 235.00

DINNER BELL - See Cottage Pattern

DORIC - See Feather Pattern

DOUBLE LEAF & DART - See Leaf & Dart Pattern

DOUBLE LOOP - See Ribbon Candy Pattern

DOUBLE RIBBON

Bread plate 24.00
Butter dish, cov.....45.00
Creamer.....45.00
Goblet.....27.50
Lamp, kerosene-type, frosted, dated 1872.....135.00
Relish.....12.50

DOUBLE WEDDING RING (Wedding Ring)

*Goblet.....70.00
Sauce dish.....25.00
Spooner.....70.00
Syrup pitcher w/original top, 6" h. 165.00
Tumbler, bar 70.00
Wine 89.00

DRAPERY

Creamer, applied handle 35.00
Goblet.....28.00
Plate, 6" d. 23.00
Spooner.....35.00
Sugar bowl, cov. 40.00

EGG IN SAND

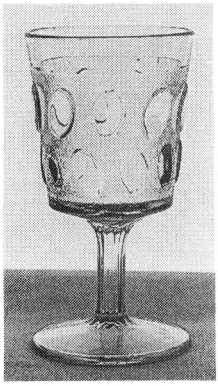

Egg in Sand Goblet

Bread tray, handled 36.00
Creamer.....32.00
Dish, flat, swan center, 7" d. 48.00
Goblet, blue 46.00
Goblet, clear (ILLUS.).....32.00
Pitcher, milk.....45.00
Pitcher, water.....35.00
Platter, 12½" oblong 42.00
Relish, 5½ x 9".....18.50
Spooner, amber.....45.00
Spooner, blue 35.00
Spooner, clear 26.00
Sugar bowl, cov. 35.00
Tumbler 30.00

EGYPTIAN

Egyptian Spooner

Bread platter, Cleopatra center, 9 x 12".....57.00
*Bread platter, Salt Lake Temple center.....248.00
Butter dish, cov.....73.00
Celery vase.....75.00 to 100.00
Compote, cov., 6" d., 6" h., sphinx base .....100.00 to 125.00
Compote, cov., 7" d., high stand, sphinx base.....195.00

Compote, cov., 8" d., high stand, sphinx base 225.00
Creamer 45.00
Goblet 45.00
Pickle dish 20.00
Pitcher, water ....200.00 to 225.00
Plate, 10" d. 65.00
Plate, 12" d., handled 85.00
Relish, 5½ x 8½" 32.50
Sauce dish, flat 18.50
Sauce dish, footed 16.50
Spooner (ILLUS.) 45.00
Table set, 4 pcs. 295.00

EMERALD GREEN HERRINGBONE - See Paneled Herringbone Pattern

EMPIRE COLONIAL - See Colonial Pattern

EMPRESS

Bowl, master, berry, 8½" d. 40.00
Butter dish, cov., green 130.00
Compote, open, 6" d., high standard, emerald green 125.00
Creamer & cov. sugar bowl, green w/gold, pr. 200.00
Cruet w/original stopper, emerald green 195.00
Salt & pepper shakers w/original tops, emerald green, pr. 195.00
Spoonholder, emerald green 68.00
Table set, 4 pcs. 650.00
Toothpick holder, emerald green w/gold 195.00
Tumbler, water, emerald green 69.00

ENGLISH HOBNAIL CROSS - See Klondike Pattern

ESTHER

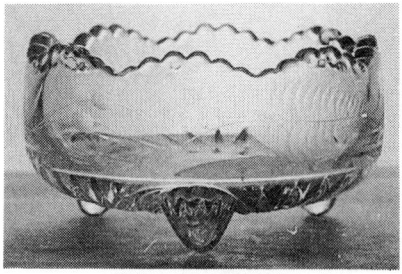

Esther Sauce Dish

Berry set: master bowl & 5 sauce dishes; green, 6 pcs. 215.00
Bowl, 8" d., clear 35.00
Bowl, 8" d., green w/gold 72.50
Butter dish, cov., amber-stained 125.00
Butter dish, cov., clear 75.00
Butter dish, cov., green 145.00
Cake stand, 10½" d., 6" h. 50.00
Celery vase, amber-stained 125.00
Celery vase, clear 35.00
Celery vase, green 85.00
Compote, open, jelly, 5" d., amber-stained w/enamel decoration 135.00
Compote, open, jelly, 5" d., green 60.00
Creamer, green 90.00
Cruet w/original stopper, clear, miniature 30.00
Cruet w/original stopper, green, miniature ....200.00 to 275.00
Cruet w/ball-shaped stopper, clear 35.00
Cruet w/ball-shaped stopper, green ....250.00 to 300.00
Goblet, amber-stained w/enamel decoration ....125.00 to 150.00
Goblet, clear 60.00
Pitcher, water, amber-stained ....200.00 to 250.00
Plate, 10¼" d. 30.00
Relish, clear, 4½ x 8½" 22.50
Relish, green, 4½ x 8½" 36.00
Relish, green, 5½ x 11" 42.50
Salt & pepper shakers w/original tops, clear, pr. 65.00
Salt & pepper shakers w/original tops, green, pr. 130.00
Sauce dish, clear, engraved (ILLUS.) 15.00
Sauce dish, green 25.00
Sauce dishes, amber-stained, set of 6 ....150.00
Spooner, clear 35.00
Spooner, green 68.00
Sugar bowl, cov., green 125.00
Toothpick holder, amber-stained ....100.00 to 150.00
Toothpick holder, green 115.00
Tray, ice cream, clear 67.50
Tray, ice cream, green 145.00
Tumbler, clear 32.00
Tumbler, amber-stained 45.00
Tumbler, green 55.00
Tumbler, green w/gold 65.00
Water set: pitcher & 6 tumblers; green, 7 pcs. 545.00
Wine, amber-stained 75.00
Wine, ruby-stained, souvenir 75.00

EUREKA (McKee's)

Butter dish 80.00
Creamer 40.00
Egg cup 30.00
Goblet 28.00
Salt dip, master size 22.00
Spooner 50.00

EXCELSIOR

Bar bottle, flint, qt. 70.00
Cake stand, flint, 9¼" h. 150.00
Celery vase, flint 78.00
Champagne 85.00
Cologne bottle w/faceted stopper 95.00
Creamer, applied handle 275.00
Egg cup 47.50
Egg cup, double, fiery opalescent, flint 295.00

Excelsior Goblet

Goblet, flint (ILLUS.) 68.00
Platter, 9¼" l. 22.00
Spillholder, flint 76.00
Sugar bowl, cov. ....100.00 to 125.00
Tumbler, bar, flint, 3½" h. 60.00
Wine, flint 50.00

EYEWINKER

Banana boat, flat, 8½" 90.00
Banana stand 115.00
Bowl, cov., 9" d. 85.00
Bowl, 6½" d. 25.00
Bowl, master berry or fruit, 9" d., 4½" h. 70.00
*Butter dish, cov. 72.50
Cake stand, 8" d. 58.00
Cake stand, 9½" d. 65.00
Celery vase, 6½" h. 55.00
*Compote, cov., 6" d., high stand 50.00
Compote, open, 4" d., 5" h., scalloped rim 32.50
Compote, open, 5½" d., high stand 60.00
Compote, open, 8½" d., high stand 75.00
Compote, open, 9½" d., high stand 82.00
Creamer 45.00
*Goblet 25.00
Pitcher, milk 70.00
*Pitcher, water 80.00
Plate, 7" sq., 1½" h., turned-up sides 24.00
Salt shaker w/original top 35.00
*Sauce dish, round 34.00
Sauce dish, square 12.00
*Spooner 45.00
Sugar bowl, cov. 52.00
Syrup pitcher w/silver plate top 135.00
*Tumbler 28.00

FEATHER (Doric, Indiana Swirl or Finecut & Feather)

Berry set, master bowl & 6 sauce dishes, 7 pcs. 120.00
Bowl, 7 x 9" oval 24.00
Bowl, 8" d. 25.00
Bowl, 8½" oval, flat 25.00
Butter dish, cov., clear 60.00
Butter dish, cov., green 195.00
Cake stand, 8½" d. 32.50
Cake stand, clear, 9½" h. 47.00
Cake stand, green, 9½" h. ..125.00 to 150.00
Cake stand, 11" d. 60.00
Celery vase 40.00
Compote, open, jelly, 5" d., 4¾" h., amber-stained 110.00
Compote, open, jelly, 5" d., 4¾" h., clear 23.00
Compote, open, 8" d., low stand 45.00
Compote, open, 8" d., high stand 38.00
Cordial 43.00
Creamer, clear 38.00
Creamer, green 75.00
Cruet w/original stopper, clear 37.00
Cruet w/original stopper, green 250.00
Doughnut stand, 8" w., 4½" h. 36.00
Goblet, amber-stained 140.00

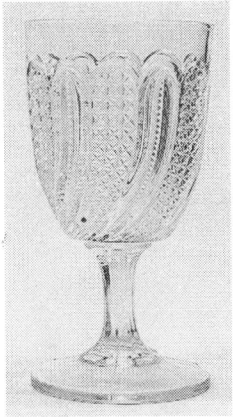

Feather Goblet

Goblet, clear (ILLUS.) 60.00
Pickle dish 15.00
Pitcher, milk 47.50
Pitcher, water, clear 60.00
Pitcher, water, green ....175.00 to 200.00
Plate, 10" d. 40.00
Relish, 8¼" oval, amber-stained 75.00
Relish, 8¼" oval, clear 18.00
Salt & pepper shakers w/original tops, green, pr. 225.00
Sauce dish, flat or footed, clear 14.50
Sauce dish, flat or footed, green 45.00
Spooner 30.00
Sugar bowl, cov., clear 46.00
Sugar bowl, cov., green 150.00
Syrup pitcher w/original top, clear 135.00
Syrup pitcher w/original top, green 315.00
Toothpick holder 85.00
Tumbler, clear 45.00
Tumbler, green 85.00
*Wine 37.50

FESTOON

Bowl, berry, 8" rectangle 23.00
Bowl, berry, 5½ x 9" rectangle 25.00
Butter dish, cov. 42.00
Cake stand, high pedestal, 9" d. ....30.00 to 40.00

Compote, open, 9" d., high stand 56.00
Creamer.....30.00
Marmalade jar, cov. 32.00
Mug, handled.....58.00
Pitcher, water.....60.00
Plate, 7" d. 36.00
Plate, 8" d. 42.00
Plate, 9" d. 47.50
Sauce dish.....10.00
Spooner 35.00

Festoon Sugar Bowl

Sugar bowl, cov. (ILLUS.).....55.00
Tray, water, 10" d. 36.00
Tumbler 24.50
Waste bowl 53.00

FINECUT

Bread tray, handled, canary, 7½ x 14½".....55.00
Cake stand, amber, 10" d., 7¼" h. 45.00
Cake stand 35.00
Creamer.....28.00
Goblet, canary 35.00
Goblet, clear 22.50
Pickle castor, canary, w/Reed & Barton silver plate frame & fork 275.00
Pitcher, water, canary.....100.00
Plate, 7" d. 15.00
Plate, 10" d., amber 42.50
Plate, 10" d., canary 45.00
Relish, boat-shaped, apple green.....35.00
Salt & pepper shakers w/original tops, canary, pr. 48.00
Salt & pepper shakers w/original tops, clear, pr. 35.00
Toothpick holder, hat shape on plate, blue 25.00
Tray, water, canary, 9¼" d.....48.00

FINECUT & BLOCK

Bowl, round, handled, pink blocks 50.00
Butter dish, cov., two-handled 55.00
Celery tray, clear w/amber blocks, 11" l. 85.00
Champagne, amber.....70.00
Cordial 35.00
*Creamer, clear 30.00
Creamer, clear w/amber blocks.....70.00
Creamer, clear w/pink blocks 75.00
Egg cup, double.....29.00
*Goblet, amber 50.00
*Goblet, clear.....40.00
Goblet, clear w/blue blocks.....55.00
Goblet, clear w/yellow blocks 52.00
Pitcher, water, clear w/amber blocks....85.00
Pitcher, water, clear w/blue blocks 125.00
Pitcher, water, clear w/pink blocks 110.00
Punch cup, clear w/yellow blocks 55.00
Salt dip.....12.00
Sauce dish, amber.....15.00
Sauce dish, clear w/amber blocks 13.00
Sauce dish, clear w/blue blocks 22.50
Spooner, clear 40.00
Spooner, clear w/amber blocks 45.00
Tumbler, clear w/blue blocks 40.00
*Wine, amber.....58.00
*Wine, blue 58.00
*Wine, clear 24.00
Wine, clear w/amber blocks.....48.00
Wine, clear w/blue blocks 45.00
Wine, clear w/pink blocks 60.00
Wine, clear w/yellow blocks.....35.00

FINECUT & DIAMOND - See Diamond Medallion Pattern

FINECUT & FEATHER - See Feather Pattern

FINECUT & PANEL (Paneled Finecut)

Finecut & Panel Plate

Bread tray, amber, 9 x 13".....47.50
Bread tray, clear, 9 x 13" 29.00
Cake stand, square, blue.....75.00
Celery vase.....25.00
Compote, open, high stand, amber 45.00
Compote, open, high stand, blue.....50.00

Creamer, amber 42.50
Goblet, amber 32.00
Goblet, clear 18.00
Goblet, vaseline 27.50
Pitcher, water, amber 100.00
Plate, 6" d., amber (ILLUS.) 25.00
Plate, 6" d., blue 28.00
Plate, 6" d., clear 13.00
Plate, 6" d., vaseline 22.50
Relish, blue, 3½ x 7" 22.50
Relish, vaseline, 3½ x 7" 21.50
Salt shaker w/original top, amber 37.50
Salt shaker w/original top, clear 35.00
Sauce dish, amber 12.00
Sauce dish, clear 8.00
Sauce dish, vaseline 14.00
Sugar bowl, cov., vaseline 60.00
Tray, water, vaseline, 12" w. 95.00
Tumbler, amber 18.00
Waste bowl, vaseline 29.50
Wine, amber 30.00
Wine, blue 28.00
Wine, clear 20.00
Wine, vaseline 36.00

FINECUT BAND - See Cottage Pattern

FISHSCALE

Fishscale Compote

Bowl, cov., 7" d. 55.00
Bowl, 6" d. 39.00
Butter dish, cov. 40.00
Cake stand, 9" d. 25.00
Cake stand, 10" d. 35.00
Celery vase 31.00
Compote, cov., 7½" d. 85.00
Compote, open, jelly 18.00
Compote, open, 6" d. 20.00
Compote, open, 7" d., high stand (ILLUS.) 31.00
Creamer 27.50
Goblet 34.00
Mug 35.00
Pickle dish 18.00
Pitcher, milk 35.00
Pitcher, water 50.00
Plate, 7" d. 28.50
Plate, 8" d. 32.50
Plate, 9" sq. 35.00
Relish, 5 x 8½" 22.50
Sauce dish, flat or footed 10.00
Spooner 21.00
Sugar bowl, cov. 38.00
Tray, water, round 35.00
Tumbler 95.00
Waste bowl 50.00

FLORIDA - See Paneled Herringbone Pattern

FLOWER FLANGE - See Dewey Pattern

FLUTE

Flute Claret

Bar bottle, clear, flint, qt. 72.00
Bar bottle, pewter closure w/marble stopper, emerald green, flint, 11" h. 1,700.00
Claret (ILLUS.) 22.00
Compote, open, 8¼" d., 3" h. 35.00
Egg cup, single 35.00
Goblet 26.00
Mug, applied handle 135.00
Pitcher, water 75.00
Relish 30.00
Tumbler, whiskey, handled 55.00
Wine 35.00

FLYING ROBIN - See Hummingbird Pattern

FOUR PETAL FLOWER - See Delaware Pattern

FROSTED CIRCLE

Bowl, 8" d., 3¼" h. 20.00
Butter dish, cov. 65.00
Cake stand, 9½" d. 47.50
Champagne 48.00
Claret 45.00
Compote, open, 9" d., 6" h. 46.50
Compote, open, 10" d., high stand, scalloped rim 55.00

Creamer....46.00

Frosted Circle Goblet

*Goblet (ILLUS.)....28.00
Pitcher, water, tankard....80.00
Plate, 7" d....22.50
Plate, 9" d....37.50
Sauce dish....12.00
Spooner....45.00
Sugar bowl, cov....60.00
Tumbler....26.00

FROSTED LEAF

Celery vase....100.00 to 125.00
Champagne....225.00
Egg cup....100.00
Goblet....95.00
Goblet, flint....125.00
Goblet, lady's....160.00
Salt dip....50.00
Sauce dish....25.00
Tumbler, footed....120.00
Wine....140.00

FROSTED LION (Rampant Lion)

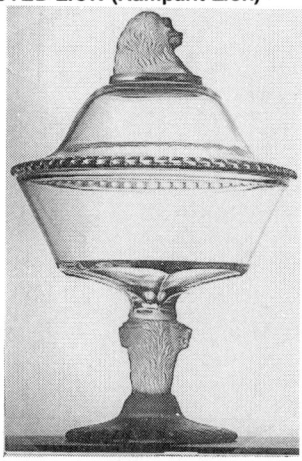

Frosted Lion Compote

Bowl, cov., 3⅞ x 6⅞" oblong, collared base....80.00
Bowl, cov., 4⅝ x 7 7/16" oblong, collared base....110.00
*Bread plate, rope edge, closed handles, 10½" d....78.00
*Butter dish, cov., frosted lion's head finial....90.00
Butter dish, cov., rampant lion finial....140.00
*Celery vase....70.00
Cheese dish, cov., rampant lion finial....425.00
Compote, cov., 5" d., 8½" h....175.00
*Compote, cov., 6¾" oval, 7" h., collared base, rampant lion finial....150.00 to 175.00
Compote, cov., 7" d., 11" h., lion head finial....150.00
Compote, cov., 7¾" oval, low collared base, rampant lion finial....128.00
Compote, cov., 8" d., 13" h., rampant lion finial....165.00
Compote, cov., 8¼" d., high stand, frosted lion head finial (ILLUS.)....145.00
Compote, cov., 5½ x 8¾" oval, 8¼" h., rampant lion finial....185.00
Compote, open, 5" d., low stand....62.00
Compote, open, 7" d., 6¼" h....125.00
Compote, open, 7" oval, 7½" h....135.00
Compote, open, 8" d....175.00
Creamer....75.00
*Egg Cup....90.00
*Goblet....93.00
Marmalade jar, cov., rampant lion finial....145.00
*Pitcher, water....525.00 to 550.00
Platter, 9 x 10½" oval, lion handles....95.00
Salt dip, cov., master size, collared base, rectangular....295.00
*Sauce dish, 4" to 5" d....25.00
*Spooner....54.00
*Sugar bowl, cov., frosted lion's head finial....50.00
Sugar bowl, cov., rampant lion finial....80.00
Table set, cov. sugar bowl, creamer & spooner, 3 pcs....225.00

FROSTED RIBBON (Duncan's No. 150)

Butter dish, cov....60.00
Celery vase....40.00
Compote, cov., 8" d., 11" h....95.00
Goblet....35.00
Pitcher, water....75.00
Sauce dish....12.00
Spooner....33.00
Sugar bowl, cov....54.00
Wine....65.00

FROSTED ROMAN KEY - See Roman Key Pattern

FROSTED STORK

Bowl, 9" oval, 1-0-1 border....45.00
*Bread plate, round....55.00
Compote, open, 8" d....45.00

Creamer....45.00
*Goblet....65.00
Jam jar, cov. 350.00
Plate, 9" d., 1-0-1 border 58.00
Platter, 8 x 11½" oval, 1-0-1 border....70.00
Platter, 8 x 11½" oval, deer & dog border 81.00
Sauce dish....28.00
Spooner....40.00
Tray, water, 11 x 15½"....100.00
Waste bowl....50.00

GALLOWAY (Mirror or misnamed Virginia)
Bowl, 9½" d., flat....30.00
Butter dish, cov....55.00
Cake stand, 9¼" d., 6" h. 52.00
Compote, open, 4¼" d., 6" h....33.00
Compote, open, 8½" d., 7" h....60.00
Compote, open, 8¾" d., flared, rose-stained 85.00
Creamer, clear....22.00
Creamer, rose-stained....75.00
Creamer, individual size, clear 19.00
Goblet....90.00
Mug, 4½" d. 37.50
Olive dish, 4 x 6"....19.00
Pitcher, milk....70.00
Pitcher, water....45.00
Punch cup....10.00
Relish, 8¼" l....14.50
Salt shaker w/original top 20.00
Salt & pepper shakers w/original tops, gold trim, 3" h., pr....47.50
Sauce dish, flat or footed....11.00
Spooner, clear 22.50
Spooner, rose-stained 80.00
Sugar bowl, cov., rose-stained 85.00
Sugar shaker w/original top....35.00
Syrup pitcher w/metal spring top 75.00
Table set, 4 pcs. ....225.00 to 275.00
*Toothpick holder, clear....22.50
*Toothpick holder, green 50.00
Tumbler 25.00
Vase, 9½" h. 32.00
Waste bowl....38.00
Water set: pitcher & 4 tumblers; rose-stained, 5 pcs....495.00
Wine 41.00

GARFIELD DRAPE
Bowl, 6" d....42.50
Bread plate, "We Mourn Our Nation's Loss," 11½"8 d....58.00
Butter dish, cov....78.00
Cake stand, 9½" d. 85.00
Celery vase, pedestal base 50.00
Compote, cov., 8" d., 12½" h. 185.00
Creamer....50.00
Goblet (ILLUS. top next column) 45.00
Pitcher, milk....85.00
Pitcher, water....95.00
Sauce dish, flat or footed....12.00

Garfield Drape Goblet

Spooner....40.00
Sugar bowl, cov. 80.00

GEORGIA - See Peacock Feather Pattern

GIANT BULL'S EYE
Bottle, brandy, original stopper, 7½" h....48.00
Butter dish, cov....45.00
Goblet....60.00
Pitcher, water....85.00
Toothpick holder....35.00
Tray, round, wine....32.00
Wine 25.00

GODDESS OF LIBERTY - See Ceres Pattern

GOOD LUCK - See Horseshoe Pattern

GOOSEBERRY
Cake stand 52.00
Creamer....40.00
*Goblet....30.00
*Mug 45.00
Spooner....25.00
Tumbler, bar 40.00
Tumbler, water....32.00

GOTHIC
Butter dish, cov....100.00 to 125.00
Castor bottle 29.50
Castor set: mustard, cruet & shaker & original wire holder....165.00
Celery vase....145.00
Champagne....195.00
Compote, open, 7" d., 3½" h....62.50
Compote, open, 8" d., 4" h....62.50
Creamer, applied handle 100.00
Egg cup, 3½" h. (ILLUS. top next page)....50.00
Goblet....62.00
Sauce dish....18.00

Gothic Egg Cup

Spooner 56.00
Sugar bowl, cov. 125.00
Wine, 3¾" h. 108.00

GRAND - See Diamond Medallion Pattern

GRAPE & FESTOON

Butter dish, cov., stippled leaf 40.00
Compote, cov., 8" d., low stand, acorn finial, stippled leaf 55.00
Compote, cov., large, high stand, w/bird's nest finial 85.00
Creamer, stippled leaf 42.00
Egg cup, stippled leaf 20.00
Goblet, stippled leaf 23.00
Goblet, veined leaf 25.00
Mug 20.00
Pitcher, water, stippled leaf 90.00
Relish, stippled leaf 10.00
Salt dip, footed, stippled leaf 22.00
Sauce dish, flat, stippled leaf, 4" d. 9.00
Spooner, stippled leaf 25.00
Spooner, veined leaf 25.00
Wine, stippled leaf 50.00

GRAPE & FESTOON WITH SHIELD

Compote, cov., 8¼" d., 10½" h. 140.00
Goblet, w/American shield 60.00
Mug, 1⅞" h. 35.00
Mug, sapphire blue, 2½" h. 48.00

GRASSHOPPER (Locust)

Bowl, cov., 7" d., footed 50.00
Butter dish, cov., no insect, clear 45.00
Butter dish, cov., w/insect, clear 70.00
Celery vase, w/insect 75.00
Compote, cov., 8¼" d. 65.00
Creamer, amber 65.00
Creamer, w/insect 45.00
Pitcher, water, w/insect 85.00
Plate, 7½" d., footed 18.00
Plate, 8½" d., footed 18.00
Plate, 10½" d., footed 28.00
Salt dip, master size 38.00
Sauce dish, footed, no insect 14.00
Spooner, no insect, clear 60.00
Spooner, w/insect, clear 75.00
Sugar bowl, cov., no insect 40.00
Sugar bowl, cov., w/insect 70.00

GUARDIAN ANGEL - See Cupid & Venus Pattern

HAIRPIN (Sandwich Loop)

Celery vase 60.00
Champagne 80.00
Decanter w/stopper, qt. 90.00
Egg cup, clear 35.00
Goblet 45.00
Salt dip, master size 20.00
Sauce dish, amethyst, 4" d. 85.00
Sauce dish, clear, 4" d. 15.00
Spooner 50.00
Tumbler 55.00
Wine 55.00

HALLEY'S COMET

Celery vase 42.00
Goblet 32.00
Pitcher, water, tankard 92.00
Pitcher, water, tankard, engraved 95.00
Spooner 50.00
Wine 18.00

HAMILTON

Hamilton Compote

Butter dish, cov. 75.00
Compote, open, 7" d., low stand 46.00
Compote, open, 8" d., 5½" h. (ILLUS.) 70.00
Compote, open, 8" d., 8" h. 325.00
Creamer 60.00
Egg cup 38.00
Goblet 60.00
Honey dish, 3½" d. 20.00
Sauce dish 14.00
Spooner 40.00
Sugar bowl, cov. ..... 100.00 to 125.00
Tumbler, whiskey, applied handle 95.00

HAMILTON WITH LEAF

Butter dish, cov., frosted leaf 85.00

Compote, open, 8" d., 8" h., frosted leaf 95.00
Egg cup, clear leaf....63.00
Goblet, clear leaf 45.00
Sugar bowl, cov., clear leaf 95.00
Tumbler, bar, clear leaf....90.00
Tumbler, bar, frosted leaf 135.00
Tumbler, whiskey, handled, clear leaf 100.00
Wine 70.00

HAND (Pennsylvania, Early)

Hand Goblet

Bread plate, 8 x 10½" oval....38.00
Butter dish, cov....125.00
Cake stand, 12¼" d., engraved 175.00
Celery vase....42.00
Claret....85.00
Compote, cov., 7" d., high stand....95.00
Compote, open, 7¾" d., 6¾" h....40.00
Compote, open, 9" d., low stand....36.00
Creamer....40.00
Goblet (ILLUS.)....55.00
Marmalade jar, cov. 65.00
Mug....95.00
Pitcher, water....68.00
Relish....22.50
Sauce dish, 4½" d....12.50
Spooner....45.00
Sugar bowl, cov. 65.00
Tumbler, water....97.00
Wine 69.00

HARP

Bowl, 6" d....45.00
Goblet, flared sides (ILLUS. top next column) 950.00
Lamp, kerosene, hand-type w/applied finger grip ....125.00 to 175.00
Lamp, kerosene, hexagonal font, shaped base, brass collar, flint, 9½" h. 475.00
Salt dip, master size 70.00
Spillholder....100.00

Harp Goblet

HEARTS OF LOCH LAVEN - See Shuttle Pattern

HEART WITH THUMBPRINT

Heart with Thumbprint Creamer

Banana boat, 6½ x 7½" 115.00
Banana boat, 6½ x 11" 145.00
Barber bottle w/original pewter stopper 163.00
Berry set, master bowl & 5 sauce dishes,6 pcs. 125.00
Bowl, 7" sq., 3½" h....37.50
Bowl, 8" d., 2" h., flared rim 25.00
Bowl, 9" d....35.00
Bowl, 10" d., scalloped rim 45.00
Butter dish, cov....125.00
Cake stand, 9" d., 5" h. ....150.00 to 175.00
Card tray, clear 19.00
Card tray, green....55.00
Celery vase....53.00
Compote, open, jelly, two handles, green....25.00
Compote, open, 7½" d., 7½" h., scalloped rim....145.00
Cordial, 3" h. ....200.00 to 250.00
Creamer....39.00
Creamer, individual size, clear (ILLUS.) 30.00

Creamer & open sugar bowl, individual size, green w/gold, pr. 65.00
Cruet w/original stopper 65.00
Goblet, clear 55.00
Goblet, green w/gold 125.00
Ice bucket 75.00
Lamp, kerosene-type, green, 9" h. ..... 250.00 to 275.00
Nappy, heart-shaped 42.50
Olive dish 19.50
Plate, 6" d. 25.00
Plate, 10" d. 34.00
Plate, 12" d. 65.00
Punch cup, clear 22.50
Rose bowl, 3¾" d. 55.00
Sauce dish 15.00
Spooner 55.00
Sugar bowl, cov., large 95.00
Sugar bowl, open, individual size, green w/gold 45.00
Syrup jug w/original pewter top 108.00
Syrup jug w/original pewter top, miniature, 4" h. ..... 100.00 to 125.00
Tray, 4¼ x 8¼" 30.00
Tumbler, water, clear w/gold 45.00
Vase, 6" h., trumpet-shaped, clear 41.00
Vase, 6" h., trumpet-shaped, green 75.00
Vase, 10" h., trumpet-shaped 65.00
Waste bowl 85.00
Wine, clear 48.00
Wine, green w/gold 135.00

HEAVY PANELED FINECUT (Paneled Diamond Cross)
Goblet, clear 28.00
Goblet, vaseline 35.00

HERCULES PILLAR (Pillar Variant)
Champagne 135.00
Egg cup, double 65.00
Goblet 55.00
Syrup jug w/pewter top, amber, 8" h. 125.00
Syrup jug w/original top, clear 85.00

HERO (*Called Ruby Rosette when ruby-stained*)
Berry set; master bowl & 5 sauce dishes; Ruby Rosette, 6 pcs. 165.00
Butter dish, cov., Ruby Rosette 51.00
Creamer, Ruby Rosette 40.00
Pitcher, clear, ½ gal. 65.00
Spooner, clear 15.00
Spooner, Ruby Rosette 62.00
Table set, Ruby Rosette, 4 pcs. 265.00
Tumbler, Ruby Rosette 39.00

HERRINGBONE (Herringbone with Star & Shield Motif)
Berry set, master bowl & 6 sauce dishes, 7 pcs. 125.00
Celery vase 30.00
Creamer 25.00
Goblet 20.00
Mustard jar, cov. 12.00
Pitcher, milk 85.00
Spooner 35.00
Sugar bowl, cov. 32.00

HERRINGBONE BAND
Goblet 20.00
Spooner, pedestal base, scalloped rim 22.00
Sugar bowl, open 20.00
Wine 22.00

HERRINGBONE WITH STAR & SHIELD MOTIF - See Herringbone Pattern

HICKMAN (Le Clede)

Hickman Creamer

Bowl, 6" d., green 25.00
Bowl, 8" d. 25.00
Butter dish, cov. 35.00
Cake stand, 8½" to 9½" d. 38.00
Celery dish, boat-shaped, green 22.00
Celery tray 18.00
Compote, cov., 5" d. 42.00
Compote, cov., 7" d., high stand 82.00
Compote, open, 8½" d., 12" h. 65.00
Compote, open, 9½" d., 8" h. 45.00
Condiment set, miniature, salt & pepper shakers & cruet w/original stopper on cloverleaf-shaped tray, 4 pcs. ..... 75.00 to 100.00
Creamer, clear w/gold 25.00
Creamer, green (ILLUS.) 27.00
Creamer & open sugar bowl, individual size, oval, green, pr. 38.00
Cruet w/triple pouring spout & faceted stopper 31.00
Goblet, clear 35.00
Goblet, green 85.00
Ice tub, clear 45.00
Ice tub, green 60.00
Pitcher, water 45.00
Plate, 6" d. 11.00
Punch cup, clear 8.00
Punch cup, green 18.50
Relish, green 22.50
Salt dip 22.50
Sauce dish, green 12.50
Sauce dish, ruby-stained 18.50

Sugar bowl, cov. 65.00
Toothpick holder 42.00
Vase, 8" h., trumpet-shaped, green 18.00
Vase, 10" h., green 37.50
Wine, clear 27.00
Wine, green 45.00

HIDALGO (Frosted Waffle)

Bowl, 9" sq., clear & frosted 24.00
Butter dish, cov. 50.00
Celery dish, boat-shaped, 13" l. 35.00
Celery vase, amber-stained 49.00
Celery vase, clear 30.00
Compote, open, 7" sq., high stand 45.00
Creamer 35.00
Goblet, clear 20.00
Goblet, engraved 22.00
Goblet, frosted 35.00
Goblet, ruby-stained 75.00
Pitcher, water, ...43.00
Sauce dish, handled 15.00
Sugar shaker w/original top 45.00
Tray, water 55.00
Tumbler, frosted 35.00
Waste bowl 25.00

HINOTO (Diamond Point with Panels)

Hinoto Creamer

Champagne 90.00
Creamer, applied handle (ILLUS.) 90.00
Egg cup, handled 45.00
Goblet 85.00
Tumbler, footed 47.50

HOBNAIL

*Butter dish, cov., clear 85.00
Celery vase, footed, square, clear 20.00
*Cologne bottle, amber, 6½" h. 37.50
*Cologne bottle, clear, 6½" h. 22.00
*Creamer, fluted top, applied handle, amber, 2 x 3" 25.00
Creamer, three-footed, blue 25.00
*Creamer, individual size, amber 31.00
*Cruet w/original stopper, 4½" h. 45.00
Egg cup, single 28.50
Egg cup, double 15.00
*Goblet 15.00
Mug, amber 30.00
Mug, blue 21.00
Mug, clear 8.00
Pitcher, 7" h., blue 80.00
Pitcher, 8" h., square top, amber 235.00
Pitcher, 8" h., square top, sapphire blue 265.00
Pitcher, water, blue 125.00
*Punch cup 22.50
*Rose bowl, 6" d., 5½" h. 85.00
Salt shaker w/original top, blue 35.00
Spooner, ruffled rim, amber 35.00
*Spooner, clear 30.00
Spooner, frosted 35.00
*Sugar bowl, cov. 20.00
*Toothpick holder, amber 39.00
*Toothpick holder, blue 25.00
Toothpick holder, vaseline 30.00
Tray, water, amber, 11½" d. 55.00
Tray, water, blue, 11½" d. 55.00
Tumbler, amber 30.00
Tumbler, seven-row, amber 20.00
*Tumbler, eight-row, amber 22.50
*Tumbler, ten-row, amber 30.00
*Tumbler, ten-row, blue 28.00
*Tumbler, clear 15.00
Tumbler, ten-row, ruby-stained 110.00
Tumbler, vaseline 38.00
*Vase, 5½" h., cone-shaped, ruffled rim, vaseline 45.00

Hobnail Wine

*Wine, amber 25.00
*Wine, clear (ILLUS.) 25.00
Wine, green 22.50

HOBNAIL WITH THUMBPRINT BASE

Butter dish, cov., child's, blue 95.00
Creamer, amber (ILLUS. top next page) 29.00
Creamer, blue 35.00
Creamer, child's, amber 20.00
Pitcher, 7" h., clear 30.00
Pitcher, 7" h., ruby-stained rim 65.00
Pitcher, 8" h., blue 80.00
Spooner, blue 35.00

Hobnail w/Thumbprint Base Creamer

Sugar bowl, cov., child's, blue 85.00
Waste bowl, amber.....35.00
Waste bowl, blue 35.00

HONEYCOMB

*Butter dish, cov., non-flint, clear.....45.00
Butter dish, cov., non-flint, clear w/gold 75.00
Cake stand, 9" d., 5¾" h., cable border 35.00
Celery vase, flint.....60.00
Celery vase, non-flint.....22.00
Celery vase w/frosted Roman Key etching, flint.....75.00
Celery vase, New York Honeycomb, flint 45.00
Celery vase, New York Honeycomb, non-flint 28.00
Champagne, flint 40.00
*Champagne, non-flint.....30.00
Claret, flint 50.00
Claret, New York Honeycomb, flint.....45.00
Compote, open, 7" d., 7" h., flint.....55.00
Compote, open, 8" d., 6¼" h., flint.....110.00
*Creamer, non-flint 45.00
Decanter w/bar lip, flint, 10½" h.....110.00
Decanter w/original stopper, flint, 13" h.....110.00
Egg cup, flint.....30.00
Egg cup, New York Honeycomb, flint...30.00
Goblet, flint 36.00
Goblet, flint, engraved 65.00
*Goblet, non-flint.....14.00
Goblet, Laredo Honeycomb.....45.00
Goblet, New York Honeycomb, flint.....22.00
Mug, flint.....28.00
Mug, child's.....35.00
Mustard pot, w/original pewter lid, etched, flint 75.00
Pitcher, milk, flint 90.00
Pitcher, water, 8½" h., molded handle, polished pontil, flint .....150.00 to 175.00
*Salt & pepper shakers w/original tops, non-flint, pr.....75.00
Sauce dish, flint 12.50
Spillholder, flint 40.00
Spooner, non-flint 23.00
Tumbler, bar 24.00
Tumbler, Vernon Honeycomb, flint.....65.00
Wine, flint.....35.00
*Wine, non-flint 10.00

HORN OF PLENTY (McKee's Comet)

Horn of Plenty Spillholder

Bar bottle w/original stopper, qt.....150.00
Bowl, 7½" d.....70.00
Bowl, 8" oval 110.00
Butter dish, cov.....125.00
Butter pat.....16.00
Celery vase.....200.00
Champagne 195.00
Compote, cov., 6¼" d., 7½" h. 250.00
Compote, open, 6" d.....75.00
Compote, open, 7" d., 3" h.....125.00
Compote, open, 7" d., 5½" h.....225.00
Compote, open, 7" d., 7½" h., waffle base 110.00
Compote, open, 8" d., 6" h.....130.00
Compote, open, 8" d., 8" h.....124.00
Compote, open, 9" d., low stand.....100.00
Compote, open, 9" d., 8½" h.....195.00
Compote, open, 10½" d., 9¾" h.....350.00
Creamer, applied handle, 7" h. 158.00
Creamer & cov. sugar bowl, pr. 325.00
Decanter, bar lip, pt. 110.00
Decanter w/original stopper, pt. 150.00
Decanter w/original stopper, qt. 175.00
Dish, 6¾ x 10", 2¼" h. 140.00
Egg cup, 3¾" h. 48.00
*Goblet.....73.50
*Hat whimsey.....350.00
Honey dish.....18.00
*Lamp, w/whale oil burner, all-glass, 11" h.....200.00 to 250.00
Peppersauce bottle w/stopper.....168.00
Plate, 6" d., canary yellow 247.50
Plate, 6" d., clear 95.00
Relish, 5 x 7" oval 95.00
Salt dip, master size, oval.....85.00
Sauce dish, 3½" to 5" d. 17.00
Spillholder, 4½" h. (ILLUS.) 80.00

Sugar bowl, cov. 120.00
*Tumbler, water, 3⅝" h. 85.00
Tumbler, whiskey, 3" h. 130.00
Tumbler, whiskey, handled 220.00
Wine 175.00

HORSESHOE (Good Luck or Prayer Rug)

Horseshoe Goblet

Bowl, cov., 5 x 8" oval, flat, triple horseshoe finial 295.00
Bowl, open, 7" d., footed 47.50
Bowl, open, 5 x 8" oval, footed 30.00
Bowl, open, 6 x 9" oval 27.50
*Bread tray, single horseshoe handles 50.00
Bread tray, double horseshoe handles 87.00
Butter dish, cov. 115.00
Cake stand, 7" d. 35.00
Cake stand, 8" d., 6½" h. 76.00
Cake stand, 9" d., 6½" h. 69.00
Cake stand, 10" d. 87.00
Cake stand, 10¾" d. 127.00
Celery vase 87.00
Cheese dish, cov., w/woman churning butter in base 275.00
Compote, cov., 7" d., high stand 75.00
Compote, cov., 8" d., low stand 210.00
Compote, cov., 8" d., high stand 175.00
Creamer 35.00
Doughnut stand 95.00
Goblet, knob stem 40.00
Goblet, plain stem (ILLUS.) 27.50
Marmalade jar, cov. 225.00
Pitcher, milk 90.00
Pitcher, water 128.00
Plate, 7" d. 45.00
Plate, 8" d. 80.00
Plate, 10" d. 86.00
Relish, 5 x 8" 5.00
Salt dip, individual size 17.50
Salt dip, master size, horseshoe shape 100.00
Sauce dish, flat or footed 14.00
Spooner 35.00
Wine 295.00

HUBER

Ale glass 45.00
Celery vase 50.00
Champagne, straight sides 45.00
Egg cup, single 30.00
Egg cup, double, engraved 90.00
Goblet, barrel-shaped, clear 25.00
Goblet, engraved, clear 42.50
Goblet, straight-sided, clear 25.00
Spooner 28.50
Sugar bowl, cov. 56.00
Tumbler, bar 22.50
Wine, clear 15.00
Wine, engraved 40.00

HUMMINGBIRD (Flying Robin or Bird & Fern)

Butter dish, cov., blue 110.00
Butter dish, cov., clear 49.00
Celery vase 32.50
Creamer, amber ....75.00 to 100.00
Creamer, blue 85.00
Creamer, clear 45.00
Goblet, amber 65.00
Goblet, blue 65.00
Goblet, clear 50.00
Pitcher, water, amber 150.00
Pitcher, water, clear 90.00
Spooner, amber 40.00
Spooner, clear 30.00
Sugar bowl, cov., blue 110.00
Tray, water, amber 155.00
Tray, water, clear 50.00
Tumbler, amber 60.00
Wine 64.00

ILLINOIS

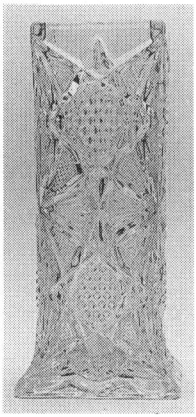

Illinois Straw Jar

Basket, applied handle, 7 x 7" 95.00
Bowl, 6" sq. 26.00
*Butter dish, cov., 7" sq. 75.00
Celery tray 35.00
*Celery vase 37.50
Cheese dish, cov., square 60.00
Creamer, small 25.00

Creamer, large....40.00
Cruet w/original stopper....110.00
Doughnut stand, 7½" sq., 4¼" h. 65.00
Pitcher, water, tankard....75.00
Pitcher, water, tankard, w/glass lid 125.00
Pitcher, water, squatty, silver plate rim, clear....95.00
Pitcher, water, squatty, silver plate rim, green....175.00
Plate, 7" sq. 25.00
Relish, 3 x 8½"....17.50
Sauce dish....14.00
Soda fountain (straw-holder) jar, cov., 12½" h. 250.00
Soda fountain (straw-holder) jar, no lid, 12½" h. (ILLUS.)....110.00
Sugar shaker w/original pewter top 65.00
Toothpick holder....30.00
Vase, 6" h. 25.00
Vase, 9" h., 4" d. 41.00

INDIANA
Cruet w/original stopper....28.00
Spooner....20.00
Toothpick holder....25.00

INDIANA SWIRL - See Feather Pattern

INVERTED FERN

Inverted Fern Sugar Bowl

Bowl, 7" d....45.00
Butter dish, cov....85.00
Creamer, applied handle 150.00
Egg cup 38.00
*Goblet....46.00
Pitcher, water....360.00
Salt dip, master size, footed 40.00
Sauce dish, 4" d....17.50
Spooner....50.00
Sugar bowl, cov. (ILLUS.)....60.00
Wine 45.00

INVERTED LOOPS & FANS - See Maryland Pattern

IOWA (Paneled Zipper or Zippered Block)
Compote, jelly....24.00
Cruet w/original stopper....50.00
Lamp, kerosene-type....105.00
Olive dish, handled....22.50
Pitcher, water, gold trim....95.00
Punch cup....22.00
Salt & pepper shakers w/original tops, clear, pr. 45.00
Salt & pepper shakers w/original tops, ruby-stained, pr. 150.00
Sauce dish, flat....15.00
Toothpick holder, clear 21.00
Toothpick holder, ruby-stained 60.00
Wine 30.00
Wine, w/gold trim 35.00

IRISH COLUMN - See Broken Column Pattern

IVY IN SNOW

Ivy in Snow Sauce Dish

Bowl, 7" d....22.00
*Cake stand, 8" to 10" d....42.00
*Celery vase, 8" h. 35.00
*Creamer, clear 25.00
Creamer, ruby-stained ivy sprigs....85.00
*Goblet, clear....50.00
Goblet, green & red ivy sprigs & gold band at top & base....175.00
Honey dish, cov., amber-stained ivy sprigs 87.50
Plate, 10" d. 30.00
*Sauce dish, flat or footed (ILLUS.) 12.00
*Spooner, clear....28.00
Sugar bowl, cov., clear 30.00
Sugar bowl, cov., ruby-stained 135.00
Syrup jug w/original top, clear 70.00
Syrup jug w/original top, ruby-stained ivy sprigs....295.00
Tumbler, clear....30.00
Tumbler, ruby-stained....40.00
Wine, clear....38.00

JACOB'S LADDER (Maltese)
Bowl, 7½ x 10¾" oval 25.00
Bowl, 9" d., flat....40.00
Butter dish, cov., Maltese Cross finial ..55.00
Cake stand, 8" to 12" d. 52.00
Celery vase....38.00

Compote, cov., 8¼" d., high stand.....128.00
Compote, open, 7" d., high stand.....35.00
Compote, open, 8" d., high stand.....42.00
Compote, open, 10" d., 5" h.....42.00
Compote, open, 10" d., high stand.....55.00
*Creamer.....35.00
Cruet w/original stopper, footed.....85.00
Dish, 8" oval.....18.00
Goblet.....65.00
Honey dish, open.....9.00
Marmalade jar, cov.....100.00 to 135.00
Pickle dish, Maltese Cross handle.....18.00
Pitcher, water, applied handle.....185.00
Plate, 6" d., amber.....105.00
Plate, 6" d., clear.....35.00
Plate, 6" d., purple.....110.00
Relish, Maltese Cross handles, 5½ x 9½" oval.....20.00
Salt dip, master size, footed.....25.00
Sauce dish, flat or footed, blue.....20.00
Sauce dish, flat or footed, canary.....72.00
Sauce dish, flat or footed, clear.....8.00
Spooner.....25.00
Sugar bowl, cov.....65.00
Syrup jug w/metal top.....100.00 to 125.00
Wine.....32.00

JEWEL & CRESCENT - See Tennessee Pattern

JEWEL & DEWDROP - See Kansas Pattern

JEWEL & FESTOON (Loop & Jewel)
Butter dish, cov.....60.00
Compote, 6½" d.....60.00
Creamer.....24.00
Creamer, individual size.....35.00
Relish, 4¼ x 8¼" rectangle.....17.00
Table set, creamer, cov. sugar & cov. butter dish, 3 pcs.....125.00

JEWEL BAND - See Scalloped Tape Pattern

JEWELED DIAMOND AND FAN - See Tacoma Pattern

JEWELED MOON & STAR (Moon & Star with Waffle)
*Banana boat, w/amber & blue staining.....225.00
Butter dish, cov., w/amber & blue staining.....70.00
Cake stand, w/amber & blue staining, 10" d.....235.00
Carafe.....38.00
Celery vase, clear.....25.00
Celery vase, frosted w/amber & blue staining.....82.50
*Compote, open, 9" d., high stand, clear.....52.00
*Goblet.....38.00
Pitcher, water, bulbous, applied handle, w/amber & blue staining.....175.00
Salt shaker w/original top, w/amber & blue staining.....125.00
Spooner, w/amber & blue staining.....48.00
Tumbler, clear.....22.50
Tumbler, w/amber & blue staining.....60.00
*Wine.....42.50

JOB'S TEARS - See Art Pattern

JUMBO and JUMBO & BARNUM

Jumbo Marmalade Jar

Butter dish & cover w/frosted elephant finial, oblong.....700.00
Castor holder (no bottles).....100.00
Creamer.....185.00
Creamer, w/Barnum head at handle...295.00
Marmalade jar w/Barnum head handles & cover w/frosted elephant finial (ILLUS.).....450.00
Spoon rack.....600.00 to 750.00
Sugar bowl w/Barnum head handles & cover w/frosted elephant finial.....350.00 to 450.00

KAMONI - See Pennsylvania Pattern

KANSAS (Jewel & Dewdrop)
Banana bowl.....55.00
Bowl, 7½" d.....22.00
Bowl, 8½" d.....35.00
Bread tray, "Our Daily Bread", 10½" oval.....42.50
Butter dish, cov.....65.00
Cake stand, 8" to 10" d.....48.00
Cake tray, "Cake Plate," 10½" oval.....78.00
Celery vase.....45.00
Compote, cov., 7" d., high stand.....125.00
Compote, open, jelly, 5" d.....42.00
Compote, open, 8" d., high stand.....57.50
Creamer.....47.00
Goblet.....62.50
Mug, small, 3½" h.....30.00

Pitcher, milk 72.00
Pitcher, water....60.00
Relish, 8½" oval....28.00
Sauce dish, 4" d....13.50
Spooner....75.00
Toothpick holder....55.00
Tumbler, water, footed....55.00
Wine 55.00

KENTUCKY

Kentucky Sauce Dish

Celery tray 25.00
Nappy, handled, green 15.00
Punch cup, clear....7.00
Punch cup, green 28.00
Sauce dish, footed, blue w/gold (ILLUS.) 32.00
Sauce dish, footed, clear....7.00
Sauce dish, footed, green....14.00
Toothpick holder, clear 30.00
Toothpick holder, green....100.00
Tumbler, green 50.00
Wine, clear....24.00
Wine, green 45.00

KING'S CROWN (Also see Ruby Thumbprint)

Banana stand 130.00
Bowl, berry or fruit, 8¼" d., flared rim ...27.00
Bowl, 9¼" oval, scalloped rim, round base 67.50
Butter dish, cov....65.00
*Cake stand, 9" d....85.00
Cake stand, 10" d. 85.00
Castor bottle, w/original top 16.50
Castor set, salt & pepper shakers, oil bottle w/stopper & cov. mustard jar in original frame, 4 pcs. 325.00
Celery vase, engraved....60.00
Celery vase, plain 48.00
*Compote, cov., 5" d., 5½" h., engraved....30.00
Compote, cov., 7" d., 7" h. 95.00
Compote, cov., 8" d., 12" h. 92.00
Compote, cov., 11" d. 145.00
Compote, open, jelly....45.00
Compote, open, 7½" d., high stand 42.00
Compote, open, 8½" d., high stand 85.00
*Cordial....50.00
Creamer, clear....40.00
*Creamer, individual size, clear 16.50
Creamer, individual size, clear w/gold ..29.50
Creamer, individual size, w/green thumbprints 35.00
*Cup and saucer....55.00
*Goblet, clear....30.00
Goblet, clear w/engraved moose, doe & dog 95.00
Goblet, w/green thumbprints 25.00
Goblet, w/green thumbprints, souvenir 18.00
Lamp, kerosene-type, low hand-type w/finger hold 120.00
*Lamp, kerosene-type, stem base, 10" h....180.00
Mustard jar, cov. 62.00
Pitcher, 5" h., souvenir....40.00
Pitcher, tankard, 8½" h. 110.00
Pitcher, tankard, 13" h., engraved 122.50
Pitcher, tankard, 13" h., plain....195.00
Pitcher, bulbous....125.00
*Plate, 8" sq. 70.00
Punch bowl, footed....225.00 to 250.00
Punch cup....22.50
Relish, 7" oval....10.00
Salt dip, individual size 37.50
Salt & pepper shakers w/original tops, pr....65.00
Sauce dish, boat-shaped....22.00
*Sauce dish, round 17.00
Spooner....38.00
Toothpick holder, clear 28.00
Toothpick holder, clear, souvenir....50.00
Toothpick holder, rose stain, souvenir..30.00
Tray, square 29.00
*Tumbler, clear 22.00
Water set, bulbous pitcher & 6 goblets, 7 pcs. ....250.00 to 300.00
*Wine, clear 25.00
Wine, cobalt blue....100.00 to 150.00
Wine, cobalt blue, souvenir 165.00
Wine, w/green thumbprints....15.00

KLONDIKE (Amberette or English Hobnail Cross)

Klondike Butter Dish

Bowl, 6" sq., frosted w/amber cross ...200.00
Bowl, 7¼" sq., scalloped top, clear w/amber cross 185.00
Bowl, master berry or fruit, 8" sq., clear w/amber cross 85.00

Bowl, master berry or fruit, 8" sq., frosted w/amber cross 250.00
Bowl, 11" sq., frosted w/amber cross 255.00
Bread plate, clear w/amber cross, 8½ x 11" oval 120.00
Butter dish, cov., clear 150.00
Butter dish, cov., clear w/amber cross .....225.00 to 250.00
Butter dish, cov., frosted w/amber cross (ILLUS.) .....450.00 to 475.00
Butter pat, clear w/amber cross 35.00
Celery vase, clear w/amber cross 138.00
Celery vase, frosted w/amber cross ...225.00
Champagne, frosted w/amber cross...700.00
Condiment set: tray, cruet, salt & pepper shakers; frosted w/amber cross, 4 pcs. 1,350.00
Creamer, clear w/amber cross 90.00
Creamer & open sugar bowl, frosted w/amber cross, pr. 200.00
Cruet w/original stopper, clear w/amber cross 425.00
Cruet w/original stopper, frosted w/amber cross .....700.00 to 750.00
Dish, oval, flat, shallow, clear w/amber cross 130.00
Goblet, clear 95.00
Goblet, clear w/amber cross 195.00
Jam dish, frosted w/amber cross, 4¾" sq., 5½" h., in silver plate holder 125.00
Pitcher, water, clear 50.00
Pitcher, water, clear w/amber cross .....250.00 to 275.00
Punch cup, frosted w/amber cross 85.00
Relish, boat-shaped, clear, 4 x 9" 40.00
Relish, boat-shaped, clear w/amber cross, 4 x 9" 115.00
Relish, boat-shaped, frosted w/amber cross, 4 x 9" 146.00
Salt shaker w/original top, clear w/ambercross 68.00
Salt shaker w/original top, frosted w/amber cross .....75.00 to 100.00
Salt & pepper shakers w/original tops, clear 150.00
Salt & pepper shakers w/original tops, frosted w/amber cross, pr. .....200.00 to 250.00
Sauce dish, flat or footed, clear w/amber cross 22.50
Sauce dish, flat or footed, frosted w/amber cross 72.00
Spooner, clear 40.00
Spooner, clear w/amber cross 85.00
Spooner, frosted w/amber cross .....275.00 to 300.00
Sugar bowl, cov., clear 95.00
Sugar bowl, cov., clear w/amber cross, 6¾" h. 165.00
Sugar bowl, open, clear w/amber cross 75.00
Table set, frosted w/amber cross, 4 pcs. 950.00
Toothpick holder, clear 125.00
Toothpick holder, clear w/amber cross 375.00
Tray, clear w/amber cross, 11" sq. 45.00
Tumbler, clear 25.00
Tumbler, clear w/amber cross 90.00
Tumbler, frosted w/amber cross 145.00
Vase, 7" h., trumpet-shaped, clear 35.00
Vase, 8" h., trumpet-shaped, clear 50.00
Vase, 8" h., trumpet-shaped, clear w/amber cross 130.00

LACY MEDALLION - See Colorado Pattern

LEAF - See Maple Leaf Pattern

LEAF & DART (Double Leaf & Dart)

Bowl, 8¼" d., low foot 20.00
Butter dish, cov., pedestal base 90.00
Celery vase, pedestal base 35.00
Creamer, applied handle 45.00
Egg cup 21.00
Goblet 28.00
Honey dish, 3½" d. 5.00
Lamp, kerosene-type, applied handle ..75.00
Pitcher, water, applied handle 95.00
Salt dip, cov., master size 95.00
Salt dip, open, master size 32.00
Sauce dish 9.00
Spooner 25.00
Sugar bowl, cov. 55.00
Sugar bowl, open 25.00
Tumbler, footed 30.00
Wine 36.00

LE CLEDE - See Hickman Pattern

LIBERTY BELL

Liberty Bell Plate

Bowl, berry or fruit, 8" d., footed 95.00
*Bread platter, "Signer's", twig handles 100.00

Bread platter, w/thirteen original states, twig handles, 8¼ x 13" 85.00
Butter dish, cov. 100.00
Butter dish, cov., miniature 150.00
Compote, open, 8" d. 75.00
Creamer, applied handle 110.00
Creamer, miniature 86.00
*Goblet 45.00
Mug, miniature, 2" h. 125.00
Mug, snake handle 300.00
Pickle dish, closed handles, 1776-1876w/thirteen original states, 5½ x 9¼"oval 50.00
Plate, 6" d., closed handles, scalloped rim, w/thirteen original states 75.00
Plate, 6" d., no states, dated 62.50
Plate, 8" d., closed handles, scalloped rim, w/thirteen original states 60.00
Plate, 10" d., closed handles, scalloped rim, w/thirteen original states (ILLUS.) 95.00
Relish, shell handles, 7 x 11¼" 70.00
Salt dip 55.00
Salt shaker w/original pewter top 110.00
Sauce dish 25.00
Spooner 62.00
Sugar bowl, cov. 105.00
Table set, 4 pcs. ..... 400.00 to 450.00

LILY-OF-THE-VALLEY

Bowl, 5½ x 8" oval 32.50
Butter dish, cov. 115.00
Celery vase 68.00
Champagne 39.00
Compote, cov., 8" d., low stand 128.00
Compote, cov., 8½" d., high stand 130.00
Compote, open, 7" d., low stand 47.50
Creamer, three-footed, molded handle 65.00
Creamer, plain base, applied handle 58.00
Cruet w/original stopper ..... 150.00 to 200.00
Egg cup 43.00
Goblet 75.00
Pitcher, milk, applied handle 112.00
Pitcher, water, bulbous, applied handle 120.00
Relish, 4½ x 7" 25.00
Relish, 5½ x 8" 28.00
Salt dip, open, master size, three-footed 60.00
Sauce dish 17.50
Spooner, plain base 45.00
Spooner, three-footed 75.00
Wine 155.00

LINCOLN DRAPE & LINCOLN DRAPE WITH TASSEL

Compote, open, 6¾" d., 5¼" h. 85.00
Compote, open, 7⅛" d., 5" h. 110.00
Compote, open, 7½" d., 3½" h. 50.00
Compote, open, 8" d., medium stand 110.00
Compote, open, 8¼" d., 5⅛" h., domed foot 87.50
Creamer 200.00

Lincoln Drape Egg Cup

Egg cup (ILLUS.) 75.00
Goblet ..... 125.00 to 150.00
Goblet w/tassel ..... 225.00 to 275.00
Salt dip, master size 55.00
Salt dip, master size, w/tassel 125.00
Sauce dish, 4" d. 22.50
Spillholder 54.00
Sugar bowl, cov. 165.00
Syrup pitcher w/original pewter top, clear 150.00
Syrup pitcher w/original top, opaque white 600.00

LION - See Atlanta Pattern

LION, FROSTED - See Frosted Lion Pattern

LION'S LEG - See Alaska Pattern

LOCUST - See Grasshopper Pattern

LOG CABIN

Log Cabin Compote

Butter dish, cov. 295.00
Compote, cov. (ILLUS.) 350.00

Compote, cov., "Lutteds Cough Drops" 325.00
*Creamer, 4¼" h. 132.00
Sauce dish, flat oblong 85.00
*Spooner, clear 125.00
Spooner, sapphire blue 395.00
*Sugar bowl, cov., 8" h., clear 250.00

LOOP (Seneca Loop)
Butter dish, cov., flint 195.00
Celery vase, flint 75.00
Celery vase, non-flint 27.50
Compote, cov., 7" d., 9" h., flint 75.00
Compote, open, 7" d., 5¾" h., flint 94.00
Compote, open, 7⅝" d., 6¾" h., flint 65.00
Compote, open, lobed rim, 8" d., 6" h., canary, flint 1,760.00
Compote, open, 8" d., 6" h., non-flint 75.00
Compote, open, 8" d., 8" h., flint 85.00
Compote, open, 8" d., 8¼" h., milk white w/fiery opalescence 600.00
Compote, open, 9¼" d., 6½" h., flint 65.00
Compote, open, 9½" d., 7" h., flint 275.00
Compote, open, 10" d., 8" h., flint ....275.00 to 300.00
Compote, open, 12¼" d., 9½" h., flint 400.00
Cordial, 2¾ h., non-flint 35.00
Creamer, clear, flint 60.00
Decanter, w/original stopper, flint, pt. 130.00
Egg cup, flint 22.00
Goblet, flint 25.00
Goblet, non-flint 12.00
Pitcher, water, applied handle, flint 195.00
Salt dip, master size, flint 25.00
Spooner, flint 32.00
Sugar bowl, cov., flint 100.00
Tumbler, footed, non-flint 35.00
Vase, 9⅝" h., flint 75.00

LOOP & DART

Loop & Dart Compote

Bowl, 5 x 8" oval, round ornaments 37.50
Butter dish, cov., diamond ornaments, non-flint 38.00
Butter dish, cov., round ornaments, flint 80.00
Butter pat, round ornaments 35.00
Celery vase, diamond ornaments 32.00
Celery vase, round ornaments, flint 50.00
Celery vase, round ornaments, non-flint 35.00
Champagne, round ornaments, flint 85.00
Compote, cov., 6½" d., high stand, round ornaments 90.00
Compote, cov., 7" d., 10" h., diamond ornaments 65.00
Compote, cov., 8" d., 10" h., round ornaments (ILLUS.) 95.00
Compote, cov., 8" d., low stand, round ornaments 74.00
Creamer, applied handle, round ornaments 45.00
Egg cup, round ornaments 24.00
Goblet, diamond ornaments 50.00
Goblet, round ornaments 30.00
Pitcher, water, round ornaments 125.00
Plate, 6" d., round ornaments 35.00
Salt dip, master size, round ornaments 45.00
Spooner, diamond ornaments 15.00
Spooner, round ornaments 32.00
Sugar bowl, cov., diamond ornaments 45.00
Sugar bowl, cov., round ornaments, flint 75.00
Tumbler, flat or footed, diamond ornaments 25.00
Wine, diamond ornaments 32.00
Wine, round ornaments 45.00

LOOP & JEWEL - See Jewel & Festoon Pattern

LOOP & PILLAR - See Michigan Pattern

LOOP WITH DEWDROPS
Celery vase 30.00
Compote, cov., 9" d. 55.00
Creamer 50.00
Goblet 35.00
Sugar bowl, cov. 25.00
Wine 27.00

LOOP WITH STIPPLED PANELS - See Texas Pattern

LOOPS & DROPS - See New Jersey Pattern

LOOPS & FANS - See Maryland Pattern

LOUISIANA
Bowl, cov., round, 6" d. 125.00
Bowl, open, square, 7" w. 20.00
Cake stand, high stand, 10" d. 68.00

Compote, open, deep bowl, jelly, 5½" d. 18.00
Compote, open, deep bowl, 6" d. 19.00

Louisiana Goblet

Goblet (ILLUS.) 45.00
Mug 12.00
Spooner 38.00
Tumbler, water 28.00

MAGNET & GRAPE

Magnet & Grape Goblet

Champagne, frosted leaf, flint 176.00
Champagne, stippled leaf, non-flint 45.00
Cordial, 4" h., frosted leaf, flint 150.00
Creamer, stippled leaf, non-flint 35.00
Egg cup, clear leaf, non-flint 33.00
*Egg cup, frosted leaf, flint 83.00
Goblet, clear leaf, non-flint 18.00
*Goblet, frosted leaf, flint (ILLUS.) 77.00
Goblet, frosted leaf & American Shield, flint 375.00
Goblet, stippled leaf, non-flint 30.00
Salt dip, master size, footed, non-flint ..24.00
Sauce dish, frosted leaf, flint 18.50
Spooner, frosted leaf, flint 68.00
Spooner, stippled leaf, non-flint 28.00
Sugar bowl, cov., frosted leaf & American Shield, flint 325.00
*Wine, frosted leaf, flint 225.00

MAINE (Stippled Flower Panels)

Bowl, 6" d. 30.00
Bread plate 26.00
Butter dish, cov. 55.00
Cake stand, 8½" d., green 65.00
Compote, open, jelly, 4¾" d. 28.00
Compote, open, 7" d., clear 32.00
Compote, open, 7" d., green 52.00
Compote, open, 8" d., clear 35.00
Compote, open, 8" d., green 42.50
Creamer 28.00
Pitcher, water, clear 85.00
Pitcher, water, w/red & green stain 115.00
Platter, oval 38.00
Relish, 7¼" l. 14.00
Salt & pepper shakers, w/original tops, pr. 63.00
Spooner 32.00
Syrup pitcher w/original top 70.00
Table set, 4 pcs. 275.00
Wine, clear 42.50
Wine, green 65.00

MALTESE - See Jacob's Ladder Pattern

MANHATTAN

*Basket, applied handle, 7 x 10", 11½" h. 145.00
*Bowl, 8¼" d. 25.00
Bowl, 9" d. 22.00
Bowl, 10½" d. 15.00
Bowl, master berry, pink-stained 40.00
Bread plate 20.00
Butter dish, cov. 48.00
Cake stand ....35.00 to 40.00
Carafe, water, pink-stained 65.00
Celery tray 26.00
Compote, open, large 47.50
Cracker jar, cov., pink-stained 55.00
Creamer 27.50
Creamer, individual size 25.00
Creamer & open sugar bowl, pr. 42.00
Cruet w/original stopper 47.50
*Goblet 25.00
Marmalade jar, cov. 37.50
Pickle castor in silver plate frame, w/tongs 110.00
Pitcher, water, pink-stained 100.00
Pitcher, water, w/silver rim 90.00
Plate, 5" d., pink-stained 25.00
*Plate, 10¾" d. 20.00
*Punch cup 20.00
Salt shaker w/original top 24.50
Sauce dish, flat, amber or pink-stained 12.50
*Sauce dish, flat, clear 12.00
Spooner 20.00
Toothpick holder, blue-stained 55.00
Toothpick holder, clear 32.00
Toothpick holder, purple-stained eyes..30.00
*Tumbler 12.50

Tumbler, clear w/gold trim 25.00
Tumbler, footed 30.00
Tumbler, pink-stained 16.00
Vase, 6" h. 20.00
*Wine 25.00

MAPLE LEAF (Leaf)
Berry set: oval master bowl & 10 footed sauce dishes; canary yellow, 11 pcs. 145.00
Bowl, 5½" oval, clear 24.00
Bowl, 9" oval, footed 24.00
Bowl, 6 x 10" oval, footed, blue 60.00
Bowl, 6 x 10" oval, footed, canary yellow 55.00
Bowl, 6 x 10" oval, footed, clear 52.00
Bowl, 10" sq., canary yellow 48.00
Bread plate, Grant, "Let Us Have Peace," blue, 9½" d. 85.00
Bread tray, canary yellow, 9¼ x 13¼" ..55.00
Bread tray, clear, 9¼ x 13¼" 32.00
Bread tray, clear & frosted, 9¼ x 13¼" 40.00
Celery vase 36.00
Compote, cov., 8" d., four log feet, clear & frosted 175.00
Compote, cov., 9" d., high stand, canary yellow 163.00
Compote, open, 8 x 10½" 65.00
*Creamer, canary yellow 65.00
Goblet, canary yellow 75.00
*Goblet, clear 38.00
Pitcher, milk, canary yellow 74.00
*Pitcher, water 45.00
Plate, 9" d., canary yellow 37.50
Platter, 10½" oval, blue 55.00
Platter, 10½" oval, canary yellow 39.00
Sauce dish, leaf-shaped, canary yellow, 5½" l. 16.00
*Spooner, blue 45.00
Spooner, green 45.00
Sugar bowl, cov., canary yellow 75.00
*Toothpick holder 30.00
Tumbler, clear, frosted 40.00
Tumbler, clear, plain 35.00
Waste bowl, canary yellow 30.00
Wine 28.00

MARYLAND (Inverted Loops & Fans or Loops & Fans)
Banana bowl, flat, 5 x 11¼" 36.00
Bread platter 25.00
Cake stand, 9" d. 65.00
Celery vase 30.00
Compote, cov., jelly 32.00
Compote, cov., 7" d., high stand 35.00
Compote, open, medium 28.00
Dish, oval, large 25.00
Goblet (ILLUS. top next column) 33.00
Pickle dish 14.00
Pitcher, milk 42.00
Pitcher, water, clear 48.50
Pitcher, water, ruby-stained 105.00

Maryland Goblet

Plate, 7" d. 22.50
Platter 30.00
Relish 30.00
Sauce dish 18.00
Syrup pitcher 55.00
Toothpick holder 35.00
Tumbler 28.00
Wine 50.00

MASCOTTE
Bowl, cov., 7" d. 90.00
Butter dish, cov., engraved 85.00
Butter pat 12.50
Cake basket w/handle 70.00
Cake stand, 10" d. 48.00
Celery vase 40.00
Cheese dish, cov. 65.00
Compote, cov., 5" d. 44.00
Compote, cov., 7" d. 45.00
Compote, cov., 8" d., 12" h. 90.00
Compote, open, jelly 20.00
Creamer 35.00
Goblet 30.00
Jar, cov., globe-type, embossed patent date, milk white 265.00
Pitcher, water 125.00
Salt shaker w/original top 14.00
Sauce dish, flat or footed, each 11.00
Spooner, clear 30.00
Spooner, vaseline 135.00
Sugar bowl, cov., engraved 48.00
Sugar bowl, cov., plain 39.00
Tray, water, clear 58.50
Tray, water, engraved 75.00
Tumbler, clear 28.00
Tumbler, engraved 34.00
Wine, clear 26.00
Wine, engraved 35.00

MASSACHUSETTS
Banana boat, 6½ x 8½" 55.00
Bar bottle, bar lip, 11" h. 50.00
Bar bottle, green, 11" h. 60.00

Bar bottle w/original pewter top, 11" h. 80.00
Bowl, 6" sq. 18.00
Bowl, 8" l., pointed sides 37.50
Bowl, master berry, 9" sq. 32.00

Massachusetts Butter Dish

*Butter dish, cov., clear (ILLUS.) 55.00
Butter dish, cov., green 65.00
Champagne 45.00
Cologne bottle w/stopper 48.00
Cordial 45.00
Creamer 32.00
Cruet w/original stopper 42.00
Decanter w/stopper 88.00
Goblet 45.00
Mug, 3½" h., clear 20.00
Mug, 3½" h., clear w/gold trim 24.00
Plate, 6" sq., w/advertising 90.00
Plate, 8" sq. 35.00
Punch cup 14.00
Relish, 8½" l. 12.50
Rum jug, 5" h. 100.00
Sauce dish 15.00
Spooner 20.00
Sugar bowl, cov. 35.00
Toothpick holder 50.00
Tumbler, juice 19.00
Tumbler, water 25.00
Vase, 6½" h., trumpet-shaped, clear 22.00
Vase, 7" h., clear w/gold 24.00
Vase, 9" h., trumpet-shaped, clear 32.50
Vase, 9" h., trumpet-shaped, green 38.00
Vase, 10" h., trumpet-shaped, green 60.00
Whiskey shot glass, clear 16.00
Wine, blue 110.00
Wine, clear 35.00

MEDALLION

Cake stand, high stand, amber, 9¼" d. 40.00
Cake stand, high stand, 9¼" d. 36.00
Creamer, amber 35.00
Creamer, canary yellow 42.50
Creamer, clear 18.00
Goblet, amber 34.00
Goblet, green 45.00
Pitcher, water, amber, ½ gal. 65.00
Pitcher, water, blue, ½ gal. 75.00
Pitcher, water, clear, ½ gal. 85.00
Relish tray, amber 20.00
Spooner, green 40.00
Tumbler, water, green 35.00

MEDALLION SPRIG

Butter dish, cov., amethyst/clear 70.00
Cruet 265.00
Pitcher, water, green/clear 80.00
Syrup pitcher, green 345.00

MELROSE

Cake stand, 8" to 10" d. 29.50
Celery vase, ruby-stained 65.00
Compote, open, jelly, 5½" d. 29.00
Compote, open, 7" d., 7" h. 25.00
Goblet 20.00
Pitcher, milk 42.50
Pitcher, water 32.00
Salt shaker w/original top 20.00
Wine 18.00

MICHIGAN (Paneled Jewel or Loop & Pillar)

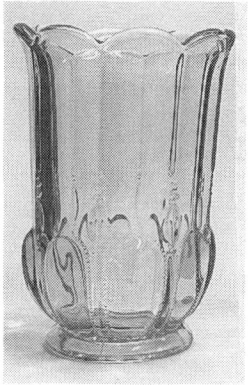

Michigan Celery Vase

Bowl, 8" d., clear 36.00
Bowl, 8" d., pink-stained w/gold trim 75.00
Bowl, 8¾" d., scalloped & flared rim 28.00
Bowl, 10" d. 35.00
Butter dish, cov., blue-stained 175.00
Butter dish, cov., clear 60.00
Butter dish, cov., pink-stained 375.00
Butter dish, cov., yellow-stained, enameled florals ....150.00 to 175.00
Celery vase (ILLUS.) 45.00
Compote, open, jelly, 4½" d., blue-stained 125.00
Compote, open, 8½" d., high stand 65.00
Compote, open, 9¼" d. 85.00
Compote, open, flared, 9¾" d., pink-stained, enameled florals 425.00
Creamer, 4" h. 30.00
Creamer, individual size 45.00
Creamer, individual size, yellow-stained, enameled florals 55.00
Goblet, clear 35.00
Goblet, clear w/blue stain 40.00
Goblet, clear w/gold 40.00

Goblet, clear w/green stain, w/enamel 49.00
Mug, clear 25.00
Mug, yellow-stained, enameled florals 28.00
Pitcher, water, 8" h. 48.00
Pitcher, water, tankard, 12" h., clear 75.00
Pitcher, water, tankard, 12" h., pink-stained 245.00
Plate, tea, 6" d., yellow-stained w/pink florals 25.00
Punch cup, clear 6.00
Punch cup, enameled decoration 25.00
Punch cup, pink-stained 30.00
Relish, clear 18.00
Relish, pink-stained 24.00
Salt shaker w/original top 27.50
Salt & pepper shakers w/original tops, individual size, pr. 75.00
Sauce dish, clear 13.00
Sauce dish, yellow-stained 19.50
Spooner, blue-stained 125.00
Spooner, clear 40.00
Spooner, pink-stained 71.00
Sugar bowl, cov., blue-stained 150.00
Sugar bowl, cov., clear 75.00
Sugar bowl, cov., pink-stained, gold trim ....100.00 to 125.00
Sugar bowl, cov., child's, 4¾" h. 40.00
Sugar bowl, individual size 22.00
Syrup jug w/pewter top 165.00
Table set, pink-stained, 4 pcs. ....350.00 to 375.00
Toddy mug, tall 45.00
Toothpick holder, blue-stained on top w/yellow enameled dots ....100.00 to 125.00
*Toothpick holder, clear 37.50
Toothpick holder, clear, enameled florals 45.00
Toothpick holder, pink-stained, gold trim ....275.00 to 300.00
Toothpick holder, yellow-stained 55.00
Toothpick holder, yellow-stained, enameled florals 90.00
Tumbler, clear 28.00
Tumbler, pink-stained, gold trim 55.00
Tumbler, yellow-stained, enameled florals 35.00
Vase, 6" h., clear 35.00
Vase, 6" h., pink-stained, enameled florals 40.00
Vase, 8" h., green-stained, white enameled dots 60.00
Vase, 12" h. 24.00
Waste bowl 68.00
Water set: pitcher & 3 tumblers; yellow-stained, enameled florals, 4 pcs. 225.00
Wine, blue-stained 40.00
Wine, clear 35.00
Wine, yellow-stained 50.00

MIKADO - See Daisy & Button with Crossbars Pattern

MINERVA

Minerva Compote

Bread tray, 13" l. 60.00
Butter dish, cov. 80.00
Cake stand, 8" d. 82.50
Cake stand, 9" d. 95.00
Cake stand, 10½" d. 115.00
Compote, cov., 8" d., low stand 175.00
Compote, cov., 8" d., high stand ....150.00 to 175.00
Compote, open, 8" d., 8½" h. (ILLUS.) 90.00
Creamer 45.00
Goblet 99.00
Marmalade jar, cov. 150.00
Pickle dish, "Love's Request is Pickles," oval 28.00
Pitcher, water 200.00
Plate, 8" d., Bates (J.C.) portrait center, scalloped rim 75.00
Plate, 9" d., handled, plain center 56.00
Platter, 13" oval 60.00
Relish, 5 x 8" oblong 32.00
Relish, 6 x 9" oblong 59.00
Sauce dish, footed, 4" d. 20.00
Sauce dish, flat, 5" d. 20.00
Spooner 42.00
Sugar bowl, cov. 70.00
Table set, creamer, cov. butter dish & spooner, 3 pcs. 195.00

MINNESOTA

Basket w/applied reeded handle 75.00
Bowl, 6" sq. 32.00
Bowl, 6 x 8¼" 38.00
Bowl, 8" sq. 32.00
Bowl, 8½" d., clear 40.00
Bowl, 8½" d., ruby-stained 100.00
Bowl, 7½ x 10½" 38.00
Butter dish, cov. 44.00
Carafe 48.00
Celery tray, 13" l. 40.00
Cheese dish, cov. 58.00
Compote, open, 7" 40.00

Compote, open, 9" sq. 50.00
Cracker jar, cov. 125.00
Creamer, 3½" h. 40.00
Creamer, individual size 15.00
Creamer, individual size, w/gold trim....18.00
Cruet w/original stopper.....50.00
Goblet.....30.00

Minnesota Goblet

Goblet, clear w/gold (ILLUS.) 35.00
Mug.....25.00
Nappy, 4½" d. 12.00
Pickle dish 12.00
Pitcher, water, tankard.....50.00 to 75.00
Plate, 7⅜" d., turned-up rim.....17.00
Relish, 3 x 5".....10.00
Relish, 6½ x 8¾" oblong.....26.00
Salt shaker w/original top, ruby-stained 50.00
Sauce dish.....10.00
Spooner, clear 35.00
Spooner, clear w/gold.....52.50
Sugar bowl, cov. 45.00
Syrup pitcher w/original top 65.00
Toothpick holder, three-handled, clear 32.50
Toothpick holder, three-handled, green.....125.00
Tumbler 18.00
Wine 23.00

MIRROR - See Galloway Pattern

MISSOURI (Palm & Scroll)

Bowl, 8" d.....22.00
Bowl, 8¾" d., green 41.00
Butter dish, cov., green.....85.00
Cake stand, 9" d., 4¾" h. 40.00
Cake stand, 10" d. 62.50
Compote, jelly.....32.00
Creamer.....35.00
Doughnut stand, 6" d. 55.00
Pitcher, milk, clear 45.00
Pitcher, milk, green.....125.00
Pitcher, water, clear.....52.00
Pitcher, water, green 125.00
Sugar bowl, cov. 47.00
Syrup pitcher 68.00
Table set, green, 4 pcs. .....250.00 to 300.00
Tumbler, green 35.00
Wine, clear.....36.00
Wine, green 55.00

MONKEY

Butter dish, cov. 195.00
Mug, amethyst 360.00
Mug, clear.....90.00
*Spooner, clear.....125.00
Spooner, white opalescent 175.00
Sugar bowl, open.....90.00

MOON & STAR

Bowl, cov., 6" d. 30.00
*Bowl, cov., 7" d.....38.00
*Bowl, master berry, 8¼" d., 4" h.....35.00
Bowl, fruit, 9" d., footed.....35.00
Bread tray, scalloped rim, 6½ x 10¾"...65.00

Moon & Star Butter Dish

*Butter dish, cov. (ILLUS.) 46.00
*Cake stand, 9" d. 65.00
Cake stand, 10" d. 95.00
Celery vase.....38.00
*Compote, cov., 6" d., high stand 55.00
*Compote, cov., 6" d., low stand.....50.00
Compote, cov., 7" d., 9" h. 45.00
Compote, cov., 7" d., 11" h. 70.00
Compote, cov., 13½" h. 125.00
Compote, open, 7" d., 7½" h.....30.00
Compote, open, 8" d., 8" h.....58.00
Compote, open, 9" d., 6½" h.....35.00
*Creamer 52.00
*Cruet w/original stopper, applied handle 125.00
*Egg cup 35.00
*Goblet.....45.00
Pickle dish, 8" l. 17.00
*Pitcher, water, 9¼" h., applied rope handle 150.00
Relish, oblong.....20.00
Salt dip, individual size, footed 32.00
*Salt shaker w/original top 30.00

*Sauce dish, flat or footed, each.....20.00
*Spooner.....45.00
*Sugar bowl, cov.....60.00
*Syrup pitcher w/original top.....125.00
*Toothpick holder.....21.00
*Tumbler, flat.....85.00
*Wine.....45.00

MOON & STAR WITH WAFFLE - See Jeweled Moon & Star Pattern

MORNING GLORY

Champagne, flint.....375.00
Compote, 7¾" d., 5" h., flint.....300.00
Compote, 9" d., 8" h., flint.....425.00
Egg cup, flint.....225.00 to 325.00
Honey dish, 3½" d., flint.....60.00
Salt dip, individual size, flint.....130.00
Salt dip, master size, pedestal, flint....225.00
Spooner, flint.....300.00 to 350.00
Sugar bowl, open, flint.....190.00
*Wine, flint.....75.00 to 100.00

NAIL

Bowl, berry, master, ruby-stained.....85.00
Butter dish, cov.....72.50
Cake stand.....42.50
Celery tray, flat, 5 x 11".....22.50
Celery vase, engraved.....50.00
Celery vase, plain.....26.00
Celery vase, ruby-stained.....65.00
Compote, jelly, 5¼", clear.....67.50
Compote, jelly, ruby-stained.....85.00
Compote, 7" d., ruby-stained.....155.00
Cordial.....55.00
Creamer, clear, engraved.....35.00
Creamer, clear, plain.....50.00
Goblet, clear, engraved.....65.00
Goblet, clear, plain.....48.00
Goblet, ruby-stained.....95.00
Pitcher, water, clear.....85.00
Pitcher, water, ruby-stained.....200.00 to 225.00
Salt shaker w/original top, w/engraving.....65.00
Sauce dish, flat or footed.....12.00
Spooner, clear.....45.00
Spooner, clear, engraved.....35.00
Spooner, ruby-stained.....60.00
Sugar bowl, cov., clear.....50.00
Sugar bowl, cov., clear w/engraved cover.....40.00
Sugar bowl, open.....17.00
Syrup jug w/original top.....28.00
Table set, spooner, creamer & cov. butter dish, 3 pcs.....175.00
Tumbler, clear.....15.00
Tumbler, ruby-stained.....60.00
Tumbler, ruby-stained, souvenir.....42.50
Wine, clear, engraved.....55.00
Wine, clear, plain.....52.00
Wine, ruby-stained, souvenir.....59.00

NAILHEAD

Bowl, 7¾" d., 2⅝" h.....50.00
Butter dish, cov.....46.50
Cake stand, 9" d.....30.00
Cake stand, 10½" d.....45.00
Celery vase.....42.00
Compote, cov., 8½" d., 12" h.....90.00
Compote, cov., 12" d.....65.00
Creamer.....26.00
Goblet, plain.....38.00
Pitcher, water.....40.00
Plate, 6" or 7" d.....18.50
Plate, 7" sq.....15.00
Plate, 9" sq.....22.50
Plate, 9" d.....22.00
Sauce dish, 4".....7.00
Spooner.....19.00
Sugar bowl, cov.....45.00
Tumbler, ruby-stained.....35.00
Wine.....25.00

NEPTUNE - See Queen Anne Pattern

NESTOR

Nestor Butter Dish

Berry set: master berry bowl & 4 sauce dishes; purple, 5 pcs.....165.00
Berry set: master berry bowl & 6 sauce dishes; blue, 7 pcs.....275.00
Bowl, master berry, green w/gold & enameling.....65.00
Butter dish, cov., blue w/gold & enameling (ILLUS.).....150.00
Butter dish, cov., blue w/gold trim.....125.00
Butter dish, cov., purple w/enameling.....125.00
Compote, jelly, blue w/enameling.....45.00
Compote, jelly, green w/enameling.....35.00
Compote, jelly, purple.....32.50
Creamer, blue w/enameling.....75.00
Creamer, green w/gold & enameling....40.00
Creamer, purple.....75.00
Cruet w/original stopper, blue w/enameling.....125.00
Cruet w/original stopper, green.....85.00
Cruet w/original stopper, purple.....95.00
Salt shaker w/original top, purple.....55.00

Sauce dish, blue w/gold trim & enameling 35.00
Sauce dish, green w/enameling 34.00
Sauce dish, purple w/gold trim 25.00
Spooner, blue w/gold & white enameling 50.00
Spooner, green w/gold & enameling 35.00
Spooner, purple w/gold trim....30.00
Sugar bowl, cov., green w/gold & enameling 60.00
Sugar bowl, cov., purple w/enameling....125.00
Toothpick holder, blue 100.00
Toothpick holder, blue w/gold & enameling 225.00
Toothpick holder, green w/gold & enameling 150.00
Toothpick holder, purple w/gold & enameling 145.00
Tumbler, green 30.00
Water set: pitcher & 6 tumblers; green w/gold & enameled decoration, 7 pcs. 315.00

NEW ENGLAND PINEAPPLE

Champagne, flint 190.00
Compote, open, 5" d., low stand....85.00
Compote, open, 9" d., flint 145.00
Compote, open, high stand, 10½" d., 9⅜" h. (rim chips) 350.00
*Cordial, flint, 4" h. 119.00
Creamer, applied handle, flint....235.00
Decanter w/bar lip, flint, qt. 175.00
Decanter w/original stopper, flint, qt. ..205.00
Egg cup, flint....55.00
*Goblet, flint....72.00
Goblet, lady's, flint 135.00
Honey dish, flint....35.00
Pitcher, water....310.00
Plate, 6" d., flint....195.00
Salt dip, master size, flint....50.00
Sauce dish, flint 30.00
Spillholder, flint 60.00
Sugar bowl, cov., flint 155.00
Tumbler, bar, flint....105.00
Tumbler, water, flint....85.00
*Wine, flint 245.00

NEW HAMPSHIRE (Bent Buckle)

Creamer....25.00
Creamer, individual, 3¼" h. 25.00
Cruet w/original stopper, clear....60.00
Cruet w/original stopper, rose-stained 289.00
Goblet, clear 30.00
Goblet, rose-stained 60.00
Mug, medium size 18.50
Olive dish, diamond shaped, 6⅝" w., rose-stained 20.00
Sauce dish, round, 4" d., rose-stained..14.00
Sugar bowl, cov., breakfast size, clear 13.50
Sugar bowl, cov., breakfast size, rose-stained 17.00
Sugar bowl, open, individual, double-handled, rose-stained 21.00
Toothpick holder, clear 19.50
Toothpick holder, rose-stained 65.00
Tumbler, water....18.00
Vase, 6" h., thick stem, rose-stained 22.50
Wine, flared bowl, clear 19.00
Wine, flared bowl, rose-stained 55.00

NEW JERSEY (Loops & Drops)

Berry set, master bowl & 3 sauce dishes, 4 pcs. 75.00
Berry set: master bowl & 6 sauce dishes, 7 pcs. 175.00
Bowl, 9" d....28.00
Bread plate 28.00
Butter dish, cov., ruby-stained ....150.00 to 200.00
Butter dish, cov., w/gold trim 75.00
Carafe, water....75.00
Celery tray, flat 25.00
Compote, open, jelly....32.00
Compote, open, 7" d., low stand....32.00
Compote, open, 7" d., high stand 60.00
Creamer, clear....36.00
Creamer, ruby-stained....65.00
Creamer, w/gold trim 60.00
Cruet w/original stopper....45.00
Goblet, clear 32.50
Goblet, ruby-stained 195.00
Goblet, w/gold trim....30.00
Pitcher, water, bulbous ....150.00 to 175.00
Plate, 10½" d. 30.00
Relish....12.50
Salt shaker w/original top 35.00
Salt & pepper shakers w/original tops ..40.00
Sauce dish, flat....13.00
Spooner, clear 27.50
Spooner, ruby-stained 65.00
Sugar bowl, cov. 53.00
Syrup pitcher w/original lid....115.00
Table set, 4 pcs. 215.00
Toothpick holder, clear 48.00
Toothpick holder, w/gold trim....65.00
Tumbler, clear....28.00
Vase, 8" h., green 26.00
Vase, 10" h. 20.00
Water set, pitcher & 6 tumblers, 7 pcs. 175.00
Wine 40.00

NOTCHED RIB - See Broken Column Pattern

OAKEN BUCKET (Wooden Pail)

Butter dish, cov., amber....70.00
Butter dish, cov., blue 85.00
Butter dish, cov., clear 65.00
Creamer, amber 45.00
Creamer, amethyst ....75.00 to 100.00
Creamer, blue....65.00
Creamer, clear....32.00

Creamer, vaseline 45.00
Pitcher, water, amber 80.00

Oaken Bucket Pitcher

Pitcher, water, amethyst
(ILLUS.) .....125.00 to 150.00
Pitcher, water, blue.....100.00
Pitcher, water, clear.....55.00
Pitcher, water, vaseline 120.00
Spooner, blue 55.00
Spooner, clear 35.00
Spooner, vaseline.....48.00
Sugar bowl, cov. 50.00
Toothpick holder, amber.....30.00
Toothpick holder, blue 22.50
Toothpick holder, clear 20.00

OLD MAN OF THE MOUNTAIN - See Viking Pattern

OLD MAN OF THE WOODS - See Queen Anne Pattern

ONE-HUNDRED-ONE

Bread plate, 10" d. 75.00
Butter dish, cov. 55.00
Celery 47.50
Compote, cov., 7" d., high stand.....85.00
Compote, open 25.00
Creamer, 4¾" h. 32.00
*Goblet.....42.00
Pitcher, water.....125.00
Plate, 7" d. 20.00
Plate, 8" d. 20.00
Relish.....16.50
Sauce dish.....13.50
Spooner 22.50

OPEN ROSE

Butter dish, cov. 65.00
Creamer.....40.00
Egg cup 22.00
*Goblet.....32.00
Goblet, lady's.....35.00
Salt dip, master size 24.00
Sauce dish.....10.00

Open Rose Spooner

*Spooner (ILLUS.) 30.00
Tumbler 41.00

OREGON No. 1 - See Beaded Loop Pattern

OREGON No. 2 - See Skilton Pattern

OWL IN FAN - See Parrot Pattern

PALM & SCROLL - See Missouri Pattern

PALMETTE

Palmette Goblet

Celery vase.....55.00
Compote, open, 8" d., low stand.....24.00
Creamer, applied handle 58.00
Cruet.....95.00
Cup plate, 3⅜" d. 45.00
Goblet (ILLUS.).....45.00
Lamp, kerosene-type, table model
w/stem 82.00
Pitcher, water, applied
handle .....100.00 to 125.00
Relish.....17.50
Salt dip, master size, footed 20.00
Sauce dish.....10.00

Spooner 35.00
Tumbler, water, flat 75.00
Tumbler, water, footed 47.50
Wine 50.00

PANELED CANE
Goblet, amber 35.00
Goblet, blue 30.00
Goblet, clear 25.00
Spooner 18.00
Tray, water 12.00

PANELED DAISY
Berry set, master bowl & 6 sauce dishes, 7 pcs. 85.00
Bowl, 5 x 7" oval 20.00
Butter dish, cov. 45.00
Cake stand, 8" to 11" d., high stand 44.00
Celery vase 35.00
Compote, cov., 8" d., 12½" h. 125.00
*Goblet 25.00
Plate, 9" sq. 28.00
Relish, 5 x 7" oval 17.50
Spooner 30.00
Sugar bowl, cov. 45.00
Tray, water 31.00

PANELED DEWDROP
Bread platter, 9½ x 12½" 50.00
Celery vase 38.00
Cordial, 3¼" h. 45.00
Creamer 25.00
Goblet 45.00
Sugar bowl, cov. 40.00
Wine 28.00

PANELED DIAMOND CROSS - See Heavy Paneled Finecut Pattern

PANELED FINECUT - See Finecut & Panel Pattern

PANELED FORGET-ME-NOT

Paneled Forget-Me-Not Compote

Bread platter, 7 x 11" oval 35.00
Butter dish, cov. 40.00
Cake stand 45.00
Celery vase 40.00
Compote, cov., 7" d., 10" h. 67.50
Compote, cov., 8" d., high stand (ILLUS.) 78.00
Compote, open, 7" d., high stand 50.00
Compote, open, 8½" d., high stand 40.00
Creamer 32.00
Cruet w/original stopper 55.00
Goblet, amethyst 750.00
Goblet, clear 35.00
Mustard jar, cov. 40.00
Pitcher, milk 60.00
Pitcher, water, amethyst 175.00
Pitcher, water, clear 65.00
Relish, handled, 4½ x 7¾" 21.00
Relish, scoop-shaped, 9" l. 19.50
Sauce dish, flat or footed 11.00
Spooner 30.00
Sugar bowl, cov. 35.00
Wine 125.00

PANELED 44 - See Reverse 44 Pattern

PANELED GRAPE
*Butter dish, cov. 46.00
*Compote, cov., 4" d., high stand 30.00
*Creamer 30.00
Creamer, individual size 25.00
*Goblet 30.00
Parfait 35.00
*Pitcher, water, 8¾" h. 55.00
*Sauce dish 15.00
*Spooner 25.00
Sugar bowl, open 28.00
Toothpick holder 38.00
Tumbler 25.00
Water set, cov. pitcher & 6 goblets, 7 pcs. ..... 200.00 to 250.00
*Wine 16.00

PANELED HEATHER
Creamer 17.00
Cruet w/original stopper 30.00
Goblet 28.00
Sauce dish, flat 8.00
Sauce dish, footed 17.00
Spooner 20.00
Table set, h.p. florals, gilt trim, 4 pcs. 158.00
Tumbler 25.00
Vase, 6½" h. 17.50

PANELED HERRINGBONE (Emerald Green Herringbone or Florida)
Bowl, 6" d., ruby & amber-stained 55.00
Bowl, master berry, 9" sq., green 30.00
Butter dish, cov., clear 50.00
Butter dish, cov., green 73.00
Compote, open, jelly, 5½" sq., green 35.00
Cruet w/original stopper, green ..... 100.00 to 125.00
*Goblet, clear 35.00

*Goblet, green 75.00
Pitcher, milk, green.....75.00
Pitcher, water, clear.....42.00
Pitcher, water, green 85.00
*Plate, 9", green.....35.00
Relish, 4½ x 8" oval, green.....15.00
Sauce dish, green.....12.50
Spooner, green.....25.00
Syrup pitcher w/original top, green.....150.00 to 200.00
Tumbler, green 21.00
Wine, clear.....22.50
Wine, green 48.00

PANELED JEWEL - See Michigan Pattern

PANELED STAR & BUTTON - See Sedan Pattern

PANELED THISTLE
*Bowl, 8" d. 18.50
*Bowl, 8" d., w/bee.....35.00
Bowl, 9" d., deep, w/bee 29.00
*Butter dish, cov., w/bee.....50.00
Cake stand 38.00
Cake stand, w/bee.....60.00
Candy dish, cov., footed, 5" sq., 6¼" h. 30.00
Celery vase.....45.00
Compote, open, 5" d., low stand.....19.00
*Compote, open, 6" d., high stand.....45.00
Cordial 18.00

Paneled Thistle Creamer

*Creamer (ILLUS.).....45.00
*Creamer, w/bee.....60.00
Cruet w/stopper 45.00
*Goblet.....34.00
*Honey dish, cov., square.....60.00
Honey dish, open.....10.00
Pitcher, milk.....31.00
*Plate, 7" sq. 28.00
*Plate, 7" sq., w/bee 23.00
Plate, 9½" d. 26.00
*Relish, w/bee, 4 x 9½".....24.00
Rose bowl, 5" d., 2¾" h. 40.00
Salt dip, individual size 17.50
*Salt dip, master size.....12.50
*Salt & pepper shakers w/original tops, pr. 65.00
*Sauce dish, flat or footed 14.00
*Spooner, handled.....45.00
*Sugar bowl, cov.....45.00
*Tumbler.....30.00
Vase, 9¼" h., fan-shaped 25.00
Vase, 13½" h., pulled top rim.....35.00
*Wine 24.00
*Wine, w/bee 30.00

PANELED ZIPPER - See Iowa Pattern

PARROT (Owl in Fan)
*Goblet.....50.00
Pitcher, water.....75.00
Wine 75.00

PAVONIA (Pineapple Stem)

Pavonia Tumbler

Butter dish, cov., clear, engraved.....85.00
Butter dish, cov., clear, plain 72.00
Cake stand, 10" d. 60.00
Celery vase, engraved.....45.00
Celery vase, plain 40.00
Compote, cov., 6" d., high stand.....55.00
Compote, cov., 7" d., engraved 100.00
Compote, cov., 8" d., engraved 125.00
Compote, open, 7" d. 48.00
Creamer, engraved.....41.00
Creamer, plain 38.00
Goblet, engraved 36.00
Goblet, plain 35.00
Pitcher, water, tall tankard, clear, engraved 75.00
Pitcher, water, tall tankard, clear, plain 60.00
Pitcher, water, tall tankard, ruby-stained .....125.00 to 150.00
Salt dip, master size 16.50
Salt shaker w/original top 28.00
Sauce dish, flat or footed.....14.00
Spooner, clear 39.00
Spooner, ruby-stained 45.00

Sugar bowl, cov., clear 50.00
Sugar bowl, cov., ruby-stained 85.00
Tray, water 73.00
Tumbler, clear, acid-etched (ILLUS.) 35.00
Tumbler, clear 32.00
Tumbler, ruby-stained 40.00
Tumbler, ruby-stained, engraved 45.00
Waste bowl 58.00
Water set: tankard pitcher & 6 tumblers; ruby-stained, 7 pcs. 375.00
Wine, clear, engraved 32.00
Wine, clear, plain 21.00
Wine, ruby-stained 39.00

PEACOCK FEATHER (Georgia)
Bonbon dish, footed 22.50
Bowl, 6 x 8" oval 27.50
Bowl, 8" d. 30.00
Butter dish, cov. 45.00
Cake stand, 8½" d., 5" h. 31.00
Compote, open, 6" d. 18.00
Compote, open, 6¾" d., low stand 25.00
Creamer 22.50
Cruet w/original stopper 40.00
Goblet 25.00
Lamp, kerosene-type, low hand-type w/handle, 5½" h. 95.00
Lamp, kerosene-type, table model w/handle, 9" h., blue 220.00
Lamp, kerosene-type, table model w/handle, 9" h., clear 85.00
Lamp, kerosene-type, table model, 10" h., amber 275.00
Lamp, kerosene-type, table model, 12" h., amber 325.00
Mug 40.00
Pitcher, water 52.00
Relish, 8" oval 14.00
Salt & pepper shakers w/original tops, pr. 85.00
Sauce dish 12.50
Spooner 37.00
Sugar bowl, cov. 38.00
Tumbler 35.00
Water set, pitcher & 6 tumblers, 7 pcs. ....250.00 to 275.00

PENNSYLVANIA (Balder or Kamoni)
Bowl, berry or fruit, 8½" d., clear w/gold trim 30.00
Butter dish, cov., clear 58.00
Butter dish, cov., green 85.00
Cake stand 45.00
Carafe 45.00
Celery tray, 4½ x 11" 28.00
Celery vase 22.50
Creamer, 3" h., clear w/gold trim, small 25.00
Creamer, 3" h., green w/gold trim, small 75.00
Cruet w/original stopper 44.00
Decanter w/original stopper, 10¾" h. 75.00
Goblet, clear 27.00
Goblet, clear w/gold 30.00
Pitcher, water 50.00
Punch cup, clear 10.00
Punch cup, clear w/gold 20.00
Salt & pepper shakers w/original tops, pr. 65.00
Sauce dish, round or square 12.50
*Spooner 21.00
Sugar bowl, cov., child's, green w/gold trim 145.00
Syrup pitcher w/original top 55.00
Table set, child's, 4 pcs. 250.00
Table set, 4 pcs. 225.00
Toothpick holder, clear 38.00
Toothpick holder, clear w/gold 69.00
Toothpick holder, green 140.00
Tumbler, juice 16.00
Tumbler, water, clear 23.00
Tumbler, water, clear w/gold trim 25.00
Tumbler, water, ruby-stained 49.00
Tumbler, whiskey, clear 16.50
Tumbler, whiskey, green w/gold trim 25.00
Vase, 5¾" h., green 60.00
Whiskey shot glass, clear 19.50
Whiskey shot glass, green 25.00
Wine, clear 16.00
Wine, green 25.00

PENNSYLVANIA, EARLY - See Hand Pattern

PETAL & LOOP
Bowl, 8" d., flat, flint 85.00
Compote, open, 9" d., 6" h., flint 65.00

PICKET

Picket Sauce Dish

Butter dish, cov. 60.00
Compote, cov., 6" d., high stand 80.00
Compote, open, 6" d., high stand 60.00
Creamer 36.00
Goblet 45.00
Pitcher, water 72.00
Salt dip, master size 42.50
Sauce dish, flat (ILLUS.) 10.00
Sauce dish, footed, 4½" d. 17.50
Spooner 50.00
Sugar bowl, cov. 50.00

PICKET BAND (Staves With Scalloped Band)
Goblet 45.00
Spooner 30.00

PILLAR
Bitters bottle 40.00
Celery vase, 9⅜" h. 90.00

Champagne, flint, 6" h. 60.00
Decanter w/bar lip, pt. 55.00
Decanter w/bar lip, qt. 205.00
Goblet 85.00

PILLAR & BULL'S EYE

Pillar & Bull's Eye Goblet

Bar bottle 60.00
Decanter w/bar lip, 10" h. 75.00
Flip glass, 5" d., 7½" h. 175.00
Goblet (ILLUS.) 85.00
Wine 75.00

PILLAR VARIANT - See Hercules Pillar Pattern

PILLOW & SUNBURST

Creamer, cov., individual size 15.00
Creamer & sugar bowl, pr. 42.00
Sugar bowl, cov. 20.00
Toothpick holder, clear w/gold trim 25.00

PILLOW ENCIRCLED

Bowl, 8" d., ruby-stained 51.00
Celery vase 35.00
Creamer, clear 25.00
Cruet w/original stopper, clear w/enameled floral decoration 35.00
Lamp, kerosene, finger-type 75.00
Mug 35.00
Pitcher, water, tankard, clear 42.00
Pitcher, water, tankard, ruby-stained ..102.00
Salt shaker w/original top 35.00
Salt & pepper shakers w/original tops, ruby-stained, pr. 85.00
Sauce dish, footed 11.50
Spooner, ruby-stained 62.00
Sugar bowl, cov., clear 35.00
Sugar bowl, cov., ruby-stained 125.00
Tumbler, clear 25.00
Tumbler, ruby-stained 42.00

PINEAPPLE & FAN

Bowl, 9" d. 45.00
Celery tray 36.00
Creamer 35.00
Cruet, w/original stopper, green 235.00
Rose bowl 30.00
Salt dip, individual 8.00
Salt & pepper shakers, w/original metal tops, pr. 40.00
Sugar bowl, cov. 45.00
Sugar shaker 43.00
Toothpick holder, clear 75.00
Toothpick holder, green w/gold 125.00
Tumbler, green w/gold 25.00
Wine 12.50

PINEAPPLE STEM - See Pavonia Pattern

PLEAT & PANEL (Darby)

Pleat & Panel Goblet

Bowl, 5 x 8" 32.00
Bowl, 6" sq., flat 28.00
Bowl, 7" d., 4½" h., footed 21.50
Bowl, 8" sq., flat 45.00
Bowl, cov., 8" rectangle, flat 90.00
Bowl, 8" rectangle, footed 35.00
Bread tray, closed handles, 8½ x 13" ...45.00
Bread tray, pierced handles 35.00
Butter dish, cov., footed, tab handles .....75.00 to 100.00
Cake stand, 8" sq. 40.00
Cake stand, 9" to 10" sq. 75.00
Celery vase, footed 38.00
Compote, cov., 7" sq., high stand 85.00
Compote, cov., 8" d., high stand 98.00
Compote, open, 8" d., high stand 35.00
Creamer 25.00
*Goblet (ILLUS.) 28.00
Lamp, kerosene-type, stem 125.00
Marmalade jar, cov. 100.00
Pitcher, milk 180.00
Pitcher, water 125.00
Plate, 5" sq. 22.00
Plate, 6" sq. 22.50
Plate, 7" sq., canary 48.00
Plate, 7" sq., clear 19.00
Plate, 8" sq. 32.00
Relish, cov., oblong, handled 65.00

Relish, open, handled, 5 x 8½".....35.00
Salt shaker w/original top 35.00
Sauce dish, flat, handled 18.00
Sauce dish, footed.....22.50
Spooner 35.00
Sugar bowl, cov. 85.00
Sugar bowl, open.....20.00
Tray, water, 9½ x 14".....45.00

PLEAT & TUCK - See Adonis Pattern

PLUME

Plume Compote

Berry set, 8½" sq. master bowl & five 4½" sq. sauce dishes, 6 pcs. 95.00
Bowl, cov., 8" d. 42.50
Bowl, open, 6" d.....24.00
Bowl, open, 8½" sq. master berry.....35.00
Bowl, open, 9" d.....30.00
Butter dish, cov. 48.00
Cake stand, 9" d., high stand.....50.00
Celery vase.....38.00
Compote, open, 6" d., collared base 36.00
Compote, open, 7" d., collared base (ILLUS.) 40.00
Compote, open, 8" d., high stand 40.00
Creamer, applied handle, clear 28.00
Creamer, ruby-stained.....60.00
Cruet w/original stopper.....38.00
*Goblet, clear.....32.50
Goblet, engraved 45.00
Goblet, ruby-stained & engraved.....75.00
Pitcher, water, bulbous, clear, engraved.....75.00
Pitcher, water, bulbous, clear, plain.....65.00
Pitcher, water, bulbous, ruby-stained .....200.00 to 250.00
Relish.....22.00
Sauce dish, flat or footed.....10.00
Spooner, clear 31.00
Spooner, ruby-stained 60.00
Tumbler, clear.....35.00
Tumbler, ruby-stained, souvenir 40.00

POINTED THUMBPRINT - See Almond Thumbprint Pattern

POLAR BEAR

Polar Bear Waste Bowl

*Goblet, clear.....125.00
Goblet, clear & frosted.....175.00
Pitcher, water, clear.....525.00
Tray, water, clear, 16" l. 165.00
Tray, water, frosted, 16" l. 250.00
Waste bowl (ILLUS.).....90.00

POPCORN

Popcorn Cake Stand

Cake stand, 11" d. (ILLUS.).....70.00
Creamer.....20.00
Goblet 40.00
Goblet w/raised ears of corn.....41.00
Wine 35.00

PORTLAND

Bowl, 8" d.....25.00
Bowl, 10" d., flared.....25.00
Butter dish, cov. 48.00
Cake stand, 10½" 55.00
*Candlestick.....110.00
*Celery tray.....25.00
Celery vase.....42.50
Compote, cov., 6½" d., high stand.....125.00
Compote, cov., 7" d., high stand.....100.00
Compote, cov., 8" d., high stand.....40.00
Compote, open, 7" d., high stand 45.00

Cordial 25.00
Creamer.....40.00
*Creamer, individual size.....18.00
Cruet w/original stopper.....45.00
Goblet.....39.00
Pitcher, water.....52.50
Pitcher, water, miniature.....26.00
Punch bowl, 15" d., 8½" h...150.00 to 175.00
Punch cup.....18.00
Salt shaker w/original top 16.00
Sauce dish, 4½" d.....10.00
Spooner.....25.00
Sugar bowl, cov. 55.00
Sugar shaker w/original top 50.00
Table set, clear w/gold trim, 4 pcs. 350.00
Toothpick holder.....27.00
Tumbler 25.00
Vase, 6" h., scalloped rim 28.00
Wine 29.00

PORTLAND MAIDEN BLUSH - See Banded Portland Pattern

PORTLAND WITH DIAMOND POINT BAND - See Banded Portland Pattern

POST (Square Panes)

Berry set, 7½" d. master bowl & 3 sauce dishes, 4 pcs. 47.50
Butter dish, cov. 67.50
Cake stand, 9½" d. 55.00
Celery vase.....32.00
Compote, cov., 5" sq., 10" h. 68.00
Compote, cov., 8" d. 85.00
Creamer.....35.00
Goblet, engraved 55.00
Goblet, plain 35.00
Lamp, kerosene-type, collared, 3½" h. 125.00
Lamp, kerosene-type, collared, 5" h. ..125.00
Lamp, kerosene-type, collared, engraved, 5" h. 125.00
Lamp, kerosene-type, 7½" h. 110.00
Lamp, kerosene-type, 8½" h. 125.00
Pitcher, milk 75.00
Pitcher, water.....90.00
Salt dips, individual size, set of 6.....37.50
Spooner.....30.00
Sugar bowl, cov. 40.00

POWDER & SHOT

Compote, open, 7⅞" d., low stand.....95.00
Creamer, applied handle, flint.....95.00
Egg cup, flint.....45.00
Goblet, flint (ILLUS. top next column)...62.00
Honey dish, flint.....10.00
Salt dip, master size 44.00
Sauce dish.....15.00
Spooner.....40.00
Sugar bowl, cov. 95.00
Sugar bowl, open.....50.00

Powder & Shot Goblet

Wine, flint, 3½" h. 55.00

PRAYER RUG - See Horseshoe Pattern

PRESSED DIAMOND

Butter dish, cov., amber.....45.00
Butter dish, cov., blue 95.00
Creamer, amber, 4¾" h. 38.00
Creamer, canary, 4¾" h. 40.00
Goblet, blue 30.00
Salt shaker w/original top, tall, blue 47.50
Sauce dish, flat, round, blue 24.50
Sauce dish, flat, round, canary 22.50
Spooner, flat, amber 40.00
Spooner, flat, canary 35.00
Spooner, flat, clear 30.00
Tumbler, water, flat, blue 28.00

PRESSED LEAF

Butter dish, cov. 60.00
Champagne 45.00
Compote, cov., acorn finial, low stand..45.00
Egg cup 30.00
Goblet.....45.00
Pitcher, water, applied handle 95.00
Salt dip, master size 31.00
Spooner.....30.00
Sugar bowl, cov. 45.00
Wine 48.00

PRIMROSE

Bread plate 30.00
Cake stand, clear, 10" d. 48.00
Creamer.....30.00
Goblet.....30.00
Pickle dish 13.00
Pitcher, milk, blue 65.00
Pitcher, milk, clear 42.00
Pitcher, water.....45.00
Plate, 4½" d., amber or blue 15.00
Plate, 4½" d., clear 13.00
Plate, 6" d., amber 16.50
Plate, 7" d., amber 22.50
Plate, 7" d., blue 16.00

Relish, amber, 5 x 9¼" 22.50
Relish, clear.....12.50
Sugar bowl, cov. 40.00
Tray, water, 11" d. 34.00
Wine, blue.....45.00

Primrose Wine

Wine, clear (ILLUS.) 25.00

PRINCESS FEATHER (Rochelle)

Bowl, cov., 8" d. 85.00
Bowl, 5 x 7" oval 25.00
Butter dish, cov. 50.00
Celery vase.....40.00
Compote, cov., 8" d., low stand 100.00
Creamer.....60.00
Goblet, flint 32.00
Lamp, kerosene-type, 12" h. 75.00
Lamp, kerosene, hand-type w/finger grip handle 120.00
Plate, 6" d., non-flint 29.00
Plate, 7" d., amber, flint 225.00
Plate, 7" d., clear, non-flint.....22.00
Plate, 8" d., non-flint 24.00
Plate, 9" d., non-flint 32.50
Spooner, clear, non-flint 26.00
Spooner, milk white, flint.....48.00
Sugar bowl, cov., clear, non-flint 60.00
Sugar bowl, cov., milk white, flint.....135.00

PRISCILLA (Alexis)

Banana stand 95.00
Bowl, 8" d., 3½" h., straight sides, flat ..38.00
Bowl, 8" d., 3½" h., w/pattern on base..45.00
*Bowl, 10¼" to 10½" d. 35.00
Butter dish, cov. 95.00
Cake stand, 9" to 10" d., high stand 65.00
Compote, cov., jelly 55.00
*Compote, cov., 8" d. 100.00
Compote, cov., 12" d. 145.00
*Compote, open, 8" d., 8" h. 55.00
*Creamer 45.00
Creamer, individual size 28.00
Cup & saucer.....32.00
*Goblet.....38.00
Pitcher, water, bulbous 120.00
Plate, 10½" d., turned-up rim 25.00
Relish.....23.00
*Sauce dish, flat, 4½" to 5" d. 25.00
Spooner.....35.00
Sugar bowl, cov. 45.00
Sugar bowl, cov., individual size.....31.00
Syrup pitcher w/original pewter top, clear 115.00
Syrup pitcher w/original pewter top, green w/gold 450.00
Table set, 4 pcs. .....200.00 to 225.00
Toothpick holder 32.00
Tumbler 45.00
*Wine 40.00

PSYCHE & CUPID

Psyche & Cupid Goblet

Celery vase.....38.00
Creamer.....40.00
Goblet (ILLUS.).....50.00
Pitcher, water.....85.00
Table set, spooner, cov. sugar bowl & creamer, 3 pcs. 185.00

PYGMY - See Torpedo Pattern

QUEEN (Daisy & Button with Pointed Panels)

Queen Goblet

Bowl, 8" d., footed, amber 25.00
Butter dish, domed cover, blue.....75.00
Dish, flat, 7" oval, amber.....22.50
Goblet, amber.....33.00
Goblet, apple green (ILLUS.).....25.00
Sauce dish, flat, 4" d., amber.....12.50
Spooner, amber.....25.00
Spooner, blue 45.00
Toothpick holder.....25.00
Tumbler, water, flat, amber.....32.50
Wine 21.00

QUEEN ANNE (Bearded Man, Neptune, Old Man of the Woods)
Butter dish, cov.....65.00
Celery vase, amber 65.00
Celery vase, clear.....40.00
Creamer.....47.50
Pitcher, water, 2 qt.....70.00
Spooner.....40.00
Sugar bowl, open.....50.00
Syrup pitcher 95.00

QUEEN'S NECKLACE
Cologne bottle, w/stopper, 3½" h.....75.00
Condiment set w/toothpick center, pepper & cruet w/stopper.....145.00
Goblet.....70.00
Spooner.....33.00
Toothpick holder.....60.00

RAMPANT LION - See Frosted Lion Pattern

RED BLOCK
Bowl, berry or fruit, 8" d. 85.00
Butter dish, cov.....95.00
Celery vase, 6½" h. 135.00
Creamer, large.....80.00
Creamer, small, applied handle.....35.00
Cruet w/original stopper.....150.00
Decanter, whiskey, w/original stopper, 12" h.....175.00
Dish, rectangular, 5 x 7½" 55.00
*Goblet.....40.00
Mug, plain, 3" h.....26.00
Mug, souvenir, 3" h.....42.00
Pitcher, 8" h., bulbous.....225.00
Pitcher, tankard, 8" h. .....175.00 to 200.00
Salt shaker w/original top 49.00
Sauce dish, 4½".....35.00
Spooner.....35.00
Sugar bowl, cov. 70.00
Tumbler, souvenir.....32.00
Tumbler 35.00
*Wine 35.00

REVERSE 44 (Paneled 44, U.S. Glass "Athenia")
Berry set: master bowl & 6 sauce dishes; clear w/gold or platinum stain, 7 pcs.....225.00
Bowl, 8" d., shallow sides, clear w/gold or platinum stain 75.00
Butter dish, cov., clear w/gold or platinum stain.....135.00
Champagne, clear w/platinum stain 75.00
Compote, jelly, clear w/gold or platinum stain.....80.00
Compote, open, 5½" d., high standard, clear 32.00
Creamer, after dinner, clear.....45.00
Creamer, berry, clear w/gold or platinum stain.....95.00
Creamer, table size, clear w/gold or platinum stain.....30.00
Creamer, tankard, clear w/gold or platinum stain.....30.00
Cruet w/original stopper, clear.....58.00
Goblet, clear 30.00
Goblet, clear w/gold or platinum stain ..60.00
Pitcher, tankard-type, footed, clear.....105.00
Pitcher, tankard-type, footed, clear w/gold or platinum stain 150.00
Sauce dish, 4" d., straight sides, clear w/gold or platinum stain 20.00
Spoonholder, handled, clear w/gold or platinum stain 55.00
Sugar bowl, open, after dinner, clear....45.00
Table set: creamer, cov. sugar bowl & spooner; clear w/platinum stain, 3 pcs. 295.00
Toothpick holder, footed, handled, clear 35.00
Toothpick holder, footed, handled, clear w/gold or platinum stain 85.00

REVERSE TORPEDO (Diamond & Bull's Eye Band)
Banana stand 135.00
Basket, high stand 160.00
Bowl, 7" d., ruby-stained.....22.50
Bowl, 7½" d.....48.00
Bowl, 9" d., piecrust rim 75.00
Bowl, 10¼" d., piecrust rim 65.00
Butter dish, cov.....75.00
Cake stand 95.00
Celery vase.....55.00
Compote, cov., 6" d., high stand.....85.00
Compote, open, jelly.....40.00
Compote, open, 5" d., flared rim, high stand 50.00
Compote, open, 7" d., smooth rim, high stand 55.00
Compote, open, 8" d., piecrust rim, high stand 100.00
Compote, open, 10" d., piecrust rim, high stand 125.00
Creamer.....67.50
Goblet.....85.00
Goblet, w/engraved flower.....100.00
Lamp, kerosene-type, 9" h.....145.00
Pitcher, water.....125.00 to 150.00
Pitcher, water, tankard w/engraved flowers 225.00
Salt shaker w/original top 40.00
Sauce dish.....22.00

Spooner 52.00
Sugar bowl, cov. 72.50
Tumbler 50.00

RIBBED FORGET-ME-NOT

Creamer 35.00
Creamer, individual size 25.00
Mug 20.00

RIBBED GRAPE

Ribbed Grape Plate

Compote, open, 8" d., 5" h. 85.00
Goblet 60.00
Plate, 6" d. (ILLUS.) 36.00
Sauce dish, 4" d. 20.00
Spooner 45.00

RIBBED PALM

Bowl, 8" d., footed 65.00
Butter dish. cov. 88.00
Celery vase 75.00
Champagne 125.00
Compote, open, 7¼" d., 4¼" h. 45.00
Creamer ..... 125.00 to 150.00
Egg cup 45.00
*Goblet 45.00
Pitcher, water, 9" h., applied handle ..... 250.00 to 300.00
Salt dip, master size 35.00
Salt dip, master size, footed 50.00
Sauce dish 14.00
Spillholder 50.00
Tumbler 120.00
*Wine 65.00

RIBBED IVY

Butter dish, cov. 95.00
Champagne ..... 150.00 to 200.00
Compote, cov., 6" d., high stand 250.00
Compote, open, 7½" d., high stand, rope edge rim 100.00
Compote, open, 8" d., 5" h. 75.00
Compote, open, 8½" d., 7½" h., high stand 95.00
Creamer, applied handle 145.00
Egg cup 40.00

Ribbed Ivy Goblet

Goblet (ILLUS.) 55.00
Spooner 50.00
Sugar bowl, cov. 110.00
Sweetmeat, cov. 325.00
Tumbler, water 100.00
Tumbler, whiskey 85.00
Wine 80.00

RIBBON (Early Ribbon)

Ribbon Waste Bowl

Bread tray 35.00
Butter dish, cov. 72.50
Celery vase 38.00
Compote, cov., 8" d. 96.00
Compote, open, 8" d., low stand 40.00
Compote, open, 8" d., 8" h., frosted dolphin stem on dome base 295.00
*Compote, open, 5½ x 8" rectangular bowl, 7" h., frosted dolphin stem on dome base 295.00
Compote, open, 8½" d., 4½" h. 50.00
Compote, open, 10½" d., frosted dolphin stem on dome base 395.00
Creamer 34.00
Dresser bottle w/stopper 125.00
*Goblet 35.00
Pitcher, water 120.00
Plate, 7" d. 34.00
Platter, 9 x 13" 60.00

Sauce dish, flat or footed.....12.50
Spooner.....30.00
Sugar bowl, cov., 4¼" d., 7¾" h.....72.00
Table set, 4 pcs. .....200.00 to 225.00
Waste bowl (ILLUS.).....42.50

RIBBON CANDY (Bryce or Double Loop)
Butter dish, cov., flat.....48.00
Butter dish, cov., footed.....50.00
Cake stand, child's, 6½" d., 3" h. 125.00
Cake stand, 8" to 10½" d. 38.00
Celery vase.....45.00
Compote, cov., 7" d. 95.00
Creamer.....32.00
Doughnut stand 32.00
Goblet.....50.00 to 75.00
Pitcher, milk.....42.00
Plate, 8½" d. 30.00
Relish, 8½" l.....14.00
Sauce dish, flat, 3½" d. 10.00
Sauce dish, footed, 4" d.....12.00
Spooner.....24.00
Sugar bowl, cov. 48.00
Wine 95.00

RISING SUN

Rising Sun Wine

Butter dish, cov., green suns 85.00
Butter dish, cov., pink suns.....50.00
Celery vase, gold suns 55.00
Compote, open, jelly, pink suns.....18.00
Compote, open, 7" d., 6" h.....18.00
Cruet w/stopper 65.00
Goblet, clear 35.00
Goblet, gold suns.....25.00
Goblet, green suns 21.00
Goblet, pink suns.....25.00
Goblet, purple suns 25.00
Pitcher, water, clear.....50.00
Pitcher, water, gold suns 44.00
Sugar bowl, open, three-handled, pink suns w/gold trim 25.00
Sugar dispenser, mechanical, in silver plate frame (worn).....65.00
Toothpick holder, three-handled, clear 28.00
Toothpick holder, three-handled, green suns 32.50
Toothpick holder, three-handled, pink suns.....38.00
Toothpick holder, three-handled, red suns 45.00
Tumbler, red suns.....25.00
Vase, 6½" h., 4½" d., gold suns.....25.00
Vase, 6½" h., 4½" d., pink suns.....35.00
Water set: pitcher & 4 tumblers; clear, 5 pcs. 120.00
Water set: pitcher & 4 tumblers; green suns, 5 pcs.....154.00
Wine, clear.....25.00
Wine, gold suns 23.50
Wine, green suns.....28.00
Wine, pink suns (ILLUS.) 29.00

ROCHELLE - See Princess Feather Pattern

ROMAN KEY (Roman Key with Flutes or Ribs)
Frosted unless otherwise noted

Roman Key Goblet

Celery vase.....70.00
Champagne 120.00
Compote, open, 7¾" sq., 7¼" h.....65.00
Compote, open, 8" d., 6" h.....60.00
Decanter w/stopper, qt. 252.00
Egg cup 30.00
Goblet (ILLUS.).....45.00
Salt dip, master size 35.00
Sauce dish.....13.00
Spooner 32.00
*Sugar bowl, cov.....125.00
Tumbler, bar 98.00
Tumbler, footed 63.00
Wine 50.00

ROMAN ROSETTE
Bowl, 8" d.....24.00
Bread platter, 9 x 11".....28.00
Butter dish, cov.....55.00
Cake stand, 9" to 10" d. 58.00

Celery vase, ruby-stained.....95.00
Compote, cov., 6" d., high stand.....70.00
Compote, open, jelly, 5" d.....22.50
Cordial.....47.50
Creamer.....35.00
*Goblet.....42.50
Marmalade dish, footed, clear.....24.00
Mug, 3" h.....20.00
Pitcher, milk.....60.00
Pitcher, water.....78.00
Plate, 7" d.....33.00
Relish, 3½ x 8½".....10.00
Sauce dish.....20.00
Spooner.....21.00
Sugar bowl, cov.....40.00
Wine, clear.....48.00
Wine, ruby-stained.....65.00

ROMAN ROSETTE, EARLY

Cup plate, opalescent, flint, 3½" d.....77.00
Honey dish, clear, 4⅛" d., flint.....20.00
Honey dish, cobalt blue, flint, 4⅛" d.....55.00
Honey dish, purple, flint, 4⅛" d.....200.00
Plate, 5" d., cobalt blue, flint.....375.00
Plate, 6" d., deep amethyst, flint.....400.00
Sauce dish, cobalt blue, 4" d.....55.00
Sauce dish, reddish amber, 5⅜" d.....100.00 to 150.00
Toddy plate, purple, flint, 5½" d.....325.00

ROSE IN SNOW

Bitters bottle w/original stopper.....100.00
Bowl, 7" d., footed, canary.....38.00
Butter dish, cov., round.....55.00
Butter dish, cov., square.....50.00
Cake plate, handled, amber, 10" d.....45.00
Cake plate, handled, blue, 10" d.....35.00
Cake plate, handled, clear, 10" d.....22.50
Cake stand, 9" d.....100.00 to 150.00
Cologne bottle w/original stopper.....95.00
Compote, cov., 6" d., 8" h.....85.00
Compote, cov., 7" d., 8" h.....95.00
Compote, cov., 7" d., low stand.....125.00
Compote, cov., 8" d., 10" h., canary.....155.00
Compote, open, 5" d., blue.....110.00
Compote, open, 6" d., canary.....42.00
Compote, open, 6" d., low stand.....50.00
Compote, open, 8" sq., low stand.....110.00
Compote, open, 8" d., high stand.....70.00
Creamer, round.....35.00
Creamer, square.....39.00
Dish, 8½ x 11" oval, 1½" h.....130.00
*Goblet, amber.....45.00
*Goblet, blue.....85.00
*Goblet, clear.....70.00
*Goblet, vaseline.....32.00
Mug, blue, large.....110.00
Mug, clear, 3½" h.....40.00
*Mug, applied handle, "In Fond Remembrance," yellow.....35.00
Pitcher, water, applied handle.....132.00
Plate, 5" d.....32.00
Plate, 6" d.....30.00
*Plate, 9" d., amber.....40.00
*Plate, 9" d., clear.....30.00
*Relish, 5½ x 8" oval, blue.....65.00
*Relish, 5½ x 8" oval, clear.....23.00
Relish, 6¼ x 9¼".....19.00
Sauce dish, flat or footed.....10.00
Spooner, round.....25.00
Spooner, square.....28.00
Sugar bowl, cov., round.....37.50
*Sugar bowl, cov., square.....51.00
Tumbler.....38.00

ROSE SPRIG

Rose Sprig Goblet

Bowl, 6 x 9" oblong.....27.50
Bread tray, two-handled, canary.....40.00
Bread tray, two-handled, clear.....32.00
Cake stand, amber, 9" octagon, 6½" h.....68.00
Cake stand, blue, 9" octagon, 6½" h.....125.00
Cake stand, clear, 9" octagon, 6½" h.....70.00
Cake stand, 10" octagonal.....72.00
Celery vase.....39.00
Compote, open, 7" oval, amber.....58.00
Compote, open, 7" d., 5" h., canary.....47.50
Compote, open, 8" oval.....50.00
Compote, open, 9" oval, high stand, blue.....22.00
*Goblet, amber.....50.00
*Goblet, blue.....55.00
*Goblet, canary.....60.00
*Goblet, clear (ILLUS.).....40.00
Pitcher, milk, amber.....80.00
Pitcher, milk, blue.....95.00
Pitcher, milk, canary.....75.00
Pitcher, milk, clear.....45.00
Pitcher, water, amber.....50.00
Pitcher, water, clear.....48.00
Plate, 6" sq., blue.....45.00
Plate, 6" sq., clear.....27.50
Relish, boat-shaped, amber, 8" l.....35.00
Relish, boat-shaped, blue, 8" l.....45.00
Relish, boat-shaped, canary, 8" l.....40.00
Relish, boat-shaped, clear, 8" l.....32.50

Sauce dish, flat 13.00
Sauce dish, footed, amber 18.50
Sauce dish, footed, canary 20.00
Sauce dish, footed, clear 17.50
Tumbler 39.00
Whimsey, sitz bath-shaped bowl, blue, 7 x 10" 85.00
Whimsey, sitz bath-shaped bowl, canary, 7 x 10" 47.50
*Whimsey, sleigh (salt dip), amber, 4 x 4 x 6" 47.00
Wine 36.00

ROSETTE

Bowl, 7½" d. 16.00
Butter dish, cov. 40.00
Cake stand, 8½" to 11" d. 28.00
Celery vase 28.00
Compote, cov., 11½" h. 50.00
Compote, open, jelly, 4½" d., 5" h. 17.50
Compote, open, 7¼" d., 6" h. 30.00
Creamer 32.00
Goblet 32.50
Pitcher, milk 50.00
Pitcher, water, tankard 55.00
Plate, 7" d. 20.00
Plate, 9" d., two-handled 21.00
Relish, fish-shaped 12.00
Sauce dish 7.50
Spooner 31.00
Sugar bowl, cov. 32.00
Tumbler 16.00
Wine 25.00

ROYAL CRYSTAL

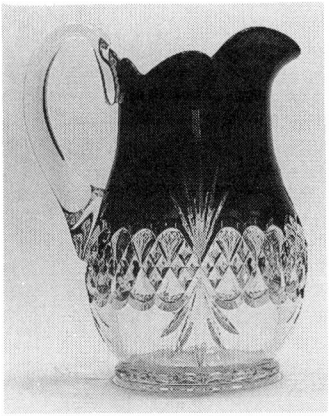

Royal Crystal Pitcher

Bowl, round, flat, 8" d., flared sides 12.00
Bread plate 25.00
Cake stand, high standard, 9" d. 25.00
Creamer, 5¼" h., ruby-stained 59.00
Cruet w/original stopper, 5 oz. 35.00
Pitcher, bulbous, milk, 1 qt., ruby-stained (ILLUS.) 250.00
Salt shaker w/original top, ruby-stained 65.00

ROYAL IVY (Northwood)

Royal Ivy Sugar Shaker

Berry set: master bowl & 3 sauce dishes; craquelle, (cranberry & vaseline spatter), 4 pcs. 175.00
Berry set: master bowl & 6 sauce dishes; frosted rubina crystal, 7 pcs. 310.00
Bowl, 8" d., frosted rubina crystal ..... 150.00 to 200.00
Bowl, fruit, 9" d., craquelle (cranberry & vaseline spatter) 235.00
Bowl, fruit, 9" d., frosted craquelle 150.00
Butter dish, cov., rubina crystal ..... 150.00 to 175.00
Creamer, clear & frosted 45.00
Creamer, rubina crystal 165.00
Creamer, frosted rubina crystal 185.00
Cruet w/original stopper, clear & frosted 135.00
Cruet w/original stopper, craquelle (cranberry & vaseline spatter) 495.00
Cruet w/original stopper, rubina crystal 295.00
Cruet w/original stopper, frosted rubina crystal ..... 350.00 to 375.00
Marmalade jar, w/original silver plate lid, clear & frosted 100.00
Pickle castor, frosted rubina crystal insert,complete w/silver plate frame ..... 350.00 to 375.00
Pickle castor, cased spatter (cranberry & vaseline w/white lining) insert, complete w/silver plate frame & tongs ..... 300.00 to 350.00
Pitcher, water, cased spatter (cranberry & vaseline w/white lining) 325.00
Pitcher, water, clear & frosted 90.00
Pitcher, water, craquelle (cranberry & vaseline spatter) 350.00
Pitcher, water, rubina crystal 250.00
Pitcher, water, frosted rubina crystal 300.00
Rose bowl, clear & frosted 60.00
Rose bowl, rubina crystal 78.00
Rose bowl, frosted rubina crystal 95.00
Rose bowl, craquelle (cranberry & vaseline spatter) 180.00

Salt shaker w/original top, cased spatter (cranberry & vaseline w/white lining) 125.00
Salt shaker w/original top, rubina crystal 48.00
Salt shaker w/original top, frosted rubina crystal 78.00
Salt & pepper shakers w/original tops, cased spatter (cranberry & vaseline w/white lining), pr. 225.00
Sauce dish, craquelle (cranberry & vaseline spatter) 50.00
Spooner, clear & frosted 50.00
Spooner, craquelle (cranberry & vaseline spatter) 150.00
Spooner, rubina crystal 65.00
Spooner, frosted rubina crystal 80.00
Sugar bowl, cov., frosted rubina crystal 200.00
Sugar shaker w/original top, cased spatter (cranberry & vaseline w/white lining) 300.00
Sugar shaker w/original top, rubina crystal 130.00
Sugar shaker w/original top, frosted rubina crystal (ILLUS.) ....200.00 to 250.00
Syrup pitcher w/original top, cased spatter (cranberry & vaseline w/white lining) 490.00
Syrup pitcher w/original top, clear & frosted ....100.00 to 150.00
Syrup pitcher w/original top, frosted rubina crystal ....500.00 to 525.00
Toothpick holder, cased spatter (cranberry & vaseline w/white lining) 145.00
Toothpick holder, clear & frosted 47.50
Toothpick holder, craquelle (cranberry & vaseline spatter) 235.00
Toothpick holder, rubina crystal 85.00
Toothpick holder, frosted rubina crystal 125.00
Tumbler, cased spatter (cranberry & vaseline w/white lining) 85.00
Tumbler, clear & frosted 52.50
Tumbler, craquelle (cranberry & vaseline spatter) 76.00
Tumbler, rubina crystal 66.00
Tumbler, frosted rubina crystal 70.00
Water set: pitcher & 5 tumblers; rubina crystal, 6 pcs. 595.00
Water set: pitcher & 6 tumblers; cased spatter (cranberry & vaseline w/white lining), 7 pcs. 955.00

ROYAL OAK (Northwood)

Berry set: master bowl & 4 sauce dishes; rubina crystal, 5 pcs. 290.00
Bowl, berry, 7½" d., frosted crystal 65.00
Butter dish, cov., frosted crystal 55.00
Butter dish, cov., frosted rubina crystal 250.00
Creamer, frosted crystal 75.00
Creamer, rubina crystal ....150.00 to 175.00
Creamer, frosted rubina crystal ....200.00 to 225.00
Cruet w/original stopper, frosted rubina crystal 250.00
Pickle castor, rubina crystal insert, w/resilvered frame & tongs 450.00
Pitcher, 8½" h., frosted crystal 82.00
Pitcher, water, rubina crystal ....300.00 to 350.00
Salt shaker w/original top, rubina crystal 100.00
Sauce dish, rubina crystal 50.00
Spooner, frosted crystal 48.00
Spooner, frosted rubina crystal 95.00
Sugar bowl, cov., frosted rubina crystal 180.00
Sugar shaker w/original top, frosted crystal 95.00
Sugar shaker w/original top, rubina crystal 138.00
Sugar shaker w/original top, frosted rubina crystal ....145.00 to 165.00
Table set, frosted rubina crystal, 4 pcs. 595.00
Toothpick holder, frosted crystal 60.00
Toothpick holder, rubina crystal 150.00
Tumbler, frosted rubina crystal 90.00

RUBY ROSETTE - See Hero Pattern

RUBY THUMBPRINT

*Bowl, 8½" d. 90.00
Bowl, master berry or fruit, 10" l., boat shaped 125.00
Butter dish, cov., engraved 225.00
Celery vase 100.00
Champagne, souvenir 45.00
*Claret 65.00
Compote, open, jelly, 5¼" h. 49.00
Compote, open, 7" d., engraved 150.00
Compote, open, 7" d., plain 145.00
Compote, open, 8½" d., 7½" h., scalloped rim ....200.00 to 225.00
Cordial, engraved 40.00
Creamer, engraved 85.00
*Creamer, plain 60.00
Creamer, individual size 30.00
Cup, engraved 35.00
*Cup, plain 30.00
Cup & saucer, engraved 65.00
*Cup & saucer, plain 60.00
*Goblet, plain 40.00
Goblet, souvenir 42.00
Pitcher, milk, 7½" h., bulbous 100.00
Pitcher, milk, tankard, 8⅜" h. 125.00
*Pitcher, water, tankard, 11" h. 132.00
Pitcher, water, tankard, 11" h., w/engraved leaf band 190.00
*Plate, 8¼" d. 22.00
Sauce dish, boat-shaped 28.00
*Sauce dish, round 20.00
*Sherbet 20.00

Spooner 65.00
Toothpick holder, engraved 47.50
Toothpick holder, plain 38.00
Tumbler, engraved 55.00
*Tumbler, plain 36.00
Water set, bulbous pitcher & 6 tumblers,w/engraved family names & dated 1897, 7 pcs. 595.00
*Wine 40.00

SANDWICH LOOP - See Hairpin Pattern

SANDWICH STAR

Compote, open, 9¾" d., 8½" h., scalloped rim 220.00
Decanter w/patented stopper, pt. 135.00
Decanter w/bar lip, pt. 75.00
Decanter w/bar lip, qt. 125.00
Spillholder, canary yellow 275.00
Spillholder, clambroth 300.00
Spillholder, clear 65.00
Spillholder, electric blue 1,200.00
Spillholder, sapphire blue 770.00
Toddy plate 25.00

SAWTOOTH

Sawtooth Covered Egg Cup

Butter dish, cov., clear, flint 78.00
*Butter dish, cov., clear, non-flint 50.00
Butter dish, cov., sapphire blue, non-flint 230.00
Cake stand, non-flint, 7½" d., 6" h. 30.00
*Cake stand, non-flint, 9½" d., 4½" h. 75.00
Celery vase, knob stem, flint 45.00
Celery vase, knob stem, non-flint 42.50
Celery vase, stepped pedestal base, notched rim, flint 125.00
Champagne, knob stem, flint 85.00
Champagne, non-flint 35.00
Compote, open, 7½" d., 5½" h. 38.00
Compote, open, 7½" d., 7½" h., flint 55.00
Compote, open, 8" d., low stand, blue, flint 250.00
Compote, open, 8" d., low stand, canary, flint 200.00
Compote, open, 9½" d., 10" h., flint 100.00
Creamer, applied handle, clear, flint 75.00
Creamer, applied handle, cobalt blue, flint 230.00
Creamer, miniature, non-flint 29.00
Decanter w/original stopper, flint, 14" h. 145.00
Egg cup, cov., canary, flint 192.50
Egg cup, cov., clear, flint (ILLUS.) 100.00
Goblet, knob stem, flint 35.00
Goblet, knob stem, non-flint 25.00
Goblet, plain stem, non-flint 18.00
Lamp, whale oil, w/marble base 150.00
Pitcher, water, applied handle, flint 215.00
Pomade jar, cov. 60.00
Salt dip, cov., master size, footed, flint 100.00
Salt dip, cov., master size, footed, milk white, flint 75.00
Salt dip, cov., master size, footed, non-flint 35.00
Salt dip, master size, flint 45.00
Salt dip, master size, non-flint 22.00
Spillholder, flint 48.00
Spillholder, jagged sawtooth rim, sapphire blue, flint, 5½" h. 700.00
Spooner, clear, non-flint 50.00
Spooner, cobalt blue, non-flint 85.00
Spooner, milk white, flint 75.00
Tumbler, bar, flint, 4½" h. 58.00
Tumbler, bar, non-flint 32.50
Wine, flint 45.00
Wine, non-flint 18.00

SAWTOOTH BAND - See Amazon Pattern

SCALLOPED TAPE (Jewel Band)

Scalloped Tape Creamer

Bread platter ....35.00 to 45.00
Cake stand, 9½" d. 32.00
Celery vase, 8" h. 28.00
Compote, cov., 8¼" d., 12" h. 55.00
Creamer (ILLUS.) 25.00
Egg cup 25.00
Goblet 16.00

Pitcher, water, 9¼" h. 55.00
Sugar bowl, cov. 35.00
Wine, blue.....55.00
Wine, clear.....15.00

SEDAN (Paneled Star & Button)

Sedan Sauce Dish

Creamer.....27.00
Goblet.....22.00
Mug, miniature.....15.00
Sauce dish, flat, 4½" d. (ILLUS.) 4.00
Wine, clear.....23.00
Wine, blue.....85.00

SENECA LOOP - See Loop Pattern

SHELL & JEWEL (Victor)

Shell & Jewel Pitcher

Bowl, 10" d.....25.00
Compote, open, 7" d., 7½" h.....55.00
Creamer.....22.50
Pitcher, milk.....32.00
Pitcher, water, blue.....82.00
Pitcher, water, clear (ILLUS.) 45.00
Pitcher, water, green 90.00
Sauce dish.....8.00
Spooner.....30.00
Tumbler, amber 32.00
Tumbler, blue.....40.00
Tumbler, clear.....18.00
Tumbler, green 44.00
Water set, pitcher & 6 tumblers, 7 pcs. .....170.00 to 190.00

SHELL & TASSEL

Bowl, 7½" l., shell-shaped, three applied shell-shaped feet 55.00
Bowl, 9" oval, clear 50.00
Bowl, 9" oval, vaseline.....175.00
Bowl, 10" oval, amber.....90.00
Bowl, 10" oval, clear 55.00
Bowl, 6½ x 11½" oval, amber 90.00
Bowl, 6½ x 11½" oval, blue 125.00
Bowl, 6½ x 11½" oval, clear 50.00
Bread tray, 9 x 13".....55.00
Bride's basket, 8" oval bowl in silver plate frame.....150.00
Bride's basket, 5 x 10" oval amber bowl in silver plate frame.....250.00 to 275.00
Bride's basket, 8" oval blue bowl in silver plate frame 350.00
Butter dish, cov., round, dog finial .....150.00 to 175.00
Butter pat, shell-shaped.....16.00
Cake stand, shell corners, 8" sq. 42.50
Cake stand, shell corners, 9" sq. 62.00
Cake stand, shell corners, 10" sq. .....100.00 to 150.00
Celery vase, round, handled.....85.00
Compote, cov., 4¼" sq., 8" h. 45.00
Compote, cov., 5¼" sq. 60.00
Compote, open, jelly.....85.00
Compote, open, 6½" sq., 6½" h. 45.00
Compote, open, 7½" sq., 7½" h. 95.00
Compote, open, 8" sq., 7½" h. 56.00
Compote, open, 9½" d., 9" h. 90.00
Compote, open, 10" sq., 8" h. 70.00
Creamer, round 45.00
Creamer, square.....50.00
Dish, 7 x 10" rectangle.....35.00
Doughnut stand, 8" sq., signed.....225.00
*Goblet, round, knob stem.....65.00
Mug, miniature, blue .....100.00 to 125.00
Oyster plate, 9½" d. .....225.00 to 250.00
Pickle jar, cov. .....150.00 to 175.00
Pitcher, water, round 225.00
Pitcher, water, square.....125.00
Plate, shell-shaped w/three shell-shaped feet, large 70.00
Platter, 8 x 11" oblong 52.00
Platter, 9 x 13" oval.....56.00
Salt dip, shell-shaped 16.00
Salt & pepper shakers w/original tops, pr. 260.00
Sauce dish, flat or footed, 4" to 5" d. 20.00
Sauce dish, footed, w/shell handle 15.00
Spooner, round.....51.00
Spooner, square 50.00
Sugar bowl, cov., round, dog finial 110.00
Table set, 4 pcs. 495.00

Tray, ice cream 125.00
Vase ..... 175.00 to 200.00

SHERATON

Bread platter, amber, 8 x 10" 40.00
Bread platter, blue, 8 x 10" 55.00
Bread platter, clear, 8 x 10" 30.00
Butter dish, cov. 40.00
Cake stand, 10½" d. 42.00
Celery vase 28.00
Compote, open, 8" d., high stand 32.50
Creamer, amber 35.00
Creamer, blue 42.00
Goblet, amber 35.00
Goblet, clear 25.00
Pitcher, milk 32.50
Pitcher, water, blue 85.00
Pitcher, water, clear 42.50
Plate, 7" sq., amber 20.00
Plate, 8½" sq, ... 20.00
Relish, handled, blue 22.50
Relish, handled, clear 16.00

SHOSHONE

Shoshone Jelly Compote

Banana bowl, clear, 8¼ x 10½" 45.00
Bowl, 8" d., ruffled, green 30.00
Butter dish, cov., clear w/gold trim 70.00
Cake stand, clear 45.00
Cake stand, green 48.00
Carafe 38.00
Celery vase, ruby-stained 95.00
Compote, jelly (ILLUS.) 30.00
Compote, open, 7 x 9", scalloped rim 38.00
Creamer, clear w/gold trim 35.00
Cruet w/original stopper, clear 55.00
Cruet w/original stopper, green 135.00
Cruet w/original stopper, ruby-stained 195.00
Pitcher, tankard-type 50.00
Plate, 7½" d., green 28.00
Relish, 7½" l. 30.00
Salt & pepper shakers w/original tops, ruby-stained, pr. 125.00
Salt dip, individual size 20.00
Sauce dish, ruby-stained 23.00
Spooner, amber-stained 45.00
Spooner, clear 35.00
Sugar bowl, cov., clear w/gold trim 58.00
Table set, clear w/gold trim, 4 pcs. 200.00
Toothpick holder, clear w/gold trim 40.00
Toothpick holder, ruby-stained 95.00
Wine, clear 45.00
Wine, ruby-stained 55.00

SHRINE

Butter dish, cov. 75.00
Compote, open, jelly 22.50
Goblet 50.00
Pickle dish 19.50
Pitcher, beer, 1 gal. 200.00
Pitcher, water 75.00
Tumbler, 4" h. 40.00

SHUTTLE (Hearts of Loch Laven)

Butter dish, cov. 110.00
Cake stand 125.00
Celery vase 46.00
Cordial, small 32.00
Creamer, tall tankard 30.00
Goblet 60.00
Mug, amber 300.00
Mug, clear 28.00
Pitcher, water 140.00
Salt shaker w/original top 60.00
Spooner, scalloped rim 50.00
Tumbler 50.00
Wine 18.00

SKILTON (Early Oregon)

Bowl, 8" d., 2½" h., ruby-stained 30.00
Bread tray 32.00
Butter dish, cov., ruby-stained 97.50
Cale stand, 9" d. 43.00
Compote, open, 7" d. 55.00
Compote, open, 8½" d., low stand, ruby-stained 67.50
Creamer, ruby-stained 40.00
Goblet 33.00
Pitcher, water, tankard, ruby-stained 115.00
Sauce dish 11.00
Spooner, clear 28.00
Spooner, ruby-stained 44.50
Sugar bowl, cov., ruby-stained 82.50
Syrup pitcher w/original top 65.00
Tumbler, ruby-stained 38.00

SNAIL (Compact)

Banana stand, 10" d., 7" h. ..... 125.00 to 150.00
Bowl, 7" d., low 35.00
Bowl, 5¼ x 8", oval 35.00
Bowl, 9" d., 2" h. 50.00
Butter dish, cov. 95.00
Cake stand, 10" d. 100.00
Celery vase 45.00
Cheese dish, cov. 125.00
Compote, cov., 7" d., 8" h., engraved 185.00
Compote, cov., 7" d., 11½" h. 145.00
Compote, open, 8" d., 6" h. 85.00

Compote, open, 10" d., 7" h. 145.00
Cracker jar, cov., 8" d., 9" h. 295.00
Creamer, clear 58.00
Creamer, ruby-stained 70.00
Cruet w/original stopper 125.00
Goblet 100.00
Pitcher, water, tankard 110.00
Pitcher, wine, tankard 295.00
Plate, 7" d. 46.00
Punch cup 32.50
Relish, 7" oval 22.50
Relish, 9" oval 31.50
Rose bowl, miniature, 3" h. 36.00
Rose bowl, 4½" h. 43.00
Rose bowl, double, miniature 35.00
Rose bowl, medium 55.00
Rose bowl, large 85.00
Salt dip, individual size 25.00
Salt dip, master size, 3" d. 40.00
Salt shaker w/original top, clear 40.00
Salt shaker w/original top, ruby-stained 65.00
Sauce dish 18.00
Spooner, clear 42.00
Spooner, ruby-stained 75.00
Sugar bowl, cov., individual size 75.00

Snail Sugar Bowl

Sugar bowl, cov., plain (ILLUS.) 68.00
Sugar bowl, cov., ruby-stained 95.00
Sugar shaker w/original top 115.00
Syrup jug w/original brass top 110.00
Tumbler 45.00
Vase, 12½" h., scalloped rim 75.00

SPIKED ARGUS - See Argus Pattern

SPIREA BAND

Berry set: master bowl & 6 footed sauce dishes; blue, 7 pcs. 150.00
Bowl, 8" oval, flat, amber 20.00
Butter dish, cov. 45.00
Cake stand, amber, 8½" d. 45.00
Cake stand, blue, 10½" d. 80.00
Celery vase 25.00
Compote, cov., 7" d., low stand, amber 55.00
Creamer, amber 32.00
Creamer, blue 35.00
Creamer, clear 32.00
Goblet, amber 34.00
Goblet, blue 33.00

Spirea Band Goblet

Goblet, clear (ILLUS.) 20.00
Pitcher, water 45.00
Platter, 8½ x 10½", amber 24.00
Platter, 8½ x 10½", blue 35.00
Relish, blue, 4½ x 7" 32.50
Salt shaker w/original top, blue 54.00
Spooner, amber 24.00
Spooner, vaseline 30.00
Sugar bowl, cov., blue 50.00
Sugar bowl, cov., clear 28.00
Wine, amber 23.00
Wine, blue 28.00
Wine, clear 15.50

SPRIG

Bowl, 7" oval 25.00
Bowl, 8" oval, footed 35.00
Bread platter, 11" oval 35.00
Butter dish, cov. 65.00
Cake stand 44.00
Celery vase 42.50
Compote, cov., 6" d., low stand 50.00
Compote, cov., 6" d., high stand 90.00
Compote, cov., 8" d., low stand 76.00
Compote, cov., 8" d., high stand 95.00
Compote, open, 6" d. 32.50
Compote, open, 7" d., low stand 38.00
Compote, open, 8" d., high stand 39.00
Creamer 37.00
Goblet 31.00
Pickle castor, resilvered frame & tongs 85.00
Pitcher, water 55.00
Relish, 6¾" oval 14.00
Relish, 7¾" oval 18.00
Relish, 8¾" oval 22.00
Sauce dish, flat or footed 12.00
Spooner 25.00
Sugar bowl, cov. 55.00

Sugar bowl, open....20.00
Wine....45.00

SQUARE LION'S HEAD - See Atlanta Pattern

SQUARE PANES - See Post Pattern

SQUIRREL - See "Animals & Birds on Goblets & Pitchers"

S-REPEAT
Berry set, apple green....85.00
Butter dish, cov., amethyst w/gold....125.00
Butter dish, cov., clear....125.00
Butter dish, cov., sapphire blue w/gold....150.00
Compote, jelly....40.00
Condiment set, apple green....200.00 to 250.00
Condiment set, clear....190.00
Condiment set, sapphire blue....200.00 to 250.00
Condiment tray, amethyst....37.50
Condiment tray, apple green....35.00
Cruet, amethyst....195.00
*Cruet, apple green....95.00
Decanter w/stopper, wine, amethyst..175.00
Decanter w/stopper, wine, apple green w/gold....125.00
Decanter w/stopper, wine, sapphire blue w/gold....195.00
Pitcher, green....85.00
Punch cup, clear....16.00
Salt shaker w/original top, sapphire blue....40.00
Salt & pepper shakers, apple green, pr....70.00
Salt & pepper shakers, clear, pr....38.00
Sauce dish, amethyst w/gold....30.00
Sauce dish, apple green w/gold....27.50
Syrup pitcher w/original top....70.00
*Toothpick holder, amethyst....62.00
*Toothpick holder, apple green....50.00
*Toothpick holder, sapphire blue....55.00
Tumbler, amethyst....40.00
Tumbler, sapphire blue....38.00
*Wine, apple green....40.00
*Wine, sapphire blue....57.50

STAR ROSETTED
Butter dish, cov....55.00
Cake (or bread) plate, "A Good Mother Makes A Happy Home"....45.00
Compote, open, 6½" d....16.00
Compote, open, 7½" d....18.00
Creamer....30.00
Goblet....30.00
Plate, 7" d., amber....45.00
Plate, 7" d., apple green....35.00
Plate, 7" d., blue....12.00
Plate, 7" d., clear....10.00
Sauce dish, flat or footed....5.00
Sugar bowl, cov....42.00
Sugar bowl, open....12.00

STATES (THE)
Bowl, 7" d., three-handled....50.00
Bowl, 7½" d....22.50
Bowl, 9" d....35.00
Butter dish, cov....56.00
Cocktail, flared....22.00
Compote, open, 5 x 5½"....34.00
Creamer....27.00
Creamer, individual size....30.00
Creamer & sugar bowl, pr....65.00
Cruet w/stopper....55.00
Goblet....35.00
Punch bowl, 13" d., 5½" h....95.00
Punch cup....15.00
Salt & pepper shakers w/original tops, pr....60.00
Sauce dish....10.00
Spooner....23.00
Sugar bowl, cov....46.00
Tumbler....25.00
Wine, clear....27.00
Wine, clear w/gold trim....29.00
Wine, green....60.00

STAVES WITH SCALLOPED BAND - See Picket Band Pattern

STIPPLED CHAIN
Butter dish, cov....30.00
Creamer....30.00
Goblet....22.00
Relish, 6⅛ x 8¼"....10.00
Spooner....22.50
Sugar bowl, cov....29.50

STIPPLED CHERRY
Bread platter....26.00
Butter dish, cov....62.00
Celery....35.00
Pitcher, water....44.00
Plate, 6" d....25.00

STIPPLED FLOWER PANELS - See Maine Pattern

STIPPLED FORGET-ME-NOT
Cake stand, 8" to 9" d....90.00
Celery vase....31.00
Compote, open, 6" d., 6½" h....32.50
Cup & saucer....35.00
Goblet....45.00
Pitcher, milk....37.00
Pitcher, water....42.00
Plate, 7" d....22.50
Plate, 7" d., w/baby in tub reaching for ball on floor center....65.00
Plate, 9" d., w/kitten center, handled....65.00
Plate, 9" d., w/star center, handled....55.00
Plate, 11" d., w/stork center....85.00
Relish....13.00
Tray, water....88.00

Stippled Forget-Me-Not Wine

Wine (ILLUS.) 35.00

STIPPLED GRAPE & FESTOON

Butter dish, cov., w/clear leaf....65.00
Celery vase....39.50
Compote, 8" d., low stand, w/clear leaf....110.00
Creamer....32.00
Goblet....30.00
Pitcher, water....95.00
Spooner....30.00
Spooner, w/clear leaf....28.00
Sugar bowl, cov., w/clear leaf....70.00

STIPPLED IVY

Goblet....25.00
Salt dip, master size....30.00
Spooner....29.00
Sugar bowl, open....25.00
Tumbler, water....24.00

STRIGIL

Bowl, flared, 9" d....24.50
Celery....24.00
Plate, 5¼" d. 6.50
Plate, 8" d. 22.50
Plate, 11" d. 26.50
Sauce dish, 4" to 4¼" (plain or flared) 6.50
Spooner....15.00
Tumbler 32.50
Wine, clear....14.50
Wine, gilt trim....30.00

SUNK HONEYCOMB (Corona)

Bowl, 8¼" d., ruby-stained w/h.p. floral decoration....75.00
Cake stand, ruby-stained....125.00
Celery, ruby-stained 72.50
Cheese dish, cov., ruby-stained 170.00
Compote, cov., 7" d., 11" h. 165.00
Creamer, ruby-stained, 4½" h....52.50
Creamer, ruby-stained, souvenir 45.00
Cruet w/original stopper, clear....30.00
Cruet w/original stopper, ruby-stained 110.00
Cruet w/original stopper, ruby-stained, souvenir "Mother, World's Fair, 1893"....95.00
Cup & saucer, ruby-stained....35.00
Goblet, clear 39.00
Goblet, ruby-stained 45.00
Mug, clear, souvenir 25.00
Mug, ruby-stained, 3" h....34.00
Pitcher, tankard, 8¼" h. 150.00
Pitcher, water, bulbous, ruby-stained 95.00
Punch cup....22.00
Salt dip, individual size 17.50
Salt shaker w/original top, ruby-stained 37.50
Sugar bowl, cov., hotel size, ruby-stained, engraved 195.00
Syrup pitcher w/original top, clear 135.00
Syrup pitcher w/original top, ruby-stained 175.00
Table set: cov. butter dish, cov. sugar bowl, creamer & spooner; ruby-stained, 4 pcs....350.00
Toothpick holder, ruby-stained, souvenir 42.50
Tumbler, clear, engraved....24.00
Tumbler, ruby-stained....50.00
Water set, pitcher & 6 goblets, 7 pcs. 350.00
Wine, clear....14.00
Wine, clear, engraved....22.00
Wine, ruby-stained....35.00
Wine, ruby-stained, engraved....40.00

SWAN

Swan Creamer

Celery vase, etched....38.00
Compote, cov., w/swan finial, 8" d.....365.00
Compote, open, 8½" h....85.00
Creamer, amber 55.00
Creamer, clear (ILLUS.) 42.50
*Creamer, milk white 38.00
Cup, handled 35.00
Marmalade jar, cov. 110.00
Pitcher, water....200.00 to 250.00

Sauce dish, flat or footed.....20.00
Spooner.....42.00
Sugar bowl, cov. 185.00

TACOMA (Jeweled Diamond and Fan)
Banana dish, flat.....35.00
Butter dish, cov., amber-stained.....95.00
Celery vase.....22.50
Creamer.....60.00
Pitcher, water, ruby-stained.....120.00
Punch cup.....22.00
Sauce dish, ruby-stained.....24.00
Toothpick holder.....20.00

TEARDROP & TASSEL

Teardrop & Tassel Salt Shaker

Berry set: master bowl & 6 sauce dishes; teal blue, 7 pcs. 395.00
Bowl, 7½" d.....38.00
Bowl, 8¼" d.....55.00
Butter dish, cov., clear.....65.00
Butter dish, cov., cobalt blue 150.00
Butter dish, cov., emerald green.....200.00
Compote, cov., 5" d., 7½" h. 85.00
Compote, cov., 7" d., 11½" h. 95.00
Compote, cov., 9½" d. 95.00
Compote, open, 5" d. 25.00
Compote, open, 6" d.....35.00
Compote, open, 8½" d.....42.00
Creamer, amber 175.00
Creamer, clear.....45.00
Creamer, cobalt blue 125.00
Creamer, Nile green .....150.00 to 200.00
Creamer, white opaque 75.00
Creamer & cov. sugar bowl, emerald green, pr. 325.00
Creamer & cov. sugar bowl, white opaque, pr.....175.00
Goblet, clear 150.00
Goblet, emerald green.....225.00
Pickle dish, amber 90.00
Pickle dish, clear.....29.00
Pitcher, water, clear.....70.00
Pitcher, water, cobalt blue 225.00
Pitcher, water, emerald green.....250.00 to 275.00
Relish, clear.....35.00
Relish, emerald green 100.00
Relish, Nile green 175.00
Relish, teal blue 175.00
Salt shaker w/original top, clear (ILLUS.) 125.00
Salt & pepper shakers w/original tops, Nile green, pr. 350.00
Sauce dish, clear.....13.50
Sauce dish, cobalt blue 30.00
Sauce dish, emerald green.....75.00
Spooner, clear 50.00
Spooner, cobalt blue.....90.00
Spooner, Nile green.....175.00
Spooner, white opaque.....65.00
Sugar bowl, cov., clear 60.00
Sugar bowl, cov., cobalt blue.....135.00
Sugar bowl, cov., Nile green.....300.00
Tumbler, clear.....37.00
Tumbler, cobalt blue 58.00
Tumbler, emerald green 165.00
Water set, pitcher & 6 tumblers, 7 pcs. 285.00

TENNESSEE
Butter dish, cov.....90.00
Cake stand, 8½" d., high stand.....32.00
Compote, open, 8" d., flared rim, shallow round bowl, high stand.....48.00
Pitcher, milk, 1 qt. 125.00
Relish tray.....20.00
Sauce dish, flat, round.....12.00
Toothpick holder.....200.00
Wine 125.00

TEXAS (Loop with Stippled Panels)

Texas Toothpick Holder

Cake stand, 9½" to 10¾" d. 62.50
Celery vase.....75.00
Compote, open, jelly.....100.00
Compote, cov., 6" d., 11" h. 165.00
Creamer.....26.00
*Creamer, individual size.....18.00
Goblet, clear 38.00
Goblet, ruby-stained 110.00
Relish, handled, 8½" l. 20.00
Salt dip, master size, footed, 3" d., 2¾" h. 22.00
Sauce dish, flat or footed.....25.00

Spooner, ruby-stained 95.00
Toothpick holder, clear (ILLUS.).....35.00
Toothpick holder, clear w/gold.....55.00
Vase, 7½" h., trumpet-shaped, pink-stained 95.00
Vase, bud, 8" h. 30.00
Vase, 9" h. 35.00
Vase, 10" h. 30.00
*Wine 115.00
Wine, ruby-stained.....125.00

TEXAS BULL'S EYE (Bull's Eye Variant)

Butter dish, cov. 40.00
Celery vase.....50.00
Cordial 25.00
Goblet 30.00
Pitcher, water, ½ gal. 55.00
Sugar bowl, open.....32.00
Tumbler 25.00
Wine 24.00

THISTLE, PANELED - See Paneled Thistle Pattern

THOUSAND EYE

Thousand Eye Butter Dish

Bowl, 8" d., 4½" h., footed, amber 35.00
Bowl, 11" rectangle, shallow, amber.....32.00
Bread tray, amber.....32.00
Bread tray, apple green 52.00
Bread tray, blue 40.00
Bread tray, clear 28.00
Butter dish, cov., amber.....115.00
Butter dish, cov., blue 145.00
Butter dish, cov., clear (ILLUS.).....50.00
Cake stand, blue, 8½" to 10" d. 88.00
Cake stand, blue, 12½" d. 60.00
Celery vase, three-knob stem, amber ..48.00
Celery vase, three-knob stem, apple green 55.00
Celery vase, three-knob stem, clear.....40.00
Celery vase, three-knob stem, clear to opalescent w/purple tint 130.00
Celery vase, plain stem, amber 45.00
Compote, cov., 12" h. 115.00
*Compote, open, 6" d., low stand, amber.....22.00
*Compote, open, 6" d., low stand, blue 38.00
Compote, open, 6½" d., three-knob stem, blue 30.00
Compote, open, 7½" d., 5" h.....35.00
Compote, open, 8" d., 3¾" h., apple green.....40.00
Compote, open, 8" d., 6" h., three-knob stem, amber 38.00
Compote, open, 8" d., 6" h., three-knob stem, apple green 65.00
Compote, open, 8" d., 6" h., three-knob stem, blue 65.00
Compote, open, 8" d., high stand, three-knob stem, vaseline.....58.00
Compote, open, 8" sq., low stand, apple green 65.00
Compote, open, 9½" d., low stand, amber.....27.00
Compote, open, 10" d., 6½" h., three-knob stem, blue 85.00
Creamer, amber 42.00
*Creamer, clear 35.00
Creamer, clear opalescent 95.00
Creamer & cov. sugar bowl, amber, pr.....100.00
Cruet w/original three-knob stopper, amber.....135.00
Cruet w/original three-knob stopper, apple green 135.00
Cruet w/original three-knob stopper, blue .....125.00 to 150.00
Cruet w/original three-knob stopper, clear 32.00
Cruet w/original three-knob stopper, vaseline.....100.00 to 125.00
Egg cup, blue.....65.00
Egg cup, clear.....25.00
*Goblet, amber 30.00
*Goblet, apple green.....40.00
*Goblet, blue.....32.00
*Goblet, clear.....28.00
*Goblet, vaseline 32.00
Lamp, kerosene-type, pedestal base, amber, 14" h. to collar.....225.00
Lamp, kerosene-type, pedestal base, blue font, amber base, 12" h. 195.00
Lamp, kerosene-type, pedestal base, blue, 12" h. 155.00
Lamp, kerosene-type, flat base, ring handle, amber 325.00
Lamp, kerosene type, flat base, ring handle, clear 110.00
*Mug, amber, 3½" h. 28.00
*Mug, blue, 3½" h. 28.00
*Mug, clear, 3½" h. 20.00
*Mug, vaseline, 3½" h. 32.00
Mug, miniature, amber.....30.00
Pickle dish, apple green 25.00
Pitcher, water, three-knob stem, blue...95.00
*Pitcher, water, clear 75.00
Pitcher, water, vaseline 60.00
Plate, 6" d., amber 22.50

Plate, 6" d., apple green 17.00
Plate, 6" d., blue 18.00
*Plate, 6" d., clear 14.50
Plate, 8" d., amber 26.00
Plate, 8" d., apple green 25.00
*Plate, 8" d., clear 28.00
Plate, 8" d., vaseline 32.00
Plate, 10" sq., w/folded corners, blue ...28.00
Plate, 10" sq., w/folded corners, clear ..28.00
Platter, 8 x 11" 30.00
Salt & pepper shakers w/original tops, blue, pr. 75.00
*Salt & pepper shakers w/original tops, clear, pr. 65.00
Sauce dish, flat or footed, amber.....12.50
Sauce dish, flat or footed, blue 16.00
*Sauce dish, flat or footed, clear.....10.00
Spooner, three-knob stem, amber.....52.00
Spooner, three-knob stem, clear 38.00
Spooner, three-knob stem, vaseline.....42.00
Sugar bowl, cov., three-knob stem, amber.....55.00
Sugar bowl, cov. 37.50
*Sugar bowl, open, three-knob stem 25.00
Syrup pitcher w/original top, amber 100.00
*Toothpick holder, amber 38.00
*Toothpick holder, blue.....40.00
*Toothpick holder, clear.....24.00
*Toothpick holder, vaseline 38.00
Tray, water, amber, 12½" d. 65.00
Tray, water, blue, 12½" d.....120.00
Tray, apple green, 14" oval.....60.00
*Tumbler, apple green 39.00
*Tumbler, blue 30.00
*Tumbler, clear 18.00
*Wine, amber.....20.00
*Wine, apple green 42.50
*Wine, blue 42.50
*Wine, clear 20.00
*Wine, vaseline.....38.00

THREE FACE

Three Face Creamer

Butter dish, cov., engraved.....200.00 to 225.00
Butter dish, cov., plain 185.00
*Cake stand, 8" to 10½" d.....150.00
Celery vase.....100.00 to 125.00
*Champagne.....165.00
Claret.....152.00
Claret, engraved 265.00
Compote, cov., 4½" d., 6½" h. 100.00
*Compote, cov., 6" d. 125.00
Compote, cov., 7" d. 285.00
Compote, cov., 8" d., 13" h. 315.00
Compote, open, 6" d., high stand 80.00
Compote, open, 7" d., high stand 90.00
Compote, open, 8½" d., high stand 125.00
Compote, open, 9½" d., high stand 160.00
*Cracker jar, cov. 1,250.00
Creamer (ILLUS.) 90.00
*Creamer w/mask spout 150.00
Goblet, engraved 150.00
*Goblet, plain 82.00
*Lamp, kerosene-type, pedestal base, 8" h. 165.00
Marmalade jar, cov. 350.00
Pitcher, water.....450.00
*Salt dip 44.00
*Salt shaker w/original top 65.00
*Sauce dish 30.00
*Spooner.....60.00
Spooner, engraved 100.00
*Sugar bowl, cov.....155.00
*Sugar shaker, w/original top.....155.00
*Wine 85.00

THREE PANEL

Three Panel Creamer

Bowl, 7" d., footed, blue.....30.00
Bowl, 7" d., footed, vaseline 31.50
Bowl, 9" d., footed, blue.....25.00
Bowl, 10" d., amber 49.00
Bowl, 10" d., blue.....65.00
Bowl, 10" d., clear.....20.00
Bowl, 10" d., vaseline 45.00
Butter dish, cov., vaseline.....50.00
Celery vase, amber 47.50
Celery vase, clear.....35.00
Celery vase, vaseline 55.00
Compote, open, 7" d., low stand, amber.....32.00
Compote, open, 7" d., low stand, vaseline.....27.50

Compote, open, 8½" d., low stand, blue 40.00
Compote, open, 9" d., 4¼" h., amber ...40.00
Compote, open, 9" d., vaseline....45.00
Compote, open, 10" d., low stand, blue 65.00
Creamer, amber 35.00
Creamer, blue (ILLUS.) 45.00
Creamer, clear....20.00
Creamer, vaseline 38.00
Cruet w/original stopper....155.00
*Goblet, amber 32.00
*Goblet, blue....42.00
*Goblet, clear....25.00
*Goblet, vaseline 40.00
Lamp, kerosene-type, amber....145.00
Mug, amber 35.00
Mug, clear....30.00
Pitcher, milk, 7" h....44.50
Pitcher, water, vaseline 110.00
Sauce dish, footed, amber....17.00
Sauce dish, footed, blue 19.50
Sauce dish, footed, clear....11.50
Sauce dish, footed, vaseline....15.00
Spooner, amber....32.00
Spooner, blue 38.00
Spooner, clear 15.00
Spooner, vaseline....35.00
Sugar bowl, cov., blue 75.00
Sugar bowl, cov., clear 55.00
Sugar bowl, cov., vaseline....65.00
Sugar bowl, open....25.00
Table set, blue, 4 pcs. 245.00
Table set, clear, 4 pcs. 175.00
Tumbler, amber 35.00
Tumbler, blue....40.00
Tumbler, clear....12.00

THUMBPRINT, EARLY (Bakewell, Pears & Co.'s "Argus")

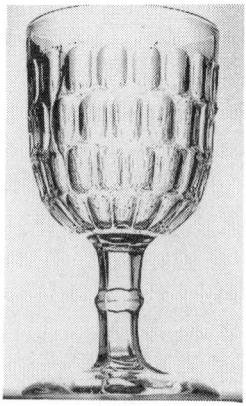

Early Thumbprint Goblet

*Butter dish, cov. 115.00
*Cake stand, 8" to 9½" d....275.00
*Celery vase, plain base....110.00
Celery vase, scalloped rim, pattern in base 155.00
*Compote, open, 6" d., low stand, scalloped rim....35.00
Compote, open, 7½" d., low stand....55.00
*Compote, open, 8" d., high stand....100.00
Compote, open, 8½" d., high stand, scalloped rim, flint ....125.00 to 150.00
Compote, open, 14" d., 12" h....600.00
*Creamer 90.00
Goblet, plain stem (ILLUS.) 38.00
Inkwell....350.00
Pickle dish 40.00
Pitcher, milk....90.00
*Pitcher, water, 8¼" h. ....300.00 to 400.00
*Sauce dish, clear....8.00
Sauce dish, milk white 75.00
Spillholder....48.00
*Sugar bowl, cov....60.00
Sweetmeat bowl, 6½" d., 7" h....190.00
*Wine, baluster stem 60.00

TONG

Celery vase....95.00
Sugar bowl, cov. 100.00

TORPEDO (Pygmy)

Bowl, 7" d., flat, clear 15.00
Bowl, 8" d....32.50
Bowl, 9" d....32.00
Bowl, 9½" d....42.50
Butter dish, cov....75.00
Celery vase....40.00
Compote, cov., jelly 43.00
Compote, cov., 6" d. 78.00
Compote, cov., 7" d., 7¼" h. 65.00
Compote, cov., 8" d., 14" h. 135.00
Compote, open, jelly, 5" d., 5" h. 47.50
Compote, open, 7" d., high stand 52.00
Compote, open, 8" d., high stand, flared rim 110.00
Compote, open, 8 x 10½", 8" h., ruffled rim 145.00
Creamer, collared base 55.00
Creamer, footed....37.50
Cruet w/original faceted stopper....75.00
Cup & saucer....65.00
Goblet, clear 50.00
Goblet, ruby-stained 80.00
Lamp, kerosene, hand-type w/finger grip, w/burner & chimney 125.00
Lamp, kerosene-type, 10" h....185.00
Pickle castor, silver plate cover & tongs 250.00
Pitcher, milk, 8½" h....95.00
Pitcher, water, tankard, 12" h. 75.00
Salt dip, individual size, 1½" d. 26.00
Salt dip, master size 45.00
Salt & pepper shakers w/original tops, pr....95.00
Sauce dish....17.50
Spooner....40.00
Sugar bowl, cov. 95.00
Syrup jug w/original top, clear ....100.00 to 125.00

Syrup jug w/original top, ruby-stained 250.00
Tumbler, clear....38.00
Tumbler, clear, engraved....55.00
Tumbler, ruby-stained....48.00
Wine, clear....90.00
Wine, ruby-stained....95.00

TREE OF LIFE - PORTLAND

Butter dish, cov....110.00
Butter pat, green....20.00
Celery vase....100.00
Celery vase, in silver plate holder....135.00
Champagne....75.00
Compote, open, 7" d., high stand, w/applied red serpent on stem....245.00
Compote, open, 7½" d., scalloped rim....45.00
Compote, open, 7¾" d., 11" h., Infant Samuel stand, signed "Davis"....125.00
Compote, open, 8½" d., 5" h., signed "Davis"....60.00
Compote, open, 8¾" d., in two-handled Meriden silver plate holder, bowl signed "Davis"....185.00
Compote, open, 10" d., 6" h., signed "Davis"....100.00 to 125.00
Creamer, signed "Davis"....55.00
Creamer, blue, in silver plate holder....175.00 to 200.00
Creamer, clear, in silver plate holder....85.00
Creamer, cranberry in silver plate holder....190.00
Epergne, single lily, red snake around stem, 18" h....450.00
*Goblet....50.00
Goblet, signed "Davis"....90.00
Ice cream set, tray & 6 leaf-shaped desserts, 7 pcs....150.00
Mug, applied handle, 3½" h....45.00
Pitcher, water, applied handle, clear 78.00
Plate, 7¼" d....50.00
Powder jar, cov., red coiled snake finial on cover....350.00
Salt dip, individual size, footed, amber....65.00
Salt dip, footed, "Salt" embossed in bowl, clear....135.00
Sauce dish, leaf-shaped, blue 18.00
Sauce dish, leaf-shaped, clear 15.00
Spooner....30.00
Spooner, in handled silver plate holder w/two Griffin heads 110.00
Sugar bowl, cov., blue, in silver plate holder....175.00 to 200.00
Sugar bowl, cov., clear, in silver plate holder....88.00
Sugar bowl, cov., clear 63.00
Syrup pitcher w/original metal top, blue opaque 100.00
Table set: cov. sugar bowl, creamer & spooner; in ornate silver plate holders, the set 180.00
Toothpick holder, apple green 125.00
Tray, ice cream, 14" rectangle....48.00
Waste bowl, amber....50.00
Waste bowl, blue 52.00
Waste bowl, blue, in ornate silver plate holder 175.00
Waste bowl, clear 30.00
Waste bowl, green....45.00

TREE OF LIFE WITH HAND (Tree of Life-Wheeling)

Tree of Life with Hand Creamer

Butter dish, cov....125.00
Cake stand, frosted base, 11½" d. 85.00
Celery vase....47.00
Compote, open, 5½" d., 5½" h., clear hand & ball stem 48.00
Compote, open, 5½" d., 5½" h., frosted hand & ball stem 65.00
Compote, open, 8" d., clear hand & ball stem 55.00
Compote, open, 9" d., frosted hand & ball stem 80.00
Compote, open, 10" d., 10" h., frosted hand & ball stem 95.00
Creamer, w/hand & ball handle (ILLUS.) 75.00
Mug, applied handle, 3" h....125.00
Pitcher, water, 9" h. 68.00
Sauce dish, flat or footed....19.00
Spooner....42.00

TRIPLE TRIANGLE

Butter dish, cov., handled, ruby-stained 85.00
*Goblet, clear....50.00
*Goblet, ruby-stained....40.00
Mug, ruby-stained....25.00
Tumbler, water, ruby-stained....25.00
*Wine, clear 60.00
*Wine, ruby-stained 35.00

TULIP WITH SAWTOOTH

Celery vase, flint....85.00
Celery vase, non-flint....45.00

Champagne, non-flint 75.00
Compote, cov., 6" d., low stand, flint 75.00

Tulip with Sawtooth Compote

Compote, cov., 7" d., 12½" h. (ILLUS.) 247.50
Compote, open, 8" d., low stand, flint 75.00
Compote, open, 9" d., 7⅜" h., flint 78.00
Compote, open, 9" d., 10" h., flint 135.00
Cruet w/original stopper, flint, 8⅝" h...165.00
Egg cup, flint 35.00
*Goblet, flint 50.00
Goblet, non-flint 25.00
Pitcher, 9¾" h., flint 250.00
Salt dip, cov., flint, 5½" h. 285.00
Salt dip, master size, scalloped rim, flint 35.00
Salt dip, open, non-flint 15.00
Spooner, flint 65.00
Spooner, non-flint 28.00
Sugar bowl, open, non-flint 32.50
Toothpick holder 39.00
Tumbler, bar, flint 80.00
Tumbler, flint 45.00
Wine, flint 45.00
*Wine, non-flint 25.00

TURKEY TRACK - See Crowfoot Pattern

TWO PANEL (Daisy in Panel)

Bowl, cov., 7" oval, vaseline 75.00
Bowl, 6 x 8" oval, blue 38.50
Bowl, 7½ x 9" oval, apple green 36.00
Butter dish, cov., blue 85.00
Butter dish, cov., vaseline 50.00
Celery vase, clear 30.00
Celery vase, vaseline 45.00
Compote, cov., 6½ x 8", 11" h., vaseline 85.00
Compote, cov., high stand, apple green 135.00
Compote, cov., high stand, blue 85.00
Compote, open, 9" oval, 4" h., apple green 60.00
Compote, open, 9" oval, 4" h., vaseline 45.00
Creamer, amber 45.00
Creamer, apple green 45.00
Creamer, blue 45.00

Two Panel Goblet

*Goblet, amber (ILLUS.) 35.00
*Goblet, apple green 35.00
*Goblet, blue 42.00
*Goblet, clear 20.00
*Goblet, vaseline 32.00
Lamp, kerosene-type, pedestal base, blue, 7¾" h., No. 1 burner 145.00
Pitcher, water, blue 90.00
Pitcher, water, clear 36.00
Relish, blue 30.00
Salt dip, master size, apple green 28.00
Salt dip, individual size, apple green 24.00
Sauce dish, flat or footed, amber 10.00
Sauce dish, flat or footed, apple green 13.50
Sauce dish, flat or footed, clear 9.50
Spooner, amber 38.00
Spooner, blue 35.00
Spooner, vaseline 35.00
Sugar bowl, cov., amber 50.00
Sugar bowl, cov., apple green 55.00
Sugar bowl, cov., vaseline 54.00
Tray, water, blue 60.00
Tumbler, vaseline 40.00
Waste bowl, amber 36.00
*Wine, amber 35.00
*Wine, apple green 40.00
*Wine, blue 35.00
*Wine, clear 29.00
*Wine, vaseline 35.00

U.S. COIN

*Bowl, berry, 6" d., frosted coins, plate rim 400.00
Bowl, berry, 7" d., frosted quarters, plain rim .....300.00 to 350.00
Bowl, berry, 8" d., frosted half dollars, plain rim 400.00

Bowl, berry, 9" d., frosted dollars, plain rim 800.00
Bowl, berry, 6" d., frosted coins, scalloped rim.....800.00
Bowl, berry, 7" d., frosted quarters, scalloped rim.....800.00
Bowl, berry, 8" d., clear half dollars, scalloped rim.....320.00
Bowl, berry, 8" d., frosted half dollars, scalloped rim.....900.00
Bowl, berry, 9" d., frosted dollars, scalloped rim.....1,200.00
Bread tray, frosted quarters & half dollars 230.00

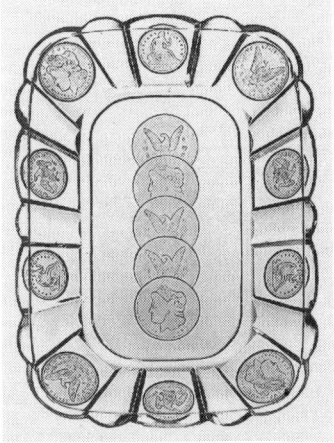

U.S. Coin Bread Tray

*Bread tray, frosted dollars & half dollars (ILLUS.).....350.00 to 395.00
Butter dish, cov., clear dollars & half dollars 490.00
Butter dish, cov., frosted dollars & half dollars .....400.00 to 500.00
Cake plate, frosted dollars & quarters, 7" d.....400.00 to 450.00
Cake stand, clear dollars, 10" d.....375.00
Cake stand, frosted dollars, 10" d.....425.00 to 450.00
Celery tray, clear quarters 195.00
Celery tray, frosted quarters.....300.00
Celery vase, clear quarters.....245.00
Celery vase, frosted quarters.....350.00 to 375.00
Champagne, flared rim, frosted half dimes 800.00
Claret, flared rim, frosted half dimes...600.00
Claret, straight rim, frosted half dimes 600.00
Compote, cov., 6" d., high stand, quarters on lid, twenty cent pieces on base 495.00
*Compote, cov., 6" d., high stand, frosted dimes & quarters..350.00 to 400.00
Compote, cov., 7" d., high stand, clear dimes & quarters.....300.00
Compote, cov., 7" d., high stand, frosted dimes & quarters..500.00 to 550.00
Compote, cov., 8" d., high stand, frosted quarters & half dollars.....475.00 to 500.00
Compote, cov., 9" d., high stand, frosted dollars 600.00
Compote, cov., 9" d., high stand, frosted dollars & quarters.....1,500.00
Compote, cov., 6" d., low stand, clear twenty cent pieces & quarters.....350.00
Compote, open, 7¼" d., high stand, straight rim, frosted quarters.....495.00
Compote, open, 7½" d., high stand, straight rim, frosted dimes & quarters.....300.00
Compote, open, 7½" d., high stand, straight rim, frosted quarters.....495.00
Compote, open, 8¼" d., high stand, straight rim, frosted quarters.....522.50
Compote, open, 8½" d., high stand, straightrim, frosted dimes & quarters.....350.00 to 400.00
Compote, open, 8½" d., high stand, straight rim, frosted quarters.....522.50
Compote, open, 9¾" d., high stand, straightrim, frosted quarters & half dollars .....350.00 to 400.00
Compote, open, 10½" d., straight rim, frosted quarters & half dollars.....500.00
Compote, open, 7" d., high stand, flared rim, frosted dimes & quarters.....300.00 to 350.00
Compote, open, 8¼" d., high stand, flared rim, frosted dimes & quarters.....350.00 to 400.00
Compote, open, 9½" d., high stand, flared rim, frosted quarters & half dollars 600.00
Compote, open, 10½" d., high stand, flared rim, frosted quarters & half dollars 700.00
Compote, open, 7¼" d., high stand, flared & scalloped rim, frosted dimes & quarters.....750.00
Compote, open, 6" d., low stand, flared & scalloped rim, frosted twenty cent pieces 800.00
Compote, open, 7" d., low stand, straight top w/scalloped rim, frosted twenty cent pieces 450.00
Compote, open, 7" d., low stand, flared & scalloped rim, frosted twenty cent pieces 600.00
*Creamer, frosted quarters 450.00
Cruet w/original stopper, frosted quarters, 5½" h. .....625.00 to 650.00
Epergne, clear quarters & dollars 632.00
Epergne, frosted quarters & dollars....800.00
Finger bowl, straight rim, frosted coins 500.00
Finger bowl, flared rim, frosted coins 500.00
Goblet, straight top, frosted dimes, 6½" h.....250.00 to 300.00
Goblet, straight top, frosted half dollar, 7" h. 400.00

Goblet, flared top, frosted half dollars, 7" h. 450.00
Lamp, kerosene-type, square font, frosted quarters & half dollars, 8½" h. ....300.00 to 350.00
Lamp, kerosene-type, square font, frosted dollars & quarters, 9½" h. ....400.00 to 450.00
Lamp, kerosene-type, square font, frosted half dollars & dollars, 10¼" h. 500.00
Lamp, kerosene-type, square font, frosted half dollars & dollars, 11" h. 550.00
Lamp, kerosene-type, square font, frosted half dollars & dollars, 11½" h. 675.00
Lamp, kerosene-type, round font, frosted quarters, 8" h. ....300.00 to 400.00
Lamp, kerosene-type, round font, frosted quarters, 8½" h. 350.00
Lamp, kerosene-type, round font, frosted quarters, 9" h. 400.00
Lamp, kerosene-type, round font, frosted half dollars, 9½" h. 400.00
Lamp, kerosene-type, round font, frosted half dollars, 10" h. ....400.00 to 450.00
Lamp, kerosene-type, round font, frosted half dollars, 10" h. ....400.00 to 450.00
Lamp, kerosene-type, round font, frosted half dollars, 11½" h. 450.00
Lamp, kerosene-type, round font, frosted dollars, 11½" h. ....750.00 to 800.00
Lamp, kerosene-type, flaring font, frosted quarters, 8½" h. 600.00
Lamp, kerosene-type, flaring font, frosted quarters, 9" h. 600.00
Lamp, kerosene-type, flaring font, frosted quarters, 9½" h. 600.00
Lamp, kerosene-type, flaring font, frosted quarters, 10" h. 600.00
Lamp, kerosene-type, handled, frosted twenty cent pieces, 5" h. 500.00
Lamp, kerosene-type, handled, clear quarters, 5" h. ....450.00 to 500.00
Lamp, kerosene-type, handled, frosted quarters, 5" h. 350.00
Mug, frosted dollars 350.00
Pickle dish, frosted half dollars, 3¾ x 7½" ....200.00 to 225.00
Pitcher, milk, frosted half dollars ....600.00 to 650.00
Pitcher, water, frosted dollars ....600.00 to 700.00
Preserve dish, clear half dollars in rim, dollars in base, 5 x 8" ....300.00 to 350.00
Preserve dish, frosted half dollars in rim, dollars in base, 5 x 8" ....300.00 to 350.00
Salt & pepper shakers w/original tops, frosted coins, pr. 300.00
Sauce dish, flat, plain rim, frosted quarters, 3¾" d. ....125.00 to 150.00
Sauce dish, flat, plain rim, clear quarters, 4¼" d. 110.00
Sauce dish, flat, plain rim, frosted quarters, 4¼" d. 150.00
Sauce dish, flat, scalloped rim, frosted quarters, 4" d. 350.00
Sauce dish, flat, scalloped rim, frosted quarters, 4½" d. 400.00
Sauce dish, footed, plain top, frosted quarters ....150.00 to 195.00
Sauce dish, footed, scalloped rim, frosted quarters 350.00
Spooner, clear quarters ....225.00 to 250.00
*Spooner, frosted quarters ....275.00 to 300.00
*Sugar bowl, cov., frosted quarters & half dollars ....350.00 to 400.00
Syrup jug w/original dated pewter top, frosted coins ....500.00 to 550.00
Toothpick holder, clear dollars ....150.00 to 175.00
*Toothpick holder, frosted dollars ....150.00 to 175.00
Tumbler, frosted dime on side ....150.00 to 200.00
Tumbler, dollar in base, clear sides w/clear 1879 coin ....200.00 to 225.00
Tumbler, dollar in base, clear sides w/frosted 1882 coin 250.00
Tumbler, dollar in base, paneled sides w/clear 1878 coin ....150.00 to 200.00
Waste bowl -- See FINGER BOWL
Water tray, frosted coins 500.00
Wine, frosted half dimes 600.00

VALENCIA WAFFLE (Block & Star)

Bread platter 30.00
Butter dish, cov., apple green 55.00
Celery vase, clear 30.00
Compote, cov., 7" sq., low stand, amber 64.00
Compote, cov., 7" sq., low stand, blue ....50.00 to 75.00
Compote, cov., 7" sq., low stand, clear 40.00
Compote, cov., 8" sq., low stand, clear 125.00
Compote, cov., 8" sq., 9" h., amber 90.00
Compote, open, 7" sq., low stand, amber 32.50
Compote, open, 7" sq., light blue 55.00
Compote, open, 8" d., 8" h., amber 60.00
Goblet, amber 35.00
Goblet, blue 45.00
Goblet, clear 25.00
Pitcher, water, 7½" h., amber 60.00
Pitcher, water, blue 72.00
Relish, amber, 5⅜ x 9" 22.50
Salt dip, master size, blue 45.00
Salt shaker w/original top, apple green 30.00

Spooner, amber....38.00
Spooner, yellow....35.00
Tray, water....25.00
Tumbler, ruby-stained....30.00

VICTOR - See Shell & Jewel Pattern

VICTORIA

Compote, cov., 6½" d. 67.50
Compote, cov., 8" d., high stand....200.00
Tumbler 25.00
Wine 27.50

VIKING (Bearded Head or Old Man of the Mountain)

Viking Sugar Bowl

Apothecary jar w/original stopper 75.00
Bowl, cov., 8" oval 100.00
Bowl, 8" sq. 45.00
Butter dish, cov., clear 75.00
Butter dish, cov., frosted 85.00
Celery vase 55.00
Compote, cov., 7" d., low stand 82.00
Compote, cov., 9" d., low stand 110.00
Creamer 60.00
Egg cup 65.00
Marmalade jar, cov., footed 75.00
Mug, applied handle 62.50
Pickle jar w/cover 95.00
Pitcher, water, 8¾" h., clear 115.00
Pitcher, water, 8¾" h., clear & frosted 310.00
Relish 25.00
Salt dip, master size 35.00
Sauce dish, footed 18.00
Spooner 30.00
Sugar bowl, cov. (ILLUS.) 65.00

VIRGINIA - See Banded Portland Pattern

WAFFLE

Celery vase 85.00
Champagne 135.00
Creamer, applied handle 125.00
Egg cup 45.00
Goblet 95.00
Sugar bowl, cov. 125.00
Syrup pitcher, applied handle 85.00
Tumbler, bar 80.00
Wine 110.00

WAFFLE AND THUMBPRINT

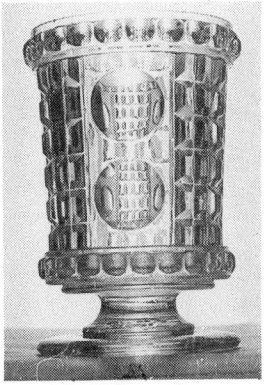

Waffle & Thumbprint Spillholder

Bowl, 6 x 8¼", flint 45.00
Compote, open, 6" d., 6" h., flint 195.00
Compote, open, 7" d., high stand, non-flint 55.00
Decanter w/bar lip, flint, pt. 100.00
Decanter w/matching stopper, pt. 325.00
Decanter w/matching stopper, qt. 375.00
Decanter w/bar lip, qt. 75.00
Egg cup, flint 30.00
Goblet, flint 100.00
Lamp, w/original whale oil burner, flint, 11" h. 153.00
Pitcher, 9½" h., tapering body w/arched wide spout, applied strap handle, made from decanter mold, flint 460.00
Salt dip, master size, flint 29.00
Spillholder, flint (ILLUS.) 100.00
Sugar bowl, cov., flint 195.00
Tray, 8¼" l. 66.00
Tumbler, bar, flint 70.00
Tumbler, whiskey, handled, flint, 3" h. 275.00
Wine, flint 95.00

WASHBOARD - See Adonis Pattern

WASHINGTON CENTENNIAL

Bread platter, Carpenter's Hall center 100.00
Bread platter, George Washington center 84.00
Bread platter, George Washington center, frosted 130.00
Bread platter, Independence Hall center, frosted 95.00
Cake stand, 8½" to 11½" d. 75.00
Celery vase 52.00

Champagne 68.00
Compote, open, 7" d., low stand 45.00
Egg cup 39.00
Goblet 50.00
Pickle dish 34.00
Pitcher, water 110.00
Relish, bear paw handles, dated 1876 ..... 35.00
Salt dip, master size 60.00
Sauce dish, flat or footed 11.00
Spooner 35.00
Sugar bowl, cov. 72.50
Sugar bowl, open 20.00
Syrup pitcher, w/dated pewter top w/tiny figural finial 165.00
Tumbler 58.00
Wine 48.00

WASHINGTON, EARLY

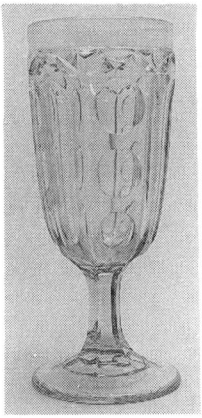

Early Washington Celery Vase

Butter dish, cov., flint 55.00
Celery vase, flint (ILLUS.) 125.00
Egg cup, flint 55.00
Salt dip, individual size, flint 20.00
Spooner, flint 29.00

WASHINGTON (State)

Creamer w/colored enameling 45.00
Pitcher, milk, ruby-stained 95.00
Toothpick holder, clear w/enamel decoration 49.00

WEDDING BELLS

Creamer, four-footed, pink-stained 65.00
Pitcher, water 47.00
Sauce dish, clear w/gold trim 18.00
*Sugar bowl, cov., clear 55.00
Toothpick holder, pink-stained 90.00
Wine, amethyst-stained 55.00

WEDDING RING - See Double Wedding Ring Pattern

WESTMORELAND (Gillinder's)

Celery tray 37.50
Celery vase 37.50
Cologne bottles, original stoppers, pr. 85.00
Compote, cov., low footed 27.50
Compote, jelly 25.00
Creamer 25.00
Cruet, 5" h. 35.00
Lamp, finger, one-handle, 3½" h. (no shade) 115.00
Lamp, 7½" h. 255.00
Lamp, 8½" h. 125.00
Pitcher, tall, scalloped rim 65.00
Water bottle, 8¼" h. 45.00

WESTWARD HO

Westward Ho Compote

Bowl, 8" 125.00
Bowl, 9" oval 95.00
Bread platter 115.00
*Butter dish, cov. ..... 125.00 to 150.00
*Celery vase 135.00
*Compote, cov., 4" d., low stand 100.00
Compote, cov., 5" d., high stand 95.00
*Compote, cov., 6" d., low stand 120.00
Compote, cov., 6" d., high stand 325.00
*Compote, cov., 4 x 6¾" oval, low stand 150.00
Compote, cov., 5 x 7¾" oval, high stand ..... 200.00 to 225.00
Compote, cov., 8" d., low stand (ILLUS.) 325.00
Compote, cov., 8" d., high stand ..... 275.00 to 325.00
Compote, cov., 5½ x 8" oval, high stand 440.00
Compote, cov., 8" d., 14" h. 350.00
Compote, cov., 6½ x 10" oval, low stand ..... 225.00 to 250.00
Compote, open, 7" d., low stand 175.00
Compote, open, 9" oval, high stand 100.00
*Creamer ..... 125.00 to 150.00
*Goblet 75.00
Marmalade jar, cov. 295.00
Mug, child's, clear, 2½" h. 250.00
Mug, child's, milk white, 2½" h. 175.00
Pickle dish, oval 65.00

Pitcher, milk, 8" h. 495.00
Pitcher, water 405.00
Platter, 9 x 13" 170.00
Relish, deer handles 100.00
Sauce dish, footed ....35.00 to 40.00
Spooner ....75.00 to 100.00
*Sugar bowl, cov. ....125.00 to 150.00
*Wine 225.00

WHEAT & BARLEY

Wheat & Barley Tumbler

Bowl, cov., 7" d. 42.50
Bowl, open, 7" d. 16.50
Bread plate, amber 30.00
Bread plate, clear 35.00
Butter dish, cov. 35.00
Cake stand, amber, 8" to 10" d. 40.00
Cake stand, blue, 8" d. 55.00
Cake stand, clear, 8" to 10" d. 38.00
Cake stand, 11½" d. 40.00
Compote, open, jelly, amber 20.00
Compote, open, jelly, blue 40.00
Compote, open, jelly, clear 25.00
Compote, open, 8¼" d., amber 65.00
Creamer, amber 45.00
Creamer, blue 55.00
Creamer, clear 25.00
*Goblet, amber 45.00
*Goblet, blue 75.00
*Goblet, clear 40.00
Mug, amber 45.00
Mug, clear 19.00
Pitcher, milk, amber 60.00
Pitcher, milk, clear 45.00
Pitcher, water, amber 125.00
Pitcher, water 53.00
Plate, 6" d. 30.00
Plate, 7" d. 21.00
Plate, 9" d., closed handles, amber 45.00
Plate, 9" d., closed handles, vaseline 35.00
Salt shaker w/original top, blue 38.00
Salt & pepper shakers w/original tops, pr. 38.00
Sauce dish, flat, handled, amber 13.00
Sauce dish, flat, handled, clear 10.00
Sauce dish, footed, amber 14.00
Sauce dish, footed, clear 11.50
Spooner, amber 45.00
Spooner, clear 30.00
Sugar bowl, cov., blue 65.00
Sugar bowl, cov., clear 40.00
Tumbler, amber 32.00
Tumbler, clear (ILLUS.) 20.00

WILDFLOWER

Wildflower Sauce Dish

Basket, cake, oblong w/metal handle 145.00
Bowl, 6½" sq., blue 35.00
Bowl, 7" sq. 17.50
Bowl, 8" sq., 5" h., footed, amber 22.50
Bowl, 8" sq., 5" h., footed, apple green 32.50
Bowl, 8" sq., 5" h., footed, vaseline 20.00
Butter dish, cov., flat, blue 50.00
Cake stand, apple green, 9½" to 11" 66.00
Cake stand, clear, 9½" to 11" 46.00
Cake stand, blue, w/bail handle 225.00
Celery vase, amber 50.00
Celery vase, apple green 65.00
Celery vase, blue 75.00
Celery vase, clear 35.00
*Champagne, amber 50.00
*Champagne, blue 50.00
*Champagne, clear 30.00
Compote, cov., 6" d., amber 40.00
Compote, cov., 6" d., clear 49.00
Compote, cov., 8" d., amber 90.00
Compote, cov., 8" d., clear ....75.00 to 100.00
Compote, open, 10½" d., 7½" h., blue 125.00
Compote, open, 10½" d., 8¼" h., amber 78.00
*Creamer, amber 35.00
*Creamer, blue 45.00
*Creamer, clear 35.00
*Creamer, vaseline 42.00
*Goblet, amber 36.00
*Goblet, apple green 40.00
*Goblet, blue 37.00
*Goblet, clear 30.00
*Goblet, vaseline 30.00
Pitcher, water, amber 65.00
Pitcher, water, apple green 95.00
Pitcher, water, blue 85.00
Pitcher, water, clear 42.50
Pitcher, water, vaseline 76.00

Plate, 10" sq., blue....45.00
Plate, 10" sq., clear....21.00
Plate, 10" sq., vaseline....28.00
Platter, 8 x 11", apple green....47.50
Platter, 8 x 11", blue....45.00
Platter, 8 x 11", vaseline....47.50
Relish, vaseline....27.50
*Salt dip, turtle-shaped, amber....45.00
*Salt shaker w/original top, amber....35.00
Salt shaker w/original top, apple green....30.00
Salt shaker w/original top, blue....55.00
Salt shaker w/original top, vaseline....55.00
Salt & pepper shakers w/original tops, vaseline, pr....110.00
*Sauce dish, flat or footed, amber....13.50
*Sauce dish, flat or footed, apple green....22.50
*Sauce dish, flat or footed, blue....17.00
*Sauce dish, flat or footed, clear (ILLUS.)....12.00
*Sauce dish, flat or footed, vaseline....14.50
Spooner, amber....30.00
Spooner, blue....35.00
Spooner, clear....22.00
Spooner, vaseline....34.00
*Sugar bowl, cov., vaseline....45.00
Sugar bowl, open, amber....25.00
Sugar bowl, open, blue....30.00
Syrup pitcher w/original top, amber....140.00 to 160.00
Syrup pitcher w/original top, blue....350.00
Tray, dresser, blue, 4 x 9"....45.00
Tray, dresser, vaseline, 4 x 9"....28.50
Tray, water, amber, 11 x 13"....45.00
Tray, water, blue, 11 x 13"....75.00 to 100.00
Tray, water, vaseline, 11 x 13"....50.00
Tumbler, amber....38.00
Tumbler, apple green....40.00
Tumbler, blue....45.00
Tumbler, clear....22.00
Tumbler, vaseline....35.00
Vase, 10½" h....58.00
Waste bowl, amber....48.00
Waste bowl, clear....28.00
Water set: pitcher, tray & 5 tumblers; apple green, 7 pcs....318.00
*Wine, clear....50.00

WILLOW OAK

Bowl, cov., 7" d., flat....42.50
Bowl, 7" d., amber....14.00
Bowl, 7" d., blue....47.50
Bowl, 7" d., clear (ILLUS. top next column)....35.00
Bread plate, clear, 9" d....40.00
Bread plate, amber, 11" d....42.00
Bread plate, clear, 11" d....32.00
Butter dish, cov., amber....65.00
Butter dish, cov., clear....55.00
Cake stand, amber, 8" to 10" d....57.00
Cake stand, blue, 8" to 10" d....65.00
Cake stand, clear, 8" to 10" d....35.00

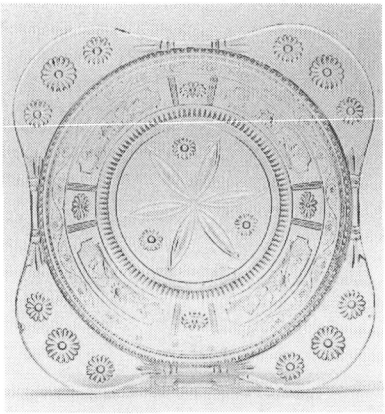

Willow Oak Bowl

Celery vase, amber....45.00
Celery vase, blue....125.00
Celery vase, clear....48.00
Compote, cov., 6" h....75.00
Compote, cov., 8" d....65.00
Compote, open, 6" d., scalloped top....40.00
Compote, open, 8" d., low stand, amber....65.00
Creamer, amber....35.00
Creamer, blue....65.00
Creamer, clear....32.00
Creamer, vaseline....45.00
Goblet, amber....42.50
Goblet, blue....36.00
Goblet, clear....32.00
Pitcher, milk, amber....95.00
Pitcher, milk, clear....40.00
Pitcher, water, amber....80.00
Pitcher, water, blue....75.00
Pitcher, water, clear....48.00
Plate, 7" d., clear....26.00
Plate, 9" d., handled, amber....38.00
Plate, 9" d., handled, blue....47.50
Plate, 9" d., handled, clear....45.00
Salt shaker w/original top, amber....40.00
Salt shaker w/original top, blue....66.00
Salt shaker w/original top, clear....28.00
Sauce dish, flat or footed....15.00
Spooner, amber....35.00
Spooner, blue....50.00
Spooner, clear....28.00
Sugar bowl, cov....41.00
Table set, amber, 4 pcs....350.00 to 375.00
Table set, clear, 4 pcs....300.00
Tray, water, clear, 10½" d....32.00
Tumbler, amber....32.00
Tumbler, blue....65.00
Waste bowl, amber....48.00
Waste bowl, clear....29.00

WINDFLOWER

Butter dish, cov....45.00
Compote, cov., 8½" d., low stand....70.00
Compote, open, 8" d....30.00

Creamer....32.00
Egg cup....32.50
Pitcher, water....65.00
Salt dip, master size....20.00
Sauce dish....12.50
Spooner....34.00
Sugar bowl, cov.....39.00

WISCONSIN (Beaded Dewdrop)

Wisconsin Wine

Banana stand, turned-up sides, 7½" w., 4" h.....72.00
Bonbon, handled, 4"....24.00
Bowl, 6½" d.....35.00
Bowl, 8" d.....42.00
Butter dish, cov.....90.00
Cake stand, 8¼" d., 4¾" h.....42.50
Cake stand, 9¾" d.....45.00
Celery tray, flat, 5 x 10"....42.50
Celery vase....47.00
Compote, cov., 10½" d.....64.00
Compote, open, 6½" d., 3½" h.....30.00
Compote, open, 6½" d., 6½" h.....26.00
Compote, open, 7½" d., 5½" h.....42.00
Compote, open, 7" d., 4" h., tricornered, medium....25.00
Creamer, individual size....35.00
Cruet w/original stopper....40.00
Cup & saucer....55.00
Dish, cov., oval....26.50
Doughnut stand, 6" d.....40.00
Marmalade jar, cov.....125.00
Mug, 3½" h.....34.00
Nappy, handled, 4" d.....20.00
Pitcher, milk....75.00
Pitcher, water, 8" h.....65.00
Plate, 5" sq.....24.00
Plate, 6½" sq.....26.00
Punch cup....16.50
Relish, 4 x 8½"....20.00
Salt shaker w/original top....55.00
Sauce dish....14.00
Spooner....38.00
Sugar bowl, cov., 5" h.....95.00
Sugar shaker w/original top....63.00
Syrup pitcher w/original top, 6½" h.....75.00
*Toothpick holder....41.00
Tumbler....45.00
Vase, 6" h.....58.00
Wine (ILLUS.)....95.00

WOODEN PAIL - See Oaken Bucket Pattern

WYOMING

Bowl, 7" d., footed....42.50
Cake stand, 9" d., high stand....57.00
Cake stand, 10" d., high stand....55.00
Compote, open, 8" d., shallow bowl....40.00
Creamer, open, individual, tankard shape....30.00
Mug....65.00
Pitcher, water, pressed handle, 3 pt.....55.00
Relish tray....28.00
Sauce dish, flat, round, 4" d.....18.00

X-RAY

Berry set: 8" d. master bowl & 6 sauce dishes; emerald green, 7 pcs.....155.00
Berry set: 8" d. master bowl & 8 sauce dishes; amethyst, 9 pcs.....295.00
Butter dish, cov., emerald green w/gold....100.00 to 150.00
Carafe, large, emerald green w/gold..135.00
Celery vase, emerald green....50.00
Compote, cov., high stand, emerald green....65.00
Compote, jelly, clear....42.00
Compote, jelly, emerald green....47.00
Creamer, breakfast size, emerald green w/gold....55.00
Cruet w/original stopper, emerald green w/gold....100.00
Pitcher, water, 9½" h., emerald green ½ gal.....65.00
Rose bowl, emerald green w/gold....68.00
Salt shaker w/original top, amethyst.....50.00
Salt shaker w/original top, clear....18.50
Sauce dish, clear, 4½" d.....12.00
Sauce dish, emerald green, 4½" d.....22.50
Spooner, emerald green w/gold....45.00
Sugar bowl, cov., emerald green w/gold....54.00
Sugar bowl, cov., breakfast size, emerald green w/gold....65.00
Syrup pitcher, clear w/gold....225.00
Table set, emerald green, 4 pcs.....300.00
Toothpick holder, emerald green....60.00
Tray, condiment....37.50
Tumbler, amethyst....42.50
Tumbler, emerald green....25.00
Water set: pitcher & 4 tumblers; emerald green w/gold, 5 pcs.....225.00

YALE - See Crowfoot Pattern

ZIPPER

Butter dish, cov.....39.00
Butter dish, cov., ruby-stained....100.00
Cheese dish, cov.....45.00

Creamer.....35.00
Cruet w/original stopper.....36.00
Goblet.....25.00
Pitcher, milk.....55.00
Relish, 6 x 9½".....45.00
Sauce dish, flat or footed.....6.00 to 8.00
Sugar bowl, cov.....35.00
Sugar bowl, cov., ruby-stained.....65.00
Toothpick holder, green w/gold.....45.00
Wine, clear.....30.00
Wine, ruby-stained.....37.50

ZIPPERED BLOCK - See Iowa Pattern

(End Of Pattern Glass Section)

PHOENIX

Phoenix Bluebell Vase

This ware was made by the Phoenix Glass Co. of Beaver County, Pennsylvania, which produced various types of glass from the 1880s. One special type that attracts collectors now is a molded ware with a vague resemblance to cameo in its "sculptured" decoration. Similar pieces with relief-molded designs were produced by the Consolidated Lamp & Glass Co. (which see) and care must be taken to differentiate between the two companies' wares. Some Consolidated molds were moved to the Phoenix plant in the mid-1930s but later returned and used again at Consolidated. These pieces we will list under "Consolidated."

Candy dish, cov., Phlox patt., tan on milk white ground.....$125.00
Compote, cov., Lacy Dewdrop patt., blue decoration on a milk white ground.....125.00
Platter, 14" d., Jonquil patt., pearlized white on white satin ground.....190.00
Vase, 6" h., 5" d., bulbous base w/short flaring neck, Aster patt., green on milk white ground.....125.00
Vase, 6" h., 5" d., bulbous base w/short flaring neck, Aster patt., tan on milk white ground.....95.00
Vase, 7" h., bulbous base w/trumpet-form sides, Bluebell patt., brown on milk white ground.....115.00
Vase, 7" h., bulbous base w/trumpet-form sides, Bluebell patt., pearlized finish.....63.00
Vase, 7" h., bulbous base w/trumpet-form sides, Bluebell patt., pink pearlized finish (ILLUS.).....75.00
Vase, 8¾" h., footed, tapering cylindrical body w/flaring rim, Primrose patt., green background w/frosted design.....125.00

Wild Geese Vase

Vase, 9¼" h., pillow-shaped, Wild Geese patt., white birds on a blue ground (ILLUS.).....185.00
Vase, 9½" h., baluster-form, Wild Rose patt., burgundy ground w/pearlized design.....300.00
Vase, 10½" h., ovoid body, Wild Rose patt., pearlized flowers on a rose ground.....225.00
Vase, 10½" h., ovoid body, Wild Rose patt., white pearlized finish.....160.00
Vase, 11½" h., baluster-form, Dancing Girls line, brown shadow figures on brown ground.....495.00
Vase, 11½" h., Dancing Girls line, clear w/frosted nudes.....195.00
Vase, 11½" h., baluster-shaped, Philodendron patt., sky blue ground w/pearlized white leaves.....200.00
Vase, 18" h., tall ovoid body, Thistle patt., pearlized white thistles on white ground.....400.00
Vase, 18" h., tall ovoid body, Thistle patt., white thistles on a pale blue ground, w/original paper label.....550.00

PILLAR-MOLDED

This heavily ribbed glassware was produced by blowing glass into full-sized ribbed molds and then finishing it by hand. The technique evolved from earlier "pattern moulding" used on glass since ancient times but in pillar-molded glass the ribs are very heavy and prominent. Most examples found in this country were produced in the Pittsburgh, Pennsylvania area from around 1850 to 1870, but similar English-made wares made before and after this period are also available. Most American pieces were made from clear flint glass and colored examples or pieces with colored strands in the ribs are rare and highly prized. Some collectors refer to this as "steamboat" glass believing that it was made to be used on American riverboats but most likely it was used anywhere that a sturdy, relatively inexpensive glassware was needed, such as taverns and hotels.

Decanter w/bar lip, eight-rib, clear, tapering conical form w/applied neck rings, 9¾" h. $82.50
Decanters w/matching ribbed pear-shaped stoppers, eight-rib, clear, bell-shaped body w/notched ribs tapering to ringed cylindrical neck, cut panels between the ribs on the shoulder, pr. 14" h. 412.50
Decanter w/original blown stopper w/airtrap, eight-rib, clear, 12⅝" h. 200.00
Pitcher, 5⅝" h., eight-rib, clear, rounded conical body tapering to a flaring rim w/pinched spout, applied strap handle w/curl end 550.00
Pitcher, 7¼" h., eight-rib, deep amethyst, slightly tapering cylindrical body w/neck ring & wide slightly flaring rim, applied strap handle, tiny broken blister inside, wear, scratches 8,800.00
Pitcher, 8⅝" h., eight-rib, clear, bulbous base w/deeply waisted sides to a flared rim w/a wide spout, applied strap handle 330.00
Pitcher, tankard, 9½" h., eleven-rib, clear, applied handle 385.00
Pitcher, 10½" h., eight-rib, clear, bulbous base tapering in at mid-section & out at top, applied foot & handle 605.00
Sugar bowl, cov., eight-rib, clear, deep rounded bowl w/galleried rim, tall slender pyramidal cover w/button finial, on slender waisted applied stem & round foot, 10⅝" h. (small flake on top of finial at pontil) 1,870.00
Syrup jug w/original metal neck & cover, eight-rib, clear, ovoid footed base tapering to a cylindrical neck fitted w/hinged metal rim & spouted cover, applied strap handle, 11¼" h. 247.50

Pillar-Molded Syrup Pitcher

Syrup pitcher w/original hinged metal lid, twelve-rib, amber, footed pear-shaped body w/applied strap handle, Pittsburgh, mid-19th c., 7" h. (ILLUS.) 2,640.00
Vase, 8" h., eight-rib, clear, tall flaring tulip-form bowl w/swirled ribs at the top, applied knopped stem & disc foot (shallow chip on one rib) 440.00
Vase, 9¾" h., 5½" d., eight-rib, clear, deep tulip-form bowl w/the ribs swirled at the top, on an applied pedestal w/knob at base above the disc foot 214.50
Vase, 11½" h., 5" d., eight-rib, tall flaring tulip-form bowl applied w/a wafer to a knopped octagonal pressed pedestal base, soft bluish opalescence at the rim, probably New England Glass Company 550.00

RUBY-STAINED

This name derives from the color of the glass - a deep red. The red staining was thinly painted on clear pressed glass patterns and refired at a low temperature. Many pieces were further engraved as souvenir items and were very popular from the 1890s into the 1920s. This technique should not be confused with "flashed" glass where a clear glass piece is actually dipped in molten glass of a contrasting color. Also see PATTERN GLASS.

Berry set: master bowl & four sauce dishes; Bar & Flute patt., 5 pcs. $160.00
Berry set: master bowl & six sauce dishes; Riverside's Victoria patt., 7 pcs. 265.00
Berry set: master bowl & six sauce dishes; Spearpoint Band patt., 7 pcs. 175.00
Bowl, berry, individual, Bar & Flute patt. 20.00
Bowl, master berry, Bar & Flute patt.....80.00
Butter dish, cov., Duncan's Empire patt., 5¼" h. 110.00
Butter dish, cov., Heavy Gothic patt. ..155.00
Butter dish, cov., Lenore patt. 95.00

Majestic Ruby-Stained Butter

Butter dish, cov., Majestic patt., 7½" d., 6" h. (ILLUS.) 110.00
Butter dish, cov., Tacoma patt. 80.00
Butter dish, cov., Tarentum's Atlanta patt. 90.00
Butter dish, cov., Triple Triangle patt....90.00

Melrose Celery Vase

Celery vase, Melrose patt., engraved blossom & leaf band, 6¼" h. (ILLUS.) 110.00
Compote, 8¼" x 8½", open, Scroll with Cane Band patt. 220.00
Creamer, Almond Thumbprint patt., 4½" h. 20.00
Creamer, Arched Ovals patt. 45.00

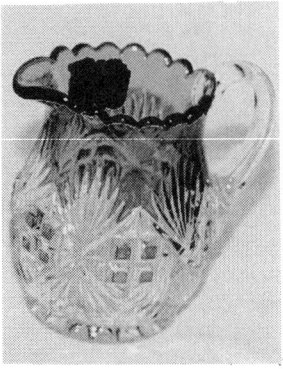

Majestic Creamer

Creamer, Majestic patt., 4½" h. (ILLUS.) 75.00
Creamer, Prize patt. 85.00
Creamer, Puritan patt. 39.00
Creamer, individual, Truncated Cube patt. 30.00
Cruet w/original stopper, Button Panel patt. 369.00
Cruet w/original stopper, National's Eureka patt. 250.00
Cruet w/original stopper, The Prize patt. 350.00
Cruet w/original stopper, Zippered Swirl & Diamond patt. 85.00
Cup, Arched Ovals patt., souvenir.....27.50
Goblet, Beaded Dart Band patt. 25.00
Goblet, Diamond Band w/Panels patt...25.00
Goblet, Swag Block patt. 50.00
Pitcher, tankard, Hexagon Block patt. 110.00
Pitcher, water, Carnation patt., w/gold trim 265.00
Pitcher, water, Foster Block patt.....225.00
Pitcher, water, Ladder with Diamond patt. 250.00
Pitcher, water, Leaf & Star patt., w/gold trim 300.00
Pitcher, water, Triple Triangle patt.....75.00
Sauce dish, Millard patt. 25.00

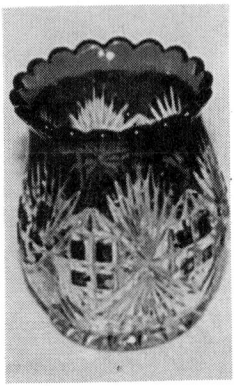

Majestic Spooner

Spooner, Majestic patt., 4⅛" h. (ILLUS.) 65.00
Spooner, Triple Triangle patt. 55.00
Straw holder, The Prize patt. 95.00
Sugar bowl, cov., Heavy Gothic patt. 125.00
Sugar shaker w/original top, Late Block patt. 295.00
Syrup pitcher w/original top, Beauty patt. 395.00
Syrup pitcher w/original top, Millard patt. 275.00
Syrup pitcher w/original top, Zippered Corner patt. 395.00
Table set: cov. butter dish, creamer, cov. sugar bowl & spooner; Diamond Band with Panel patt., 4 pcs. 190.00
Toothpick holder, Box-In-Box patt., w/enameled floral decoration 145.00
Toothpick holder, National's Eureka patt. 95.00
Toothpick holder, Summit patt., souvenir 50.00
Toothpick holder, Tarentum Thumbprint patt., dated "1914" 24.00
Tumbler, Arched Ovals patt., souvenir 45.00
Tumbler, Diamond & Sunburst Variant patt. 29.00
Tumbler, Late Block patt. 15.00

Blocked Thumbprint Water Set

Water set: 10½" h., 5½" d. pitcher, four 3" d., 4" h. tumblers; Blocked Thumbprint patt., ruby & clear frosted bands, 5 pcs. (ILLUS.) 225.00
Water set: pitcher & six tumblers; Diamond Band with Panel patt., 7 pcs. 145.00
Wine, Block Band patt. 24.00
Wine, Riverside's Esther patt. 28.00
Wine, Rustic Rose patt. 25.00
Wine, Teardrop & Thumbprint patt. 30.00
Wine, Triple Triangle patt. 25.00

SANDWICH

Sandwich Columnar Candlestick

Numerous types of glass were produced at The Boston & Sandwich Glass Works in Sandwich, Massachusetts, on Cape Cod, from 1826 to 1888. Those listed here represent a sampling. Also see PATTERN GLASS and LACY.

All pieces are pressed glass unless otherwise noted.

Bowl, 6" d., lacy, Rayed Peacock Eye patt., clear $135.00
Candlestick, the hexagonal tulip-shaped socket above a ring-and-knob shaft applied w/a wafer to the flaring hexagonal base, medium green, ca. 1840, 7" h. (minute flake in side of socket) 1,210.00
Candlestick, Dolphin patt., the petal-form dark blue socket on a short knob stem applied w/a wafer to the milky clambroth figural dolphin pedestal on a double-step square foot, ca. 1850, 9¾" h. 715.00
Candlesticks, dark blue petal socket atop a milky clambroth columnar standard w/stepped, square base, ca. 1850, minor base chips, heat check in one socket, 9¼" h., pr. (ILLUS. of one) 1,320.00
Candlesticks, Acanthus Leaf patt., opaque blue hexagonal leaf-molded socket applied w/a wafer to the baluster-form acanthus leaf-molded milky clambroth pedestal & domed, leaf-molded hexagonal foot, 10⅞" h., pr. (very minor flakes under foot 1,870.00
Candlesticks, Petal & Loop patt., clear, pr. 120.00
Celery tray, footed, Diamond Point patt., applied gold on rim & feet 125.00
Cologne bottle w/original lily-shaped stopper, urn-shaped body raised on

a pedestal base, black amethyst body decorated w/a h.p. stork in a circle of flowers, base & stopper w/matching numbers, 7½" h. 250.00
Cologne bottle w/original steeple-shaped stopper w/air trap, ring-necked bottle, dark green 250.00
Compote, open, 8¼" h., 8" d., Ribbon patt., upright reticulated sides on the bowl, thick wafer joining bowl to large flaring hexagonal base, clear..770.00
Compote, open, 9½" d., 6¾" h., Petal & Loop patt., moonstone 1,650.00
Egg cup, Diamonds in Oval patt., starch blue, ca. 1840-50 .....385.00
Lamp, kerosene table-type, cut overlay, the inverted pear-shaped font in blue cut to white cut to clear w/a band of oblong cartouches above a band of thumbprints, on a reeded brass pedestal & a stepped white marble foot w/brass trim, ca. 1860-75, 12" h.....977.50

Rare Sandwich Lamp

Lamp, kerosene table-type, lavender blown-molded ribbed onion-form font w/a metal connector ring to the ribbed matching pedestal base, attributed to Sandwich, ca. 1865-80, 12¼" h. (ILLUS.) 6,900.00
Salt shaker, "Christmas" salt w/dated metal top w/agitator, amber, lid signed "Dana K. Alden, Boston" 65.00
Salt shakers, "Christmas" salt w/dated metal top w/agitator, in original box labeled "Dana K. Alden's World Renowned Table Salt Bottles," two amethyst, one each cobalt blue, pale aqua blue, vaseline & amber, set of 6 (one top & agitator badly corroded) 715.00
Salt & pepper shakers, "Christmas" salt w/dated metal top w/agitator, amber, 2⅝" h., pr. 247.50
Salt & pepper shakers, "Christmas" salt w/dated metal top w/agitator, deep cobalt blue, 2⅝" h., pr. 275.00
Spill holder, Sandwich Star patt., clear 75.00
String holder, domical, overlay, cut thumbprint design w/cobalt blue cut to clear 275.00
Sugar bowl, cov., lacy, octagonal Acanthus Leaf patt., deep emerald green, 5½" h. (usual mold roughness) 17,600.00
Sugar bowl, cov., lacy, Gothic Arch patt., opaque blue w/lightly 'sanded' surface, 5¼" h. (small chips).....1,375.00
Sugar bowl, cov., lacy, octagonal Gothic Arch patt., opaque starch blue, 5⅜" h. (three shallow chips on upper rim of base & finial) 1,430.00
Sugar bowl, cov., lacy, Gothic Arch patt., octagonal flaring sides w/arches on a low foot, matching domed cover w/button finial, canary yellow, ca. 1840 (minor roughness inside cover) 1,100.00
Vase, 9¼" h., ovoid opaque moonstone Sawtooth patt. body raised on a blown jade green pedestal foot & w/a tall blown jade green slender trumpet neck w/flattened ruffled rim, ca. 1860....1,980.00
Vase, 10" h., "Trevaise" art glass, baluster-form body tapering to a flat mouth, opaque green w/gold iridescent heart-shaped leaf & vine decoration, recessed button pontil, Alton Manufacturing Co. of Sandwich, late 19th c.....920.00
Vases, 10½" h., tulip-type, flaring paneled bowl above a knopped stem & flaring octagonal base, canary yellow, ca. 1850, pr. (traces of mold roughness) 1,430.00

STIEGEL & STIEGEL-TYPE

This glass was made at the American Flint Glass works of "Baron" Henry W. Stiegel at Manheim, Pennsylvania, from 1765 until the 1770's. It is difficult to attribute pieces positively to Stiegel.

Bottle, half post-type, blown, clear w/polychrome floral enameling on one side & barrel, compass & tools on the other, pewter cap, 6⅜" h.....$132.00
Bottle, pocket-type, blown, molded Daisy & Diamond design above thirty vertical ribs, sheared & fire polished lip, amethyst, 4¾" h. (ILLUS.) 126.50

Stiegel-Type Bottle

Bottle, pocket-type, blown, Ogival pattern, sheared & fire polished lip, amethyst, 5½" h. (slight roughness on bottom edge).....3,850.00
Creamer, ovoid body tapering to a short cylindrical neck w/flared rim & pinched shoulder, applied strap handle, overall diamond quilted patt., brilliant sapphire blue, 3⅜" h.....1,430.00
Mug, blown w/applied handle, clear w/polychrome floral enameling one side & deer on the other, 5⁵⁄₁₆" h. (check at handle) 412.50
Salt dip, mold-blown in the expanded diamond design, bell-shaped bowl w/incurved rim on a short round base, cobalt blue.....132.00
Sugar bowl, cov., circular footed body, the domed cover w/flanged rim & acorn finial, blue, possibly Manheim, Pennsylvania, late 18th c., 7" h.....1,265.00

STRETCH

Collectors have given this name to a glassware related to Carnival Glass which features a lightly iridized finish somewhat resembling the skin of an onion. It is most often found on pastel-colored wares in light blue, green, amethyst, amber and pink. Stretch wares, popular in the 1920s, were produced by many American glass firms including Fenton, Northwood and Imperial.

Bowl, 10½" d., blue.....$25.00
Candleholders, blue, 7½" h., pr.....65.00 to 75.00
Candy dish, cov., blue 60.00
Candy dish, cov., dolphin-shaped base, blue 75.00

Northwood Stretch Compote

Compote, open, deep flaring bowl raised on a tall paneled stem w/double knobs above a round foot, blue, Northwood Glass Co. (ILLUS.) 55.00
Plate, 9" d., amethyst.....14.00
Plate, luncheon, pearl iridescent w/green trim 45.00
Powder jar, cov., vaseline.....40.00
Vase, 8" h., fan-shaped, No. 857, Celeste Blue, Fenton Art Glass Co....50.00
Vase, 8" h., fan-shaped, No. 857, Tangerine, Fenton Art Glass Co. 90.00
Whipped cream bowl w/matching ladle, footed, green, 6¾" d., 2 pcs. 68.00

TIFFIN

Tiffin Glass Label

A wide variety of fine glasswares were produced by the Tiffin Glass Company of Tiffin, Ohio. Beginning as a part of the large U.S. Glass Company early in this century, the Tiffin factory continued making a wide range of wares until its final closing in 1984. One popular line is now called "Black Satin" and included various vases with raised floral designs. Many other acid-etched and hand-cut patterns were also produced over the years and are very collectible today. The three "Tiffin Glassmasters" books by Fred Bickenheuser are the standard references for Tiffin collectors.

Basket, flower, No. 6553, clear.....$85.00
Candlesticks, Black Satin, No. 82, 8½" h., pr. 45.00
Candy dish, cov., coralene florals decoration on Black Satin ground.....88.00
Candy dish, cov., heart-shaped, decorated w/pink flowers, green.....58.00
Carafe, etched Roses patt., clear.....72.00
Champagne, etched Flanders patt., pink 36.00
Champagne, etched June Night patt., clear, 6 oz. 18.00
Cocktail, etched Cordelia patt.....10.00
Compote, 7½", twist stem, No. 315, vaseline satin 55.00
Console set: 13" d. bowl w/deep everted rim & pair of candleholders; Fontaine etching, bowl No. 8153, candleholders No. 9758, twilite, 3 pcs. 385.00
Creamer & sugar bowl, etched Fuchsia patt., clear, pr. 50.00
Creamer & sugar bowl, etched June Night patt., clear, pr. 40.00
Flower bowl, cut Twilight patt., No. 9153-108, clear, 10" d. 165.00
Goblet, etched Cherokee Rose patt., clear, 8" h. 18.00
Goblet, etched Classic patt., clear.....28.00
Goblet, Diamond Optic patt., All Rose-Pink, 10 oz. 30.00
Goblet, etched Flanders patt., pink.....42.00
Goblet, Franciscan patt., citron.....10.00
Goblet, water, etched Fuchsia patt., clear, 7⅝" h. 24.00
Goblet, etched Persian Pheasant patt., clear 35.00
Parfait, etched Byzantine patt., clear....22.00
Plate, 8" d., etched Flanders patt., yellow 11.50
Plate, 8⅛" d., etched Fuchsia patt., clear 22.00
Rose bowl w/three ball feet, Copen blue, medium 45.00
Sherbet, etched Classic patt., clear.....22.00
Sherbet, etched Fuchsia patt., clear.....25.00
Tumbler, iced tea, footed, Fuchsia patt., clear 30.00
Tumbler, footed, etched June Night patt., clear, 10½ oz. 30.00
Tumbler, juice, footed, etched Persian Pheasant patt., clear, 5 oz. 15.00
Vase, 5" h., etched Poppy patt., black amethyst 85.00
Vase, 6" h., four-footed, cut Twilight patt., clear 85.00
Vase, 6½" h., Black Satin ground w/alternating glossy stripes.....55.00
Vase, bud, 10" h., etched Cherokee Rose patt., clear.....45.00
Vase, 11" h., footed, etched June Night patt., clear.....75.00
Vase, 19" h., free-form, No. 17424, Desert Red.....75.00
Wine, etched June Night patt., clear.....35.00

VASELINE

Vaseline Cologne Bottle

Vaseline *is a term used to describe a wide range of pressed, free-blown and mold-blown glasswares popular since the mid-19th century. It refers to the yellowish green color of such wares which resembles the hue of petroleum jelly. The color was obtained by adding uranium salts to the glass batch and the term is fairly modern. Originally the yellow color was called "canary" by glass manufacturers.*

Popular in Victorian pressed glass and early 20th century decorative glasswares, the color was not widely produced after the 1930s.

For additional background see Yellow-Green Vaseline! A Guide to The Magic Glass *by Jay L. Glickman (Antique Publications, 1991).*

Cologne bottle w/original facet-cut vaseline stopper, cylindrical body w/embossed oval ring pattern on sides, 19th c., 2" d., 4¾" h. (ILLUS.) $110.00
Compote, open, 8" d., footed, three-panel design 65.00
Cruet w/original stopper, Big Button patt. 85.00
Cruet w/original stopper, Ranson patt. 175.00
Dish, opalescent, oval w/scalloped rim, pressed paneled cane design, England, ca. 1900, 6½ x 8½" 75.00
Salt dip, master-size, opalescent, in silver plate frame w/spoon, 2⅛" d., 4½" h. 75.00
Salt dip, master-size, opalescent, scalloped edge, vaseline shell trim applied around sides, in silver plate footed frame, 3¼" d., overall 2" h.....125.00
Toothpick holder, petticoat style, Radiant patt., gold trim.....110.00

VICTORIAN COLORED GLASS

There are, of course, many types of colored glassware of the Victorian era and we cover a great variety of these in our various glass categories. However, there are some pieces of pressed, mold-blown and free-blown Victorian colored glass which don't fit well into other specific listings, so we have chosen to include a selection of them here.

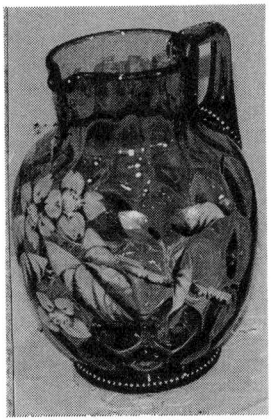

Inverted Thumbprint Pitcher

Animal covered dish, Cow on oval paneled base, black opaque.....$500.00

Animal covered dish, Lion on picket base, opaque blue w/white head, 5½" l.....85.00

Box w/hinged cover, free-blown, cobalt blue, lacy-style, decoration w/enameled dainty white leaves & gold flowers around sides w/gold dots, scallops w/dainty white leaves in reserves, 2" d., 1¼" h.....145.00

Box w/hinged lid, free-blown, cobalt blue, decorated w/white enameled daisies & leaves on cover, 2" d., 1¼" h.....135.00

Cracker jar, cov., free-blown, barrel-shaped, lime green enameled w/overall decoration of dainty blue forget-me-nots, green leaves & lavender foliage, resilvered cover, rim & bail handle, 4¾" d., 6½" h.....225.00

Cracker jar, cov., free-blown, barrel-shaped, lime green decorated overall w/sprays of dainty pink & blue flowers & green leaves, resilvered rim, handle & cover, 5" d., 6¾" h. 225.00

Cracker jar, cov., pressed, rectangular shape, Water Lilies & Cattails patt., opaque chartreuse, silver plate lid, rim & bail handle, 6" d., 9" h.....150.00

Creamer, mold-blown, bulbous body w/squared mouth, Inverted Thumbprint patt., amber body & applied amber handle, ca. 1880s, 5" h.....30.00

Decanter w/original spear-shaped amethyst cut to clear bubble stopper, bulbous amethyst cut to clear body w/eight-cut panels, short cylindrical neck, pattern cut under scalloped foot, 3⅞" d., 11" h. 145.00

Pitcher, 8" h., 5½" d., mold-blown Inverted Thumbprint patt., footed ovoid body tapering to a short cylindrical neck, applied angular handle, aqua blue decorated w/large white & yellow blossoms & green leaves & branch (ILLUS.).....165.00

Salt dip, master-size, chartreuse green w/green threaded decoration, clear applied snail feet, 1¾" d., 1¼" h.....65.00

Salt shaker w/original top, Challinor's Forget-Me-Not patt., Nile green.....40.00

Salt & pepper shakers w/original tops, Inverted Thumbprint patt., blue, pr...120.00

Sugar shaker w/original top, Argus Swirl patt., peach bloom 250.00

Syrup pitcher w/original top, Inverted Thumbprint patt., blue, Hobbs, Brockunier & Co.....140.00

Toothpick holder, Jefferson Optic patt., blue 65.00

Tumble-up (water carafe w/tumbler lid), free-blown, footed spherical body w/cylindrical neck fitted w/a tumbler, sapphire blue enameled w/large white flowers & leaves, 4⅞" d., 7¾" h., 2 pcs.....195.00

Vase, 6⅞" h., 6½" d., ovoid melon-ribbed body w/widely flaring rolled & crimped rim w/applied clear edging, clear applied feet w/gold trim, sapphire blue, decorated overall w/dainty pink & white flowers & tan leaves 325.00

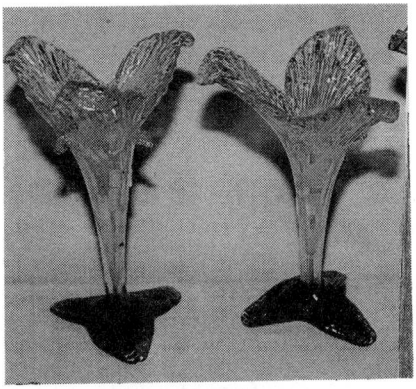

Flower-Form Vases

Vase, 8" h., 4" d., trumpet-form w/vaseline petals applied around the rim, body sharply tapering to four applied vaseline petal-shaped feet, cased creamy body w/chartreuse lining 95.00

Vases, 4¼" h., 2¾" d., squatty bulbous bases tapering to a trumpet-form neck w/slightly flaring & scalloped rim, cobalt blue decorated w/white daisies w/yellow centers, pink buds & green leaves, pr. 125.00

Vases, 8⅛" h., 5⅜" w., flower-form w/large flaring triple-petal rim w/pink opalescent tips spattered w/pink specks then shading to yellow & clear, green three-leaf applied foot, pr. (ILLUS. bottom of previous page).....185.00

WESTMORELAND

Westmoreland Cat on Lacy Base Dish

The Westmoreland Specialty Company was founded in East Liverpool, Ohio in 1889 and relocated in 1890 to Grapeville, Pennsylvania where it remained until its closing in 1985.

During its early years Westmoreland specialized in glass food containers and novelties but by the turn of the century they had a large line of milk white items and clear tableware patterns. In 1925 the company name was shortened to The Westmoreland Glass Company and it was during that decade that more colored glasswares entered their line-up. When Victorian-style milk glass again became popular in the 1940s and 1950s, Westmoreland produced extensive amounts in several patterns which closely resemble late 19th century wares. These and their figural animal dishes in milk white and colors are widely collected today but buyers should not confuse them for the antique originals. Watch for Westmoreland's "WG" mark on some pieces. A majority of our listings are products from the 1940s through the 1970s. Earlier pieces will be indicated.

Early Westmoreland Label & Mark

Animal covered dish, Cat on a lacy base, glass eyes, opaque blue, copied from the Atterbury original (ILLUS.) $55.00

Animal covered dish, Cat on a lacy base, glass eyes, purple slag, copied from the Atterbury original.....70.00

Animal covered dish, Chick and Eggs, milk white, copied from the Atterbury original 95.00

Animal covered dish, Duck on a wavy base, purple slag, copied from the Challinor, Taylor & Co. original 110.00

Animal covered dish, Hen on nest, chocolate brown w/iridizing, gold yellow & green trim, copied from antique original 125.00

Animal covered dish, Hen on nest, red & yellow slag, copied from antique original 75.00

Animal covered dish, Lamb on picket base, Green Marble, copied from antique original, 5½" l. 65.00

Animal covered dish, Rabbit on picket base, chocolate, copied from antique original, 5½" l. 40.00

Animal covered dish, Robin on Twig Nest, light blue, copied from antique original 75.00

Animal covered dish, Rooster on ribbed base, milk white w/blue head, copied from antique original, 5½" l.....95.00

Animal covered dish, Rooster on ribbed base, purple slag, copied from antique original, 5½" l. 118.00

Ashtray, Beaded Grape (No. 1884) patt., milk white, 6½" 9.00

Banana stand, Doric (No. 3) patt., milk white 30.00

Banana stand, Paneled Grape (No. 1881) patt., milk white 90.00

Banana stand, Ring & Petal (No. 1885) patt., clear 38.00

Basket, oval w/open handle, Paneled Grape (No. 1881) patt., milk white 28.00

Batter pitcher, Old Quilt (No. 500) patt., milk white 35.00

Bowl, cov., 9" d., Beaded Grape (No. 1884) patt., milk white 55.00

Bowl, 13" d., Thousand Eye (No. 1000) patt., clear 35.00

Butter dish, cov., Old Quilt (No. 500) patt., milk white, ¼ lb. 34.00
Candleholders, Old Quilt patt., milk white, pr. 20.00
Candlesticks, model of a dolphin w/hexagon base, milk white, 9" h., pr. 125.00
Candy dish, cov., English Hobnail (No. 555) patt., clear 28.00
Candy dish, cov., Old Quilt patt., clear 22.50
Celery tray, Old Quilt patt., milk white, 10" l. 30.00
Celery vase, Old Quilt patt., milk white, 6½" h. 35.00
Cheese dish, cov., Old Quilt patt., milk white 60.00
Compote, 8", ball stem, Della Robia (No. 1058) patt., colored trim 85.00
Compote, 8" h., shell-shaped bowl w/dolphin base, Mother of Pearl Dolphin & Shell line, milk white w/mother of pearl finish 77.00
Compote, 11" d., 6½" h., Lattice Edge (No. 1890) patt., milk white 75.00
Console set: 9½ x 12" oval, footed bowl w/flared rim & two 4" h. candlesticks; Paneled Grape patt., milk white, 3 pcs. 85.00
Creamer, Old Quilt patt., milk white 14.00
Creamer & open sugar bowl, Della Robbia patt., milk white, pr. 24.00
Cruet w/original stopper, Della Robbia patt., milk white 18.00
Cup & saucer, English Hobnail patt., milk white 15.00
Cup & saucer, Old Quilt patt., milk white 30.00
Cup & saucer, Paneled Grape patt., milk white 16.50
Decanter w/original stopper, Paneled Grape patt., milk white 125.00
Dresser set: two cologne bottles w/original stoppers, cov. puff box & oval tray; Paneled Grape patt., clear, 4 pcs. 215.00
Goblet, water, American Hobnail (No. 77) patt., milk white 14.00
Goblet, water, Della Robbia patt., colored trim, 6" h., 8 oz. 37.50
Goblet, water, Della Robbia patt., milk white 16.00
Goblet, Paneled Grape patt., Honey Amber Carnival 12.00
Goblet, water, Paneled Grape patt., milk white 13.00
Goblet, brandy or wine, Princess Feather (No. 201) patt., blue 17.00
Gravy boat & underplate, Paneled Grape patt., milk white, 2 pcs. 52.50
Honey dish, cov., Beaded Grape patt., milk white 14.00
Honey dish, cov., Old Quilt patt., milk white 20.00
Pitcher, water, 12" h., Paneled Grape patt., milk white, 1 qt. 50.00
Planter, Paneled Grape patt., milk white, 4½" sq. 30.00
Plate, 7" d., Beaded Edge patt., clear...12.00
Plate, dinner, 10½" d., Beaded Edge patt., clear 20.00
Plate, dinner, 10½" d., Paneled Grape patt., milk white 25.00
Punch cup, Old Quilt patt., milk white 8.00
Punch cup, Paneled Grape patt., Brandywine blue 10.00
Punch cup, Paneled Grape patt., milk white 9.00
Punch set: 5 qt. punch bowl, 18" d. underplate, twelve cups & ladle; Paneled Grape patt., milk white, 15 pcs. 550.00
Salt & pepper shakers w/original tops, Old Quilt patt., milk white, pr. 14.00
Salt & pepper shakers w/original tops, footed, Paneled Grape patt., milk white, pr. 18.00
Sherbet, American Hobnail patt., milk white 15.00
Sherbet, Della Robbia patt., milk white 12.00
Spooner, Paneled Grape patt., milk white 20.00
Sugar bowl, cov., Old Quilt patt., milk white 9.00
Syrup pitcher w/original top, Old Quilt patt., milk white 30.00
Table set: cov. butter dish, cov. sugar bowl, creamer & spooner; Ring & Petal (No. 1875) patt., cobalt blue, 4 pcs. 600.00
Tumbler, pilsner-type, American Hobnail (No. 77) patt., clear 18.00
Tumbler, iced tea, footed, Della Robbia patt., milk white 18.00
Tumbler, Old Quilt patt., clear, 9 oz. 10.00
Tumbler, iced tea, Paneled Grape patt., milk white, 12 oz. 18.00
Tumbler, water, Paneled Grape patt., clear 15.00
Vase, 6" h., Paneled Grape patt., milk white 10.00
Vase, 9" h., fan-shaped w/octagonal foot, Old Quilt patt., milk white 20.00
Vase, 9" h., flared rim, Paneled Grape patt., milk white 29.00
Vase, bud, 11" h., Paneled Grape patt., milk white 25.00
Vase, 12" h., Paneled Grape patt., milk white 50.00
Vase, 16" h., "swung"-type, Paneled Grape patt., milk white 30.00
Water set: 9" h. pitcher & six 6" h. tumblers; Paneled Grape patt., clear, 7 pcs. 200.00
Wine set: decanter w/original stopper & eight 2 oz. wines; Paneled Grape patt., milk white, 9 pcs. 185.00

GLOSSARY OF SELECTED GLASS TERMS

Applied - A handle or other portion of a vessel which consists of a separate piece of molten glass attached by hand to the object. Most often used with free-blown or mold-blown pieces but also used with early pressed glass.

Banana stand - A dish, usually round, with two sides turned-up to form a valley and resting atop a pedestal base. A *banana bowl* is usually an oblong or boat-shaped bowl with deep sides. Popular form in late Victorian pattern glass.

Bar lip - A style of lip used on early pressed and mold-blown decanters where a thick ring of applied glass forms the rim of the piece.

Berry bowl - A small dish, most often round, used to serve individual helpings of ripe berries but also used for ice cream or other desserts. It was usually part of a set which included a large (master) berry bowl and several small ones. A popular form in pressed glass.

Celery vase - A tall vase-form vessel, often with a pedestal base, used to serve celery in the Victorian era. It was a common pressed glass piece used in most homes.

Crimping - A method of decorating the rims of bowls and vases. The glassworker used a special hand tool to manipulate the nearly-molten pressed or blown glass and form a ribbon-like design.

Crystal - A generic term generally used today when referring to thin, fine quality glass stemware produced since the early 20th century. Derived from the Italian term *cristallo* referring to delicate, clear Venetian blown glass produced since the 14th century.

Egg cup - A small footed cup, sometimes with a cover, that was meant to hold a soft-boiled egg at breakfast. Most commonly found in early pressed flint glass patterns of the 1840-70 era.

Elegant glass - A modern collector's term used when referring to the better quality 20th century glasswares of such companies as Heisey, Cambridge or Fostoria. Meant to differentiate these wares from the less expensive Depression glass of the same era.

Epergne - A French term used to describe a special decorative vessel popular in the 19th century. It generally consists of one or more tall, slender trumpet-form vases centering a wide, shallow bowl base. The bowl base could also be raised on a pedestal foot. It sometimes refers to a piece with a figural pedestal base supporting several small bowls or suspending several small baskets. Also made from silver or other metals.

Etching - A method of decorating a piece of glass. The two main types are *acid etching* and *needle etching*. In acid etching a piece is covered with an acid-resistant protective layer and then scratched with a design which is then exposed to hydrofluoric acid or acid fumes, thus leaving a frosted design when the protective layer is removed. Needle etching is a 20th century technique where a hand-held or mechanized needle is used to draw a fine-lined design on a piece. Ornate repetative designs were possible with the mechanized needle.

Fire-polishing - A process used to finish early American mold-blown and pressed glass where a piece is reheated just enough to smooth out the mold seams without distorting the overall pattern.

Flint glass - The term used to refer to early 19th century glass which was produced using *lead oxide* in the batch, thus producing a heavy and brilliant glass with a belltone resonance when tapped. When first developed, powdered flints were used instead of lead oxide, hence the name. Nineteenth century American glassmakers used "flint" to describe any quality glass, whether or not it was made with lead.

Galleried rim - A form of rim most often used in early free-blown or mold-blown glass objects, usually sugar bowls. The rim is turned-up around the edge to form a low shelf or gallery which will support the cover.

Knop - Another term for 'knob,' usually referring to a finial on a lid or a bulbous section on the stem of a goblet or wine glass.

Marigold - The most common color used in Carnival glass, generally a bright iridescent orange.

Milk white glass - Also known as *milk glass*; an opaque solid white color popular in the late 19th century for some glass patterns, novelties and animal covered dishes. Glassmen referred to it as *opal* (o-pál).

Mold-blown - A method of glass production where a blob of molten glass (called a "gather") is blown into a patterned mold and then removed and further blown and manipulated to form an object such as a bottle.

Novelty - A pressed glass object generally made in the form of some larger item like a hatchet, boat or animal. They were extremely popular in the late 19th century and many were meant to be used as match holders, toothpick holders and small dresser boxes.

Opal - Pronounced o-pál, this was the term used by 19th century glassmen to describe the solid white glass today known as milk glass.

Pattern glass - A term generally referring to the popular pressed glass tablewares produced from the mid-19th century into the early 20th century.

Pontil mark - The scar left on the base of a free-blown, mold-blown and some early pressed glass by the pontil or punty rod. The hot glass object was attached at the base to the pontil rod so the glassworker could more easily handle it during the final shaping and finishing. When snapped off the pontil a round scar remained which, on finer quality pieces, was polished smooth.

Pressed glass - Any glass produced by a pressing machine. First widely produced in the 1820s in a limited range of pieces, by the turn of the century it was possible to produce dozens of different objects by mechanical means.

Rose bowl - A decorative small spherical or egg-shaped bowl, generally with a scalloped or crimped incurved rim, which was designed to hold rose petal potpourri. It was widely popular in the late 19th century and was produced in many pressed glass patterns as well as more expensive art glass wares such as satin glass.

Scalloping - A decorative treatment used on the rims of plates, bowls, vases and similar objects. It was generally produced during the molding of the object and gave the rim a wavy or ruffled form.

Sheared lip - A type of lip sometimes used on early American free-blown or mold-blown pieces, especially bottles and flasks. It refers to the fact that the neck of the piece is snipped or sheared off the blow pipe.

Sickness - A term referring to cloudy staining found in pressed or blown glass pieces, especially bottles, decanters and vases. It is caused when a liquid is allowed to stand in a piece for a long period of time causing a chemical deterioration of the interior surface. Generally it is nearly impossible to remove completely.

Spall - A shallow rounded flake on a

glass object, generally near the rim of a piece.

Spill holder - Also called a 'spill,' is a small vase-form glass holder used in the 19th century to hold *spills*. The spill was a rolled up thin tube of paper which had been placed under an oil lamp during filling to catch any drips or 'spills' of oil. Once rolled up it could be used as a punk to light lamps. What collectors today call spill holders were produced mainly in flint glass in the 1850s and 1860s, however, research shows that the manufacturers listed them as *spoon holders,* not spills, a term that doesn't appear until the 1870s.

Spooner - A vase or goblet-form glass piece which was meant to hold a bunch of spoons at the center of a table. It was part of the table set common in Victorian pattern glass.

Stemware - A general term for any form of drinking vessel raised on a slender pedestal or stemmed base.

Strap handle - An early form of applied handle on glass objects. It is a fairly thick ribbon of glass generally terminating at the base with a decorative squiggle or curlique. It is flattened where later applied handles are round.

Table set - A matching set of four pieces commonly produced in late 19th century pressed pattern glass. The set included a spooner (spoon holder), creamer, covered sugar bowl and covered butter dish.

Vaseline - A greenish yellow color of glass which was popular in Victorian pressed and blown glass. It was named by collectors for its resemblance to vaseline petroleum jelly. In original glass company catalogs or advertisements this color was simply called "canary" (canary yellow).

Waste bowl - A small, deep bowl commonly part of a ceramic tea set, but also produced in glass. It was made to hold the dregs from the bottoms of tea cups or the teapot.

Whimsey - A glass or ceramic novelty item. Generally in Victorian glass it is a free-blown or mold-blown object, often made by a glassworker as a special present and not part of regular glass production. Glass shoes, pipes and canes are examples of whimseys.

APPENDIX I

GLASS COLLECTORS' CLUBS

Types of Glass

Akro Agate
Akro Agate Art Association
Joseph Bourque
Box 758
Salem, NH 03079

Akro Agate Collector's Club, Inc.
Roger Hardy
10 Bailey St.
Clarksburg, WV 26301-2524

Cambridge
National Cambridge Collectors
P.O. Box 416
Cambridge, OH 43725-0416

Candlewick
National Candlewick Collector's Club
c/o Virginia R. Scott
275 Milledge Terrace
Athens, GA 30606

Carnival
American Carnival Glass Association
c/o Dennis Runk
P.O. Box 235
Littlestown, PA 17340

Collectible Carnival Glass Association
c/o Wilma Thurston
2360 N. Old S.R. 9
Columbus, IN 47203

Heart of America Carnival Glass Association
c/o C. Lucile Britt
3048 Tamarak Dr.
Manhattan, KS 66502

International Carnival Glass Association
c/o Lee Markley, Secretary
R.R. 1, Box 14
Mentone, IN 46539

New England Carnival Glass Club
c/o Eva Backer, Membership
12 Sherwood Rd.
West Hartford, CT 06117

Depression
National Depression Glass Association
P.O. Box 69843
Odessa, TX 79769

20-30-40 Society, Inc.
P.O. Box 856
LaGrange, IL 60525

Western Reserve Depression Glass Club
c/o Ruth Gullis, Membership
8669 Courtland Dr.
Strongville, OH 44136

Duncan
National Duncan Glass Society
P.O. Box 965
Washington, PA 15301

Fenton
Fenton Art Glass Collectors of America
P.O. Box 384
Williamstown, WV 26187

National Fenton Glass Society
P.O. Box 4008
Marietta, OH 45750

Findlay
Collectors of Findlay Glass
P.O. Box 256
Findlay, OH 45839-0256

Fostoria
The Fostoria Glass Society of America
P.O. Box 826
Moundsville, WV 26041

Fry
H.C. Fry Glass Society
P.O. Box 41
Beaver, PA 15009

Greentown
National Greentown Glass Association
LeAnne Milliser, PR.
19596 Glendale Ave.
South Bend, IN 46637

Heisey
Heisey Collectors of America
P.O. Box 4367
Newark, OH 43055

Imperial
National Imperial Glass Collector's Society
P.O. Box 534
Bellaire, OH 43906

Milk Glass
National Milk Glass Collectors Society
c/o Helen Storey
46 Almond Dr.
Hershey, PA 17033

Morgantown
Old Morgantown Glass Collectors' Guild
P.O. Box 894
Morgantown, WV 26507

Morgantown Collectors of America, Inc.
c/o Jerry Gallagher
420 1st Ave. N.W.
Plainview, MN 55964

Phoenix & Consolidated Glass Collectors
c/o Jack D. Wilson
P.O. Box 81974
Chicago, IL 60681-0974

Stretch Glass
Stretch Glass Society
c/o Joanne Rodgers
P.O. Box 770643
Lakewood, OH 44107

Tiffin
Tiffin Glass Collectors' Club
P.O. Box 554
Tiffin, OH 44883

Westmoreland
National Westmoreland Glass Collectors' Club
P.O. Box 372
Westmoreland City, PA 15692

Westmoreland Glass Collectors Club
c/o Harold Mayes
2712 Glenwood
Independence, MO 64052

Special Glass Clubs

Antique and Art Glass Salt Shaker Collectors' Society
2832 Rapidan Trail
Maitland, FL 32751

Glass Knife Collectors' Club
P.O. Box 342
Los Alamitos, CA 90720

Marble Collectors' Society
P.O. Box 222
Trumbull, CT 06611

National Reamer Collectors
c/o Larry Branstad
Rt. 1, Box 200
Grantsburg, WI 54840

National Toothpick Holder Collectors' Society
c/o Joyce Ender, Membership
Red Arrow Hwy., P.O. Box 246
Sawyer, MI 49125

Pairpoint Cup Plate Collectors
P.O. Box 52D
East Weymouth, MA 02189

Paperweight Collectors Association
P.O. Box 468
Garden City Park, NY 11010

Perfume and Scent Bottle Collectors
c/o Jeanne Parris
2022 E. Charleston Blvd.
Las Vegas, NV 89104

General Glass Clubs

Glass Collectors Club of Toledo
2727 Middlesex Dr.
Toledo, OH 43606

Glass Museum Foundation
1157 N. Orange, Box 921
Redlands, CA 92373

Glass Research Society of New Jersey
Wheaton Village
Millville, NJ 08332

National Early American Glass Club
P.O. Box 8489
Silver Spring, MD 20907

APPENDIX II

Museum Collections of American Glass

Many local and regional museums around the country have displays with some pressed glass included. The following are especially noteworthy.

New England

Connecticut: Wadsworth Atheneum, Hartford.

Maine: Jones Gallery of Glass and Ceramics (June - October), Sebago; Portland Museum of Art, Portland.

Massachusetts: Old Sturbridge Village, Sturbridge; Sandwich Glass Museum (April-November), Sandwich.

New Hampshire: The Currier Gallery of Art, Manchester.

Vermont: Bennington Museum (March-November), Bennington.

Mid-Atlantic

Delaware: Henry Francis du Pont Winterthur Museum, Winterthur.

New Jersey: Museum of American Glass, Wheaton Village, Millville.

New York: Corning Museum of Glass, Corning; Cooper-Hewitt Museum, the Smithsonian Institution's National Museum of Design (by appointment), New York; Metropolitan Museum of Art, New York; New-York Historical Society, New York.

Pennsylvania: Historical Society of Western Pennsylvania, Pittsburgh; Philadelphia Museum of Art, Philadelphia; Westmoreland Glass Museum, Port Vue.

Southeast

Florida: Lightner Museum, Saint Augustine; Morse Gallery of Art (Tiffany glass), Winter Park.

Louisiana: New Orleans Museum of Art, New Orleans.

Tennessee: Houston Antique Museum, Chattanooga.

Virginia: Chrysler Museum of Norfolk, Norfolk.

Washington, D.C.: National Museum of American History, Smithsonian Institution.

West Virginia: The Huntington Galleries, Inc., Huntington; Oglebay Institute - Mansion Museum, Wheeling.

Midwest

Indiana: Greentown Glass Museum, Greentown; Indiana Glass Museum, Dunkirk.

Michigan: Henry Ford Museum, Dearborn.

Minnesota: A.M. Chisholm Museum, Duluth.

Ohio: Cambridge Glass Museum, Cambridge; Milan Historical Museum, Milan; National Heisey Glass Museum, Newark; Toledo Museum of Art, Toledo.

Wisconsin: John Nelson Bergstrom Art Center and Mahler Glass Museum, Neenah.

Southwest and West

California: Los Angles County Museum of Art, Los Angeles; Wine Museum of San Francisco and M.H. de Young Museum, San Francisco.

Texas: Mills Collection, Texas Christian University, Fort Worth.

AMERICAN PRESSED GLASS & BOTTLES

INDEX

Akro Agate....1
General Line....1
Children's Dishes....1
Animals....2
Blown Three Mold....3
Bottles & Flasks....6
Bitters....6
Figurals....11
Flasks....11
Inks....21
Medicines....22
Milk....26
Mineral Waters....27
Nursing....27
Pickle Bottles & Jars....28
Poisons....29
Whiskey & Other Spirits....29
Cambridge....31
Carnival Glass....35
Acanthus, 35; Acorn, 35; Acorn Burrs, 35; Advertising & Souvenir Items, 36; Amaryllis (Dugan), 37; Apple Blossoms, 37; Apple Blossom Twigs, 37; Apple Tree, 37; April Showers (Fenton), 37; Australian, 37; Banded Drape, 38; Basket (Fenton's Open Edge), 38; Basket (Northwood) or Bushel Basket, 38; Beaded Bull's Eye (Imperial), 38; Beaded Cable (Northwood), 38; Beaded Shell (Dugan or Diamond Glass Co.), 39; Beauty Bud Vase, 39; Big Fish Bowl (Millersburg), 39; Bird with Grapes, 39; Blackberry (Fenton), 39; Blackberry Bramble, 40; Blackberry Miniature Compote, 40; Blackberry Spray, 40; Blackberry Wreath (Millersburg), 40; Bouquet, 40; Broken Arches (Imperial), 40; Bushel Basket, 38; Butterfly (Northwood), 40; Butterfly & Berry (Fenton), 41; Butterfly & Fern (Fenton), 41; Buzz Saw, 47; Captive Rose, 41; Carnival Holly, 63; Caroline, 42; Cattails & Water Lily, 100; Chatelaine, 42; Cherry (Dugan), 42; Cherry or Cherry Circles (Fenton), 42; Cherry or Hanging Cherries (Millersburg), 42; Cherry Circles, 42; Christmas Compote, 43; Chrysanthemum or Windmill & Mums, 43; Cobblestones Bowl (Imperial), 43; Coin Dot, 43; Coin Spot (Dugan), 44; Comet or Ribbon Tie (Fenton), 44; Concave Diamond, 46; Constellation (Dugan), 44; Coral (Fenton), 44; Corn Bottle, 44; Corn Vase (Northwood), 44; Cornucopia, 44; Cosmos, 44; Crab Claw (Imperial), 44; Crackle, 45; Crucifix, 45; Cut Cosmos, 45; Daisy & Plume, 45; Daisy Cut Bell, 45; Daisy Squares, 45; Daisy Wreath (Westmoreland), 45; Dandelion (Northwood), 45; Dandelion Paneled (Fenton), 46; Diamond & Rib Vase (Fenton), 46; Diamond Concave or Concave Diamond (Dugan), 46; Diamond Lace (Imperial), 46; Diamond Point Columns, 46; Diamond Ring (Imperial), 47; Diamonds (Millersburg), 47; Diving Dolphins Footed Bowl (Sowerby), 47; Dogwood Sprays, 47; Double Dutch Bowl, 47; Double Star or Buzz Saw (Cambridge), 47; Double Stem Rose, 48; Dragon & Lotus (Fenton), 48; Dragon & Strawberry Bowl or Dragon & Berry (Fenton), 48; Drapery (Northwood), 48; Embroidered Mums (Northwood), 49; Estate (Westmoreland), 49; Fan (Dugan), 49; Fanciful (Dugan), 49; Fantail, 49; Farmyard (Dugan), 49; Fashion (Imperial), 49; Feather & Heart, 50; Feather Stitch Bowl, 50; Feathered Serpent, 50; Fentonia, 50; Fenton's Flowers Rose Bowl, 75; Fern, 50; Field Flower (Imperial), 50; Field Thistle (English), 50; File (Imperial), 50; File & Fan, 51; Finecut & Roses (Northwood), 51; Finecut Flowers, 51; Fine Rib (Northwood & Fenton), 51; Fisherman's Mug, 51; Fishscale & Beads, 51; Fleur De Lis (Millersburg), 51; Floral & Grape (Dugan or Diamond Glass Co.), 52; Floral & Wheat Compote (Dugan), 52; Flowers & Beads, 52; Flowers & Frames, 52; Flute (Imperial), 52; Flute (Northwood), 53; Flute & Cane, 53; Fluted Scroll, 53; Formal, 53; Four Flowers, 83; Four Seventy Four (Imperial), 53; Frolicking Bears (U.S. Glass), 53; Frosted Block, 53; Fruit Salad, 53; Fruits & Flowers (Northwood), 53; Garden Path, 54; Garland Rose Bowl (Fenton), 54; God & Home, 54; Goddess of Harvest (Fenton), 55; Golden Harvest or Harvest Time (U.S. Glass), 55; Good Luck, 55; Grape & Cable,

55; Grape & Gothic Arches (Northwood), 59; Grape Arbor (Northwood), 59; Grape Delight, 59; Grape Leaves (Northwood), 60; Grapevine Lattice, 60; Greek Key (Northwood), 60; Hammered Bell, 60; Hanging Cherries, 42; Harvest Flower (Dugan or Diamond Glass), 60; Harvest Time, 55; Hattie (Imperial), 60;
Heart & Horseshoe (Fenton's Good Luck), 61; Heart & Vine (Fenton), 61; Hearts & Flowers (Northwood), 61; Heavy Grape (Dugan, Diamond Glass or Millersburg), 61; Heavy Grape (Imperial), 61; Heavy Iris (Dugan or Diamond Glass), 62; Hobnail (Millersburg), 62; Hobnail Swirl, 94; Hobstar (Imperial), 62; Hobstar & Feather (Millersburg), 62; Hobstar Band, 62; Holly, Holly Berries & Carnival Holly (Fenton), 63; Holly Sprig, 64; Holly Whirl or Holly Sprig (Millersburg & Dugan), 64; Homestead, 74; Honeycomb, 65; Horse Heads or Horse Medallion (Fenton), 65; Horseshoe Curve, 97; Illinois Soldier's & Sailor's Plate, 65; Illusion (Fenton), 65; Imperial Grape (Imperial), 65; Inverted Coin Dot, 66; Inverted Feather (Cambridge), 66; Inverted Strawberry (Cambridge), 66; Inverted Thistle (Cambridge), 67; Iris, 67; Iris, Heavy, 62; Jeweled Heart (Dugan or Diamond Glass), 67; Kittens (Fenton), 67; Lattice & Grape (Fenton), 67; Lattice & Poinsettia (Northwood), 68; Lattice & Points, 68; Leaf & Beads (Northwood), 68; Leaf & Flowers or Leaf & Little Flowers (Millersburg), 68; Leaf Chain (Fenton), 68; Leaf Rays Nappy, 69; Leaf Swirl Compote, 69; Leaf Tiers, 69; Lily of the Valley (Fenton), 69; Lined Lattice Vase, 69; Lion (Fenton), 69; Little Barrel Perfume, 69; Little Daisies (Fenton), 70; Little Fishes (Fenton), 70; Little Flowers (Fenton), 70; Little Stars Bowl (Millersburg), 70; Loganberry Vase (Imperial), 70; Long Hobstar, 70; Long Thumbprints, 70; Lotus & Grape (Fenton), 70; Louisa (Westmoreland), 71; Lustre Flute (Northwood), 71; Lustre Rose (Imperial), 71; Many Fruits (Dugan), 72; Many Stars (Millersburg), 72; Maple Leaf (Dugan), 72; Marilyn (Millersburg), 72; Mary Ann Vase (Dugan), 72; Mayan (Millersburg), 72; Memphis (Northwood), 72; Mikado (Fenton), 73; Milady (Fenton), 73; Millersburg Pipe Humidor, 83; Millersburg Trout & Fly, 97; Mirrored Lotus, 73; Morning Glory (Millersburg), 73; Multifruits & Flowers (Millersburg), 73; My Lady, 73; Nautilus (Dugan), 73; Nesting Swan (Millersburg), 74; Night Stars (Millersburg), 74; Nippon, 74; Nu-Art Chrysanthemum Plate (Imperial), 74; Nu-Art Homestead Plate (Imperial), 74; Octagon (Imperial), 74; Ohio Star (Millersburg), 75; Orange Peel, 75; Orange Tree (Fenton), 75; Orange Tree Orchard (Fenton), 76; Orange Tree Scroll, 76; Oriental Poppy (Northwood), 76; Palm Beach (U.S. Glass Co.), 76; Paneled Dandelion, 46; Paneled Holly (Northwood), 77; Panther (Fenton), 77; Peach (Northwood), 77; Peach & Pear Oval Fruit Bowl, 77; Peacock & Dahlia (Fenton), 77; Peacock & Grape (Fenton), 78; Peacock & Urn (Millersburg, Fenton & Northwood), 78; Peacock at Fountain (Northwood), 79; Peacock, Fluffy (Fenton), 80; Peacock Tail (Fenton), 80; Peacocks on Fence (Northwood Peacocks), 81; Perfection (Millersburg), 81; Persian Garden (Dugan), 81; Persian Medallion (Fenton), 82; Petal & Fan (Dugan), 82; Petals (Northwood), 83; Peter Rabbit (Fenton), 83; Pillow & Sunburst (Westmoreland), 83; Pineapple (Sowerby, England), 83; Pine Cone (Fenton), 83; Pipe Humidor (Millersburg), 83; Plaid (Fenton), 83; Plume Panels Vase (Fenton), 83; Pods & Posies or Four Flowers (Dugan), 83; Poinsettia (Imperial), 83; Poinsettia & Lattice, 84; Polo, 84; Pond Lily, 84; Pony, 84; Poppy (Millersburg), 84; Poppy (Northwood), 84; Poppy Show (Northwood), 84; Poppy Show Vase (Imperial), 84; Prayer Rug (Fenton), 84; Primrose Bowl (Millersburg), 85; Princess Lamp, 85; Prisms, 85; Pulled Loop, 85; Puzzle, 85; Question Marks, 85; Quill (Dugan or Diamond Glass Co.), 85; Raindrops (Dugan), 85; Rambler Rose (Dugan), 85; Ranger, 86; Raspberry (Northwood), 86; Rays & Ribbons (Millersburg), 86; Ribbed Funeral Vase, 86; Ribbon Tie, 44; Ripple Vase, 86; Rising Sun, 86; Robin (Imperial), 86; Rococo, 86; Rosalind (Millersburg), 86; Rose Show, 87; Roses & Fruit (Millersburg), 87; Rosette, 87; Round Up (Dugan), 87; Rustic Vase, 87; Sailboats (Fenton), 88; Sailing Ship Plate, 88; Scale Band, 88; Scales, 88; Scotch Thistle Compote, 88; Scroll Embossed, 88; Seacoast Pin Tray (Millersburg), 88; Seaweed (Millersburg), 89; Shell (Imperial), 89; Shell & Jewel, 89; Shell & Sand, 89; Shell & Wild Rose, 89; Ship & Stars Plate, 89; Singing Birds (Northwood), 89; Single Flower, 89; Six Petals (Dugan), 89; Ski Star (Dugan), 90; Soutache (Dugan), 90; Springtime (Northwood), 90; "S" Repeat (Dugan), 90; Stag & Holly (Fenton), 90; Star & File (Imperial), 91; Starfish, 91; Star Flower, 91; Star Medallion; 91; Star of David (Imperial), 91; Star of David & Bows (Northwood), 92; Stippled Flower (Dugan),

92; Stippled Petals, 92; Stippled Rays, 92; Stork (Imperial), 92; Stork & Rushes (Dugan or Diamond Glass Works), 92; Strawberry (Fenton), 93; Strawberry (Millersburg), 93; Strawberry (Northwood), 93; Strawberry Scroll (Fenton), 93; Stream of Hearts (Fenton), 93; Sunflower Bowl (Northwood), 93; Sunflower Pin Tray (Millersburg), 94; Swan Pastel Novelties (Dugan), 94; Swirl Hobnail (Millersburg), 94; Swirl Rib, 94; Target Vase (Dugan), 94; Ten Mums (Fenton), 94; Thin Rib Vase, 94; Thistle (Fenton), 95; Thistle & Thorn (Sowerby's, England), 95; Three Fruits (Northwood), 95; Tiger Lily (Imperial), 96; Tornado Vase (Northwood), 96; Town Pump Novelty (Northwood), 96; Tracery (Millersburg), 96; Tree Trunk Vase (Northwood), 97; Trout & Fly (Millersburg), 97; Tulip & Cane, 97; Twig Vase, 97; Twins or Horseshoe Curve (Imperial), 97; Two Flowers (Fenton), 97; Two Fruits, 98; Venetian Giant Rose Bowl (Cambridge), 98; Victorian, 98; Vineyard, 98; Vintage or Vintage Grape, 98; Vintage Band, 99; Vintage Grape, 98; Waffle Block, 99; Water Lily (Fenton), 99; Water Lily & Cattails, 100; Whirling Leaves Bowl (Millersburg), 100; White Oak Tumbler, 100; Wide Panel, 100; Wild Rose, 100; Wild Strawberry (Northwood), 101; Windflower, 101; Windmill or Windmill Medallion (Imperial), 101; Windmill & Mums, 43; Windmill Medallion, 101; Wine & Roses, 101; Wishbone (Northwood), 102; Wishbone & Spades, 102; Wreathed Cherry (Dugan), 102; Wreath of Roses, 103; Zig Zag (Millersburg), 103; Zippered Heart, 103; Zippered Loop Lamp (Imperial), 103

Consolidated....104
- Bulging Loops....104
- Cone....104
- Florette....104
- Guttate....105
- Later Lines....105

Cruets....106
Cup Plates....108
Depression Glass....108
Adam, 108; American Sweetheart, 109; Block, 110; Bubble, 111; Cameo, 112; Cherry Blossom, 113; Cloverleaf, 114; Colonial, 114; Columbia, 115; Cube, 115; Daisy, 116; Diamond Quilted, 116; Diana, 117; Dogwood, 117; Doric, 118; Doric & Pansy, 119; English Hobnail, 119; Floral, 120; Florentine (Old), 121; Florentine, 122; Georgian, 123; Hobnail, 123; Holiday, 124; Homespun, 124; Iris, 124; Lace Edge, 125; Lorain, 125; Madrid, 126; Manhattan, 127; Mayfair, 128; Miss America, 129; Moderntone, 129; Moonstone, 130; Moroccan Amethyst, 131; Normandie, 131; Number 612, 132; Old Cafe, 132; Oyster & Pearl, 132; Parrot, 133; Patrician, 133; Petalware, 134; Pineapple & Floral, 135; Princess, 135; Queen Mary, 136; Raindrops, 136; Ribbon, 137; Ring, 137; Roulette, 138; Royal Lace, 138; Royal Ruby, 139; Sailboats, 139; Sandwich; 140; Sharon, 140; Sierra, 141; Spiral, 141; Swanky Swigs, 141; Swirl, 142; Tea Room, 142; Twisted Optic, 143; Waterford, 143; Windsor Diamond, 144

Duncan & Miller....145
Fenton....147
Fostoria....149
Fry....152
Goofus....153
Greentown....153
Heisey....154
Historical & Commemorative....157
Imperial....160
- Candlewick Pattern....160
- Cape Cod Pattern....161
- Free Hand Ware....162
- Jewels Line....162
- Miscellaneous Patterns & Lines....162

Iowa City Glass....162
Lacy....162
McKee....167
- Kitchenwares....167
- Pres-Cut Lines....167
- Miscellaneous Patterns & Pieces....168

Milk White....168
New Martinsville....172
Northwood....172
Paden City....175
Pattern Glass....175
Actress, 176; Adonis, 176; Alabama, 176; Alaska, 176; Alexis, 234; Almond Thumbprint, 177; Amazon, 177; Amberette, 216; Animals & Birds on Goblets & Pitchers, 177; Apollo, 178; Argus, 178; Art, 178; Ashburton, 179; Atlanta, 179; Atlas, 179; Aztec, 179; Baby Thumbprint, 196; Balder, 230; Baltimore Pear, 180; Bamboo, 184; Banded Beaded Grape Medallion, 180; Banded Buckle, 180; Banded Portland, 180; Barberry, 180; Barley, 181; Basketweave, 181; Beaded Band, 181; Beaded Bull's Eye with Drape, 176; Beaded Dewdrop, 259; Beaded Grape, 181; Beaded Grape Medallion, 182; Beaded Loop, 182; Beaded Tulip, 182; Bearded Head, 255; Bearded Man, 235; Bellflower, 182; Bird & Fern, 213; Bird & Strawberry, 183; Bleeding Heart, 183; Block & Fan, 183; Block & Star, 254; Bluebird, 183; Bohemian, 184; Bow Tie, 184; Broken Column, 184; Bryce, 237;

Buckle, 184; Buckle with Star, 185; Bull's Eye, 185; Bull's Eye Variant, 248; Bull's Eye with Diamond Point, 185; Bull's Eye with Fleur De Lis, 185; Button Arches, 185; Cabbage Rose, 186; Cable, 186; Cable with Ring, 186; California, 181; Cameo, 188; Canadian, 186; Cane, 186; Cannon Ball, 179; Cape Cod, 187; Cardinal Bird, 187; Cathedral, 187; Ceres, 187; Chain with Star, 187; Chandelier, 187; Checkerboard, 188; Classic, 188; Classic Medallion, 188; Collins, 191; Colonial, 188; Colorado, 188; Columbian Coin, 189; Compact, 243; Cord & Tassel, 189; Cord Drapery, 189; Corona, 246; Cottage, 190; Croesus, 190; Crowfoot, 190; Crown Jewel, 187; Crystal Ball, 179; Crystal Wedding, 191; Cupid & Venus, 191; Currier & Ives, 191; Curtain, 192; Curtain Tieback, 192; Cut Log, 192; Dahlia, 193; Daisy & Button, 193; Daisy & Button with Crossbars, 194; Daisy & Button with Narcissus, 195; Daisy & Button with Thumbprint Panels, 195; Daisy & Button with "V" Ornament, 196; Daisy in Panel, 252; Dakota, 196; Dart, 196; Deer & Dog, 197; Deer & Pine Tree, 197; Delaware, 197; Dew & Raindrop, 198; Dewdrop, 198; Dewdrop with Star, 198; Dewey, 199; Diagonal Band, 199; Diagonal Band & Fan, 199; Diamond & Bull's Eye Band, 235; Diamond & Sunburst, 199; Diamond Medallion, 199; Diamond Point, 200; Diamond Point with Panels, 211; Diamond Quilted, 200; Diamond Thumbprint, 201; Dinner Bell, 190; Doric, 203; Double Leaf & Dart, 217; Double Loop, 237; Double Ribbon, 201; Double Wedding Ring, 201; Drapery, 201; Egg In Sand, 201; Egyptian, 201; Emerald Green Herringbone, 228; Empire Colonial, 188; Empress, 202; English Hobnail Cross, 216; Esther, 202; Eureka, 202; Excelsior, 202; Eyewinker, 203; Feather, 203; Festoon, 203; Finecut, 204; Finecut & Block, 204; Finecut & Diamond, 199; Finecut & Feather, 203; Finecut & Panel, 204; Finecut Band, 190; Fishscale, 205; Florida, 228; Flower Flange, 199; Flute, 205; Flying Robin, 213; Four Petal Flower, 197; Frosted Circle, 205; Frosted Leaf, 206; Frosted Lion, 206; Frosted Ribbon, 206; Frosted Roman Key, 237; Frosted Stork, 206; Galloway, 207; Garfield Drape, 207; Georgia, 230; Giant Bull's Eye, 207; Goddess of Liberty, 187; Good Luck, 213; Gooseberry, 207; Gothic, 207; Grand, 199; Grape & Festoon, 208; Grape & Festoon with Shield, 208; Grasshopper, 208; Guardian Angel, 191; Hairpin, 208; Halley's Comet, 208; Hamilton, 208; Hamilton with Leaf, 208; Hand, 209; Harp, 209; Hearts of Loch Laven, 243; Heart with Thumbprint, 209; Heavy Paneled Finecut, 210; Hercules Pillar, 210; Hero, 210; Herringbone, 210; Herringbone Band, 210; Herringbone with Star & Shield Motif, 210; Hickman, 210; Hidalgo, 211; Hinoto, 211; Hobnail, 211; Hobnail with Thumbprint Base, 211; Honeycomb, 212; Horn of Plenty, 212; Horseshoe, 213; Huber, 213; Hummingbird, 213; Illinois, 213; Indiana, 214; Indiana Swirl, 203; Inverted Fern, 214; Inverted Loops & Fans, 221; Iowa, 214; Irish Column, 184; Ivy In Snow, 214; Jacob's Ladder, 214; Jewel & Crescent, 247; Jewel & Dewdrop, 215; Jewel & Festoon, 215; Jewel Band, 241; Jeweled Diamond & Fan, 247; Jeweled Moon & Star, 215; Job's Tears, 178; Jumbo and Jumbo & Barnum, 215; Kamoni, 230; Kansas, 215; Kentucky, 216; King's Crown, 216; Klondike, 216; Lacy Medallion, 188; Leaf, 221; Leaf & Dart, 217; LeClede, 210; Liberty Bell, 217; Lily-of-the-Valley, 218; Lincoln Drape & Lincoln Drape with Tassel, 218; Lion, 179; Lion, Frosted, 206; Lion's Leg, 176; Locust, 208; Log Cabin, 218; Loop, 219; Loop & Dart, 219; Loop & Jewel, 215; Loop & Pillar, 222; Loop with Dewdrops, 219; Loop with Stippled Panels, 247; Loops & Drops, 226; Loops & Fans, 221; Louisiana, 219; Magnet & Grape, 220; Maine, 220; Maltese, 214; Manhattan, 220; Maple Leaf, 221; Maryland, 221; Mascotte, 221; Massachusetts, 221; Medallion, 222; Medallion Sprig, 222; Melrose, 222; Michigan, 222; Mikado, 194; Minerva, 223; Minnesota, 223; Mirror, 207; Missouri, 224; Monkey, 224; Moon & Star, 224; Moon & Star with Waffle, 215; Morning Glory, 225; Nail, 225; Nailhead, 225; Neptune, 235; Nestor, 225; New England Pineapple, 226; New Hampshire, 226; New Jersey, 226; Notched Rib, 184; Oaken Bucket, 226; Old Man of the Mountain, 255; Old Man of the Woods, 235; One-Hundred-One, 227; Open Rose, 227; Oregon No. 1, 182; Oregon No. 2, 243; Owl In Fan, 229; Palm & Scroll, 224; Palmette, 227; Paneled Cane, 228; Paneled Daisy, 228; Paneled Dewdrop, 228; Paneled Diamond Cross, 210; Paneled Finecut, 204; Paneled Forget-Me-Not, 228; Paneled 44, 235; Paneled Grape, 228; Paneled Heather, 228; Paneled Herringbone, 228; Paneled Jewel, 222; Paneled Star & Button, 242; Paneled Thistle, 229; Paneled Zipper, 214; Parrot, 229; Pavonia, 229; Peacock Feather, 230; Pennsylvania, 230; Pennsylvania, Early, 209; Petal & Loop, 230; Picket, 230; Picket Band, 230; Pillar, 230; Pillar & Bull's Eye, 231; Pillar Variant, 210; Pillar & Sunburst,

231; Pillow Encircled, 231; Pineapple & Fan, 231; Pineapple Stem, 229; Pleat & Panel, 231; Pleat & Tuck, 176; Plume, 232; Pointed Thumbprint, 177; Polar Bear, 232; Popcorn, 232; Portland, 232; Portland Maiden Blush, 180; Portland with Diamond Point Band, 180; Post, 233; Powder & Shot, 233; Prayer Rug, 213; Pressed Diamond, 233; Pressed Leaf, 233; Primrose, 233; Princess Feather, 234; Priscilla, 234; Psyche & Cupid, 234; Pygmy, 250; Queen, 234; Queen Anne, 235; Queen's Necklace, 235; Rampant Lion, 206; Red Block, 235; Reverse 44, 235; Reverse Torpedo, 235; Ribbed Forget-Me-Not, 236; Ribbed Grape, 236; Ribbed Palm, 236; Ribbed Ivy, 236; Ribbon, 236; Ribbon Candy, 237; Rising Sun, 237; Rochelle, 234; Roman Key, 237; Roman Rosette, 237; Roman Rosette, Early, 238; Rose In Snow, 238; Rose Sprig, 238; Rosette, 239; Royal Crystal, 239; Royal Ivy, 239; Royal Oak, 240; Ruby Rosette, 210; Ruby Thumbprint, 240; Sandwich Loop, 208; Sandwich Star, 241; Sawtooth, 241; Sawtooth Band, 177; Scalloped Tape, 241; Sedan, 242; Seneca Loop, 219; Shell & Jewel, 242; Shell & Tassel, 242; Sheraton, 243; Shoshone, 243; Shrine, 243; Shuttle, 243; Skilton, 243; Snail, 243; Spiked Argus, 178; Spirea Band, 244; Sprig, 244; Square Lions Head, 179; Square Panes, 233; Squirrel, 177; S-Repeat, 245; Star Rosetted, 245; States (The), 245; Staves with Scalloped Band, 230; Stippled Chain, 245; Stippled Cherry, 245; Stippled Flower Panels, 220; Stippled Forget-Me-Not, 245; Stippled Grape & Festoon, 246; Stippled Ivy, 246; Strigil, 246; Sunk Honeycomb, 246; Swan, 246; Tacoma, 247; Teardrop & Tassel, 247; Tennessee, 247; Texas, 247; Texas Bulls's Eye, 248; Thistle, Paneled, 229; Thousand Eye, 248; Three Face, 249; Three Panel, 249; Thumbprint, Early, 250; Tong, 250; Torpedo, 250; Tree of Life - Portland, 251; Tree of Life - With Hand, 251; Triple Triangle, 251; Tulip with Sawtooth, 251; Turkey Track, 190; Two Panel, 252; U.S. Coin, 252; Valencia Waffle, 254; Victor, 242; Victoria, 255; Viking, 255; Virginia, 180; Waffle, 255; Waffle & Thumbprint, 255; Washboard, 176; Washington Centennial, 255; Washington, Early, 256; Washington (State), 256; Wedding Bells, 256; Wedding Ring, 201; Westmoreland, 256; Westward Ho, 256; Wheat & Barley, 257; Wildflower, 257; Willow Oak, 258; Windflower, 258; Wisconsin, 259; Wooden Pail, 226; Wyoming, 259; X-Ray, 259; Yale, 190; Zipper, 259; Zippered Block, 214

Phoenix....260
Pillar-Molded....261
Ruby-Stained....261
Sandwich....263
Stiegel & Stiegel-Type....264
Stretch....265
Tiffin....265
Vaseline....266
Victorian Colored Glass....267
Westmoreland....268